International Business Information
How to Find It, How to Use It

International Business Information
How to Find It, How to Use It

by Ruth A. Pagell and Michael Halperin

Oryx

1994

The rare Arabian Oryx is believed to have inspired the myth of the unicorn. This desert antelope became virtually extinct in the early 1960s. At that time several groups of international conservationists arranged to have 9 animals sent to the Phoenix Zoo to be the nucleus of a captive breeding herd. Today the Oryx population is nearly 800, and over 400 have been returned to reserves in the Middle East.

Library of Congress Cataloging-in-Publication Data

Pagell, Ruth A.
    International business information : how to find it, how to use it
    / by Ruth A. Pagell and Michael Halperin.
        p. cm.
    Includes bibliographical references and index.
    ISBN 0-89774-736-4
    1. Business information services—Handbooks, manuals, etc.
2. Business—Bibliography—handbooks, manuals, etc. I. Halperin,
Michael, 1940– .   II. Title.
    HF54.5.P33   1994
    332.1'753—dc20   93-49000
                                                CIP

Contents

List of Exhibits

List of Tables

Preface

"The emerging global economy," "transnational corporations," "the world market place"—these phrases define the business environment of the 1990s. The practical impact of the new world economic order is illustrated by a quote from Robert Reich, which appeared in the *Wall Street Journal* on July 5, 1991, before Mr. Reich became secretary of labor.

> A sports car is financed in Japan, designed in Italy and assembled in Indiana, Mexico and France, using advanced electronic components invented in New Jersey and fabricated in Japan.

The advent of the global economy has required librarians and business researchers to learn about new sources of information and expand their understanding of international business subjects. From any national perspective, much international business information is truly foreign. The sources are different, the language is different, the coding is different, the definitions are different. This book is designed to help its users overcome the obstacles to finding and understanding international business information.

International Business Information: How to Find It, How to Use It describes key international business publications and databases, and provides the subject background needed to understand them. The book is designed to be a practical guide for the researcher and librarian. Many of the print and electronic sources we describe are widely available in medium or large libraries worldwide. Although written from a U.S. perspective, the information and sources we describe should be of value to all librarians and business researchers.

Users of Michael Lavin's *Business Information: How to Find It, How to Use It* (Oryx, second edition, 1992), will see its format and approach (and title) reflected in this volume. We are great admirers of Mr. Lavin's approach to writing about business topics.

International Business Information is not a bibliography. We have been highly selective in the sources included. No publication or database is highlighted that we have not examined or searched. We have attempted to examine a wide range of sources and to acquire or access newly released sources. We have attended several international business conferences to examine sources not yet available in the U.S. and to obtain a broader perspective on the uses and application of non-U.S. products. Because both printed publications and electronic files are necessary for comprehensive business research, we have described a mix of these formats. Our emphasis is on what we consider the core of business research: companies, industries, markets, and finance. Most of the sources we describe are serial publications.

In screening the vast number of possible international business sources for inclusion, we looked for materials that were authoritative, available, and affordable. Most of the sources we described are in English or have at least partial English translations. We recognize that English language business sources may not be the most complete or authoritative for non-English-speaking countries. Many countries have their own prominent business publishers or information providers. An example is Hoppenstedt in Germany. As a practical matter, we have focused our presentation on English language directories, yearbooks, reports, and electronic files.

Each chapter of this book consists of subject background followed by a description of the subject's information sources. We occasionally strayed from this plan when it seemed appropriate to describe a source while discussing a business subject. Most of the chapters stand alone and can be consulted as needed. While we recommend that you read the introductory information in each chapter, you can use this book simply to identify sources.

Inclusion of a source in this book should not necessarily be seen as a recommendation for its use or purchase. We occasionally describe a source with a recommendation that it not be purchased. The prices we give for publications are approximate and are designed as a general aid for purchase decisions.

In our description of sources, we have presented hundreds of extracts of entries, tables, and records. Seeing an actual record, or even a partial record, will often give a better sense of the contents of a source than the most elaborate description. (To save space, we have often truncated records reproduced in the text.)

We believe that it is important for publishers of business information to give dates for the information they describe. For this reason, we include the dates of the editions we examined and the electronic information we extracted. Most of the sources we describe provide data. The indexes, abstracts, and full-text databases we describe should be adequate to identify material that treats theoretical or conceptual issues.

Printed and electronic sources for international business are proliferating. Printed sources may have one or more CD-ROM and time-sharing versions. We have attempted to list and, in many cases, describe the electronic versions of key print sources. We realize that electronic publishing is in such a state of flux that our descriptions may date quickly. The Internet is becoming popular as an access route to commercial and local time-sharing systems. We describe the Internet when its use is appropriate for access to international data sources. At this stage of its development, the best use of the Internet may be as a way to tap into the collective knowledge of colleagues through E-mail and list-serves.

Throughout this book, we emphasize the need for care in the use and interpretation of international business data. Business vocabulary often changes meaning when it crosses a border. Terms and concepts familiar in the U.S., such as CPI, current ratio, SIC number, and disclosure, may not be used or have different definitions abroad. Something as apparently simple as comparing the GDP of two countries has pitfalls.

An important goal for us has been to provide the reader with the information and techniques needed to evaluate and select information products for interna-

tional business research. We believe that identifying and explaining the problems in relationship to existing international business sources will help the reader evaluate new sources that will appear after this book is published.

While writing this book, the Soviet Union, Yugoslavia, and Czechoslovakia divided to form a score or so of new countries, while Germany reunited. As the number of countries in the world increased, the number of information providers we were researching shrank. IAC purchased Predicasts, and Reed purchased National Register. As we were doing our final editing, DIALOG purchased DATA-STAR. Even the merger databases merged. IDD Enterprises purchased ADP Data Services. IDD's merger database was then purchased by Securities Data Company (SDC), a Thomson Corporation subsidiary.

Research guides are by their nature incomplete. New editions of publications continually appear with new information, additional company listings, and changes in structure. Business researchers need information that varies in complexity, from single facts to grand theories, and in accessibility, from common knowledge to state secrets. Secondary sources can describe only a portion of this information universe. Sometimes the answers to apparently simple and plausible questions are nowhere to be found. Having said this, it is important to note that the scope, availability, and currency of published business information has never been greater. Despite the volatility of publishing, many of the core titles in international business have been in existence for decades. We believe that our selection and description of sources in *International Business Information* will serve you well as the foundation for international business research.

Ruth A. Pagell
Michael Halperin
Philadelphia, PA

Acknowledgments

Our thanks to all the people who have helped us in writing this book. We thank Michael Lavin for allowing us to model this book's form and title after his guide to U.S. sources (*Business Information: How to Find It, How to Use It*). We thank him as well for demonstrating how a guide to the business literature should be written.

The help of the staff of the Lippincott Library was crucial for the book's completion. We drew heavily on the entire staff's reference experience, technical processing skills, detailed knowledge of sources, computer skills, and published articles. Several of our colleagues read portions of the manuscript. Our thanks to Steven Bell, Marie Bridy, Linda Eichler, and Jean Newland. Their comments and suggestion were invaluable. We thank, too, John Ganley of the New York Public Library and Ray Lester of the London Business School Library for sharing their knowledge and their collections with us.

Publishers and database producers were generous in providing review copies, test CD-ROMs, and access to time-sharing systems. They were generous as well with explanations of their data gathering and data processing techniques. We owe special thanks to the following information providers: CIFAR, DATA-STAR, DataStream, DIALOG, Disclosure, Dun & Bradstreet, Euromonitor, Extel, Gale Research, LEXIS AND NEXIS SERVICES, Moody's, Securities Data Company, SilverPlatter, Predicasts, and UMI.

Finally, our thanks to John Wagner for his meticulous editing and many excellent suggestions.

PART I
Introduction

CHAPTER 1
General Sources for International Business Research

TOPICS COVERED

1. U.S. Sources of International Information
2. Non-U.S. Business Bibliographic Sources
3. Online Full-Text Sources
4. General Finding Aids
5. Searching for New International Subjects
6. International Conferences
7. Conclusion
8. Note

MAJOR SOURCES DISCUSSED

- *Predicasts* Publications
- *ABI/Inform*
- *Business Periodicals Index*
- *Business Index/General Business File*
- *PAIS International*
- *Index to International Statistics*
- *European Directory of Non-official Statistical Sources*
- *Directory of International Sources of Business Information*

In this chapter, we describe the use of several standard sources of U.S. business information for international research as well as discuss the use of general finding aides for a variety of international business sources and subjects.

Michael Lavin devotes the first chapters of *Business Information: How to Find It, How to Use It* (2nd ed., Oryx Press, 1992) to describing the sources and forms of business information, including guides for locating people, organizations, and publications. Although Mr. Lavin's emphasis is on U.S. business research, his explanations and many of the sources he describes are appropriate for international business research. Rather than repeat Lavin's descriptions of many standard U.S. sources, we refer the reader to the appropriate sections of *Business Information.**

U.S. SOURCES OF INTERNATIONAL INFORMATION

Despite the globalization of business and the development of the transnational corporation, the individual nation state is still the paramount political and economic force. International business research frequently has a national point of view. Consequently, sources for national and international business research often overlap. For example, the U.S. researcher might be interested in the following topics:

- Japanese investment in the U.S. chemical industry
- Availability of German company stocks in the U.S.
- The effect of EC regulations on U.S. trade with Europe

---

*We found the following chapters of *Business Information* especially useful as background information for international business research:

Chapter 1: Sources and Forms of Business Information
Chapter 2: Locating Experts
Chapter 3: Finding Reference Materials
Chapter 4: Finding Books, Documents, and Statistical Reports
Chapter 5: Searching Journals, Newspapers, and News Services
Chapter 13: Introduction to Statistical Reasoning

Many useful sources for U.S. business information and news also have international information. For example, standard U.S. business indexes and abstracts, while emphasizing U.S. business and U.S. publications, often include bibliographic information about international issues. Listed below are examples of standard U.S. business indexes and abstracts useful for international research.

* *ABI/Inform*
* *Business Periodicals Index*
* *Business Index*
* *PAIS International*
* *PTS PROMT*
* *Wall Street Journal Index*

Some U.S. business sources have international companion volumes, often by the same publisher. Many of these parallel sources are described throughout this volume, and a few pairs are listed below.

U.S. Business Source	Companion International Business Source
Encyclopedia of Associations	*Encyclopedia of Associations. International Organizations*
American Statistics Index	*Index to International Statistics*
F&S Index	*F&S Europe/F&S International*
Predicasts Forecasts	*WorldCasts*
Brands and Their Companies	*International Companies and their Brands*
Consultants and Consulting Organizations Directory	*European Consultants Directory*
Polk's Bank Directory	*Polk's International Bank Directory*
D&B Million Dollar Directory	*Dun's Principal International Business*
Pratt's Guide to Venture Capital	*Guide to European Venture Capital Sources*
Best's Life/Health and *Best's Property/Casualty*	*Best's Insurance Reports (International Edition)*
Moody's Industrial Manual	*Moody's International Manual*
Encyclopedia of Business Information Sources	*Encyclopedia of Business Information Sources: Europe*

U.S. government publications are often an excellent and inexpensive source of international business information. In later chapters, we describe the international research value of several U.S. government publications, including the *Survey of Current Business, Foreign Economic Trends, Foreign Labor Trends,* the *Monthly Labor Review,* and the *National Trade Databank CD-ROM.* The *Statistical Abstract of the United States,* described in this chapter, is a useful finding aid to a wide range of international data.

Indexing and Abstracting Services

There are several U.S. indexing and abstracting services useful for international business research. Some of the more important ones are discussed below.

Predicasts Publications (Information Access Company)

The *Predicasts* publications have the largest set of international articles. The print *F&S Indexes* are divided into three parts: U.S., Europe, and International (which includes Canada and Mexico). All three parts appear online as one database.

PROMT (*P*redicasts *O*verview of *M*arkets and *T*echnology) is available both in print and online. It includes fewer publications than the *F&S Indexes,* but all entries have abstracts. The *PROMT* file online may also have extracts or full text. *PROMT* is available on the following databanks:

> BRS Information Technologies and COLLEAGUE
> DATA-STAR
> DIALOG Information Services, Inc.
> NIFTY Corporation, NIFTY-Serve Japan
> MEAD DATA CENTRAL, Inc. (MDC) NEXIS
> THOMSON FINANCIAL NETWORKS INC, Investext/Plus Direct
> MAID
> BIOSIS Life Science Network

Finally, Predicasts produces a CD-ROM that combines aspects of the *F&S Indexes* and *PROMT.* Called *Predicasts F&S + Text,* it is composed of separate U.S. and International files. Both files have two CD-ROMs, a backfile for 1990, and a current set from January 1, 1991. The discs, using SilverPlatter software, are sold to public and academic libraries in the U.S. and to most libraries in developing countries.

The Predicasts' definition of what makes a record "international," is based on where the activity takes place. A description of a U.K. company in the *Wall Street Journal* is an international record; a description of a U.S. company in the *Financial Times* is a U.S. record. About 1,000 publications, including magazines, newspapers, and trade publications, are indexed. *F&S Plus International* will provide a German view of Europe or a Japanese view of Asia. Only Predicasts would index an article such as the following: "Dairy Farming in the Baltic States," *East-Europe and USSR Agriculture and Food,* Sept. 1991. Exhibit 1-1 presents an extract of a sample record from *F&S + Text International.*

Many of the publications indexed in *F&S + Text* are not in English, although an English *abstract* summarizing the article is provided. In addition, many of the sources Predicasts indexes are not readily available in

> **EXHIBIT 1-1. Record from *F&S + Text International***
>
> TI: DAIRY FARMING IN THE BALTIC STATES
> USSR: Baltics produce 6.5 mil m tons of milk in 1989
> SO: East-Europe-and-USSR-Agriculture-and-Food.
> September, 1991, page N/A
> IS: 0263-3205
> TX: Natural conditions in the three newly-independent
> Baltic States (Lithuania, Latvia and Estonia) are
> generally favourable for the production of milk and
> meat, with 35%-40% of the agricultural land of these
> countries consisting of meadows and pasture land. In
> 1989, the three Baltic states produced 6.5 million
> tonnes of milk, or 6% of the total milk output of the
> former Soviet Union....
> Table reports dairy production in 1989 in Lithuania,
> Latvia and Estonia by product and state.
> TX: THIS IS AN EXCERPT: Copyright 1991 Agra
> Europe (London) Ltd.
> PN: Bulk Fluid Milk (2026100)
> CN: USSR (6USS)
> EN: Production Information (62)
> TA: YES
> AN: 3063844

Reprinted with permission from Information Access Company.

print. All articles contain at least an abstract. Some, such as the example above, contain *excerpts*, selected portions of text offered verbatim because they characterize the major points of the article. Very short articles contain the full text. As seen in Exhibit 1-1, the excerpts include relevant data. Therefore, not having access to the full text is disappointing but not fatal.

Predicasts' files feature a useful coding system with hierarchical codes for products, events, and geographic areas. Table 1-A presents the number of records for selected geographic areas, using DIALOG File 16 as the source.

Predicasts was purchased by Ziff Communications in November 1991 and is now part of the IAC Group. As long as Predicasts maintains its individual identity and philosophy, it will remain one of the premier international business publishers.

ABI/Inform (UMI/Data Courier, Inc.)

ABI/Inform was one of the first online business databases, dating back to mid-1971. There is no print equivalent. *ABI/Inform* is available on several systems, including BRS, DATA-STAR, and DIALOG, and is also produced as a CD-ROM. Most of the 800 journals indexed and abstracted by Data Courier are published in the U.S. Some 200 non-U.S. English language management publications were added to the file in 1993. The full text of selected articles has been added to the online database. *ABI/Inform* does not index journals cover-to-cover. However, UMI Data Courier has a CD-ROM image product, *Business Periodicals on Disc*, which contains complete image facsimiles of about half the journals abstracted in *ABI/Inform*.

ABI/Inform has both geographic descriptors for countries and regions and a numeric classification system that has codes for geographic regions.

Business Periodicals Index (H.W. Wilson)

Business Periodicals Index, the original business index, is available in print, online direct from Wilson, and on Wilsondisc CD-ROM. A companion product, *Business Periodicals Abstracts*, is available on CD-ROM and online.

BPI has been a standard index in many small and medium-sized libraries. *BPI* is known for the quality of its indexing and its sensitivity to users' collections. However, *BPI* does not have broad coverage of international business topics.

Business Index/General Business File (Information Access Group)

Business Index is available as a microfilm loop, on CD-ROM (under the name *InfoTrac*), or as the *Trade and Industry* online database. None of these forms have

Table 1-A. Predicasts Geographic Codes

No of Records	Code	(definition)	No of Records	Code	(definition)
711,108	*4	(ALL EUROPE)	422,083	9	(ALL ASIA)
23,664	4 EC	(EUROPEAN COMMUNITY)	1,222	9 11	(FAR EAST)
24,256	4B		240	9 2AT	(ASEAN)
749	4BEJ	(BENELUX)	799	9 2T	(SOUTHEAST ASIA)
1,174	4BEK	(BELG-LUX ECON UNION)	954	9 50	(OCEANIA)
22,374	4BEL	(BELGIUM)	8,683	9 THA	(THAILAND)
12,240	4DEN	(DENMARK)			

Source: DIALOG File 16

identical contents. IAC now has an expanded CD-ROM, *General Business File,* that includes *Business Index* and Investment Bank Reports from the *Investext* database.

Business Index has been adding abstracts to its file and making changes to its CD-ROM software. Unfortunately, the changes have made the product more difficult to use, although it is still a good source for locating company information.

IAC makes the full text of some of the articles it indexes available in two formats, online and in microfilm. Selected articles are available online on several databanks such as LEXIS/NEXIS SERVICES, BRS, DOW JONES NEWS RETRIEVAL, DIALOG, and DATA-STAR. Articles are available as well in *Business Collection*, a microfilm system linked by a numeric code to *Business Index* citations.

IAC is adding abstracts of European journals to its databases. *Trade and Industry* (File 148 on DIALOG and INDY on DATA-STAR) added titles as diverse as *Bank of England Quarterly* and *Electrical Contractor*. Few of IAC's new titles are duplicated by *ABI/Inform*.

PAIS International (Public Affairs Information Service)

PAIS International is another multi-format bibliographic source, available in print, online, and on CD-ROM. Many of the sources indexed in *PAIS* are written in French, German, Spanish, Italian, or Portuguese. Though more a social science than a business database, *PAIS* indexes many business-related articles.

Economic Literature Index (American Economics Association)

Economic Literature Index contains international business articles of interest to academic researchers. It is available in print, online (DIALOG File 139), and on CD-ROM.

NON-U.S. BUSINESS BIBLIOGRAPHIC SOURCES

Management and Marketing Abstracts (PIRA International, U.K.)

A European competitor to *ABI/Inform, Management and Marketing Abstracts* is available both in print and online in DATA-STAR *(MMKA).* The focus of the database is on management issues and case studies. Finance is covered only as it relates to management. Only 175 publications are abstracted, the majority from the U.K. About 10% of the entries are non-English and approximately 20% are from North America. Many of

the English language titles in *MMKA* were added to *ABI/Inform* in 1993.

HELECON (Helecon Online Services, Helsinki, Finland)

This European bibliographic CD-ROM combines seven European management and business databases. The seven are listed in Table 1-B. References are to books, periodical articles, research papers, and dissertations. Less than 50% of the articles are in English. It is updated semi-annually.

Institute of Management International Database Plus (Bowker-Saur—quarterly)

A new European-based product, primarily for the U.K. market, is the *Institute of Management International Database Plus,* a CD-ROM collection of management resources produced in conjunction with Bowker-Saur. The disc, which was released in December 1992, contains six databases:

1. **Journals:** 35,000 abstracts from 220 U.K., U.S., and European journals
2. **Books:** Index to 22,000 English language management titles
3. **Company Practice:** Over 1,000 examples of company employment and personnel documents
4. **Short Courses:** 2,100 short courses from 60 U.K. and European organizations; records contain source, language, objectives, and content
5. **Audio-visual Material:** Over 1,000 abstracts and indexes to training videos, films, and mixed media packages
6. **Training Exercises:** Details of 150 commercially available exercises for managers

Bowker-Saur UK maintains a document delivery service that supplies the materials listed on the disc.

Table 1-B. Databases Included in *HELECON*

Database Name	Language	No of Records (1992)	Entry Format	Starting Date
Delphes	French	140,000	abstracts	1980
Econis	German	300,000	references	1980
Fonds Quetelet	Belgium	115,000	references	1980
IMA-NCOM	Nordic	22,000	references	1975
SCANP	Scandinavia	29,000	references	1980
SCIMP	W. Europe	90,000	references*	1980
BISSE	Europe		index	

*Some abstracts in recent years

According to the Institute, the goal of the product is to serve as an aid rather than a substitute for course work, attending conferences, or reading books. The system should save time wasted in choosing the wrong seminar or book. The disc costs £799 (£699 for Institute members).

An evaluation of a similarly designed Bowker-Saur CD-ROM for education revealed that the education product was not up to the quality standards that librarians expect from bibliographic research products. However, this is not the target audience for the Institute.

ONLINE FULL-TEXT SOURCES

Full-text business sources online are in great demand. Many business researchers will gladly trade the breadth of coverage and depth of indexing of bibliographic files for the convenience of having the complete text of an article for immediate use. Full-text newspapers are often online within a day of their publication, and newswire services are usually updated continuously. Bibliographic files, in contrast, often lag behind the publications they index by several months. Databanks with full-text news are listed below. Full-text sources are described more extensively in Chapter 6.

Databanks with Primarily Full-Text News:
 DOW JONES NEWS RETRIEVAL
 LEXIS AND NEXIS SERVICES
 DATATIMES
 NEWSNET
Databanks with Some Full-Text News Files:
 DATA-STAR
 DIALOG
Data bases with Full-Text and/or Translated News:
 Textline—on DATA-STAR, DIALOG, NEXIS, M A I D,
  CD-ROM (Worldwide news)
 Comline—DATA-STAR, NEXIS (Japanese news),
  CD-ROM

GENERAL FINDING AIDS

The general finding aids described in this section will help you locate books, serials, periodicals, and data sources on all international business subjects. (For finding aids on a specific topic, see the chapter covering that topic.) Several of these general finding aids, such as *Ulrich's International Periodicals Directory* and the *OCLC Online Union Catalog,* are described in detail in Michael Lavin's *Business Information.* Two books were published too late in 1993 for us to examine. One is Lorna

Daniells' third edition of *Business Information Sources*, published by the University of California Press. Another bibliography that was published too late for our inclusion is the *Encyclopedia of Business Information Sources: Europe*, edited by M. Balachandran and published by Gale Research.

Locating Books, Serials, and Periodicals

Union catalogs of library holdings, such as the *OCLC Online Union Catalog* and RLIN (Research Library Information Network), are useful for establishing ownership of particular books and serials. But when used for subject searching, they may overwhelm with detail. Often, a subject search of the holdings of one strong collection is more productive. The availability of many individual library catalogs on the Internet has made them easily accessible. The online catalog of the New York Public Research Library, for example, has proven particularly valuable for its listings of current holdings of international material.

Ulrich's International Periodicals Directory and *Books in Print* use general subject headings that in the printed versions are too restrictive. These two aids can be used more effectively in their online version on DIALOG, Files 480 and 470, respectively.

DIALOG's *Journal Name Finder* (File 414) allows you to search DIALOG bibliographic files to identify journal names. The file allows quick identification of files that include a particular journal or have the most comprehensive coverage of a journal. It is particularly useful if you have abbreviations or an incomplete title. The form of the journal name appears as it does in the original database index, including abbreviations, punctuation, and spelling variations. Two other DIALOG name finder files (*DIALOG Company Name Finder,* File 416, and *DIALOG Product Name Finder,* File 413) are also useful as online finding aids.

Locating Electronic Files

The availability of full-text journals online can be established from *Full Text Online*, published by BiblioData. The Internet (the worldwide "network of networks") has thousands of potentially useful files. However, finding what you need can be tedious. AT&T provides a "directory of directories" for access to information sources on the Internet. It is freely accessible to all Internet users through Wide Area Information Service (WAIS) Archie, telnet, anonymous FTP, Gophers, or electronic mail.[1]

Statistical Sources

Business research questions often center on finding numbers. Many of the sources we describe in this book are statistical sources for a particular subject area. Described in the following section are general sources of statistics. In addition, several of the guides described by Lavin, such as *Statistics Sources* (Gale Research, Inc.), are useful for international research.

Index to International Statistics (Congressional Information Service—Monthly)

IIS is the one general index to the publications of international organizations. It indexes and abstracts the publications of about 100 intergovernmental organizations. It includes the statistical publications of the United Nations and U.N. affiliates such as the International Monetary Fund and the General Agreement on Tariffs and Trade, as well as those of the European Community and the Organization of Economic Cooperation and Development (OECD). Virtually all of the publications indexed are published in English. Updated monthly, with quarterly, annual, and multiple year cumulations, *IIS* has been published since 1983.

IIS is arranged by issuing agency. It has five separate indexes:

1. By subjects, names, and geographic areas
2. By categories:
   age
   commodity
   country
   individual company or enterprise
   industry
   sex
3. By issuing source
4. By title
5. By agency publication number for EC, OAS, and U.N. publications

In addition to its indexing, *IIS* has several other useful features:

- Membership lists for major international organizations such as the OECD and the EC
- Addresses and phone numbers for the sources of the publications
- Outlines of selected standard classification codes such as the SITC and NACE

The full texts of publications identified in *IIS* are available on microfiche from the publisher.

IIS has been available since 1989 on CD-ROM, updated quarterly. The print version of *IIS,* although detailed, does not usually index to the level of the individual economic series appearing in the publications *IIS* covers. For example, using *IIS* indexes, you will not be able to determine that import elasticity growth rates for Mexico are reported in the World Bank's annual *Trends in Developing Economies.* However, searching the CD-ROM version of *IIS* for "Mexico and elasticity and imports" would retrieve the appropriate record, a truncated version of which appears in Exhibit 1-2.

European Directory of Non-official Statistical Sources (Euromonitor, 1993)

The second edition of this directory provides details of the key non-official statistical sources in Western Europe. It mainly covers statistical sources on particular markets, industries, products, and sectors, plus general economic data. The sources include trade associations, professional bodies, research organizations, trade journals, and market research companies. Only regularly produced statistical sources are included. Arranged by issuing body, the *Directory* is indexed under 75 broad subject groups with publisher and country subdivisions. Exhibit 1-3 gives an example of a record.

Statistical Abstract of the United States (U.S. Bureau of the Census—Annual)

The *Statistical Abstract*'s section on "Comparative Economic Statistics" contains more than 50 tables giving figures for the world as a whole and for many countries on a comparative basis with the U.S. The tables often give several years of data. The tables in *Statistical Abstract* are a useful index to more detailed information. For example, a table on health expenditures gives these two sources: *OECD Health Data* and *OECD Health Systems Facts and Trends.*

The Appendix to the *Statistical Abstract* lists the sources used for the tables. A separate "Guide to Foreign Statistical Abstracts" presents recent statistical abstracts by country, noting the language of the publication. Examples of data on comparative economic statistics in *Statistical Abstract* include:

- Central bank discount rates/money market rates
- Civilian employment
- Communications (number of telephones, newspapers, televisions)
- Consumer prices
- Demographic statistics (population and vital statistics)
- Energy consumption and production
- Foreign trade
- Foreign exchange rates (20-year time series of 30 currencies)

EXHIBIT 1-2. Record from *Index to International Statistics* (CD-ROM)

```
TITLE: Trends in Developing Economies, 1991
PUB. DATE: 1991.  <0/91>
PERIODICITY: Annual.
COLLATION: vii+614 p.
ISSUING SOURCE: International Bank for Reconstruction and Development
LANGUAGE: En
LC CARD NO: 90-640763
ISSN: 1014-7004
ISBN: 0-8213-1922-1
AVAILABILITY: IBRD (Washington DC; Paris; Tokyo), $25.95.
MICROFICHE STATUS: IIS/MF

Annual report on economic trends in developing countries, varying periods
1965-90. Includes data on GDP/GNP; trade; private consumption; investment;
savings; national income; inflation; population changes; labor force;
balance of payments, by component; currency exchange rates; national
budget and deficit financing; and international financial flows and
external debt,  with IMF accounts position, and shares of IBRD and IDA
lending in debt; by   country.

Data sources: IBRD sources.
   Format and data presentation: Foreword, contents listing, and
introduction (p. iii-vii); 99 country or economic grouping sections, each
generally with 1 table (p. 1-611); and notes (p. 612-614).
   Monetary values are expressed in national currencies or US$. Trade data
include imports by product group, and exports by major commodity. Labor
force and selected GDP data are shown by sector. Not all data are shown
for each country.
   Note: Report complements World Development Report...
     MAIN TERMS (and Content Notations):
      Subjects and Authors
      -ECONOMIC.INDICATORS
        (Developing countries basic econ indicators, by country, 1960s-90..
        -ECONOMIC.AND.ECONOMETRIC.MODELS
      (Econ basic indicators, including elasticity of imports to GDP, by
       developing country, 1960s-90, IBRD annual rpt)
      -GOLD
        (Econ basic indicators, with intl reserves including/excluding gold,
        by
        developing country, 1980s-90, IBRD annual rpt)
      -MANUFACTURING
        (Trade of developing countries, by product group and commodity,
        1980s-90, IBRD annual rpt)
      Category Breakdowns
      -BY.FOREIGN.COUNTRY
        (Econ basic indicators, by developing country, 1960s-90, IBRD annual
        rpt)
      -BY.COMMODITY
        (Trade of developing countries, by product group and commodity,
        1980s-90, IBRD annual rpt)
```

- Gross Domestic Product (GDP) per capita
- Gross National Product (GNP) in constant dollars
- Growth rates of Gross Domestic Product (GDP)
- Health expenditures
- Hourly compensation for production workers in manufacturing
- Industrial production
- Labor force participation rates
- Mineral commodities (world production)
- Public debt
- Reserve assets and international transaction balances
- Tax revenues

Business Information Sourcebooks

Sometimes the information we seek is too unusual or detailed to be found in standard print or electronic sources. In such cases, it is helpful to contact people who have specialized knowledge. Often they can be found in

EXHIBIT 1-3. Sample Record from *European Directory of Non-official Statistical Sources*

ASSOCIATION OF THE GERMAN CLOCK
INDUSTRY
VERBAND DER DEUTSCHEN UHRENINDUSTRIE
**Address: Daschinger Strasse 20, 7730 Villingen-
Schwenningen, Germany**
Telephone: +49 7720 7005
Fax: +49 7720 7707

Title: Einfur-und Ausfuhr Statisik
Frequency: Various issues per year
Contact: Statistics, based on central government data, on the
imports and exports of watches and clocks.

Reprinted with permission from Euromonitor.

professional associations, research organizations, and government. Information brokers also may have knowledge of esoteric sources of information. Sourcebooks provide the information we need in this area.

Directory of International Sources of Business Information (Pitman Publishing—1989)

Written by Sarah Ball from a U.K. perspective, the *Directory* concentrates on companies, markets, finance, and economics. Because the book was published in 1989, there is nothing on Eastern Europe. A typical country entry gives names and addresses for banks, chambers of commerce, stock exchanges, securities traders, professional associations, market research organizations, and organizations providing economic and statistical data. Publications listed include company directories, major newspapers, and journals. The work is organized in several sections.

- *European Business Information Brokers* provides descriptions of business information brokers in Western Europe.
- *Country Data Sources* describes 30 mostly industrialized and newly industrialized countries, with a few surprising inclusions such as Sri Lanka.
- *Industry Data Sources* is arranged in 11 general industry groups with area and country breakdowns; this section lists trade associations, directories, market research reports, and journals.
- *Online Data Sources* offers detailed descriptions of hundreds of business time-sharing databases and their providers. Each database is given a full-page description. This section of the *Directory* is becoming obsolete as new databanks appear, as old databanks merge or go out of business, and as CD-ROMS compete with time-sharing systems.

The *Directory* contains an impressive collection of

information sources but is aging rapidly, and a new edition will be welcome.

Sources on Conducting International Business

One area of international business of importance to businesspeople, business researchers, and academics is personal conduct. Roger E. Axtell has written a series of inexpensive books published by John Wiley which cover all aspects of business protocol. The basic book in the series is *The Do's and Taboos Around the World: A Guide to International Behavior* (1990). Axtell also has written guides on hosting international visitors, cultural barriers to international trade, and understanding international body language.

SEARCHING FOR NEW INTERNATIONAL SUBJECTS

Political changes affect the way we search for business information. The political changes in Eastern Europe have scrambled the controlled vocabularies of all social science databases. It is instructive to see how business databases have reacted to these rapid and momentous changes. We use the examples of Europe, Eastern Europe, and Russia to demonstrate how databases incorporate new or changing subjects. To put these changes in context, we give a brief chronology of recent changes in Eastern Europe.

November 1989	Berlin Wall falls
October 1990	German reunification
June 1991	Slovenia and Croatia declare independence from Yugoslavia
August 1991	Baltic states (Latvia, Lithuania, and Estonia) declare independence
September 1991	USSR recognizes Baltic independence
December 1991	CIS is founded
January 1992	USSR ceases to exist
January 1, 1993	Czech and Slovakia become independent countries

It takes time for indexers to integrate changes in vocabulary into a thesaurus. New vocabulary appears first in titles and abstracts of articles. If the changes in terminology appear significant and permanent, they will be adopted as descriptors (indexing terms). New indexing terms often will appear online or on disc before they are used in print indexes. The subject vocabularies of institutions such as the Library of Congress are the slowest to change. How did the business databases handle the changing geography of Eastern Europe?

Table 1-C lists various identifying terms for Europe as a region on *ABI/Inform*. Notice the transition in the fall of 1988 from the descriptor "EEC" to the descriptor "EC." This reflects the general change from "European Economic Community" to the broader "European Community." Although the descriptors have changed, both abbreviations and both terms still appear in article titles and abstracts and can be retrieved with free-text searching.

Researchers are interested in an efficient way to identify both records about Eastern Europe and the newly emerging nations. By the end of 1991, Lithuania, Latvia, and Estonia—but not Russia—had been added to *ABI*'s descriptor field. At the beginning of 1992, *ABI* added the rest of the former Soviet republics, based on the forms used by the Associated Press.

Armenia	Russia
Azerbaijan	Tajikistan (formerly
Belarus (formerly Byelorussia)	Tadzhikistan)
Georgia	Turkmenistan (formerly
Kazakhstan	Turkmenia)
Kyrgyzstan (formerly Kirgizia)	Ukraine
Moldova (formerly Moldavia)	Uzbekistan

While it is easy to retrieve some articles on geographic areas, you often must use more than one term to find all articles. Because geography is changing rapidly, it is helpful to know when free-text words became descriptors.

Predicasts has taken a conservative approach to adding new codes. They do not want to change codes constantly and they have no mechanism for retroactively changing codes. The coding in *F&S + Text International* is *cc6* for Eastern Europe and *cc6uss* for USSR. In January 1993, *cc6uss* continued to be the Predicasts' code for the new Republic of Russia and will remain in the database for retrospective searching no matter what changes are made in the future.

PAIS has always had strong European coverage. Its commitment to worldwide coverage of social, economic,

Table 1-C. Searching for European Terms on *ABI/ INFORM*

	Free Text	Descriptor
European Community	5,199	0
EC	6,345	2,807 *
European Economic Community	1,759	0
EEC	1,868	0
EFTA	211	0
European Free Trade Association	202	0
Europe	60,309	8,774
cc 9175[code for Europe]		47,187
Eastern Europe	6,075	1,046
cc 9176 [code for Eastern Europe]		4,4,17
cc 9175 OR cc 9176		50,994
Russia	1,052	272 **
USSR	3,661	2,052 **
CIS	244	0 ***
Commonwealth of Independent States	228	0 ***
Lithuania	92	13
Estonia	90	3
Latvia	77	18
Asia [included for comparison]	28,980	1,778
cc 9179 [code for Asia]		26,845

*Added October 1988; both EC and EEC still appear in articles
**Russia first appeared at the end of January 1992; both Russia and USSR are still being used as descriptors
***CIS has multiple meanings, e.g., "customer information system"
Source: DATA-STAR, January 10, 1993

and political activities resulted in the merging of its two paper products—*PAIS Foreign Language Index* and *PAIS Bulletin*—into *PAIS International in Print* in 1991. Because *PAIS* covers social science and historical topics, the "new" nations were already used as subject headings. For example, "Slovenia" appeared in the descriptor field as early as 1980 and "Russia-Federative-Republic" has been in use for the entire time span of the CD-ROM, although few articles were given this description until recently. Exhibit 1-4 shows a *PAIS* record using the "Russia (Federative Republic)" descriptor.

EXHIBIT 1-4. *PAIS* Record

```
Fessler, Pamela.  Russia's Yeltsin charms Congress, but aid
    is another questions.  i. Congressional Quarterly Weekly
    Report. 49:1685-6 Je 22 1991

    Visit of Boris N. Yeltsin, newly elected president of...

Subject headings: 1. Yeltsin, Boris Nikolayevich. 2.
United States - Foreign relations - Soviet Union..
5.  Russia (Federative Republic)
```

PAIS' strength as an academic product is a weakness in a general library setting. Many of the articles are in foreign languages. For example, more than 60% of the articles coded "European-Economic-Community" are *not* in English. Unlike the full text and abstracts in *F&S + Text*, foreign language articles in *PAIS* are only citations.

What terms do you use to search for current information about business in Russia? Searches done on DATA-STAR in four online databases using free-text and controlled vocabulary revealed the variation in terms. The four databases are *ABI/Inform, PAIS International, Trade & Industry,* and *Textline.* DATA-STAR uses the tag .CN. to indicate controlled vocabulary for a country name. As Table 1-D illustrates, databases have always handled the USSR in different ways and continue to do so. Generally, the term "Russia" is used to refer exclusively to the nation Russia, while the term "Commonwealth" refers to the group of states making up the former USSR. *Textline* uses "Commonwealth-of-Independent-States" as its country term and "USSR" as the code. *PAIS* has a unique term, "Russian-Federative-Republic"; it does not appear in the other three databases. Geographic field codes are an important feature when using standard indexes and abstracts for international applications. Controlled vocabulary for geographic areas allows precise retrieval.

INTERNATIONAL CONFERENCES

One way to keep on top of all of the changes in international business information and the sources supporting it is to read as much as possible—the daily newspapers, the business literature, and the information literature. Another helpful, though expensive, means is to attend an international business information conference.

One such conference is the European Business Information Conference (EBIC), organized by the Task Force Pro Libra (TFPL) in London. This conference is held each spring in a major European city. The speakers include representatives from the business community, academia, and the information industry. Another conference is ORBIS, sponsored by Learned Information and CERVED, the Italian Chambers of Commerce, in September in Rome.

The International Online Meeting in London each December, sponsored by Learned Information Ltd, is an excellent source for European online and CD-ROM products. Many products displayed at this show are not yet readily available in the U.S.

Table 1-D. Vocabulary for Searching "Russia"

	ABI/ INFO	PAIS	TRADE & INDUSTRY	TEXT- LINE
USSR	3,661	959	6,229	117,252
USSR.CN.	2,048	0	350*	104,381
COMMONWEALTH INDEPENDENT	250	138	1,997	108,775
COMMONWEALTH IND ST.CN.	2	127	1,000	104,335
SOVIET UNION	1,884	10,210	43,585	106,902
SOVIET UNION.CN.	0	9,466	22,592	0
RUSSIA	1,052	992	11,822	57,280
RUSSIA.CN.	272	221	3,197	31,225
FORMER SOVIET UNION	528	4	2,358	13,058
CIS	244	22	1,792	9,927
CIS AND (RUSSIA OR SOVIET)	104	11	793	7,197
FORMER USSR	158	0	322	2,121
UNION SOVIET SOCIALIST	17	68	123	312
PAIS USES ONLY Descriptors (.DE.)				

* USSR is used as descriptor (DE) not country name (CN)
Source: DATA-STAR, January 1993

CONCLUSION

This chapter described several standard sources of U.S. business information for international business research and the use of general finding aids. In addition, we discuss some of the issues involved in searching international subjects. We compare retrieval on several major bibliographic databases using a variety of indexing terms and "free text."

Standard sources of U.S. business information can often be used as well for international research. U.S. business sources sometimes also have international companion volumes. A key finding aid for statistical sources is the *Index to International Statistics*. It is the one general index to the publications of international organizations.

NOTE

1. "AT&T to Provide Directory & Database Services on the Internet," *DATABASE* (June 1993): 9.

PART II
Company Information

CHAPTER 2
Accounting Standards and Practices

TOPICS COVERED

1. Multinational Issues
2. Role of the European Community
3. Accounting Practices in Selected Non-EC Countries
4. Emerging Markets
5. International Accounting Bodies
6. Solutions to Accounting Differences
7. Resources
8. Using Indexes to Find International Accounting Information
9. Conclusion
10. Notes

MAJOR SOURCES DISCUSSED

* *European Accounting Guide*
* *International Accounting and Reporting Issues*
* *International Accounting and Auditing Trends*
* *The Handbook of International Accounting*
* *Accounting Certification, Educational, & Reciprocity Requirements*
* *European Financial Reporting Series*
* *Accounting and Tax Index*

The purpose of accounting is to provide *information* on business activities in order to facilitate decision-making by users of financial statements.[1]

Accounting provides the tools, rules, and language of communication for financial disclosure. The information published as an outgrowth of accounting standards and practice affects the decision making of shareholders, potential investors, workers, consumers, host and partner governments, and the general public.

Accounting standards grow out of the economic and legal infrastructure of a nation's business. Within a country, sources of finance, relative importance of shareholders and creditors, and the role of government and taxation all influence accounting standards. Financial statements of companies from different countries, therefore, have major variations.

A researcher trying to compare three companies— Amstrad, IBM, and DEC—questions why Amstrad's performance based on "net income" varies greatly from its American counterparts.

This apparently straightforward question brings up a host of problems. What is net income? How is it measured? Is net income reported for Amstrad in the U.S. the same as net income reported for the company in the U.K.?

Which line of the British financial statement is the "right answer"?

Familiarity with accounting standards is essential for business research. We might not all need to know that the price earnings ratio for a Japanese company understates stockholder earnings or that the French value costs at replacement value. However, we should all be aware of potential differences in standards, practices, filing, and language in our own research or when presenting data to a client.

U.S. accounting standards, for example, provide a uniform platform for company and industry analysis. The regulations that accompany accounting and auditing principles and procedures provide the basis for internal managerial decision making, investor analysis, bank lending, and client-supplier relationships. In the U.S., accounting standards and Securities and Exchange Commission disclosure requirements are the rules for preparing financial statements. Because companies follow the same set of accounting regulations, we can make reasonable assumptions about the comparable performance of Ford, General Motors, and Chrysler by analyzing their financial statements. But can we make the same assumptions about Daimler Benz, Volvo, Renault, Fiat, and Toyota?

Pressure from North American investors and the European Community has increased the availability of company information worldwide and is slowly increasing the comparability of that information. Despite the movement for international harmonization of accounting standards, country differences in accounting standards, filing formats, and disclosure requirements directly affect the financial information presented in published and online sources.

There are also country differences between accounting standards and accounting practices, and between accounting standards and public disclosure of financial information. The growth of cross-border trading increases the need for disclosure for three reasons:

1. To maintain confidence in capital markets
2. To protect investors
3. To increase the supply of reliable information from a central source

MULTINATIONAL ISSUES

In 1989, U.S. SmithKline Beckman merged with U.K. Beecham PLC. Net income for SmithKline Beecham in 1989, according to U.K. Generally Accepted Accounting Principles (GAAP), was £130.1 million; according to U.S. GAAP, it was £87.0 million.

What country's accounting rules take precedent for a company operating in more than one country or within the EC? In preparing reports, companies have a range of choices of action to accommodate international users. These choices include:

* Doing nothing
* Preparing convenience translations
* Preparing convenience statements
* Restating on a limited basis
* Preparing secondary statements
* Preparing statements according to world standards[2]

Convenience translations are statements translated from the filing language into another language, usually English. They retain all the original accounting principles and the original currency. When translating into "English," it must be understood that "American English," as illustrated below, is different from British accounting English.

U.S.	U.K.
Sales	Turnover
Income statement	Profit and loss account
Common stock	Ordinary shares
Inventories	Stocks
Treasury stock	Own shares
Receivables	Debtors
Reserve for doubtful accounts	Provision for bad debts
Included in equity	Taken to reserves
Leverage	Gearing

Not all the translations from another language are reliable. Many accounts translated into English are different from the original language and are basically marketing brochures. A statement issued for informational purposes in a second language anywhere other than its home country does not have to obey any disclosure rules.

Convenience statements not only translate the language but also convert the currency. However, they still maintain local standards. For example, a convenience statement from a Japanese company for the U.S. investment market will be written in English and present financials in U.S. dollars, but maintain Japanese accounting standards and definitions. It is difficult to identify a convenience statement.

Restatements modify net income and balance sheet figures to meet another country's requirements. The language may be translated, but the figures are in the original currency. A company needs two sets of accounting records to issue restatements. Disclosure of restated financials appears in footnotes.

Secondary statements completely restate the annual accounts for the foreign reader. The Japanese have adopted this approach. All non-U.S. companies traded on U.S. exchanges (20-F filings) must follow this format.

World standards reporting is a rare approach. A company adopts one set of statements to meet all user needs. The accounting standards used will have universal applicability.

If you request an annual report directly from a foreign company that is not traded in your country, you will not be able to tell in advance what form of translation is used.

ROLE OF THE EUROPEAN COMMUNITY

Much of the focus of this chapter is on the European Community (EC). It is within the EC that legislated harmonization is being required. The EC, in preparation for 1992, harmonized company filing requirements and accounting standards for its 12 member countries through a series of directives, some of which are discussed in more detail in Chapter 3.

EC Directives and Harmonization Standards

EC member states have been required to incorporate these directives into their own legal frameworks. However, each state also has flexibility in exactly how the laws are enacted. No additional accounting standards will be drafted. An overview of the EC situations will give a sense of the complexity of the accounting issues researchers and investors are facing. Even where standardization has occurred, dates of implementation differ greatly, making time-series analysis for the same company risky. Three of the most important EC Company Law Directives are the Second, Fourth, and Seventh.

The *Second EC Directive* addresses public companies, including naming of companies and setting minimum capital requirements. It is discussed in detail in Chapter 3.

The *Fourth Directive* applies to public and private companies. It sets standard accounting formats, provides exemptions for small companies, and introduces accounting principles based on the U.K. Company Law principle of "true and fair value." It defines small, medium, and large companies and what *types* of information each must disclose. The Directive sets standards for types of information, but not for the actual data items. Article 2 of this Directive states the following:

1. The annual accounts shall comprise the balance sheet, the profit and loss account and the notes on the accounts. These documents shall constitute a composite whole.
2. They shall be drawn up clearly and in accordance with the provisions of this Directive.
3. The annual accounts shall give a true and fair view of the company's assets, financial position and profit or loss.

Despite the Directive, country differences still exist. In the U.K., for example, small companies must be audited; in Germany they are exempt. The meaning of "true and fair" is not defined. A good source for clarifying who must file where, and what printed and online sources are available for each country, is the *Sourceguide to European Company Information,* prepared by the London Business School and published by Gale.[3]

The *Seventh EC Directive* concerns "Group Accounting" or consolidated statements. The U.S. has been preparing consolidated figures since the beginning of the twentieth century. The U.K. and the Netherlands, which have many holding companies, also require consolidated reporting. Other countries did not require consolidated statements prior to 1985.

All groups above "medium-sized" must prepare consolidated statements and must include domestic and foreign subsidiaries. However, the directive offers many options, including how to define subsidiaries and which

to include. For example, three major European breweries used different accounting methods for consolidation in calculating greater than 50% long-term investment (1990 annuals):

Heineken NV — *Domestic* subsidiaries are consolidated; others on cost basis
Guinness PLC — *All* subsidiaries consolidated
Holsten Brauerei — Consolidation for *significant* subsidiaries; others on cost basis

Chris Nobes, who writes and speaks extensively on the subject of EC accounting, calculates that there are 51 yes/no options for the Seventh Directive alone, amounting to "2 zillion" possible ways to handle group accounting![4]

Table 2-A shows the year when each country adopted the Fourth and Seventh Directives into national law. The dates of adoption vary by as much as a decade.

Table 2-A. National Adoption Dates for the Fourth and Seventh EC Directives

	Fourth	Seventh
Drafts published	1971,1974	1976,1978
Adoption by EC Council	1978	1983
Belgium	1985	1990
Denmark	1981	1990
France	1983	1985
Germany	1985	1985
Greece	1987	1987
Ireland	1986	1992
Italy	1991	1991
Luxembourg	1984	1988
Netherlands	1983	1988*
Portugal	1989	1991
Spain	1989	1989
U.K.	1981	1989*

* Consolidated accounting predated implementation of EC Directive

Standardization Problems in the EC

Despite the Directives and country company laws, there are still unresolved issues.[5] These include:

- Availability of published accounting data
- Language problems
- Extent and type of audit
- Format or presentation of financial statements
- Frequency of reports
- Quantity of data disclosed
- Different currencies
- Biases in the accounting data
- User friendliness of annual reports
- Valuation of assets
- Measurement of profits
- Cultural differences

Publication and Audit. There is universal audit in the U.K. for all companies filing with the national registration body, Companies House. In Germany, only large companies are audited. Because banks are major shareholders in Germany and Switzerland, there has been less pressure for public disclosure in these countries. Table 2-B shows the variation in size criteria used to exempt companies from some or all reporting and auditing requirements. For example, U.K. companies with sales of less than about $3 million are exempt from publication, but not from audit.

European annual reports are often filed and published many months after the year-end closing date. However, in the U.K., companies must file news releases with the Official Companies Register, an arm of Companies House, so data are available in sources such as *Extel Cards* or in news databases well before they are available in the annual report.

Format or Presentation. The presentation format for accounts is based on national choice. There is no single standard template. Frequency of filing, terminology used, and the quantity of data required also vary among countries. The physical layout of reports also vary. French and German company reports are horizontal while British reports are vertical. The order of presentation also varies. On a U.S. balance sheet, the most liquid assets, current assets, come first. In other countries they come last. See Appendix D for sample U.K. and French balance sheets.

Currency Translation in Accounting Practice. The EC has no directives on currency translation. The U.K., Ireland, and the Netherlands have standards but no laws. France and Germany have neither standards nor laws. What exchange rate does a company use to record its international transactions? These transactions can include purchases, sales, or subsidiary activities. What do multinational corporations do in practice? There are different approaches for different financial items:

1. Items on a company's own accounts are frozen on the date of purchase. For example, a French company buys a German computer system and records the cost of the asset in francs per date of purchase. This is called the "temporal" exchange rate.
2. Long-term liabilities use fiscal year-end date. Therefore, a U.K. company with a December 31 year-end date should translate U.S. debt at 1.87 dollars per pound sterling in 1991 and 1.52 dollars per pound sterling in 1992.
3. Losses usually are translated immediately into profit and loss accounts as in Item #1 but gains may be handled differently.
4. Balance sheets for the foreign subsidiaries of multinationals use the fiscal year-end rate as in Item #3, where the pound to dollar rate for December 31, 1992 was 1.52. Profit and loss statements for the foreign subsidiares may apply average rates for the fiscal year or median rates. For 1992, the exchange rate using the average method was 1.72, while using the median, it was 1.92.

Several questions arise. When a temporal exchange rate is used, debits and credits do not balance. The difference is placed in the reserve account. In the next

Table 2-B. Size Criteria Exempting Companies from Reporting and Auditing (recalculated in millions of U.S. dollars for week ending December 25, 1992 for comparison)

	U.K.	France	Netherlands	Germany
Small:				
Turnover (Sales)	3.128	1.867	4.539	5.105
Employees	50	50	50	50
Balance Sheet Total	1.525	.933	2.269	2.489
Medium:				
Turnover (Sales)	12.512	*	19.857	20.419
Employees	250		250	250
Balance Sheet Total	6.100		9.645	9.890

Exemptions in U.K.:
—Small companies exempt from publication, but not from audit; provide profit and loss account and directors' report; publish abbreviated balance sheet for shareholders
—Medium companies publish abbreviated profit and loss

Notes:

* France	—Abridged accounts and notes may be published for small and medium companies
Netherlands	—Small companies file abbreviated formats from statements; exempt from audit
	—Medium companies file abbreviated profit and loss
Germany	—Small companies exempt from audit
	—Medium companies audited by a different body

Source: Baring Securities Guide to International Financial Reporting (Oxford: Basil Blackwell, 1991), p. 4

section we will look at valuing fixed assets, but from a currency perspective the question becomes what exchange rate do you use for fixed assets? U.S. multinationals use the balance sheet date for the balance sheet exchange and a yearly average for the income statement. This is also recommended international practice.

Valuation of Assets and Measurement of Profit. Researchers interested in analyzing European balance sheets and income statements may be unaware of the different methods of valuation of assets and measurement of profits. As Table 2-C shows, fixed asset valuation (property, plant, and equipment) varies from strict historical costs, to revaluation, to current costs.

Table 2-C. How European Countries Value Assets

Germany	Historical costs; no revaluation; often based on post-World War II figures (1946-48; e.g., Daimler Benz)
France	1976 prices
Italy	1983 prices
Spain	1984 prices
Greece	Frequent revisions
U.K., Ireland	Company choice
Netherlands	Some company choice based on replacement costs

The conservative German approach, using historical cost set at 1946 prices, results from the banking sector's use of the lowest figures.

Conservatism also affects the measurement of profit. In France, Germany, Belgium, and Italy, companies must set aside about one percent of annual profit in a statutory reserve fund. There are also hidden reserves. For example, most German companies do not account for "goodwill." Knowledgeable analysts will inflate German profit figures to be used in comparisons.[6]

Other EC Accounting Issues

Segment data for both line of business and geographic segments is generally accepted accounting practice in the U.S. Segment data are still not widely reported outside the U.S. The EC requires that sales be split by sector and market. The 1985 U.K. Companies Act assesses pretax profit by sector and U.K. accounting practice adds turnover and capital employed as other data items reported by segment.

Goodwill is another accounting item handled in a variety of ways. The valuation of goodwill, especially in mergers and acquisitions, affects the balance sheet, shareholders equity, and income statements. Anyone interested in an in-depth analysis of goodwill, with examples of different accounting practices, should read the *Abacas*

article by Brunovs and Kirsch, "Goodwill Accounting in Selected Countries and the Harmonization of International Accounting Standards."[7]

Unique European disclosure components, which do not appear on statements of companies from other regions, include value added statement, employees, and environmental or social issues. Flow of funds and earnings, however, are often excluded.

Inflation is another important accounting issue. It does not affect the EC as much as other parts of the world. Accounting based on historical costs is obviously distorted in times of inflation. One approach to accounting for inflation is general price level or constant dollar accounting. In this method, assets and liabilities reflect the currency's purchasing power; the balance sheet is reported in units. A second approach is the current value method in which assets and liabilities are changed to current dollars. The former approach has been used in South America and in Israel and has been recommended for international practice.[8]

Financial Culture

The underlying financial culture in a country affects financial statements, accounting principles, and disclosure practices. Legal systems and tax law both have an impact on accounting and disclosure. All discussions of accounting standards describe the dichotomy between common law and roman law countries. Common law countries include the United Kingdom, members of the British Commonwealth, and the United States. Most of the European continent uses roman law. Table 2-D categorizes countries by their legal systems. This categorization will be referred to in discussing other regulatory issues throughout this book.

Table 2-D. Categorization of Countries by Type of Legal System

Common Law	*Roman Law, codified*
United States	Germany
United Kingdom	France
Ireland	Italy
Canada	Spain
Australia	Netherlands
New Zealand	Japan (commercial)

Source: *Baring Securities Guide to International Financial Reporting* (London: Basil Blackwell, 1991), p. 10

Common Law. Common law is English in origin and is grounded in concepts of the "reasonable man" and "true and fair view." The financial culture in common law countries has been shaped by company demands and a principle of "true and fair value." "True and fair value" has been incorporated into EC law. In theory that means that firms go beyond the legal requirements in presenting their accounts. There has been a history in common law countries of widespread share ownership, separate financial and taxation accounting theory, and an unimportance of theory. Enforcement is only through court action, after a complaint is filed. Accounting regulations are prepared by professional bodies. There is a limited amount of government control.

Roman Law. Countries with legal systems based on roman law, such as France and Spain, depend on extensive government involvement. Roman law systems are based on detailed, codified law, rather than common practice. Accounting regulations are prepared by government-run committees. In Germany and Switzerland, the financial culture is driven by banks, which, rather than individual investors, are the primary sources of corporate funding.

Reporting for Taxation

Reporting for taxation is a description of past performance necessary to compute tax obligations. It differs from financial reporting which is both a description of present conditions and an aid to future decision making. There are three models of tax regulations relative to financial disclosure

- Uniformity of reporting, where tax rules and accounting regulations are the same
- Separation of reporting (the U.S. model), where reporting for taxation is separate from financial reporting
- Adjustment in reporting, where one set of rules is modified to apply to taxation and financial disclosure

Table 2-E categorizes countries by those in which tax rules have little influence on accounting, as in the U.S., and those in which tax rules have a heavy influence on accounting, as in Germany.

Table 2-E. Tax Rules and Accounting

U.K. Model (Little direct influence of tax rules on accounting)	*Continental Model* (Heavy influence of tax rules on accounting)
U.S.	Germany
U.K.	Japan
Ireland	Belgium
Canada	Italy
Australia	Spain
New Zealand	Portugal
Hong Kong	Switzerland
Singapore	Sweden

Source: Baring Securities Guide to International Financial Reporting (London: Basil Blackwell, 1991), p. 11

The tax rules for the EC are well documented. Publications are available in EC depository libraries and in many online databases.

ACCOUNTING PRACTICES IN SELECTED NON-EC COUNTRIES

Europe

Switzerland does not require disclosure. The country is not a member of the EC and is not controlled by EC company directives. In addition, full disclosure is not required because Switzerland is a country in which the banks rather than the shareholders have the greater influence. However, disclosure requirements are changing as the result of a revision in Swiss company law in July 1992. Quoted companies are being required to come into line with international accounting practices.

Austria is not a member of the EC, but is incorporating the Fourth, Seventh, and Eighth, EC directives into its Corporation Law and will require consolidated accounts from 1994. Tax law supplements corporation law and historical costing is used.

Norwegian companies comply with a 1976 Companies Act and a 1977 Accounting Act. All companies with control exercised by voting shares prepare consolidated accounts based on historic costs. The accounts are filed with the Central Registrar of Companies and are available for public inspection.

Swedish groups follow the 1975 Companies Act and prepare consolidated accounts filed with the Royal Patent and Registration Office within seven months of year-end and are available for public inspection. Historic cost conventions are used but revaluations are allowed.

Japan

Japanese accounting standards are hybrid. They derive from medieval double-entry bookkeeping, borrow from German and French commercial codes of the late nineteenth century, and incorporate U.S. post-World War II securities legislation. Table 2-F categorizes the origins of Japanese accounting standards.

Table 2-F. Origins of Japanese Accounting Standards

From the German Style	*From the U.S. Style*
Accounting controlled by government	Special rules for public companies
Uniform formats like Fourth EC Directive	Full consolidated accounts for public companies

Table 2-F. Origins of Japanese Accounting Standards *(continued)*

From the German Style	From the U.S. Style
Dominance of tax rules in depreciation	U.S. balance sheet order
Historical cost valuation (also U.S.)	Amortization of goodwill
Form over substance	U.S. terminology
Requirement for legal reserve	Disclosure of earnings per share

There are three forms of government influence on accounting practice in Japan: the commercial code, the Securities and Exchange Law, and the tax law.

1. **The Japanese Commercial Code**, under the Ministry of Justice, applies to the one million joint stock companies, called *kabushiki kaisha* (KK). While these companies must file statements to the ministry, the statements are generally not available to the public.
2. **The Securities and Exchange Law (SEL)**, from the Ministry of Finance, applies to the 3,000 companies that have raised more than 100 million yen from the public, have their shares listed on a Japanese stock exchange, or are traded over the counter. The law is modelled on the U.S. SEC. Independent audit, public filings, and consolidated accounts are all required. These filings are available to the public.

   The Commercial Code favors protection of creditors over shareholders, while the SEL favors the protection of the investor. Because the largest companies are under the jurisdiction of the SEL, it is powerful in shaping accounting practice.
3. **Tax law** is another government influence on accounting practice, especially in the area of depreciation. Japanese companies, unlike U.S. companies, do not prepare separate tax filings.

Accounting principles and the equivalent of Japanese GAAP are presented in *Financial Accounting Standards for Business Enterprises*, from Business Accounting Deliberation Council. BADC advises the Ministry of Finance and has sole responsibility for establishing accounting and financial reporting standards.

Japanese companies trading in the U.S. follow U.S. SEC guidelines; other English language accounts may be convenience translations. Many companies produce reports in "American English," in dollars as well as yen, and adjust for either GAAP or IAS. However, the convenience translations are not always an accurate translation of the statutory account.[9]

Table 2-G lists the financial items Japanese companies are required to file.

Table 2-G. Required Japanese Filings

Commercial Code Parent: Kabushiki Kaisha	Securities and Exchange Law Parent: Stock exchange Company
Balance Sheet	Balance Sheet
Income Statement	Income Statement
Business Report	including cost of goods manufactured
Proposal for appropriation of retained earnings	Statement of appropriation of retained earnings
Supporting Schedules	Supporting Schedules
Consolidated Accounts	

Source: Frederick Choi, *Handbook of International Accounting*, pp. 5.12-5.13

The BADC has prescribed a set of standards for foreign currency translation, for short-term transactions, long-term transactions, and for foreign branches and foreign subsidiaries. There is no reporting for either business or geographic segments.[10]

Australia and New Zealand

Australia and New Zealand are part of the common law accounting model. Australia introduced a revised Corporations Law and new valuation accounting standards in late 1991. As of mid-1992, there was still confusion over methods of valuation and filing requirements for small companies. The Corporations Law now requires consolidated accounting, and compliance of financial accounts with accounting standards in order that balance sheets have some "connection with reality" and with "true and fair value." The Australian Accounting Standards Board issued "Accounting for the Revaluation of Non-current Assets" which revised the method for revaluing non-current assets to reflect their recoverable amount. However, because companies interpret the standard in different ways, valuation of company assets in Australia is more art than science.[11]

The effect of all these changes and the inconsistent manner of their adoption indicates that comparison with past statements or with other Australian companies is, as the *Australian Financial Review* says, "not straightforward."[12]

January 1, 1993 marked the date of major revisions to New Zealand's financial reporting and accounting standards based on the Company's Bill first introduced in 1990. An accounting standards review board was established. New standards, applying to private and public sector entities, are being drafted under a new name: Financial Reporting Standards. In addition, the

Accountant's Society has issued exposure drafts dealing with differential reporting for small entities (companies with under $1.5 million New Zealand in sales and less than 10 employees).

EMERGING MARKETS

If there are accounting snares within the well-legislated, well-regulated industrialized countries, there are landmines in the financial accounts from emerging nations. The accounting problems common to new markets include:

- Lax accounting
- Poor liquidity
- Slow and difficult settlement
- Share price manipulation
- Insider dealing
- Scarcity of accurate and timely information[13]

Many emerging nations have not yet developed internal standards or Western accounting and filing systems. One exception is Chile, which has been issuing a series of "Circulars" on accounting and disclosure practices. Circular Nos. 869, 922, and 931, for example, stipulate the information to be given to the public.[14] South Korean companies, in contrast, have a relaxed accounting system, with no consolidated filing.

In general, insider trading is both legal in emerging markets and common in some Southeast Asian markets. Therefore, there is less need or demand locally for reliable public information.

Eastern Europe

New financial markets and privitized companies in Eastern Europe and the former Soviet Union are trying to cope with Western accounting and filing rules. The reform process underway varies in the individual countries, depending on whether it is being driven by joint ventures, as in the former USSR, or by privatization, as in Poland and Hungary.

In the past, the objective of accounting was to provide information for the centrally planned economy. Accounting was "bookkeeping," based on detailed instructions from the appropriate ministry. Since prices and exchange rates were controlled by the government, there was no measurable profit or loss.

Information about the new accounting standards in Eastern Europe is available online through the LEXIS AND NEXIS SERVICES from articles found in the ALLEUR file of the EUROPE library, NEXIS CURRNT,

and in the *Textline* database. The newsletter *World Accounting Report* has a quarterly update on Eastern Europe.

By the end of 1992, *Russian* companies had to prepare accounts based on procedures established by the Ministry of Finance. The latest version appears in the "Instructions on the Use of the Plan of Accounts for Financial and Business Accounting of Enterprises," effective as of January 1, 1992. With the exception of banks and "budget supported agencies," all enterprises using double-entry bookkeeping, including joint ventures and foreign-owned companies, must comply.[15]

An outline of the new *Hungarian* law was published in the January 1, 1992 issue of *Accountancy*. Hungary is incorporating EC principles and international standards to gain quick acceptance from the West. All economic organizations must prepare annual reports ranging from a consolidated statement to a simplified balance sheet for small companies. Some of the accounting laws still use "bookkeeping" terminology and address the form of the books themselves. "Share companies" (public companies), large limited liability companies, and issuers of bonds must publish annual reports. These new laws go into effect January 1, 1994 for large companies, January 1, 1996 for medium companies, and January 1, 1998 for the majority of enterprises.

In *Poland* a decree issued in January 1991 introduced accounting requirements for profit and loss statements and assets and liabilities. The Ministry of Finance has published a sample, but not mandatory, accounts format. The Commercial Code requires that joint stock companies have an annual audit, but the audit is concerned with adherence to tax regulations, not "true and fair" value. Over the next few years, Poland will phase in new auditing procedures, meeting international accounting standards.[16]

INTERNATIONAL ACCOUNTING BODIES

In the U.S., a private body, the Financial Accounting Standards Board (FASB), issues accounting standards. A governmental body, the Securities and Exchange Commission (SEC), enforces the standards as they apply to companies required to file with it. Professional associations, such as the American Institute of Certified Public Accountants, contribute to the formulation of standards. The U.S. differs from the EC in that only companies filing with the SEC have to be audited and to publish reports.

There are many associations concerned with the harmonization of accounting and auditing standards and practices. In addition to the legal approach toward harmonization taken by the EC, the International Accounting Standards Committee, International Federation of Accountants, the Organization for Economic Cooperation and Development (OECD), and the United Nations are all working both independently and cooperatively to harmonize accounting standards. Some major accounting organizations and their acronyms are listed below.

Acronym	Organization
IASC	International Accounting Standards Committee
IFAC	International Federation of Accountants
IOSCO	International Organization of Securities Commissions
FASB	Financial Accounting Standards Board (U.S.)
AICPA	American Institute of Certified Public Accountants
SEC	Securities and Exchange Commission (U.S.)
BADC	Business Accounting Deliberations Council (Japan)
ISAR	Intergovernmental Working Group of Experts on International Standards of Accounting and Reporting (UN)
FEE	Fédération des Experts Comptables Européens

International Accounting Standards Committee

The International Accounting Standards Committee (IASC) was founded in 1973 as a result of an agreement by the accountancy bodies in the following countries:

Australia	Mexico
Canada	Netherlands
France	United Kingdom
Germany	Ireland
Japan	U.S.

By 1990, this London-based organization was supported by more than 100 professional accounting bodies from 80 countries. It functions like the U.S. FASB with its stated role being to

> contribute to the development and adoption of accounting principles that are relevant, balanced and comparable internationally and to their observance in the presentation of financial statements (IASC Objectives and Procedures).

Therefore, the IASC provides a framework for *harmonized* standards that are *non*-binding. It issues "world class" standards, which must be approved by three-quarters of the members. It also prepares exposure drafts that must be approved by a two-thirds majority of the IASC Board before being distributed to members. The language of approved exposure drafts and standards is English. National members of IASC are responsible for translating the documents into local languages.

The regulations governing the IASC are contained in the 1983 "International Accounting Standards Committee Objectives and Procedures," the full text of which is available on the *NAARS* database through the LEXIS AND NEXIS SERVICES.

Member bodies agree to support the standards and encourage their local organizations to incorporate them into accounting practice. Some countries, such as Malaysia, which had not had standards of their own, have adopted IASC standards as national standards. In general, however, enforcement has been a problem. IASC's goal is to complete its international standards by the end of 1993.

The titles of standards released by the IASC as of September 1993 are listed in Table 2-H. No new standards have been adopted since December 1990.

Table 2-H. IASC Standards in Effect September 1993

IAS 1	Disclosure of accounting policies
IAS 2	Valuation and presentation of inventories in the context of the historical cost system
IAS 4	Depreciation accounting
IAS 5	Information to be disclosed in financial statements
IAS 7	Statement of changes in financial position
IAS 8	Unusual and prior period items and changes in accounting policies
IAS 9	Accounting for research & development activities
IAS 10	Contingencies and events occurring after the balance sheet date
IAS 11	Accounting for construction contracts
IAS 12	Accounting for taxes on income
IAS 13	Presentation of current assets and current liabilities
IAS 14	Reporting financial information by segment
IAS 15	Information reflecting the effects of changing prices (superceded IAS 6)
IAS 16	Accounting for property, plant and equipment
IAS 17	Accounting for leases
IAS 18	Revenue recognition
IAS 19	Accounting for retirement benefits in the financial statement of employers
IAS 20	Accounting for government grants and disclosure of government assistance
IAS 21	Accounting for the effects of changes in foreign exchange rates
IAS 22	Accounting for business combinations; includes treatment of positive and negative goodwill and valuing acquisitions
IAS 23	Capitalization of borrowing costs
IAS 24	Related party disclosure

Table 2-H. IASC Standards in Effect September 1993 *(continued)*

IAS 25	Accounting for investments
IAS 26	Accounting and reporting by retirement benefit plans
IAS 27	Consolidated financial statements and accounting for subsidiaries (superseded IAS 3)
IAS 28	Accounting for investments in associates
IAS 29	Financial reporting in hyperinflationary economies
IAS 30	Disclosure in the financial statements of banks and similar financial institutions
IAS 31	Financial reporting interests in joint ventures

The full text of the IASC standards are published in *International Accounting Standards: The Full Texts of All International Accounting Standards Extant at 1 January 1990.*[17] The full text of all the standards is also available on *NAARS.*

Other Accounting Bodies

The International Federation of Accountants (IFAC) was created in 1977 to serve as the professional organization for accountants from IASC bodies. The IFAC is similar to the American Institute of Certified Public Accountants (AICPA). All members of the IFAC are members of the IASC. According to its constitution, the IFAC's broad objective is "the development and enhancement of a coordinated worldwide accountancy profession with harmonized standards."

The IFAC currently sponsors the World Congress of Accountants, which has met every five years since 1962. The 14th Congress met in Washington D.C. in October 1992. The IFAC itself was formed after the 11th Congress, as the result of an agreement signed by 63 accountancy bodies representing 49 countries.

The OECD Working Group on Accounting Standards was set up by the Committee on International Investment and Multinational Enterprises in 1979. Its goal is to promote harmonization of accounting practices in OECD countries. It also cooperates with the other multinational accounting bodies, such as the IASC and the Fédération des Experts Comptables Européens (FEE). OECD guidelines are not legally enforceable and are not intended to supersede national requirements. The guidelines may be more strict than national rules. Multinational enterprises from OECD countries are encouraged to voluntarily supply any additional information. The guidelines have several objectives.

1. To address all categories of companies with "complex structure"
2. To focus on *information* in consolidated financial statements

3. To set objectives for information disclosure to meet the needs of all categories of users of financial statements[18]

The Fédération des Experts Comptables Européens (FEE) is the coordinating organization for the accountancy profession in Europe. It was founded in 1987 by the merger of two other European accounting bodies. It comprises national accounting bodies of 34 member states, including all the countries in the EC. It has taken on the role of spokesperson for the European accountancy profession in the IFAC.

The Intergovernmental Working Group of Experts on International Standards of Accounting and Reporting (ISAR) was founded by the United Nations in 1977 and is part of the United Nations Centre on Transnational Corporations. Its central role is in developing guidelines for transnational corporations in the area of information disclosure and accounting practices. It participates in discussions on harmonization, writes technical papers, and publishes an annual review, which is discussed below. At the end of 1990, it had 28 members from developing countries as well as developed countries. Membership is on a rotating basis. The United States and Canada are not members.

The International Organization of Securities Commissions (IOSCO), founded in the 1970s and based in Montreal, is another player. It focuses on the free flow of cross-border capital and the harmonization of securities markets. IOSC has been working with 36 emerging markets. It has been pressuring the IASC to reduce options allowable in its standards and it will pressure quoted companies to comply with IASC Standards. IASC Exposure Draft 32, discussed below, was introduced in response to the IOSCO interaction.

Effect of International Standards on Local Practice

The IASC standards, if widely adopted internationally, will present problems for U.S. multinationals. IASC Exposure Draft 32, *Comparability of Financial Statements*, introduced in 1989, has proposed amendments to many standards and would affect the way U.S. companies handle their accounts.

There are three major areas of concern for U.S. firms in three standards. For all three standards, listed below, the IAS practice differs from standard U.S. practice.

- IAS 22 addresses business combinations and the amortization of goodwill as part of mergers and acquisitions
- IAS 2 addresses "Inventory accounting" and disallows the use of LIFO (last in, first out), widely applied in the U.S.

- IAS 9 requires a method of accounting for research and development activites which is different from U.S. practice

The new standards will also affect the German practice of hidden reserves and the U.K.'s method of handling goodwill.

We have noted that international companies trading in the U.S. must modify their accounts to meet U.S. standards and that other multinationals may prepare convenience reports to meet U.S. practices. Now U.S. companies will have to prepare reports to meet international standards when reporting to European or Japanese shareholders.

Accountancy Profession

Most countries have accounting and auditing bodies. The number of accountants per country varies. Some differences in numbers are a result of the types of legal systems and sources of funds. Those countries whose accounting standards are based on common law tend to have more accountants than the roman law countries. According to *Morningstar Japan*, in Japan "the ratio of accountants to the population is about 1 to 12,000. In the U.S. the ratio is 1 to 800."[19]

The pressure to harmonize international accounting standards has affected the accounting profession. One result of required filings of audited statements has been a need for more accountants worldwide. Another side effect is the issue of reciprocity of licensing.

- Can a U.S. CPA practice in France?
- Should a Japanese CPA be able to audit statements in the U.S.?

In the U.S. each state sets its own standards for licensing CPAs. On the other hand, the EC, through the Eighth EC Company Law Directive and the *Directive on the Mutual Recognition of Professional Qualifications,* now has transcontinental professional practice.[20] The FEE has proposed supplemental requirements to the EC, including a written or oral exam for candidates wishing to practice in other member states.

The Institute of Chartered Accountants of England and Wales has reciprocal agreements with other commonwealth chartered accountants, including those in Australia, Canada, New Zealand, Scotland, and Northern Ireland. A selected list of countries' reciprocity practices appears in Gupta's January 1992 article in the *Journal of Accountancy.*[21] He cites various volumes in the Price Waterhouse *Doing Business In...* series as his source. A more complete list is published in Jack Fay's *Accounting*

Certification, Educational, & Reciprocity Requirements: An International Guide, described later in this chapter.

In 1990, the U.K. Accounting Standards Committee (ASC), the British equivalent of the AICPA, was replaced by the Accounting Standards Board, and given more power. The Accounting Standards Board issues fewer standards with less detail than did the ASC. The standards apply to all companies. The *Statements of Standard Accounting Practice* (SSAP) are the U.K. equivalent of the U.S. Financial Accounting Standards Board's *Statements of Financial Accounting Standards.* The Board intends to use the IASC conceptual framework. Germany and France also have separate state-run auditing bodies whose members act as regulators. Appendix A in Jack R. Fay's *Accounting Certification, Educational, & Reciprocity Requirements: An International Guide* has an extensive list of major accounting organizations. Addresses for the major auditing and accounting organizations for European countries are included in the *European Accounting Guide,* discussed below.

Big Six Accounting Firms

What effect has globalization had on the accounting and auditing profession? The U.S. "Big Six" (who had for years been the "Big Eight" until mergers reduced the number) dominate the international scene. Ranked by worldwide fee income, they are KPMG Peat Marwick, Ernst & Young, Coopers & Lybrand, Arthur Andersen, Deloitte Touche Tohmatsu, and Price Waterhouse. These firms audit 494 of the U.S. Fortune 500 and 96 out of the 100 biggest U.K. companies.[22]

In non-Western cultures, demand for accountants is increasing with growth in the capital markets and joint ventures. An example is Saudi Arabia, which has about 255 CPA offices, with 15 large firms. The large firms include the international Big Six, whose partners are primarily from the U.S. The Big Six firms account for 75% of the revenue generated by the accounting firms.

Accountancy reported in April 1992 that the "Big Six accountancy firms are establishing themselves in the Commonwealth of Independent States (CIS) at the speed that would impress McDonalds."[23] The first professional organization in Russia is the Moscow Audit Chamber, designed to promote auditing practices and improve training. *BizEcon* reported more than 150 different auditing organizations just in Moscow by October 1992.[24]

SOLUTIONS TO ACCOUNTING DIFFERENCES

Ratios

Ratio analysis is often recommended as a way to circumvent problems created by different languages, currencies, principles, and practices. Unfortunately, ratio analysis has its own set of problems. Ratios are computed on raw data. Accounting definitions vary widely as do the perceptions of what constitutes a "good" or "bad" ratio. For example, in Japan, a high debt/assets ratio is considered good because it indicates the company is able to get money from a bank. Japanese banks consider a low debt/assets ratio a sign that no one will lend to the company.

As a business researcher, it is important to be aware that you cannot compare the performance of companies among countries against a uniform standard, even if you use ratio analysis. What is considered acceptable practice in Germany, based either on financial culture or accounting standards and practice, may not be acceptable in Japan or the United States. Sources of ratios are discussed in Chapter 5.

Footnotes to Financial Statements and Company Accounting Practices

As an aid to interpreting financial statements, researchers and analysts need the footnotes from the annual statements as well as accounting standards. Access to the footnotes is important to researchers using convenience statements, in order to determine how the company has compiled its accounts. They are also important to researchers using commercial sources of financial information, which restate data to fit into standard formats. Three of the major commercial sources of worldwide financial information—EXTEL, Worldscope, and CIFAR—attempt to deal with accounting and format differences by presenting standardized data items, as well as data "as reported." For example, an EXTEL brochure states that

> to allow searches on financial data regardless of the accounting principles, currency, country of origin or reporting structures used by an individual company, EXTEL has selected 39 elements of key financial data for the Annual Card and presents each element in local currency, pounds sterling and in U.S. dollar equivalents.

In other words, many commercial financial sources standardize the output structure of the data they present, but do not standardize either the data or the data measure-

ment! Standard and Poor's, however, in its *Global Vantage* product, recalculates the data as well. Access to the footnotes of financial statements is important for understanding how the data have been standardized. For examples of footnotes on CD-ROM products, see Chapter 5, Exhibit 5-3.

RESOURCES

Four scholars whose research and writing on international accounting are helpful for the non-accountant are Christopher Nobes, Vinod Bavishi, Gerhard G. Mueller, and Frederick D.S. Choi. Christopher Nobes, a British accounting professor, writes extensively on international accounting standards and practices. Vinod Bavishi began collecting international annual reports when he was a professor at the University of Connecticut and has since established the Center for International Financial Research and Analysis (CIFAR), which conducts extensive research into these accounting and financial issues. Gerhard G. Mueller and Frederick D.S. Choi also have written books and articles that are both informative and understandable to a non-accountant. Some of their publications are listed below.

Sources of Information about Accounting Practices

European Accounting Guide (distributed in the U.S. by Harcourt Brace Jovanovich, 1st ed., 1991)

One of the standard accounting sources in the United States is the *Miller GAAP Guide* (Guide to U.S. Generally Accepted Accounting Principles). The *European Accounting Guide*, edited by David Alexander and Simon Archer, was first published in 1991 as a companion to *Miller*. As we have seen, company law, rather than generally accepted accounting principles, determines accounting practice in most countries. Although there are no generally accepted accounting principles for all Europe, there are standards within each country and similar issues that need to be addressed.

The *European Accounting Guide* is arranged by country. The first edition covers the EC, five other European countries, and four Eastern European countries. Each country chapter includes sections on background, published financial statements, valuation and income measurement, future developments, and specimen financial statements, both in the original language and in English. In the spirit of European accounting, the content of standard chapter sections varies by country.

The chapters have been written by local experts and are moderately easy to understand. You do not need to be a CPA to read the book. The *European Accounting Guide* is useful for any library offering international financial information. Sample chapter subheadings include information about the accounting profession, the form and content of published reports, accounting policies and practices with implications for the analyst, and accounting for specific requirements, such as group accounts, goodwill, and foreign currency translation.

The chapters for the Eastern European countries—Czechoslovakia [sic], Hungary, Poland, and the USSR [sic]—follow a similar format, though each chapter is considerably shorter than those for the rest of the continent. Exhibit 2-1 is a sample financial report from the *European Accounting Guide* presented to illustrate Polish financial statements.

International Accounting and Reporting Issues (United Nations Transnational Corporations and Management Division—Annual)

International Accounting and Reporting Issues is a record of the accomplishments of the Intergovernmental Working Group of Experts on International Standards of Accounting and Reporting (ISAR). It also contains developments in accounting and reporting in more than 40 countries ranging from the U.K. to Zaire, and from Bolivia to Myanmar. Not all countries are covered in each issue. The coverage varies from a paragraph to a few pages. For example, the entry on Bolivia sets down filing requirements for all public and private enterprise. The entry on Kenya presents a table of Kenyan Accounting Standards (KAS), with KAS number, description, issue, and effective date. At the other end of the procedural spectrum, the entry for Myanmar states that not only are there no legal requirements or accounting standards but

also "no professional body has been given the authority to set corporate accounting or reporting standards." Prior to the 1992 editon, the work was published by the United Nations Centre for Transnational Corporations.

The UN's Transnational Division has a Working Group that also reviews special topics. Exhibit 2-2 is from a survey of financial statements of transnational corporations. The survey included the degree of compliance with international accounting standards. Breakdowns for compliance are given by accounting item, by country, and by industry sector.

EXHIBIT 2-2. Compliance with International Accounting Standards

Table 2. Degree of compliance, by country

Country	Yes	No
	(Percentage)	
Australia	63	37
Belgium	44	56
Canada	67	33
France	61	39
Germany, Federal Republic of	58	42
Italy	62	38
Japan	49	51
Netherlands	61	39
Sweden	63	37
Switzerland	46	54
United Kingdom	72	28
United States	68	32
Average	61	39

Source: *UNCTC International Accounting and Reporting Issues: 1990 Review* (New York: U.N., 1991), p. 49. Reprinted with permission.

The 1991 edition has chapters on "Accounting and Reporting During and After the Transition from Public to

---

EXHIBIT 2-1. Sample Report from *European Accounting Guide*

```
Format of Polish Financial Statements
(from 1991)

Balance Sheet

Aktywa                              Assets
A.  Aktywa zmniejszajace kapitaly   A.  Assets decreasing equity
        wlasné
    1. Nalezne wplaty na poczet          1. Subscribed capital
       kapitalu                             unpaid

B.  Majatek trwaly                  B.  Fixes assets
    1. Rzeczowe i zrownane z nimi       1.  Tangible assets
       skladnik
```

Source: European Accounting Guide, 1st ed., p. 33. Reprinted with permission from Academic Press, Ltd.

Private Enterprise" and "Accounting for Environmental Protection Measures." Finally, the publication contains a table on the IASC proposals for the comparability of financial statements, including the IAS number, the issues the proposal addresses, the required benchmark, the alternative accounting methods that would be eliminated, and status as of December 1990.

Spicer & Oppenheim Guide to Financial Statements Around the World (John Wiley & Sons, 2nd ed., 1989)

This guide has standardized information on 37 individual countries, plus international standards, EC information, and a glossary. Its stated purpose is to "give a brief description and explanation of the accounting and reported practices in selected countries." It is designed to be used to compare procedures among countries.

It has information on all EC and EFTA (European Free Trade Association) countries except Iceland; other major industrial nations, such as the U.S. and Japan; five countries from Latin America and the Caribbean; most of the Asian newly industrialized countries; Nigeria; and South Africa.

For each country, the following information is included:

Form and Content	Capital and Reserves
Public Filing Requirements	Group Financial
Audit Requirements	Statements
Valuation Principles	Foreign Currency
Depreciation	Translation
Leasing	Taxation
Research and Development	Unusual and Prior Period
Inventories	Items
Retirement Benefits	Price Level Changes

A similar format is used to present accounting standards from the International Accounting Standards Commission and the EC. While this guide has neither as much detail for individual countries as *European Accounting Guide* nor specimen financial statements, its standard format is easier to use for comparisons.

International Financial Reporting and Auditing: A Guide to Regulatory Requirements (Coopers & Lybrand, 1989)

This review includes more countries, 102, with less information, than the other sources we have described. Its target audience is multinational companies doing business in one or more of these countries. It is not an authoritative source, but a brief comparison. New editions are issued irregularly. The two-page entry for each country includes securities law agencies, requirements of regulatory bodies, the types of reports that need to be filed, and the items that the reports should contain. It also specifies whether a licensed auditor is required.

Coopers & Lybrand also issues a report entitled *Euroscope*, which is available electronically on the LEXIS AND NEXIS SERVICES in the EUROPE Library as the *EURSCP* file. Certain issues of the report update EC company law in detail, explain the EC Directives, and give the current status of the Directives.

International Accounting and Auditing Trends (CIFAR, 3rd ed., 1993)

In the U.S., the AICPA publishes the annual *Accounting Trends and Techniques*, which examines how publicly traded companies handle various accounting issues. CIFAR publishes *International Accounting and Auditing Trends*, which examines the accounting and disclosure practices of thousands of international companies. In addition, *International Accounting and Auditing Trends* lists regional and country accounting and auditing bodies, as well as the changes in accounting and auditing standards issued since the previous edition.

Volume 1, "International Accounting Trends," has information based on audits performed in 46 countries. The objective of Volume 1 is to provide an understanding of the discrepancies in accounting standards and practices among the world's leading companies. See Appendix D for a chart of accounting standards in different countries. The book answers such questions as:

- How do companies in the food/beverage industry comply with international standards?
- Is there an Accounting Standards Board in Mexico?
- Do Mexican companies file audited interim reports?

Rather than presenting examples of how individual companies handle accounting practices, CIFAR has developed what it calls the *International Financial Reporting Index (IFRI)*, which quantifies disclosure of 90 key items, divided into the seven following categories:

A. General Information	E. Accounting Policies
B. Income Statement	F. Shareholder's Information
C. Balance Sheet	G. Other Items
D. Flow of Funds Statement	

Data are then presented for countries, industries, and companies by country in tabular format.

Exhibit 2-3 shows the *IFRI* for three well-known food/beverage companies. The numbers refer to the degree of conformity to international standards for each of the seven categories.

According to the CIFAR *Index*, the U.K. company Guinness has the highest rate of compliance to international accounting standards of the three beer companies.

EXHIBIT 2-3. *International Financial Reporting Index*

Index Company	A	B	C	D	E	F	G	TI*	TI*=Total CN
Anheuser Busch	63	73	93	80	80	53	58	71	US
Guinness PLC	75	73	100	80	85	65	82	80	U.K.
Heineken N.V.	75	82	86	40	50	53	55	63	NE
Industry Average	76	76	91	76	74	55	66	73	

Source: *International Accounting and Auditing Trends,* 3rd ed. Exhibit C—International Financial Reporting Index of Industrial Companies by Industry, vol.1, pp. 68-71. Reprinted with permission from the Center for International Financial Analysis & Research, Inc. (CIFAR).

Volume 1 also contains summaries of accounting standards, reporting practices, and interim reports for the 46 countries. Examples of consolidated financial statements and footnotes for a multinational industrial, commercial bank, and insurance company are also presented in tabular form. Finally, tables present variation in stock and bond price reporting in specific newspapers.

Volume 2, "International Auditing Trends," studies the global audit marketplace, including audit fees and clients of major accounting firms.

- What insurance firms does Ernst & Young International audit in Australia?
- Who audits Singapore Airlines? What was the fee that Singapore Airlines paid for the audit?

Information is arranged in tables by accounting firm, country, industry, and company.

The summaries of accounting standards for countries from *International Accounting and Auditing Trends* is also available online as the INTACC library in the LEXIS AND NEXIS SERVICES. In April 1993, the second edition was still online even though the third edition had been distributed to libraries.

Survey of International Accounting Practices (AICPA, 1991)

This summary compares U.S. accounting practices with other countries. It is an inexpensive and brief survey prepared by the SEC, the AICPA, and the Big Six

accounting firms. In 1991, the Office of the Chief Accountant of the U.S. Securities and Exchange Commission asked the Big Six accounting firms to survey and compare key accounting standards and practices in the U.S. to major countries and the International Accounting Standards. The survey concluded that U.S. standards are relatively more complex than those in the other countries. Of all the differences noted, accounting for goodwill was singled out as one difference with significant impact on earnings. The summary results of this survey are presented in *Survey of International Accounting Practices* published by the AICPA. Six related detailed studies may also be purchased.

There is also a brief overview of different accounting issues. What is unique is a paragraph for each standard on the "Cost of Compliance with U.S. Standards." International accounting practices (IAS) are compared to those in the U.S., Australia, Canada, France, Germany, Italy, Japan, The Netherlands, and the U.K. in a series of tables. Exhibit 2-4 is an example of one of the tables.

FEE European Survey of Published Accounts (Fédération des Experts Comptables Européens—Biannual)

This is a comparative study based on a 1989 survey of more than 400 companies in nine EC countries as well as Finland, Norway, Sweden, and Switzerland. All the EC companies had adopted the Fourth EC Directive

EXHIBIT 2-4. Sample Table from *Survey of International Accounting Practices*

BUSINESS COMBINATIONS, GOODWILL AND INTANGIBLES

United States	International	Australia	Canada	France
PURCHASE ACCOUNTING Cost				
Fair value of consideration given or received	Similar to U.S.	Fair value of consideration given	Fair value of consideration given unless not evident.	Acquisition cost as stated in the contract

Source: *Survey of International Accounting Practices,* p. 18. Reprinted with permission from the American Institute of Certified Public Accountants (AICPA).

(described above). This survey gives greater detail than the AICPA *Survey of International Accounting Practices* for the following areas:

Fixed assets: intangibles   Fixed assets: tangibles
Fixed assets: financial   Inventories
Marketable securities   Pension provision
Deferred taxation   Foreign currencies
Off-balance sheet   Leasing
  commitments   Government grants
Complex financial
  instruments

For each issue, the relevant portion of the EC Fourth or Seventh Directive is presented with data showing the number of companies following each practice. Exhibit 2-5 is an example of data presentation from the FEE *Survey*. The survey concludes that there is more variation within countries complying with the EC directives than within those outside the EC.

The Handbook of International Accounting, Frederick D.S. Choi, ed. (John Wiley & Sons, 1991)

Frederick Choi has published many books and articles on international accounting. The *Handbook* is a more academic approach to worldwide accounting issues than the other sources we have discussed. The first edition, published in 1991, is divided into eight sections.

I.   Internationalization of the Accounting Function
II. World Scene of Accounting Practices
III. International Financial Analysis
IV. International Accounting Harmonization
V.   Technical Issues in International Accounting
VI. Financial Reporting and Disclosure
VII. Analysis, Planning and Control Issues
VIII. International Transfer Pricing and Taxation

Chapters are written by individual authors who are academics or members of Bix Six accounting firms.

Three chapters are especially useful to librarians and information specialists coping with international financial statements. One is "Worldwide Regulatory Disclosure Requirements," written by Shahrokh M. Saudagaran, from Santa Clara University, and Morton B. Solomon of KPMG Peat Markwick. It examines several issues involved with finance and disclosure, presents financial reporting from selected countries, including Japan, and lists "salient" disclosure requirements of major stock exchanges.

Two other key chapters are "1992 and Harmonization Efforts in the EC," written by Gerhard G. Mueller, and "International Accounting Standards and Organizations: Quo Vadis?," by Arthur R. Wyatt. These chapters give a detailed examination of the IASC and the issue of harmonization and standardization. See Appendix E for a chart on disclosure requirements from Choi.

Accounting Certification, Educational, & Reciprocity Requirements: An International Guide by Jack R. Fay (Quorum Books, 1992)

The *Guide* contains data on reciprocity for professional accountants, certification requirements, activities

---

EXHIBIT 2-5. Sample Tables from *FEE European Survey of Published Accounts*

Sample size	Bel	Den	Fra	Ger	Gre	Ire	Lux	Net	U.K.	
Total	50	32	40	49	30	38	12	40	50	341
Evidence of land and buildings	38	29	33	48	27	35	12		39	311
Valuation basis used for land:*										
Cost, purchase price	5	5	28	1	25	8	4	6	–	82
Cost, purchase less amortization	–	–	–	–	–	3	–	1	–	4
Replacement value	1	–	–	–	–	–	–	2	–	3
Independent expert valuation	–	–	–	–	–	4	–	1	–	5
Other	–	1	16	–	2	–	–	1	–	20
Not separate disclosure	4	2	1	1	–	4	–	2	–	14

. . .
(*more than one possible answer)

Non-compliance countries: (Tables 5.23, 5.28)

	Ita	Spa	Total		Fin	Nor	Swe	Swi	Total
Sample size	30	30	60		10	9	11	11	40
Evidence of land and buildings	27	27	54		9	9	8	11	37
Valuation basis used for land:									
Cost, purchase price	4	7	11		5	5	7	4	11
Other	1	5	6		1	–	1	3	5
No separate disclosure	–	1	1		1	–	–	–	1

Source: FEE European Survey of Published Accounts, Tables 5.23, 5.28. Reprinted with permission from Routledge.

and responsibilities for professional accountants, continuing education requirements, and accounting organizations. The data are a result of a worldwide survey of governmental agencies, accounting firms, and accounting organizations. The guide is arranged by the subject areas described and then by country for each subject. Results are also summarized in tables such as "Summaries of Reciprocity Policies in Asia/Pacific Basin." An appendix lists over 100 Professional Accounting Organizations and Standard-Setting Bodies worldwide.

European Financial Reporting (Routledge, 1993)

Routledge, in conjunction with the Institute of Chartered Accountants in England and Wales, issued the series *European Financial Reporting* in 1993, with an individual volume for each EC country. Each volume is organized in the same manner. Part I, "Business Environment," presents fiscal, legal, and financial background. Part II, "Accounting, Auditing and Financial Reporting," describes the current practice. In Appendices, each volume includes illustrative financial statements; differences in financial reporting among the country, the U.S., and the U.K.; and the manner in which the country has incorporated EC Directives. Finally, there is a bi-lingual glossary and a bibliography.

Other Selected Accounting Publications for the Specialist

Many of the organizations mentioned previously in this chapter publish works for the specialist. A sample of these are listed below, arranged by the organization.

The United Nations Transnational Corporations and Management Division, previously the Centre for Transnational Corporations (New York and Geneva), published a series of accounting studies plus a variety of other titles. Examples are presented below.

* *Joint Venture Accounting in the USSR: Direction for Change,* 1990, part of the United Nations Centre for Transnational Corporations (UNCTC) Advisory Studies. Series B; no. 7.
* *Accounting for East-West Joint Ventures,* 1992.
* *Conclusions on Accounting and Reporting by Transnational Corporations* prepared by the Intergovernmental Working Group of Experts on International Standards of Accounting and Reporting, 1989.

The OECD Working Group on Accounting Standards (Paris and New York) publishes different series on accounting and auditing issues. Those listed below are representative titles.

* *Accounting Standards Harmonization* Series, selected titles
  1. Foreign currency translation 1986. 32p.
  2. Consolidation policies in OECD countries 1987. 63p.
  5. Consolidated financial statement 1988. 42p.
  6. New Financial Instruments 1991. 40p.

* *Working Documents of the Working Group on Accounting Standards*
  Availability of Financial Statements c1987.
  The Qualification of Auditors. c1988.
  Accounting Reform in Central and Eastern Europe, 1991, from a conference sponsored by: Centre for Cooperation with European Economies in Transition, in conjunction with Fédération des Experts Comptables Européens.

The following United Kingdom-based organizations are good sources for up-to-date accounting information.

* **European Accounting Association** in London publishes the quarterly journal, *European Accounting.*
* The **Institute of Chartered Accountants** in London has published the quarterly journal *Accounting and Business Research* since 1970. It also publishes *Accounting Standards,* the annual full-text compilation of all U.K. exposure drafts and accounting standards, and the long-standing accounting journal *Accountancy,* which started in 1889 under the title Society of Incorporated Accountants and Auditors and Society of Incorporated Accountants.
* The **Japanese Institute of Certified Public Accountants** in Tokyo published three books in English in 1987. (There is no record of any more recent editions):
  Corporate Disclosure in Japan: Auditing
  Corporate Disclosure in Japan: Overview
  Corporate Disclosure in Japan: Reporting

USING INDEXES TO FIND INTERNATIONAL ACCOUNTING INFORMATION

Print Indexes

Accounting and Tax Index (University Microfilms—Quarterly)

Some of the indexes we discussed in Chapter 1 have articles about international accounting. For more comprehensive lists of articles and books, use the *Accounting and Tax Index* and its predecessor the *Accountants' Index.*

Accountants' Index, a product of the AICPA, suffered from a lack of timeliness in publishing a print edition, a lack of access to the online file (exclusively on

ORBIT), and a lack of abstracts. In 1992, UMI/Data Courier took over the *Index* from the AICPA, renamed it *Accounting and Tax Index*, and changed its indexing, its accessibility, and, we hope, its timeliness.

The new print index continues to include books, journal articles, and reports. The Data Courier thesaurus, used for online databases such as *ABI/Inform,* has replaced the old AICPA Library of Congress-based subject headings. AICPA continues to supply citations for books, but all the indexing is now being done by Data Courier. More accounting and tax-specific subject headings are being added. In addition to the print version, an online version has been loaded on DIALOG. The annual printed version appears about six months after the end of the year.

When using *Accountants' Index* for retrospective research, you will find subject headings such as:

> ACCOUNTING—International
> ACCOUNTING—Principles and standards—Bulgaria

Accounting and Tax Index is introducing more specific terms, and will continue to use such geographic subheadings as:

> ACCOUNTING FIRMS—New Zealand
> CORPORATIONS—Accounting—France

International Accounting Articles Online

Accounting and Tax Database (DIALOG File 485)

The new *Accounting and Tax Database* provides comprehensive coverage to accounting information in journals, books, newspapers, and other business publications. Its international coverage is basically the same as *ABI/Inform.*

While the print index includes only books and journals, the online database is an amalgam of all accounting and tax information appearing in UMI's other online databases, including:

> *ABI/Inform* (Abstracts and some full text)
> *Dissertation Abstracts*
> *Newspapers Abstracts*
> *Periodicals Abstracts*
> *Business Dateline* (Full text)
> *Accounting and Tax Index* (some full text)
> *Accountants' Index* (historical citations)

Any full text in the original database will also appear in File 485. Examples of full-text international newsletters are *Australian Tax Forum* and *World Accounting Report. Accounting and Tax Database* will be updated one week after *ABI/Inform,* based on the time it will take to pull all the sources together. You should not need to use any other UMI database except File 485. Despite the number of indexes and online files used to create the database, the number of articles about non-U.S. subjects in *Accountants and Tax Database* is not great. However, there is more material here than can be found in *ABI/Inform* or other bibliographic sources.

To demonstrate the comparative strength of databases in retrieving information on international accounting, we searched 11 databases on DIALOG, including all the UMI files. Table 2-I shows the retrieval results from three searches. The table indicates the name of the

Table 2-I. International Accounting in Online Databases

	Accounting/de and International/de	Russia or USSR or Soviet	International Accounting Standard?
UMI Files:			
***Accounting & Tax Database* (485)**	**2,098**	**12**	**1036**
ABI/Inform (15)	305	2	197
Newspaper & Periodical Abs (484)	21	1	9
Business Dateline (635)	4	0	3
Other DIALOG Databases:			
Textline (777)	1,566	7	576
EconLit (139)	242	2	5
FINIS (268)	141	2	6
PAIS International (49)	112	0	18
PTS F&S (18)	4	0	0
PTS Newsletter (636)	0	0	177
PTS PROMT (16)	0	0	63

All searches were performed January 20, 1993.

file searched and its DIALOG file number. The first column shows the number of records retrieved with the search of the word "Accounting" combined with the word "International." Both words were searched as descriptors (indexing terms). The second column shows the number of records retrieved when we combined the "international accounting" set (column one) with the words "Russia or USSR or Soviet." The search was designed to emphasize recall rather than precision. Finally, we searched for the phrase "International accounting standard(s)."

The retrieval results indicate the relative strength of the *Accounting and Taxation Database* and *Textline* in the area of international accounting. The results also demonstrate the weakness of most of the Predicast databases and of some of the newspaper files for this subject. The search also indicates the small amount of material currently available on the former Soviet Union. Finally, it points up the problems with trying to perform the same search across dissimilar databases, since by using descriptors we would have missed all of the articles in *PTS Newsletter* database.

Exhibit 2-6 gives examples of records from two of the databases combined for File 485.

Textline is a good source for news articles on the status of accounting practices in different countries. It is especially useful for Eastern Europe and the former Soviet Union and emerging markets. A sample article retrieved from *Textline* is "Russia: Finance Minister Simplifies Accounting Procedures" from the June 18, 1993 publication *Novecon.*

World Accounting Report is a monthly publication of Financial Times Business Information Ltd. It costs about £300 in print and is accessible online full-text on DATA-STAR in *Financial Times Business Reports* (FTBR). It is also a part of several other databases on a variety of systems: in the Predicasts *PTS Newsletter* and *PROMT, Accounting and Tax Database,* in NEXIS (WAR), as part of the DOW JONES //Text International selection, and on DATIMES and the WESTLAW gateway to DIALOG. The most complete file of the report is on NEXIS WAR, with more than 2,100 articles (as of September 1993), dating back to 1989.

The descriptor field is divided into region or country and subject such as:

Bahrain, Company-law, Regulations.
New-Zealand, Company-law, Draft-regulations.

World Accounting Review is an excellent source for the latest information on changing accounting practice.

Online Sources of EC Accounting Information

The same databases that provide access to all EC legislation can be used to follow the EC directives and

---

> **EXHIBIT 2-6. Records from *Accounting & Tax Database***
>
> 2.6A: Record from *Accountants Index in File 485:*
> 00311827   DIALOG FILE 485 Accounting & Tax Database
> Challenge of change for Soviet accounting
> Coombs, Hugh; Liberman, Lev
> Public finance and accountancy, Eng P p. 12–15. March 8, 1991
> **JRNL CODE: AICP**
> DESCRIPTORS: Accounting—Union of Soviet Socialist Republics; Cooperatives—Accounting—Union of Soviet Socialist Republics; Joint ventures—Accounting—Union of Soviet Socialist Republics
>
> 2.6B: Record from *Newspaper Abstracts in File 485:*
>
> 00378015 DIALOG FILE 485 Accounting & Tax Database
> Polish Tax Police, Like Taxpayers, Can Be a Bit Evasive
> Newan, Barry
> Wall Street Journal PP: A, 1:4 Nov 6, 1992 ISSN: 0099-9660
> JRNL CODE: WSJ
> DOC TYPE: Newspaper article LANGUAGE: English
> AVAILABILITY:Dow Jones & Co, Inc, 200 Liberty Street, NY
> ABSTRACT: The methods of Poland's Tax Police, which often skirt the edges...
> COMPANY NAMES:
> Tax Police-Poland
> GEOGRAPHIC NAMES: Poland
> DESCRIPTORS: Police; Law enforcement; Tax evasion; Organizational profiles

decisions involving company law, accounting standards, and professional qualifications.

Spearhead (SPHD on DATA-STAR), a product of the U.K. Department of Trade and Industry, summarizes all current and prospective EC measures regarding the single market or other areas having implications for business. *Spicers Centre for Europe Database* (SPCE on DATA-STAR) covers all issues discussed by the European Community institutions. *Celex* (Computerized Documentation System on European Community Law) is the official database for every area of EC legislation. All three may be used to track EC activities.

LEXIS AND NEXIS SERVICES

Many of the LEXIS AND NEXIS SERVICES libraries contain information important to international accounting. The largest number of articles about international accounting and auditing is retrieved in the NEXIS library. The actual International Accounting Standards are included in *NAARS* (IAS) as part of the Accounting and Audit Literature Files, and there are selected articles in BANK. The book mentioned above, *International Accounting and Auditing Trends* (INTACC), is a separate library and is included as well in the geographic libraries, such as WORLD and COMPNY.

DOW JONES NEWS RETRIEVAL

Dow Jones MENUS contain predominately North American articles related to accounting firms. In //TEXT the majority of articles coded "accounting" in Dow Jones' own files (*Wall Street Journal*, Dow Jones News, and *Barrons*) are also predominately related to U.S. accounting practices and focus on U.S. accounting firms. For international articles, choose //TEXT International News which includes the *Asian Wall Street Journal* and the *Wall Street Journal Europe*. As shown below, different Dow Jones codes are necessary to retrieve all relevant information.

Codes for Accounting on Dow Jones News Retrieval

News/Retrieval Category	WIRES/ CLIP	DJNEWS	TEXT 1, 2,3,11	TEXT 9, 13
Accounting	N/ACC	.I/ACC	ACC.NS. ACC.IN.	ACC.NS.

CONCLUSION

An extreme statement of the problems surrounding company comparisons comes from a British expert on European Community accounting: "not only can you not compare companies across countries, you cannot even compare companies within countries!" Although this may be an overstatement designed to make a point, it emphasizes the effect of accounting standards on comparative company analysis.

Researchers performing competitive intelligence, financial analysis, and industry comparisons can use the resources described in this chapter to keep up on the changes in international accounting standards and the move toward harmonization.

NOTES

1. *Accounting Reform in Central and Eastern Europe* (Organisation for Economic Cooperation and Development, 1991), p. 11.
2. Gerhard G. Mueller, Helen Morsicato, and Gary Meek, *Accounting—An International Perspective: A Supplement to Introductory Accounting Textbooks* (Homewood, IL: Irwin, 1987), p. 26.
3. *Sourceguide to European Company Information* (Detroit: Gale, 1993).
4. Christopher Nobes, "EC Group Accounting: Two Zillion Ways to Do It," *Accountancy* (U.K.) *106* (December 1990): 84–85.
5. *The Baring Securities Guide to International Financial Reporting*, Christopher Nobes, ed. (Oxford: Basil Blackwell, 1991), p. 3
6. *Baring Securities Guide*, p. 74.
7. Rudolf Brunovs and Robert J. Kirsch, "Goodwill Accounting in Selected Countries and the Harmonization of International Accounting Standards," *Abacus* 27 (September 1991): 135–61.
8. International Accounting Standard 29.
9. Christopher Nobes and Sadayoshi Masada, "Japanese Accounting: Interpreters Needed," *Accountancy* (U.K.) *106* (September 1990): 83.
10. *Baring Securities Guide*, Chapter 7, 1108; Frederick Choi, *Handbook of International Accounting* (New York: John Wiley & Sons, 1991), p. 5.12; Nobes and Masada, "Japanese Accounting," pp. 82–83.
11. Mark Lawson, "Reluctance to Bite Revaluation Bullet," *Australian Financial Review* (September 29, 1992). DATA-STAR, *Textline*
12. "The Public Affairs of Private Companies," *Australian Financial Review* (June 30, 1992): 25. DATA-STAR, *Textline*.
13. Rupert Bruce, "Pitfalls Lurk in Emerging Market Craze, "*International Herald Tribune* (January 25, 1992). LEXIS AND NEXIS SERVICES
14. *International Accounting and Reporting Issues* (New York: United Nations Centre on Transnational Corporations, 1990), p. 36.
15. *World Accounting Report*, August 1992.
16. "Accounting and Auditing in Poland," *PAP Polish Press Agency*, Business News from Poland (June 6, 1992). LEXIS AND NEXIS SERVICES

17. *International Accounting Standards: The Full Texts of all International Accounting Standards Extant at 1 January 1990.* (London: Institute of Chartered Accountants in England and Wales, 1989).

18. OECD *Accounting Reform*, p. 134.

19. *Morningstar Japan*, (February 28, 1992).

20. Eighth Council Directive 84/253/EEC of 10 April 1984 based on Article 54(3)(g) of the Treaty, *Official Journal* Reference L126 of 12 May 1984.

21. Parveen Gupta, "International Reciprocity in Accounting," *Journal of Accountancy*, *173* (January 1992): 46–54.

22. "Accountancy: All Change," *Economist* 325 (October 17, 1992): 19–23.

23. "Accountancy Firms Are Establishing Themselves in the Commonwealth of Independent States at a Rapid Rate," *Accountancy* (April 7, 1992).

24. *BizEcon News*, October 21,1992, on LEXIS AND NEXIS SERVICES from an article in *Moskovskaya Pravda,* No. 206, p.3.

CHAPTER 3
Company Information: Issues

TOPICS COVERED

Questions about companies are basic to business research. They can be the most straightforward business research questions, but answering them can often prove to be complex and involved. They can range from finding an address, to finding "everything" about a known company; from screening a set of companies to meet specific criteria, such as finding gas springs manufacturers in Europe, to ranking companies, such as listing the largest food companies in the world. Since there are 25 million companies in the U.S. and the European Community, the number of possible company questions is immense.

This chapter provides a framework for our discussion of companies in future chapters. We describe the types of company sources and their applications, and discuss the issues of interpreting their contents.

CHARACTERISTICS OF COMPANY INFORMATION SOURCES

Company information sources fall into several categories, which can be usefully grouped as follows:

- Types of information included about the company
- Types of companies included
- Location of the companies
- Format/Access method

The categories overlap and no clear line divides, for example, a basic directory from a more specialized source. As an aid to understanding the variety of company information sources, we give below examples of sources from each group. An additional checklist of specific data elements appears in Appendix A.

Types of Information

Based on the types of information they provide, company information sources can be categorized as follows:

1. **Basic Directory:** Provides name, address, telecommunications numbers
   Applications: To locate the address/phone number of a known company; To find a list of companies in a given location
   Example: Duns Principal International Businesses
2. **Product Directory:** Provides a description of the business and its classification codes
   Applications: To identify a company's specific product lines; To determine the companies within a given market segment
   Example: KOMPASS publications in print and online
3. **Financial Directory:** Provides balance sheet and income statement data
   Applications: To examine the financial performance of a company
   Example: Moody's International Manual
   Applications: To screen companies for a set of characteristics; e.g., companies with return on investment greater than 15% and sales greater than $U.S. 100M
   Example: Disclosure/Worldscope CD-ROM
4. **Director's Directory:** Provides names of officers
   Applications: To get a list of a company's major officers

or board members; To find out what position an individual holds

Example: Directory of Directors

5. **Rankings Directory:** Provides listings of companies arranged by size

Applications: To see where a particular company ranks in its market; To identify the top companies in an industry or geographic location

Example: Times 1000

Types of Companies

Directories use some of the following different criteria to select companies for inclusion:

1. **Legal Status:** Companies listed on a stock exchange, incorporated, registered nationally

Applications: To determine if any French company has the name Pagell; To find the addresses of all corporations traded on the Paris Bourse

Example: Telefirm (FRCO) on DATA-STAR

2. **Size:** Large, medium, small, or micro companies

Applications: To locate companies with less than 100 employees; To identify medium-sized companies

Example: Medium Companies in Europe

3. **Special Features:** Import/export, multinationals, members of associations

Applications: To find a list of potential trading partners

Example: Sell's British Exporters

Location of Companies

Geographic location is a special type of criteria for including companies in a directory. Some large publishers, such as Dun & Bradstreet or Moody's, issue directories covering countries worldwide. In addition, many countries have their own directories, which could be published by an international publisher, such as KOMPASS, or the local chamber of commerce.

1. **International:** May include or exclude the U.S. or North America

Example: World Business Directory

2. **Pan-continental:** Includes companies on one or more continents

Example: Major Companies of Australasia

3. **Regional:** Includes selected countries within a region

Example: SIBD—Business Directory for the Soviet Region

4. **National:** Includes companies from one country

Example: French Company Handbook

Format and Access Method

Data Formats. Data formats for directories include print, microform, magnetic disks and tapes, and CD-

ROM. Directories in electronic format are accessed through commercial and local time-sharing systems, as well as through stand-alone systems. Some sources of company information are available in a wide range of formats. Moody's *International Manual*, for example, is in print and on CD-ROM. EXTEL company financials are available on cards, through commercial time-sharing, on CD-ROM, and on locally loaded magnetic disk. Some sources are more exclusive. For example, Japanese company data on credit ratings, rankings, and officers' educational backgrounds are only available from one time-sharing database in the United States.

1. **Print:** All types of directories available
2. **Microforms:** Financial filings from listed companies
3. **Commercial Time-Sharing:** All type of directories available online
4. **CD-ROM:** A growing number of files, especially European directories
5. **Local Time-Sharing:** Commercial time-sharing files sometimes make their databases available on magnetic tape for local loading

Access to Company Information. Most libraries have core collections of national directory information. In the U.S., these include *Standard & Poor's Register of Corporations* and Dun & Bradstreet's *Million Dollar Directory*. Moody's *Manuals* and *Standard and Poor's Corporate Records* dominate the scene for financial information. D&B's *American Corporate Families* and National Register's *Corporate Affiliations* provide corporate family trees. *Thomas Register* identifies large and small manufacturers.

Business researchers in the U.S. have developed a tool-kit of sources to handle basic reference queries. They know the limitations of disclosure in the U.S. and the resulting public availability of information and have built their information expectations accordingly. They will not waste time looking for the current ratio of Godiva Chocolate or the current assets of Miller Beer.

Do the same rules of disclosure apply when we are seeking information about a British or Japanese company? Are the same publishers prominent on the international scene? The answer to the first question is maybe; the answer to the second is sometimes. Many of the factors that allow us to immediately determine the level of difficulty of questions about our national companies apply to all enterprises worldwide.

There is an information continuum from macro "multinational" parent companies listed on major exchanges to micro enterprises exempted from filing requirements. The level of overall business activity in a country also affects the amount of company information that is available. Obviously, more information is available about companies in the EC than in emerging markets.

As Table 3-A shows, we can form reasonable expectations about how much information is available on a given company by determining its country of incorporation; its size (multinational, large, medium, or small); if it is listed or non-listed; if it is a parent or subsidiary, affiliate or branch; and its major industry. We know that we will have an easier time finding in-depth information about Daimler-Benz than about Clear Car Autoservice in Duesseldorf.

We consider next some of the questions researchers may encounter when interpreting international company information.

UNDERSTANDING INTERNATIONAL COMPANY INFORMATION

The information needed to answer a question about a company may be found in one or several sources. With some sources it is often difficult to understand the information once we have found it. These problems of understanding range from the transliteration of a company name to interpreting foreign financial accounts.

Directory Features

There are several features of international company information that may be difficult to interpret. We outline these issues below. We will examine some of these features in more detail in relation to specific types of directories in Chapter 4.

Table 3-A. Company Information Availability Continuum

BUSINESS INFORMATION AVAILABILITY CONTINUUM

	WIDELY AVAILABLE *In Print/CD/Online*		GENERALLY AVAILABLE *In Print/Online*		AVAILABLE *Online*	SPECIALIZED *Online/CD*
COMPANY						
Ownership	Public		Incorporated		Partnership	Single
For Public:						
Exchange	New York	American	NMS		NDQ	OTH
Size	Large		Medium		Small	Micro
Affiliation	Parent		Subsidiary/Affiliate		Branch	Single location
COUNTRY	US	EC	Europe/Japan (non-EC)	Pacific Rim	Emerging Markets	LDCs
INDUSTRY						
Type	Consumer Products		Manufacturing	Retail	Wholesale	Professional Services
Level	Industry		SIC Code	Product		Brand
DEMOGRAPHICS						
Regional	State/MSA		City	Zip		Block
Segment	Age or Sex or Race or Income					Age or Sex or Race
Lifestyles	"Middle America"		Affluent			Poor
FINANCIAL/ECONOMIC DATA						
Frequency	Annual		Monthly	Quarterly	Daily	Real Time
MACHINE READABLE TEXT						
Content	Citations	Abstracts	Selected Text		Full Text	Full Text Image

Company Coverage. The number of companies listed in a source is a fundamental, if obvious, part of our evaluation.

- How many companies are in the source? The more information given about a company in any source, the fewer the companies listed. For example, there will be many more companies in *Duns Principal International Businesses*, a basic directory, than in *Moody's International Manual.* ICC's full-text annual reports (online and on CD-ROM) have the fewest companies but the most information of these three sources.

- What are the criteria for inclusion? Companies may be included in a directory because they fit a certain size category, be in a particular industry group, operate in certain countries, or be willing to fill out a questionnaire to be listed. A key question here is does the publisher solicit the company or vice versa?

- How is the information compiled? Does the publisher collect information by questionnaire or phone? Does the publisher use other external sources such as registration records, phone books, or news reports? Is there double-checking? How long will a company listing remain in the source if the company does not respond to requests for verification?

- How frequently is the source updated? A record updated? A printed directory might be published annually and an electronic database updated monthly, but neither of these facts necessarily indicates that each record is updated regularly. Individual records may go unchanged for longer than the publishing or updating cycle.

Product/Industry Classifications. Most sources include at least some basic description of a company's business.

- Is the classification system standard or is it generated by the producer?

- Is the classification numeric, text, or both? Is it in English?

- What is being categorized? The company's primary industry group? An establishment's product line?

- What criteria are used for assigning classifications? Does the company describe its business? Does the producer assign a code based on sales, income, or the description?

Financials. Understanding and interpreting international financial statements are the subjects of many books and are covered more fully in Chapter 2, "Accounting Standards and Practices." Briefly, here are some fundamental characteristics of financial sources to be aware of.

- Are the companies in a directory "listed" on a stock exchange, privately held, government owned, or of all types?

- What financial items are being reported? For how many years? In what monetary unit?

- What is the fiscal year-end date? The date of the reported financials?

- Has an exchange rate been used to convert local figures to a standard currency? If so, what rate and date were used?

- What are the accounting standards the company follows?

- Are the data "as reported" or "standardized"?

Language. The most appropriate sources may not be in English. Often, the most detailed company information for a company in a non-English-speaking country is in a native language source.

- What is the language of the source? Is the source multi-lingual? Some print sources, such as those from the UN, OECD, or EC have multi-lingual introductions and data labels. Some computer readable files can be searched in more than one language. For example, the CD-ROM *DIANE* (Bureau Van Dijk) may be searched either in French or English.

- Is language an obstacle if you are looking only for an address or a provider of a product?

- Are there any standard coded fields? For example, using a standard two-letter country code alleviates the problem of whether to look for "Deutschland" or for "Germany." Knowing that U.S. SIC codes are used in Hoppenstedt's German language products may simplify the search for products.

- How are the meanings of key terms translated? It is sometime difficult even to distinguish between British and American financial English. American "stocks" are British "equities" and British "stock" are American "inventories."

- How are non-Roman alphabets handled? Are names translated? Transliterated? For example, the name of the president of a Japanese company is transliterated as Minoru Ohnishi in Worldscope and as Minoru Onishi in Hoover; the company's senior marketing director is Hirozo Ueta in Worldscope and Hirozo Ueda in Hoover.

Quality. A source might list the types of companies you need, from the countries required with the appropriate data items. The publisher may even be well known. However, these facts in themselves do not mean that the information is of high quality.

- How can you judge the quality of the data? Do the results "make sense"? Is the source free of misspellings and typos? Are data elements dated? Are there references?[1]

Our classic example of results that did not make sense is a search for major food companies in Europe in 1990 that listed Yugoslavian companies as the largest because of discrepancies between the sales figure dates and the exchange rate dates.[2]

Publisher Issues

Standard U.S. business publishers and databank providers, such Dun & Bradstreet, Moody's, DIALOG, DOW JONES, or LEXIS AND NEXIS SERVICES, provide an extensive array of international company information. However, non-U.S. publishers, such as KOMPASS, Graham & Trotman, EXTEL, and the databanks DATA-STAR or FT PROFILE , often have unique company information. The variety of publishers and formats necessitates another set of decisions.

1. Multiple formats and multiple systems
- If a source is in print, online, and on disc, which format do you use?
- What is the best way to access these sources?
- When a database is available on several systems, which system do you use?

Moody's International is a standard print source with a "mirror image" on CD-ROM. Its news volume is also available online (DIALOG). The British Jordan's U.K. company file is a book, an online database on DATA-STAR, and a CD-ROM with enhanced financial analysis software (FAME). *Financial Times* is available in print with a printed index or as abstracts or full text online through several online systems.

2. Unfamiliar sources/systems
- Do you only use the systems you know best?
While many databases appear on multiple systems, some databases are unique to non-U.S. hosts. For example, the Swiss-based DATA-STAR specializes in European directories.

3. Documentation
- Does the printed documentation answer data-related questions?
- Whom do you call for customer service and how much does that person know about database content?

The print source *D&B Europa* is well documented and will provide answers for most of the questions relating to its use and interpretation. However, online Dun & Bradstreet files have little or no documentation. When you are using European files, you may find that you call a local customer service representative who doesn't necessarily know the answers to your questions. For example, you are retrieving U.K. financial data from a numeric online database and your client asks for a definition of the data item. You call your representative in New York who phones or faxes your question to London for the answer. Your client must wait for London to get back to New York and New York to get back to you.

4. Cost
- What is the purchase price of the directory or CD-ROM vs. the cost of retrieving a company record online?

Because of the number of directories and their expense, it is important that you weigh carefully the alternatives of owning a printed directory or its CD-ROM equivalent vs. accessing individual company records online as needed.

Print vs. Electronic Sources

Online and on disc company sources are well known for their speed and ability to screen for combinations of variables. Printed sources have their advantages as well. They are usually easier to use than online sources. A printed directory has documentation that tells us basic facts such as how the companies have been selected, how the information has been collected, and inconsistencies the publishers may have encountered. When we search electronic company files, the documentation is usually sketchy or absent, and the file arrangement is hidden. The complications of searching online files make understanding the data presented in the files more difficult.

IDENTIFYING COMPANIES

Companies, like people, have identifying characteristics. We may be interested in a company's name, legal status, and size.

Company Names

Searching for company names may not be straightforward. Companies have legal names and "traded as" names, which are often more familiar. Different companies may have the same or similar names. It can be difficult to tell if they are part of the same corporate family. For example, Sears PLC, the retail chain in the United Kingdom, has no relationship to Sears and Roebuck in the U.S. Over 500 companies have the word Nestle in their name in DIALOG databases. There are over 50 Mitsubishis just in the Japanese *Teikoku* database. And DIALOG's company namefinder (File 416) has 261 Alcatels. Exhibit 3-1 lists a few of the Alcatels in the DIALOG files. The location may indicate city, county, state, or country.

Textline, Reuters' international business news database, has a separate name finder database that is updated

EXHIBIT 3-1. Partial List of "ALCATEL" Companies in DIALOG Files

```
Company / Location
-----------------------------------------------------------------------
 1  ALCATEL                           BELGIUM
 2  ALCATEL (AUSTRIA)                  17  ALCATEL BELL TELEPHONE
 3  ALCATEL (BELGIUM)                  18  ALCATEL BELL TELEPHONE / BELGIUM
 4  ALCATEL (NETHERLANDS)              19  ALCATEL BELL-SDT / BELGIUM
 5  ALCATEL (NETHERLDS)                20  ALCATEL BELL-TELEPHONE
 6  ALCATEL (SPAIN)                    21  ALCATEL BUS
 7  ALCATEL (W GERMANY) / WEST GERMANY 22  ALCATEL BUSINESS SYS (FRANCE)
 8  ALCATEL - CIT / FRANCE             23  ALCATEL BUSINESS SYSTEMS / MANCHESTER
 9  ALCATEL AB / SWEDEN                / UNITED KINGDOM
10  ALCATEL ALSTHOM                    24  ALCATEL BUSINESS SYSTEMS / ENGLAND &
11  ALCATEL ALSTHOM CGE               WALES
12  ALCATEL AUSTRIA / J--              25  ALCATEL BUSINESS SYSTEMS FRANCE
13  ALCATEL BELGIUM                    26  ALCATEL BUSINESS SYSTEMS LTD / BARNET
14  ALCATEL BELL                       / UNITED KINGDOM
15  ALCATEL BELL / BELGIUM             27  ALCATEL BUSINESS SYSTEMS LTD (U.K.
16  ALCATEL BELL BUSINESS SYSTEMS /   HEAD OFFICE) / ROMFORD / UNITED
                                      KINGDOM
```

Source: DIALOG Company Name Finder

weekly. The file contains the names and codes of companies appearing in *Textline*. If an article is about an independent company or a subsidiary quoted separately on a stock exchange, the article is indexed with the company's name and a unique code. When the press reports that a company has been acquired by another company, or has changed its name, the *Textline* name finder records these facts with appropriate dates. The file reports names as they appear in the press. It does not attempt to be an exhaustive guide to corporate relationships. Exhibit 3-2 is an example of a search of the name Alcatel on DATA-STAR's *Textline* name finder file (TXCO). Alcatel appeared in 30 records with 11 unique codes.

EXHIBIT 3-2. ALCATEL Sample Record

AN   210547.
CO   Name: ALCATEL-S-T-NORW.
     Code: **STKNOR**.
NT   QUOTED SUB> OF ALCATEL NV (NETH) (ALCATEL ALSTHOM)
     THIS IS A QUOTED SUBSIDIARY
     CGE can be used instead of STKNOR
     ALCTEL can be used instead of STKNOR
     FIRST CODE: STKNOR
     SECOND CODE: ALCTE
     THIRD CODE: **ALCTEL**

Source: Reuter Textline (TXCO) via DATA-STAR, October 4, 1992. Reprinted with permission from Reuters.

On October 4, 1992, there were 1,654 articles in DATA-STAR's *Textline* that used both ALCTEL and CGE as codes. Other Alcatel companies in TXCO include

SEMI-CONDUCTOEURS-ALCATEL-FRA ALCATEL-ALSTHOM-FRA

ALCATEL-S-E-L-AG GFR
ALCATEL-CABLE-SA-FRA

ALCATEL-TELECOMUNICACOES-BRAZ ALCATEL-NV-NETH

RONEO-ALCATEL-LTD
ALCATEL-C-I-T-MAROC-MOROC

ALCATEL-CAVI-ITALY
ALCATEL-CIT-POKSKA-POL

Another difficulty in searching company names is related to language. Obviously, all the world's companies do not have English language names. Less obvious is that the legal names of companies from countries using the Roman alphabet may be different than the English language version. Some examples for Renault are listed below.

If you are an experienced DIALOG searcher and *expand* on the French company names RENAULT, PERRIER, and AIR FRANCE in the *Extel* database, you will get no hits. However, these companies are in the file.

D&B France on DATA-STAR	Renault SA.
Extel online	Regie Nationale Des Usines Renault SA formerly Renault (Regie Nationale des Usines)
WORLDSCOPE CD-ROM	Renault (Regie Nationale Des Usines) SA
Directory of French Cos on DATA-STAR (FRCO)	Regie Nationale Des Usines Renault
Global Companies Handbook	Renault (Regie Nationale des Usines)

Dun's Europa for 1992 states in its introduction that all company names are in their local languages—except Greek. "In Switzerland and Belgium, the local language chosen is governed by postal code, except in Brussels, where the company states its preference." Many directories do not tell us which form of the name is being used.

The difficulties of searching for company names are magnified if the company is Asian or Russian. Some Asian companies have two names—local and English. Others have to be *translated* or *transliterated.*

The Japanese *Teikoku* database (DIALOG File 502) originally had only those Japanese companies that "have official English-language names" out of approximately 950,000 companies in *Teikoku's* Japanese databank. For instance, the company whose English name is *Stanley Electric Co. Ltd.* has the transliterated name *Sutanre Denki KK.*

On the DIALOG system, the English name appears in the company field (CO). The transliterated name appears in the romanized company field (RC). *Teikoku* has added over 120,000 companies without English language names. *Teikoku* now places the same transliterated name in the English company field with an asterisk next to the name and the note "* in company name indicates English name is not available." An example is KOKUMIN KINYUKOKO.

In September 1992, C. Itoh and Co. Ltd., listed in some rankings as the world's largest company, changed its Western name to Itochu Corporation. Its official Japanese name is ITOCHU SHOJI KK and it wants to have international name identity.

How then, can we guarantee that we have the company we actually want? Various numbering systems and ticker symbols may help us track an individual company. Just as U.S. stock issues are assigned CUSIP numbers, international companies receive numbers such as a SEDOL or VALOR. (These numbering systems are discussed in more detail below.)

Standard Numbers

A variety of systems are used for both listed and unlisted companies. In the United States, and worldwide, one company, Dun & Bradstreet, assigns D-U-N-S numbers (Dun & Bradstreet Information Services' Data Universal Number System) to companies. European countries, such as the United Kingdom and France, have central registration systems that assign unique numbers to all companies. More than three million French companies have *SIRENE* numbers, which are issued by INSEE, the state statistical agency. The company's number must appear in its letterhead. Table 3-B lists major company registration systems.

The United Nations has recommended establishment of the D-U-N-S number as one of the standard worldwide identifiers for businesses involved in cross-border electronic data interchange.[3]

Establishment Level Codes. A D-U-N-S number is given to an individual establishment. The number moves with the business; if the business changes name, address, or ownership, the number remains. It is used to identify linkages within company families. It is a unique 9-digit code, randomly selected within blocks. An example of a D-U-N-S number is *30-021-0119,* the number for the Austrian company 3 Pagen Handelsgmbh.

A D-U-N-S number, according to Dun & Bradstreet, is a social security number for business establishments. A D-U-N-S number is assigned when D&B creates a record or investigates a company. The first two digits of the D-U-N-S number indicate the country. Examples are:

Austria	30-0	Brazil	89-
Denmark	30-5	Colombia	88-
France	26- ,76 (1990)	Congo	86-
Germany	31-	Peru	93-
Greece	42-	Venezuela	88-
Ireland	21-, 98 (1991)	Zambia	55-
Italy	44-	Zimbabwe	56-
Luxembourg	40-	Israel	60-

Table 3-B. Major Company Registration Systems

NUMBER	ASSIGNOR	ASSIGNEE	COUNTRY
Duns Number	Dun & Bradstreet	Public and Private Companies in D&B files	International
Registration	Companies House	All U.K. Companies	U.K.
Registration	Chambres de Commerce	All French Companies	France
Ticker Symbol	Stock exchanges, Information providers	Quoted companies	
CUSIP	American Banking Assn.	Equity issues on U.S. exchanges	U.S.
SEDOL	London Stock Exchange	Securities traded in the U.K.	International
VALOR	Telekurs N.A.	Securities	Swiss & Intl
ISIN	Telekurs and S&P	Quoted companies	International

Netherlands	40-	Thailand	65-
Portugal	45-	Japan	69-
Spain	46-, 47-	Philippines	70-
Switzerland	48-	Indonesia	79-
U.K.	21-		

Establishments within the U.K., France, Italy, and Germany are all assigned unique official registration numbers. However, most print and online sources outside the home country do *not* use these numbers.

Listed Companies. While the symbols and codes discussed below are assigned as a way of tracking a company's equities issues, they can also be used as a means of identifying a company. Codes may be assigned to an individual company or to a specific equity issue.

Ticker Symbols. We are familiar with the use of ticker symbols to identify companies traded on U.S. stock exchanges. Originally, the symbols were the identifying labels for stock prices that came across the "ticker tape." In the U.S., companies get to choose their ticker symbols. Many U.S. database providers, including IAC, UMI/Data Courier, and Predicasts, include tickers in U.S. company records.

Use of tickers is not standardized internationally. Symbols may be alphabetic or numeric. We associate the ticker symbol with one company, but the alphabetical ticker symbol is *not* unique to one company. As Table 3-C shows, different companies, trading on different exchanges, may have the same symbol.

Table 3-C. Examples of Non-Unique Ticker Symbols in the *Extel* Database

Company Name	Country Symbol	Ticker
Ameritech Corporation	United States	AIT
Anglo American Investment Trust	South Africa	AIT
Allied-Signal Inc	United States	ALD
Aldus Ltd	Australia	ALD
Coca-Cola Amatil Ltd	Australia	CCL
Celanese Canada Inc	Canada	CCL
CSR Ltd	Australia	CSR
City Sports and Recreation Co	Thailand	CSR

Companies that are traded on exchanges outside their home countries may have different symbols on foreign exchanges.

	ATTWOODS PLC	ABITIBI— PRICE INC
Home exchange	London	Toronto, Vancouver, Montreal
Home exchange symbol	ATWL	A, ABPR
NYSE	A	ABY

Commercial sources of company information may use different designations for a company ticker. ABITIBI-PRICE INC tickers in online databases include the following

Database	Symbol	Exchange
EXTEL	ABY	
DISCLOSURE	ABY	NYS
CANCOPR	A, ABPR	Toronto, Montreal, NYS
STANDARD & POOR'S	ABY	NYS

REUTERLINK is an online service covering a wide range of exchanges. Depending on the exchange, Reuters uses its own ticker symbols (RICS, i.e., Reuters Instrument Codes), the local stock exchange symbols, or EXTEL symbols.

ATTWOODS PLC in REUTERLINK:	
London	A.L
London International (ADR)	ATWLy.L
NYSE (ADR)	NA*
NY(Reuters Consolidated)	A.NY
NY Floor (Reuters)	A.N

*NA is the code, not Not Available

Japanese companies have numeric ticker symbols assigned by the Securities Identification Code Conference. The ticker for Mitsubishi Corporation is 8058.

Equities Numbers. At the securities level, various numbering systems are used for companies and individual equities: CUSIP, SEDOL, VALOR, ISIN.

A CUSIP is a number assigned to companies and their securities traded on U.S. exchanges by the American Bankers Association Committee on Uniform Securities Identification Procedures.

The SEDOL is the Stock Exchange Daily Official List, developed by the London Stock Exchange. Similar to the U.S. CUSIP, it is assigned to individual equity issues. The first digit is a continent designator: all SEDOLs beginning with 0 are U.K., 2 North America, 4 Europe, and 6 Asian markets. For example, a SEDOL for Kirin Brewery Co. Ltd. is 6493745, while Hong Kong's AMOY Properties Limited is 6030506.

VALOR is produced by Valor Inform, a Swiss company. There are approximately 300,000 VALORS for Swiss and non-Swiss financial instruments.

The ISIN is the International Securities Identification Number and is a product of ISO, the International Standards Organization. It is designed to help with cross-border identification of international securities. Presently, there are about 200,000 numbers.

The ISIN numbers and the *International Securities Identification Numbers Directory* are a joint product of Telekurs N.A. and Standard and Poor's, Inc. Telekurs and S&P participate in the ISO Committee on global trading. Telekurs A.G. is owned by more than 300 Swiss banks and stock exchanges and is chartered to collect and distribute information on securities in all markets around the world. It maintains the Swiss Register of Securities and issues Swiss VALOR numbers to identify securities. S&P is under license from the American Bankers Association to administer the CUSIP number system for the U.S. and Canada.

Telekurs assigns numbers to companies in countries that lack national securities numbering systems or authorities. In the U.S., S&P has adopted the national CUSIP for inclusion in the CINS (CUSIP International Numbering System), a 9-character number that is an extension of the CUSIP. *Worldscope* (Table 3-D) is one source that uses all of these numbering systems. Note from the highlighted numbers in Table 3-D that the ISIN incorporates the CUSIP for U.S. and Canadian companies, the SEDOL for British companies, and the VALOR for Swiss companies.

Legal Status

Legally, companies may be proprietorships, partnerships, or "limited" corporations. They may also be cooperatives or government-operated. In the United States, we use "public" to refer to companies that trade stock and are registered with the Securities and Exchange Commission. In international company research, we may also see "public" used as the designation for government-owned enterprises.

We may find more financial information about non-U.S. "private" companies than U.S. private companies. Two models for collecting and maintaining company information are the United Kingdom and Italy.

In the United Kingdom, all companies register with Companies House. It holds the records to more than one million companies and registers about four million documents each year. It was first established in England and Wales and separately in Scotland by the Joint Stock Companies Act of 1844. There have been many amendments to the act, the most recent based on EC directives discussed below. A new company has 18 months to file an initial annual accounts statement. It is the responsibility of Companies House to incorporate and dissolve companies, examine and file the required documents, and make the documents available to the public. Documents include accounts and annual returns, changes to directors' details and registered office addresses, secured loans taken out by a company, and liquidators' and receivers' documents.

In the U.K., two or more persons may form an incorporated company which can be one of four types.

1. Private company limited by shares
2. Private company limited by guarantee (based on contributions to company assets)
3. Private unlimited company (no limit to liability)
4. Public company with a minimum of £50,000 of share capital.[4]

In the U.K., the term "limited" is applied to both listed and private companies that are registered as legal entities. The distinction is that the listed company's shares are sold in a market. A listed company is required by law to include PLC in its name.

Table 3-D. Sample Numbers from *Worldscope*

COMPANY NAME	CUSIP NO	SEDOL NO	ISIN NO	VALOR NO
AALBORG PORTLAND HOLDING A/S		4001979	DK0000013616	460403
ABBOTT LABORATORIES	002824100	2002305	US0028241000	903037
ABITIBI-PRICE INC	003680105	2003900	CA0036801052	676657
ABERFOYLE LTD.		6003100	AU0008652598	640005
ACCIAIERIE FERRIERE LOMBARDE		4330907	IT0000078003	565642
ACATOS & HUTCHENSON PLC		0005607	GB0000056076	368880
ACCOR SA		4112321	FR0000120404	485822
ACEC-UNION MINIERE SA		4005001	BE0003626372	439007
ACERINOX		4005238	ES0132105034	466304
ACHILLES CORPORATION		6496045	JP3108000005	761402
ATTWOODS PLC	000G061261	0062323	GB0000623230	371003
BE KANTONALBANK		4483016	CH0001333308	133330
YEO HIAP SENG LIMITED		6986160	SG0008735854	824347

In Italy, all companies must register with their local chamber of commerce. The Italian Chamber of Commerce has the legal responsibility to maintain and update all public data on *all* Italian enterprises, both companies and sole "traders (of whom there are about 4.5 million). The information is available in electronic form in Italian through CERVED, the Italian Chamber of Commerce Database. Profile information and balance sheets, as well as listings of directorships and defaults are all part of the databank. Definitions of different terms used to describe companies appear in Appendix B.

EC DIRECTIVES

In the United States, we cannot determine from a company's name whether it is a listed or private company. Either type of company name may end in Corp., Inc., or Co. Within the EC, you can tell immediately by the abbreviation at the end of the enterprise's name whether or not it is listed. Laws for these companies are set down in EC directives.

Table 3-E lists the EC directives on company law. The EC has been moving toward harmonization of company law, based on the EEC Treaty (Article 54(3)g). The law has been promulgated as a set of EC directives that have then been adopted as the law of the individual EC countries. A similar approach has been taken toward the harmonization of financial markets. It is important to be aware of the directives that are directly related to company names, size, and disclosure because they affect the availability of information.

A directive, according to Article 189 of the Treaty of the European Community, "shall be binding, as to the result to be achieved, upon each Member State, but shall leave to the national authorities the choice of form and methods." Member states have flexibility in how and when they implement directives.

Table 3-E. EC Company Law Directives

COMPANY LAW	Date Adopted	Current Status

First Directive
8/151/EEC OJ Special Edition 1968(1) p. 41-45
  Mandatory publication of specified
  company documents
	1968	In force in all
		member states

Second Directive 77/91/EEC OJ V20 L26 31 Jan 1977 p. 1-13 Safeguards in respect to formation of public companies	1976	In force in all member states
Third Directive 78/855 EEC OJ V21 L295, 20 Oct 1978 p. 36-43 Mergers between two public companies in member states	1978	Exceptions: Italy, Spain, Belgium

Fourth Directive
78/660 EEC OJ V21 L222 14 Aug 1978 p. 11-31
  Annual accounts of individual companies complemented by
  the 7th Directive
	1978	Exceptions: Italy,
		Spain, Portugal

Proposed Fifth Directive OJ V26 L240 L240 p. 2-38 Structure of Management of PLCs		Proposals 1983, 1989-
Sixth Directive 82/891 EEC OJ V25 L378 31 Dec 1982 p. 47-54 Splitting PLCs	1982	Exceptions: Italy, Spain, Belgium, not applicable in West Germany, Denmark, or The Netherlands
Seventh Directive 83/349 EEC OJ V26 L193 18 July 1983 p. 1-17 Consolidated accounts	1983	Partially implemented
Eighth Directive 84/253 EEC OJ V27 L126 12 May 1984 p. 20-26 Qualification of auditors	1984	Exceptions: Italy, Denmark, France, Portugal, Ireland

Table 3-E. EC Company Law Directives *(continued)*

COMPANY LAW	Date Adopted	Current Status
Proposed Ninth Directive Conduct of groups containing PLCs		1984; no action

Draft Tenth Directive
    OJ V28 C23 25 Jan 1985 p. 11-15
    International mergers of public companies
	1985; no further action	

Eleventh Directive   1989
    OJ V32 L395 30 Dec 1989 p. 36-39
    Disclosure requirements of branches
		Implementation:
		1992 for 1993

Twelfth Directive   1989
    OJ V32 L395 20 Dec 1989 p. 40-42
    Single member private limited companies
		Implementation:
		January 1992

Another method for implementing harmonization measures in the EC has been through regulations. Article 189 states that a regulation "shall have general application. It shall be binding in its entirety and directly applicable in all Member States. A regulation can supplant or supplement national law." Even though regulations carry with them tighter structure than directives, the anticipated level of harmonization has not occurred for the following reasons:

1. Member states, in enacting national law, interpret directives differently
2. It may be difficult to incorporate directives into national law
3. Harmonization requires general agreement on the definition of terms and concepts
4. Directives and regulations rely on company law of member states
5. A range of options may be included in the directive
6. Harmonization in company law depends on harmonization in other areas, which may not be in place.[5]

As a result of the First and Second Directives, official information about both listed and unlisted EC companies is now readily available. We are able to find official registration information and financial information about companies whose shares are not traded on markets.

The First Directive sets down legal requirements for registered listed and private companies in member states. It provides for establishing company registries in the countries. It specifies that companies must publish information on capital, annual accounts, details of directors, registered office, company statutes, and details pertaining to liquidation. The types of repositories for company registration used by EC members are shown in Table 3-F.

Table 3-F. EC Repositories for Company Registration

Central Repository	*Regional Repositories*
U.K. (Companies House)	Spain(1991): provincial registry
Portugal (based on size)	Luxembourg: local court
Ireland	Italy (CERVED): chambers of commerce
Denmark	Greece (1991)
	Germany, Netherlands, France, Belgium: local courts and chambers of commerce

The Second Directive specifies harmonized standards for the formation and maintenance of capital of public companies with a view to protect shareholders and creditors. Standards include naming of companies and setting a minimum capital requirement of 25,000 ECU. Companies must include information on registered office and nominal value of shares. More information about the Fourth and Seventh Directives appears in Chapter 2, "Accounting Standards and Practices."

Table 3-G shows commonly used EC abbreviations to designate legal company type. Many countries use the "Ltd" designation for all corporations that have shareholders, whether they are traded or not.

D&B Europa 1993 identifies over 30 legal types of organizations among the 19 countries it covers and gives each legal type a code. It presents a table for each country. Table 3-H is an example of the legal status of Belgian companies.

OTHER COUNTRY REQUIREMENTS

Once we move outside the EC, there are no standard regulations for reporting information. It is necessary to

Table 3-G. European Company Name Designations

```
Country          Public                          Private

Belgium          SA(Société Anonyme) or          SPRL (Société de Personnes a
                 NV (Naamloze                      Responsibilité Limitée) or
                    Vennootschap                  PVBA (Personenvennootschap met
                                                    heperkte aansprakelijkheid)
Denmark          A/S (Aktieselskab)              ApS (Anpartsselskab)
Finland          OY  Osakeyhtio                  OY  Osakeyhtio
France           SA (Société Anonyme)            SARL (Société a Responsibilité
Luxembourg                                           Limitée)
Switzerland

Germany          AG (Aktiengesellschaft)         GmbH (Gesellschaft mit beschrankter
  Austria                                             Haftung)
  Switzerland
Greece           AE (Anonymous Eteria)           EPE (Eteria Periorismenis Efthinis)
Italy            SpA (Societa per Azioni)        SRL (Societe a Responsibilita
                                                     Limitata)
Netherlands      NV (Naamloze                    BV (Besloten Vennootschap met
                    Venootschap                      beperkte
Portugal         SARL or SA (Sociedade           LDA (Sociedade por Quotas de
                    Anonima de Resonsabilidade        Responsabilidade Limitada)*
                    Limitada)
Spain            SA (Sociedad Anonima)           SA (Sociedad de Resonsabilidad
                                                     Limitada)
U.K.             PLC (Public Limited Company) Ltd (Private Limited Company)**
Ireland
_____

* Also used in overseas territories
** Adopted in Commonwealth countries
***S.A. and SpA designations - [anonymous] - companies issue bearer shares and owners are
nameless.
```

check on a country-by-country basis. Although many companies have mandatory filing rules, that does not guarantee that this information must be made available to the public. Two examples of the variety of country treatment of filing requirements are Scandinavia and Australia.

Scandinavian countries have strict registration and reporting procedures. Companies must report an annual

Table 3-H. Legal Status Tables for Belgium

Belgium

Code	Legal Status	
2	Société de personnes a responsabilité limitée	SPRL
	Personenvennotschap met beperkte aansprakelijkheid	PVBA
3	Société anonyme	SA
	Naamloze venootschap	NV
4	Société en commandite	SCS
	Vennootschap bij wijze van eenvovolige geldschieting	VEG
6	Foreign Registered Company	
8	Société cooperative	SC
	Samenwerkende vennootschap	SV
18	Société en nom collectif	SNC
	Vennootschap onder gemeenschappelijke naam	VGN
19	Besloten venootschap met beperkte aansprakelijkehid	BVBA

balance sheet from the previous year to the government but there is no obligation to make this information public. The rules vary among countries. Nordic Databases 1990, compiled by SCANNET, provides information about Scandinavian company files.

In Australia, all companies register with the Australian Securities Commission (G.P.O. Box 4866, Sydney, NSW 2001, Australia). Private companies are also to be listed with the ASC. Searches are conducted on company name to insure a unique name within a line of business. The ASC maintains a central databank.

Disclosure Requirements: Sources of Information

The *Directory of World Stock Exchanges* has a summary of requirements for listed companies for individual exchanges. More in-depth coverage may be found in two sources: CIFAR'S *International Accounting and Auditing Trends* for listed companies and Business International's *Investing, Licensing and Trading in...* which has requirements for listed and private companies. These two sources are in print and on LEXIS AND NEXIS SERVICES.

Exhibit 3-3 describes disclosure practices for two emerging markets—Argentina and Thailand. The information is from the "Reporting Practices" section of *International Accounting and Auditing Trends*, 1991 (LEXIS AND NEXIS SERVICES, Nov. 1992). Included are some items we would expect to see in an annual or 10K filing but which are either optional or *not* required in these countries.

EXHIBIT 3-3. Extracts from *International Accounting and Auditing Trends*

ARGENTINA: REPORTING PRACTICES

- Product segmentation is not disclosed.
- Geographic segmentation is not disclosed.
  Exports are reported by some.
- Earnings per share is not disclosed.
- Dividend per share is reported by some.
- Shareholders
  Major shareholding is not disclosed.
- Subsidiary information is reported with name, domicile and percent held by parent.
- Number of employees is not disclosed.
- Management information
  Names and titles of principal officers are reported by many.
  List of board members is reported by many.
  Company shares owned by directors/officers are not disclosed
  Remuneration to directors/officers is not disclosed
- Research and development expenses are not disclosed.

THAILAND: REPORTING PRACTICES

- Foreign exchange gains/losses are reported by some.
- Changes in shareholders' equity are not reported at all.
- Appropriation of retained earnings is disclosed by most.
- Product segmentation is disclosed by some.
- Geographic segmentation is disclosed by some, exports by many.
- Earnings per share is reported by most.
- Shareholders
  Major shareholding and names of shareholders are reported by some.
- Number of employees is reported by many on domestic companies only.
- Management information
  Names and titles of principal officers are reported by most.
  List of board members is not reported at all.
  Company shares owned by directors/officers are not reported at all.
  Remuneration to directors/officers is not reported at all.
- Research and development expenses are not disclosed at all.

Reprinted with permission from the Center for International Financial Analysis & Research, Inc. (CIFAR).

Business International's *Investing, Licensing and Trading (IL&T)* includes company requirements for all the countries it covers. Exhibit 3-4 is from the *IL&T* report on Argentina; it distinguishes between unlisted (SRL) and listed (S.A.) requirements.

Businesses may be established as sole proprietorships, general or limited partnerships, cooperatives, branches, corporations (*sociedades anonimas*—SAs), or limited-liability companies (*sociedades de responsabilidad limitada*—SRLs). The SA is the only entity that may issue shares to the public. The SRL is in effect a partnership, but the liability of the partners is limited to their subscribed capital. If one partner is a foreign company, the SRL is taxed in the same manner as a branch. The Argentine affiliates of Abbott Laboratories, Miles Laboratories, Ralston Purina, Timken, and Dun & Bradstreet, among others, are organized as SRLs.

Table 3-I shows the abbreviations used for Latin American companies. They are not, however, specified by law, as in the EC.

Table 3-I. Latin American Company Name Designations

Country	Abbreviation/ Definition	Type of Company
General Usage:	**S.A.** Sociedad Anonima	Corporation
	Ltda Limitada	Limited Liability
Alternatives: Ecuador, Venezuela	**C.A.** Compania Anonima	Corporation
Dominican Republic	**C for A** Compania for Acciones or **CXA**	Corporation

Source: Dun's Latin America (1991, p. IX). Copyright © 1991 Dun & Bradstreet, Inc. All rights reserved. Reprinted with permission.

SIZE OF COMPANIES

Most companies are small, and the smaller the company, the less information that is available. Therefore, we cannot expect to find much more than an address for the great majority of enterprises worldwide. Within the EC, company size categories are specified by law: large, medium, small, and micro. Over 90% of all EC enterprises fall into the micro category.

Multinationals

Outside the range of official size categories are companies referred to as "multinational" companies. In Chapter 9 we examine the concept of multinationality as it applies to how a company operates abroad. Here, however, we are interested in the definition of a multi-

EXHIBIT 3-4. *IL&T* **Report on Argentina**

	SRL	S.A.
Capital	No minimum	P17,500 minimum but may be changed
Founders, Shareholders	2–50 Partners	Minimum of 2 shareholders
Disclosure	If capital > P16,000 an annual report with balance sheet and P&L statement must be submitted for publication in the official bulletin Auditor required	Annual P&L statement and balance sheet submitted to Justice Inspectorate, or to provincial authorities, for publication in the official bulletin. Annual balance sheets must be adjusted for inflation and audited. There should be one or more *syndic* a type of independent auditor.
Types of shares	Shares or quotes must be of equal book value.	Shares may be registered or bearer, and common or preferred.

3.10 Establishing a local company. Businesses may be established sole proprietorships, general or limited partnerships, cooperatives, branches (3.11), corporations (*sociedades anónimas*—SAs) or limited-liability companies (*sociedades de responsabilidad limitada*—SRLs). The SA is the only entity that may issue shares to the public. The SRL is in effect a partnership, but the liability or partners is limited to their subscribed capital. If one partner is a foreign company, the SRL is taxed in the same manner as a branch.

Source: Investing, Licensing and Trading Conditions Abroad, Argentina, June 1992, p. 6; the Economist Intelligence Unit. Reprinted with permission.

national corporation. The multinational is referred to by a variety of terms: Multinational Corporation (MNC), Multinational Enterprise (MNE), or, as used by the U.N., Transnational Company/Enterprise (TNC/TNE).

No standard definition of a multinational corporation exists. An early review of the literature and status of multinationals was written by Yair Aharoni in the *Quarterly Review of Economics and Business* in 1971.[6] Aharoni credits David E. Lilienthal for first using the term "multinational" in April 1960 when he suggested the definition of "multinational corporations" as "corporations which have their home in one country but operate and live under the laws and customs of other countries as well." These first "multinationals" were firms with management operations in more than one country.

In 1982, Richard Caves published a review of the literature of the 1970s about the multinational enterprise. In it he defined an MNE as an enterprise that controls and manages production establishments—plants—located in at least two countries.[7]

The definitions that have evolved in the past 10 years have become more complex. The first multinational directory, the 1981 *World Directory of Multinational Enterprises*, included 500 of the largest industrial corporations with "significant international investments." Companies were included that had manufacturing or mining activities in at least three foreign countries, 5% of sales attributable to foreign investments, and $75 million sales from foreign manufacturing operations.

In 1992, John H. Dunning, one of the authors of the *World Directory*, gave a different broad definition of a multinational enterprise as one that "owns and controls value-adding activities in more than one country."[8]

A synthesis of the characteristics of a multinational includes:

1. Number of countries in which a firm is operating
2. Number of countries in which a firm makes products/services available
3. Composition of management operating the firm, both in terms of nationality and outlook
4. Financial performance: absolute or relative share of assets, employees, and sales in a foreign country are "significant portion"[9]

Vinod Bavishi, from CIFAR, suggests three variables as good measures of multinationality: foreign sales, foreign income, and foreign assets.[10] He also suggests using the number of active foreign subsidiaries, percent of common shares owned by foreign-based shareholders, and number of employees abroad as other measures.

John D. Daniels, author of one of the standard textbooks on international business, *International Business: Environment and Operations*, distinguishes between the multinational and the transnational. For Daniels, the multinational has an integrated philosophy toward home country and overseas operations. Daniels' has a narrow view of the transnational, as a company owned and managed by nationals in a different country.[11]

Lee Preston and Duane Windsor in *The Rules of the Game in the Global Economy* suggest a framework in which multinationals are part of a continuum that ranges from purely domestic companies to possible stateless enterprises (*see* Exhibit 3-5). They also distinguish investor-owned companies from those which are partly or totally state-owned.[12]

EXHIBIT 3-5. Multinational Enterprises Classification

	Multinational Enterprises			
	Purely Domestic Enterprises	National-Base Enterprises	Joint Venture Strategic Alliance Enterprise Networks	Stateless Global Enterprises
Investor-Owned Enterprises	Canadian Pacific	Nestle SA Union Carbide (US)	Caltex(US) Auto Companies --------------->	BCCI Likely
Jointly-Controlled Enterprises and Private-Government Combinations	Conrail(US)	British Petroleum (BP)	Union Carbide India Ltd SAS (Sweden, Norway,Denmark) ------------->	Possible
State-Owned Enterprises	Amtrak(US) Canadian National	Quantas (Australia)	Renault (France) ------------------>	Unlikely

Source: *Rules of the Game in the Global Economy*, p. 26. Reprinted with permission.

Cyrus Freidheim, vice-chairman of the management consulting Booz, Allen & Hamilton, suggests that the enterprise of the twentieth-first century will be a "relationship-enterprise," a network of strategic alliances among big firms from different countries and different industries. Freidheim also notes that today's global companies still have a domestic base, a home-country bias, and are restrained by national laws.[13]

Forbes magazine has published a special report on U.S. multinationals since 1979, using a measure of foreign revenues, income, and assets. Companies are ranked based on total foreign revenue. *Forbes* calculates foreign revenue, profit, and assets as a percent of total revenue, profit, and assets. Exhibit 3-6 includes the data for the top 25 companies listed by *Forbes*. The table as it appears in *Forbes* also has data for total assets.

The United Nations states that a multinational corporation owns or controls economic resources in two or more countries. According to the U.N.'s Centre on Transnational Corporations, the world's largest industrial transnational corporations, with annual sales of more than one billion dollars, account for more than one-fifth of the value-added in the production of goods worldwide. These corporations met the following criteria:

1. Parent company engaged in manufacturing or extractive sectors
2. One or more foreign affiliates
3. Total annual sales over one billion $U.S.

Table 3-J shows the geographical distribution of transnational corporations according to the UN's definition.

The United Nations Centre on Transnational Corporations is a major source for information about transnationals. The Centre's objective is to help developing countries understand and negotiate with transnational corporations. Below are examples of the Centre's publications.

Transnational Business Information: A Manual of Needs and Sources (1991) is a simple, clear book that will help researchers better understand and identify information about transnationals. The chapters are organized by type of information one should know about transnationals and the publicly available sources that provide the information.

Transnational Corporation: A Selective Bibliography 1983-1987 and *1988/1990* are two bibliographies

Table 3-J. Transnational Corporations by Country (1991)

Country	Number of enterprises	Share (Percentage)
United States of America	301	39.4
Japan	141	18.5
United Kingdom	80	10.5
Germany	61	8.0
France	33	4.3
Canada	23	3.0
Netherlands	20	2.6
Sweden	18	2.4
Switzerland	13	1.7
Italy	9	1.2
Republic of Korea	8	1.0
Belgium	8	1.0
Australia	6	0.8
Spain	6	0.8
Finland	5	0.7
Other countries (20)	31	4.1
Total	**763**	**100.0**

Source: *International Accounting & Reporting Issues: 1991 Review*, pp.170-171

EXHIBIT **3-6.** *Forbes* **100 Largest Multinationals**

1991 Rank	Company	Revenue foreign ($ mil)	Revenue total ($ mil)	foreign as % of total	Net profit n1 foreign ($ mil)	Net profit total ($ mil)	foreign as % of total
1	Exxon	78,073	102,847	75.9	4,717	5,600	84.2
2	IBM	40,358	64,792	62.3	1,909	-564	P-D
3	General Motors	39,083	123,056	31.8	2,534	-4,992	P-D
4	Mobil	n2 38,778	n2 56,910	68.1	n3 2,101	n3 2,435	86.,3
5	Ford Motor	34,477	88,286	39.1	-811	-2,258	35.9
6	Texaco n4	24,754	49,648	49.9	n3 1,046	n3 1,817	57.6
7	Chevron n4	17,180	44,984	38.2	1,130	1,293	87.4
8	El du Pont de Nemours	17,086	38,151	44.8	740	1,403	52.7
9	Citicorp	16,848	31,839	52.9	437	-914	P-D
10	Philip Morris Cos	13,152	48,064	27.4	999	3,927	25.4
11	Procter & Gamble	12,327	27,026	45.6	402	1,773	22.7
12	Dow Chemical	9,728	18,807	51.7	n6 280	n6 1,178	23.8
13	General Electric	n2 8,671	n2 60,236	14.4	443	4,435	10.0
14	Xerox n4	8,590	19,372	44.3	292	454	64.3
15	Eastman Kodak	8,537	19,419	44.0	221	17	NM
16	Digital Equipment	8,325	13,911	59.8	145	-617	P-D
17	Hewlett-Packard	8,104	14,949	54.2	251	755	33.2
18	United Technologies	n2 8,029	n2 21,262	37.8	n6 225	n6 -968	P-D
19	Coca-Cola	7,401	11,572	64.0	1,139	1,618	70.4
20	American Intl Group	n7 7,322	16,884	43.4	n7 670	1,553	43.1
21	Minn Mining & Mfg	6,465	13,340	48.5	n6 401	n6 1,186	33.8
22	Amoco	n2 6,372	n2 25,647	24.8	200	1,173	17.1
23	Motorola	6,340	11,341	55.9	304	454	67.0
24	ITT	6,310	20,421	30,9	n6 411	n6 868	47.4
25	Johnson & Johnson	6,199	12,447	49.8	787	1,461	53.9

n1 From continuing operations.
n2 Includes other income.
n3 Net income before corporate expense.
n4 Includes proportionate interest in unconsolidated subsidiaries or affiliates.
n5 Average assets.
n6 Net income before minority interest.
n7 Excludes Canadian operations.
D-P: Deficit to profit.
P-D: Profit to deficit.
NA: Not available.

Source: "100 Largest U.S. Multinationals," *Forbes*, July 20, 1992. The list published in the July 19, 1993, *Forbes* has the same companies in the top 25, with only minor changes in order. Reprinted by permission of *Forbes* magazine, July 20, 1992. Copyright © Forbes Inc., 1993.

published by the Centre. About one-third of the titles are from languages other than English. Citations are arranged by broad category, according to the Centre's classification scheme. There are also subject, title, and author indexes.

United Nations Library on Transnational Corporations is a series to be published by Routledge beginning in late 1993. The series is published on behalf of the Transnational Corporations and Management Division of the United National Department of Economic and Social Development. Sample titles that have been announced include *Transnational Corporations in Services, Transnational Corporations and Regional Economic Integration,* and *Transnational Corporations and Human Resources.*

Size of Enterprises

Enterprises in Europe (Commission of the European Communities)

In 1986, the EC began systematic data collection to count the number of establishments within the EC market by country and by size category. There were about 13.4 million enterprises employing 92.4 million people in 1986.

The EC itself has special programs to encourage a favorable business environment for the creation and development of "small and medium enterprises" (SMEs). Toward this end, the Commission has collected and published data on the size distribution of enterprises by sector. The first report, published in 1990, was *Enterprises in the European Community*. The second report, *Enterprises in Europe*, was released at the end of 1992.

Official data, similar to the economic censuses in the U.S., have been collected every five years and were limited in scope. The first report used 1983 data and covered only 10 of the 12 countries. The more specific the industrial classification code, the fewer the countries supplying data. The newer release has data through 1989 and covers not only the EC but also EFTA, with some comparative U.S. and Japanese figures as well.

The second report has two chapters. Chapter One is an analysis at the EC level, with international comparisons to Japan and the United States. Chapter Two contains descriptions for the 17 countries for which data are available. The report tries to follow a common format. However, there is variation based on the amount of information available from the different countries. There

is more emphasis in the second report on SMEs as well as industry analysis.

Data are collected from public and private sources. The first choice of source is a country's national statistics office. The reporting unit is the enterprise. The classification system is NACE, the official industrial classification of economic activities within the EC, established by Eurostat in 1970. Data are collected for three economic variables: employment (paid and unpaid), turnover (total sales), and value added. Size classification has been based on number of employees. Table 3-K shows the EC classification for enterprise size.

Table 3-K. EC Classification of Enterprise Size

Classification	Number of employees
Large Business Sectors	500 or more
SME Business Sectors	10–499
Small	10–99
Medium	100–499
Micro Sectors	0–9

For comparison, in the U.S., an SME is defined as an enterprise with less than 500 employees, and U.S. SMEs account for 60% of the nation's total employment.

In the 1986 count, micro enterprises comprised 91.34% of all enterprises in the EC. SMEs constituted 8.56% and large enterprises made up the difference. Micro enterprises provided 27% of all jobs, SMEs 45%, and large enterprises 28%. Exhibit 3-7 displays the percentages for number of enterprises and employment by size class in 1986 for the EC. Additional data on company size appears in Appendix F.

EXHIBIT 3-7. Percentage of Number of Enterprises and of Employment by Size Class 1986 for the EC 12

	Micro		SMEs	Large
	(0)	(1-9)	(10-499)	(500+)
Enterprises:				
All	52.0	39.34	8.56	0.10
Manufacturing	37.0	45.70	16.91	0.39
Construction	47.0	44.28	8.68	0.04
Services	56.0	37.03	6.92	0.06
Employment				
All	7.56	19.34	45.02	26.10
Manufacturing	2.15	8.95	45.95	42.91
Construction	9.35	30.15	50.75	9.90
Services	10.72	23.98	43.44	21.82

Source: Enterprises in the European Community, Table 3.4a, p. 3.8, 1986. Reprinted with permission from the Office for Official Publications of the European Communities.

SPECIAL CASES

EC law affects the structure of EC companies and the information flow about those companies. Japanese and Korean culture and practice serve the same function.

Japanese Companies

The unique structure of Japanese companies affects Japanese company information, industry analysis, marketing data, and international trade. Major Japanese companies are organized in *keiretsu* [kay-rhet-sue] or company coalitions. The keiretsu are business alliances in which companies have interlocking directors and joint stock holdings. They form trading groups that may be vertical or horizontal. Mutual stockholding, two-way flow of capital and personnel, and a predisposition to buy from and sell to one another are characteristics of current keiretsu. The six largest corporate families account for about 25% of Japan's GNP.

For example, Mitsubishi is a horizontal keiretsu with about 190 member companies and sales of $300 billion. Toyota is a vertical keiretsu with 175 primary suppliers and 4,000 secondary ones. Distribution alliances also exist with other manufacturers and retailers. DKB group is comprised of Dai-Ichi Kangyo, the world's largest bank in 1992 based on assets; Asahi Chemical, one of the world's largest chemical companies; and Fujitsu, one of the world's largest computer companies. The group also includes Isuzu Motor.

What distinguishes the keiretsu is the way in which the companies do business together. They differ from U.S. subsidiary or affiliate relationships where the parent company owns a controlling share. Three members of the DKB group are listed as major shareholders in Fujitsu: Dai-Ichi Kangyo Bank Ltd., Asahi Mutual Life Insurance Co., and Dai-Ichi Mutual Life Insurance Co. They hold 4.6%, 6.4%, and 1.3%, respectively.

Some companies are members of more than one group. For example, Nippon Express, a company primarily involved in shipping and transportation, has shareholders from five of the six major keiretsu mentioned by Rapoport: Mitsubishi, Mitsui, Sumitomo, Fuyo, DKB, and Sanwa. The groups have members from the financial services industry, electronics, automobiles, food, construction, real estate, chemicals, industrial equipment, and shipping and transportation. Exhibit 3-8 shows these Keiretsu interrelationships.

Identifying keiretsu relationships is difficult. Although the Japanese have changed disclosure requirements to reveal more interrelationships, the Japanese press does not publicize these groupings. The keiretsu are part of what the U.S. considers Japanese unfair trade practices, but in Japan, this is accepted procedure. Japanese companies manufacturing in the United States depend on these affiliated suppliers to provide the parts for products built in the U.S., rather than using U.S. suppliers.

Japanese joint stock companies are referred to as KK—*Kabushiki Kaishas*. There are about one million joint stock companies in Japan. The very large general trading companies are called *sogo shosha*. Examples are C. Itoh & Co (Itochu Shoki KK), Sumitomo, Marubeni, Mitsubishi, and Mitsui & Co. They are the largest companies in the world.

Korean Companies

Chaebol are Korean conglomerates similar to keiretsu. The major chaebol are Samsung (48 affiliates), Hyundai (42 affiliates), Lucky Goldstar International (62 affiliates), and Daewoo Corp. (24 affiliates). The sales of all the affiliate companies and the revenues of the top 30 chaebol came to 127 trillion won ($180 billion) in 1990, equivalent to 76% of the country's GNP. Like Japan's pre-war zaibatsu, the four chaebol started out as family

---

EXHIBIT 3-8. Keiretsu Relationship Extracted from *Extel* Record

```
NIPPON EXPRESS CO LTD.
MAJOR  SHAREHOLDERS in the Company at 31-03-92:
  Asahi Mutual Life Insurance Co  92,381,000  (8.6%)
  The Dai-Ichi Kangyo Bank Ltd 50,146,000 (4.7%);
  The Sanwa  Bank  Ltd  35,329,000 (3.3%);
  The Koa Fire & Marine Insurance Co Ltd 31,512,000 (2.9%);
  The Industrial Bank of Japan Ltd 29,356,000 (2.7%);
  The Long-Term  Credit Bank of Japan Ltd 28,184,000 (2.6%);
  Japan Railways Group Mutual  Aid  Assoc  26,780,000  (2.5%);
  The  Mitsui Trust & Banking Co Ltd 25,439,000  (2.4%);
  The Toyo Trust & Banking Co Ltd 25,316,000  (2.4%);
  The Sumitomo  Trust  &  Banking  Co  Ltd  23,626,000  (2.2%);
  Total 368,069,000
  (34.3%).
```

Source: *Extel* online, DATA-STAR, February 1993. Reprinted with permission from EXTEL Financial Ltd.

businesses but, unlike Japan's biggest companies today, they remain family-dominated.

Company Structure in the Former Soviet Union

From the few official State Trading Organizations and state enterprises in existence prior to 1988, many types of business now co-exist in the CIS. About 30,000 organizations are dealing in international trade. The main forms of business arrangement are

- **State Enterprises:** pre-existing enterprises run by the government
- **Joint Ventures:** started in 1987
- **Cooperatives:** legalized in May 1988, 250,000 were registered as of May 1991; these first nonpublic Soviet enterprises had to be worker-owned
- **Private Sector:** small independent entrepreneurs (*malyye predpriyatiya*), legalized in June 1989
- **Joint Stock Companies and Limited-Liability Corporations:** legalized in mid-1990
- **State Trading Companies (FTOs):** limited in number, these former official organizations for trade have been disbanded

CONCLUSION

This chapter was designed to provide the background needed to begin evaluating sources of company information and to understand the difficulties associated with international company information. It has described characteristics of company information sources that we use to categorize materials in later chapters. It has presented techniques to identify companies. It has introduced concepts such as disclosure and size of enterprises, which influence the amount of information available in secondary sources. We hope that it will provide a basis for sources that we examine in the following five chapters.

FOR FURTHER READING

Selected Reading on Multinationals

Organisation for Economic Co-operation and Development (Working Group on Accounting Standards). *Disclosure of Information by Multinational Enterprises—Survey of the Application of the OECD Guidelines*, 1987.

Pearce, John A., II and Roth, Kendall. "Multinationalization of the Mission Statement," *Advanced Management Journal 53*(Summer 1988): 39-44

Porter, Michael E. "Changing Patterns of International Competition." *California Management Review 28*(2) (Winter 1986): 9-40.

Porter makes a distinction between companies that operate in "multi-domestic" industries (in which competition is independent across countries of operations) and those that operate in global industries (in which competition in each country affects competition in other countries).

Stafford, David C. and Purkis, Richard H.A., eds. *Directory of Multinationals,* 3rd ed. 2 vols. (New York: Stockton Press, 1990).

Includes companies that had $1billion in sales in 1987 with "significant" foreign investments. Includes 450 parent companies and uses 1987 data.

"Survey: Multinationals,"*Economist* (March 27, 1993): 5-20.

Selected Reading on Keiretsu and Chaebol

"Japan Keiretsu System Growing Weaker, JFTC Study Finds," *BNA International Trade Daily* (April 30, 1992). NEXIS, CURRNT.

The Japan Fair Trade Commission concludes that the keiretsu relationships are growing weaker.

Kearns, Robert L. *Zaibatsu America: How Japanese Firms Are Colonizing Vital U.S. Industries* (New York: Free Press/Macmillan, 1992).

The book examines the grip Japanese conglomerates have on American industry. This contrasts with the report from the Japan Fair Trade Commission.

"South Korea's Conglomerates: Do or Be Done For," *Economist 31*(December 9, 1989): 74, 79.

The conglomerates must restructure to survive. Chaebol need to raise funds on international capital markets. This will dilute family control and cross holdings.

"South Korea's Conglomerates: Spoiled Rotten," *Economist 31* (June 8, 1991): 76.

Chaebol dominate the South Korean economy, and this has become a problem. The companies pursue market share at all costs.

Udagawa, Hideo. "Dawning of a New Age for the Sogo Shosha Traders," *Tokyo Business Today* 60 (January 1992): 54-57.

Sogo Shosha are setting up production subsidiaries worldwide and getting involved in energy and information communications.

Weimer, George. "Keiretsu, Kudzu, Zaibatsu, and You: Are We Japan's New Colony," *Industry Week* (March 16, 1992): 68-.

Zaibatsu were the 30 giant trading conglomerates that ran most of pre-World-War II Japanese industry and were the forerunners of keiretsu and sogo shosha.

NOTES

1. Anne Mintz, "Quality Control and the Zen of Database Production" *Online 14* (November 1990): 15–23.
2. Ruth A. Pagell, "Sorry Wrong Number," *Online 14,* (November 1990): 20-23.

3. *D&B News*, (December 1991): 9.

4. *FAME User Manual* (London: FAME, 1991), p. 9.

5. *EEC Directive on Company Law and Financial Markets* (Oxford University Press, 1991), pp. 2-89.

6. Yair Aharoni, "On the Definition of a Multinational Corporation," *Quarterly Review of Economics and Business 11* (1971): 27-37.

7. Richard E. Caves, *Multinational Enterprise and Economic Analysis* (Cambridge: Cambridge University Press, 1982).

8. Christopher Nobes and Robert Parker, eds., *Comparative International Accounting*, 3rd ed. (Hempel, U.K.: Prentice Hall Ltd., 1991).

9. S.J. Grey, *Handbook of International Business and Management* (Oxford: B. Blackwell, 1990).

10. Vinod Bavishi, *Analyzing International Financial Statements: A Systematic Approach* (Princeton, NJ: CIFAR, 1987). Presented at SLA conference.

11. John D. Daniels, *International Business: Environments and Operations,* 6th ed. (Reading, MA: Addison-Wesley, 1992).

12. Lee E. Preston and Duane Windsor, *The Rules of the Game in the Global Economy: Policy Regimes* (Boston: Kluwer Academic Publishers, 1992).

13. "The Global Firm: R.I.P.," *Economist* (February 6, 1993): 69.

CHAPTER 4
Company Information: Directory Sources

TOPICS COVERED

1. Selecting International Directories
2. Basic Company Directories
3. Industry Directories
4. Product Directories
5. Directors and Officers
6. Company Histories
7. Company Information When the Company Is Not Known
8. Other Selected Directories

MAJOR SOURCES DISCUSSED

- *Principal International Businesses*
- *World Business Directory*
- *D&B Europa*
- *Directory of the World's Largest Service Companies*
- *KOMPASS International Editions*
- *International Directory of Company Histories*

In Chapter 3, we described the problems of finding and identifying company information. We categorized directories by the types of information they include. A general understanding of the concepts in Chapter 3 will be helpful in evaluating directories. This chapter discusses several categories of basic directories and describes some recent publications.

Although Chapter 6 gives an overview of online and ondisc sources, electronic sources are included in the discussion of print sources when relevant.

SELECTING INTERNATIONAL DIRECTORIES

Until recently, very few company directories offered worldwide coverage. One of the first, *Moody's International Manual*, was published in 1971. Dun & Bradstreet's *Principal International Businesses (PIB)* followed in 1974. Publications from individual countries, such as *Kelly's Business Directory*, *Bottin International*, and the KOMPASS International Editions were available for libraries that needed detailed product level information from individual countries. International organizations such as the United Nations and the World Bank limited their publications to statistical sources.

Today, however, there are many company directories, both international and country specific, from U.S.

publishers, non-U.S. publishers, and international organizations. These publications often are expensive. In rapidly changing areas, such as the former USSR, what you order today may be out of date before it arrives.

No single library can own all or even a large fraction of the published directories. No single research guide can discuss all directories in any depth. However, all libraries will need at least a few basic sources for company information. As an aid to decisions about purchasing, we have identified some important characteristics for an international directory.

- Who is the publisher? Because the market for international business information is now profitable, both new publishers and traditional reference publishers, such as Gale, are entering the international directory market. Whatever the size of your materials budget, stay away from unknown publishers and publications unless they are recommended by a reputable reviewer. Non-U.S. sources are not automatically more accurate than U.S. sources or vice versa. Check the publisher's pricing history and its continuations record.
- What does the book cost? Are you asked for information about international companies often enough to purchase a $500 volume, or would it be more efficient to search online for the occasional question?
- How many organizations/companies/people/products/ countries are covered? Some directories cost more than others, but the more expensive sources may have more entries and more data items.

- How is the book organized? Most of the sources we will be discussing have at least three dimensions: country, company, and product/industry. What is the primary arrangement? How are the additional indexes arranged? Can you find what you need?
- If the book contains sales data, is the date for those figures given? Are sales reported in local currency (e.g., French francs), converted to U.S. dollars, or reported in a standard currency (ECUs) or some combination of these methods? If the local figures are converted, is the exchange rate given?
- How well is the book documented? Are the criteria for inclusion presented? Are the methods of collecting the data described? One advantage of printed sources over machine-readable information is the quality and accessibility of the documentation.
- How timely is the material? How current is the information compared with the date of the publication?
- Who has actually compiled or collected the information? If it comes from other printed sources, are they clearly cited?
- Is there value added? Has the editor included additional information about the countries? Are there summary statistical data?

It is difficult to determine a directory's quality without examining it and using it. Ask the publisher for a 30-day trial. The cost of returning a volume is much less than the cost of buying and processing the wrong directory. Appendix A contains a checklist of directory data items.

BASIC COMPANY DIRECTORIES

Directories should be more than address books. Here are the pieces of information a basic company directory should contain.

- **Name:** legal or trading name, translated or transliterated
- **Address:** preferably with postal code
  Telecommunications: telephone, telex, fax, cable
- **Principal Officers and Directors**
- **Lines of Business Using a Standard Coding System**
- **Other Data:** sales/turnover and number of employees

International Directories

Principal International Businesses (Dun and Bradstreet—Annual)

The basic international company directory is *Principal International Businesses* (*PIB*). Published annually by Dun & Bradstreet, it includes basic information on more than 50,000 companies in 140 countries. The directory is easy to use and its layout is familiar to most U.S. users because of its similarities to the *Million Dollar*

Directory. The 1994 edition remained one volume, divided into three sections.

The introduction is in four languages: English, French, Spanish, and German. The directory has three sections:

Section I, Businesses Geographically (white pages): alphabetically by country and by company within the country

Section II, Businesses by Product Classification (yellow pages): by U.S. SIC codes and alphabetically by country, city, and then company within each code, with name, address, and all SIC codes

Section III, Businesses Alphabetically (blue pages): one alphabetical listing of all companies with name and address

In 1993, Dun and Bradstreet created one mega-international database which will be the basis for their international products. *Principal International Businesses* is one subset of this file. Information is gathered by non-U.S. affiliates of Dun & Bradstreet and maintained by Dun & Bradstreet Information Services North America. These reports also serve as the basis for the Dun's online files discussed below. A listing in this directory is not a credit endorsement by D&B. *PIB* is designed for use as a marketing tool.

D&B selects companies for *PIB* on the basis of size, national prominence, and international interest to businesses outside their own country. No firm solicits a listing. The entire range of industries are represented, including communications, power generation and distribution, real estate firms, and other services. A sample entry can include as many as 13 data items.

1. D-U-N-S number
2. Import/export designation
3. Business name (complete or "acceptable" abbreviation)
4. Parent company name
5. Business address
6. Cable and telex
7. Telephone
8. Annual sales volume for latest year in local currency (M represents thousands); the year is *not* given
9. Total number of employees
10. Year started
11. SIC code(s)
12. Lines of business
13. Chief executive, name and title

Exhibit 4-1 gives a sample entry from the section on Argentina in the 1994 edition of *PIB*. The information for this company in the 1994 edition is the same as the entry in the 1989 edition.

EXHIBIT 4-1. Sample Entry from *Principal International Businesses (PIB)*

```
    D-U-N-S 97-000-3778                    IMP EXP

  ACEROS BRAGADO SACIF
  Bernardo De Irigoyen 190, Buenos Aires 1072
  Telephone 222911          Cable/Telex 222911
  Ownership Date 1969       Emp Total 1,700
  SIC  3312 Blast furnaces & steel mills
  Presidente: Bernardo Abel Coll, Presidente
```

Source: Principal International Businesses, 1994, p.11. Copyright © 1993 Dun & Bradstreet, Inc. All rights reserved. Reprinted with permission.

For *PIB,* how is D&B handling the changing international scene and keeping its files updated? Not as well as expected. The 1993 entries for Yugoslavia are the same as the 1992 entries and little changed from most 1989 entries. Companies in the independent countries of Slovenia and Croatia are listed as being in Yugoslavia. The monetary unit given is the new dinar, Yugoslavia's currency. Slovenia now has its own currency.

While records for the major industrialized countries indicate frequent updating, the same is not true for many of the other countries covered. Although D&B acknowledges data collection problems in selected countries, this information is not included in *PIB.* It appears that the move to one Global File for all of D&B's publications and databases will improve updating.

World Business Directory (Gale—Annual)

The first important competitor to *PIB* appeared in mid-1992, Gale's *World Business Directory (WBD).* It is compiled in conjunction with the World Trade Centers Association (WTCA). This four-volume set has information on more than 100,000 businesses in 190 countries. Gale's criteria for inclusion are vague: companies that are important to or interested in international trade. The number of companies per country is approximately proportionate to each country's participation in world trade. Companies of all sizes are included.

Company information in *WBD* is collected from World Trade Centers, chambers of commerce, and trade officials. Companies responded to questionnaires and information was gathered or verified by reviewing annual reports and through telephone interviews.

Financial data are presented in the currency in which they are provided to Gale. Gale warns that "Accounting practices differ significantly from firm-to-firm and country-to country as do fiscal year configurations" (p. xii). Volumes 1-3 are arranged by country. Each entry may have the following information:

- Telephone, fax, and telex numbers
- Executive officers' names and titles
- Financial data
- Employee figures
- Company type
- Fiscal year-end
- Founding year
- Products traded
- Industry activity
- Parent information
- WTC affiliation
- WTC Network Code

Exhibit 4-2 displays a sample entry from *WBD.*

EXHIBIT 4-2. Sample Entry from *World Business Directory (WBD)*

Aceros Bragado SA
Bernardo de Irigoyen 190
1072 Buenos Aires, Argentina
Tel: 3345952, 3341687, 3347001
3349350 **Fax:** 3341226 **Tx:** ACERBA
17414
Officer(s): Bernardo Abel Coll, President; José Coll, Vice President; Héctor Pottí, Secretary. **Revenue:** 100,000,000,000-1,000,000,000,000 A (1990). **Employees:** 1,300(1991). **Activities:** Manufacturing-General. **Products:** Iron and Steel.
Source: *WBD* p.21

Source: World Business Directory, 1992, vol. 1, p. 26. Reprinted with permission from Gale Research.

Volume 4 of *WBD* has three indexes.

1. Alphabetical by product grouping from 2- and 4-digit Harmonized System codes, country, and company, to be replaced by SIC codes in the second edition.
2. Industry grouping based on company's principal business activities. Within this breakdown are several categories important to international business, such as freight forwarder agents, customhouse brokers, and manufacturers representatives.
3. Alphabetical list of companies.

Gale has announced that *WBD* will be available on CD-ROM by the end of 1993 on a disc entitled *Companies International:Ward's and World Business Directories on CD-ROM*. The CD-ROM will include 250,000 companies in 190 countries, including the U.S.

WBD covers more countries and more companies than *PIB* and costs less, but *WBD* has its share of errors. The entry for Yugoslavia has the note, "Including Macedonia, Montenegro, and Serbia," but the first company listed is from Slovenia. *WBD* does include dates for sales figures; however, those figures may be either in U.S. dollars or the currency of the country.

The first edition of *WBD* was a positive addition to the category of international business directories. The second edition, with 30,000 additional companies, primarily from Latin America and Russia, has an announced publication date of November 1993. Because we have not seen it, we have no way to judge the quality of the updating. *WBD* does not have the experience of D&B and the D&B staff to back it; nor does it have the huge financial and credit database behind it. If D&B, with its worldwide network, has difficulty maintaining the quality of data for all countries, we wonder if Gale, with no grounding in international research, will be able to do better.

There is very little overlap among the companies covered in *PIB* and *WBD*. For a library that needs one international company directory, *WBD* will be an alternative to *PIB* if it establishes a regular update frequency for both publication and data quality. Many libraries will find both publications useful. Table 4-A compares features of the two directories. Comparisons are based on 1993 *PIB* and the first edition of *WBD*.

Regional Directories

Two major publishers of regional international directories are Dun & Bradstreet and Graham Trotman.

In addition to *PIB*, Dun & Bradstreet publishes continental directories and a series of "Key" directories for individual countries.

Key Business Directory of Latin America 2 vols. 1993/ 94- (Dun & Bradstreet—Annual)

One example is *Key Business Directory of Latin America* which replaced *Duns Latin America's Top 25,000 Companies* in 1993. Business in this directory were selected from Duns Global File based on employee size within 35 Latin American countries. There are more companies listed per country in *Key Business* than in *PIB*. The directory is published annually, but not all records are updated regularly due to problems with reporting.

Table 4-A. Comparison of *Principal International Businesses* and *World Business Directory*

	PIB	WBD
Number of entries	over 50,000	100,000
Number of countries	143	190
Size of firms	"large"	all sizes
Fax number	No	Yes
Products	SIC	Verbal description and harmonized code; SIC added to 2nd ed.
Financials— Sales	All entries	Some entries, may be a range
Date for financials	Not given	Given
Currency	Local	Local or U.S. Dollars
Number of volumes	1	4
Purchase agreement	Lease	Buy

This directory is arranged in two volumes: Volume 1 has the alphabetical entries by country and businesses within the countries and an alphabetical listing to all companies. Volume II is a cross-reference by U.S. SIC codes and employee rankings.

Key Business Directory has added a telephone number to the ACEROS entry in Exhibit 4-1, changed the wording from "year started" to "ownership date," spelled out the words in the SIC code definition, and, most important, added a credit rating, instead of a sales figure. (See Chapter 8 for an explanation of Duns credit ratings.)

Given the spotty updating schedule for individual company records, a major concern with the Latin American directory is the absence of a year for the sales figure. In countries with high rates of inflation and unstable currency, not knowing the year of the sales figure makes comparisons among companies suspect.

D&B Europa (Dun & Bradstreet International—Annual)

A third D&B source is *D&B Europa*, first published in 1989 by Dun & Bradstreet International. This four-volume set includes approximately 60,000 companies from 19 countries. In the 1993 edition, 15,000 more companies and an additional country, Israel, were added. The 1993 edition also marked a change in title from *Dun's Europa* to *D&B Europa*.

Volumes 1-3 are listings of companies by country. Countries are arranged alphabetically by country codes. Volume 4 has European statistics, rankings, and indexes.

The set may be purchased in English, German, Spanish, French, Italian, or Portuguese.

The number of companies chosen for each country is based on the country's 1990 gross domestic product. The largest companies in each country have been selected based on annual sales, except for banks, where total assets are used for selection, and insurance companies, which are selected by amount of commissions.

D&B Europa describes more companies than do online databases of public corporations. It lists fewer companies per country than do many country-level directories or Dun's online file *European Market Identifiers.* Table 4-B displays the number of companies listed in *D&B Europa* for 19 countries it covers.

Table 4-B. *D&B Europa*: **Companies Listed by Country**

OS	Austria	1,347	LX	Luxembourg	77
BL	Belgium	1,701	NL	Netherlands	2,252
DK	Denmark	1,239	NO	Norway	852
SF	Finland	1,001	PO	Portugal	559
FR	France	10,694	ES	Spain	4,222
DE	Germany	13,052	SW	Sweden	453
GR	Greece	496	CH	Switzerland	2,005
IR	Ireland	441	TK	Turkey	963
IS	Israel	442	UK	United Kingdom	9,096
IT	Italy	7,959			

Source: D&B Europa, 1993

Companies are assigned one of nine major industry/commercial sectors, with the largest group in manufacturing (more than 24,000) and the next largest in wholesale (more than 12,000). Communications and insurance were new to the 1993 edition. Table 4-C shows the approximate number of companies listed for each of the nine industry/commercial sectors in *D&B Europa.*

Table 4-C. Industry Sectors in *D&B Europa*

Commercial/ Industrial Sector	Approximate number of companies listed
Agriculture	397
Mining	389
Construction	2,625
Manufacturing	24,003
Transport/Communication	3,324
Wholesale	12,412
Retail	3,836
Finance/Insurance	9,761
Services	3,764

Source: D&B Europa, 1993

Exhibit 4-3 is a sample record from *D&B Europa* displaying 23 potential data items.

Table 4-D shows the number of companies in selected Dun & Bradstreet international regional directories as well as the purchase or annual lease price of each directory.

International Dun's Market Identifiers is D&B's electronic collection of non-U.S. reports on DIALOG. Individual country data are standardized and records are matched against worldwide corporate affiliation data.

In addition to its many print directories, Dun and Bradstreet also offers a wide range of electronic databases. Both the print and electronic products are now derived from Duns Global File. Individual country data are standardized and records are matched against worldwide corporate affiliation data.

There are currently four non-U.S. D&B Files on DIALOG: File 518, *International Market Identifiers (IDMI)*; File 521, *European Market Identifiers (EDMI)*; File 520, *Canadian Market Identifiers;* and File 522, *Asia/Pacific Market Identifiers.* An example of an *IDMI* record is shown in Exhibit 4-4. A version of the Global File is also available on Dow Jones Menus.

DATA-STAR contains 14 individual European directory Duns files, one for each of the present EC countries plus Austria and Switzerland. DATA-STAR combines the directories in one file (DBZZ). D&B has three additional international files on DATA-STAR: *D&B Eastern Europe, D&B Canada,* and *D&B Israel.*

European Dun's Marketing Identifiers (EDMI), available on DIALOG, is a subset of *IDMI. EDMI* has the same data fields and coverage as *IDMI.* The European marketing files on DATA-STAR had been produced directly by Dun & Bradstreet Information Services—Europe. The DATA-STAR files may have different data fields, coverage, and standardization than does *EDMI.* For example, Ireland and the U.K. have both U.K. and U.S. SIC codes, and the French database includes the French APE product codes. About half the DATA-STAR records include sales. Where sales are given, they appear in three currencies: U.S. dollars, local currency, and ECUs (a standard European Currency Unit). Statement profit, also in three currencies, and statement year may also be in a record. Another data item appearing for companies designated as exporters or importers is "% export sales."

DATA-STAR records also include a standard registration number in those countries where "public limited company" is a legal type: the United Kingdom, Ireland, France, Spain, Luxembourg, and Portugal. Two other extra data items in the DATA-STAR records are "single location" and "employees here." Because all records will now be derived from the same database, there should be

---

Exhibit 4-3. Record Structure and Sample Record from *D&B Europa 1993*

1/2	DUNS No. 62-812-0446 Imp-Exp. 2	1	DUNS NO.
3	ADEL KALEMCILIK TICARET VE SANAYI A.S	2	Importer/Exporter
4	ANKARA ASFALTI, SOGANUKOY KARSISI KARTAL 81411 ISTANBUL	3	Company name
5/6	Te(901)353 36 46 Fx(901)353 42 90	4	Trading address
		5/6	Phone/Fax
7		7	Telex
8	Legal Status: 1	8	Code for Public/Private
9	Executives:	9	Principal directors or executives
	SUKUTI ARAS 10	10	Codes for function(s)
	YUSUF OLNAMAK 12	11	Activity indicated by US SIC Code
10	ZIYA NURBILGIN 21	12	1972 US SIC designation
	YUNUS CELIK 25	13	Import/Export
	OSMAN BAYIKSEL 16	14	% annual sales in export
	RUHI AKSOY 25	15	Parent information; may include
11	Principal Business Activity:		DUNS No.
	LEAD PENCILS, CRAYONS & ARTIST MTRLS	16	Nominal capital
12	SIC: 3952	17	Issued capital, where it exists
13	Importer-Exporter	18	Net Profit/Loss
14	Export Sales: 20%	19	Annual sales or revenues
15	Subsidiary of:	20	Number of staff employed
	ANADOLU ENDUSTRI HOLDING A.S. ISTANBUL (TK)	21	Bankers
16	Nominal Capital: TL 13,000,000,000		[Not in this record]
17	Issued Capital: TL 13,000,000,000		Year founded
18	Net Profit/Loss: TL 1,552,926,000		Sales ranking from TOP list
19	Annual Sales: (90) TL 56,000,000,000		Employee ranking from TOP list
20	Employees: 225		
21	Bankers: TURKYE IS BANKASI A.S.		

Source: D&B Europa, vol. 3, 1993, p. 571. Copyright © 1993 Dun & Bradstreet, Inc. All rights reserved. Reprinted with permission.

Table 4-D. 1992 Selected International Titles from Dun & Bradstreet

Title	No of Companies	Price $
Asia/Pacific Key Business Enterprises	22,000	400
Brazil Dez Mil	10,000	395 *
Canadian Key Business Directory	20,000	410
Czechoslovakia: Major Businesses	4,000	365
Hungary: Major Businesses	5,000	NA **
Key British Enterprises	50,000	875
Dun's 15,000 Netherlands	15,000	280
Poland: Major Businesses	4,500	NA **
Dun's PEP—Principal Companies in Portugal	3,500	370

* outright purchase; others, annual lease

** new in 1992—information not available

```
EXHIBIT 4-4. Sample IDMI Record


  File 518:D & B-INTL MARKET IDENTIFIERS   07/93
         (Copr. 1993 D&B)


  2635581  DIALOG File 518: D&B International DMI
  ADEL KALEMCILIK TICARET VE SANAYI A S
  ANKARA ASFALTI SOGANLI KOYU MEVKI
  ISTANBUL, TURKEY

  TELEPHONE: 9013871938
  TELEX: TR29265

  BUSINESS:  STATIONERY PRODUCTS

  PRIMARY SIC:    2678   STATIONERY PRODUCTS
  SECONDARY SIC: 3951   PENS AND MECHANICAL PENCILS
  SECONDARY SIC: 3952   LEAD PENCILS AND ART GOODS
  SECONDARY SIC: 3069   FABRICATED RUBBER PRODUCTS, NEC

  YEAR STARTED:            1967

  EMPLOYEES TOTAL:         500

  SALES (LOCAL CURRENCY):   48,700,000,000
  SALES (U.S. CURRENCY):     4,520,000

  DUNS NUMBER:            62-812-0446

  EXECUTIVE NAME :        SELAHATTIN DEMIRCI

         Copyright 1993 Dun & Bradstreet
```

Source: IDMI/EMDI DIALOG Files 518 or 521, searched September 1993. Copyright ©
1993 Dun & Bradstreet, Inc. All rights reserved. Reprinted with permission.

more standardization between D&B on DATA-STAR and DIALOG in the future.

Comparison of D&B Print and Electronic Records. There are variations in the amount of information recorded for the same company in different D&B products. To illustrate this, Exhibit 4-4 shows the entry for the Turkish company as it appears in *IDMI/EDMI*. Exhibit 4-3 shows the record for the same Turkish company in the printed *D&B Europa*. This is one example where the printed source includes more information than the online one. The record in Exhibit 4-4 does not have a fax number, has only one officer rather than six, and does not indicate any corporate affiliations.

D&B Europa lists six executives, with coded positions, none of whom are Mr. Demirci, the executive identified in the *IDMI* record. The print version also includes nominal and issued capital and net loss and an export sales figure.

D&B Europa is also available on CD-ROM, through Lotus OneSource. An extract of the full report on CD-ROM for our Turkish company is presented in Exhibit 4-5.

Other potential fields, for which no information is available for this particular company include Other Subsidiaries (up to 10), Line of Business (English), Line of Business (local language), Growth Rates, Balance Sheet (current and noncurrent assets and liabilities in local currency), Profit & Loss (for X years in local currency), Reconciliation (in local currency), Business Ratios, and Footnotes.

Table 4-E compares the various Dun and Bradstreet products. Though all the information is derived from the same database, each product contains a different set of data items.

Major Companies of Europe (Graham Trotman—Annual)

Major Companies of Europe is one directory in a series published by Graham Trotman. The directory is in three volumes.

Volume I	Continental European Community
Volume II	United Kingdom
Volume III	Western Europe Outside the EC

A companion volume, *Medium Companies of Europe,* is also available. The entire set has 8,000 companies with

Table 4-E. Comparison of D&B Products for Company Profile Information

	PIB Print 1993	IDMI Online (9/93)	D&B Europa Print 1993	CD-ROM 12/92
Company Name	X	X	X	X
Alternate Name				X
Address:				
Street	X	X	X	X
City	X	X	X	X
Region		X		
Country	X	X	X	X
Postal Code			X	X
Registered Office				
Address				(1)
Telecommunications				
Telephone	X	X	X	X
Telex/Cable	X	X		
Fax			X	X
Business	X	X	X	(1)
CODES				
Primary Code	X	X	X*	X
Secondary Codes	X	X		X
Year Started	X	X	X	NA
Employees	X	X	X*	X
Financials				
Sales, Local	X	X	X*	X
Sales U.S.		X		
Nominal Capital			X	X
Issued Capital			X	X
Net gain/loss			X	X
Legal status			X	X
Subsidiary				
Private				
Parent name	X			X
Parent address	X		X	X
D-U-N-S Number	X	X	X	X
Parent D-U-N-S				
Officers				
Executives	CEO	CEO	6*	6
Import-Export			X	X
Export Sales			X	X
Banker			X	
Credit Rating				(1)

(1) Users may screen on credit ratings in Europa CD-ROM. However, the ratings are not displayed in the record.

*—Data elements differ between the *PIB/IDMI* entry and the *D&B Europa* entries.

more financial information than you find in D&B sources. It is also considerably more expensive than *D&B Europa*, but you may purchase individual volumes.

Entries are arranged by country indexes, alphabetical index to all companies, and a business activity index, with more than 80 categories. Professional services not in the D&B directories, such as accountants and lawyers, architecture and town planning, art and industrial design,

and developmental agencies, appear in the Graham Trotman Major Company series.

Companies submit information for inclusion. A company record consists of the name, address, telecommunications numbers, chairperson and managing director, principal activities, parent company (where applicable), and one or two years of brief financial information. The financial information may include turnover, profits, au-

EXHIBIT 4-5. Extract of Record from *CD/Europa*

DUNS Number: 628120446

Adel Kalemcilik Ticaret Ve Sanayi A.S.
Ankara Asfalti, soganlikoy Karsisi, kartal
Istanbul 81411
Turkey
Alternate Name: Adel Kalemcilik

Tel: (901) 353 36 46 Fx: (901) 353 42 90 Tx:

Reg Office Address:

Financials are not Consolidated

Legal Form: Public Limited Company
Year Started: N/A

Turnover, Profit, Nominal and Issued Capital figures in TKL '000

Nominal Capital: 13,000,000	FYE: 12/31/90
Issued Capital: N/A	Turnover: 56,000,000
Employees—Actual: 225	Profit/(Loss): -1,552,926
Importer/Exporter	Export Sales (%): 20
Overall Rank (Empl): 31,326	**Overall Rank (Sales): 55,341**
	Turnover ECU: 14,008

PARENT SUMMARY
Parent Duns Number: N/A
Anadolu Endustri Holding A.S.
Istanbul TK
BUSINESS ACTIVITY
Primary SIC Code: 3952   Pencil & Crayon Manufacturers
SIC Category:
  3900 - 3999 Miscellaneous Manufacturing Industries
SIC Category Rank   **Sales**   **270**
                                    Employees   **429**
MANAGEMENT STRUCTURE

Executive	Function
Sukuti Aras	General Manager
Yusuf Olnamak	Financial Director
Ziya Nurbilgin	Sales Director
Yunus Celik	Manager
Osman Bayiksel	Personnel Director
Ruhi Aksoy	Manager

KEY FINANCIALS

	Fiscal Individual 12/31/90 TKL '000	Fiscal Individual N/A TKL '000	Fiscal Individual N/A TKL '000
Turnover	56,000,000	N/A	N/A
Exports	N/A	N/A	N/A
Profit/ (Loss)	-1,552,926	N/A	N/A
Net Worth	N/A	N/A	N/A
Fixed Assets	N/A	N/A	N/A
Total Assets	N/A	N/A	N/A
Current Assets	N/A	N/A	N/A
Current Liabilities	N/A	N/A	N/A
Working Capital	N/A	N/A	N/A
L.T. Debt	N/A	N/A	N/A
Employees—Actual	225	N/A	N/A

Note: Employee figures are not in '000s
Source: CD/Europa, December 1992 disc. Copyright © 1993 Dun & Bradstreet, Inc. All rights reserved. Reprinted with permission.

Table 4-F. Graham & Trotman Series

	Number of Companies	Number of Countries	Price per Volume ($US)	Price per Set ($US)	Year	Edition
Major Companies of Europe	8,000			$1,250	91/92	11
Vol 1 Continental Europe EC		11	$630			
Vol 2 United Kingdom		1	310			
Vol 3 Western Europe outside EC			310			
Medium Companies of Europe	7,000			1,080	91/92	2
Vol 1 Continental Europe EC		11	540			
Vol 2 United Kingdom		1	270			
Vol 3 Western Europe outside EC			270			
Major and Medium Companies of Europe	15,000			1,740		
Continental Europe EC			1,170			
United Kingdom			580			
Western Europe outside EC			580			
Major Companies of the Arab World	7,000	20		700	91/92	15
Major Companies of the Far East and Australasia	1,700	13		1,030	91/92	8
Vol 1 Southeast Asia		6	380			
Vol 2 East Asia		5	380			
Vol 3 Australia and New Zealand		2	270			
Major Business Organizations of Eastern Europe and the Soviet Union	4,000	8		599	1991*	1
Major Financial Institutions of Europe (excluding U.K.)	1,000	16		350	92/93+	4
U.K. Business Finance Directory	1,500	1		265	1990*	4

*no date in title;+ listed as 92/93 editions, published in 1991. Minimum price for 9 volumes: $3,470; Minimum price for entire set: $4,085. Prices from Gale distributor's brochure, February 1992.

thorized capital, paid-up capital, total balance, and total assets. Principal shareholders, bankers, date of establishment, and number of employees are also listed.

Table 4-F lists the titles in the series, with companies, prices, and edition dates included for comparison with Dun and Bradstreet publications.

Directory of European Business (Bowker-Saur)

A new European entrant in the international directory market is the *Directory of European Business*, published by Bowker-Saur U.K. The publication combines information on 33 countries with directory information for 4,000 companies. Countries covered are the EC, EFTA, and also those from the former Soviet Union and former Yugoslavia. The companies include the top five to ten firms in selected product categories.

The User's Guide clearly states the criteria for inclusion and ranking of companies. The 60 companies for the

U.K. are listed companies, private companies, and local and foreign subsidiaries. Entries are brief, containing company name, address, activities, senior personnel, turnover (sales), and staff. The records for some of the listed companies, PLCs, also include information on major shareholders and major subsidiaries.

Arrangement is by country and subject within the country. Each country chapter comprises the following subjects, in addition to manufacturing company directory entries:

Country Political/Economic Information:
Key indicators
Political system
Government
Economic policy
Recent performance
Business culture
Trade regulations

Principal cities
Banking & business hours
Legal system
Currency
Tax system
Foreign investment
Business incentives
Accounting rules and standards
Sources of finance
Business information
Business Service Companies:
Accounting
Advertising
Banking
Insurance
Law
Management consulting
Market research
Public relations
Venture capital
Business Organizations:
Chambers of commerce
Professional bodies
Trade associations
Government:
Foreign representatives
Ministries
Regulatory agencies
Business Information:
Market intelligence
Business periodicals
Statistical sources
National newspapers

There is only one index, an alphabetical listing of all organizations. This directory is puzzling. It is a potpourri—a little of this, a little of that, but not much of anything. Libraries that do not need individual listings for any of the categories mentioned above but want some broad European coverage could consider this.

Eastern Europe/Former Soviet Union Company Information

The breakup of the USSR and the move toward market economies has led to increased interest in this region for business researchers. However, the demand for information and the supply of accurate, reliable information are still far apart.

We hesitate to recommend that any library purchase directories for companies in Eastern Europe. We are unsure about the reliability of the data, the use of translation or transliteration for company names, and even the continued existence of companies once the directories are published. As one publisher states about the former

Soviet Union: "The present is confusing. It is contradictory. It is risky." (FYI, publisher of *SIBD*, p.vi).

FYI, a consulting firm active in the former Soviet Union, recommends that clients ask the following questions when researching companies in this region for potential business partners:

* If they are private, why did they become private?
* How independent are they?
* Do they set their own prices?
* Do they choose their own suppliers?

SIBD 92-93: The Business Directory for the Soviet Region (Washington D.C.: FYI Information Resources for a Changing World; Ukraine: IIA Sistema-Reserve)

This unique title is a joint venture between two business information consulting firms that specialize in the former Soviet Union, one in the U.S. and one in the Ukraine. The 1992/93 two-volume set is the second edition. The Russian language version of this book sells more copies than the English edition.

Volume One is in two parts: an alphabetical listing of 6,500 enterprises with a maximum of 18 data items, and an alphabetic listing of products, as provided by the producers themselves. Volume Two has a business activities index, geographic index, index of leaders, and a list of the 500 largest enterprises.

Inclusion in the directory is self-selected. Companies responded to television and trade publication advertisements that asked them to fill out questionnaires. All entries are supposed to be checked by follow-up phone calls. Companies that had been in the first edition were called again for the second edition and dropped if they did not respond.

Company names are both transliterated if they are proper nouns and translated if they are products. The example for the tractor company in Exhibit 4-6 is transliterated, but other types of names that appear are *14 Rented Shop* or *DINA * Stock Society*. The U.S. Board of Geological Names is used as the basis for transliteration. Company names often include the legal name and than a descriptive extension, which follows the * in the listing.

The six parts that make up the two volumes of *SIBD* contain the following types of information:

* **Part 1 (Volume One): Data Items for Companies**
1. S-R-N-S: Sistema-Reserve Registration Number
2. State
3. Symbols for importer/exporter status
4. Symbols for form of ownership
5. Symbol for 500 largest
6. Name of organization
7. Date of founding or registration
8. Number of employees and trade turnover (sales) in rubles

```
┌─────────────────────────────────────────────────────────────────┐
│                                                                   │
│     EXHIBIT 4-6. Sample Entry from SIBD                           │
│                                                                   │
│                                                                   │
│     S-R-N-S  3803              EXP        IMP                      │
│     Russia                     ♦ ○        ♦ ○                      │
│     ○● CHEBOKSARKY ZAVOD                                           │
│                                                                   │
│     PROMYSHLENNYKH TOVAROV  * PA                                   │
│                                                                   │
│     Date established                     07/08/1980               │
│      Number of employees: 22000    Turnover:597,000,000           │
│     Bank account: 000267701  v Chuvashskom                        │
│         upravlenii PSB g. Cheboksary  MFO 28352                   │
│     Address:  428033  ChSSR   g.Cheboksary                        │
│                                                                   │
│       Telephone:  (8350) 23-02-36                                 │
│       Fax:  (8350) 23-35-38                                       │
│       Director general               23-78-42                     │
│       MINGAZOV Khanif Khaydarovich                                │
│       Technical director             23-12-68                     │
│       KOSMIN Gennady Danilovich                                   │
│         Foreign Trade registration:  PP-1197/6                    │
│                                 of 04/12/1989                     │
│                                                                   │
│       Hard currency account  : 67089212/001                       │
│                     Vneshekonombank                               │
│                                                                   │
│     Business activities: Output of produce for production         │
│     technical purposes *Consumer goods production                 │
│                                                                   │
│     Main products:  Industrial tractors * Parts for tractors      │
│     Main services: Electroplating and heat treatment *Non-standard│
│     equipment production *Services to the public in manufacture   │
│     of metal structures, wooden articles. household appliances, repairs│
└─────────────────────────────────────────────────────────────────┘
```

Source: Reprinted from *SIBD, 1992/93,* p. 50

9. Bank account information
10. Address
11. Telecommunications: phone, teletype, Fax, cable
12. Names, titles, and telephone numbers of key employees
13. Foreign trade registration number with USSR ministry of foreign economic regulations (no longer required)
14. Hard currency account information
15. Existing branches/subsidiaries
16. Main business activities
17. Main products
18. Main services

• **Part 2 (Volume One): Index of Products**
The index contains the product name, registration number, and page. Most products have only one or two entries. Because products are as reported by companies, there is no standardization.

• **Part 3 (Volume Two): Business Activity Index**
Enterprises are grouped into 10 broad categories and subdivided into 146 narrower types of activities, which have been given alpha-numeric codes. The codes are a variant of the SITC codes, described in Chapters 14 and 15. More than one code may be given an enterprise. Enterprises are arranged alphabetically by republic within each section.

• **Part 4 (Volume Two): Geographic Index**
Enterprises are listed alphabetically according to republic, region, and city. Each entry includes name, address, telephone, business activity code, symbol for form of ownership, and page in Part 1.

• **Part 5 (Volume Two): Index of Leaders**
This index lists, in alphabetical order, the leaders of the enterprises and organizations that appear. Included are the position, individual's name, company, region, telephone, and page in Part 1.

• **Part 6 (Volume Two): 500 Largest Enterprises**
This listing of large producers of goods and services is based only on those companies that are listed in the directory and that have provided the publishers with turnover (sales or revenue) figures. Many enterprises do not reveal these figures. Companies are ranked in decreasing order of turnover. The entry includes the company name, leader, number of employees, turnover (sales), and page in Part 1.

World Business Directory, which we discussed in detail above, also has entries for companies from the former Soviet region under the new country names. We estimate about a 20% overlap between *WBD* and *SIBD*, although issues of translation, transliteration, and the order of words in company names make comparison difficult.

The Cheboksary tractor company, whose record from *SIBD* is illustrated in Exhibit 4-6, is also listed in *WBD*. There are many differences in the entry; the most important is that the company name is translated rather than transliterated: *Cheboksary Tractor Plant, Production Association.* The revenue figure is reported as 2,460,200,000 Rb. Neither source provides a date for the sales figure.

Eastern European Business Directory, 1st ed. (Gale)

Eastern European Business Directory (EEBD) is a pan-Eastern Europe directory. We examined this publication in detail because it is distributed by a major provider of library publications. The first edition, published in 1991, covered Bulgaria, Czechoslovakia, the former East Germany, Hungary, Poland, Romania, and the western Soviet Union.

The introduction states that company data was gathered from government sources and private organizations. Companies were chosen based on "size, importance of the company to the country's economy and possible interest to the Western businessman" (p. xv).

Company names are generally transliterated from the native language but occasionally have been translated. The transliteration from the Cyrillic to the Roman alphabet used the nearest phonetic spelling rather than a standard source.

The 8,000 organizations appear in one volume, arranged in four sections.

1. Products and services arranged alphabetically by industry and country and then company. Entries provide name, address, telecommunications, contact and title, and trade mark and founding date, where available. No standard classification system is followed.
2. Geographic listing arranged alphabetically by country, city or region, and company with separate listings if a company has multiple addresses.
3. Company listing arranged alphabetically by company name for almost 6,000 individual organizations with the same information as Part 1, plus a list of products or services.
4. Former East German section with about 1,300 companies with a listing by product/service and an alphabetical list of companies.

We do *not* recommend this directory as a source of company information in the former Soviet Union. Despite the introductory documentation on compilation and coverage, the organizations listed are heavily concentrated in the publishing, hotel, and mineral industries; many entries are listed at the same address; and the company names are transliterated or translated in a manner that makes any comparison with other sources almost impossible. There are scattered entries from cities in new countries, such as the Ukraine, but the country name is not provided. These facts make us question the quality of the data.

Other Print Directory Sources. *U.S.-Soviet Trade Directory* and *U.S.-East European Trade Directory: An Invaluable Reference for Conducting Business in Poland, Hungary, Czechoslovakia, Bulgaria, Yugoslavia, Romania, & Albania* were two sources issued in 1991 by Probus, a publisher not generally known for directories. Both have the same editor and arrangement. They list U.S. organizations doing business with the Eastern European countries, including consultants, trading companies, lawyers, government agencies, financing sources, advertising, insurance, shipping, travel, and exhibitions.

Each book sells for under $50, which is a plus. However, many firms have jumped into the former Eastern bloc arena with little experience. If these sources are not updated, we would not recommend purchasing the 1991 editions.

Yellow Pages Moscow (Hannover, Germany: Claudius Verlagsgesellschaft—Annual)

Yellow Pages Moscow is another new source just for Moscow. Compiled by Moscow City Telephone Network-Moscow Information Service, the book is issued in Russian as well as English. It is arranged by products with an index to advertisers, subject headings, and lists of chambers of commerce. No indication is given if the names are translated or transliterated.

An entry includes name, address and phone number. A sample entry from the 1992/93 *Yellow Pages Moscow* under the subject heading "Joint Ventures" is:

> Flora Service (USSR -Yugoslavia)..address, phone and fax

Obviously, the appearance of both USSR and Yugoslavia in a 1992-1993 edition makes us wary of this product.

Individual Country Directories

There are a wide range of company directories published for individual countries. Sources such as *European Markets, Asian Markets,* and the new *Latin American Markets* from Washington Researchers, and the *Sourceguide to European Company Information* compiled by the London Business School and published as of 1993 by Gale, list pan-continental and individual country directories.

Bottin. Bottin, founded in 1796, has been publishing business directories for many years. Its current entry is *Qui Decide.* It lists 100,000 enterprises and more than 350,000 "decision makers," company officers who have some budgetary authority. It is arranged in three volumes by geographic regions: Ile de France (the region around Paris), Eastern France, and Western France. The entries are short, including basic directory information, the French APE code and business description, and the type of computers in use. What distinguishes *Qui Decide* from most directories is the fact that the date of verification for each entry is listed. Verification dates for the 1992 edition ranged throughout 1991, with many falling in July.

Finding Aids

European Markets: A Guide to Company and Industry Information Sources (Washington Researchers Publishing)

European Markets is recommended for general collections, and is a good choice for small businesses willing to do their own research at the source. The cost is $275 for information on 18 countries in the EC and EFTA. Washington Researchers also publishes companion guides for Asia-Pacific and Latin America.

Sourceguide to European Company Information (Gale)

The fifth edition of the London Business School's *Guide to Company Information: EC* was the first edition published by Gale with the slight title change to *Sourceguide*. Country coverage has been expanded to include Austria, Finland, Norway, Sweden, Switzerland and Turkey, in addition to the EC countries. The *Sourceguide* covers pan-European sources and country-by-country sources in print and electronic formats. A companion publication, *Sourceguide to East European Information,* will be issued by Gale in conjunction with the London Business School in mid-1994.

Latin America—A Directory and Sourcebook 1993, 1st ed. (Euromonitor, 1993)

This finding aid and source for company and marketing information is new to the Euromonitor series of publications, which, along with the Washington Researcher publications, are discussed in more detail in Chapter 9. This book provides sources of information about eight countries in Latin America: Argentina, Brazil, Chile, Mexico, and Venezuela, the major markets, plus Colombia, Ecuador, and Peru. It lists companies in these countries by type of industry.

Manufacturers of Consumer Goods
Heavy and Light Industrial Companies
Key Retailers
Service Companies
Passenger and Cargo Transport Companies
Banks and Finance Companies

There is also a brief Statistical Factfile for each of the countries. Company data are brief. All records have

name, address, telecommunications, and business activity, while some may include an officer and a sales figure, with or without its date. *Latin America* uses the same format as *Eastern Europe: A Directory and Sourcebook* and *Asia: A Directory and Sourcebook*. These books are more useful as marketing tools and finding aids than as directories.

A selected list of other directory titles appears at the end of this chapter.

INDUSTRY DIRECTORIES

All the directories discussed so far include companies representing a range of business activities. There is another set of specialized directories arranged by business activity. The directories may include only companies within a broad industry grouping or within a specific activity. Coverage may be international, regional, or country specific. Table 4-G lists different types of industry directories with a sample title for each type.

Table 4-G. Types of Industry Directories

Country	Sector	Activity
International	*Directory of the World's Largest Service Companies*	*Intl Directory of Advertising Agencies*
Regional	*European Wholesalers*	*European Consultants*
National	*Manufactured Products (South Africa)*	*Wine and Beer (Australia/New Zealand)*

International Industry Directory

Directory of the World's Largest Service Companies (Moody's, in conjunction with the United Nations Centre on Transnational Corporations, 1990)

The *Directory of the World's Largest Service Companies* is designed to include those industry sectors generally omitted from major international directories. 1990 marked the premier edition. No other edition is presently planned.

Services are now the largest economic sector in most developed countries. According to the U.N. Centre on Transnational Corporations, an estimated $100 billion flowed from transnational direct investment from service corporations. The Centre developed this directory as part of its role in analyzing the impact of these companies on international economic development.

The *Directory* lists 200 companies in the following 14 services:

Accounting	Legal Services	Retail Trade
Advertising	Market Research	Securities and
Air Transport	Publishing	Diversified
Construction	Rail Transport	Financial Services
Hotels	Restaurants and	Shipping and Trucking
	Fast Food	Wholesale Trade
	Chains	

The *Directory* is arranged by sector with the company profiles alphabetical within their sector. Each section contains rankings for the top 50 to 200 companies in the sector, and profiles of up to 15 companies, the 10 largest companies plus five additional firms chosen in order to expand geographical coverage.

Entries (*see* Exhibit 4-7) include name and address, legal name and status, industry classification and product and ISIC class, directors, ownerships where identifiable, major shareholders, and a textual profile including background, history, structure, products and markets, financial data, and countries of operation. The 1990 edition has data from 1983-1988. There are as many as four standard tables.

- Table 1: Traditional financial performance: (5-year consolidated income and balance sheet data)
- Tables 2 & 3: Performance and standing by geographic region and country
- Table 4: Subsidiaries and affiliates with performance measures, where available

There is also an alphabetical index of all companies. Information is derived from published reports for public companies and direct information from privately owned firms and partnerships. Articles were also consulted. Companies were given an opportunity to verify their profiles.

EXHIBIT 4-7. Extracted Entry from *Directory of the World's Largest Service Companies*

BECHTEL GROUP, INC ,   **Corporate Information**

Legal status: Private corporation. Incorporated in the
    State of Delaware in 1925.

Home country: United States of America

Headquarters:
    50 Beale Street
    San Francisco, California 94105
    United States of America

Phone: 415-7068-1234
Inc.

Fiscal year: 1 January - 31 December

Industry/ISIC:
Inc.

Architectural & engineering activities and related technical consultancy	7421
Site preparation	4510
Building of complete constructions; civil engineering	4520
Mining of non-ferrous metal ores	1320

Ownership: Privately owned, predominately by the
    Bechtel family
Inc.

Board of Directors:

Name	Title/Affiliation
S.D. Bechtel	Chairman, Bechtel Group, Inc. and Bechtel Corp.
R.P. Bechtel	President, Bechtel Group, Inc. and Bechtel Corp.; Chairman, Bechtel Power Corporation and Bechtel National, Inc.
D.M. Slavich	Senior Vice President & Treasurer Bechtel Group, Inc., Bechtel Power Corp and Bechtel National, Inc.

Board of Directors: (continued)

Name	Title/affiliation
C.W. Hull	Executive VP, Bechtel Group, Inc. & Corp.
J. Neerhout, Jr.	Executive VP, Bechtel Group, Inc. & Corp.
J.D. Carter	Senior VP & Secretary Bechtel Group, Inc. Corp, Power Corp & Bechtel National
W.L. Friend	Senior VP, Bechtel Group, Corp, Pres. Bechtel National
D.J. Gunther	Senior VP, Bechtel Group, Inc. & Corp.
H.J. Haynes	. . .
L.G. Hinkelman	Senior VP, Bechtel Group Inc. & Corp.
J.M. Komes	President, Becon Construction Comp,
J.L. Moore. Jr.	Senior VP, Bechtel Group Inc. & Corp.
R.L. Polvi	. . .
G.P. Shultz	. . .
H.W. Wahl	Senior VP, Bechtel Group Inc. & Corp.
J.W. Weiser	Senior VP, Bechtel Group, Inc. & Corp.
A. Zaccaria	Senior VP, Bechtel Corp and Pres. Bechtel Power

Source: Directory of the Worlds Largest Service Companies, 1990, p. 196, with modifications. Reprinted with permission from Moody's Investors Service.

EXHIBIT 4-7. Extracted Entry from *Directory of the World's Largest Service Companies* *(continued)*

BACKGROUND

Bechtel Group Inc ranks as one of the world's leading global construction and engineering contractors. The company was founded by Warren A. Bechtel in 1906...

nuclear power projects. By 1960, Bechtel claimed the first United States commercial nuclear facility in Dresden, Ill.

Structure

Bechtel has been under the leadership of its founding family for four generations, and since its founding, Bechtel has remained a privately-owned company...

National;Bechtel Limited;Bechtel Construction; and Becon. Another unit, Bechtel Enterprises, provides

Products and markets

Bechtel has handled diverse projects in more than 100 countries on all continents of the world.

scale construction projects typically performed in developing countries...

Consolidated Data, world-wide
1983-1988 [A]
(millions of dollars)

Item	1983	1984	1985	1986	1987
1988					
Contract[B]	13,810.0	8,220.0	7,3464.0	7,079.0	7,954,1
10,877.0					
Domestic...					

[A] Source is *Engineering News Record*(ENR) for entire contracts category
[B] Figures includes prime construction contracts, shares of joint ventures,subcontracts, ..

Countries or areas where company has operations and/or contract
1988[A]

Region/country or area	Region/country of area
DEVELOPED MARKET ECONOMIES	Iraq
North America	Jordan
United States	Qatar
Western Europe	Saudi Arabia...

[A] In addition, the company has contracts in the Arctic and the Antarctic.

Subsidiaries and affiliates
1988

Bechtel Power Corporation
Bechtel Petroleum, Chemical &
  Industrial...

Bechtel Construction

Sources: "The top 400 U.S. contractors," *Engineering News Record;* Derdak, Thomas, et.al.

Source: Directory of the World's Largest Service Companies, 1990, p. 196, with modifications. Reprinted with permission from Moody's Investors Service.

Exhibit 4-7 presents extracts from the *Directory* entry for Bechtel Group, Inc., a private, U.S.-based company in the construction industry.

Regional Industry Directories

European Wholesalers and Retailers. Three English language directories cover the European wholesale and retail industries. Although the coverage of the directories overlap to some extent, they each have unique features. *The European Directory of Retailers and Wholesalers* covers both sectors. *European Wholesalers and Distributors Directory* emphasizes wholesalers and what and where they distribute. The Directory of European Retailers looks at retailers and their worldwide buyers.

European Directory of Retailers and Wholesalers (Euromonitor, 1988-)

This directory and sourcebook gives as much emphasis on where to locate additional information on the retail and wholesale industry as on the major companies. It lists 3,000 companies from 17 countries. Many of the companies are department stores or retail chains.

European Wholesalers and Distributors Directory (Gale, 1992)

This directory has entries from 20 Western European countries, five former Eastern bloc countries, and countries from the former USSR. Many of the companies are also listed in Gale's *World Business Directory. European Wholesalers and Distributors* has four parts.

• Section 1: main entries arrange companies by 3-digit U.S. SIC code and then by country; each company has an annotation number

- Section 2: lists companies alphabetically by product line
- Section 3: this *unique* aspect of the book arranges companies by the countries to which they distribute and then by SIC code
- Section 4: an alphabetical listing of companies; there is no alphabetical list by country

According to the introduction, information is compiled from questionnaires, chambers of commerce, Infodesign Information and Advertising Centre in Moscow, and the National Trade Data Bank. The concerns we expressed about Gale's ability to collect and maintain a quality international publication in relationship to *World Business Directory* also apply here. Organizations needing this level of detailed information about wholesalers and distributors should consider online databases and chamber of commerce CD-ROMS mentioned later in this chapter and in Chapter 12.

Directory of European Retailers (Newman Books, 18th biennial edition, 1992-93)

This directory covers major retailers in 22 countries. Although the publisher is not well known in the United States, the book has been published for many years. The contents contain:

- Trade associations and other professional bodies
- Buying agents worldwide
- Commercial representatives overseas
- Retail journals by country

"All the significant companies involved in retailing in Europe" are said to be in this volume (p.19). All entries for the companies contain address and telephone number. Additional data items may be proprietors, trading names, head and buying office, type of trade, employees, selling area, chief executives and buyers, and number and location of stores. Town names are given in their native form. Exhibit 4-8 presents a sample entry from the *Directory of European Retailers*.

Possible subject headings for types of retail establishments within a country listing in the *Directory of European Retailers* include:

- Department & Variety Stores & Large Specialty Shops
- Specialty Chains in Non-Food
- Hypermarkets & Superstore Chains & Groups
- Restaurant & Fast Food Chains
- Mail Order Firms, Home Shopping, & Catalogue Showrooms
- Franchising
- Wholesaling of Food & Non-Food (including Cash & Carry Warehouses)
- Voluntary Groups & Chains (Wholesale & Retail)
- Retail Buying & Services Groups
- Consumer Cooperative Societies

EXHIBIT 4-8. Sample Entry for Andorra from *Directory of European Retailers*

CASA PEREZ SA, (Prop. Family Perez) **T/A** Grands Magasins Pyrenees. Automobils Pyrenees. Avenue Meritxell 9, **P.O.** Box 23 Andorra la Vella. Principaute Andorra. **Tel.** (628_ 20414; **Telex** 205; **C.A.** Pyrenees Andorra; **Fax** (628) 26978; Retailing activities include supermarket chain and department stores; **Staff** 1400 (Casa Perez 800 Pyrenees 600) **Man. Dir. & Administrator** Philippe Bergeron; **Financial Man.** A. Garcia; DPM X. Muchart; **Commercial Man.** J. Llosada; **Personnel Man/** A. Delincak; **Tech. Man.** J. Bonnet; **Security Off.** J. Lluch; **Distribution Man.** J. Gonzales

Source: Directory of European Retailers, 1992/93, p. 63. Reprinted with permission.

Information is collected by questionnaire. There is no charge for inclusion, though there are advertisements. Mailing lists may be purchased directly from the publisher.

European Consulting Firms. Two European titles cover consulting, an activity of interest to many business clients. The first edition of the *European Directory of Management Consultants* appeared in 1990; it is published by Task Force Pro Libra (TFPL), itself a U.K. consultancy. The TFPL directory describes consulting firms from 18 countries in the EC or EFTA, plus a listing of international professional bodies. In 1991 Gale issued *European Consultants Directory*, with 5,500 consultancies in 34 countries.

European Directory of Management Consultants (Task Force Pro Libra)

In the TFPL directory, English translations may be provided for firms with non-English names. Each consultancy has supplied the information for each entry. Addresses and phone numbers have been standardized. There are three indexes: alphabetically by organization, with the company name, entry number, and country; by key areas of specialization (up to 10 per consultancy); and by industry area of specialization. Entries are brief as shown in Exhibit 4-9. European business school students are familiar with the *European Directory of Management Consultants* from TFPL and recommend it for their job-hunting.

EXHIBIT 4-9. *European Directory of Management Consultants*

1489 Cosmos GmbH Unternehmensberatung fur Organisation & Datenverabeitung

Hauptstr 2	Business enquiries: Mr Glusa
8132 Tutzing	Established: 1984
West Germany	No. of consulting staff: Between 10–50
Tel: +49 81 583044	

Coverage: Nationally; Worldwide

Source: European Directory of Management Consultants, 1990, p. 371. Reprinted with permission from Task Force Pro Libra.

PRODUCT DIRECTORIES

The directories listed above are arranged by broad industry grouping, but our clients often need lists of companies arranged by very specific product grouping.

Who manufactures gas springs in Europe?
Where are the breweries in the United Kingdom?

There is no international equivalent of the *Thomas Register of American Manufacturers* but there are sources that give detailed lists of a company's products as well as categorizing products by type. The detailed product grouping makes these publications useful.

KOMPASS Publications

Kompass, part of Reed Information Services, is probably the most widely known publisher of product directories. By the end of 1992, there were 45 individual KOMPASS directories covering about one million companies in Europe, the Middle East, Asia, and northern Africa. Each publication has volumes arranged by product/service with unique charts and by companies. Many are published in conjunction with sponsors, such as the Export Council of Norway or the Confederation of British Industry. The first KOMPASS directory was published for France 60 years ago.

Table 4-H lists the KOMPASS international editions available through March 1994. KOMPASS has been adding new editions every year. Most editions are updated annually, while some, like Brunei and Thailand, have been updated less frequently. To own the entire series would cost over $10,000.

As an example of a typical KOMPASS directory, we will describe the *UK Kompass Register* in detail. The 30th edition of the *UK Kompass Register* is in five volumes, with the first two standard to the series. It is published in conjunction with the Confederation of British Industry. Industrial or industrial service companies with 10 or more employees, doing business nationally, are included in the *Register*.

- Volume I: Details of 41,000 different products and services offered by British industrial companies
- Volume II: Corporate information on 42,000 leading companies in British industry
- Volume III: Latest three years of financial information for 30,000 companies
- Volume IV: 100,000 parents and their subsidiaries
- Volume V: Details on 25,000 companies and 100,000 registered trade names

Using a KOMPASS directory is awkward. First go to the alphabetical product index to find a unique seven-digit code. Second, locate the five-digit table. The final two digits reference the column in the product grid. Exhibit 4-10 presents a sample entry. Then go to the company index to find more information about the company.

Companies are arranged alphabetically by town, within county. Exhibit 4-11 is a sample company entry from *UK Kompass Register*. Other possible data elements in *UK Kompass Register* entries include:

- Names of Ultimate and Holding Companies
- Employees for the Group
- Agents for Firm's Products
- Trade Names
- Locations: registered, sales, branches, and factory
- Products for which the Firm Acts as Agent in U.K. and Overseas
- Group Details
- Other Information: i.e., type of computer
- Quality Assessment Awarded

KOMPASS has its own coding system, organized on a two-, five-, and seven-digit level. Note in Table 4-I that the first few categories resemble U.S. SIC codes. Also note the emphasis on the manufacturing sectors.

KOMPASS is also available online as four DIALOG files:

KOMPASS Europe	File 590
KOMPASS UK	File 591
KOMPASS Asia/Pacific	File 592
KOMPASS Canada	File 594

Table 4-H. KOMPASS Registers 1992-1994

COUNTRY	1992 EDITION	NUMBER OF COMPANIES	PRICE OF 93/94 EDITION
Australia	22nd	20,000	$495
Austria	1st	14,000	415
Bahrain	2nd*	1,500	225
Belgium	30th	24,000	425
Brazil	1st	NA	515
Brunei	3rd	700	185
Bulgaria	1st	5,000	305
Canada	2nd	30,000	465
Czechoslovakia	1st*	11,500	425
Denmark	32nd	16,500	325
Egypt	1st	15,500	NA
Finland	3rd	15,000	325
France	59th	102,600	525
Germany	20th	48,000	525
Greece	28th	17,000	375
Holland	27th	24,500	425
Hong Kong	2nd	50,000	NA
Hungary	1st	20,000	NA
Iceland	2nd	2,000	200
India	2nd	50,000	525
Indonesia	8th	12,000	NA
Ireland	5th	12,000	325
Israel	6th	5,000	325
Italy	31st	40,000	525
Japan	1st	110,000	675
Korea	3rd	20,000	360
Luxembourg	13th	1,700	275
Malaysia	15th	20,000	350
Malta	1st	1,700	NA
Mexico	1st	20,000	NA
Morocco	13th	8,000	305
New Zealand	5th	12,000	NA
Norway	23rd	16,000	375
Philippines	3rd	15,000	325
Poland	1st	20,000	375
Portugal	1st	5,000	325
Saudi Arabia	1st	20,000	NA
Singapore	15th	16,000	350
Spain	22nd	26,000	425
Sweden	25th	18,000	375
Switzerland	42nd	36,000	425
Taiwan	2nd	20,000	375
Thailand	1st*	NA	325
Tunisia	1st	4,500	325
Turkey	10th	27,000	400
United Arab Emirates	2nd	3,000	300
United Kingdom	30th	41,500	625

*Current edition prior to 1992

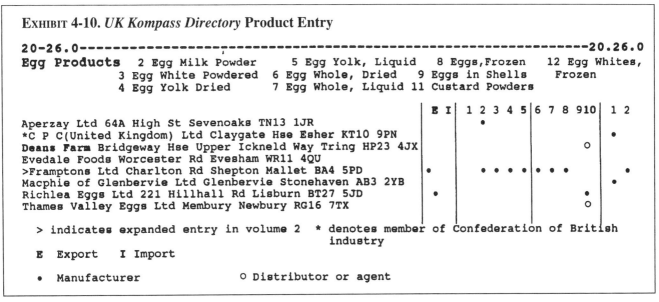

EXHIBIT 4-10. *UK Kompass Directory* Product Entry

Source: Extracted from *UK Kompass Register*, vol. I, 1992, p. 36. Reprinted with permission from KOMPASS.

EXHIBIT 4-11. *UK Kompass Register* Company Entry

Tring

Deans Farm,
Bridgeway Hse, Upper Ickheld Way, Tring HP23 4JX
Tel: (0442) 891811
Telex: 826916 DEANS G
Facsimile No: (0442) 891880
Bank: National Westminster, 15 Bishopgate, London
Directors: P.D. Dean (MD) N Dean (Ops) P D Challands (Mktg) J W Grundy (Sales)
Co Reg No: 672991 **Turnover** £20-£50M
Employees: 990 (Estb)
Product Groups: 20

Reprinted with permission from KOMPASS.

By the end of 1993, three KOMPASS CD-ROMS were on the market: U.K., Europe, and a new Asia-Pacific disc. What is unique to the electronic versions of KOMPASS is their very detailed product listings at a 5- or 7-digit product level; an indication if the company is a producer, distributor, supplier, importer, or exporter for each product; the language spoken; and the date the record was updated.

An oddity in the KOMPASS family is that there is some variation in coding among databases. EKOD, the European CD, and File 590 both use almost the same 5-digit codes. KOMPASS UK, Asia, and Canada use 7-digit codes, but definitions at the 7-digit level may vary.

KOMPASS UK (File 591): **3617024 Springs, Gas ...**
KOMPASS Asia-Pacific (File 592): **3617024 Springs for the Electrical Industry Prod Exp**

Table 4-I. KOMPASS Product Codes

Codes	Industry Group
01-09	Agriculture and Fisheries
11-19	Raw Material Extraction Industries
20-21	Food and Beverages
22-24	Textiles and Apparel
25-28	Wood, Paper, and Publishing
29-32	**Rubber, Plastics, and Chemicals**
33-36	Metal, Glass, and Ceramics
37-38	Electrical, Electronics, and Optics
39-47	Machinery and Transport Equipment
48	Engineering Sub-contractors
51-59	Construction and Public Utilities
61-69	Wholesale and Distribution
71-79	Transport Services
80-89	Service Industries

30 Plastic Products	
30010	**Synthetic Resins**
30020	Misc. Resins
30080	Pre-processing of plastics
30090	Recycling and reprocessing of plastics
30100	Semi-finished plastics
• • •	
30950	Plastics Industry Sub-contractors x work
30955	Plastics Industry Sub-contractors x article

Country Product Directories

Individual countries have product registers. There are at least three in the U.K.: KOMPASS UK, *Kelly's Business Directory*, and *Sell's British Exporters*. The latter two began publication in the late 1800s.

Kelly's Business Directory (Reed Information Services—Annual)

One of the oldest product registers is *Kelly's Business Directory*. Though it has experienced some name changes, the 1994 edition, copyright in 1990, was the 107th edition. It includes three sections: classified, which is the largest, company, and exporters. Under the classified heading "Egg Packers or Merchants" is a listing for the company Deans Farm with a full mailing address. The company entries in the classified section are very brief, just name and address. The cross-references for companies in the "Company Information" also include a phone number and abbreviation classification. Commercial, professional, and industrial organizations in the U.K. are in *Kelly's*. The slender yellow section, "International Exporters & Services," contains entries "inserted by special arrangement with the publishers."

Other product directories are advertised in *Kelly's*. There is a large ad from one of the major pan-European import/export guides, *ABC Europe-Export/Import*, a two-volume set with 100,000 manufacturing companies from 32 countries. *ABC/Europe* is also available online on DATA-STAR. Indexing is in English, German, Spanish, and French.

Sell's British Exporters (Sell's Publications Ltd.—Annual)

Sell's British Exporters, which has been published for more than 100 years, also has three main sections: Products and Services, with more than 9,500 headings arranged alphabetically by company name and county location; the largest section is Company data, 44,000 commercial and industrial companies in Great Britain in alphabetical order with addresses and telecommunications; and Trade Names, listed alphabetically. Again, the entries are brief. Under the classified heading "Egg Packers" is the entire entry "Deans Farm Bucks." The Company entries have an address and full description of business.

KOMPASS UK on DIALOG and CD-ROM includes *Kompass UK Register, Kelly's*, and *Sell's British Exporters*. It also has additional U.K. sources, such as *Dial Industry*, which covers engineering, electronics, and computing; *U.K. Trade Names;* and *Directory of Directors*, which we discuss below.

Product directories accessible online are described in Chapter 6.

DIRECTORS AND OFFICERS

Selected Print Country Sources

Questions are often asked about company officers and directors. What are the international equivalents of the biographical volume of Standard & Poor's *Register* or D&B's *Reference Book of Corporate Managers*? Typical questions are:

* Who is the CEO of Unilever? Is his biography available?
* Who are Nestle's general managers?
* What is the average age of a Japanese CEO?
* I am looking for Wharton alumni outside the U.S.

Listed below are biographical sources for selected offices and also sources with extensive lists of officers and directors.

Financial Post Directory of Directors (Financial Post— Annual)

The Canadian *Financial Post Directory of Directors* is one national print source of information on officers and directors. The *Directory* was first published in 1947. It is divided into two sections. Section One is an alphabetical list of directors and executives of Canadian companies who reside in Canada. The basic listing includes name, gender, position, company name, and address. Additional information may include birthdate and schools attended.

Section Two is an alphabetical listing of almost 2,000 Canadian companies with their boards of directors and executives, regardless of place of birth.

Directory of Directors: Key Data on the 60,000 Directors Who Control Britain's Major Companies (Reed Information Services—Annual)

Directory of Directors has been published for over 110 years. Again there are two parts. Volume 1 lists directors and Volume 2 lists the 16,000 companies and their 85,000 board members. Note that the *Directory* does *not* include executives.

Criteria for an individual to be included are based on company size, with minimum turnover set at £50,000. Company secretaries supply the initial information. The basic entry in Volume 1 includes name, business address, title, honors, awards, education, and main type of business interest. According to the brochure for the 1993 edition, "three quarters of all entries (are) updated each year."

Volume 2 is arranged alphabetically by company name, with address, main business, corporate family, detailed list of board members, and financial highlights.

The Arthur Andersen Corporate Register, 1991– (Hemmington Scott Publishers—Semi-annual)

Corporate Register is the source for U.K. executives, directors, and advisers. The main body of the book is arranged by company. Directory information consists of address, telecommunications numbers, sector, subsector (group), activities, market cap, and turnover. There is then a list of executive directors and non-executive directors, with appointment date, position, and number of ordinary and incentive shares; directors' pay; number of employees and total payroll; names of internal staff, such as treasurer, accountant, and personnel officer; and external advisers, such as bankers, auditors, and solicitors.

The entry for GLAXO holdings also includes pictures of the members of the board with their ages and very brief biographical information. A sample biographical entry is shown in Exhibit 4-12.

EXHIBIT 4-12. *The Arthur Andersen Corporate Register,* **September 1993**

HENDERSON, Sir Denys Hartley, LLB FIMgt FRSA FCIM. Imperial Chemical Industries PLC, Imperial Chemical House, 9 Millbank, London SW1P 3JF. Tel: (071) 834 4444. Fax: (071) 8342042. SEC: Miss Margaret A Jonas. **COMPANIES SECTION:** Barclays (dir*) *p 41;* Imperial Chemical Industries (ch) *p 236*; RTZ Corporation (The) (dir*) *p 372.* **PAST CAREER:** 1990 to date, The RTZ Corporation PLC (dir*); 1987 to date, ICI PLC (ch); 1985 to date, Barclays PLC (dir*); 1983 to date, Barclays Bank PLC (dir*); 1986 - 87, ICI PLC (dch); 1967 - 86, ICI PLC (var); 1955 - 57, Army (RASC & Directorate Army Legal Services) (staff capt); 1952 - 55, Esslemont & Cameron (advocate) **PROF:** The Advertising Association (cttee mem); Soler. **OTHER INTERESTS:** Henley Management College (ch, court of gov's); The Prince's Youth Business Trust (advy cncl); CBI (president's cttee); British Malaysian Soc (cncl); The Save the Children Fund (ind & commi gp); Natural History Museum (trustee); Japan Festival 1991 (cncl mem). **EDUC:** Aberdeen Univ; Aberdeen Grammar School. **RECR:** Family Life; Swimming; Reading; Travel; Gardening; Golf. **CLUB(8):** Athenaeum Club; RAC. BORN: 11 Oct 1932 (60). MATR: 1957, Doreen Mathewson (nee Glashan), 2 dtrs.

Source: The Arthur Andersen Corporate Register, September 1993, Hemmington Scott Publishing Ltd. Reprinted with permission.

International Corporate Yellow Book: Who's Who at the Leading Non-U.S. Companies (Monitor)

International Corporate Yellow Book, formerly the *International Corporate 1000,* includes extensive listings of directors and managers for each company in the directory. A sample entry has company name, address, telecommunications numbers, a description of business, and an annual sales or revenue figure. It does not have any unique financial or statistical information, nor biographies. It is a companion to the Yellow Books Monitor publishes for the U.S., such as the *Corporate Yellow Book.*

The directory is arranged by region, by major country within region, and then alphabetically by company within country. Officers' titles and responsibilities differ among countries. In countries not using a U.S. model, boards of directors do not differ from officers.

Who's Who in European Business 1st ed, 1993 (Bowker-Saur)

Entrants come from 35 countries, including Eastern Europe. Information is from questionnaires. A basic entry includes only name, mailing address, and position, but other potential data items include career, education, language spoken, family, honors, and publications. The entrants are all directors or senior executives from

- Top 100 companies by turnover in a particular country
- European top 500 companies by turnover
- 100 largest firms, by number of partners, for the service sector

Who's Who in European Business is divided into two sections. Part One lists biographies alphabetically by surname. Part Two contains a country index, with name and company, and a company index, with country and officers. A companion publication, now in its sixth edition, is *Who's Who in International Banking.*

Because of the obvious lack of information in print sources, electronic formats must fill in the gaps.

Online Files on LEXIS AND NEXIS SERVICES

Who's Who Edition European Business and Industry (Who's Who Edition—Biannual)

When the most recent print edition of the German publication *Who's Who Edition European Business and Industry* was for 1990-91, the directory was available on LEXIS AND NEXIS SERVICES as the *WHOEUR* file in the "World," "Europe," and "People" libraries, updated through mid-November 1992. About 5,500 entries provide name, company, address, position, family, education, career, nationality, birthdate, and may also have recreation, languages, home address, honors, and publications.

Teikoku, a Japanese database described in detail in Chapters 6 and 8, has a small amount of biographical information on chief executives: birthdate, birthplace, and education. All non-Japanese universities are grouped together as "univ abroad."

Both the *Financial Post Directory of Directors* and Standard and Poor's *Register of Directors and Executives* are available on LEXIS AND NEXIS SERVICES. Both contain Canadian company directors. As illustrated in Exhibit 4-13, the records of the Financial Post and S&P publications are very similar.

EXHIBIT 4-13. Comparing *Directory of Directors* and *Register of Directors and Executives* on LEXIS AND NEXIS SERVICES

	The Financial Post Company *Directory of Directors*	Standard and Poor's Corporation *Register of Directors and Executives*
Name	Posluns, David	POSLUNS, DAVID
Position:	Senior vice-president, corporate development and strategic planning, secretary-treasurer and chief financial officer	Senior Vice-President, Secretary, Treasurer & Chief Financial Officer
Company:	Dylex Ltd.	Dylex Limited
Address:	637 Lake Shore Blvd. W Toronto, Ontario, Canada M5V 1A8	637 Lake Shore Blvd. W. Toronto Canada M5V 1A8
GENDER:	Male	
DEGREES:	B.S., M.B.A.	
ALUMNI:	Wharton School of Business, U. of Pennsylvania, B.S. U. of Chicago, M.B.A.	Univ. of [Pennsylvania] (Wharton Sch.), 1982 Univ of Chicago[sic], 1984
BIRTHDATE:	December 12, 1959	1959, Toronto, Ont.,Canada
LOAD-DATE:	September 4, 1992	

Source: LEXIS AND NEXIS SERVICES, January 1993. Reprinted by permission of Standard & Poor's and Financial Post Datagroup.

Listed Company Reports

Selected company annual reports are another source for selected biographical information about directors and officers. Use SEC filings 20-F for non-U.S. companies that trade on U.S. stock exchanges, and ICC's full-text annual reports files for companies that trade on the London exchange. Both these files can be used to search for officers and directors of a company, for an individual, or to screen for specific educational background.

Examples of using the SEC filings *20-F* file on LEXIS AND NEXIS SERVICES and ICC *Full-Text Annual Reports* (ICAC) on DATA-STAR are presented. Exhibit 4-14 displays a record from *SEC Online*: 20-F.

Example 1:

Q: What Harvard graduates are on boards of directors of foreign companies filing in the U.S.?
A: Search file *20-F* for Harvard.

The record in Exhibit 4-14 also tells us (not shown) that Kolber is 29 years old, has been a director since 1990, and is the beneficiary of a trust.

The full-text ICC annual report files, either online or on CD-ROM, can be used to locate U.K. directors and officers and some background information.

Example 2:

Q. How do I find what Wharton school grads are presidents or CEOs of U.K. companies?
A. Use ICC full-text company reports.

An ICC record is displayed in Exhibit 4-15.

COMPANY HISTORIES

A search for a "company history" often results in little or no results. Some very large international companies have had monographs written about them. However, there is no Library of Congress subject heading that readily identifies all of the histories in a collection, let alone all those in print. The *Moody's Manuals*, including the *International Manual,* have brief overviews of a

---

EXHIBIT 4-14. Record from *SEC Online*: 20-F

Company: Teva Pharmaceutical Industries, Ltd.
Filing-Date: 08/14/91   Document-Date: 12/31/90
(searched 01/08/93)

Jonathan B. Kolber is the President of Claridge Israel Inc
.....He received his B.A. from Harvard University in 1983.
Mr. Kolber serves as a director of ECI Telecom Ltd.,
Optrotech Ltd. and Luz International Limited.

Reprinted from *SEC Online.*

EXHIBIT 4-15. *ICC Full Text Company Reports and Accounts*

```
                ICAC
AN    084942 9212.
TI    WICKES PLC - 1989 Annual Report and Accounts.
SO    Wickes PLC
      19 - 21 Mortimer Street,
      London W1N 7RJ
      TEL: (071) 631 - 1018
      FX: (071) 637 - 1784
      PUBLICATION DATE: 891231;
      TOTAL PAGES OF DOCUMENT: 27.
TX    8 OF 27 DIRECTORS' BIOGRAPHIES
Henry Sweetbaum (52), Chairman and Chief Executive, is a
graduate of The Wharton School, University of Pennsylvania.
He has been Chairman and Chief Executive of the Wickes
Group since 1982 and is also a non-executive director of
Ashton Tate Corporation...
```

company's acquisitions, name changes, etc., which often is all we can offer as history.

International Directory of Company Histories (St. James—Semi-annual)

This is the one comprehensive source. The work was originally published as a five-volume set between 1988 and mid-1992. It had 1,200 companies arranged by industry grouping (*see* Table 4-J). However, the publishers began adding semi-annual updates in December 1992. The updates cover additional companies and new information about original companies. The first update added 200 more companies.

Companies are included based on sales and influence in their industry or geographical location. State-owned enterprises and subsidiaries that were independent within the preceding five years and are still prominent in their own right are included in addition to their parent firms. Companies read their entries to check facts.

Each entry has directory information, including company's legal name in English, with its native language followed in parentheses; headquarter's address; telecommunications numbers; ownership status; incorporation date; employees; and a sales figure in local currency and U.S. dollars (with no date). Finally, the entries have a bibliography and the name of the author(s). Each volume has a single cumulative index to people and companies.

Magazines, books, and annual reports, as well as information provided by the companies themselves, are used to compile the histories. Entries are several pages long.

Although generally a useful source for any collection, the *International Directory* has some shortcomings.

* No index by country
* Quality of entries varies
* No index to subsidiaries; only companies mentioned in text are indexed
* Histories of Asian companies almost exclusively Japanese
* About 50% of companies from the U.S.

In order to see just how international this source is, we counted the number of companies by region by industry. About half are from the U.S., though distribution varies by industry. Table 4-K shows the geographical distribution of companies by industry.

COMPANY INFORMATION WHEN THE COMPANY IS NOT KNOWN

Questions about companies are usually of two types:

1. Finding information about a specific known company
2. Finding a group of companies that meet specific criteria

Table 4-J. Industries Included in *International Directory of Company Histories* as of April 1993

VOLUME 1	VOLUME 2	VOLUME 3	VOLUME 4	VOLUME 5
Advertising	Electrical & Electronic	Health & Personal Care	Mining & Metals	Retail & Wholesale
Aerospace	Entertainment & Leisure	Health Care Systems	Paper & Forestry	Rubber & Tire
Airlines	Financials: Banks	Hotels	Petroleum	Telecommunications
Automotive	Financials: Nonbanks	Information Technology	Publishing & Printing	Textiles & Apparel
Beverages	Food Products	Insurance	Real Estate	Tobacco
Chemicals	Food Services & Retailers	Manufacturing		Transport Services
Conglomerates		Materials		Utilities
Construction				Waste Services
Containers				
Drugs; Pharmaceuticals				

Table 4-K. Number of Companies by Industry by Country in *International Directory of Company Histories*

Industry	U.S.	Europe	Asia	Other*	Percent Total	Percent U.S.
Retail	36	21	18	2	77	0.47
Rubber & Tire	2	3	3		8	0.25
Telecommunications	11	11	1	2	25	0.44
Textiles	8	2	4		14	0.57
Tobacco	4	3	1	1	9	0.44
Transportation	15	9	13	1	38	0.39
Utilities	41	14	11	2	68	0.60
Waste Services	2				2	1.00
	119	63	51	8	241	0.49

* All other are Canada

The second application is used most often for marketing or trade applications, for investing purposes, or for job-hunting. To answer questions of this type, printed directories should have a variety of access points or indexes. Again, our ideal directory will have a listing by industry or product code, a geographical index and an alphabetical index by company name. In some printed directories, the most information about a company is listed in the alphabetical section. Additional indexes may only list the company name, or give a name and address. Dun's *Principal International Businesses* is an example of this type of directory. In other directories (*Kelly's*, *Sell's,* and KOMPASS, for example) the main information is found in the product index.

Printed directories are useful for finding information about a few companies in a single category. They quickly become impossible to use when we are screening for companies in multiple categories, for example, a list of French companies in computer manufacturing with sales of more than $100 million. This type of question must be answered with directories available through time-sharing or on CD-ROM, which are discussed in Chapter 6.

OTHER SELECTED DIRECTORIES

There are hundreds of company directories in print which we have not mentioned. The list below includes some other major sources. See Chapter 6 for additional online directory sources and Chapter 13 for directories of companies involved primarily in importing and exporting. Appendix A has a check list of characteristics to use when evaluating other directories.

Regional Directories

Duns Asia/Pacific Key Business Enterprises (Dun & Bradstreet—Annual)

This basic directory covers 22,000 leading companies in 14 countries with annual sales over $10 million or with more than 500 employees. Countries include Japan, Korea, the People's Republic of China, Hong Kong, Australia, India, Taiwan, and Thailand. The introductory text is in English, Japanese, and Chinese.

Pan-Continental Directories

Asia's 7500 Largest Companies (ELC International—Annual)

This British directory covers Hong Kong, Japan, Malaysia, Philippines, Taiwan, Indonesia, South Korea, Singapore and Thailand. In addition to manufacturing and trading companies, it has banks, insurance companies, investment companies, and privately owned companies. It is arranged in five sections: two rankings of business, an alphabetical index, trade index, and company directory. Rankings include the 100 largest quoted companies by "profit"; 500 most profitable companies by "profit margin" and money losers; and the largest quoted companies by country and by business activity.

Jobson's Year Book of Public Companies (Dun & Bradstreet—Annual)

Jobson's has more than 2,000 public companies which are listed on the Australian and New Zealand stock exchanges. Entries include corporate structure, five-year financial tables, and operating results. It also has articles and a "Directory of Directors."

Country Directories

Brazil

Brazil Dez Mil [Brazil's Top 10,000] (distributed by Dun & Bradstreet—Biennially)

This basic directory, written in Portuguese, covers over 10,000 companies.

Bulgaria

100 Bulgarian Companies (Sofia, Bulgaria: IS Information Services Corporation, 1991-92)

This is a very specialized basic directory of Bulgarian state-owned and private companies. Entries include company name, address, telecommunications, and description of activities. There is an index by company name and by 25 industry groupings.

Canada

Canadian Key Business Directory (Dun & Bradstreet—Annual)

This *Directory* lists 20,000 major businesses in Canada that have $20 million in sales, employ 100 individuals, have net worth of $1 million (measured in Canadian dollars), or have branches with more than 500 total employees. Almost 80,000 executives are included. The *Directory* is arranged alphabetically, geographically, and by line of business.

Financial Post 500 (Financial Post—Annual)

This publication covers Canada's largest companies in industry and finance. The Financial Post also publishes the annual *Financial Post Survey of Industrials,* which has over 2,000 Canadian public, listed, and unlisted industrials (non-resource) corporations. Entries include names, addresses, telephone numbers, stock symbols, transfer agents, details of operations, management, financial data, and subsidiaries. Access is only by company name. A companion volume to the *Survey of Industrials* is the *Financial Post Survey of Mines and Energy Resources.* This volume has enhanced coverage of 35 companies. Financial Post publications are also available online on LEXIS/NEXIS, Telerate, and Infomart Online.

China

China Phonebook & Address Directory (New York: Croner Publications Inc.—Annual)

The *Phonebook* is a product directory, arranged alphabetically by city/region and then alphabetically by company within industry groupings. There are over 20 major industry groups, though not all are used for all locations. Places names indexing is in English and Chinese stroke count. There is also a company index. An entry includes the English and Chinese company name and address.

3W Register of Chinese Business (3W International Digital Publishing—Annual)

The Register covers 30,000 Chinese companies. It also has Chinese provincial information. It uses an international "standard sic code" with up to 20 categories per company. Entries include name, address, telecommunications (phone, fax, telex), officers (president, contact), owner, assets, date started, employees, sales in use, stock, import, export, products: SIC codes. Arrangement is alphabetical by company with SIC code index and product name index. Output is also available on CD-ROM or diskette (updated twice a year).

Poland

General Trade Index & Business Guide, Poland (Business Foundation Co., 1991)

This export directory contains 3,500 Polish businesses and firms seeking trade opportunities. There are sections on Polish economy and laws, banking and finance, and culture. Entries include trade names, full name, address, year of establishment, contact person and language spoken, line of business, number of employees, and estimated turnover. The *Index* uses EC classification codes. Advertisements are included.

United Kingdom

Key British Enterprises (Dun & Bradstreet Ltd.—Annual)

This multi-volume set covers 50,000 large and medium size companies which employ more than one-third of the U.K. work force and account for 65% of U.K. business activity. Manufactures, wholesalers, retailers, distributors, and service companies with minimum annual sales of 1 million pounds are included. The set is arranged alphabetically and by line of business. Entries include 30 data items: name, headquarters, telecommunications, officers, total and export sales, geographic markets, employees, branches, formation date, legal status, registration and Duns number, description of trading activity, trading styles and trade names, and U.K. SIC code. Information comes from questionnaires, telephone surveys, personal communication, published information, and official sources. Output is available online, offline, on diskette, or by mailing list.

UK's 10,000 Largest Companies (ELC; distributed in U.S. by Dun & Bradstreet—Annual)

This publication covers companies in manufacturing, distribution, and the service industries. It ranks largest companies by sales, profit, profit margin, money losers, and employees.

CHAPTER 5
Company Information: Financial Sources

TOPICS COVERED

1. Availability of Financial Information
2. Sources of Financial Information
3. Providers of Financial Information
4. Finding Financial Footnotes on CD-ROM
5. Where to Find International Annual Reports
6. Text Sources of Company Financial Information
7. Notes

MAJOR SOURCES DISCUSSED

- *Moody's International Manual* and *International Company Data* CD-ROM
- *Hoover's Handbook of World Business*
- *Global Company Handbook*
- *Morningstar Japan*
- *Best's Insurance Reports, International Edition*
- CIFAR and Worldscope
- EXTEL Cards

AVAILABILITY OF FINANCIAL INFORMATION

As discussed in Chapter 3, the amount of financial information available about a company depends on its size and its country of registration, not only on whether it is traded on an exchange. An understanding of what reports a company must file will help you and your clients have more realistic expectations concerning what data can be obtained.

In this chapter we will look at specific sources of corporate finance. Some typical questions about company financial information are:

- How is a company performing financially this year? in previous years?
- Is a full financial report (with balance sheet and income statement) available? Does the report contain text?
- Is the company profitable?
  What is the company's credit rating?

Registration Requirements

Companies within the European Community have clearly stated registration and disclosure directives. These can be found in the EC directives, in articles by Nobes,[1,2] and in *SourceGuide to European Company Information.*[3] Filing and disclosure requirements for non-EC countries may be found in Business International's *Investing Li-censing and Trading*, either in print or on LEXIS AND NEXIS SERVICES. More information about registration can be found in Chapters 2 and 3.

Often, companies listed on exchanges are faced with some set of filing or disclosure requirements. The requirements may not, however, be as frequent, complete, or timely as those required by the U.S. stock exchanges and the Securities and Exchange Commission. For example, there is no international equivalent of the U.S. 10K or 10Q reports. Quarterly reports may not be required nor in many countries are any interim financial statements necessary or forthcoming.

Pressure from the international investor community has increased the amount of information that is disclosed and how it is presented by the companies. Providers of international financial filings are therefore continually increasing the number of companies whose financial filings they present.

The form and contents of published annual reports by industrial companies from different countries varies widely. The Center for International Financial Analysis and Research (CIFAR) categorized countries by the comprehensiveness of their annual reports, as presented below in Table 5-A.

Quoted companies may be tracked in financial print and online sources by their ticker symbols or by using other standard numbering systems (see Chapter 3).

Table 5-A. Level of Comprehensiveness and Relevant Data in Annual Reports

Most Comprehensive	Reasonably Good	Below Average
Australia	Hong Kong	Austria
Canada	Malaysia	Belgium
France	South Korea	Denmark
Ireland	Singapore	Germany
New Zealand		Japan
Scandinavian Countries		Netherlands
(except Denmark)		Spain
South Africa		
United Kingdom		
United States		

Source: International Accounting and Auditing Trends, vol. 1, 1989, p.21

Problems in using company financial reports include the language and monetary unit (e.g., pounds or francs) of the original document, fiscal year-end dates, and delays in publication of reports. Some companies will publish a modified report in English for the investment community.

companies for which reports are available has been growing rapidly as well. Table 5-B lists different sources and the number of companies with financial balance sheet and income statement data available by country. Dates and numbers are used for comparison purposes. Every update brings more companies.

Country Coverage in International Sources

Many sources include extracts of listed company filings or the actual reports themselves. The number of

Table 5-B. Coverage of International Financial Statements for Companies in Multi-Country Sources

Source	Extel DIALOG	Moody's INTL	Global Vantage	World- Scope	Laser D INTL	Cifar (Lexis)	S&P
DIALOG							
Type	Online	CD-ROM	CD-ROM	CD-ROM	Disc	Online	Online
Date	4/93	2/93	1/93	2/93	1991 FY	3/93	4/93
Argentina		14		4	39	33	1
Australia	172	364	175	216	457	136	34
Austria	44	110	74	70	122	37	
Bahamas	1	6				1	1
Bahrain	23	6					
Barbados		3					
Belgium	59	107	82	148	253	69	1
Bermuda	56	45	31		19		18
Bolivia		1					
Botswana	1	1					1
Brazil		61		15	225	68	2
British West Indies		1					4
Bulgaria		1					
Canada	92	1155	400	454	634	396	980
Cayman Islands	38	12	2		23		
Central African Republic		2					
Chile		15		17	103	136	2

Table 5-B. Coverage of International Financial Statements for Companies in Multi-Country Sources (*continued*)

Source	*Extel* DIALOG	*Moody's* INTL	*Global* Vantage	*World-* Scope	*Laser D* INTL	*Cifar* (Lexis)	S&P
DIALOG Type	Online	CD-ROM	CD-ROM	CD-ROM	Disc	Online	Online
Date	4/93	2/93	1/93	2/93	1991 FY	3/93	4/93
China		3					
Colombia		15		8	14	47	
Cook Islands	1						
Costa Rica		2					
Cyprus		2			1		
Czechoslovakia		1					
Denmark	49	122	102	117	127	73	2
Djibouti		1					
Dominican Republic							
Ecuador		2					
Egypt		2			4		
Finland	39	115	76	89	131	73	1
France	209	420	328	484	1249	324	9
Germany	210	488		455	107	371	11
Greece		14		27	56	14	2
Guatemala		2					
Guyana		2					
Honduras		1					
Hong Kong	107	167	89	97	207	140	23
Hungary		2			11		
Iceland		3			3	1	
India	4	33			628	566	
Indonesia		17			2	4	2
Ireland	105	52	73	49	103	49	7
Israel	2	50			32	20	35
Italy	79	247	214	234	319	122	8
Jamaica		3					
Japan	142	518	777	1222	1268	1350	42
Jordan		1			5	3	
Kenya	1	9			12	8	
Korea, South	50	47	47	51	153	492	1
Kuwait	25	6			8		
Liechtenstein	1	5	3				
Luxembourg	22	30	6		30	15	3
Malawi		2					
Malaysia	338	133	123	66	118	87	
Malta		2					
Mauritius		1					
Mexico		40		32	51	70	14
Morocco		2					
Netherlands	84	182	117	146	611	177	14
Netherlands Antilles	16	8	2		1		4
New Zealand	19	29	54	47	67	23	2
Nigeria		3			16	72	
Norway	36	107	66	114	124	54	4
Oman	5						
Pakistan		49			29	64	

Table 5-B. Coverage of International Financial Statements for Companies in Multi-Country Sources *(continued)*

Source	*Extel* DIALOG	*Moody's* INTL	*Global* Vantage	*World-* Scope	*Laser D* INTL	*Cifar* (Lexis)	*S&P*
DIALOG							
Type	Online	CD-ROM	CD-ROM	CD-ROM	Disc	Online	Online
Date	4/93	2/93	1/93	2/93	1991 FY	3/93	4/93
Panama	1	3	3		1		2
Papua New Guinea	2	3	1				
Peru		5			3	2	
Philippines	1	31			29	19	6
Poland		2					
Portugal		13		38	62	10	1
Qatar	3						
Saudi Arabia	16	4					
Singapore	179	82	97	49	84	108	2
South Africa	102	344	191	142	405	163	27
Spain	44	109	123	124	120	59	7
Sri Lanka		5			7	26	
Suriname		2					
Swaziland		1					
Sweden	69	226	146	150	186	104	6
Switzerland	115	217	151	187	389	91	5
Taiwan	2	25			44	67	1
Thailand	303	75	51		30	41	2
Trinidad & Tobago		3					
Turkey	1	10			35	18	
United Arab Emirates	14	3			4		
United Kingdom	4553	957	855	1522	2483	1453	95
United States	327	28	3096	3210	164	4355	8696
Uruguay					21	2	
Venezuela		10		2	33	28	4
Yugoslavia		2			17		
Zaire		1					
Zambia	1	1			2		1
Zimbabwe	3	11			16		
Total No of Companies	7766	7020	7555	9588	11498	11640	10083
Total Non-U.S.	7439	6992	4459	6378	11334	7285	1387
Total countries	50	92	31	33	61	50	44

While finding financial information has become easier, interpreting what we find has not. See Chapter 2 for a discussion of the effects of international accounting standards and practices on financial statements.

SOURCES OF FINANCIAL INFORMATION

Sources of financial information can be categorized in a variety of ways—by format, financial content, types of listings, and place of publication or coverage. Finan- cial information may be published in books, on fiche or cards, online, or on CD-ROM. A report may be in the form of the primary filing, extensive extracts from the filing, or a standardized restatement of the financial filing. In countries where nonlisted as well as listed companies must file financial statements, sources can be further categorized by whether they include only listed or traded companies, or whether they include unlisted companies as well. Finally, sources can be examined according to their scope: international, pan-continental, regional, or single country.

There is no clear distinction between a basic directory and a "financial source," such as *Moody's International Manual*. Most financial sources will include basic directory information just as many basic directories include sales (or turnover) and income (or profit) and in Europe often a "capital" figure. Financial sources also include detailed company accounts, consisting of

- balance sheet information, stating assets, liabilities, and shareholders equity;
- an income or profit and loss statement;
- stock market performance measures such as book value, earnings per share and a price earnings ratio for a given date;
- an annual flow of funds statement; and
- other performance measures, such as standard ratios.

Most researchers would prefer to have financial accounts for multiple years of three, five, or even ten years. In addition to the financial data, the textual footnotes that explain the accounting standards used in presenting the information should be provided, along with a list of company officers and directors, major shareholders, and subsidiaries. A description of the company with any corporate structural changes is also welcome.

Finally, the financial information should be presented in two ways: "as reported" by the company for its local exchange, and "restated" to allow us to look at the data items in a standardized format. Having the option of restatement into a familiar accounting standard, using a currency of the researcher's choice would be preferable. Ideally, we could manipulate the data in models of our choosing to predict the growth and performance of companies and their industries.

These characteristics are available with varying degrees of completeness in sources presently or soon to be available. The most advanced products, intended for the investment banking community, exist in electronic form only. They consist of CD-ROMS or workstations connected to modems, with special front-end software.

Many of us, however, will find that printed sources covering extracts of financial filings for companies in a wide range of countries will be sufficient.

The rules of thumb are the same for financial sources as for basic directories.

- Sources of worldwide information often cover fewer companies than one-country sources.
- The more information given for each company, the fewer companies listed.
- Online time sharing systems cover more companies and may be more timely than print sources.
- Information providers make the same information available in a variety of print and electronic sources.

International Financial Sources

Moody's International Manual (Moody's Investors Service—Annual)

The major international print source of extracted financial information is *Moody's International Manual*, first published in 1981. The multi-volume *International Company Manual* plus the News Reports volume are similar in record content to other Moody's manuals. It has information on more than 7,000 major corporations, as well as national and supranational institutions from 105 countries.

The *Manual* is arranged alphabetically by country. A section for "world corporations" includes regional development banks, such as the Asian Development Bank, as well as major international organizations, such as the International Monetary Fund and the World Bank (International Bank for Reconstruction and Development.) Some of the institutions found in Moody's are *not* listed companies. See Table 5-B for countries for which Moody's has unique coverage. The unique entities are usually banks.

The data are compiled by Moody's Investors Service, which has been collecting company data since 1900. The international company information is derived from the corporation itself, using stockholders' reports and filing documents. A full entry has a brief corporate history; a list of corporate changes, such as acquisitions and restructuring; a description of the business; an extensive list of subsidiaries; a list of directors; and such facts as the number of employees and the name of the company's auditors. Financial information includes two years of income statements and balance sheet data in the reported currency. Long-term debt and the Moody's rating, where available, are also part of a company's record.

Moody's has modified the financial information to achieve *uniformity* among entries, but it has not reworked the numbers. The introduction warns readers that "accounting standards and terminology vary from country to country and ... direct comparisons of figures, even when the terms appear to be the same, can be misleading."

There is an extensive special features section in the blue paper insert in the middle of Volume 1. The section includes a geographical index, an industry classification index, stock and bond data, and international economic statistics. Companies are divided into more than 100 industry groupings.

Inclusion in Moody's is based on size of the company, exchanges on which the company is traded, and importance as an international entity. Some enterprises pay Moody's a fee to have an enhanced entry. As in the U.S. manuals, Moody's gives ratings on debt securities, though the number of companies rated in the *International Manual* is limited. The issuers of the securities have paid Moody's a fee for the ratings.

Moody's International Company Data, released in early 1993, is the CD-ROM version of the *International Manual*. According to a Moody's spokesperson, the disc is a mirror image of the three company volumes and the news update volume. Some interesting features on the CD-ROM are the ability to search and display in over 100 currencies, to compare results in two currencies, and to convert the as-reported balance sheet or income statement to a standard, U.S.-based accounting structure.

Exhibit 5-1 illustrates both currency conversion and the use of local financials and cross-border financials. The example is taken from Moody's *International Company Data* on CD-ROM for the Czech-Slovak foreign trade bank, Ceskoslovenska Obchodni Banka A.S. The local country chart in local currency is the default display. The cross-border chart takes the local income statement and reworks the data into U.S. accounting format. U.S. currency may be selected in place of Czech Koruna (Crowns).

Moody's Corporate News-Intl, DIALOG File 557, covers the articles and financial filings that appear in the print news updates. Records in the online file date back to 1983. The file is useful to search for name changes and new ventures. The news records also appear on the CD-ROM.

Standard & Poor's Corporate Register/Standard & Poor's Corporate Records (Standard and Poor's Corporation—Annual)

Standard & Poor's is regarded as the main competitor to Moody's in the U.S. print financial market. However, S&P is keeping a lower profile in the international print market. About 1,000 international companies are now listed in its directory, *S&P Corporate Register,* and its financial reports, *S&P Corporate Records*, both in print and online (DIALOG Files 527 and 133, respectively). More than 950 of the non-U.S. companies are Canadian.

At present, S&P itself does not have plans to expand its international print coverage. However, Standard & Poor's has been involved with a joint venture with EXTEL Financial (discussed below) to provide a high-end CD-ROM product, *Global Vantage*, based on Compustat PC Plus software.

EXHIBIT 5-1. *Moody's International Company Data* **Report**

CESKOSLOVENSKA OBCHODNI BANKA A.S.

Annual income statement in local country charts and local currency
Annual income statement in cross-border charts and converted currency

ANNUAL INCOME STATEMENT

	Local Country Chart Czech Koruna (000) 12/31/90		Cross-Border Chart Czech Koruna (000) 12/31/90	U.S. $
Exchange			0.0357	
Interest received	10,960,037	Investment revenue	10,960,028	391,273
Commiss rec from fgn	5,421,736	Service revenue	5,421,737	193,556
exh deals & others		Total revenue	16,381,765	584,829
Total earnings	16,381,773	Direct investment		
Interest paid	8,999,810	expense	8,999,804	321,293
Commiss paid & other	14,832	Total direct exp	8,999,804	321,293
expenses		Selling general &		
Salaries	55,478	administrative ex	55,490	1,981
Material expenses	112,676	Other s g a ex	127,507	4,552
Rates & taxes	4,679,908	Total s g a ex	182,997	6,533
Net income	2,519,069	Total other income	-4,679,916	-167,073
		& losses		
		Net Income	2,519,076	89,931
(slight difference due to rounding)				

Source: Moody's International Company Data, February 1993. Reprinted with permission from Moody's Investors Service.

Hoover's Handbook of World Business (Reference Press—Annual)

Moody's is the standard international print financial directory. It is required for most medium and large libraries with business clients. For those libraries that only need financial information on major international companies, a recent publication, *Hoover's Handbook of World Business*, may be adequate.

The second edition of *Hoover's* (c.1993) cost $21.95 (including shipping and handling). *Hoover's* has two-page profiles of 191 major companies of the world. The cost per company in *Hoover's* is about the same as many of the more expensive directories.

Hoover's also includes profiles for 60 countries, rankings, and a plethora of lists. Companies are selected based on six criteria:

1. Exporters or producers known in the U.S.
2. Global firms—including the Big 6 accounting firms
3. Businesses that dominate big industries or lead the industry in their countries
4. Representative companies worldwide, e.g., one company from India is included
5. Representative companies from 24 industry groupings
6. Companies with high profiles to consumers

While most companies in *Hoover's* are public, there are also some listings for private companies and government-owned companies. Many of the public companies are those traded in the U.S. Information comes from a variety of other publicly available sources such as Standard & Poor's for company financials and Economist Intelligence Unit reports for country information. Hoover makes the following interesting disclaimer in its inside cover:

> Readers should not rely on any information contained herein in instances where such reliance might cause loss or damage.

Hoover's Handbook of World Business uses a standard format for each company entry, using the following headings:

Overview
When: A brief history of the company
Who: Executives, directors, and auditors
Where: Address and general foreign locations
What: Product information by segment; major joint ventures and subsidiaries
Key Competitors
How Much: Key financials, including 10 years of sales, net income, earnings, stock prices, and dividends

Hoover's is available on LEXIS AND NEXIS SERVICES in the COMPNY library and also the country

libraries as file HVRWDL. The 1993 edition was available online before it was available in print.

Should you purchase *Hoover's*? It's hard to resist a bargain. Obviously, *Hoover's Handbook* will not substitute for a collection of international company sources. However, for the high school library, small company, or public library, or any library with $22 to spare, this book does give you your money's worth.

Global Company Handbook (Center for International Financial Analysis and Research [CIFAR], 2nd ed., 1993).

For basic financial data on a maximum number of companies and countries in print form, consider *Global Company Handbook: An Analysis of the Financial Performance of the World's Leading 10,000 Companies.* The second edition of the *Handbook* will be in four volumes. Volume I contains company rankings and industry and country averages. Volumes II, III, and IV have profiles for each of the 10,000 companies. Each volume can be purchased separately for $145 while the entire four-volume set costs $495. The 1993 edition has a minimum of 25 companies from each of 46 countries, representing 32 industry groupings.

Based on the first edition, we recommend *Global Company Handbook* for its breadth of coverage. It is strong in its coverage of companies from emerging markets, while weaker in its coverage of Europe. However, we question the decision to include "round numbers" of companies based on both country and industry, i.e., at least 25 companies per country and at least 50 companies per industry. It means that some companies have been included or excluded based on category specifications rather than company size or prominence. Table 5-C displays the regional and industry coverage found in the second edition of the *Global Company Handbook.*

Each company profile includes 48 data items and "latest" news. Data items are divided into the following eight categories:

- General information, including directory information and stock market data
- General financial data, including product and geographic segmentation data
- Basic financial data (last five years in local currency), including income statement and balance sheet data
- Selected data in US$ (latest year only) of sales, income, assets, and market value
- Key company news from the past year
- Per share data (last five years in local currency)
- Key financial ratios (last five years)
- Special industry-specific ratios

Table 5-C. Coverage in *Global Company Handbook* (2nd edition)

COVERAGE BY REGION			COVERAGE BY INDUSTRY		
Continent	No. of Countries	No. of Companies	Major Industry	No. of Sectors	No. of Companies
Vol II			Basic Industries	6	1,600
Asia/Pacific	14	3,000	Capital Goods	7	3,100
Vol III			Consumer Goods	8	2,500
Europe	18	2,700	Financial &		
Africa/Middle East	5	300	Other Services	11	2,800
Vol IV					
North America	3	3,700			
South America	6	300			

Regional Print Financial Sources

In addition to international sources of financial information, more specialized regional sources are also published.

Asia Company Handbook (Toyo Keizai—Annual)

Toyo Keizai, publisher of the *Japan Company Handbook*, began publishing the companion *Asian Company Handbook* in 1991. In 1992 the *Asian Company Handbook* included information on more than 760 selected corporations on stock exchanges in the following countries:

No. of Companies	Country
100	Hong Kong
68	Malaysia
300	Korea (Republic)
53	Singapore
150	Taiwan
92	Thailand

According to the introduction, companies are selected based on the recommendations of "Acclaimed research organizations in the six nations."

Companies are listed alphabetically. A Securities Code Number, if the country assigns one, is provided as are Chinese characters, where applicable. The *Asian Company Handbook* includes the following data elements:

- **Establishment Date:** Usually when a company first registered as a joint-stock company
- **Head Office:** Except Hong Kong, the place that controls the companies' activities and is registered as Head Office. NA not available; "-" none
- **Financial Data:** Generally uniform item; some national differences due to terminology or preference of the research agency. For example, Korea uses "Bank Borrowing" for long- and short-term debt issued by banks and other corporations

- **Sales Breakdown** (segment data): percent
- **Overseas Business** (the ratio of overseas work to total work)
- **Stock and Share Price:** Number of shareholders, major shareholders, foreign ownership, and a chart showing three years of monthly share price highs and lows
- **Subsidiaries and Affiliates:** Stockholding ratio of company and its subsidiaries and affiliate companies
- **Special Feature:** Export destinations

Price Waterhouse European Companies Handbook (Euromoney—Annual)

The *Price Waterhouse European Company Handbook* is a pan-European financial source. It contains national companies with securities traded on the stock exchanges in European countries (OTC excluded). Beginning in 1991, the *Handbook* was issued in four volumes: (1) Northern Europe; (2) Western Europe; (3) Central & Southern Europe; and (4) Indices.

The *Handbook* has the top 2,000 companies ranked by market capitalization with a minimum of 25 companies per country. Information is gathered from the local stock exchanges. Entries indicate if the accounts are restated or nonconsolidated. The *European Company Handbook* includes the following data items:

Basic Data: Name, country, sector, registered office, phone, directory, major shareholders (5%), and business summary

Financial Data: Market capitalization in local currency and U.S. dollars, five years of data giving seven measures of profit and loss, and seven data items from the balance sheet; ratios include current ratio and ROE; market data include per share price, price range, high/low, net dividends, gross yield, and eps

Rankings: Top 10 companies by market capitalization in each country; top 20 companies by market capitalization in each sector; pan-European comprises all of the companies by market capitalization

Market capitalization is a criteria frequently used in non-U.S. directories. It is the number of ordinary (common) shares in an issue times the closing share price on a given date.

The advantage of a source such as the *European Company Handbook* is that it gives comparable information about the major companies on the European markets. However, the limited amount of financial data is a drawback.

European Handbook (EXTEL—Annual)

EXTEL, discussed in detail below, publishes a series of financial directories, similar in content to CIFAR's *Global Companies Handbook*. An example is the two-volume *European Handbook*, published two times a year. This *Handbook* has more than 2,000 companies from 15 European countries. Information is collected directly from the companies. Companies are arranged alphabetically by country with an alphabetical index and an index by broad sector. A companion publication is the *Asia Pacific Handbook*.

Country-Specific Financial Sources

French Company Handbook (International Business Distribution and the International Herald Tribune—Annual)

The *French Company Handbook* is a multi-purpose, single-country directory. It has two pages of information on about 80 major listed French companies. Thirty-eight industry segments are included, with companies listed in more than one segment. The *French Company Handbook* also includes a brief summary of the French economy, industry evaluations, and information about investing in France.

Sample Data Items in the French Company Handbook

Sample company data includes name, address, telecommunications, management, major activities, employees at home and abroad, consolidated turnover breakdown by sector, company background, major brand names, major known shareholders, principal French subsidiaries and holdings, exports, research/innovation, strategy and trends, and important developments.

Financial highlights contain 6 years of tabular data for 17 items from the income statement, balance sheet and price data, and a verbal description of the prior year. For example, the 1991 edition had data for 1985-1989 with a verbal summary of 1990.

There are now two major English language print sources for financial information on Japanese compa-

nies. The *Japan Company Handbook,* formerly the *Japan Company Directory,* has been published since 1957. The first issue of *Morningstar Japan* appeared February 28, 1992.

Japan Company Handbook (Toyo Keizai—Quarterly)

Since 1987, the *Japan Company Handbook* has been published quarterly in two parts. The First Section provides financial information on the more than 1,264 companies on the first sections of the Tokyo, Osaka, and Nagoya stock exchanges and the Second Section provides the financial information for the 770 companies on the second section of the same exchanges. Entries in the *Japan Company Handbook* are similar to those in the companion *Asia Company Handbook*, described above.

Morningstar Japan (Morningstar—Bi-weekly)

Morningstar, a U.S. investment company, has increased its information profile in the past few years with the publication of mutual funds books and a CD-ROM. In 1992, it introduced *Morningstar Japan*, which looks remarkably like the U.S. *Valueline Investment Service. Morningstar Japan* publishes two parts bi-weekly. The first includes a summary of the investment climate in Japan, and an index listing high-low securities performance and summary data for all companies in the file. Data items include price per share, price/earnings ratio, percent change in price for one and three months and one year, earnings per share data, a beta, and yield.

The second part features 70 companies in each issue, arranged by major industry grouping. Reports are updated on a 20-week cycle. There is one page per company, with the layout following the *Valueline* format, as illustrated in Exhibit 5-2.

Table 5-D compares data elements in *Japan Company Handbook* and *Morningstar Japan.*

Companies by Industry

Less prevalent are international financial sources arranged by industry group. Two are described below.

Best's Insurance Reports:International Edition (A.M. Best—Annual, with updates)

An example of an international sector financial directory is *Best's Insurance Reports International*, published since 1985. Best is probably the best known publisher of insurance company information in the United States. The company is to be commended for the care it has taken in its introductory remarks to remind the user of the pitfalls of using international financial information.

Table 5-D. Comparison of Data Elements in *Japan Company Handbook* and *Morningstar Japan*

	Japan Company Handbook	*Morningstar Japan*
• Arrangement	By Security Code	By industry
• Updates	Quarterly	Biweekly summary 20-week cycle
• Number of companies	1234 1st section	700
• English, Japanese, and Transliterated Names	Yes	Yes
• Text	Profile, Outlook	Profile, Analysis
• Time series & forecasts	3 yrs, 7 items, 2 yr forecast	10 yrs, 28 items, 10 yr growth
• Sales segments	Business	Business & region
• Stock price	5 yrs with graph	10 yr graph, Alpha & Beta
• Ownership/Shareholders	10 major holders; % foreign	10 major; % all categories
• Finance	Balance Sheet Borrowing; R&D	Balance sheet
• Miscellaneous	Bank, exchanges, underwriters	Relationships, incl. lenders; # of shareholders
• Years	Established; listed	
• Employees	Number	Number; % union; avg salary
• Officers	Chairman, president	Chairman, president (with age)
• Addresses	Principal	Japanese and U.S.
• Group membership	In profile	In Relationships

These statements are presented in accordance with the custom or regulatory requirements of the country of domicile and there are significant variations in the method or reporting from one country to another. These differences are not only in the accounting principle used, but in the valuation of assets and liabilities and the treatment of taxes. (Introduction, 1991 Fall Edition)

Best's includes more than 900 insurers and reinsurers, and the number of companies is growing. Companies are classified in one of 15 size categories, from up to $1,000,000 adjusted policy holder surplus to more than $2 billion.

Reports contain the source of information, investment results, taxes, consolidated and group reports, history, management, and operations. An "English-Foreign Index" of companies and a "Foreign-English Index" are followed by an alphabetical list of rated companies. Company reports are then arranged alphabetically. A country index lists 59 nations ranging from Argentina to Zimbabwe.

Information is received directly from the company either as annual reports to stockholders or policyholders, or as statements presented to the regulatory bodies having jurisdiction in the various countries in which the companies operate. Reports also may include supplemental information obtained by Best from questionnaires, examination of other reports, and meetings with company management.

Data items include balance sheet, income, and expenditures data, reported in the currency of the country and also in U.S. dollar equivalents. An exchange rate table is included. Entries vary in length but most are at least two columns. Best is trying to standardize headings for each company and note differences in footnotes. Exhibit 5-3 presents excerpts from a sample entry.

Polk World Banking Profile (R.L. Polk & Co.—Triennial)

Polk International Banking Directory has been published since 1895. In 1993 Polk added *Polk World Banking Profile*, compiled by Bankers Trust Company and subtitled "2000 major banks of the world; 3-year analytical reports showing financial data & key ratios." This 2,000-page directory contains financial data about the world's major banks, taken from annual reports and other sources "Bankers Trust regards as reliable." Banks are located in about 100 countries worldwide. The International Section of the *International Banking Directory* answers such questions as:

• What banks are in Bangkok? Do any have correspondents in New York?

• Who are the officers of Banque Privee Edmond de Rothchild SA?

The *World Banking Profile* answers questions such as:

• What are the profitability ratios for Banque Privee Edmond de Rothchild SA?

• How does that compare to other Swiss banks? to U.S. banks?

EXHIBIT 5-2. *Morningstar Japan*

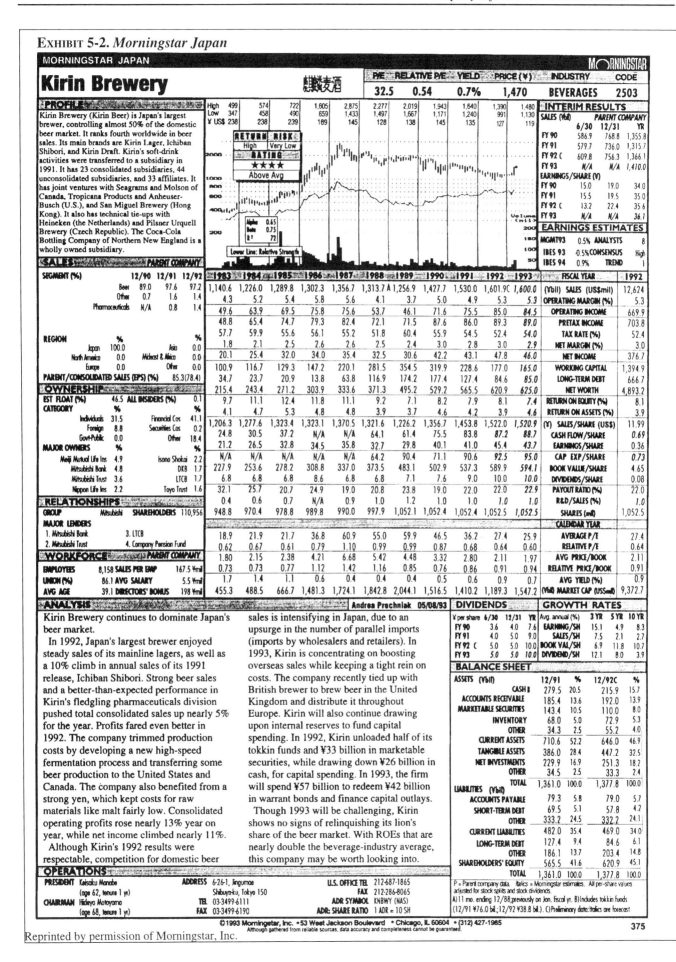

Reprinted by permission of Morningstar, Inc.

EXHIBIT 5-3. Excerpt from *Best's Insurance Reports*, *International Edition*
GRE (UK) LIMITED

GRE (UK) LIMITED
Royal Exchange
London EC3V 3LS, England
Tel: 44 71 283-7101   Telefax: 44 71 623-3587
Telex: 883232   AMB: 85550

1992 Best's Rating

Based on our current opinion of the consolidated financial condition and operating performance of the property/casualty members of the Guardian Royal Exchange Assurance plc, which operate under a group structure, each group member is assigned a Best's Rating of A (Excellent). The company is assigned the Financial Size Category of Class XIV, which is the Financial Size Category of the group. Refer to the Preface for a complete explanation of Best's Rating system and procedure.

OPERATING COMMENTS

Underwriting losses increased relative to 1990 as the combined ratio rose nearly 5.5 points to 135.2 in 1991. The adverse conditions in 1991 was due to loss activity driven by arson and robbery claims attributed to the recession. The company paid a dividend of GBP 192,000,000 in 1991 which reflected the transfer of their holdings in The Metropolitan Trust plc to Guardian Royal Exchange Assurance plc. Large realized capital gains and a change in revaluation reserves mitigated, to some extent, the losses from underwriting and the large dividend payment leading to a 9.3% decline in shareholders' funds.

The performance of non-life contracts issued by the company is guaranteed by Guardian Royal Exchange Assurance plc. With the approval of the Department of Trade and Industry, the company, its holding company and certain of its fellow subsidiaries have entered into a mutual guarantee whereby each company guarantees payment of all liabilities incurred by the others in respect of non-life business.

SOURCE OF INFORMATION: Company Annual Report

Summarized Accounts as of December 31, 1991
US$ per Local Currency Unit 1.8695=1 British Pound (GBP)

ASSETS

	12/31/91 GBP(000)	12/31/91 %	12/31/91 US$(000)
Preferred stocks	89,200	4.4	166,759
Common stocks	284,500	14.0	531,873
Debentures & debenture stocks	278,000	13.6	519,721
Foreign securities	185,000	9.1	345,858
Government securities	265,200	13.0	495,791
Mortgages & loans	41,600	2.0	77,771
Real estate investments	59,500	2.9	111,235
Investment in subsidiaries	102,500	5.0	191,624
Cash & bank deposits	55,400	2.7	103,570
Agents' balances	218,600	10.7	408,673
Reinsurance balances	38,900	1.9	72,724
Receivable from affiliates	61,600	3.0	115,161
Accounts receivable	154,900	7.6	289,586
Taxes recoverable	126,600	6.2	236,679
Deferred policy acquisition cost	76,800	3.8	143,578
Total assets	2,038,300	100.0	3,810,602

LIABILITIES, SURPLUS & OTHER FUNDS

	12/31/91 GBP(000)	12/31/91 %	12/31/91 US$(000)
Loss reserve	1,328,300	65.2	2,483,257
Unearned premiums	397,300	19.5	742,752
Reinsurance accounts payable	3,600	0.2	6,730
Payable to agents	11,800	0.6	22,060
Accounts payable	49,200	2.4	91,979
Other liabilities	3,300	0.2	6,169
Total liabilities & other funds	1,793,500	88.0	3,352,948
Capital	258,200	12.7	482,705
Revaluation reserve	93,200	4.6	174,237
Retained income	-106,600	- 5.2	-199,289
Total capital & surplus	244,800	12.0	457,654
Total	2,038,300	100.0	3,810,602

STATEMENT OF INCOME

	12/31/91 GBP(000)	12/31/91 US$(000)
Gross premiums written	1,008,900	1,886,139
Reinsurance ceded	58,800	109,927
Net premiums written	950,100	1,776,212
Net operating income after tax	-162,100	-303,046

CAPITAL & SURPLUS ACCOUNT
Changes

	12/31/91 GBP(000)	12/31/91 US$(000)
Capital & surplus beginning of year	269,800	504,391
Capital & surplus end of year	244,800	457,654

HISTORY

The company was incorporated in England on October 15, 1915 as the United British Insurance Company Limited, for the purpose of writing all classes of non-life insurance business. The name of the company was changed from United British Company Limited to GRE (UK) Limited on May 13, 1987.

MANAGEMENT

All of the outstanding issued shares are directly held by Guardian Royal Exchange Assurance plc. The ultimate holding company is Guardian Royal Exchange plc (incorporated in England) which ultimately controls all members of the Guardian Royal Exchange Group of which GRE (UK) Limited is a member. This group operates on a worldwide basis and offers comprehensive financial services through its many subsidiaries and affiliates. (For more information about these companies, please refer to their reports which appear in this publication.)

Officers: Managing director, J. Sinclair; general manager, A. Thompson; secretary, J. Clayton.
Directors: S. A. Hopkins (chairman), J. Sinclair (managing director), Miss C. M. Burton, P. G. Edwards, N. L. Feldman, B. Fothergill, J. T. McDonough, J. Morley, M. J. Sissons, A. Thompson.

OPERATIONS

The principal activity of the company is the writing of non-life insurance business other than certain reinsurance business. The performance of non-life contracts issued by the company is guaranteed by Guardian Royal Exchange Assurance plc. On January 1, 1988 the United Kingdom non-life insurance business of Guardian Royal Exchange Assurance plc, other than certain reinsurance business, was transferred together with the related assets and liabilities to the company.

Affiliations/Associations: The company is a member of the Institute of London Underwriters (ILU).

*By-Line Distribution of Premiums Written

	12/31/91 Net	12/31/91 %	12/31/90 Net
Commercial lines	385,400	40.5	360,900
Marine	44,300	4.7	35,200
Personal lines	520,400	54.8	447,800
Total	950,100	100.0	843,900

*Currency: GBP thousands.

*Geographical Distribution of Premiums Written

	12/31/91 Net	12/31/91 %	12/31/90 Net
United Kingdom	928,700	97.8	831,100
Other	21,400	2.2	12,800
Total	950,100	100.0	843,900

*Currency: GBP thousands.

*Underwriting Experience

Year	Gross Premiums Written	Net Premiums Written	Net Premiums Earned	Losses & Loss Adj Exp Inc'd	Commission & Underw Exp Inc'd	Under writing Income	Net Income A/T
1988	716,900	689,700	652,500	461,100	151,500	27,700	82,700
1989	843,800	813,100	759,500	603,800	181,500	-25,800	65,000
1990	915,300	844,000	837,200	877,600	209,900	-250,300	5,800
1991	1,008,900	950,100	930,800	1,033,900	229,000	-332,100	-162,100

*Currency: GBP thousands.

COMPARATIVE FINANCIAL AND OPERATING EXHIBIT
FINANCIAL DATA

Year	Gross Premiums Written	Net Premiums Written	Net Investment Income	Net Operating Inc (B/T)	Total Admitted Assets	Policy-holders' Surplus	Adj Policy-holders' Surplus
1988	716,900	689,700	65,200	110,300	1,638,700	476,600	476,600
1989	843,800	813,100	88,400	86,300	1,982,700	642,500	642,500
1990	915,300	844,000	81,000	-50,100	1,891,800	269,800	269,800
1991	1,008,900	950,100	86,500	-229,500	2,038,300	244,800	244,800

Profitability Tests

Year	Loss Ratio	Expense Ratio	Combined Ratio	Net Invest. Income to NPE	Net Operating Ratio	NOI (B/T) to NPW	Return on Adj PHS	NPW to GPW
1988	71.0	22.0	92.9	10.0	82.9	16.0	....	96.2
1989	79.5	22.3	101.8	11.6	90.2	10.6	13.6	96.4
1990	104.8	24.9	129.7	9.7	120.0	-5.9	0.9	92.2
1991	111.1	24.1	135.2	9.3	125.9	-24.2	-60.1	94.2

Leverage Tests / Liquidity Tests

Year	NPW To Adj PHS	Change In NPW	Tech Res To Adj PHS	Tech Res To GPW	Current Liquidity	Overall Liquidity	Invested Assets & Cash to Tech Res	Agents Balances to Assets
1988	1.4	....	2.2	1.5	77.2	141.0	86.2	12.1
1989	1.3	17.9	1.9	1.4	80.2	147.9	89.3	11.9
1990	3.1	3.8	5.6	1.7	57.1	116.6	60.8	14.0
1991	3.9	12.6	7.0	1.7	70.2	113.6	72.9	10.7

Best's Insurance Reports, International Edition, reprinted with permission from A.M. Best Company.

The major portion of the *Profile* is arranged alphabetically by bank within country. There is a one-page standardized financial summary for each bank with four sections of information: three years each of assets, liabilities, and income statement data in home currency plus one year in U.S. dollars with a three-year average, as well as ratio data.

Basic directory information is given for each bank, including address, telecommunications, type, establishment date, and exchange rate used. *World Banking Profile* has two additional features, credit ratings and rankings, which will be discussed in Chapter 8. This directory is useful if you need data on a wider range of banks than are included in the other financial sources described here.

PROVIDERS OF FINANCIAL INFORMATION

CIFAR and Worldscope

In 1990, there were two additional major providers of listed international company financial data in the U.S. One was CIFAR, the Center for International Financial Analysis and Research, located in Princeton, New Jersey; the other was Worldscope, a product of Wright Investors Services, a Connecticut investment firm. Some corporate history is necessary to understand the products on the market today.

CIFAR began as an innovation of Professor Vinod Bavishi, when he was at the University of Connecticut collecting international annual reports. Because no such service existed, Professor Bavishi had his reports microfilmed and sold to libraries in microfiche. CIFAR has been building its collection since 1984, based originally on companies of interest to Professor Bavishi. As the collection grew, it was marketed for a short time by University Microfilms and then came back to CIFAR.

In 1988, selected information from the international annual reports was published in a multi-volume looseleaf set called *Worldscope Manuals.* The *Manuals* were a joint venture with Wright Investors Services, which provided U.S. information to supplement the international file. Patterned after the *Standard and Poor's Report* services (the "tear sheets"), the *Manuals* offered a page of financial data per company, in standardized format.

In mid-1990, CIFAR and Worldscope parted company. CIFAR continued to collect international annual reports gathered by individuals located in targeted countries and to do research on international accounting and finance. Disclosure Inc. had the rights to distribute the

microfiche collection through fiscal 1991. CIFAR continues to create its own database and is marketing a CD-ROM product as well. CIFAR publishes its own directory, *Global Companies Handbook,* described above.

Disclosure now has entered into a joint venture with Wright to provide the Disclosure/Worldscope CD-ROM. The first disc became available in 1991, replacing *Disclosure Europe*, which had appeared the year before. Worldscope data are also available on CD-ROM through LOTUS CD/International and online from LEXIS AND NEXIS SERVICES and DOW JONES NEWS RETRIEVAL. On DOW JONES, access is only by company name. Disclosure also sells the data on magnetic tape.

These changes have been confusing, especially for information professionals who must maintain a standard set of international financial information that has value as a time series. The proliferation of formats and vendors also complicates evaluation.

Because of its Disclosure joint venture, Wright is now an important player in the information market. In early 1993, the *Worldscope* database contained approximately 9,000 companies from more than 30 countries, including 3,000 from the U.S. Not all the companies in the database are publicly traded. Ten years of historical data is available. Companies are arranged in 24 industry groupings in the database.

CIFAR offers a service called CfarQuest that provides individual reports in the language, currency, and delivery method of the client's choice. The price for one full company profile, with more than 250 data items in English with local currency, is $50.

Company reports in both CIFAR and Worldscope are presented in a standard format, which differs based on major industry grouping. The different formats are listed below:

Worldscope	CIFAR
Industrials	Industrials
Bank	Banks
Insurance	Insurance
Brokerage	Financial
Other Financial Companies	

The Worldscope joint venture will print special "industry studies" on demand for the 20 industries listed below. The studies resemble the old Worldscope printed manual in format. There is one page of information per company, plus rankings and averages. The *World Food, Beverage & Tobacco Industry Study*, which we examined, had more than 400 major food manufacturers, agricultural producers of major products, wholesalers, and retailers. The word "study" is misleading since there was no analysis in these reports. We have been informed by the producer that news stories are being added to these reports. The cost is $295 for commercial organizations or $195 for academic and public libraries. This is, however, a good new source to consider for a client who needs financial information for individual companies within large industry groupings.

Worldscope Industry Studies

Computer Hardware
  and Software
Automotive
Banking
Chemical
Apparel and Textile
Construction and
  Engineering
Drugs, Healthcare, and
  Cosmetics
Electrical and Electronic
  Equipment
Energy
Food, Beverage, and
  Tobacco

Forest Products,
  Paper, and Packaging
Insurance
Machinery and Equipment
Mining, Metal Products,
  and glass
Print, Publishing, Broad-
  casting, and Advertising
Real Estate and Financial
  Services
Recreation
Retailing
Transportation
Utility

European Providers of Financial Information

Extel. EXTEL Financial Ltd. is an information institution in the U.K. Known for its "annual cards" (similar in concept to microfiche), it was founded in 1872 as the Exchange Telegraph Company. In 1919, it began disseminating financial data about British companies. At the end of 1992, EXTEL was tracking more than 8,000 companies, with about half from the U.K. Its goal is to collect information on the more than 10,000 equity trading companies in Europe and Japan, and to add the emerging markets in Asia and Latin America. EXTEL cards also contain the nonfinancial companies in the S&P 500 for comparison with its international companies. In late 1993, EXTEL was purchased by Financial Times.

The card service includes cards with financial statements and cards of news information. Because most international companies do not file quarterly reports, the most up-to-date financial information appears in these news cards.

EXTEL services are available in a variety of formats on a wide range of databanks as indicated by the April 1993 EXTEL brochure in Table 5-E.

Table 5-E. EXTEL Financial

THIRD PARTY HOSTS AND SELECTED PROVIDERS OF EXTEL FINANCIAL DATA

EXTEL CARD DATABASE

ONLINE	CD ROM	TERMINAL PROVIDERS
MAID SYSTEMS MEAD DIALOG DATASTAR FT PROFILE	LOTUS ONE SOURCE	BRIDGE INFORMATION FIRST CALL

EXSTAT DATABASE

GLOBAL VANTAGE
IDC
NIKKEI

EXSHARE DATABASE

RE-VENDORS	BUREAU/PACKAGE INTERFACES	ADDED VALUE APPLICATIONS	HOSTS
IDC MULLER DATA REUTERS MERRILL LYNCH	SEI CORP. FINANCIAL MODELS DATASTREAM SHAW DATA PREMIER ADP	FACTSET IDD TRADELINE BARRA VESTEK LYNCH JONES RYAN FIRST CALL EVALUATION ASSOC. FAME	FII TRACK DATA SHARK COMPUSERVE

EXTEL data may be purchased directly from EXTEL on tape, diskette, or as a CD-ROM product running on a 486 workstation using Windows software. Weekly and monthly updates are available for the CD-ROM. Data may also be stored on a hard disk and updated online daily. Information in the workstation is from the EXTEL annual and news cards. The workstation also has an Equity database with seven years of daily stock prices.

All three of these information providers—CIFAR, Wright/Disclosure Joint Venture, and EXTEL—design their products for use by accountants and financial analysts. Files contain the footnotes that accompany the financial data and accounting standards used.

Bureau Van Dijk. Bureau Van Dijk, a management consulting firm in Brussels and Paris, has a series of financial CD-ROM databases that it offers in conjunction with local information suppliers. Examples of Bureau Van Dijk discs are *FAME*, with data from Jordan & Sons in the U.K.; *Diane*, the French disc with SCRL data; and *Dafne*, the German database with Creditreform data. All of the discs use the same sophisticated statistical analysis package. A description of the Bureau Van Dijk CD-ROM financial products appears in the March 1993 issue of *CD-ROM Professional*.[4] Bureau Van Dijk will be setting up a New York office in 1994.

In 1993, Bureau van Dijk issued a new product called *amadeus* (analyse major databases from European Sources). This pan-European database gives detailed financial information on around 100,000 of the largest companies from 17 European countries, the EC plus Sweden, Norway, Finland, Switzerland, and Austria. *amadeus* includes the top companies from products such as *FAME*, *Diane*, and *Dafne*. According to Bureau van Dijk's preview notice, a financial model has been used to standardize the income statement and balance sheet accounts for 36 financial items plus 20 ratios and 36 growth trends. Historical data are available for five years. We did not have an opportunity to preview *amadeus* for this publication.

Three other important European providers of financial and company information are worth noting.

* *Jordan and Sons* offers print directories, online and CD-ROM databases, and industry reports. Data are from Companies House. Jordan's has full financials for more than 70,000 U.K. companies with turnover greater than £1 million, pre-tax profit greater than £50,000, or shareholder funds of more than £1 million.
* *ICC Information Group* is another major U.K. provider of company and industry information, most of it available in the U.S. online either direct to ICC or through the major time-sharing systems. The range of products includes British company financials, from the same Companies House source as Jordan's; full-text annual reports, presently from the U.K.; industry reports; and brokerage house reports. ICC also provides Sharewatch on its own system; this service tracks share ownership in British quoted companies. The annual reports and ICC KEYNOTE industry reports are also available on CD-ROM through SilverPlatter and in *UK Company Factfinder* on DIALOG.
* *Companies House* itself is now accessible online through Mercury Data Network in the U.K. Profile data, including company incorporation date, registered number, date of accounts, and a history screen are on the online file. Any document filed with Companies House can be received via post in print or microform or by fax. Like the U.S. SEC, Companies House has complete microfiche collections in reading rooms.

FINDING FINANCIAL FOOTNOTES ON CD-ROM

Worldscope (Wright/Worldscope Joint Venture) and CIFAR both emphasize the availability of footnote information on their CD-ROM products and online files. Exhibit 5-4 displays a Worldscope menu.

EXHIBIT 5-4. Worldscope® Menus for Text

Would you like to search by:

C T		
	Search Text Fields by:	
F	All Text Fields Below	
T	Accounting Practices Text	
N	**Footnotes to Financials**	
O	Footnotes to Stock Report	
S	Footnotes to Ratios	
S	Description of Business	

Use Previously Saved Search
More Search Choices

Source: Copyright © Worldscope®/Disclosure Partners 1993. Reprinted with permission from Worldscope/Disclosure.

Every significant word in these fields is searchable. For example in both CIFAR and Worldscope, you can

* Search for accounting practices for French companies that use straight line depreciation.
* Search for examples of how U.K. companies handle extraordinary earnings when calculating earnings per share.
* Identify "stock splits" in the footnotes to stock reports, or "reorganizations" in the footnotes to financials.

There is no standardization for footnotes to financial statements. The text is taken directly from the company's report. CIFAR and Worldscope also include notes that indicate where the data have been reworked for the database.

In Exhibit 5-5, the French hotel conglomerate ACCOR S.A. does not report current liabilities. Therefore, Wright used other balance sheet data to calculate the figure for the *Worldscope* database.

GLOBAL VANTAGE (Standard and Poor's)

Another source aimed at both the financial and research market is *Global Vantage,* a PC-based CD-ROM product using Compustat PC Plus software. The underlying database (*see* Table 5-B) has combined industrial/commercial data from the EXTEL database with S & P's own financial services reports. The EXTEL company coverage in *Global Vantage* is not exactly the same as the EXTEL database.

The CD-ROM product has annual data items, beginning in 1982, for most companies on the disc. Items have been standardized and adapted to fit the type of company:

> Industrial/Commercial
> Bank
> Insurance
> Broker/Dealer
> Real Estate
> Other Financial Services

The file has extensive footnotes detailing accounting standards, valuation principles, and methods of consolidation.

Fifty-four currencies are used with translation rates available for month-end, monthly average, and 12-month moving average. Translations may be done from a country's native currency to other currencies. There is also a file of more than 8,800 equity issues with pricing and market-related information from 1982 to the present.

WHERE TO FIND INTERNATIONAL ANNUAL REPORTS

We have been discussing a variety of ways of getting financial data. Listed below are the major sources of annual statements in a variety of formats.

- **Print:** *Moody's International Manual*
- **Microfiche:** From CIFAR, distributed by Disclosure ** (a)
- **Cards:** EXTEL Card Service
- **CD-ROM:** Laser D/International (Disclosure)** U.K. Company Reports (ICC on SilverPlatter and DIALOG *U.K. FactFinder*), *EXTEL Workstation*, MicroEXTAT, *Moody's International Company Data*
- **Online:** ICC Annual Report file (DIALOG, DATA-STAR, LEXIS AND NEXIS SERVICES, ICC Direct); Extel (DIALOG, DATA-STAR, LEXIS AND NEXIS SERVICES, FT PROFILE)

** Actual primary documents
(a) Disclosure ceased distributing the microfiche at the end of the 1991 fiscal year cycle

TEXT SOURCES OF COMPANY FINANCIAL INFORMATION

Companies issue annual financial statements. There is often a lag of six months between the end of the fiscal year and the time the statement is published in print for

---

**EXHIBIT 5-5. Worldscope® Record—Footnotes to Financial Statements
Search for the word "reorganization"**

ACCOR S.A.

FOOTNOTES TO FINANCIAL STATEMENTS:
1: 1990, 1989 - INCLUDES OTHER TAXES
2: 1990, 1989, 1988, 1987, 1986 - *COMPANY DOES NOT REPORT CURRENT LIABILITIES; CALCULATED*
3: 1990, 1989, 1988, 1987, 1986 - SIMILAR CHARGES INCLUDED
4: 1983 - MAJOR **REORGANIZATION**. 1990, 1989, 1987, 1984 -ACQ'D(1990 - MOTEL 6 L.P. & MAJORITY SHARE IN RUHL CASINO IN 90) (1989 - 51% OF AUSTRALIAN GREETINGS GROUP LTD IN 89)(1987 - ARA FRANCE RESTAURATION COLLECTIVE, RESTOCHECK & LUNCHECK IN 87)(1984 - COMPAGNIE INT'L DE RESTAURATION IN 84)
5: 1990, 1989 - INCLUDES INVESTMENT INCOME
6: 1990, 1989, 1988, 1987, 1986 - INCLUDES SELLING, GENERAL AND ADMINISTRATIVE EXPENSE
7: 1990, 1989, 1988 - SIMILAR CHARGES INCLUDED

Source: Worldscope® CD-ROM November 1992. Copyright © Worldscope/Disclosure Partners 1993. Reprinted with permission from Worldscope/Disclosure.

the international audience. As a practical matter, researchers cannot track changes between reports by reading and clipping the extensive range of text sources about companies in newswires, newspapers, newsletters, business magazines, academic journals, investment bank reports, and market research reports. However, many of these publications are available online, in English, and are updated daily or weekly. There is no substitute for the timeliness and breadth of coverage of time-sharing systems. The material is there to read when needed.

Newspapers

Many countries have financial newspapers, similar in purpose to the *Wall Street Journal*. In addition to their native language papers, non-English-speaking countries often publish business newspapers and journals in English to reach an international audience. Some of the papers are also available in electronic format.

The *Financial Times,* the international equivalent of the *Wall Street Journal,* is now published in Philadelphia, as well as in England and Frankfort. It has a printed index and is also widely available online.

The *Wall Street Journal* includes international coverage and publishes both an *Asian Wall Street Journal* and a *European Wall Street Journal* daily on those continents. There are also weekly editions in the U.S.

EXTEL, in addition to its annual report cards, publishes news cards. McCarthy International Ltd, another U.K. information provider, also has a news card service.

All of the indexing services and online databases discussed in Chapter 2 have articles about companies. Three of the financial CD-ROM products we discussed, *Moody's International Company Data, Worldscope*, and *Extel Workstation* include brief news items associated with financial issues as part of the company records. CIFAR announced that it too was adding news to its company financial records.

NOTES

1. From a speech at the European Business Information Conference, Amsterdam, March 1991. Professor Nobes has written numerous articles on comparative accounting standards, including "Financial Reporting in the EEC: Why and How It Differs," *Management Accounting, 65* No. 40 (April 1987): 34-35 and "EC Group Accounting: Two Zillion Ways to Do It," *Accountancy* (UK), *6* No. 1168: 84-85.
2. Christopher Nobes, *Interpreting European Financial Statements: Towards 1992* (London: Butterworths, 1989).
3. *SourceGuide to European Company Information: EC Countries,* 5th ed. (Detroit: Gale, 1993).
4. Ruth A. Pagell, "European Information on CD-ROM: Part III-Individual Country Financial Information from Bureau van Dijk," *CD-Rom Professional* (March 1993): 107-17.

CHAPTER 6
Company Information: Electronic Sources

TOPICS COVERED

1. Databank Overviews
2. Company Databases with Product Codes
3. Online Information: Asian Companies
4. Online Information: East European/Former Soviet Companies
5. Company Data on CD-ROM
6. Online Text Sources of International Company Information
7. Caveat Emptor
8. Conclusion
9. Notes

MAJOR SOURCES DISCUSSED

- DIALOG
- DATA-STAR
- LEXIS AND NEXIS SERVICES
- DOW JONES NEWS RETRIEVAL

No single library owns or would want to own all the published company directories. They are expensive. They date quickly; many are out of date when published. Like all printed sources, they lack the flexibility to screen for a variety of characteristics. The information in printed directories is often available through standard time-sharing systems that are easily accessible worldwide. This online availability allows us to compare the annual cost of purchasing a specialized print directory with the annual cost of searching an online database for the same information only when needed.

The distinction between types of directories becomes less significant when they are searched online or ondisc. Many of the online and CD-ROM files include basic information, extensive product listings, officers and directors, and one or two financial data items.

Articles in publications such as *Online* and *Database*[1,2] describe current databases and common questions. For Europe, *European Markets: A Guide to Company and Industry Information Sources*[3] and *SourceGuide to European Company Information*[4] complement their print coverage of sources with a country-by-country

listing of online sources as well. The print and online database directories[5] also may be used to generate lists of international company directories.

Selecting the right source of electronic information is a difficult task in an international environment. There are thousands of databases, on hundreds of hosts, many of which are unfamiliar to us. The numbers keep growing as do the formats. Remote time-sharing, CD-ROM, locally loaded tapes, resident databases, and real-time satellite feeds are all options.

We highlight and recommend certain sources of electronic information throughout this book. However, by the time this book is published, new databases will no doubt be available and many more will come along soon after. Appendix G presents guidelines for selecting an international database.

DATABANK OVERVIEWS

There are many online company databases, from the equivalents of standard print sources, mentioned in Chapter 4, to niche databases for individual countries and applications. Detailed descriptions of these databases are provided through databank documentation. The purpose of this section is to organize the many directory titles by presenting them in tables arranged by databank provider. We discuss DIALOG, DATA-STAR, LEXIS AND NEXIS SERVICES, and DOW JONES in detail. Table 6-A provides help in finding online company information in the United States.

DIALOG

Searching for companies and news by geographic region is simplified by DIALOG's Onesearch files, for example, ASIACO and ASIANEWS. Tables 6-B and 6-C list the DIALOG databases in each geographic category as of March 1993. Dates are given for comparison.

Table 6-A. Where to Search for Company Information Online in the U.S.

U.S.-Based Hosts:

DIALOG: Best general source for manipulating data online

DOW JONES: Up-to-date news wire and company information; international financial and securities data

LEXIS AND NEXIS SERVICES: Best source for full-text Eastern European publications

European-Based Hosts:

DATA-STAR: Best source for European Company directory files (*Note*: As of March 1993, a subsidiary of DIALOG)

FT Profile: Available in the U.S. through several gateways, including DataTimes

Questel: French databank with unique files such as DMI France

Reuterlink: Current and time series data on financial markets; uses special software that links to Lotus

Datastream: Time series stock prices and financials

Table 6-B. DIALOG Company Files (XXXXXCO)

File	Name	Date	Asia	Canada	Europe	Japan	Latin America	Mideast Africa	UK
286	Biocommerce ABS	81-93 Feb			X				
479	Company Intelligence	4 Mar 93	X		X	X		X	X
491	Cancorp	93 Feb W4		X					
500	EXTEL	1992				X			
502	Teikoku	2/93	X			X			
505	FBR Asian Cos	9301	X						
513	Corporate Affil	12/92	X	X	X	X	X	X	X
518	D&B Int'l DMI	10/92	X		X		X	X	X
520	D&B Canadian DMI			X					
521	D&B Europe DMI								
522	D&B Asia-Pacific	3/93	X			X			
529	Hoppenstedt - GE				X				
561	ICC British Co								X
562	ICC British Co Financials								X
590	KOMPASS Europe				X				
591	KOMPASS UK								X
592	KOMPASSAsia/Pacific	12/92	X			X			

Table 6-C. DIALOG News Files (XXXXXNEWS)

File	Name	Date	Asia	Canada	Europe	Japan	Latin America	Mideast Africa	UK
16	PTS Promt	72-93 Mar8	X	X	X	X	X	X	X
30	Asia Pacific	Mar 1 93	X			X			
111	NTL Newspaper Index	79-93/Feb	X	X	X	X	X	X	
148	Trade & Industry	81-93 Feb	X	X	X	X	X	X	X
211	Newsearch	03/05/93	X	X	X	X	X	X	X
262	Canadian Business & Current Affairs	1982-Jan 1992		X					
465	Arab Info Bank	83 -93/Feb						X	
466	Info-South L A News	88-93/Mar					X		
481	Delphes	80-93/Feb			X				
484	Newspaper & Periodical Abs	88-93 04 Mar 1993		X				X	X
501	Extel Intl News	X		X	X			X	
545	Investext	82- Mar 93	X	X	X	X	X	X	X
560	Financial Times Abs	82-May 92							X
563	ICC Intl Brokerage House Reports	Mar 93							X
564	ICC Intl Annual Reports	23/Feb/93							X
583	Infomat Intl Bus	86-Feb 93	X	X	X	X	X	X	X
609	Knight Ridder/ Tribune Fin News	89-Mar 93	X	X	X	X	X	X	X
611	Reuters	87-Mar 93	X	X	X	X		X	
612	Japan Economic News	84-Mar 93				X			
613	PR Newswire	87/5-93/3	X	X	X				
614	Agence France -Eng	6/91-3/93			X				
622	Financial Times Full	86-Mar 93							X
627	EIU:Business Int'l	Mar 93		X	X	X	X	X	X
624	McGraw-Hill Pubs	85-Mar 93	X		X	X			
635	Business Dateline	85-Mar 93			X				
636	PTS Newsletter	87-Mar 93	X	X	X	X	X	X	X
637	Journal of Commerce	86-Mar 93			X				
645	Current Digest Soviet Press	82-1/29/92	X		X				
648	Trade & Industry ASAP	83-Feb 93	X	X	X	X	X	X	X
710	Times/Sunday Times	6/88-3/93			X				X
711	Independent (London)			X				X	
771	Textline Global News	1980-90	X	X	X	X	X	X	X
772		1990-1991							
799		1992-3/93							

Source: DIALOG, searched March 7, 1993

A helpful tip for finding alternative entries for company names when searching across DIALOG files is to use DIALOG *Company Name Finder* (File 416).

DATA-STAR

DATA-STAR presently has the largest number of country-specific databases for Europe. The files include directory files, product files, and financial statements for hundreds of thousands of European companies.

The strength of the databank is the number of databases and companies that are included. A problem for the searcher, however, is that the information is fragmented into many files each having its own file structure and field codes. Another problem for searchers is that many of the files are in the local language. Table 6-D lists company directory files found on DATA-STAR. Table 6-E lists DATA-STAR company files by geographic coverage or origin.

Table 6-D. Company Directory Files on DATA-STAR

DATABASE	LABEL	TYPE	GEOGRAPHIC COVERAGE	FILE SIZE	LANG	LAST UPDATE
ABC EUROPE	EURE	D	EUROPE	156,625	E	92-12
ABC WEST GERMANY	ABCE	D	GERMANY	78,798	E	92-12
BDI-GERMAN INDUSTRY	BDIE	D	GERMANY	23,616	E	92-04
CANCORP DATABASE	CNCO	F	CANADA	8,642	E	93-3-24
COMPANY INTELLIGENCE	INCO	D, N	NON-US	28,899	E	93-2-26
CREDITREFORM AUSTRIA	AVVC	D	AUSTRIA	36,561	G	93-3-8
CREDITREFORM W. GERMANY	DVVC	D	GERMANY	628,964	G	93-8-11
CREDITREFORM E. GERMANY	OVVC	D	GERMANY	55,414	G	ceased with 93-8-11
DUN & BRADSTREET CANADA	DNCA	D	CANADA		E	
DUN & BRADSTREET	DBZZ	D	EUROPE	2,180,359	E	93-3
DUN & BRADSTREET	DNAP	D	ASIA-PACIFIC	215,262	E	New: 93-8
DUN & BRADSTREET	DNEE	D	EASTERN EUROPE	28,770	E	1993
DUN & BRADSTREET ISRAEL	DNIS	D	ISRAEL	11,871	E	1993
DUN & BRADSTREET SWISS COMPANIES	SWCO	D	SWITZERLAND	152,393	E	92-3
DUN & BRADSTREET SWISS CO. FINANCIALS	SWFF	F	SWITZERLAND	1289	E	93-03-22
ECO REGISTER	ECCO	D	GERMANY	2,023,516	G	93-03-26
ELECTRO/ ELECTRONIC BUYERS GUIDE	ZVEE	D	GERMANY	2,342	E	92-4
EXTEL CARD DATABASE	EXTL	F	WORLDWIDE	9,549	E	93-03
FINF/NUMERIC COIN/NUMERIC	FINN COIN	F	GERMANY	8,894	G E	from 1983-
FIRMIMPORT/ FIRMEXPORT	FRIE	I/E	FRANCE	37,068	E	92-10

Table 6-D. Company Directory Files on DATA-STAR *(continued)*

FRENCH COMPANIES FULL FINANCIALS	FRFF FREF	F	FRANCE	119,976	F F E		93-1-7
GERMAN BUYERS GUIDE	E1X1	D	GERMANY	54,827	E		93-1
HOPPENSTEDT AUSTRIA	HOAU	D	AUSTRIA	5.085	G		ND
HOPPENSTEDT BENELUX	BNLU	D	BELGIUM,LUXEMBO URG,NETHERLANDS	81,405	E,G,F D,S		ND
HOPPENSTEDT E. GERMANY	HOEA	D	GERMANY	13,056	G		ND
HOPPENSTEDT GERMANY	HOPE	D	GERMANY	50,482	G		ND
ICC DIRECTORY OF UK COMPANIES	ICDI	D	ENGLAND,WALES, SCOTLAND, NO. IRELAND	2,620,000	E		1993
ICC FINANCIAL DATASHEETS	ICFF	F	GREAT BRITAIN	215,466	E		1993
ICC FULLTEXT COMPANY REPORTS & ACCOUNTS	ICAC	F	GREAT BRITAIN	appx 2500	E		93-3
INFOTRADE BELGIUM CO. DATABASE	BECO	D	BELGIUM	203,810	E,F,D		92-6-27
ITALIAN COMPANY FULL FINANCIAL DATA	ITFF	F	ITALY	4,331			93-3-23
ITALIAN TRADING COMPANIES	ITIE SDOE	I/E	ITALY	87,625	E I		93-2-23
JAPANESE CORPORATE DIRECTORY	JPCO	D	JAPAN	4,490	E		92-12-23
JORDANWATCH	JORD	F	U.K.	343,229	E		93-3-24
KEY BRITISH ENTERPRISES	DKBE	F	U.K.	49,440	E		
KREDIT- SCHUTZVER- BANK VON 1870	KSVA	D	AUSTRIA	121,434	G		93-3
TELEFIRM	FRCO	D	FRANCE	1,369.000	E		92-11-23
UK IMPORTERS	UKIM	I/E	U.K.	96,012	E		93-1
WER GEHOERT ZU WEM	WGZW	D	GERMANY	12,153	E		ND
WHO MAKES MACHINERY & PLANT	VDME	D	GERMANY	6,227	E		92-10

Table 6-D. Company Directory Files on DATA-STAR *(continued)*

WHO SUPPLIES WHAT?	WLWE	D	GERMANY	142,286	E	93-03

Types of FILES ARE:D (DIRECTORY), F (FINANCIALS),I/E (IMPORTERS/EXPORTERS), N (News)
GEOGRAPHIC COVERAGE:Number of companies in database March 28,1993
LANGUAGES ARE E (ENGLISH), G (GERMAN), F (FRENCH), D (DUTCH), S (SPANISH)
DATE OF UPDATE: Date on most recent record, March 28, 1993

Source: Adapted from Linda Eichler and Jean Newland, "Data-Star: A Galaxy of Databases," *Database*, June 1993. Used with permission from Online Inc.

Table 6-E. DATA-STAR Company Files by Geographic Coverage/Origin

GEOGRAPHIC COVERAGE	DATABASE	LABEL	TYPE	NUMBER OF COMPANIES
AUSTRIA	CREDITREFORM	AVVC	D	36,561
	KREDITSCHUTZVER BANK VON 1870	KSVA	D	121,434
	HOPPENSTEDT AUSTRIA	HOAU	D	5085
	DUN & BRADSTREET AUSTRIA	DBOS *	D	67,491
BELGIUM	DUN & BRADSTREET BELGIUM	DBBL *	D	143,211
	HOPPENSTEDT BENELUX	BNLU	D	81,405
	INFOTRADE BELGIUM	BECO	D	203,810U
CANADA	CANCORP DATABASE	CNCO	F?	8,642
	DUN & BRADSTREET CANADA	DNCA	D	143,570
DENMARK	DUN & BRADSTREET DENMARK	DBDK *	D	1,238
FRANCE	DUN & BRADSTREET FRANCE	DBFR *	D	228,694
	FRENCH COMPANIES FULL FINANCIALS INFORMATION	FRFF/ FREF	F	119,976
	FIRMIMPORT/EXPORT	FRIE	I/E	37,068
	TELEFIRM	FRCO	D	1,369,000
GERMANY	ABC W. GERMANY	ABCE	D	78,798 ++
	BDI-THE GERMANY INDUSTRY	BDIE	D	23,616 ++
	CREDITREFORM GERMANY	DVVC	D	578,220
	DUN & BRADSTREET GERMANY	DBWG	D	232,390 +
	DDR COMPANIES	DDRC	D	U
	ECO REGISTER	ECCO	D	2,023,516 +
	ELECTRO/ELECTRONIC BUYERS GUIDE	ZVEE	D	2,342 ++
	FINF-NUMERIC/COIN-NUMERIC	FINN/COIN	F	8,894
	GERMAN BUYERS' GUIDE	E1X1	D	54,827 ++
	HOPPENSTEDT E. GERMANY	HOEA	D	13,056
	HOPPENSTEDT GERMANY	HOPE	D	50,482
	WER GOHOERT ZU WEM	WGZW	D	12,153
	WHO MAKES MACHINERY & PLANT	VDME	D	6,227 ++
	WHO SUPPLIES WHAT	WLWE	D	142,286 ++
GREECE	DUN & BRADSTREET GREECE	DBHE *	D	18,388
IRELAND	DUN & BRADSTREET IRELAND	DBEI *	D	13,799
ISRAEL	DUN & BRADSTREET ISRAEL	DNIS	D	11,831
ITALY	DUN & BRADSTREET ITALY	DBIT *	D	527,841
	ITALIAN COMPANIES PROFILES	ITFF	F	4,331
	ITALIAN TRADING COMPANIES	ITIE SDOE	I/E	87,625
JAPAN	JAPANESE CORPORATE DIRECTORY	JPCO	D	4,490
LUXEMBOURG	DUN & BRADSTREET LUXEMBOURG	DBLU *	D	11,339
	HOPPENSTEDT BENELUX	BNLU	D	81,405
NETHERLANDS	DUN & BRADSTREET NETHERLANDS	DBNL *	D	216,728
PORTUGAL	DUN & BRADSTREET PORTUGAL	DBPO *	D	94,644
SPAIN	DUN & BRADSTREET SPAIN	DBES *	D	171,052

(continued next page)

Table 6-E. DATA-STAR Company Files by Geographic Coverage/Origin *(continued)*

SWITZERLAND	DUN & BRADSTREET SWISS COMPANIES	SWCO	D	152,393
	DUN & BRADSTREET SWISS COMPANIES FULL FINANCIALS	SWFF	F	1,289
	DUN & BRADSTREET SWITZERLAND	DBCH *	D	129,730
UNITED KINGDOM	DUN & BRADSTREET UNITED KINGDOM	DBGB *	D	323,814
	ICC DIRECTORY OF UK COMPANIES	ICDI	D	2,620,000
	ICC FINANCIAL DATASHEETS	ICFF	F	215,466
	ICC FULL TEXT COMPANY REPORTS AND ACCOUNTS	ICAC	F	appx 2,500
	JORDANWATCH	JORD	F	343,229
	KEY BRITISH ENTERPRISES	DKBE	F	49,440
	UK IMPORTERS	UKIM	I/E	96,012
EUROPE/EC	ABC EUROPE:EUROPEAN EXPORT INDUSTRY	EURE	D	156,625
	DUN AND BRADSTREET E. EUROPE	DNEE	D	21,660
WORLD	COMPANY INTELLIGENCE	INCO	D	28,899

* Part of DBZZ
+ Include companies from the former East Germany
++ Part of the Fiz-Technik German Databank; include coding for the former East Germany
TYPES INCLUDED ARE: D (Directory), F (Financials), I/E (Importers/Exporters)
Searched March 1993
Source: Adapted from Linda Eichler and Jean Newland, "Data-Star: A Galaxy of Databases," *Database*, June 1993. Used with permission from Online Inc.

LEXIS AND NEXIS SERVICES

The international company files found in LEXIS AND NEXIS SERVICES are listed in Table 6-F. These files are part of the COMPNY library.

These company files are complemented by scores of full-text international, regional, and country news and business publications. Walden Country Reports, which are found in such geographic libraries as WORLD or EUROPE, are an unexpected source of company listings. What is unique in the *Walden* reports are lists of top national companies for those countries where national enterprises are the most important organizations. For example, the *Walden* report for Ghana lists 17 core state enterprises that include Ghana Airways, Ghana Oil, and Ghana National Petroleum Corporation. In addition, the report lists Ghana's largest companies under government control.

Table 6-F. LEXIS AND NEXIS SERVICES: International Files in the COMPNY Library

NAME	FILE	NAME	FILE
CFAR	-CFARbase Company Financials Database	HVRWLD	-Worldwide Hoover Profiles
		HOPAUS	-Hopp. Co/Exec in Austria
CFRBNK	-CFAR Banks	HOPEGR	-Hopp. Co/Exec in E. Germany
CFRFIN	-CFAR Financials	HOPSTD	-Directory of German Companies
CFRIND	-CFAR Industrials	HOPTRD	-Hopp. German Trade Assocns
CFRINS	-CFAR Insurance	ICC	-Combined ICCCO & ICCMKT files
EXTEL	-Extel Cards Database	ICCCO	-ICC Quoted Company Annuals
SOVCO	-BizEkon News Russian Business Directory	INTACC	-Int'l Accounting & Auditing Trends
		JPNCO	-Comline Corporate Directory
TECHLN	-CHI TECH-LINE Indicators	ICCMKT	-ICC Keynote Market Rpts
WWC	-World Wide Companies (WWC)		
WLDSCP	-Worldscope		
20-F	-Annual 20-F Filings		

Source: LEXIS AND NEXIS SERVICES, April 10, 1993

Comparison of Financial Databases on LEXIS AND NEXIS SERVICES. Since so many sources of international financial data exist in electronic form, it is difficult to distinguish among them. For example, *Worldscope, Cfarbase, Extel, Standard and Poor's, 20-F SEC Filings,* and *ICC Company Reports* are all international files in the LEXIS AND NEXIS SERVICE COMPNY library. From the searcher's perspective, this is unfortunate, since the software does not lend itself to sophisticated screening and report building. Data cannot easily be saved for use in spreadsheets, as is possible with DIALOG's report format. Also, each file is constructed differently, using different segment codes for items as basic as the company name!

Listed below are some special features from these files on LEXIS AND NEXIS.

WORLDSCOPE:	CO for company name
	Standard format for every company
	Key financials in U.S. dollars
	Product and geographic segment data
	Most useful range of screen and sort segments such as sales, net income, market capital, earnings per share, and choice of output formats
CFARBASE:	One database and then individual databases by type of company; i.e., industrial, bank
	Memos or notes to financials with restatements
	Largest number of companies from emerging markets
	Screen on total revenue, net income
EXTEL:	U.K. terminology and SIC codes
	News cards as well as annual cards in one file
	Key-Financials in three currencies: U.S., U.K., and local currency
	ADR information
	Text descriptions of business ventures and a "chairman's letter"
	Segments for screening and sorting listed in the printed Product Guide
S&P SPCO:	COMPANY segment for company name
	Limited number of non-U.S. companies, mainly Canadian
	Screen on sales and employees
20-F:	COMPANY-NAME segment for company name
	Multiple years of filings
	Some ADRs
	No numeric screening
ICCCO Annuals:	Only U.K. companies
	Multiple years
	Full text

CIFAR was loaded on the LEXIS AND NEXIS SERVICES in January 1993, its first widespread commercial venture in the U.S. At that time it had over 12,000 companies of which 4,355 were U.S. CIFAR on the LEXIS AND NEXIS SERVICES is divided into five files.

CFAR—CFARbase Company Financials Database, the entire set
CFRBNK—CFAR Banks
CFRFIN—CFAR Financials
CFRIND—CFAR Industrials
CFRINS—CFAR Insurance

CFAR differs from *Worldscope* and *Extel* in the following ways:

CFAR has more companies, primarily more U.S. companies and companies from emerging markets. There are over 500 Indian companies.

CFAR generally has six years of data; however, it is loaded a line at a time, so with LEXIS AND NEXIS pricing, you may be paying for a data item a line.

CFAR has detailed ownership data for a large number of companies, which are not given elsewhere online, as shown in Exhibit 6-1.

Financial information in electronic format should give the flexibility to screen on a series of variables and to download data in a form for processing in a spreadsheet. It is disappointing, therefore, that the most comprehensive company financial databases are all loaded on a system that does not have that capability. We recommend that if you need this type of data frequently you consider purchasing these products in a CD-ROM format.

DOW JONES NEWS RETRIEVAL

DOW JONES NEWS RETRIEVAL is one of the key online tools for the U.S. financial researcher, but it does *not* play the same role for international information. Table 6-G displays the international company information found on DOW JONES NEWS RETRIEVAL.

Worldscope is the only international financial file on DOW JONES. Company reports can only be retrieved by company name. The financial data from *Worldscope* have not been included in DOW JONES multi-file //QUICK search. However, for those international companies covered in the *Disclosure* database, financial data will be in //QUICK.

A second source of international company financial information on DOW JONES NEWS RETRIEVAL is //CANADA, selected financial and markets information on 2,400 public, private, and government Canadian enterprises, supplied by Info Globe.

EXHIBIT 6-1. *CFAR* **Ownership Data**

Copyright 1993 Center for International Financial Analysis &
Research, Inc.
Cfarbase (TM), INDUSTRIAL

LOAD DATE: January 14, 1993
COMPANY: Bangkok Agro-Industrial Products Co.
LATEST ANNUAL FINANCIAL DATA: 1990

OWNERSHIP

MAJOR SHAREHOLDERS	Year	Holders	%	Shares
Bangkok Bk. Ltd. For Mutual Fund Co.	1990	1	1.4	420
Banque Int. Luxembourg SA Templeton	1990	1	2.9	870
Chase Nominees Limited	1990	1	7.0	2100
Wardley Investment Services Int'l. L	1990	1	1.2	360
Charden Pokphand Feedmill Co. Ltd.	1990	1	59.8	17940
Total Number of Shares Outstanding	1990	0	100.0	30000
COUNTRY: Thailand				

Source: CIFAR on LEXIS AND NEXIS SERVICES, May 1993. Reprinted with permission from the Center for International Financial Analysis
& Research, Inc (CIFAR).

Table 6-G. International Company Information on DOW JONES NEWS RETRIEVAL

Database	Type of Data	Number of Companies	File
Worldscope	Financial	about 7,500	//WORLD
Canadian Corporations	Financial and News	2,400	//CANADA
Dun & Bradstreet *	Directory	2.4 million	//DMI
* Menu-driven screening capabilities			

The entire U.S. and international *Duns Market Identifier Database* is available on DOW JONES as //DMI. This file is not accessible to academic subscribers.

Current news information is available in //WIRES, and DOW JONES Text has been expanding its international library.

COMPANY DATABASES WITH PRODUCT CODES

Table 6-H lists some of the major databases with product listings and the coding schemes that are used.

If you are looking for companies in a specific product line, use *DIALOG Product Name Finder*, File 413, to find out what codes are being used in the various DIALOG international company databases. Exhibit 6-2 lists some of the results from a search for "Information Services" on the *DIALOG Product Name Finder*, File 413. Notice that none of the international Dun & Bradstreet files nor Predicasts files are listed in Exhibit 6-2. In this example, the U.S. SIC codes have no real equivalent codes. *Duns International Market Identifiers* uses 7299,

"Misc. Personal Services," and 7389, "Business Services, not elsewhere classified."

ONLINE INFORMATION: ASIAN COMPANIES

Pan-Asian Databases

KOMPASS and Dun & Bradstreet provide separate company directory databases on DIALOG for the Asia-Pacific region. KOMPASS covers the 12 major Pacific Rim countries. D&B *Asia Pacific Duns Market Identifiers* has entries from more countries than KOMPASS, including such places as the People's Republic of China, the Christmas Islands, and Tahiti. Table 6-I lists the number of companies for those countries covered in both databases.

Another Asian DIALOG file is *Asia-Pacific*, File 30. The file has both journal abstracts and company records. There are several fields for company location but the indexing in these fields appears to lack authority control. For example, "PO," the field for ultimate parent country, has Bahrain entered with several variations: Bahrain,

Table 6-H. Databases Containing Product Codes

Database Name or Code	Coding Scheme	Sample Code	Product Name Category
ABCE, EURE	ABC	Vb	Chocolate
BDI- The German Industry	BDIE	43-0103	Chocolate
COIN / FINN Numeric	GBI	G2820	Food
DBFR (D & B France)	FR- APE	4031	Chocolate & cocoa product
	US SIC	2066	manufacturers
Duns Market Identifiers on DIALOG	US SIC	2066	Chocolate & cocoa
DBGB (D&B Great Britain)	UK SIC	42141	Cocoa and chocolate
E1X1-German Buyers' Guide	E1X1	36-0571-435	Chocolate
Extel	UK SIC	42141	Cocoa and chocolate
FRCO French Companies	FR- APE	4031	Chocolate, confectionery
Hoppenstedt Files	HOPE &	2870	Confectionery industry
	US SIC	2066	
ICC files	UK SIC	4214	Cocoa-chocolate-and-sugar-confectionery
	& ICC	ZCM	
ITIE/SDOE Italian	HS	HS1806	Chocolate, other food products
Trading Companies	US SIC	SIC2066200	Confectionery-type chocolate and cocoa products molded chocolate confections
KOMPASS EUROPE	KOMPASS	20740	Cocoa & chocolate
KOMPASS ASIA/PACIFIC	KOMPASS	2074034	Chocolate bars

Source: Online searches, April 1993

EXHIBIT 6-2. Extract from a Search for "Information Services" on File 413, *DIALOG Product Name Finder*

Product Name	Product Code	File	Record Count	Type of Code
INFORMATION SERVICES	8110016	592	38	KOMPASS
ECONOMIC INFORMATION SERVICES	8834001	591	28	KOMPASS
INFORMATION SERVICES ENERGY MANAGEMENT AND C	8474013	591	35	KOMPASS
COMPANY INFORMATION SERVICES	8066002	591	91	KOMPASS
INFORMATION SERVICES	8032005	591	126	KOMPASS
INFORMATION SERVICES	8110016	594	4	KOMPASS
INFORMATION SERVICES CONSUMER	72990604	516	377	SIC-DUNS
MISCELLANEOUS INFORMATION SERVICES	8529	502	148	SIC-JAPAN
RESEARCH AND INFORMATION SERVICES EXCE	8523	502	224	SIC-JAPAN

Source: DIALOG File 413, searched April 1993

Bahran and Bahrian. Consequently, it is not possible to give an accurate count of the companies described. Also, this obvious lack of quality control makes us wary of the file contents.

Asian companies are also included in File 479, *Company Intelligence,* and File 513, *Corporate Affiliations.* Table 6-J compares the data items available for the same company on three of these files, D&B *Asia/Pacific,* IAC *Company Intelligence*, and KOMPASS *Asia/ Pacific.* An "X" indicates that the data element is included in the company record.

Japanese Databases

Two databases on U.S. databanks have Japanese company information exclusively, *Teikoku* and *Comline.*

Teikoku Databank Ltd. is the largest credit reporting organization in Japan. Information on the companies in the *Teikoku* database on DIALOG (File 502) are a subset of the approximately 900,000 companies in Teikoku's COSMOS 2 databank. Unique to the Teikoku record are sales rankings within industry, major trading banks, and a credit rating. The sales rankings are based on the entire

Table 6-I. Country Comparison of KOMPASS and Dun & Bradstreet *Asia/Pacific* Files on DIALOG

	KOMPASS *Asia/Pacific* File 592	D&B *Asia/Pacific DMI* File 522
Load date	12-92	4-93
Australia	17142	73496
Brunei	683	102
Hong Kong	8161	40981
India	18707	4880
Indonesia	32107	2291
Japan	102943	38999
Korea	13179	4558
Malaysia	14975	3811
Philippines	11576	1421
Singapore	17390	16105
Taiwan	16391	6338
Thailand	9095	2671
TOTALS		
Comparable Countries	262349	195653
Total in Database	262349	213019
Total Asian Countries	12	39

Source: DIALOG, searched April 1993

databank and not just those companies in the English language file. Teikoku Databank is also available as a DIALOG ONDISC CD-ROM and on the Japanese databank NIKKEI.

DIALOG File 502 has more than 180,000 Japanese companies. You can search for English language names or translated names (CO) or for the transliterated Japanese names (RC). Japanese SICs of 3- and 4-digits are assigned to each company with an English description of business.

Comline International Corporation produces a set of databases that include both news and company financial profiles. The news files are available directly from Comline as well as on NEWSNET, LEXIS AND NEXIS SERVICES, and DATA-STAR. Articles from the news database are also available on a SilverPlatter CD-ROM.

The Comline company file is on LEXIS AND NEXIS SERVICES and DATA-STAR. The database includes only quoted Japanese companies. As in *Teikoku*, you may search both the English and transliterated names. Although the database comprises only quoted companies, the useful information provided by Comline is in the company description and in extensive lists of shareholders and subsidiaries.

Comline includes group affiliations in its business descriptions. This allows us to track such groups as the keiretsu described in Chapter 3. The extract in Exhibit 6-3 is from the version of the file on LEXIS AND NEXIS SERVICES. Note that "Mitsubishi Corp." is the translated name and "Mitsubishi Shoji K.K." is the transliterated name.

EXHIBIT 6-3. *Comline* Extract

Mitsubishi Corp
Mitsubishi Shoji K.K.
TOKYO STOCK EXCHANGE: 8058

COMPANY DESCRIPTION: Japan's largest trader and the core of the Mitsubishi group...

A large number of business databases are available in Japan and also accessible from overseas. Many are in English or Japanese and English. G-Search Corporation databank includes a wide range of Japanese language databases, including several company financial files, biographical data on Japanese CEOs, news articles, and a market research database. Another major Japanese databank with business files is NIFTY Corporation with a wide range of Japanese business newspapers and newswires, the text of *Economist* in Japanese, financial information from Japanese sources, CIFAR and other miscellaneous information, including movie and restaurant guides and a horse race tip sheet. Japanese databases are promoted in the United States through the Database Promotion Center, which exhibits on behalf of Japanese

Table 6-J. Comparison of a Company Record on Three DIALOG Files: 522, 479, and 592

DIALOG Database Name	D&B Asia Pacific	Company Intelligence	KOMPASS Asia/Pacific
File Number	522	479	592
Company Name	Boon Rawd Brewery Co. Ltd.	Boon Rawd Brewery Co. Ltd.	Boon Rawd Brewery Co. Ltd.
Address	X	X	X
Region		X	X
Country	X	X	X

Table 6-J. Comparison of a Company Record on Three DIALOG Files: 522, 479, and 592 *(continued)*

DIALOG Database Name	D&B Asia Pacific	Company Intelligence	KOMPASS Asia/Pacific
Telephone	X	2 Nos	3 Nos
Fax	X	X	X
Telex	X	X	X
Cable		X	
Description of business	X		X
Brand name		X	X
Primary SIC	U.S. SIC		KOMPASS Code
Secondary SICs	1	1 US SIC	10 Products
D-U-N-S Number	X	X	
Year Started	X	X	
Employees Total	1650	1560	1300
Sales -local		X (1990)	X (1988)
Sales - U.S. $	529,519,263	361,800,000	
Exchange rate used	25.45	25.7	
Date of conversion		910924	
Financial Information -			
Year		X	
Profits		X	
Authorized capital		X	
Paid-up capital		X	
Total assets		X	
Status: SF Field, incl			
Import and Export	X	X	
Officers - Chief Executive	X	X	X
Executives	X	X	
Subsidiaries		X	X
Principal Shareholders		X	
Bankers		X	
Citations to articles		X	
Foreign trade status			X
Languages spoken			X
Date of record change			X

databases at international online trade shows. Table 6-K lists sources of Japanese online information.

Table 6-K. Sources of Japanese Online Information

Database Promotion Center, Japan
2-4-1 Hamamatsucho, Minato-ku, Tokyo
FAX: 81-03-34327558

G-Search Corporation
8F Houkou-Kowa Bldg.
1-2-4, Tsukiji, Chuo-ku,
Tokyo 104 Japan
TEL: 81-03-5565-1480

NIFTY Corporation
U.S. Representative - CompuServe
500 Arlington Centre Blvd.
P.O. Box 20212, Columbus OH 43220
FAX: 614-457-0504

ONLINE INFORMATION: EASTERN EUROPEAN/FORMER SOVIET COMPANIES

Of the former Eastern Bloc countries, East Germany has the most online coverage. Only two German language databases on DATA-STAR remain devoted exclusively to the former East Germany. Other database providers are adding former East German companies to their Germany and Europe files.

- *Hoppenstedt East Germany* (HOEA): contains extensive product and trade information in German; the file is also on LEXIS AND NEXIS SERVICES and CD-ROM
- *DDRC Companies* from Deutsche Bank (DDRC): with 4 years of brief financial data in English

Listed below are some of the German directory databases that include companies from all of Germany.

* *EcoRegister:* Registrations published in the official gazette of the Ministry of Justice, with more than 68,000 East German companies as of November 1992
* *EcoNovo*: All legal announcements other than registrations, such as appointments and bankruptcies
* *ABC Germany* (ABCE): German companies and their products
* *Creditreform Germany* (DVVC): Ownership data for all German companies. A record for a former East German company is displayed in Exhibit 6-4.

In Exhibit 6-4 the OS field describes the type of company, which in this case is a partnership [GES="partner"]. In July 1993, *Creditreform* merged the records from the East German file *OVVC* with *DVVC* to form one database. New 5-digit German postal codes were also added to each entry.

EXHIBIT 6-4. Record from *Creditreform Germany*

DVVC
AN 333015242 930728
CO Etec Gesellschaft fuer Anwendungstechnik,
Energie und Umwelt mbH.
YR 199104.
CA STAMMKAPITAL: DM   50.000.
OS GES: Gieselmann, Wilhelm, 2804 Grabow,
STR: Berliner Str. 32, DM
20.000, 19300
GES: Etec, Hannover, DM 20.000
GES: Westfeld, Ralf, 2804 Grabow, DM 5.000, 19300
GES: Mueller, Carsten, 2804 Grabow, DM 5.000,
19300.OS GES: Etec, 3000

Reprinted from *Creditreform Germany*.

The following European databases include all Germany:
KOMPASS Europe
Dun & Bradstreet files *IDMI* and *EDMI*

Files including all Eastern Europe, including the former USSR are:

ABC Europe
Company Intelligence
Dun & Bradstreet Eastern Europe
Moody's Corporate News International
Moody's International Company Data CD-ROM (primarily banks)

Only former USSR companies are listed in BizEkon Russian Business on LEXIS AND NEXIS SERVICES and WESTLAW.

The tractor company used as the example in Chapter 4 (*see* Exhibit 4-6) appears online as well, in *BizEkon* and *ABC Europe*. In *BizEkon*, a third name is used for this company: *Cheboksary Industrial Tractors Works Production Association* (*see* Exhibit 6-5). The database enhances company profiles with a section on miscellaneous information, such as production potential, volume, R&D infrastructure, advertising and reference materials, and number of commercial deals. None of this information is available for the tractor company. However, in the miscellaneous section of the record for the Chemical Foreign Trade Association, *BizEkon* reports that the organization has 30% of the world's ammonia and 20% of the world's carbamide, methanol, and potassium fertilizer, earning 2,368 million rubles in foreign currency.

The name under which our tractor company is listed in *ABC Europe* is a translation (*see* Exhibit 6-6). The *ABC Europe* record has extensive information on the company's foreign partners and specific information on its product line. Capital rather than revenue or sales is reported.

Table 6-L compares the data elements in *ABC Europe* and *BizEkon*.

East European Financial Information and News

Moody's International Manual in print, online, and on CD-ROM has reports from Bulgaria, Czechoslovakia, Hungary, Poland, and the former Yugoslavia. The institutions reported are primarily banks.

The LEXIS AND NEXIS SERVICES include the full text of newswires from individual Eastern European countries. *Financial Times Eastern Europe Database*, another source of Eastern European news, is available on DATA-STAR and FT Profile. Coverage began in 1992 and updates are weekly. Records are full text and come from FT internal documents plus sources such as East European Markets Finance East Europe. The database uses ISO country codes, regional codes, and U.S. SIC codes.

Special Product

Reuter East European Briefing is a new end-user online database, running in a Windows environment, for those who need to focus exclusively on this region. Articles come from Reuters and numerous other sources and are translated into English from 15 different languages. The file contains current information (current within two days) that can be searched by country and by four broad news topics: general, political, economic, and

EXHIBIT 6-5. Sample Record from *BizEkon* on LEXIS AND NEXIS SERVICES

Date of entry into database: February 6, 1992
Company name: Industrial Tractors Works Production Association
Alternate name: Cheboksary Industrial Tractors Works Production Association
Address:

      Street: Traktorostroitelei Prospect,

      City and Postal Code: Cheboksary 428033,

      Region: Chuvash Autonomous Region

      Country: Russian Federation

Telecommunications:

      TELE: 23-3748

      FAX: N/A

      Telegraph: TRAKTOR

      Telex: 158131 KVANT

COMPANY DESCRIPTION: Industry (Basic Line of Activity): Tractors, other agricultural machinery, equipment and tools (18)
Basic Lines of Products/Services: - Tractors, other agricultural machinery, equipment and tools (18) - Patents, licenses, knowhow (01)
EXECUTIVE: Mingazov, Khanif Khaidarovich; director general
CONTACT: Manager for Foreign Markets: N/A,TELE: N/A
WORKFORCE: N/A
BANK:

      Foreign Currency Account: VNESHECONOMBANK of the USSR

      Ruble Account: N/A

MISCELLANEOUS:

      Production Potential: N/A

      Production Volume (total): N/A

      Export Oriented: N/A

      R&D Infrastructure: N/A

      Performance Indicators: N/A

      Advertising and Reference Materials: N/A

      Statistics Available from: August 20, 1991

      External Economic Operations: yes

      Foreign Partners (Direct): N/A

      Licenses (Short list of products): N/A

      Number of Commercial Deals: N/A

      Annual Trade Turnover (Export/Import): N/A

      Program and Area of Cooperation (Including import): N/A

      Specialization: INDUSTRIAL ENTERPRISE

COUNTRY: SOVIET UNION

Reprinted with permission from Russica Information, Inc.

EXHIBIT 6-6. Sample Record from *ABC Europe* (EURE on DATA-STAR)

Cheboksary Tractor Works Production Amalgamation.

PS	P.O. Box Yu 9055
	Tractorostroiteley Prospekt.
RE	RUS-428033 Cheboksary, Tschuwaschische ASSR
	Russian Federation.
CN	RU Russian Federation.

Exhibit 6-6. Sample Record from *ABC Europe* (EURE on DATA-STAR) *(continued)*

TL	Telephone: (08350) 233748
	Telefax: (08350) 233508
	Telex: 412627.
PF	Heavy-duty track-type tractors, models T-330P-1-01, T-500P-1, T-25.01BP-1, TT-330, TT-500 (earth moving, stripping, highway construction, open mining of ore and coal, wood and jungle cutting for culture planting, gas and oil pipe laying).
PE	Agricultural tractors. Road tractors.
IM	Imported Products: Foundry equipment, CNC machine tools, lasers, flexible production lines, welding equipment, travelling column CNC machines, precision metering machines, programmable controllers, surface grinders.
IC	Ia <* Construction of vehicles, ships and aircraft *>.
RP	Exports to: Bulgaria, Romania, Poland, Germany, Democratic People's Republic of Korea, Czechoslovakia, Yugoslavia, People's Republic of China, Mongolian People's Republic, Italy, Spain, Nigeria, Botswana, Iraq, Jordan, Zambia, Greece, Cyprus, Hungary.
	Imports from: USA, Japan, Italy, Austria, Germany, France, Sweden, Switzerland, Great Britain and N.I., Democratic People's Republic of Korea. USA, Japan, Italien, Oesterreich, Deutschland, Frankreich, Schweden, Schweiz, Grossbritannien u. Nordirland, Demokratische Volksrepublik Korea.
MM	State-owned.
	General Manager: Hanif Haidarovich Minghasov.
	Import Manager: Michael Ivanovich Skrynnik.
	Export Manager: Ghennadij Ivanovich Filatoff.
YR	Established: 1972.
EM	Employees: 2300.
CA	Capital: 1.200.000.000.-.
BK	Bankers: Vnesheconombank, International Bank for Economic Cooperation.

Source: ABC Europe, October 30, 1992. Reprinted with permission from ABC Europe.

Table 6-L. *ABC Europe* and *BizEkon*

DATA ITEM	ABC Europe	BizEkon
Company Name	Cheboksary Tractor Works Production Amalgamation	Industrial Tractors Works Production Association
Street Address	P.O. Box Yu 9055 Tractorostroiteley Prospekt	Traktorostroitelei Prospect
Town	Cheboksary	Cheboksary
Postal Code	428033	428033
Region	Tschuwaschische ASSr	Chuvashia Autonomous Region
Country	Russian Federation	Russian Federation/Soviet Union
Telephone	(08350) 233748	23-3748
Telefax	(08350) 233508	N/A
Telex	412627	158131 KVANT TRAKTOR
Telegraph		
Industry	Ia <Construction of vehicles, ships and aircraft>	Tractors; other agricultural machinery
Products	Agricultural and road tractors, models T-330P-1-01...earth moving, stripping,	Tractors, other ag machinery, equipment and tools (18)-patents, licenses, knowhow(01)
Management/ Executives	State-owned; General manager: Hanif Haidarovoch Minghasov. import and export managers	Director general: Mingazov, Khanif Khaidarovich Contact: Manager for Foreign Markets N/A
Employee/Workforce	2300	N/A
Imports from	USA, Japan, Italy, Austria, UK	N/A
Exports to	Bulgaria, Romania, Poland, PRC	
Imported Products	Foundry equipment, CNC machine.	

Table 6-L. *ABC Europe* **and** *BizEkon (continued)*

Bankers	Vnesheconombank, Intl Bank for Economic Cooperation	Vnesheconombank of the USSR -for foreign currency
Dates	Year established - 1972	Date entered in database 2/92
Financial	Capital 1,200,000,000	Sales-Turnover N/A
Miscellaneous		Production Potential -N/A
		Production Volume - N/A
		Performance Indicators - N/A
		Advertising materials - N/A
		Statistics available from 082091
		Licenses N/A
		Number of deals N/A

sports. It also has an archive of one year's worth of articles that can be accessed by countries, topics, industries, companies, (250,000 worldwide), or information sources. Users also may search by a keyword and date: 1 week; 1,3, or 6 months; 1 year; or specific date. Searches can be stored, re-executed, printed, and downloaded. The product is priced for the high-end niche market specialist.

A more complete listing of both online and print resources on Eastern Europe and the Commonwealth of Independent States is provided by Michel Bauwens in the February and March 1993 issues of *Business Information Alert.*

COMPANY DATA ON CD-ROM

Many directories and financial databases are being published in CD-ROM format. The quality of the search software varies greatly, as does the value added by purchasing the CD-ROM version. Consider purchasing CD-ROMs as a substitute for heavily used print directories if you will get increased flexibility from the CD product. If your primary clientele uses your international directories mostly to locate individual companies, then purchasing the CD-ROM counterpart is not necessary. Table 6-M lists some CD-ROM company databases.

For an in-depth discussion of many company financials on CD-ROM, see "European Information on CD-ROM Part II: Financial Information (*CD-ROM Professional*, November 1992) and "Part III" (*CD-ROM Professional,* March 1993). The word "International" can be substituted for "Europe" in Part II for the products from Worldscope and CIFAR. *Coin* and *Comline* are discussed in *CD-ROM Professional,* July 1993.[6]

D&B Europa has been available on CD-ROM using LOTUS OneSource software in Europe for more than a year. Lotus introduced it to the U.S. market in May 1993. The Lotus CD-ROM version includes the information

from the print directory plus financial data and credit ratings (*see* Chapter 4, Exhibit 4-5). For example, the CD-ROM makes it possible to search for companies in France, Germany, or Switzerland who manufacture chocolate and have a top credit rating. All financial information is stated in local currency. The most recent year's key financials are translated into six currencies: U.S. dollars, British pounds sterling, French francs, Deutschmarks, Japanese yen, and ECU. Output is in preformatted or customized reports. The data can be exported into a spreadsheet. Updates are bi-monthly. The same 60,000 companies in the 1993 print version are also on the CD-ROM. Like all Lotus CD-ROM products, D&B*Europa* is expensive. We estimate that *D&B Europa* will cost $13,000 in the United States.

ONLINE TEXT SOURCES OF INTERNATIONAL COMPANY INFORMATION

As mentioned above, news sources are important for keeping updated on company information. Numerous electronic files provide daily or weekly information about companies. Many of these are described in Chapter 1. Table 6-N offers a selected list of online sources of international company information.

CAVEAT EMPTOR

While online databases offer expanded sources and increased flexibility for company research, they also create a new set of issues concerning data quality. Online and ondisc files allow manipulation of directory data in ways not envisioned by the database producers. We sometimes retrieve results that do not make sense.

Table 6-M. Where to Find Company Information on CD-ROM

From Producers Familiar in the U.S.:
CFARBASE - Financial
DISCLOSURE/ WORLDSCOPE Global - Financial
Duns Global Families Disc - International company relationships, with family trees (released late 1993)
LOTUS OneSource - Financial, Market, and Directory
      CD/Investment International Equities (Worldscope)
      CD/Corporate UK (from Extel Financial Card Service)
      CD/Private+:UK (from ICC British Companies Database)
      CD/Europa
MOODYS INTERNATIONAL Company Database - Financial
PREDICASTS F&S International - Text
SILVER PLATTER *UK Corporations CD* (ICC) - Financial and Text
      COMLINE - Text
      COIN (from Reuter's *Textline*) - Text
DIALOG *U.K. Factfinder* - Financial, Credit, and Text
      Teikoku - Directory, Financial, and Credit
      Directory of U.S. Importers & Exporters (including Piers data) - Directory and Trade
      Corporate Affiliations, including *International Directory of Corporate Affiliations*

From European Sources:
BUREAU VAN DIJK - Financial
      Fame - Jordan, UK
      Diane - SCRL -French
      Dafne - German
      amadeus - pan-European
HOPPENTSTEDT - Directories
KOMPASS UK and *EKOD* (Europe) - Product directories
BOWKER-SAUR (Reed Intl Group)
      Corporate Affiliations, including *International Directory of Corporate Affiliations*

Table 6-N. Selected List of Online Sources of International Company Information

Database	System
Articles:	
Promt *	DIALOG, DATA-STAR
Infomat	DIALOG, DATA-STAR
Delphes	DIALOG, DATA-STAR
International libraries	LEXIS AND NEXIS SERVICES
Financial Times	FT Profile, DIALOG, LEXIS AND NEXIS SERVICES, DATA-STAR
//DJINTL	DOW JONES News Retrieval
Textline *	Reuters, DIALOG, DATA-STAR, LEXIS AND NEXIS SERVICES
Comline *	DATA-STAR, LEXIS AND LEXIS SERVICES
Investment Bank Reports:	
ICC Stockbroker Research *	FT Profile, DIALOG, DATA-STAR, LEXIS AND NEXIS SERVICES, ICC
Investext *	DIALOG, DATA-STAR, DOW JONES, Direct
Selected Newspapers:	
II Sole Ore 24	
Jerusalem Post	
Asian and European Wall Street Journals	
International Herald Tribune	
Financial Times	
South China Morning Post	

* Subsets also available on CD-ROM

Quality Issue: Exchange Rates

As an example of using a database in a way not expected by its producers, consider the case of ranking food companies by annual sales in an international directory and marketing database. Yugoslavian and then Greek food companies[7,8,9] were listed as the largest in Europe. These rankings were the result of the way the database producer uses exchange rates. Sales figures in the database are in both local currency and U.S. currency. The exchange rate used is the one "current" at the time the database is being loaded. However, this database sometimes uses sales figures in local currency that are several years old. This is often the case in countries such as the former Yugoslavia and in Argentina, where currency fluctuation is the greatest.

According to U.S. accounting standards, the conversion for annual sales figures should be the annual average rate for the year. The two examples shown below illustrate the effect of using non-current exchange rates. During the past six years, Argentina has experienced a high rate of inflation and has revalued its currency. Example 1 presents the three most recent years of sales figures for an Argentinean company as reported in *Worldscope*. U.S. dollar sales have been calculated using the average exchange rate for each year.

Example 1. The Effect of Exchange Rate Fluctuations on Reported Sales

Data Presented in *Worldscope*: Income Statement (000's)			
Fiscal Year Ending	12/31/90	12/31/89	12/31/88
Net sales (local)	169,208	18,234	354
Sales (US$)	32	13	22
Rate used by *Worldscope*	0.0002	0.0007	0.062

Suppose that in 1992 the sales figure in a company database had not been updated since 1989. The sales figure in local currency would still be 18,234,000 australs. However, using the May 1992 rate of 1.0101 australs to the dollar, instead of the 1989 rate of .0007, the company's sales in U.S. dollars would be given as $18,418,000 instead of $13,000!

Example 2. Recalculated Data Using the Procedure of Some Directory Databases

Argentinean Company: 1989 Sales	Local Currency (000 austral)	U.S. Dollars (000)	Exchange Rate
Worldscope	18,234	13	.0007
Directory Database	18,234	18,418	1.0101

Quality Issue: Date of the Data Elements

We often use online databases because they are updated more frequently than print or CD-ROM. However, online directories are not always more current than the other formats. For example, the D&B files on DIALOG are updated twice a year. Other company databases may be updated monthly. However, updating does not necessarily mean that an individual company record has been changed. In fact, even if a company record has been modified, the change might be only to one data element. The best quality online databases give us the date of the sales figure they are using. This allows us to do our own conversions using the exchange rate we select.

For instance, information on a Turkish company is available in a printed directory and in its online equivalent. By checking back issues of the printed volume, we could see that the local sales figure had not been updated between 1991 and 1993. The same sales figure appears in the current online update. Since many online directory files include only the "most recent" sales figure, the user has no way of knowing what year that is.

The online source also presents sales in U.S. dollars. The exchange rates changed so the U.S. dollar figure changed accordingly. Listed below are the figures as they appeared in the last two print editions and the last three online updates.

	DATE OF PRINT EDITION		DATE OF ONLINE UPDATE		
	1992 (c 1991)	1993 (c 1992)	11/91	6/92	10/92
Local Sales (000)	971,000	971,000	971,000	971,000	971,000
US$ Sales	NA	NA	200	143	135

Quality Issue: Confusing Answers

In November 1992 we searched two databases for a list of major Japanese banks; we found Saitama Bank Ltd; Kyowa Bank, and Kyowa Saitama Bank in database A, with Saitama Bank Ltd. listed as the second largest Japanese consumer bank. Only Kyowa Saitama Bank was listed in database B. What is the relationship among these banks?

To answer this question it became necessary to go beyond directory databases. When we checked a Japanese company news file we learned that Kyowa Bank merged with Saitama Bank 18 months before database was A loaded. When it merged, it changed its name to Kyowa Saitama Bank. Taking the search a step further, we checked a newswire file to see if there were any further developments. About two weeks before database

A was loaded the bank changed its name again, this time to Asahi Bank Ltd.

CONCLUSION

As this chapter has illustrated, there is a wide range of electronic company databases. The number of companies in these files far surpasses the number of companies in most libraries' printed directory collections. These online files give the researcher the added capability of screening for companies meeting certain criteria, selecting a customized list of companies, and downloading this information to disc.

Because of the many problems we have discussed regarding company information in Chapters 3 through 6, use electronic international company information with caution. Don't use financial information in an international online directory unless you have a good understanding of the contents and limitations of the database. Online directory information is not necessarily more timely or accurate than a printed source.

NOTES

1. See articles by Marydee Ojala, such as "Best of British: British Information Online," *Database 11* (December 1988): 15-28; and "Communing with Eastern European Business Information," *Online 15* (January 1991): 67-69.

2. Colin Hensley, "European Community Databases: Online to Europe," *Database 12* (December 1989): 45-52

3. *European Markets: A Guide to Company and Industry Information Sources, Edition III.* (Washington, DC: Washington Researchers, 1990). Washington Researchers also publishes *Asian Markets* and *Latin American Markets.*

4. *SourceGuide to European Company Information* 5th ed. (Gale, 1993).

5. *Online Business Sourcebook* (Cleveland, U.K.: Headland Press); and their monthly newsletter, *Online Business Information.*

6. Ruth A. Pagell, series of articles on European and international CD-ROM products in *CD-ROM Professional*, July and November 1992, March and July 1993.

7. Ruth A. Pagell. "It's Greek to Me! Exchange Rate Translations and Company Comparisons," *Database 14* (February 1991): 21-27.

8. Ruth A. Pagell, "Sorry Wrong Number," *Online* (November 1990).

9. Ruth A. Pagell, "What's for Dinar," *Database* (April 1991).

CHAPTER 7
Corporate Affiliations and Corporate Change

MAJOR SOURCES DISCUSSED

- *Directory of American Firms Operating in Foreign Countries*
- *Directory of Foreign Firms Operating in the United States*
- *Directory of Foreign Manufactures in the United States*
- *Directory of Corporate Affiliations*
- *Corporate Affiliations*
- *Merger and Acquisition SourceBook*
- *International Merger Yearbook*
- *Merger & Corporate Transaction Database*

This chapter discusses two specialized and often related aspects of corporate research: corporate affiliations and corporate change. Corporate affiliations are the network of subsidiaries and branches that make up a corporation. Corporate change involves events that significantly alter a company's identity. These changes can be as broad as a total corporate restructuring or as specific as a change in an executive position.

CORPORATE AFFILIATIONS

"Who owns whom?" is the central question concerning corporate affiliations. The question is about corporate parent-subsidiary relationships. Sometimes researchers need to know the names of subsidiaries owned by a parent company, and sometimes they need to know the name of the parent company owning a particular subsidiary.

Many other questions are related to these issues of ownership. For example, what is the corporate hierarchy? When and from whom were the subsidiaries that now make up the company acquired? What percentage of the subsidiary's stock is owned by the parent company? International corporate affiliations also raise questions

about the nationality of the parent and subsidiary. What U.S. companies are subsidiaries of Japanese companies?

Information about corporate affiliations, like information about corporate finance, is usually not volunteered by companies. Disclosure rules, described in Chapter 2, require that certain corporations reveal details concerning their ownership of subsidiaries. However, if a company is intent on concealing its corporate relationships, it will often succeed. For example, the Bank of Credit and Commerce International (BCCI) managed to buy a bank in Washington, D.C. without revealing its identity.

The secondary sources for corporate affiliations that we describe will not reveal the secret network of holdings of a BCCI. They will allow you to see the details of corporate structures for many of the larger companies in the world. Exhibit 7-1 lists the terms used by Dun & Bradstreet to describe corporate hierarchies; it will serve as useful background for our description of sources.

Sources for Corporate Affiliations

The first three sources we describe are helpful if we need basic information on the subsidiaries of large corpo-

EXHIBIT 7-1. Dun & Bradstreet Terms Used in Corporate Linkage

COMPONENT	DESCRIPTION
Corporate Family Location	The top-most company of a corporate family
Division	A secondary location of a company reporting to main office (i.e., the headquarters). Usually has a different distinct name or trade name.
Headquarters	The main office of a company. Implies the existence of a branch or branches reporting to it and having the same name.
Branch	A secondary location of a company. Reports to a main office. Branches carry the same name as their headquarters.
Parent	A corporation that owns more than 50% of the voting stock of another corporation (i.e., the subsidiary).
Subsidiary	A corporation in which more than 50% of its voting stock is owned by another company (i.e., the parent).

Source: DIALOG Chronolog, March 1993, 93:81. Reprinted with permission from Dun & Bradstreet Inc.

rations. However, their usefulness is limited by infrequent updates and lack of comprehensive coverage and description of corporate relationships.

Directory of American Firms Operating in Foreign Countries (Uniworld Business Publications—Triennial)

The twelfth edition of the *Directory* (1991) lists 2,600 U.S. corporations that have some 19,000 subsidiaries and affiliates in 127 countries. Included are companies in which American firms have a "substantial direct capital investment and which have been identified by the parent firms as a wholly or partially owned subsidiary affiliate or branch." Volume 1 lists U.S. firms that have operations overseas. The entries consist of the company name, address, chief officer, number of employees, and the names of the countries in which the company operates. Volumes 2 and 3 contain a listing by country, from Algeria to Zimbabwe, of American firms' foreign operations. Franchises and noncommercial enterprises are not included. Information for the *Directory* is collected mainly through questionnaires. Exhibit 7-2 displays two sample entries from the *Directory*.

Directory of Foreign Firms Operating in the United States (Uniworld Business Publications—Triennial)

This standard directory has been published every three years since 1969. The seventh edition (1992) lists more than 1,600 foreign firms in 54 countries and the nearly 2,700 businesses in the U.S. that they own, either wholly or in part. Only the American headquarters or one major location of each subsidiary or affiliate is listed. The basic arrangement is by country. Within each country the foreign firms are listed alphabetically together with the American firms owned wholly or in part. Separate indexes are provided for foreign firms and American affiliates. Exhibit 7-3 shows the form used in *Directory* records.

Directory of Foreign Manufactures in the United States, 5th ed. (Georgia State University Business Press, 1993)

EXHIBIT 7-2. Sample Entries for Thailand in *Directory of American Firms Operating in Foreign Countries*

ABBOTT LABORATORIES Abbott Park, North Chicago, IL 60064
Tel: (312) 937-6100
(Pharm & lab prdts)
  Abbott Labs., Ltd., P.O. Box 2633, Bangkok, Thailand
  Abbott Pharma Ltd. (JV), P.O. Box 2633, Bangkok, Thailand

ABERCROMBIE & KENT INTL INC 1420 Kensington Rd, Oak Brook, IL 60521 210,
Tel: (708) 954-2944
(Tour wholesaler)
  Abercrombie & Kent (Thailand) Ltd., 4th fl., Silom Plaza, 491-29 30 Silom Rd.
  Bangkok 10500, Thailand

Reprinted with permission from World Trade Academy Press.

EXHIBIT 7-3. Record from *Directory of Foreign Firms Operating in the United States*

ENGLAND

FOREIGN FIRM	AMERICAN AFFILIATE
GRAND METROPOLITAN PLC	BURGER KING CORP
	17777 Old Cutler Rd
	Miami, FL 33157
	Ian A Martin, Chrm
	Tel: (305) 378-7011
	Fax: (305) 378-7262
	Emp: 41000
	% foreign owned: 100
	Restaurants, fast food outlets
	CARILLON IMPORTERS
	Glenponte Centre W
	Teaneck, NJ 07666-6897
	Tel: (201) 836-7799
	Fax: (201) 836-3312]
	Tlx: 431329
	Emp: 60
	% foreign owned: 100
	Imp/mktg alcoholic beverages

Reprinted with permission from World Trade Academy Press.

The fifth edition of the *Directory* appeared in 1993. It is arranged by the name of the U.S. company. A company is considered foreign owned if its ultimate parent owns 10% or more of the company. In about 1% of the listings, "not available" is given under the parent company name. The *Directory* is indexed by state, parent companies, country of parent company, and four-digit standard industrial classification number. In addition to the usual manufacturing SIC numbers (2000 through 3999), companies are included whose business is in agriculture, forestry, mining, oil and gas, and software. Exhibit 7-4 displays a sample record from the *Directory*.

Directory of Foreign Investment in the U.S.: Real Estate and Businesses, Nancy Garman, ed. (Gale Research, 1991)

Real estate ownership by foreign companies is particularly easy to conceal. *DFI* lists 1,200 real estate properties and more than 10,000 key companies owned by foreign investors in all areas of U.S. trade and industry. The real estate section is arranged geographically by city within states. The business section is arranged by three-digit SIC numbers. There are three indexes: an alphabetic index to properties, foreign owners, companies, and sellers; a foreign owners by country index that lists the foreign companies owning U.S. property or companies; and a geographic index listing properties, companies, and foreign owners and sellers, arranged by state and by city within state. Exhibit 7-5 gives an example of a real estate record and a company record.

Directory of Corporate Affiliations (National Register—Annual)

This five-volume set has information for some 33,000 companies. The volumes are organized so that the subsidiaries, no matter where they are located, will be found in the same volume as the parent company. The basic form of the listings is the same in each volume. Parent company information is given first, with name, address, and telecommunications data in bold type. These entries are followed by any divisions, subsidiaries, affiliates, and joint ventures of the parent.

The volumes in the *Directory of Corporate Affiliations* set are:

EXHIBIT 7-4. Record from *Directory of Foreign Manufactures in the United States*

NTN BEARING MFG. CORP OF AMERICA
3637 Medina Rd
Medina OH 44256
SIC: 3562
    Anti-friction bearings
Parent Company:

NTN Corp
3-17 1-chome Kyomachibori
Nishi-ku Osaka 550 Japan

Reprinted with permission from Georgia State University Business Press.

EXHIBIT 7-5. Records from *Directory of Foreign Investment in the U.S.*

Phoenix

12

Anasazi Golf Course

4435 E. Paradise Valley Pkwy. S.

Phoenix, AZ

[MSA: Phoenix, AZ]

602/935-9110

Description: 17-acre golf course, plans are to build 20,000 square foot clubhouse; other partners are Mitsui and Arizona developer, Westcor Company. Purchase Price: $13,000,000. Seller: Westcor. **Owner:** Shimizu Construction Company Ltd. Japan.

1669

Alpo Pet Foods, Inc.

Rte. 309 & Pope Rd.

P.O. Box 2187

Allentown, PA 18001

215/395-3301

Franklin Krum

Description: Annual Sales: $250,000,000. Employees: 1,500. **Owner:** Grand Metropolitan PLC. Address: 11/12 Hanover Sq., London, GL W1A 1DP, England. SIC 2047.

Reprinted from *Directory of Foreign Investment in the U.S.*

- *U.S. Public Companies Volume 1:* lists U.S. public companies and their subsidiaries
- *U.S. Public Companies Volume 2:* contains geographic SIC and personnel listing for public companies
- *U.S. Private Companies:* lists U.S.-based private companies and their subsidiaries
- *International Public and Private Companies:* lists all non-U.S.-based companies whether they are public or private, and all of their subsidiaries whether they are located in the U.S. or overseas
- *Master Index:* alphabetically lists all companies, both headquarters and subsidiaries; also contains brand name index

In addition to its company listings, the *International Public and Private Companies* volume contains these features:

- Geographic index arranged by country and city within country
- SIC index
- Personnel listing, "Who's Where Internationally," that gives organization name and page reference
- A list of mergers, acquisitions, and name changes for the previous six years
- Addresses of foreign consulates
- Addresses of U.S. embassies
- Addresses of American Chambers of Commerce Abroad
- Addresses of Foreign Trade Commissions and Chambers of Commerce
- Major international public holidays
- Foreign currency exchange
- Country codes and dial instructions

Exhibit 7-6 shows a sample record from the company listing that displays subsidiary listings.

The online version of the *Directory* is available on DIALOG as *Corporate Affiliations* (File 513). The file includes more than 100,000 parent companies and their affiliates. *Corporate Affiliations* has two types of records. The first (parent company record) contains the complete corporate family tree. The second (affiliate company record) contains the portion of the corporate family tree in which a particular company fits. Exhibit 7-7 is the parent company record for the U.K. company Grand Metropolitan, owner of several widely known American companies.

As the Exhibit indicates, the information includes (in addition to a list of subsidiaries) the parent company name, address, and telephone number; ticker symbol and stock exchange; up to 20 Standard Industrial Classification (SIC) codes and descriptions; the number of employees, total assets, sales, net worth; and names of executives and members of the board of directors. The record also includes an NRPC number (National Register Parent Company) that can be used to retrieve all related companies regardless of name. The record in Exhibit 7-7 has been truncated to save space.

More information can be found on individual subsidiaries and plants by searching directly by subsidiary name. For example, to retrieve information about Pillsbury Canada Ltd., search for that company name. Exhibit 7-8 displays the results of such a search.

There are several ways to search corporation relationships in the file. Each record has a 10-digit number called the NRPC number. The first six digits of this number are the same for related companies. Searching on

EXHIBIT 7-6. Record from *Directory of Corporate Affiliations*

Sullivan Graphics, Ltd. _____ Company Name

52 Upper Fitzwilllam Bd. _____ Company Address

Dublin 1 2, Ireland

Tel: WOl 568 333 _____ Telecommunications Data

Telex: 95421

Fax: 0001 588 334

Year Founded: 1967

SULLl- (DUB LON) _____ Ticker Symbol & Stock Exchanges

Approx. SIs: $7,498,898,900_____ Financial Information

Fiscal Year End: 12/31/91

Emp: 10,800_____ No. of Employees, Including Sub-cos.

Designs, Manufacturers & Markets _____ Business Description

Electronic Design Automotion (EDA)

Software & Systems for the IC and

Systems Design Markets

S.1.C.: 3577 _____ SIC Codes

Joseph M. McGillivary (Ohm. Bd .) _____ Key Personnel

Elizabeth Mulloy (Pres. & Chief Exec. Officer)

Kevin B. O'Reilly (Chief Oper. Officer)

Simmons & Fitzgerald (Legal Firm) _____ Name and Address of Service Firm

Consheagh Bd., Dublin 17, Ireland

Subsidiary:

    Ericsson Systems, Inc. (1) _____ Reports to Parent Company (Sullivan Graphics)

    2 Wellington Bd., Killamey,

    County Kerry, Ireland

    Tel: 1 7183 48

    Telex: 96140

    Mfr. of Computer Peripheral

    Equipment

    S.1.C.: 3577

    Thomas J. McSwwney (Pres.)

Subsidiary:

    Kerngan Co., Inc. (2) _____ Reports to Level 1 Co.(Ericsson Systems)

    8 Swords Rd., Dublin 17, Ireland

    Tel: 01611778 (100%)

    Telex: 30472

    Emp.: 850

    Mfr. of Computer Printers

    S.1.C. 3577

    Tennant & McDaniel, Inc. (1)

    Greenhills Rd., Tallaght, Dublin 24,

    Ireland

    Tel: 35 3712 6832 (100%) _____ Percentage of Ownership

    Emp: 1200

    Mfr. of Computer Peripheral

    Equipment

    S.1.C.: 3577

    Raymond J. O'Sullivan (Chief Oper. Officer)

Non-U.S. Subsidiary:

    Padova Systems, Inc. (1) _____ Subsidiary not in Ireland or U.S.

    Via Laurentina 449, 1- 20097, Milan,   Reports to Parent (Sullivan Graphics)

    Italy

EXHIBIT 7-6. Record from *Directory of Corporate Affiliations (continued)*

Tel: 06 305291
Emp.: 1500
Mfr. of Computer Printers
S.l.C. 3577
Anthony Macaluso (Pres.)

Copyright © 1993 by Reed Publishing (USA) Inc.

EXHIBIT 7-7. Online Record from *Corporate Affiliations*

1948158
Grand Metropolitan Plc
20 St James's Sq
London, SW1 4RR
United Kingdom

Telephone: 071 321 6000

NRPC Number: 020659000
Ticker Symbol: GRM Stock Exchange: NYSE, ASE, PS, LON

Number of NonUS Affiliates: 93
Number of US Affiliates: 43
Total Number of Affiliates: 136

Business: Mfrs, Wholesalers & Retailers of Spirits, Wines & Foods;
    Opthamalic Products & Srvcs; Restaurant Opers

SIC Codes (Primary listed first):
   2026   Fluid milk
   2033   Canned fruits, vegetables, preserves, jams & jellies
   2037   Frozen fruits, fruit juices & vegetables
   2041   Flour & other grain mill products
   2045   Prepared flour mixes & doughs
   2051   Bread & other bakery products, except cookies & crackers
   2052   Cookies & crackers
   2086   Bottled & canned soft drinks & carbonated waters
   2091   Canned & cured fish & seafoods
   2096   Potato chips, corn chips & similar snacks
   2099   Food preparations, NEC
   5812   Eating places
   5813   Drinking places (alcoholic beverages)
   5451   Dairy products stores

Number of Employees: 152,175

Sales: $14,857,711,000

This is a(n) Parent, NonUS, Public Company

Numeric Field(s) Last Updated: 920216
Textual Field(s) Last Updated: 921124

Executives:
Chairman of the Board, Chief Executive Officer
   Sir Allen JG Sheppard/Chm Bd & Grp Chief Exec
Vice Chairman
   Sir John Harvey-Jones/Deputy Chm
•
•
•

EXHIBIT 7-7. Online Record from *Corporate Affiliations (continued)*

Controller
 Rosemary P Thorne/Controller

Corporate Family Hierarchy:

=>Grand Metropolitan Plc 1948158<=
 Grand Metropolitan Foods Europe Limited (Principal Subsidiary Company)
  1948157
 Express Foods Group (International) Ltd (Subsidiary) 1948156

  Express Dairy Ltd (Operating Division) 1948155
   •
   •
   •

 Haagen-Daz UK Ltd (Subsidiary) 1948146
 Kaysens (Subsidiary) 1948145
 Memory Lane Cakes Ltd (Subsidiary) 1948144
 Pilstral SA (Non-US Subsidiary) 1948143
   •
   •
   •

 The Paddington Corporation (Subsidiary) 1948055
 Azteca Foods Incorporated (Subsidiary) 1948054
 Burger King UK Limited (Non-US Subsidiary) 1948053
   •
   •

Source: DIALOG File 513. Copyright © 1993 by Reed Publishing (USA) Inc.

the first six digits of the NRPC number will bring together all related companies in the file. You can also search and retrieve companies reporting to the "ultimate parent" (the company at the top of the hierarchy) or companies reporting to an "immediate parent" (the company that owns the subsidiary). The DIALOG file uses the prefix "UP" for ultimate parent and "IP" for immediate parent.

Another use for the file is to find the names and characteristics of cross-border subsidiaries (for example, the names of U.S. companies owned by Japanese companies). As Table 7-A shows, DIALOG's report format allows the information to be displayed as columns and rows. *Corporate Affiliations* is also available on CD-ROM from Bowker-Saur.

Who Owns Whom (Dun & Bradstreet International— Annual)

Who Owns Whom contains information on the corporate structure of approximately 23,000 parent companies and their 300,000 subsidiaries. Approximately one-third of the companies in *Who Owns Whom* are in the U.K., one-third are in continental Europe, and one-third in the rest of the world. Information for each full company entry includes name, status as parent or subsidiary, country of incorporation, percentage shareholding (when available), an indication of whether the company is currently active

or dormant, and its position within the group. Parent company entries also include company address, telephone number, and U.S. SIC number. *Who Owns Whom* also includes many companies owned by official bodies, such as governments that have subsidiaries but are not themselves corporations.

Information is collected by annual questionnaires and telephone interviews with company secretaries (or equivalent authority). Company annual reports, major business newspapers of the world, and selected trade journals are also scanned for information on new groups to be added to the database. The printed version of the directory comprises 6 volumes.

• *Who Owns Whom. Australia Asia* (Vol. 1)
• *Who Owns Whom. North America* (Vol. 2)
• *Who Owns Whom. United Kingdom* (Vols. 3 & 4)
• *Who Owns Whom. Continental Europe* (Vols. 5 & 6)

The price for libraries is $325 for the North American edition and $295 for the other sets. The directories have two basic arrangements. The first is by country subdivided by parent company name. The second is alphabetically by parent company name. The information provided includes address, SIC codes, principal officers, and a list of subsidiaries and their countries. The index is by subsidiary name showing parent company

---

EXHIBIT 7-8. Subsidiary Record from *Corporate Affiliations*

1948027
Pillsbury Canada Ltd
243 Consumers Road Ste 1200
Willowdale, ON
Canada M2J 4Z5

Telephone: 416-494-2500

NRPC Number: 020659167

Ultimate Parent: Grand Metropolitan Plc (United Kingdom) - 1948158
Immediate Parent: Grand Metropolitan Plc (United Kingdom) - 1948158
Ownership by Parent: 100 %

Number of NonUS Affiliates: 4
Number of US Affiliates: 0
Total Number of Affiliates: 4

Business: Canadian Headquarters

SIC Codes (Primary listed first):
  6719   Offices of holding companies, NEC
Number of Employees: NA

Sales: NA

This is a(n) Affiliate, NonUS Company

Executives:
Chief Oper. Officer Sub-Company
  Richard A Peddie/Pres

Corporate Family Hierarchy:

  Grand Metropolitan Plc 1948158
  =>Pillsbury Canada Ltd (Non-US Holdings) 1948027<=
    Pillsbury Canada Ltd (Division) 1948026
    Pillsbury Canada Ltd (Division) 1948025
    Pillsbury Canada Ltd (Division) 1948024
    Pillsbury Canada Ltd (Division) 1948023

Source: DIALOG File 513. Copyright © 1993 Reed Publishing (USA) Inc.

---

and percentage of ownership when available. The sample record in Exhibit 7-9 is from the online version of the directory.

D&B-Dun's Market Identifiers (Dun and Bradstreet)

D&B-Dun's Market Identifiers may be used to find some cross-border corporate links. The DIALOG version of the file lists about 17,000 U.S. companies that have foreign ownership. The records of these companies are tagged "NON-US OWNED." On DIALOG you can retrieve these companies by selecting SF=NON-US OWNED.

Only the top-most company of a U.S. corporate family hierarchy with U.S. foreign owners has this designation. For example, Alpo Petfood is a U.S. company owned by Grand Metropolitan Inc., another U.S.-based company. Grand Metropolitan Inc. is owned by Grand Metropolitan PLC, a U.K. company. Only the record for Grand Metropolitan Inc. (the U.S. ultimate parent) is

designated by D&B as "foreign owned." Exhibit 7-10 shows three brief company records. The first two are from the DIALOG version of *D&B-Dun's Market Identifiers*. They show that the Corporate Family D-U-N-S number for Alpo links it to Grand Metropolitan Inc. The third record is from DIALOG's *D&B-INTL DUNS MARKET IDENTIFIERS*. It illustrates how the parent D-U-N-S number for Grand Metropolitan Inc. links to the ultimate parent, Grand Metropolitan PLC in the U.K. At the end of 1993, Dun & Bradstreet introduced *Global Corporate Families,* available on a D&B CD-ROM and on Dow Jones. The file has 1.7 million locations for 300,000 corporate families.

wer gehoert zu wem [**Who Belongs to Whom**] (DATA-STAR)

wer gehoert zu wem (*WGZW*) is the online version of the printed Commerzbank publication of the same name.

Table 7-A. U.S. Subsidiaries of Major Japanese Companies (1992)

Corporate Affiliations Database	
U.S.	Japanese
Company	Ultimate
Name	Parent
American Honda Motor Co Inc	Honda Motor Co Ltd
Canon USA Inc	Canon Inc
CBS Records Inc	Sony Corporation
The CIT Group Inc	The Dai-Ichi Kangyo Bank Limit
Marubeni America Corporation	Marubeni Corporation
Matsushita Electric Corporation	Matsushita Electric Industrial
MCA Universal	Matsushita Electric Industrial
Mitsubishi Electric America In	Mitsubishi Electric Corporatio
Mitsubishi International Corporation	Mitsubishi Corporation
National Steel Corporation	NKK Corporation
New United Motor Manufacturing	Toyota Motor Corporation
Omron Systems of America Inc	Omron Tateisi Electronics Co
7-Eleven Stores	Ito-Yokado Co Ltd
Sharp Electronics Corporation	Sharp Corporation
Sony Corporation of America	Sony Corporation
Sony Pictures Entertainment	Sony Corporation
The Southland Corporation	Ito-Yokado Co Ltd
Subaru of America Inc	Fuji Heavy Industries Ltd
Toshiba America Inc	Toshiba Corporation
Toyota Motor Sales USA Inc	Toyota Motor Corporation

Source: DIALOG File 513

EXHIBIT 7-9. Sample Record from *Who Owns Whom*

```
      1 WHOW
AN 000184234, Duns number: 210124764, Reg number: 291848,
    D-S
Update:
    930316.
OC  PARAGRAPH
    CO (1)
CO  Grand Metropolitan PLC.
CN  United Kingdom.
AD  20 St. James's Square,
    London,
    SW1Y 4RR.
    LONDON.
TL  071-321 6000.
CC  US SIC:
        6711    HOLDING COMPANY
        7011    HOTELS, MOTELS, AND TOURIST
                RESORTS
        5141    GENERAL GROCERY
                WHOLESALERS
        5143    DAIRY PRODUCT WHOLESALERS
        2026    FLUID MILK PROCESSORS.
```

```
CT  Ultimate parent
    (Non-dormant).
NU  Number of subsidiaries listed in SU: 626 in 49 group(s).
SU  1 OF 49.
    - Bistrial S.A., France.
    2 OF 49.
    - Burgerking (Holdings) Ltd., United Kingdom
        - Burger King (U.K.) Ltd., United Kingdom
            - King Foods Ltd. (d), United Kingdom
    - Haagen-Dazs UK Ltd., United Kingdom
    - Pillsbury U.K. Ltd., United Kingdom
        - Fiesta Foods Ltd. (d), United Kingdom
        - Green Giant Foods Ltd. (d), United Kingdom
        - Precis (1000) Ltd. (d), United Kingdom.
[an additional 12 pages of subsidiaries listings]
```

Source: DATA-STAR, *Who Owns Whom*. Reprinted with permission from Dun & Bradstreet Ltd.

EXHIBIT 7-10. D-U-N-S Number Cross-Border Links

Record #1
Alpo Petfoods Inc
DUNS NUMBER: 00-251-8090
CORPORATE FAMILY DUNS: **11-307-1799**   Grand Metropolitan Inc

Source: DIALOG File 516

Record #2
Grand Metropolitan Inc
Minneapolis, MN 55402-1416
   NON-US OWNED
DUNS NUMBER: **11-307-1799**
PARENT DUNS: **21-012-4764**

Source: DIALOG File 516

Record #3
Grand Metropolitan PLC
London, UK-England SW1y4RR
DUNS NUMBER: **21-012-4764**
Source: DIALOG File 519

Reprinted with permission from Dun & Bradstreet Inc.

WGZW contains information on the ownership of approximately 12,500 companies located in the Federal Republic of Germany with a capital stock of at least one million marks. The database covers nearly all 'AG' companies (public companies) and about two-thirds of the capital of 'GmbH' companies (private companies).

Each document contains the exact name, legal status and location of the company, its industrial sector, amount of capital, major shareholders or partners, percentage shareholdings, the country of foreign shareholders, and cross-references to shareholders entered elsewhere in the database. Several of the fields can be searched in English or German.

The information in the database is the result of direct written contact between Commerzbank and the companies concerned. The information is updated twice a year by means of official published sources and the companies' own publications.

Although the records in *WGZW* are brief, the database provides the answers required of a corporate affiliation file. For example, you can search the database to find

- Who owns whom (Who owns Union Deutsche Lebensmittelwerke?)
- Who belongs to whom (Which companies does Siemens own?)
- Corporate links (How many companies does Siemens own?)

- Country of shareholders
- How many companies are located in East Germany

A useful feature of the database is its ability to search for percentage of shareholdings. Exhibit 7-11 is a record retrieved from a search of the file for all companies that were 100% owned by U.S. firms.

CORPORATE CHANGE

Our discussion of sources for corporate change begins with a brief list of key terms and their definitions. The definitions are generally applicable internationally, although many legal, accounting, and institutional details apply only to individual countries. Some general examples of such country-specific items include:

EXHIBIT 7-11. Record from *wer gehoert zu wem*

AN 0010022329 9212, Copyright: COMMERZBANK AG.
CO Microsoft GmbH.
LO 8044 Unterschleissheim.
CA DM 5.050 Mio.
LS GmbH.
CC 305 Electrical engineering and electronics (including data processing).
OS Microsoft Corporation Redmond, Redmond/Wash, (United States of America), (10022328) - 100.00 %.

Reprinted with permission from Commerzbank AG.

- *Accounting Regulations:* German companies are not permitted to buy their own shares, which limits their defense against hostile takeovers.
- *Anti-Monopoly Laws:* Japanese law (Anti-Monoploy and Fair Trade Maintenance Act) requires a report before a merger is carried out.
- *Foreign Ownership:* Switzerland has restrictions upon the foreign ownership of corporate assets.

An overview of the legal and accounting framework of international acquisitions can be found in *International Mergers and Acquistions*, IFR Publishing, 1989.

Definitions

Acquisition: The acquiring of control of one corporation by another. The acquiring company is often referred to as the "buyer" or "acquirer"; the acquired company is referred to as the "seller" or "target." "Acquisition" is often used to describe a transaction in which both the buyer and seller are willing to make a deal. "A hostile acquisition" in which the seller is unwilling to deal is usually called a "takeover."

Bankruptcy: The conditions under which the financial position of a corporation is such as to cause actual or legal insolvency. When a bankruptcy is declared, three basic resolutions are possible: liquidation, acquisition, or reorganization.

Consolidation: A combination of two or more organizations into one to form a new entity. Consolidation, in that it creates a new corporate entity, is similar to both an acquisition and a merger. Consolidation is considered a more friendly, cooperative deal than either a merger or acquisition. It gives equal footing in the new firm to each corporation. Again, this is a classic definition, and in reality a consolidation may be no more friendly than any deal type nor is there a certainty the two firms have equality in the new entity.

Leveraged Buyout (LBO): The acquisition of a business primarily with borrowed funds that are repaid from the target company's earnings or sale of excess assets. The LBO differs from a typical acquisition in that, along with transfer of ownership, there is also a complete restructuring of the target company's balance sheet. An LBO often transforms a target company's balance sheet from a very debt-free condition to a highly leveraged state.

Liquidation: The winding up of the affairs of a business by converting all assets into cash, paying off all outside creditors in the order of their preference, and distributing the remainder, if any, to the owners in proportion, and in the order of preference, if any, of ownership.

M & A (Merger & Acquisition): This phrase is often applied to a wide range of corporate change activities, including mergers, acquisitions, partial acquisitions, leveraged buyouts, divestitures, exchange offers, stock repurchases, self-tenders, tender offers, and spinoffs.

Merger: The combining of two or more entities through the direct acquisition by one of the net assets of the other. Mergers usually involve an exchange of stock. Regardless of the format of the deal, a merger is the final legal requirement for its completion.

Recapitalization: Altering the capital structure of a firm by increasing or decreasing its capital stock. In doing so, a firm also may increase its debt or leverage. In a leveraged recapitalization, stock is exchanged for debt securities and leverage becomes a greater percentage of the total capitalization. Methods of decreasing stock, as a takeover defense or to increase stock value, are referred to as *stock buybacks* or *stock repurchases*. The stocks are bought back from existing shareholders, which shrinks outstanding shares.

Reorganization: The altering of a firm's capital structure, often resulting from a merger, that affects the rights and responsibilities of the owners. In a bankruptcy, the objectives of a reorganization are to eliminate the cause of failure, settle with creditors, and allow the firm to remain in business. Alternately, a company may undergo a nonlegal reorganization that may result only in changes to the organization chart through a shuffling of subsidiaries and divisions.

Restructuring: A collection of activities designed to increase shareholder wealth by maximizing the value of corporate assets. These activities may include divestiture of underperforming businesses, spin-offs to shareholders, stock repurchases, recapitalization, or acquisitions.

Spin-Off: The separation of a subsidiary or division of a corporation from its parent by issuing shares in a new corporate entity. Shareowners in the parent receive shares in the new company in proportion to their original holding and the total value of the shares remains about the same.

Accounting rules may affect the price that acquiring companies are willing to pay for acquisitions. Rules affecting goodwill are an example. Goodwill is the purchase price of the acquisition minus the market value of the acquisition's assets. In the U.K., for example, acquiring companies can write off goodwill against shareholders' equity. In the U.S., goodwill must be paid for out of earnings.[1]

In the EC, all large mergers, acquisitions, and joint ventures are subject to review by the EC Commission's Merger Control Task Force. The review applies to all large European Community business transactions as well as international deals meeting the community's criteria for review.

Cross-Border Transactions

Cross-border deals are M & A transactions in which the target (the company being acquired) and the acquirer (or the acquirer's ultimate parent) are based in different countries. An example of a cross-border M & A transaction is Grand Metropolitan's purchase of Pillsbury in 1988. Grand Metropolitan is a U.K.-based company and Pillsbury is based in the U.S. A domestic deal from a U.S. point of view is the acquisition of a U.S. company by another U.S. company. As Table 7-B indicates, a combination of a non-U.S. acquirer and a non-U.S. target can be either a cross-border transaction (e.g., a German company acquiring a U.K. company) or a domestic transaction (e.g., a German company acquiring another German company). Companies have several motives for becoming involved in cross-border acquisitions, including increased access to foreign markets, achieving international brand name recognition, and favorable exchange rates.

From a U.S. perspective, it is easiest to find information about M & A transactions in which either or both the parties are U.S. companies.

Sources for Corporate Change Information

M & A Yearbooks. Several important M & A Yearbooks are listed below.
Mergers and Acquisitions SourceBook (Quality Service Company—Annual)

Although primarily a reference for U.S. mergers, the *Source Book* includes a chapter describing foreign transactions. The transactions include completed transactions, negotiations, and terminated deals. The chapter has two parts. The first part, described as "Full Financial Disclosure," lists about 30 transactions. It gives seller's SIC number, sales, net income, and net worth for the previous three years. The description of the buyer gives SIC number and, when available, current sales and net income. The following facts are given concerning the purchase price: the total amount, the price as a multiple of the seller's annual sales and net worth, and its percent

of seller's annual sales. In addition, the descriptions include a brief paragraph describing the deal. Usually given are price per share offered and the common stock price at the time of the announcement.

The second part includes some 400 transactions. For each transaction, a brief paragraph describes the deal, giving SIC number; the name, industry and description of buyer and seller; and the purchase price, if disclosed.

Mergers and Acquisitions Source Book includes a section that gives trends and aggregate statistics on cross-border deals. It lists foreign acquisition of U.S. companies and U.S. acquisitions of foreign companies, broken down by year and country. The *Source Book* is handicapped by its single index of transaction—by company name only. There is no country index.

International Merger Yearbook (Securities Data Company—Annual)

The *International Merger Yearbook* first appeared in 1990, when the *Merger Yearbook* became two separate M & A annual publications, the *Domestic Merger Yearbook* and the *International Merger Yearbook*. The books are subtitled *Corporate Acquisitions, Leveraged Buyouts, Joint Ventures and Corporate Policy*. The domestic version reports only deals involving U.S. corporations. The international version includes only cross-border deals and non-U.S. domestic deals. (In 1993, the separate U.S. and International editions were combined.) The *International Merger Yearbook* will report a deal whether or not a U.S. company is a party. It also reports many more cross-border deals in a single volume (some 12,000) than were previously available in a printed source. The information in the *Yearbook* is based on the SDC *Mergers and Acquisitions Database* described below.

Organized by four-digit SIC number, each record gives basic deal information, including the value and current status of the transaction. A useful feature in each *Yearbook* entry is a code for type of deal. These deal types include private negotiations, divestitures, spinoffs, and even rumors. Bankrupt companies are included if they are seeking a buyer. The deals are indexed only by company name or investor, making it impossible to identify cross-border deals by the company's country. Despite this limitation, the *Yearbook* is the best single

Table 7-B. M & A Transactions in Relation to Nationality

	U.S. Acquirer	Non-U.S. Acquirer
U.S. Target	U.S. Domestic	U.S. Cross-Border
Non-U.S. Target	U.S. Cross-Border	Non-U.S Cross-Border *or* Non-U.S. Domestic

printed source for cross-border and non-U.S. merger information.

Aggregate figures for worldwide M & A are an important feature of the *Yearbook.* The data presented include tables for the following transactions measured in billions of U.S. dollars:

- Global Mergers and Corporate Transactions
- Global Acquisitions
- Hostile Acquisitions of Global Targets
- Acquisitions of Global Targets Valued at $1 Billion or Greater
- Global LBOs and MBOs
- Global Acquisitions of Targets with Industry Break-downs

Another unique listing is a ranking of targets and acquirers by nation. Exhibit 7-12 is derived from the *Yearbook* ranking of targets by nation. The original table included three years of data for 50 countries.

Exhibits 7-13 and 7-14 show the entries for the same transaction as they appear in the *Merger & Acquisition Sourcebook* and the *Merger Yearbook International,* respectively.

Mergerstat Review (W.T. Grimm & Co.—Annual)

Mergerstat Review contains summary data on cross-border merger transactions. It does not report the names of companies involved in a transaction, only the aggregate statistics. The *Review's* statistical tables include a section for both foreign buyers and foreign sellers. A limitation of the *Review's* coverage of cross-border deals is its requirement that a U.S. company must be involved in a transaction to be included. The foreign buyers section gives data on both the foreign purchase of domestic companies and the purchase of foreign-based subsidiaries of U.S. corporations. The foreign sellers section lists U.S. corporations' purchases of foreign companies and units of foreign companies. Ten years of data are

Exhibit 7-12. Table from *Merger Yearbook International*

Ranking of Targets by Nation (Global Acquirors)

Acquiror Nation	Value ($millions)	% of Tot.	# of Deals
United States	144,442.1	45.9	4,48
United Kingdom	48,278.8	15.3	1,17
Germany	13,026.3	4.1	52
France	12,524.7	4.0	23
Italy	11,421.9	3.6	10
Spain	11,240.5	3.6	9
Mexico	10,627.3	3.4	4
Australia	8,431.5	2.7	13
Sweden	7,901.3	2.5	8
Unknown	7,144.2	2.3	3
Canada	6,158.2	2.0	50
Hong Kong	4,706.1	1.5	8
Malaysia	3,596.6	1.1	2
Netherlands	3,035.2	1.0	9
Belgium	2,422.7	0.8	5
Portugal	2,116.2	0.7	3
South Africa	1,621.1	0.5	2
Austria	1,497.5	0.5	2
Japan	1,354.0	0.4	4

Source: *Merger Yearbook International 1992*, p. 15. Reprinted with permission from Securities Data Company.

given for most series.

The main data series for foreign buyers are

- Foreign acquisitions of U.S. companies
- Foreign acquisitions—price paid
- Average premium paid over market
- Average price/earnings ratio paid
- Industries attracting foreign buyers
- Number of transactions by country
- Dollar total by country

Exhibit 7-13. Record from *Merger & Acquisition Sourcebook*

SIC NUMBER	Seller	Buyer	Purchase Price ($Millions)
2841	80% of Pollena Bydgoszcz a Polish detergent maker, owned by the Polish government.	Unilever, Rotterdam, Netherlands, an Anglo-Dutch food, detergent, and toiletries manufacturer	$20.00

COMMENTS: Unilever said that is has agreed to purchase 80% of Pollena Bydgoszcz form the Polish government for $20 million. The Polish government, which is to retain 20% of the detergent maker, describes the planned sale as the country's largest privatization so far. Unilever said it intends to invest a further $24 million to double the Polish concern's production capacity, upgrade its technology and add equipment to make liquid products. Pollena Bydgoszcz, which employs 430 people, will be renamed **Lever Polska.**

Source: *Merger & Acquisition Sourcebook 1992*, p. 6-43. Reprinted with permission from Quality Service Company.

Exhibit 7-14. Entry from *Merger Yearbook International 1992*

Pollena Bydgoszcz(Poland)	2841 Unilever NV	$20.00 US
Manufacture detergents	Produce food and consumer prod	Acq. Maj. Int.
	Rotterdam	
Poland	Netherlands	Ancd: 06/17/91 Pending

Unilever agreed to acquire an 80% interest in Pollena Bydgoszcz from the Polish government for $20 mil US. Pollena Bydgoszcz, which was to be renamed Polska Lever, was auctioned by the Polish government. Unilever planned to invest $24 mil to double production capacity, upgrade its technology and equipment to make liquid products. Pollena was Poland's leading laundry detergents producer and the first to be privatized.

CROSS DIVEST

Source: Merger Yearbook International 1992, p. 155. Reprinted with permission from Securities Data Company.

The main data series for foreign sellers are

- U.S. acquisitions of foreign businesses—number of transactions
- U.S. acquisitions of foreign businesses—total dollar value
- Industries attracting American buyers
- Industry dollar totals
- Number of transactions by country
- Dollar total by country

M & A Journals. Journals that provide international coverage of M & A supplement the annual coverage of yearbooks.

Acquisitions Monthly (Lonsdale House—Monthly)

This journal emphasizes U.K. mergers. Each issue contains an "Acquisition Record" for the month that includes 40 pages of capsule descriptions of domestic and cross-border deals. About half the descriptions involve U.K. companies. The information is presented by company within country. A separate "sector analysis" presents the same information grouped by U.K. SIC numbers. Each issue has a company index. *Acquisitions Monthly* provides the data for the *AMDATA* M&A database. The database runs on a personal computer and is updated with diskettes. It supplies 180 data fields for each transaction. The database covers domestic and cross-border transactions for Europe, Japan, and the U.S. Historical coverage varies by country, but most have coverage from 1989 to date.

Mergers & Acquisitions (MLR Publishing—Semi-monthly)

Mergers & Acquisitions includes an "M & A Roster" giving capsule descriptions of deals taking place during the previous quarter. Two sections focusing on cross-border deals are included in the Roster. One section covers U.S. deals for foreign firms and the other covers deals for U.S. companies by foreign firms. There is no coverage of deals between two non-U.S. firms. In the

Roster, standard information, such as terms of the deal, is provided for each transaction. There is also an annual index to all deals covered in the Roster, but it is an index by company name only. The index always appears in the May/June issue of *Mergers & Acquisitions*, an issue that also includes the "Almanac," a statistical summary of the year's M & A activity. The Almanac includes the tables "Countries most active in U.S. acquisitions" and "Countries attracting U.S. buyers."

M & A Europe (MLR Publishing—Semi-monthly)

This companion publication of *Mergers & Acquisitions* focuses on deal activity among European firms. Though articles make up the bulk of the journal, lists of deals and statistical analysis of deal activity are also included. *M & A Europe* is also available as a full-text database on the LEXIS/NEXIS SERVICE, in the EUROPE Library.

Mergers & Acquisitions International (Financial Times Business Information—Monthly)

This monthly journal provides information on the mergers and acquisitions of private and public companies in the U.K., whether pending, completed, or terminated. There are also detailed sections for areas outside the U.K., and here transactions involving U.S. and European firms are recorded. Deals are indexed by company name and country, both for acquirers and targets.

Multinational Business (Economist—Monthly)

A non-U.S. perspective of deal activity may be found in the center section of each issue of *Multinational Business*. The "Acquisitions and Mergers" report provides a summary of major deals in Europe, the United Kingdom, the U.S., and other major countries (Japan, Canada, the Mideast).

Euromoney (Euromoney PLC—Monthly)

A more specialized annual report on European merger and acquisition activity is found in the February issue of *Euromoney*. The reports in this magazine emphasize adviser activity. A representative table ranks advisers by all completed deals for European countries buying into the United Kingdom. There are also summary statistical tables on cross-border deals by nation, industry breakdowns, and deal values. *Euromoney* does not provide specific information for each transaction.

Japan M & A Reporter (Ulmer Brothers Research—Monthly)

This newsletter gives brief descriptions of current acquisitions, joint ventures, and buyouts involving Japanese companies. Charts that group transactions by geographic region (e.g., Europe / Japan) are a useful feature.

World M & A Network International Executive Reports (Quarterly)

Companies interested in selling all or part of their business often make their wishes known by informing potential acquirers or by publishing their intention to sell. *World M & A Network* lists companies for sale, merger candidates, and willing buyers. A typical listing is a 100-word description of a business and the terms of the deal together with an asking price. The companies' names are not given. Leads are organized by company size, geographic region, and SIC codes. Although primarily a source of U.S. opportunities for U.S. sellers and investors, *World M & A Network* does include non-U.S. offers.

Electronic Sources for Corporate Change Information.

Finding information about cross-border M & A transactions is made easier by using M & A "transaction" databases. These databases bring together the main facts about individual M & A transactions. The databases take information about M & A activity from newswire stories, the financial press, and company reports. They combine this information in one record. Transaction databases allow you to answer such questions and complete such projects as:

- Which companies are actively buying into the German electronics industry?
- How many cross-border U.K./French deals were there from 1988 to the present?
- Define the M & A strategy of Grand Metropolitan.
- Rank U.K. financial advisors by dollar volume of their deals.

Until 1992, U.S. searchers had their choice of three transaction databases: *M & A Data Base* (ADP Data Service), IDD Enterprise's *M & A Transactions* (IDD Information Services), and the *Merger and Corporate Transaction Database* (Securities Data Company). IDD's *M & A Transactions* was available on several systems, including DIALOG and DATA-STAR. In the space of a few months in 1992, IDD bought ADP and then SDC

bought IDD's M&A and banking databases. Although IDD's *M & A Transactions* may be left on DIALOG as an historical file, Securities Data Company now is the principal transaction database producer. We describe their international corporate change databases below.

Merger & Corporate Transactions Database (Securities Data Company)

SDC's *Merger & Corporate Transactions Database* is the most comprehensive source of merger activity information. This menu-driven system is updated daily and available 24 hours a day. The database describes more than 55,000 domestic U.S. transactions dating back to 1980 and more than 40,000 international deals since 1985. Five hundred data items per transaction are provided for screening and reporting. The database covers mergers, acquisitions, partial acquisitions, leveraged buyouts, divestitures, exchange offers, stock repurchases, self-tenders, squeeze outs, tender offers, and spinoffs. The information is updated daily from SEC filings (8-Ks, l0Ks, and l0Qs), proxy statements, tender offers, annual reports, major financial publications, and company press releases. Some of the system's features include:

- *Merger Daily Activity Report:* Gives details of all merger-related activity within a given time
- *Volume Totals*: Provides online calculation of the volume of merger activity for any designated period
- *Reports*: Allows creation of customized reports, including any named variables

Exhibit 7-15 is a brief record of the acquisition of a U.K. company by a German company. It is often difficult to find published information on this type of small non-U.S. cross-border deal.

Worldwide Joint Ventures & Strategic Alliances (Securities Data Company)

This unique database gives details on cross-border and intra-nation joint ventures and strategic alliances. Transactions include new operating units, privatizations, and many types of strategic alliances, such as R&D, manufacturing, and technology licensing agreements. Updated daily, the file allows you to monitor global venturing and alliance activities by company, industry, and country; identify potential partners; and evaluate capitalization scenarios.

Financial Times M&A International (Financial Times)

FTMA provides detailed transaction reports on mergers, acquisitions, buyouts, joint ventures, pre-bid speculative announcements (rumors), and share swops in all key non-U.S. markets, as well as cross-border bids involving U.S. companies. It covers the period 1990 to date. In addition to the basic bid details, documents

EXHIBIT 7-15. Record from SDC's *Merger & Corporate Transaction Database*

Date Announced	Target Name	Acquiror Name
Date Effective	Business Description	Business Description
Date Unc	Financial Advisors(s)	Financial Advisor(s)
04/06/88	Bruce Engineers	Schade Plettenberg
04/06/88	Manufacture automotive parts	Mnfr motor vehicle components
	Form	
	Status	Acquisition
Value (mil)	Attitude	Technique(s)
0.8STG	Acq. Maj. Int.	Divestiture
	Completed	
Price/Sh	Friendly	

755,000 British pounds ($1.4 mil US) cash/50% ownership interest

Reprinted with permission from Securities Data Company.

contain, where available, names of advisors, related deals, and financial information. For U.K. and European quoted companies, comprehensive interim and five-year profit and loss data, sales analysis, share price history, and company announcements are also included. Information is collected from financial newspapers, public offering documents, and company press releases. As of May 1993, the database held about 24,000 records.

PROMT (Predicasts)

The online *PROMT* database is a good choice for international news on corporate change. Its controlled vocabulary allows precise retrieval. *PROMT* uses several "event names" to describe corporate change. They include:

- Organizational Nomenclature
- Organizational History
- Subsidiary to Parent Data
- Parent to Subsidiary Data
- Acquisitions & Mergers
- Asset Sales & Divestitures

Exhibit 7-16 is an example of an article retrieved from *PROMT* that combines the event names "Acquisitions & Mergers" and "Asset Sales & Divestitures" with the country names "France" and "United Kingdom."

NOTE

1. John J. Curran, "What Foreigners Will Buy Next," *Fortune* (February 13, 1989): 94-98.

EXHIBIT 7-16. Extract of Full-Text Record from DIALOG's Version of *PROMT*

04388199	DIALOG FILE 16:	PTS PROMT
TESCO (UK) IN FRENCH FOOD RETAILING ACQUISITION		
Multinational Service	January 15, 1993	p. N/A

TESCO, the UK's second-largest food retailer, has paid GBP 175.6 million for a 76% stake in the CATTEAU supermarket chain which operates 90 food stores in northern France. The Catteau family will retain a 24% stake. Most of the stores are located in the Nord-Pas de Calais region. Two are hypermarkets operating under the HyperCedico name, which are similar in size to TESCO's UK superstores. The 63 others, under the name Cedico, are smaller than TESCO UK stores. The CATTEAU chain also operates 25 convenience stores. The deal has been notified to the European Commission, which said on January 8 that it could come within the scope of the EC's Merger Regulation.

THIS IS THE FULL TEXT: Copyright 1993 by Europe Information Service
WORD COUNT: 112

COMPANY:
        *Tesco Stores Hldg
        Catteau
PRODUCT: *Grocery Stores (5411000); Supermarkets (5411100)
EVENT: *Acquisitions & Mergers (15); Asset Sales & Divestitures (16)
COUNTRY: *United Kingdom (4UK); France (4FRA)

Reprinted with permission from Information Access Company.

CHAPTER 8
Special Topics: International Credit Information and Rankings

TOPICS COVERED

1. International Credit Information
2. Rankings and Comparisons
3. Sources of Rankings
4. Online/Ondisc Rankings
5. Conclusion
6. Additional Sources of Information
7. Notes

MAJOR SOURCES DISCUSSED

- Dun & Bradstreet
- *Global Scan*
- *Polk World Banking Profiles*
- SCRL
- *ICC British Company Financial Datasheets*
- *Infocheck*
- *Teikoku*
- *Fortune, Forbes,* and *Business Week*
- *Times 1000*

INTERNATIONAL CREDIT INFORMATION

Finding international credit information is very important to the researcher who is considering doing business with a buyer or seller in another country. The credit worthiness of a potential partner is a vital piece of information. There are international credit services as well as services from individual countries. We will discuss a few of the larger services that make themselves known at international conferences. We cannot guarantee the level of quality of the services we are discussing.

Most countries have at least one credit reporting agency. A list of credit agencies is given in Appendix K of *The McGraw-Hill Handbook of Global Trade and Investment Financing*. The list is not complete, but it covers a wide range of countries.

International Credit Reporting Services

Dun and Bradstreet has an international credit reporting service in addition to its United States credit service. The international credit reports are collected in the individual countries Dun and Bradstreet covers. They are available online through *DunsPrint Worldwide* (the equivalent of the U.S. DunsPrint) or with a new user-friendly front-end system, D&B Access.

D&B International uses a two-part rating code in its business reports, for example *5A 4*. The first part of the rating, Financial Strength, is based on *tangible net worth* of the business, taken from the latest available audited accounts.

Standards of financial strength differ from country to country based on country practices and norms. The standards for U.K. reports are listed in Exhibit 8-1.

The second part of the rating is the Condition Code or Risk Factor. It indicates D&B's calculation of the level of risk associated with dealing with the business concern. Codes range from 1 to 4 with 1 being the lowest risk. D&B uses a scoring system based on 30 key company data elements to assign the Risk Factor. These elements come from the payment data, financial data, other public records such as court judgments, and special events such as a press release that may affect the company's trading position. D&B provides the chart in Exhibit 8-2 as a guide to interpreting the risk levels.

D&B Business Information Reports contain more than 20 million records worldwide, including 10 million across Europe and 2.5 million in the U.K. Reports include:

Exhibit 8-1. D&B Standards of Financial Strength for U.K. Companies

Indicator	Net Worth	Indicator	Net Worth
5A	£35,000,000 and above	B	£200,000–349,999
4A	£15,000,000 -34,999,999	C	£100,000–199,999
3A	£7,000,000 -14,999,999	D	£70,000–99,999
2A	£1,500,000 - 6,999,999	E	£36,000–69,999
1A	£700,000 - 1,499,999	F	£20,000–34,999
A	£350,000 - 699,999	G	£8,000–19,000
N	NEGATIVE NET WORTH	H	up to £7,999

Source: Dun and Bradstreet documentation. Reprinted with permission.

Exhibit 8-2. Interpreting Levels of Risk in D&B Credit Ratings

Risk Factor	Level of Risk	Guide to Interpretation
1	Minimal Risk	Proceed with transaction—offer extended terms if required
2	Low Risk	Proceed with transaction
3	Slightly greater than average risk	Proceed with transaction but monitor closely
4	Significant level of risk	Take suitable assurances before extending credit—i.e. Personal Guarantees
—	Insufficient information to base a decision	For example, legal form and/or location unconfirmed

Source: Documentation from D&B International U.K., 1992. Reprinted with permission.

- Financial Information, with the comprehensive report also having up to 18 key ratios
- Unique D&B Rating
- Maximum Credit Figure
- Payment Experiences, which include a payment score for the company and the industry quartiles
- Public Record Information, including court judgments and mortgages
- Background Information, such as legal structure, history, principals, subsidiaries, parents, and branches

Reports are collected in the country of origin and are translated into English.

An example of a unique D&B rating is given in Exhibit 8-3.

A report can be ordered online directly with DunsPrint or D&B Access or by telephone, speaking computer, facsimile, telex, magnetic tape, or post. DunsPrint is also available for individual countries such as France, Australia, and Canada.

Exhibit 8-3. Sample D&B Rating

D&B RATING:	2A3
CONDITION:	FAIR
TREND:	UP
MAXIMUM CREDIT:	150,000 +
LATEST STATEMENT:	31-03-91
PAYMENT SCORE:	42

Copyright © 1993 Dun & Bradstreet, Inc. All rights reserved. Reprinted with permission.

Global Scan (Infocheck Ltd.)

Global Scan is available online directly from Global Scan and through the French system Questel. Reports are available in the original language of the document as well as in English. Users may search in one of 10 languages. Reports have financial and credit data as well as descriptive summaries for more than six million public and private companies worldwide. Table 8-A lists the type of information available by country in *Global Scan*.

Coverage of companies in Taiwan, Spain, Greece, Japan, Hong Kong, Singapore, Argentina, Chile, and Ireland is expected to be added in the future.

Sources of information for *Global Scan* include reports filed with companies houses and chambers of commerce or compiled by business information specialists. Users pay for each report retrieved. Other conditions vary by gateway.

Credit Ratings for Banks

Polk World Banking Profiles (R.L. Polk—Every three years)

Polk World Banking Profiles, first published in 1993, compiles three sets of credit ratings: from Standard & Poor's, Moody's, and IBCA International Credit Rating Agency. These credit agencies rate banks from the major industrial countries.

Table 8–A. *Global Scan* **Report Information**

Country	Credit Reports	Balance Sheets	Country	Credit Reports	Balance Sheets
Austria	500		Netherlands	200,000	
Belgium		120,000	Norway	50,000	
Canada	1,500,000		Portugal	50,000	
Denmark		50,000	Sweden	100,000	
Finland	130,000		Switzerland		500
France	2,000,000 (1)		United Arab		
Germany	1,900,000	6,000	Emirates	30,000 (2)	
Italy	400,000	15,000	United Kingdom	320,000	3,200

(1) Not specified   (2) Market reports

Source: *Global Scan* documentation, December 1992

Researchers can use these ratings to answer such questions as:

- What banks in Japan have a potentially negative credit rating?
- What banks in the Asia/Pacific region have a long-term rating of Aaa?
- What is the rating for Dai-ichi Kangyo Bank? Has it changed recently? Was it downgraded or upgraded?

The *Standard & Poor's* ratings are based on fundamental credit analysis and subjective factors such as management depth and quality and business aggressiveness. Ratings are provided for long- and short-term debt and investments. Unique to S&P ratings in *Polk* is a column for "*Outlook* or *CreditWatch* Implications," taken from these two Standard and Poor's print newsletters.

Moody's Bank Credit Report Service, as reported in *Polk*, rates long- and short-term debt for banks from 30 countries. There are three listings: alphabetical by company and by country, and region by rating.

ICBA, established in the U.K. in 1978, assesses the risk that a bank or corporation may not meet its unsecured obligations in a timely fashion. ICBA uses financial performance, historical information, and meetings with management to create its ratings. ICBA ratings include ratings for long- and short-term obligations and indicate when a rating was changed and whether it was downgraded or upgraded.

Most organizations that already receive *Polk International Banking Directory* and *Moody's International Manual,* which also includes the ratings, will not need this publication.

European Credit Services

EUROGATE is an online service introduced in late 1992 and designed for the European market. It is produced by a partnership of European companies active in credit assessment, debt collection, and marketing information. It was founded by three major credit information

agencies in Europe: Graydon Holdings, Bürgel Wirtschaftsinformationen (BW), and SCRL, with backing from major credit insurers. Over eight million companies from Germany, Austria, Spain, France, the United Kingdom, the Netherlands, Portugal, and Switzerland are currently included.

Online searching is by gateway from a local European country. Searchers from non-European countries can still gain access through one of the local gateways. Searching is menu driven. Users may select the language of their choice.

A sample report from SCRL, the French credit service, includes the data items listed in Table 8-B.

Exhibit 8-4 shows the credit section of an SCRL report.

TELE INFORM 1. provides descriptive and financial data in French and English on about 2.5 million French firms. Credit data include revenues, profit history, and credit rating. An annual subscription from O.R. Telematique costs 1350 FF. This service provides current information, with historical data back to 1980.

CREDITREFORM-ONLINE from Verband der Vereine Creditreform e.V. has credit information on over

Table 8-B. Data Items in an SCRL Credit Report

Identification	Activities
Siren	Trade class
Address	Position (i.e., manufacturer)
Foundation Date	Activities (i.e., product)
Legal Type	Market
Capital	Franchising
Regulation Number	Trademarks
Town	Branch(es)
Director(s)	
Financial Details (2 yrs.)	**Shareholding**
Turnover	Shareholder(s) and %
Exports	Subsidiaries
Current Result	
Net Result	**Comments**
Employees	
Real Property	**Failures**
Accounts	
Balance Sheet	
Profit and Loss Account	
Additional Data	
Detail of fixed assets	
Profit and Loss Accounts data including subcontracting work and leasing income	
Schedule of debts: within 1 year, 1 -5 yrs, over 5 years	
Sundry information: lease commitments, discounted bills	
VAT collected	

Source: SCRL documentation, December 1992

EXHIBIT 8-4. Credit Section of SCRL Report

S O L V E N C Y

Registered defaults	:	**UNPAID BIL. 10/91**
Privilege(s)	:	**NIL**
Payments	:	**PRES. REGULAR**
Cial Reputation	:	**GOOD**
Banker (s)	:	**BNP AG. MESSINE_PARIS 8E**
		POMMIER PARIS 8E

S C R L   B A C K G R O U N D (over the 12 last months)

CREDIT RATING	:	**STABLE**
Number of requests	:	**12**
Average credit requested	:	**455 000 FRF**
Average credit opinion	:	**230 000 FRF**

S C R L ' S   O P I N I O N

Credit requested	:	**500 000 FRF**
Credit opinion	:	**300 000 FRF**

COTEXPERT
(CREDIT RATING)

2.5-

RANKING

Ranking of the company compared to 344 companies.

RATIO year 91		COMPANY	SECTOR	QUARTILE
Debt ratio (financial debts/income)	%	33.03	186.61	3
Shareholders funds/total liabilities	%	17.83	31.37	2
Liquidity ratio (net current assets—stocks/debts)	U	.68	1.36	1
Clients credit period	D	88.89	64.32	1
Suppliers credit period	D	68.55	74.77	2
Self financing capacity	U	0.05	0.02	3
Net profitability (net result/turnover)	%	-4.92	0.75	1
Value added/turnover	%	57.94	50.06	3

ND: NOT AVAILABLE U: UNIT
D: DAY

Source: SCRL sample report, December 1992. Reprinted with permission from SCRL.

1.7 million joint stock and individual trading companies in Austria, Switzerland, and Germany. In addition to profile information, company records have dates of formation or re-formation, capital, partners, and financial indicators covering capital, obligations, loan payment record, liabilities, and credit rating. The version on DATA-STAR covers 470,000 registered (e.g., AG, GmbH, KG,OHG) companies.

EUROCREDIT, the leading Italian credit company, provides status reports for companies and sole traders for between about $50 and $200 dollars, depending on delivery turn-around time.

United Kingdom Credit Services

ICC provides credit services both on and off line. According to ICC, U.K. credit services include:

- Financial Reports for trading U.K. companies with scores, limits, and credit opinion
- Status Reports for smaller companies with credit limits
- Overviews for fast credit checks with scores and ratios
- Special Premium Services with tailored credit ratings for U.K. and non-U.K. companies; also available in print

The online file, ICC *British Company Financial Datasheets* (F562, ICFF), includes both credit ratios and a credit rating score for a company for up to nine years. This information is also available on the U.K. Factfinder CD-ROM, for 1,800 major U.K. quoted companies. Exhibit 8-5 displays a listing from *British Company Financial Datasheets.*

Infocheck, the company that offers *Global Scan,* is another U.K. credit service. Infocheck reports provide full and snapshot credit profiles on about 420,000 limited companies in England, Scotland, and Wales. Credit evaluation is based on company performance and prospects. Sources of data include filings with the U.K. Registrar of Companies, newspapers, and Infocheck's own confidential database on share debtor information.

Infocheck is available by direct dial to Infocheck. It is also accessible via FT PROFILE Information Online Service, DATA-STAR, and through the local U.K. MercuryLink. The DATA-STAR version had over 285,000 records when it was loaded in May 1993. Much of the information in the Infocheck record is available on the other U.K. company files on DATA-STAR, such as basic directory and financial data, ratio analysis, and shareholders. Exhibit 8-6 is an extract from a record from *Infocheck,* as it is loaded in DATA-STAR.

Infolink calls itself the U.K.'s largest independent credit information organization. The database has data on 3.5 million organizations. Infolink company reports have three-year profit and loss accounts, supplemented with details of credit transactions and defaults. Options for Ltd. companies include a full company search, directors search, and mortgages and charges search, while public notice searches and consumer credit license searches are available for sole traders and partnerships as well. Prices range from £25 for a full search to £4.05 for a consumer credit license search. The data are supplemented by details of credit transactions and defaults. Infolink's U.K. Consumer Service offers credit searches; voter roll searches, including confirmation of residence against the Election Register; and trade references.

Asian Credit Services

Teikoku, discussed in Chapter 6 as a database available online through DIALOG and on DIALOG ONDISC,

---

EXHIBIT 8-5. ICC *British Company Financial Datasheets*

CO PRESCIENT ENGINEERING LTD

RA RATIOS:		920630	910630	900630
Credit Ratios:				
Stock Turnover	R	10.3	11.4	11.0
Credit Period	Days	83.4	60.1	81.6
Liquidity	R	3.1	2.8	2.3
Quick Ratio	R	2.4	2.1	1.6
Current Liabilities/Stock	R	1.4	1.3	1.6

ICC INDUSTRY COMPARISONS
     SIC Code: 3161 (Hand tools and implements).

CS ICC Scores

Based on an analysis of the company's financial performance and a comparison with the industry sector represented by SIC code 3161 (Hand tools and implements), the company scored as follows, out of 100, in the following years:

     1992: 100
     1991: 92
     1990: 82
     1989: 72
     1988: 54
     1987: 51
     1986: 72
     1985: 37
     1984: 52

Source: DATA-STAR search on File ICFF, March 1993. Reprinted with permission from ICC.

EXHIBIT 8-6. Extract from *INFOCHECK (CHCK)* on DATA-STAR

```
        1 CHCK
AN      Company registered number: 02589070 D-S update: 930518
Date report prepared: 09/02/93
Report status: Full report, up to date.
CO      MUNSLOW PRECISION ENGINEERING LIMITED.
AD      WEDNESFIELD
        WOLVERHAMPTON
        WV11 3RG
        UK.
AC      Accounts—DATA-STAR will list 4 years of Accounts
CM      COMMENTS
```

On 12.07.91 the Company changed its name from Positive Manufacturing Ltd. The Company's accounts are for 13 months ending 31.03.92 and are the first on file. These are modified accounts as the company is exempt from certain disclosure regulations, including the requirement to file a profit and loss account, under the 'small company' classification of Sections 246 & 249 of the Companies Act 198 .

Source: Reprinted from *Infocheck* on DATA-STAR, July 1993

---

includes credit ratings as part of each company record. Company records are updated two times a year. Custom reports in English can be ordered through DIALORDER for any Japanese company, not only those in the DIALOG database.

The companies included in *Teikoku* are a subset of those covered in the Japanese language database, *COSMOS 2*. The *COSMOS 2* source has ratings on over 850,000 Japanese companies. It corresponds in part to the Japanese language directory Teikoku Ginko Kaisha Nenkan (*Teikoku Bank and Company Yearbook*). A third product from Teikoku, also in Japanese, is *Company Credit Reports* (CCR). This has credit information on 150,000 companies in the Tokyo metropolitan area. It is available through subscription or a per-report basis.

In the *Teikoku* DIALOG database, companies are rated from A to E:

Rating	Number of DIALOG Companies
A (86-100)	244
B (66-85)	25,604
C (51-65)	130,510
D (36-50)	24,538
E (1-35)	1,266

Source: DIALOG search File 502, March 1993

Teikoku can be used to answer questions about the credit ratings of Japanese companies. Exhibit 8-7 displays a sample report from the *Teikoku* Database on DIALOG.

Taiwan On-line Business Data Services from F.B.R. DATA BASE INC. is reported to contain five files of Asian business and corporate information. One file,

Credit Reports, has descriptive and financial information on approximately 20,000 of Taiwan's largest corporations with profile information, banking references, and data on facilities, assets, capital, and turnover.

RANKINGS AND COMPARISONS

Many international business questions involve rankings or comparisons.

*   Who are the *top* 50 companies in the world?
*   What are the *biggest* companies in Japan?
*   What's the size of the *leading* chemical companies in the world?
*   Who are the *largest* food companies in Europe?

Interpreting Rankings

No matter how the question is phrased, rankings of companies and products are frequently requested. Many directories say they include the "Top 1000" or the "7,500 Largest" companies. But, as we have discussed, using international financial data to make comparisons among companies is risky.

Several years ago, we did some research on company rankings in U.S. sources.[1] We found that databases agreed on company rankings only about 25% of the time. This led us to identify a series of factors that affect rankings: type of company, industry/product classification of companies, and ranking criteria. Not only do all these factors apply to international comparisons, but there are additional problems as well.

EXHIBIT 8-7. Report from *Teikoku* Database on DIALOG

JAPANESE TEXTILE COMPANIES WITH CREDIT RATINGS OF A OR B

Top 10 Ranked by Sales

Company Name	Primary Japanese SIC	Sales (000 $)	Credit Rating
KANEBO LTD	2221	3,841,407	B
TOYOBO CO LTD	2221	2,463,898	B
NISSHINBO INDUSTRIES INC	2221	1,486,105	B
GUNZE LTD	225	1,310,109	B
NITTO BOSEKI CO LTD	2221	1,027,432	B
KURABO INDUSTRIES LTD	2221	1,025,103	B
WACOAL CORP	234	855,185	A
KAWASHIMA TEXTILE MANUFACTURER	2292	671,810	B
FUJI SPINNING CO LTD	2221	626,180	B
SUMINOE TEXTILE CO LTD	2292	610,750	B

Source: DIALOG File 502, searched November 1992. Reprinted with permission from Teikoku.

Type of Company. Is the entity being ranked the parent company, a subsidiary, or both? As we mentioned in our discussion of EC Company Directives, consolidated or group accounting is new to many European countries and is not used uniformly throughout the world. Some company rankings may include only the parent company, while other rankings may have the parent and its subsidiaries. Some sources rank only those companies listed on stock exchanges, while other sources also include government enterprises, privately held companies, and subsidiaries.

Industry Classification. Often, we are seeking rankings for competitive or financial analysis in which we compare companies within a specific industry grouping. What categories are being used and how have companies been assigned to these categories? Europe's Largest Companies (ELC), the publisher of a "Largest" series of books, uses very broad categories, i.e., industrial or trade (wholesale/retail) and service. Actual requests for industry rankings are usually much more specific, and run into the coding problems discussed previously under product listings in Chapter 4.

In most print sources, companies are ranked only by their primary industry or product grouping. If they are major participants in more than one industry, they may be ranked only in the primary industry. For example, a print source may list Philip Morris as the world's largest food company and RJR Nabisco as the world's largest tobacco company. Since Philip Morris was listed as a food company it is not included in the rankings of tobacco companies, although it may be the world's largest tobacco company as well.

Ranking Criterion. A request for a ranking of the "top" companies must include a criterion. Sales or revenue (turnover for U.K.) is frequently used, but rankings may also be of profit or income, market capitalization, or employees. Many non-North American sources use "profit" rather than net income. Keep in mind that there are several measures of profit, such as profit before taxes or after taxes.

Date of the Ranking Criterion. How current are the data used for the rankings? We might expect publications copyrighted in the current year to be using year-old data. However, because companies have different year-end dates and information is not always filed in a timely manner, it is possible that the latest filings for a group of companies could be as much as three years old. For example, a book with a 1993 copyright might have 1990, 1991, or 1992 data or a mix or all three. Some publications, such as those from ELC, generally drop back to the latest year for which most company data are available. The Times 1000 provides the filing date for each of its entries. Some sources put the dates in footnotes while others provide no dates. In countries with stable currencies and in times of economic and social stability the date effect may not be that important.

Foreign Exchange Conversions. When seeking worldwide rankings, some standard unit of currency has to be used, whether it is the U.S. dollar, the British pound, the Japanese yen, or the EC ECU. The information providers have to use some method to convert all of the financial figures into one currency. Several factors should be considered in the calculations.

- **Company Issues:** Date of sales figure (year and year-end)
- **Exchange Rate Issues:** Rate used (current rate, year-end rate, or average rate)

The rate to use in translating sales, net income (profit), or asset figures is based on accounting practices. U.S. standards require one method for income statement items, such as sales or net income, and another for balance sheet items, such as assets. The former use a weighted average for the company's fiscal year, while the latter are translated from local to reporting currency using the exchange rate at the balance sheet date of the foreign entity. The objective is to keep the same financial results and relationships as expressed in the local currency.[2]

When ranking companies within the same country and using data as reported (e.g., French franc or Japanese yen), there is no foreign exchange effect. However, we have documented the effect foreign exchange may have on international rankings.[3] If you need country level information, it is better to find a source published in that country.

Sources from Worldscope, EXTEL, or CIFAR, whose intended audience is financial analysts and accountants, use generally accepted accounting practices in their currency translations. However, some directory sources give undated financial information. If they convert financial information to dollars, the rate of exchange is not given.

In the United States, the standard ranking source is Fortune *Global 500 Industrial,* while in the U.K. it is the *Times 1000.* In fact, there is a general sense of agreement about the largest companies in the world. Table 8-F, later in the chapter, illustrates that anyone's "Top 30" list covers everyone's Top 20.

Some sources, such as the D&B International Online Files should *not* be used to create rankings. These files are designed for company identification and market applications. Attempting to get a "Top" list from D&B *International Market Identifiers* may cause anomalous results.

How do the issues we have been discussing affect the accuracy of rankings? We may be generating a ranking in which the definitions for the characteristics being ranked vary—both for the data item and the product/activity—the date of data collection varies, and the foreign exchange rates do not follow accepted accounting standards. For comprehensive analysis, we recommend using more than one source and reading the notes carefully.

Finding Aids for Rankings

European Business Rankings (Gale—Annual)

In 1992, Gale published the first edition of *European Business Rankings*, which is similar to its U.S. *Business Rankings Annual. European Business Rankings* is com-

piled by Oksana Newman and Alan Foster of the Manchester Business School Library and Information Service to serve as a *quick* guide to rankings appearing in leading *published* sources. About 800 sources, published in 1991 and received by the Manchester Business School Library, were scanned for rankings. Entries are arranged by the same Library of Congress-based subject headings used in the U.S. version.

Each entry includes the "top ten" of a category, the ranking values, remarks, and the source. Each listed company, product, and person is indexed. There is a list of all included publications, but no cross-reference from the publication title to its rankings. For example, it isn't possible to find a list of all rankings from Euromoney publications.

The first edition has obvious limitations. As the authors admit, it is heavily weighted toward the U.K. Many of the company rankings are from such standard sources as *Dun's Europa, Fortune,* and *Business Week.* It relies only on printed sources received by one library and makes no judgment of the quality or reliability of the data. For comprehensive research, this book should be used *only* as a finding aid and not as a source in itself.

Exhibit 8-8 is a sample entry from *European Business Rankings.* The book was published in 1992, written in 1991, and has a table from 1990 with data from 1989.

Researchers can find published rankings directly by using standard online databases such as *PROMT* or

---

EXHIBIT 8-8. Sample Entry from *European Business Rankings*

1156
LARGEST GROUPS IN THE FOOD INDUSTRY
Ranked by: FOOD and DRINKS SALES $bn 1989.
Number listed: 6

1.	Nestle	28.3
2.	Philip Morris Co. Inc	26.4
3.	Unilever	17.2
4.	Mars	8.0
5.	Sara Lee	7.9
6.	BSN	7.0

Source: Euromoney, Special Supplement, June 1990, p.13

Source: *European Business Rankings,* 1992, p. 165. Reprinted with permission from Gale Research.

Textline. Exhibit 8-9 presents a ranking from *PROMT.*

Gale has announced the publication of another book of European business rankings that will contain annotations about the sources rather than the actual rankings. The book will be the second edition of *Sourceguide to Market Share and Business Rankings Tables,* compiled by the London Business School Information Service.

EXHIBIT 8-9. Using *PROMT* as a Finding Aid for Rankings

AN   4328953 PROMT 930329.

SO   Electronics-Times, February 11, 1993, PAGE 5.

TI   Top ten semiconductor equipment manufacturers.

TX   Charting success: For the first time in six years a US semiconductor equipment maker tops the annual worldwide sales ranking produced by VLSI Research . . .

Top ten semiconductor equipment manufacturers

1992 rank	1992 estimated sales(*) ($m)	Company	1991 rank	
1	794	Applied Materials	2	
2	677	Tokyo Electron	1	
3	501	Nikon	3	
4	333	Canon	5	
5	327	Advantest	4	. . .

(*) Includes service and spares

($1 = Y126.1 = DFI 1.767)

THIS IS THE FULL TEXT: Copyright 1993 Morgan-Grampian PLC.

Source: PROMT on DATA-STAR, May 1993. Reprinted with permission from Information Access Company.

SOURCES OF RANKINGS

Sources may be arranged geographically (worldwide, continent, country) or by industry (industrials, service, food and drink) for all companies or just listed companies.

International Ranking Sources

Three popular U.S. business magazines, *Fortune*, *Forbes*, and *Business Week*, all publish "global" rankings in their July issues. Beginning in August 1991, *Fortune* issued a second annual international ranking, this one for service companies. *Forbes* combines industrial, service, and financial companies in one ranking but does not include U.S. companies in its 500 ranking. *Business Week* ranks the top 1,000 companies in the world but uses market capitalization instead of sales. Table 8-C shows the number of companies by country found in *Fortune*, *Forbes,* and *Business Week*.

Fortune Guide to the Global 500 (Time Inc.—Annual)

Fortune has been publishing an international industrial ranking since 1974. The title of the report has gone through a series of name changes, with the 1992 issue entitled, Fortune "Guide to the Global 500" (July 27, 1992). The 500 largest industrial companies in the world are ranked by sales; by performance, for example, profits, increases in sales, returns on sales, and assets; within 26 industries; and within countries. Table 8-D lists the Fortune industry groupings for industrials.

There are eight different categories for the "Service 500." Companies are ranked within their categories by sales/revenues or assets. For example, retail stores are ranked by sales and banks by assets. All companies are also ranked by profit and by shareholder equity. Financial statements through March 1992 are used in the

Table 8-C. Number of Companies by Country in *Fortune*, *Forbes*, and *Business Week* Rankings

	Fortune		*Forbes*	*Business Week*
	Industrial 500	Service* 500		
United States	157	139		383
Japan	119	113	195	245
Britain	43	43	74	110
Germany	33	44	37	39
France	32	31	44	48
Sweden	14	14	14	15
South Korea	13	3	10	
Switzerland	10	14	18	12
Australia	9	8	13	20
Canada	9	22	23	23
Hong Kong		3	3	21
Italy		15	11	18
Netherlands		11	14	15
Spain		16	11	16
Belgium			10	

*South Africa, China, Brazil, and Iran are some of the other countries with companies in the Fortune "Global Service 500."

Source: July and August 1992 issues

Table 8-D. *Fortune* **Industry Groupings for Industrials**

Aerospace	Furniture	Publishing, Printing
Apparel	Industrial & Farm Equipment	Rubber & Plastics
Beverages	Jewelry, Watches	Scientific & Photo Equipment
Building Materials	Metal Products	Soaps, Cosmetics
Chemicals	Metals	Textiles
Computers, Office Equipment	Mining, Crude Oil	Tobacco
Electronics, Electrical Equipment	Motor Vehicles & Parts	Toys, Sporting Goods
Food	Petroleum Refining	Transportation Equipment
Forest Products	Pharmaceuticals	

Source: "Guide to the Global 500," *Fortune* (July 27, 1992)

August 1992 issue. Table 8-E lists the categories used by *Fortune* in the "Service 500."

Table 8-E. *Fortune* **Categories for the Service 500**

Type of Service	Ranking Category	Number of Companies
Diversified Service	Sales	100
Commercial Banks	Assets	100
Diversified Financial Companies	Assets	50
Savings Institutions	Assets	50
Life Insurance Companies	Assets	50
Retailing Companies	Sales	50
Transportation Companies	Revenues	50
Utilities	Assets	50

Source: "Fortune Guide to the Global Service 500," *Fortune* (August 24, 1992)

Forbes "500 Largest Foreign Companies" (Forbes Inc.—Annual)

The companies in the *Forbes* "500 Largest Foreign Companies" are all publicly owned and are ranked by gross revenues. Additional rankings include the 25 largest nonpublic foreign companies, which are headed by China Petroleum, Korea's Samsung group, and the Italian ENI. Large subsidiaries of foreign companies and a separate listing of the U.S. multinationals (*see* Chapter 3) are two other global lists published by *Forbes*. Companies are arranged by country. Forbes also identifies a "Super Fifty," based not only on sales but also on profits, assets, and market value, with Royal Dutch Petroleum heading this list. Raw data for the rankings are supplied by Morgan Stanley International.

Business Week "Global 1000: An Investor's Guide to the Leading International Companies" (McGraw Hill—Annual)

The *Business Week* "Global 1000" measures how a company performs on the stock market, not in the marketplace. For 1992, rankings are by market capitalization,

based on the share price available on May 29, 1992 multiplied by the latest available number of shares outstanding and translated into U.S. dollars using May 29, 1992 exchange rates. Market value may include several classes of stock, price, and yield data and are based on the company's most widely held issue. A list of the top 15 by sales and profits is also included. The "Global 1000" is also compiled by Geneva-based Morgan Stanley Capital International, which tracks 2,500 companies in 22 countries in developed markets.

To show the relative consistency among the rankings for the world's largest companies based on sales, we have in Table 8-F combined the *Fortune* rankings from industrials and service and compared them to several other international ranking sources.

The *Business Week* "Global 1000" rankings illustrate the difference that can occur in rankings based upon a company's stock market performance. The *Business Week* rankings are very much a function of the market on which companies trade. Notice that 8 out of the top 10 *Business Week* companies are U.S., while 6 of the top 10 *Fortune* companies are Japanese. The major differences among *Fortune*, *Forbes*, and *Business Week* can be summarized as follows:

Fortune	All companies worldwide in two separate listings, 500 Industrial and 500 Service, ranked by sales
Forbes	500 largest non-U.S. companies in all industries, ranked by sales; separate report on U.S. multinationals
Business Week	1,000 companies worldwide, ranked by market capitalization

Other national business magazines are publishing their own "500" lists. Some examples include "500 Most Important Companies in Mexico," appearing in *Expansion*; "Les 500 Premiers Groups" in France, Europe, and Central and Eastern Europe, appearing in *Les Echos* and Canada's 500 Largest Corporations in the *Financial Post*.

Table 8-F. World's Largest Companies Ranked in 1992

(1)	(2)	(3)	(4)	(5) T	(6) W	(7) G	(8) E	(9) SALES US $mil	(10) BW MC	(11) BW S
WORLD'S LARGEST COMPANIES (Industrials and Service) from *FORTUNE* July 27, 1992, August 24, 1992										
1	S1	.C. ITOH & CO. *	JP	1	1	2	1	156,967.5	405	1
2	S2	.SUMITOMO	JP	3	2	1	2	150,813.8	252	4
3	S3	.MARUBENI	JP	5	4	4	4	140,674.7	395	3
4	S4	.MITSUBISHI	JP	4	5	5	5	136,267.6	105	6
5	S5	.MITSUI & CO.	JP	2	3	3	3	133,847.7	244	2
6	1	GENERAL MOTORS	US	6	6	6	6	123,780.1	31	5
7	2	ROYAL DUTCH/SHELL	UK/NE	8	11	8	8*	103,834.8	1	8
8	3	EXXON	US	7	7	9	7	103,242.0	3	7
9	4	FORD MOTOR	US	10	8	10	9	88,962.8	45	9
10	S6	.NISSHO IWAI	JP	9	9	7	10	86,446.8	705	10
11	5	TOYOTO MOTOR	JP	11	10	12	12	78,061.3	11	13
12	6	IBM	US	13	12	11	13	65,394.0	10	12
13	7	IRI	IT					64,095.5		
14	S7	.AMERICAN T & T	US	15	13		15	63,314.0	9	
15	8	GENERAL ELECTRIC	US	30	17	15	32	60,236.0	5	
16	S8	.TOMEN	JP	19	16	19	17	60,166.1	308	
17	9	BRITISH PETROLEUM	UK	12	15	13	12	58,355.9	32	14
18	10	HITACHI	JP	17	18	20	18	58,053.3	51	
19	11	DAIMLER-BENZ	GE	16	14	17	16	57,321.3	39	
20	R1	SEARS ROEBUCK	US	18	19	16	19	57,242.4	88	15
21	12	MOBIL	US	14	21	14	14	56,910.0	33	
22	S9	.NICHIMEN	JP	23	28	21	23	49,867.2		
23	S10	.CARGILL	US					49,148.0		
24	13	MATSUSHITA ELECT	JP	22	20	23	21	48,595.0	42	
25	S11	.NIPPON TEL & TEL	JP	25	30		26	48,206.2	2	
26	14	PHILIP MORRIS	US	20	26	18	20	48,109.0	4	
27	15	FIAT	IT	24	23	25	24	46,812.0	177	
28	S12	.KANEMATSU	JP	27	34		27	46,596.5		
29	16	VOLKSWAGEN	GE	21	22	22	22	46,042.2	206	
30	17	SIEMENS	GE	26	31	31	30	44,859.2	41	
31	R2	WAL-MART	US		32			44,289.4	6	
32	18	SAMSUNG	SK					43,701.9	NR	
33	19	NISSAN MOTOR	JP	28	24	29	24	42,905.7	106	
34	20	UNILEVER	UK/NE	29	29	28	28/31	41,262.3	24	
116		COCA COLA	US						7	
152		MERCK	US						8	

Key to Columns:

(1)   Merged *Fortune* ranking based on sales listed in Industrial and Service 500
(2)   *Fortune* ranking in either Industrial or Service
(3)   Company name
(4)   Company headquarters location
(5)   **T**: *Times 1000* 1992-1993
(6)   **W**: Worldscope CD-ROM October 1992
(7)   **G** *Global Companies Handbook, 1992*
(8)   **E**: *Extel* on DIALOG December 31, 1992
        BW: *Business Week,* July 12, 1992
(9)   MC - Market Capitalization rankings
(10) S - Sales ranking
* Name changed to Itochu Corporation (9/92)

Times 1000 (Times Books—Annual)

The *Times 1000* has been a standard source in the U.K. since 1975. Originally the *Times 300*, this is a listing of the world's "leading industrial and financial companies." In addition to seven rankings for the U.K., such as the "top 100" and the "25 largest building societies," the 1992-93 edition has the following tables, plus a company index:

Location	Number of Companies	Ranking
World	50	Industrial Companies
Europe	1000	Turnover(sales)
	50	Profit makers
	50	Capital employed
	50	Market capitalization
	50	Largest takeovers
	25	Banks
USA	100	
Japan	100	
Australia	25	
Hong Kong	50	
Malaysia	50	
Singapore	50	
Thailand	25	
South Korea	25	

Data are tabulated by EXTEL Financial. According to the introduction, the guide can be used to make comparisons of the size of companies in leading industrialized nations, at least in terms of total sales. But users are warned that any attempt to carry comparisons of size beyond this could be of doubtful validity (1992-93, p.9). The introduction also provides users with the following guidelines on what figures are used.

1. Rankings are based on consolidated accounts. Subsidiaries are listed only when parent information is not available.
2. Different measures of profit are used—profit before interest and tax and profit before tax, depending on the accounting standards used. In some countries, reported profits are just enough to cover dividends to shareholders.
3. Different year-end dates have had to be used. Most data are 1991 with nothing after June 30 1992.
4. Exchange rates used are close to individual year-ends.

Tables on South America and the "Rest of the World," which had been included in earlier editions, were discontinued in the latest edition because it was not possible to guarantee the accuracy of the information given.

Regional Rankings

FT500 (Financial Times, 11th ed., February 10, 1993—Annual)

Financial Times publishes an annual survey on the 500 largest companies in Europe, as well as the 500 largest in the U.K., with the daily newspaper. Like *Business Week, FT* uses market capitalization as its measure for identifying the 500. It also has a separate ranking for the top 200 by turnover(sales). The data used in the February 1993 ranking were current to the close of September 1992. The top five *FT* companies were Royal Dutch/Shell, Glaxo Holdings, British Petroleum, Unilever plc/NV, and Nestle. The top five by turnover were Royal Dutch/Shell, Daimler-Benz, IRI, British Petroleum, and Volkswagen.

Financial Times identifies three factors affecting the market capitalization rankings: performance of the company, movement of the company's national stock exchange, and currency fluctuations. *FT* uses market capitalization instead of sales, however, because it "avoids the difference between national accounting standards that bedevil rankings based on profitability and avoids the inconsistencies between industries that undermine rankings by revenues" (p. 2). This method underrepresents French and Italian companies, since many major enterprises are state owned. U.S. dollars in October 1992 are used as the currency for the pan-European rankings. The *FT500* is available for separate purchase directly for the *Financial Times* in London. The 1993 price is £22.

D&B Europa, which is discussed in detail in Chapter 4, includes the top 5,000 companies in Europe ranked by sales in ECUs (excluding banks and insurance companies) in its last volume. Exhibit 8-10 lists the *D&B Europa* top 10. The same companies are in the *Times 1000* top 10, but in somewhat different order.

Companies are also ranked by main (2-digit U.S. SIC Code) industry sectors. A brief example is presented in Exhibit 8-11.

A cross-country exchange rate table, which also serves as a book mark, accompanies each volume.

ELC, Europe's Large Companies, publishes three "Largest" lists distributed in the United States by Dun & Bradstreet. The 1992 titles are listed below with the date they were first published and the number of companies included in the first edition.

Titles	# of Companies	1st ed. Date
Europe's 15,000 Largest Companies	10,000	1982
UK's 10,000 Largest Companies	7,500	1985
Asia's 7,500 Largest Companies	7,500	1985

The European volume covers 16 countries: EC members, Austria, Switzerland, Sweden, and Finland. Headings are in English, German, and French. There are separate rankings for the largest Industrials, Trading

EXHIBIT 8-10. Europe's Top 5,000 Companies Ranked by Sales in ECU (millions) from *D&B Europa*

1993	1992	Company	Country	Sales	Employees	Rank	Vol:	Page
1	1	NV KON. NEDERLANDSE PETROEUM MAATSCHAPPIJ	NL	82.934	57000	140	3	84
2		IRI ISTITUTO PER LA PICOSTRUZIONE INDUSTRI	IT	51.247	407169	2	2	990
3	2	THE BRITISH PETROLEUM CO. PLC	UK	46.467	115250	46	3	726
4	4	DAIMLER-BENZ AG	DE	46.307	381511	5	1	322
5		VOLKSWAGEN AKTIEGESELLSCHAFT	DE	37.195	267009	8	1	886
6	3	FIAT SPA	IT	36.434	288500	7	2	922
7	8	UNILEVER NV	NL	33.070	9800	955	3	135
8	7	UNILEVER PLC	UK	33.004	298000	6	3	1220
9	5	ENI ENTE NAZIONALE IDROCARBURI	IT	32.819	131248	33	2	901
10	9	SIEMENS AKTIENGESELLSCHAFT(KONZERN)	DE	30.796	40600	3	1	803

Source: *D&B Europa*, 1993, vol. 4, p. 43. Copyright © 1993 Dun & Bradstreet, Inc. All rights reserved. Reprinted with permission.

EXHIBIT 8-11. Top Companies in Each Main Business Activity Ranked by Financial Size in ECU (Millions) in *D&B Europa*

2-3 Manufacturing
20 Food and Kindred Products

Rank	Company	Country	Financial Size	Employees	Rank	Vol:	Page
1	UNILEVER NV	NL	33.070	9800	49	3	135
2	UNILEVER PLC	UK	33.004	298000	1	3	1220
3	NESTLE SA	CH	27.272	7000	62	3	406
4	B S N	FR	9.485	46000	10	2	50
5	ALLIED-LYONS PLC	UK	7.637	78743	3	3	661

Source: *D&B Europa*, 1993, vol. 4, p. 185. Copyright © 1993 Dun & Bradstreet, Inc. All rights reserved. Reprinted with permission.

Companies, and Service Companies. In the 1992 edition, service companies were divided into banks, insurance, transport, advertising agencies, hotels and restaurants, and miscellaneous. Companies are ranked by sales, profit, and employees.

Data are presented in spreadsheet format. The Top 500 in Europe are ranked by sales, profit, and employees. For each company, there are 20 columns of data including this year's and last year's rank, sales, profit, assets, equity capital and employees, and sales as a percent of employees, assets, and equity capital. Sales dates are footnoted for discrepancies from the heading data. There is an alphabetical index of companies with their rank and code. The data are also currently available on diskette.

The activity coding system used in ELC publications is the ISIC, the U.N. International Coding system. The list of codes and exchange rate tables are provided in the publication.

Major Sector Rankings: Services

Directory of the World's Largest Service Companies (Moody's Investors Service and the U.N. Centre for Transnational Corporations—Irregular)

The Directory of the World's Largest Service Companies has rankings based on company data and other published data. "Appropriate" measures of size are used for different industries. For example, legal services firms are ranked by number of partners and also number of foreign offices. Airlines are ranked by revenues per passenger kilometers as shown in Exhibit 8-12.

Specific Sector Rankings: Banks

"The Euromoney 500," *Euromoney,* **June issue** (Euromoney Publications—Annual)

Euromoney has been publishing a ranking of the world's largest 500 banks since 1982. The ranking is based on shareholder equity, and includes fiscal date, total assets, and net income for each bank.

Polk World Banking Profile (R.L. Polk & Co.—Every three years)

Listed above as a source of bank credit information, *Polk World Banking Profile* also ranks the 2,000 banks it includes by total assets, total deposits, total income, shareholders equity, return on assets, and return on equity. For each item, the bank is given a world ranking

Exhibit 8-12. *Directory of the World's Largest Service Companies*

The world's 100 leading airlines by revenue passenger kilometers
1988
(millions)

Rank	Firm	Parent company[1]	Home country area	1988 Revenue passenger kilometre	1983 Revenue passenger kilometre	Rank
1	Aeroflot	-	USSR	213,717	176,480	1
2	United Airlines	UAL Corp.	USA	111,184	70,465	2
3	American Airlines	AMRS Corp.	USA	104,216	54,700	3
4	Delta Airlines	-	USA	83,266	43,071	7
5	Continental	Texas Airlines	USA	66,077	14,935	19
98	Japan Asia	-	Japan	1,994	0	80
99	Biman-Bangladesh	-	Bangladesh	1,987	0	91
100	Air Jamaica	-	Jamaica	1,935	1,552	69

Notes: [1]From International Civil Aviation Organization, *Civil Aviation Statistics of the World, ICAO Statistical Yearbook* (Geneva 1988)

Source: Directory of the World's Largest Service Companies, 1990, p.130. Reprinted with permission from Moody's Investors Service.

and a country ranking. For example, in Exhibit 8-13 Union Bank of Switzerland is ranked number 28 in the world for total assets and number 1 in Switzerland for total assets.

Listed Companies

Global Company Handbook (CIFAR—Annual)

Volume 1 of *CIFAR's Global Companies Handbook* has a series of rankings for the companies in the publication, which have been selected by market performance measures. Like the *Business Week* rankings, these are for the investor community.

The first ranking, the CIFAR 500, ranks the world's top financial performing companies measured by "global uniform standards" (p. 1). All companies have been traded for a minimum of three years. The factors used in the ranking are profitability (i.e., earnings growth), financial stability (i.e., quick ratio), growth potential (sales, assets, dividends), and shareholder-related measures (rate of return), all measured using ratios. Different market capitalization requirements were set for six major markets, other developed markets, and emerging markets. Exhibit 8-14 lists the top companies from *Global Company Handbook's* unique ranking system.

A second ranking, Global Country and Industry Rankings of the Leading 7,500+ Companies, is a more usual ranking and includes rankings by sales, assets, net income, market value, and employees. Rankings are worldwide, by industry worldwide, and within a country, as illustrated in Exhibit 8-15.

CIFAR has two unique characteristics for each company.

- **Multinationality Index (MNC):** the degree of geographic diversification of a company based on foreign sales, assets, exports, and subsidiaries; rankings are High, Medium, Low, and Non-MNC
- **Product Diversification Index (DIV):** the degree a company is diversified outside its primary industry and within its primary industry; rankings are again H, M, L and N—not diversified

I/B/E/S International 500 (Lynch, Jones and Ryan—Annual)

I/B/E/S International 500 is a ranking of listed companies of interest to the investor; it lists the 500 international firms expected to earn the most in the coming year. The publication first appeared in 1989. For 1992, *I/B/E/S* forecasted that British Telecomm would be number one, followed by Royal Dutch and Toyota Motor Corporation. U.S. companies are not included in the 500 but a list of the top 10 companies in the world is headed by Exxon, Philip Morris, and General Electric.

Management Today (December 1992)

A listing of interest to investors in Europe appeared in the December 1992 *Management Today*. It is a study by a German professor that ranks the 400 largest European quoted companies (by turnover) plus the 50 largest banks and the 50 largest insurance companies on the following criteria:

Profitability	*Financial Solidity*	*Growth*
Return on equity	Equity as a percent of capital	Annual percent growth of total assets and turnover
Cash flow as a percent of sales	Liquid assets as a percent of total assets	

EXHIBIT 8-13. Extract from *World Banking Profile*

Bank Name (City, Country; Fiscal Yr. End; Pg. No.)	Total Assets U.S.$ (000) (Ranking: World/Country)	Net Income U.S.$ (000) (Ranking: World/Country)	Return on Equity as % (Ranking: World/Country)
Dai-Ichi Kangyo Bank Limited Tokyo, Japan (3/92) (p. 1049)	$426,048,000 1/127/3	$541,000 1635/83	3.26843
The Sakura Bank, Limited Tokyo, Japan (3/92) (p. 1061)	414,387,000 2/2	675,000 19/2	2.90694 1718/94
Sanawa Bank Limited Tokyo, Japan (3/92) (p. 1032)	384,821,000 3/3	767,000 15/1	3.59466 1544/58
Industrial & Commercial Bank of China Beijing, China (12/91) (p. 272)	206,636,646 19/1	2,933,464 1/1	5.72615 907/10
Union Bank of Switzerland Zurich, Switzerland (12/91) (p. 1627)	146,980,678 28/1	719,297 18/1	6.95926 650/55

Published by R. L. Polk & Co., Bank Services Division, 2001 Elm Hill Pike, Nashville, TN 37230-5100 USA, telephone (615) 889-3350. Reprinted with permission.

EXHIBIT 8-14. *Global Company Handbook*, Vol. 1

The CIFAR 500:The World's Top Performing Companies, Measured by Global Uniform Standards by Industry

Sales Growth	Earn Growth	Assets Growth	Div Growth	Div Yield	Shrhdl Return	Industry And Company Name	Country	Rev/ Empl	Debt/ Assets	Quick Ratio	Cash to Mktcap	Mktcap to Equity	Cash to Sales
						Food/Beverages							
80.73	102.16	110.30	27.36	1.95	53.24	Albert Fisher Group	United Kingdom	0.25	56.30	1.79	0.08	3.68	5.99
25.94	49.01	12.54	NM	NM	54.65	Hoko Fishing Co Ltd.	Japan	0.79	99.09	0.49	NM	6.80	NM
90.51	370.19	118.42	NM	NM	38.17	Vons Companies Inc.	United States	0.36	81.53	0.91	0.13	1.49	2.42
27.80	102.36	39.36	28.42	4.20	120.78	Crown Seal Co. Ltd.	Thailand	0.05	54.10	0.43	0.14	3.47	10.53
40.64	413.39	71.79	34.91	1.85	86.98	Saint Louis Groupe	France	0.20	55.22	1.07	0.15	1.79	9.84
31.46	280.01	25.92	175.00	4.21	81.17	Serm Suk Co., Ltd.	Thailand	0.03	65.74	0.16	0.12	3.84	4.99
107.55	89.46	103.43	7.51	4.15	43.11	Eridania Gruppo Ferruzzi	Italy	0.53	86.13	0.33	0.33	1.11	4.81

Source: Global Company Handbook, 1992, p. 20. Reprinted with permission from Center for International Financial Analysis & Research, Inc. (CIFAR).

EXHIBIT 8-15. *Global Company Handbook*
Ranking by Sales by Industry

RANKING LIST 6: TOP INDUSTRIAL COMPANIES BY
SALES (IN MIL OF US$ BY INDUSTRY)

Company	Country	Sales	MNC	DIV
Food/Beverages (Consumer Goods)				
Philip Morris Cos	US	51,169	H	M
Unilever Group	UK/NE	39,783	H	H
Nestle SA	SW	33,714	H	H
Occidental Petroleum	US	21,694	N	H
Pepsico Inc	US	17,803	H	H
Grand Metropolitan	UK	16,048	H	H

Source: *Global Company Handbook*, vol. 1, 1992; rankings list 6, p.15. Reprinted with permission from Center for International Financial Analysis & Research, Inc. (CIFAR).

Number one in the listing is Glaxco, a British company. Other well-known European firms in the listing are Royal Dutch at 76 and British Petroleum at 226.[4]

World Economies

A look at the biggest and the best in the world appears in a 1991 article in *Across the Board*, which is taken from the Conference Board Study "Global Presence and Competitiveness of U.S. Manufacturers." This ranking is of the top 100 economies, which includes both countries and companies. The study was first performed in 1971 by the Library of Congress Congressional Research Service. In 1981, the Congressional Research Service printed an updated version. Between 1981 and 1991, more companies have been added to the list. 1981 had 61 countries and 39 industrial companies. In 1991 the number of industrial companies grew to 47.

To make international comparisons, a purchasing power parity method was used for countries; however, countries such as Russia, for which there is no reliable data, are not on the current list. The company list is arbitrarily limited to manufacturers, which leaves out mega-banks and trading companies. Exhibit 8-16 shows the top 46 economies on the list.

ONLINE/ONDISC RANKINGS

Annual financial figures are released once a year. Therefore, online databases do not have the same advan-

EXHIBIT 8-16. *Across the Board*

THE TOP 100 ECONOMIES
Rankings are based on countries'
gross national products and companies' sales.

#		(000)	#		(000)
1	United States	$5,237,707,000	24	Norway	$92,097,000
2	Japan	2,920,310,000	25	Saudi Arabia	89,986,000
3	Germany	1,272,959,000	26	Indonesia	87,936,000
4	France	1,000,866,000	27	Exxon Corp	86,656,000
5	Italy	871,955,000	28	South Africa	86,029,000
6	United Kingdom	834,166,000	29	Royal Dutch/Shell Gr	85,537,900
7	Canada	500,337,000	30	Turkey	74,731,000
8	China	393,006,000	31	Argentina	68,780,000
9	Brazil	375,146,000	32	Poland	66,974,000
10	Spain	358,352,000	33	Thailand	64,437,000
11	India	287,383,000	34	IBM Corp	63,438,000
12	Australia	242,131,000	35	Toyota Motor Corp	60,443,600
13	Netherlands	237,415,000	36	Hong Kong	59,202,000
14	Switzerland	197,984,000	37	Yugoslavia[sic]	59,080,000
15	Korea	186,467,000	38	General Electric Co	55,264,000
16	Sweden	184,230,000	39	Greece	53,626,000
17	Mexico	170,053,000	40	Algeria	53,116,000
18	Belgium	162,026,000	41	Mobil Corp	50,976,000
19	Austria	131,899,000	42	Hitachi Ltd	50,894,000
20	General Motors	126,974,300	43	British Petroleum	49,484,400
21	Finland	109,705,000	44	IRI	49,077,200
22	Denmark	105,263,000	45	Venezuela	47,164,000
23	Ford Motor Co	96,932,600	46	Israel	44,141,000

Source: *Across the Board*, December 1991, p. 18. Reprinted with permission of The Conference Board.

tage with rankings as they do with other company issues. Many of the company databases are designed as marketing tools to identify companies participating in an industry, and they should not be used for ranking applications.

However, company databases that have financial fields, such as sales or profits, and are retrieved on systems that have numeric sorting, such as DIALOG or, to a limited extent, LEXIS AND NEXIS SERVICES and DATA-STAR, may be used to produce customized rankings. It is important to know both the content and structure of the database before creating ranked lists of companies.

When using a database for rankings, look for the following:

- Can you select companies based on their fiscal year-end dates?
- Are primary industry codes, such as SIC, assigned? Can you rank on segment data?
- If the financial figures are converted into one currency, is the exchange rate or the exchange rate date provided?

The financial CD-ROM products, such as *Worldscope*, Moody's, or the Lotus-based files, are products designed for ranking applications. You may use them to produce your own rankings. In *Worldscope*, the software is easy to use. However, even with *Worldscope*, you are retrieving different year-end dates and consolidated information for the company. Exhibit 8-17 illustrates a user-defined ranking report from *Worldscope*. The ranking in francs differs from the ranking in dollars because of different year-end dates and exchange rates.

In sources providing listed company financials, such as those from EXTEL, Worldscope, or Moody's, companies are ranked based on their *total* sales or turnover, not on the sales from individual product grouping. This creates two other ranking issues—consolidated sales and industry groupings. These are both illustrated by a search on *Extel* on DIALOG (File 500) for the largest tobacco and beer companies in the database. *Extel* includes a series of financials that have been translated into U.K. pounds and U.S. dollars. Companies are assigned multiple SIC codes and sales figures are consolidated. As we can see in Exhibit 8-18, one company can be ranked first in more than one industry and the same sales figure is presented. Also, while that company is ranked first in both these industries, its primary SIC code is for neither. It has been listed as a holding company. Two different user-defined reports have been selected to present the relevant data.

The actual sales figures for the tobacco and beer segments of Philip Morris are reported in *Worldscope* and shown in Exhibit 8-19. However, most countries outside the United States do not require companies to disclose the amount of sales and profit derived from different lines of business. And the major databases have no mechanisms to search on these figures.

One database designed for ranking applications is the *Teikoku Databank of Japanese Companies* (File 502) on DIALOG. Each company record has a ranking by sales within its primary Japanese SIC group. Therefore, *Teikoku* can easily answer questions like the following:

EXHIBIT 8-17. *Worldscope* **Rankings: A Ranking of Publicly Traded French Wine Producing Companies**

The two numbers are in bold to illustrate the difference in rankings if francs rather than dollars had been used.
FRENCH COMPANIES with SIC 2084 (Wines)

A	B	COMPANY NAME	DATE	US SIC CODE	NET SALES (000S)	NET SALES ($000S)	CALCULATED EXCHANGE RATE
1	1	LVMH MOET-HENNESSY LOUI	12/31/91	2084	22036000	4254050	0.193
2	2	PERNOD RICARD SA	12/31/91	2084	15221000	2938414	0.193
3	3	LOUIS VUITTON SA	12/31/90	3111	6798542	1335642	0.196
4	5	COMPAGNIE LA HENIN SA	12/31/91	1479	**4175200**	820260	0.196
5	4	REMY & ASSOCIES	3/31/91	2084	**4418219**	769035	0.174
6	6	TAITTINGER SA	12/31/91	7011	3735030	721048	0.193
7	8	CIE. DES SALINS DU MIDI	12/31/91	2899	1816000	350579	0.193
8	7	MARTELL AND CO. SA	12/87	2084	1831781	300778	0.164
9	9	BERGER SA	12/31/91	2084	782230	151010	0.193
10	10	JEAN CLAUDE BOISSET SA	12/31/91	2084	631742	121958	0.193
11		HENRI MAIRE SA	12/31/91	2084	447649	86419	0.193
12		EXOR SA	01/31/91	6719	293000	58412	0.199

A - Ranked by sales in $US; B - Ranked by sales in Francs

Source: Worldscope ® CD-ROM, October 1992. Reprinted with permission from Worldscope/Disclosure.

EXHIBIT 8-18. Rankings of the Largest Tobacco and Beer Companies Using *Extel* on DIALOG

Largest TOBACCO Companies:

Company COMPANY NAME	(Sales) TURNOVER($000)	Actual Segment Data
PHILIP MORRIS COS INC	56,458,000	<—28,178,000
TOSHIBA CORPN	35,517,000	
B.A.T INDUSTRIES PLC	25,796,000	
GALLAHER LTD	8,734,364	
DALGETY PLC	7,568,513	
BRITISH-AMERICAN TOBACCO	7,533,000	

Largest BEER Manufacturers:

COMPANY NAME	Turnover (Sales) ($000)	Latest Annual Date	PRIMARY UK SIC	Actual Segment Data
PHILIP MORRIS COS INC	56,458,000	31 Dec 91	83962	<- 4,056,000
GRAND METROPOLITAN PLC	15,335,000	30 Sep 91	42701	
BSN	2,718,000	31 Dec 91	41301	
ANHEUSER-BUSCH COS INC	12,634,200	31 Dec 91	83962	
KIRIN BREWERY CO LTD	12,256,000	31 Dec 91	42701	
ALLIED-LYONS PLC	9,222,000	07 Mar 92	42701	
BASS PLC	8,350,000	30 Sep 90	42701	

Source: Extel on DIALOG, December 1992. Reprinted with permission of EXTEL Financial Ltd.

EXHIBIT 8-19. Philip Morris Segment Data Reported in *Worldscope*

PRODUCT SEGMENT DATA - 1991 (000'S U.S. DOLLARS)

	SALES	OPERATING INCOME	ASSETS
Food	28,178,000	2,016,000	31,622,000
Tobacco	23,840,000	6,463,000	8,648,000
Beer	4,056,000	299,000	1,608,000
Financial Services	384,000	178,000	4,538,000

Source: Worldscope ® CD-ROM, December 1992. Reprinted with permission from Worldscope/Disclosure.

- What are the 10 largest software companies in Japan?
- What are the largest Japanese companies that are No. 1 in their SIC group?

Exhibit 8-20 shows records from the *Teikoku Databank* on DIALOG that answer these two sample questions.

CONCLUSION

In this chapter, we have looked at two special aspects of company information: credit information and rankings of companies. We listed some major international, European, and Asian credit services and identified a source

that had a global listing.

Researchers often want lists of companies ranked by some measure of size globally, by geographic region or by industry grouping. There are many underlying data factors that are considerations in global rankings, such as the measurement used, the data of the data for each company, and the foreign exchange conversion rate. Major business magazines publish rankings of international companies. These sources are discussed along with other sources of international, regional, and country rankings. Finally we present online and ondisc sources of rankings and techniques for creating your own ranking.

Reference Hint: Small and medium libraries may be able to answer most of their rankings questions from the

EXHIBIT 8-20. *Teikoku* **on DIALOG**

Example 1: Top 5 software companies in Japan
Search Teikoku using PC=8521 and SR=1:10

Company Name
1. HITACHI SOFTWARE ENGINEERING C
2. NEC KOFU LTD
3. NIPPON STEEL INFORMATION & COM
4. TOYO INFORMATION SYSTEMS CO LT
5. NEC INFORMATION SERVICE LTD

Example 2: Number 1 Japanese Companies in Japan by SIC Code
A. Search for sales >10billion and SR=1

Company Name	Roman. Company Name	Primary Japanese SIC	Sales (000 $)
THE DAI-ICHI KANGYO BANK LIMIT	DAIICHI KANGYO GINKO KK	502	336,227,239
THE NORINCHUKIN BANK	NORINCHUO KINKO	511	311,174,409
C ITOH & CO LTD	ITOCHU SHOJI KK	4011	150,623,611
THE SHOKO CHUKIN BANK	CHUOKINKO SK	5214	104,363,593
JAPAN FINANCE CORPORATION FOR	KOEI KIGYO KINYUKOKO	504	100,644,678
THE ZENSHINREN BANK	ZENKOKU SI RENGOKAI	5212	90,140,538
TOYOTA MOTOR CORPORATION	TOYOTA JIDOSHA KK	3711	70,489,577**
SMALL BUSINESS FINANCE CORP	CHUSHOKIGYO KINYUKOKO	5215	59,080,814
NIPPON LIFE INSURANCE COMPANY	NIHON SEIMEI HOKEN SO	551	57,775,206
* NOT KNOWN	KOKUMIN KINYUKOKO	5216	56,620,600

* About 120,000 companies do not have English names (*see* Chapter 3).
 All sales dates 3/92 except: ** 6/92
U.S. dollars are calculated by DIALOG and are for informational purposes only.

Source: *Teikoku Databank* on DIALOG, December 1992. Reprinted with permission from Teikoku.

Fortune international lists or the *Times 1000*. Use Gale's *European Rankings*, despite its limitations, as a finding aid to special issues in your own or other libraries. Be aware of the limitations of all of these tools. If you are using ranking sources not mentioned here, be sure to read the introduction of the source to make sure that the compiler has addressed the issues we have discussed.

ADDITIONAL SOURCES OF INFORMATION

Further Reading

"Monitoring Financial Markets, Company Financial Information Services," *The Financial Times* (August 22, 1990). The various credit services available in the U.K. are described by this article.

Tursman, Cindy. "Eastern European Credit Issues Made for Top-Notch Conference in Prague," *Business Credit 94* (January 1992):18-19.

This article describes the first Foreign Credit Interchange Bureau-National Association of Credit Management conference in Prague, Czechoslovakia, October 14-15, 1991. The conference had 130 attendees.

Company Addresses

DUNSPRINT WORLDWIDE
Dun & Bradstreet Europe Ltd.
Holmers Farm Way
High Wycombe, Bucks
HP12 4UL
United Kingdom
Phone: 0494 422000
FAX: 0494 422260

GLOBALSCAN
28 Scrutton St.
London EC2A 4RQ
United Kingdom
Phone: 071-377 8872
FAX: 071-247 4194
Telex: 893530 INFO

INFOCHECK GROUP Ltd.

Godmersham Park, Godmersham Nr. Canterbury
Kent CT4 7DT
United Kingdom
Phone: +44 227 813000
FAX: +44 227 813100

SCRL

5 Quai Jayr
B.P. 9063-69255 Lyon Cedex 09
France
Phone: 33 72 20 10 00
Telex: 330903 SCRL F

ICC Information Group Ltd.

Field House, 72 Oldfield Rd.
Hampton Middlesex TW12
2HQ
United Kingdom
Phone: 081 783 1122
FAX: 081 783 0049

Infolink Ltd.

Coombe Cross
2-4 South End
Croyden CRO 1DL
United Kingdom
Phone: 081-686 7777
FAX: 081-680 8295

Telematique

7, rue de Sens
Rochecorbon, F-37210 Vouvray
France
Phone: 047 626262
FAX: 01 48973425

Creditreform-Datenbank-Dienste

Verband der Vereine Creditreform e.V.
Hellersbergstr. 12 D-4040 Neuss-1 Germany

Teikoku Databank Ltd.

5-20, Minami Aoyama 2-Chome
Minato-ku, Tokyo 107
Japan
Phone: 03 34044311

Taiwan On-line Business Data Services from F.B.R.

DATA BASE INC.
9-16 Nan Kan Hsia, 15 Lin, Nan Kan Village
Lu Chu Hsiang, Tao Yuan County
Taiwan
Phone: 886 (3) 326 2911
FAX: 886 (3) 326 2900

NOTES

1. Ruth A. Pagell and Michael Halperin, "Whose Top 20?," *Database* (1987).
2. Ruth A. Pagell, "It's Greek to Me! Exchange Rate Translations and Company Comparisons," *Database* (February 1991).
3. Ruth A. Pagell, "What's for Dinar: Foreign Exchange Rate Data Sources," *Database* (December 1990).
4. Europe's Top 500: Why Germans Like the Best of British," *Management Today* (December 1992): 38-52.

PART III
Marketing

CHAPTER 9
International Marketing:
Issues and Sources

TOPICS COVERED

1. Approaches to International Marketing
2. Environmental Scanning
3. Sources for Market Information
4. The International Four P's
5. International Marketing of Services
6. Franchising
7. Sources of International Marketing Information
8. Conclusion
9. Selected Articles on International Marketing
10. Notes

MAJOR SOURCES DISCUSSED

- *Social Indicators of Development*
- *Foreign Economic Trends*
- *Overseas Business Reports*
- *European Marketing Data and Statistics*
- *International Marketing Data and Statistics*
- Euromonitor Directories of Marketing Information Sources
- Washington Researchers Guides to Company and Industry Information

---

Companies must learn to operate as if the world were one large market—ignoring superficial regional and national differences.[1]

The 1989 Pontiac LeMans was made in eight different countries.

In order to sell ice cream in Hungary a German company had to give free refrigerators to kiosks and gas stations.

International sales are a vital part of the global economy. The value of world trade is growing twice as fast as world GNP. Although 50% of all world trade is accounted for by the Triad (the U.S., Europe, and Japan), companies in countries all over the world are looking for ways to do business beyond their borders.

All companies require planning and research before embarking on marketing abroad. However, the information needs of a small business trying to sell its product overseas are different from the large corporation that is developing an international marketing strategy. Smaller companies and new entrants into the international marketing arena are often concerned with information and issues related to exporting.

Our discussion of international marketing is divided into four parts.

1. International Marketing Concepts and Resources
2. Market Research Reports, Market Share, and Demographics
3. Advertising, Media, and Direct Marketing
4. Exporting and Importing

According to Vern Terpstra, international marketing is finding out what customers around the world want and satisfying those wants better than other domestic or international competitors.[2] International marketing research involves many of the same issues and resources discussed in previous chapters. In our home countries, research for marketing requires primary as well as secondary sources. Because primary sources are often unavailable outside their country of origin, researchers must rely on the secondary sources discussed in these chapters.

APPROACHES TO INTERNATIONAL MARKETING

Various definitions of the international firm, based on organizational and financial characteristics, are presented in Chapter 3. What constitutes an international firm from a marketing perspective? The list below presents some of the scenarios.

- **Export Mode:**
  Manufacture at home; use an intermediary to market abroad
  Manufacture at home; market abroad directly
- **Import Mode:**
  Manufacture abroad; sell at home
  Distribute goods manufactured abroad
- **International Mode:**
  Produce abroad; sell abroad
- **Corporate Affiliation Mode:**
  Joint venture between domestic and foreign companies
  Domestic company invests in a foreign firm
  Foreign firm invests in a domestic firm
  Domestic firm licenses a foreign firm
  Domestic firm issues franchise to foreign franchisee

An Export Scenario

Described below is an American-Russian export project announced in June 1990.

A Pennsylvania company builds steel-framed modular homes, equipped with American appliances and saunas. It ships the homes to suburban Moscow with all the required parts for assembly. Included with the shipment are three American assemblers. The homes are part of a joint venture between a Connecticut firm and the Russian cooperative Rosinka to provide a planned townhouse community for Western executives working in Moscow.[3]

The mode in which a company produces and distributes its products or services determines how it is described. For example, if a company manufactures abroad and markets within the U.S., it may be described as "foreign." If, however, it is operating in multiple markets, than it is described as "international."

There are different levels of "international." If a company operates in several countries, adjusting its products and practices to each, it is described as "multinational." Michael Porter refers to these companies as "multi-domestic."[4] If a company, such as Sony or Coca Cola, offers a standardized product across all markets it is described as a "global" company. Marketing in the 1990s is moving toward a global perspective. "International" marketing has been based on differences among consumers in regional and national markets; "global" marketing assumes similarities among consumers in regional and national markets.

According to marketing theory, a key decision for the larger company is where to operate on the global marketing continuum. In order to make these decisions, the corporation needs to gather a large amount of data. The major steps in information gathering lead from macro-economic analysis of the world economy to developing a specific marketing plan for the firm. We will look at these steps and the information needed for the decisions.

Step 1:   General Information—External Environment—World Economy

Step 2:   Country Information—Economic Environment—Country Economy

Step 3:   Specific Information—Market Environment—Industry Economy

Step 4:   The Marketing Plan

ENVIRONMENTAL SCANNING

World Economy

The first step for every company should be to perform macroeconomic research. The global researcher is concerned with general issues about the movement of goods between countries and must answer the following questions:

- What goods does the country trade and to whom does it trade them?
- What is the country's attitude toward trade?
- To what international trade agreements is the country a party?
- How stable is the country's currency?
- What is the global influence of the home country?

Macroeconomics is concerned with aggregate data for a country, such as total population or national income. It analyses the overall economic activity of a country, not the activity of individual companies, industries, or segments of the population. The data sources for this macro-level research are described in Chapters 13 and 15 on economics and foreign trade.

Economic Environment: Domestic Economy of Host

The economic and cultural characteristics of the host country have been referred to as "uncontrollables." These are the conditions with which companies planning to undertake international marketing must contend. Whether the company decides that the country is not suitable as a host, requires adaptation, or can be addressed with standardized marketing factors, will result from collected and analyzed data.

The economic features of the potential host country can be divided into several categories.

1. Market Size
2. Market Potential
3. Market Resources
4. Market Activity
5. Infrastructure
6. Urbanization

Market Size—Population Size and Distribution.
While the Triad—United States, Europe, and Japan—dominates the world trading market, there are many other potential markets. The United Nations had 178 members in September 1992 and counted 200 "political entities." A global company such as Singer sells sewing machines in 155 countries.

Population is the most obvious indicator of market size. According to the World Bank, there were 131 countries with populations greater than one million in 1992. Before the breakup of the Soviet Union, half the world's population lived in 10 countries, while one-third lived in countries with fewer than 10 million people.

Age distribution is another market indicator. Statistics show that 40% of the population of developing countries is under age 15, but only 20% of the population in industrial countries is under 15. Table 9-A illustrates the aging of the population in the European Community.

Table 9-A. EC Population by Age Group (%)

	0-19	20-59	>=60
1965	32.4	51.2	16.4
1990	25.5	54.9	19.6
2015	21.1	53.8	25.1

Source: Europe in Figures, 3rd ed., 1992, p. 85

Population density and distribution make up a third indicator of market size. There are, for example, 1,750 people per square mile in Bangladesh, but only 7 people per square mile in Canada, with most of Canada's population concentrated along the U.S. border.

Market Potential—Income Factors. Market potential research seeks to discover how many people in a country are able to buy a product or service.

Per capita income, such as disposable income or GDP per person, is one way of measuring market potential. Other measures use the family or the household as the unit of measurement. How comparable are such measurements among countries? In many countries, the definitions of "family" or "household" will be different from U.S. definitions. The accuracy of official economic statistics become suspect if a country has a large underground economy or if many "free" government services are provided to the population.

In addition to per capita measures, total GNP/GDP and total population are also important for understanding a market. A country with a large population and low per capita income, such as India, will have a larger number of people in more affluent segments than a small rich country like the United Arab Emirates. Table 9-B compares population and GDP per capita for India and the United Arab Emirates.

Table 9-B. Population and GDP Per Capita for India and the United Arab Emirates

	INDIA	UNITED ARAB EMIRATES
Population	850 million (1990e)	1.629 million (1991e)
GDP	$222.730 billion (1987)	$23.836 billion (1988)
GDP per Capita	$278 (1987)	$15,879 (1988)

Source: Extracted from *ABC/Clio Kaleidoscope,* 1993, on LEXIS AND NEXIS SERVICES

Income distribution measurements should be used in conjunction with the income figure. A study conducted in many countries on the relationship between the percent of income held by the richest 40% of the population and the country's per capita GDP showed no relationship.[5]

One source of income distribution figures is *Social Indicators of Development (SID),* an annual published by the World Bank. For example, a non-Spanish company planning to market a summer camp to Spanish parents could use *SID* to find income distribution figures for Spain. *SID* shows that the top 10% of Spanish households hold 25% of the income, the top 20% have 40% of the income, and the bottom 40% have only 19% of the income. This leaves the middle class (the middle 40%) with 41% of the income. The most recent GNP per household in Spain is $9,150 compared to an EC average of $18,840. Exhibit 9-1 shows that over the past generation a slight movement toward a more equitable income distribution has taken place in Spain.

Economist Intelligence Unit's (EIU) *Country Profiles* and *Country Reports* and the International Trade Administration's (ITA) *Market Reports* sometimes include distribution data. A few individual countries publish their own statistics. For example, a rich source of general market-related statistical data is the annual *Report on the Survey of Personal Income Distribution in Taiwan Area of the Republic of China.* This government source has income distribution and average disposable income by household by quintile, as well as regional data and household ownership of products. The 1991 edition of the *Report* can, for instance, tell us that there are 136.68 motor bikes owned per hundred households, when the head of the household is a laborer from the Taiwan area.

EXHIBIT 9-1. Extract from *Social Indicators of Development*

Social Indicators of Development 1990
Spain

	Unit of measure	25-30 years ago	15-20 years ago	Most Recent Estimate (MRE)	Same region/income group
					High income
INCOME AND POVERTY					
Income					
GNP per capita (mre1989)	US$	700	2,700	9,150	18,840
Total household income					
Share top 10% households	"	29	28	25	"
Share top 20% households	"	46	44	40	"
Share bottom 40%	"	17	17	19	"
Share bottom 20%	"	6	6	7	"

Source: *Social Indicators of Development*, 1990, p. 287. Reprinted with permission from the World Bank.

Finally, the sales of some goods are not related to income as witnessed in the worldwide appeal of Coke and Pepsi.

The Market Intensity Index, which measures the richness of the market or the degree of concentrated purchasing power it represents, is calculated by Business International. The world value is set at 1.00. In 1989, the North American index was 11.85, the EC index 8.37, and the Japanese index 10.43. The index for Asia as a continent was .85. This index appears in BI's annual *Indicators of Market Size*, which has been published for over 30 years.

Market Resources—Economic Geography. Topography, climate, and the presence of natural resources are all important market factors, especially in developing countries. The U.S. Department of Interior publishes reports on mineral resources worldwide in the Minerals Yearbook. The country reports mentioned in Chapter 13 or any encyclopedia provide basic information on a country's economic geography. For example, the Walden Reports on LEXIS AND NEXIS SERVICES have sections for both "Geography and Climate" and "Raw Materials and Natural Resources."

Market Activity—Agriculture vs. Industrial vs. Service. In evaluating a country's potential, the relationship among the three economic sectors and the rate of change that is occurring is another market indicator. The usual pattern of development is agriculture to industry to service.

Infrastructure. The business infrastructure will have serious implications for the distribution of goods or services. Data on the following aspects of the infrastructure are often needed:

- Modes of transportation to move goods
- Communications: telecommunications, fax
- Energy: supply and cost
- Commercial Infrastructure: banks, insurance, advertising agencies, and market research support services
- Technology: computers, networking, robotics

Urbanization. The degree of urbanization is another measure of a country's potential demand for goods and services. Highly urbanized countries usually have a higher per capita income. In Thailand, the 1989 per capita income in Bangkok was $3,700, while in the rural Northeast, it was $470.[6]

Some examples of the movement toward urbanization are presented in Table 9-C. For example, in 1970, 37.17% of the world's people lived in urbanized areas. This figure was 42.71% in 1990 and is projected to be 60.45% by the year 2025. Table 9-C shows selected urbanization patterns by world, regions, and a country.

Cultural and Lifestyle Data

Serious marketing mistakes have been made when companies have failed to consider the lifestyles and culture of the countries to which they market. For example, one U.S. firm introduced cake mix into Japan with an advertising campaign saying it was as easy as making rice. Japanese housewives take pride in their rice and do not perceive it as easy to prepare.

When seeking information about a country's culture and lifestyles, researchers should consider these factors:

1. Material culture
2. Language
3. Education

Table 9-C. *Prospects of World Urbanization*

	Percent Urbanized				
	1970	1980	1990	2000	2025
World	37.17%	32.31%	42.71%	46.65%	60.45%
Europe	66.52%	70.25%	73.24%	75.98%	82.23%
Romania	41.85%	48.14%	50.53%	53.19%	60.92%
Lesser	25.49%	29.31%	32.99%	39.51%	56.93%
Developed Regions					

Source: UN *Prospects of World Urbanization*, pp. 7, 171

4. Religion
5. Ethics and values
6. Social organization

Material Culture. Material culture includes technology, manufacturing processes, and durable goods ownership. Manufacturing processes in developing countries are labor intensive. The availability of electricity, refrigeration, and stoves is related to the manufacturing process, with the availability of media, storage facilities, and transport related directly to the marketing function.

Language. Language affects many aspects of marketing, in particular brand names, packaging, and promotion. The importance of language on marketing is discussed throughout the following chapters.

Education. Education levels and systems are indicators of the quality of the potential work force. In many countries, learning is by rote. Some countries have good systems of technical education. Companies have been interested in the former Eastern European countries as sites for foreign ventures because of the availability of a well-educated labor force. Education is also an important factor in analyzing the potential consumer.

Religion. Religion affects behavior well beyond traditional holidays and well-known consumption taboos. For example, Strohs developed nonalcoholic beer for the Saudi Arabian market, where the large Muslim majority of the population is forbidden by their religion to consume alcohol. Social structure, such as castes and the role of women, is often related to religious practices. Religion plays an important role in many societies. For example, while U.S. researchers find little readily available information about U.S. religious behavior, researchers on religious behavior in Thailand can use the *Report of the Cultural Activity Participation and Times Use Survey 1990*, which contains primarily data about Thai religious activities.

Ethics and Values. Ethics and values vary; many countries, for instance, view selling as a suspect occupation. Companies developing sales forces in these countries have to be prepared to offer incentives to workers. Officials in some countries expect "incentives"

to facilitate a deal, an activity that is illegal under U.S. law.

Social Organization. Social organization includes the composition of the family unit, family compounds, neighborhoods, or tribes. In addition, every culture has its special interest groups defined by religion, occupation, and recreational lifestyles. Class, still important in many cultures, age, and, again, the role of women are all lifestyle factors that need to be measured.

Political and Legal Environment: Home, Host, and International

Even if the economic and social conditions in a country are right for a venture, certain political issues must be addressed. These issues include the general political climate of the country and its prevailing system of laws and regulations.

Political Climate. How compatible is a company's activities with the interests of the host country? How important is national sovereignty? If a product is too important to national interests, it may not be left in the hands of foreigners and may be nationalized. *The Walden Country Reports* from Walden Publications are a good source for lists of the largest nationalized companies in a country and their primary industries. *The Walden Country Reports* are also on LEXIS AND NEXIS SERVICES.

Another aspect of political climate is the stability of the government and an assessment of the political risk associated with doing business in the country. Some sources of political risk are described in Chapter 13.

The relationship between the host country and the home country is another factor effecting assessment of political climate. Are the two countries friendly? Do they belong to the same treaty organizations? If your home country is Switzerland, your ability to function successfully in the international arena is very different than if your home country is Cuba.

Laws and Regulations. The effect of a country's legal environment on international marketing practice is similar to the effect of a country's laws on accounting practice, discussed in Chapter 2. Some countries, such as the U.S. and the U.K., are common law countries; the countries on the European continent, such as France or Germany, are code law countries. Legal trade restrictions may take the form of tariffs, currency restrictions, exchange rate controls, and operational restrictions, such as percent of foreign ownership or production quotas. Other legal considerations are patents, trademarks, brands, and packaging and labeling regulations.

In the U.S., there are export controls on destinations and products, Internal Revenue Service rulings on transfer prices, and antitrust considerations for acquisitions, joint ventures, or marketing agreements that affect a company's action in the U.S. or abroad.

SOURCES FOR MARKET INFORMATION

The Economist Intelligence Unit's *Country Profiles* and *Country Reports,* or the *Walden Country Reports* provide current information about many of the social, political, and legal issues relating to marketing. We describe these reports in Chapter 13.

More specific business applications are found in Business International's *Investing, Licensing and Trading* (both in print and online through the LEXIS AND NEXIS SERVICES) and the IMF's *Exchange Arrangements and Restrictions*. The publications of international banks and accounting firms are another source. An example is the series by Price Waterhouse entitled *Doing Business In [Country]*

The U.S. government has a wide range of sources. A summary of each is offered in the *Basic Guide to Exporting*. These government sources include export statistics, country reports, and industry reports. Many are now available on the *National Trade Data Bank*, the Commerce Department's widely promoted CD-ROM, or from individual reports that can be purchased from US&FCS (U.S. & Foreign Commercial Services) District Offices.

Two U.S. government country level series used widely by marketers are *Foreign Economic Trends and Their Implications for the United States (FET)* and *Overseas Business Reports (OBR)*.

Foreign Economic Trends (U.S. Department of Commerce)

*FET*s cover a wide range of countries, are updated on a regular basis, and contain country level economic data. While there is no standardized format, all *FET*s present key economic indicators and have a section on "Opportunities for U.S. Exports" that is reprinted in

commercial export sources, such as the *Official Export Guide* and the *Exporters Encyclopaedia*.

The *FET* for Thailand from January 1993 is typical. It included an overview of the political situation, the macro-economic situation, a review of the major sections of the economy, income distribution, investment opportunities, and sources of information.

Overseas Business Reports (U.S. Department of Commerce—Irregular)

Although they include a wealth of information, *OBR*s cover only a few countries and are updated infrequently. Only 18 *OBR*s were issued in 1992. As with the *FET*s, there is no standard format. For example, the Table of Contents from "Marketing in the Philippines," *OBR* 92-02 (superseding 87-06) listed the following topics:

I.	The Land and the People
II.	Distribution and Sales Channels
III.	Business Forms Suitable for Foreign Entities and Other Modes of Entry
IV.	Transportation, Utilities, and Living Conditions
V.	Advertising and Research
VI.	Regulatory Agencies
VII.	Trade Regulations
VIII.	Investment in the Philippines
IX.	Labor and Social Legislation
X.	Guidance for Business Travelers
Appendix I.	Multilateral Lending Institutions
Appendix II.	US&FCS's Broad Role in the Philippines

The *OBR* will answer many questions relating to a country's marketing infrastructure. In addition, it has specific marketing background and information, including names of local market research firms and the availability of advertising media. Though prepared by a U.S. government agency, the information in the *OBR*s is of value to anyone interested in doing business in the country. In addition to print distribution, *FET*s and *OBR*s are part of the "Market Report" series on the *National Trade Data Bank* CD-ROM. They can also be searched through LEXIS AND NEXIS SERVICES' International Libraries.

The United Nations, the World Bank, and the International Monetary Fund publish a wealth of data useful for marketing. Other sources of valuable information are publications from intergovernmental organizations, such as the Organization for European Economic Cooperation and Development (OECD), the European Community (EC), the Food and Agricultural Organization (FAO), the International Labor Organization (ILO), and the General Agreement on Tariffs and Trade (GATT). Many of these sources are described in Chapter 13.

Additional sources of marketing information can be found in the publications of the following types of groups and organizations:

- Business and Trade Associations
- Chambers of Commerce
- National Foreign Trade Council (association of American companies doing business abroad)
- Foreign Trade Associations (at least 50 in the U.S.)
- Service Organizations (banks, transportation companies, accounting firms, and advertising firms)

Gale's *World Business Directory* lists World Trade Centers in each country. The World Trade Centers Association Inc. is an international organization of trade service and facility providers with locations worldwide. These centers are designed to encourage international trade and provide information on business opportunities.

THE INTERNATIONAL FOUR P'S

Once a company has decided *where* to operate (the market), it must then determine *what* (product) to offer to *whom* (the consumer). Although internal company information and policy play the most important role in creating the marketing plan for the four P's (product, price, place, and promotion), secondary data are also consulted.

Product

A product can be described by size, shape, color, special features, and options. Listed below are some of the features most affected by international marketing.

1. Adaptation
2. Brands
3. Labeling
4. Warranties
5. Service
6. Product Life Cycle

Adaptation. A company can sell the same product worldwide, make minor or major adjustments, or develop different products for each country. Coke is an example of a global brand with minor adjustments to local taste. For example, Thai coke is sweeter than U.S. coke. Luxury goods such as Rolex watches are the same worldwide. Some beer, such as Heineken, is available worldwide, but almost every country has its own brand of local beer such as Kloster in Thailand or Zagorka in Bulgaria.

Brands. Brands identify and differentiate a product or service, communicate a message to the consumer, and are a piece of legal property. Brands are treated as assets on balance sheets (goodwill) and are important in merger and acquisitions valuations.

Brands that are successful in one market are increasingly likely to have appeal to consumers internationally because of:

- Improved communications
- Increased travel
- Greater use of English
- Similarity of consumer tastes
- Impact of television

International brands provide cohesion to international companies. Local brands may fragment the international company. Even small companies in niche markets can be successful using a global brand name, for example Crabtree & Evelyn.

Brands also fall into the category of international property rights along with trademarks, copyright, and patents. Many sources use the words "brand" and "trademark" interchangeably. The trademark is a distinctive word or symbol placed on a product or service to identify it. The trademark consists of two parts, the name (brand) and the physical design that appears on the product. In the U.S., trademarks are registered with the U.S. Patent and Trademark Office or a state government. Until 1989, a trademark could only be registered in the United States after it had been on the market. Now a trademark may be registered with an "intent to use." In most other countries a brand name itself can be registered, even if it is not used. There is a cost to register a brand in each country.

Kodak is an example of a trademark that is registered internationally. Kodak machines and processes are patented, Kodak artwork on packages is protected by copyright, and the shape of Kodak containers may be protected by design trademark.

The multinational company has to weigh the costs of registering its brands in many countries against the threat from pirates who will register it themselves. Before mid-1991, Indonesian companies could legally register trademarks that were well-known outside Indonesia for themselves.

World's Greatest Brands (Interbrand, Wiley, 1992)

World's Greatest Brands tracks 1,000 leading brands in the U.K., U.S., France, Benelux, Switzerland, Scandinavia, Canada, Australia, New Zealand, Hong Kong, and Japan. Brands are selected based on their leadership, stability, trend, and the markets in which they operate.

World's Greatest Brands identifies the top 10 brands in the world based on its own criteria, incorporating the qualities for inclusion listed above plus other factors such as the internationality of the brand and its legal protection through trademark or common law. An overall score is computed for each brand. Each industry grouping lists the top companies with their rankings within the industry and information about the brand.

Advertising Age's issue on world brands based on agency is discussed more fully in the advertising section below.

International Brands and Their Companies (Gale, 3rd ed., 1992-93)

This is the international companion to *Brands and Their Companies*, formerly titled *Gale Trade Names Dictionary*. First published in 1989 as *International Trade Names Dictionary*, this nonauthoritative source is designed for the personal user. Information comes from other published sources, not government offices. There is at least one brand from 130 countries worldwide, including Eastern Europe. Arrangement is alphabetical by brand name with cross-references to the company marketing the product and its address.

The primary role of both *International Brands* and its U.S. counterpart is to locate the company producing a consumer brand. However, it may serve the international marketer as a preliminary guide to trade names already in use.

The electronic versions of *International Brands and Their Companies* and *Brands and Their Companies* are on DIALOG as part of File 116, *Trade Names Database*. An entry includes the tradename, product, company, company address and phone number, and the source publication.

The *Trade Names Database* can be used to answer such questions as:

- Are there any products from the former Soviet Union with international brands?
- What unique toothpaste brands are sold in South East Asia?

Neither the print nor the online source answers this question:

- What company owns the rights to the shampoo Timotei?

Trademarkscan, a trademark of Thomson & Thomson, has files on DIALOG for Canada (127) and the U.K. (126) as well as the U.S. federal (226) and state files (246). The U.S. files are available as a DIALOG ONDISC CD-ROM. The databases display, for those with the proper software, the actual design as well as identifying the company. Any trademark that is officially registered in the U.S., U.K., or Canada, regardless of the home country of the registrant, is listed. *Trademarkscan* can answer the following questions:

- What Thai foods are registered in the U.S.?
- What are the registered trademarks for Canadian toothpaste?
- What company owns the rights to the shampoo Timotei?

A record includes the name and description of the design; product classification; status, from pending through abandoned; name and address of the applicant; registration in the country of origin; dates it was used; where it is used; legal representative in the U.K. or Canada; and registration number and type. Exhibit 9-2 displays a record from the U.S. federal file of *Trademarkscan.*

Inpadoc/Family and Legal Status Database (International Patent Documentation Center, Vienna, DIALOG File 345)

Inpadoc contains a listing of patents issued in 55 countries and patenting organizations. *Inpadoc* gives the title, inventor, and assignee for most patents. In addition, this file brings together information on priority application numbers, countries and dates, and equivalent patents (i.e., patent families) for patents issued by the 55 countries and organizations. Also, this file contains legal status information of patents from 10 countries.

Derwent World Patents Index (Derwent Publications, Ltd., DIALOG, Files 350, 351)

Derwent World Patents Index provides access to information from almost 12 million patent documents, giving details of over three million inventions from 33 patent-issuing authorities. Each record in the database describes a single "patent family" containing the data from the original "basic patent," as well as equivalent patents. Patent coverage begins in 1963, although the dates covered vary by country and by subject.

JAPIO (Japan Patent Information Organization, DIALOG File 347)

This database is based on the print *Patent Abstracts of Japan* and represents the most comprehensive English language access to Japanese patents. The file contains approximately four million records from October 1976 to the present. Abstracts are provided for applications originating in Japan.

Chinese Patent Abstracts in English (Patent Documentation Service Center, People's Republic of China, DIALOG File 344)

Chinese Patent Abstracts in English is produced by the Patent Documentation Service Center of the People's Republic of China. The file includes all patents published in the People's Republic of China since April 1,

---

EXHIBIT 9-2. *Trademarkscan—U.S. Federal* **(File 226)**

04304873 DIALOG FILE 226: TRADEMARKSCAN(R)-FEDERAL
CHAOBAN <COMMON PEOPLE> STYLIZED LETTERS
INTL CLASS: 29 (MEATS & PROCESSED FOODS)
U.S. CLASS: 46 (FOODS & INGREDIENTS OF FOODS)
STATUS: REGISTERED
GOODS/SERVICES: CANNED VEGETABLES AND FRUITS, PRESERVED
VEGETABLES AND FRUITS, DRIED VEGETABLES AND FRUITS,
PROCESSED FRUITS AND VEGETABLES, AND COCONUT MILK
SERIAL NO.: 74-304,873
REG. NO.: 1,760,093
REGISTERED: MARCH 23, 1993
FIRST USE: JUNE 15, 1983 (INTL CLASS 29)
FIRST COMMERCE: JUNE 15, 1983 (INTL CLASS 29)
FILED: AUGUST 12, 1992
PUBLISHED: DECEMBER 29, 1992
ORIGINAL APPLICANT: FIRST WORLD IMPORT & EXPORT CO., LTD.
(THAILAND CORPORATION), SATHUPRADIT ROAD, YANNAWA,
369/6 SOI WAT POMAN, BANGKOK, 10120, TH (THAILAND)
OWNER AT PUBLICATION: FIRST WORLD IMPORT & EXPORT CO.,
LTD. (THAILAND CORPORATION), SATHUPRADIT ROAD, YANNAWA,
369/6 SOI WAT POMAN, BANGKOK, 10120, TH (THAILAND)
FULL TEXT TRANSLATION: THE ENGLISH TRANSLATION OF
"CHAOBAN" IS "COMMON PEOPLE."
FILING CORRESPONDENT: DEANNE H. OZAKI, 555 SOUTH FLOWER
STREET, 23RD FLOOR, LOS ANGELES, CA 90071

Source: *Trademarkscan—U.S. Federal* database on DIALOG, May 22, 1993. Reprinted with permission of Thomson & Thomson.

1985. Records contain bibliographic information as well as English language titles and abstracts.

Labeling. Cultural issues affect product size, shape, and color, but labeling is mandated by local law and regional regulations. The EC has adopted legislation in the area of labeling; EC Directives and Regulations cover labeling of such products as hazardous substances, tobacco and smoking materials, and food additives.

Warranties. Warranties or guarantees are generally considered part of the product description. For example, the warranties for General Motors vehicles vary internationally from 3 months/2,400 miles to 24 months/unlimited miles. Labeling, warranties, and gradings in the U.S. are available in a 1993 book from Gale, *Consumers' Guide to Product Grades and Terms*. This is not a legal source and is primarily compiled to provide information for the consumer in anticipation of new 1994 U.S. labeling laws. There is no international equivalent. The export compendia discussed in Chapter 12 have general labeling provisions as do the *OBRs*.

Service. Alternatives for servicing an international product include offering no service, local service providers, local distributors who may offer training and parts, and direct on-site service.

Product Life Cycle. Finally, when introducing a product into another country, companies consider where the product is in its international product life cycle. A product typically goes through a life cycle consisting of introduction, maturity, and decline. Products are usually introduced first in highly industrialized countries and later in less industrialized countries. When a product has saturated its market in one country and is in decline, it may be transferred to another country in a different product life stage. An example is the microwave oven, which is in well over half of U.S. homes.

Price

Pricing an item for the international market is a complex issue. Many of the sources of information required for this decision are internal to the company. There is no comprehensive source that provides prices for specific manufactured and consumer goods and services sold in either the U.S. or the international market.

Factors determining the price of an item include consumer behavior based on economic demand and utility curves, competitive structure of the market, the firm's cost structure and profit objectives, and government regulations.

The different types of international pricing decisions include:

1. Export Pricing and Terms
2. Transfer Pricing
3. Foreign Market Pricing

Export Pricing and Terms. A company that is manufacturing at home but marketing abroad incurs additional expenses, including tariffs, transport, packaging, insurance, and taxes. However, increased output from the export sales may result in economies of scale that bring down the unit cost.

Different financing schemes and terms of payment may result in a discount to full cost as well.

- Is the quoted price f.o.b., c.i.f., or some combination (*see* Table 9-D)?
- In what currency is the price quoted? The buyer's currency, or the seller's, or some standard such as ECU?
- How will the deal be financed?

Chapter 12 on exporting has a more complete explanation of export financing alternatives. Table 9-D gives the definitions of standard export pricing terms.

The buyer would like the price to be c.i.f. with long payment terms. The seller, on the other hand, wants the price quoted f.o.b. with immediate payment.

Export pricing is generally higher than domestic pricing but it often does not reflect the full additional costs. A company or its agent needs to know the price range for similar products in the target market and determine if it can operate within that range. This information comes from a representative on-site, not a secondary source.

Exchange Rate Effect on Export Pricing. We have discussed foreign exchange as an economic concept, as a part of international financial markets, and as a factor affecting company financial rankings. The fluctuation in the relationships between currencies also has an impact on pricing decisions, since a company has to decide whether to price its product in its home currency or the foreign currency.

Ironically, a weak dollar (a dollar that is losing its value in relation to foreign currencies) is considered good for the U.S. economy. It results in strong exports and an improvement in the U.S. trade balance. When the dollar is weak, U.S. goods are less expensive for foreign buyers. The reverse is true for imports. A weak dollar makes imports more expensive.

In deciding on which currency to use for pricing, a researcher may wish to check time series data to see how the domestic and foreign currencies have been moving against each other, as well as forward foreign exchange data to estimate trends.

Here is a simple example of the effect of currency rates on prices. In December 1985, an American importer agreed to buy widgets from a Japanese manufacturer at the cost of $100 per widget through 1992. The American importer is protected from the 39% decrease in the value of the dollar in relationship to the yen over that time period. As seen in Table 9-E, $100 was worth 20,279 yen in 1985 and 12,404 yen in 1992.

Conversely, what if that same importer had agreed to pay 20,279 yen per unit, the exchange rate in 1985? Instead of paying $100 per unit by 1992, the importer would be paying $163.49, an increase of 63.5% per unit in dollars.

Table 9-E. Effect of Exchange Rate Fluctuations on Export Pricing

YEAR End December	Yen to buy one unit @ $100	Dollars to buy one unit @20,279 yen
1985	20,279	100.00
1986	16,205	125.14
1987	12,824	158.13
1988	12,361	164.06
1989	14,369	141.13
1990	13,389	151.46
1991	12,804	158.38
1992	12,204	163.49
% change in value of $1	-39%	63%

Table 9-D. Export Price Quotations

Abbreviation	Term	Meaning
EX	From	Applies only to point of origin: ex factory; ex dock. The seller agrees to place the goods at the disposal of the buyer at a specified place within a fixed time.
f.o.b.	Free on board	Price includes loading goods into transport vessels at a specified place: fob Philadelphia
f.a.s.	Free alongside	Price includes delivering the goods alongside a specified vessel: fas Merchant Transport
c.i.f.	Cost, insurance, freight	Price includes cost of goods, insurance, and freight
c & i	Cost & insurance	Price includes cost of goods and insurance
c & f	Cost & freight	Price includes cost of goods and freight

When the seller's currency is strong, as in our example, it is to the buyer's benefit to have the price quoted in the buyer's currency. When the seller's currency is weak, it is to the buyer's benefit to have the price quoted in the seller's currency.

Transfer Pricing. A company providing goods or services from its home country to a facility abroad, whether it is a manufacturing or a distribution arm, has to charge the receiving unit for the items. This is transfer pricing. If the producing unit is a cost center, than it wants to charge the international unit what it charges anyone else. To be competitive, the international unit only wants to pay the cost of manufacturing.

Foreign Market Pricing. Foreign market pricing is the price a company sets in another country. The actual price will depend upon:

- **Company Goals:** Profit (U.S.) or market share (Japanese)
- **Costs**: Manufacturing, transportation and distribution, marketing
- **Demand**: Number of consumers, their ability to pay, and their tastes
- **Competition**: Price, number of competitors, country attitude
- **Government**: Policy of competition, price controls, taxes and tariffs
- **Inflation**: Time between production and sale, sale and payment

Place or Channels of Distribution

Many of the issues discussed in Chapter 12 on exports deal with the transport and distribution of goods or services that originate in one country and are sold in another. A country's transport infrastructure should have been part of the initial research and decision making. At this point, the distributor needs to identify sources of wholesale and retail trade and direct marketing. Several directories of wholesalers and retailers are listed below. Country sources and export guides give overviews of the transportation infrastructure.

Promotion and Advertising

Promotion is the communication by a firm to its audience with a view toward informing and influencing the audience. Advertising is paid communication through impersonal media. Advertising as a part of the marketing plan is included here. A fuller explanation of international advertising agencies and regulations is presented in Chapter 11.

A variety of factors make up the international advertising environment: language, economic differences, tastes and attitudes, and local competition. Other factors include agency availability, media availability, and government regulations.

Even if a firm decides to market a global product, that firm must still decide whether to use standard or adapted advertising and promotional campaigns. A firm faces several areas of decision when putting together a global marketing campaign.

1. Selecting the agency—international or local
2. Choosing the message—high context/low context, language
3. Selecting the media—print, TV, satellite TV, etc.
4. Determining the budget
5. Organizing for advertising

Journal articles that address these issues disagree on how to proceed. Despite the convergence of tastes worldwide, cultural and language differences that may interfere with a global advertising campaign still exist.

Selecting the Agency. International companies often select international agencies. (See Chapter 11 on advertising for more agency information.)

Choosing the Message. In addition to local standards and tastes, cultural differences are based on the context of a culture. Table 9-F divides countries into high and low context cultures where context refers to the importance of the social situation.[7]

Product comparisons are illegal in Japan because Japanese culture finds open criticism of others unacceptable. In Thailand, effective advertisements are graphic displays rather than written text.

There are a variety of language issues beyond the obvious ones: an incorrect translation, misspellings in the translation, or different meanings for words. Other language issues are illustrated by the following examples:

- Swiss, Germans, and Japanese do not believe anything being given away free is of value
- The number 4 means death in some Asian cultures
- In judging ad space, the German language takes 20% more space than English
- Idioms or trendy words do not translate[8] (for example, many countries have been unable to translate the name of the logo for the 1996 Olympics)

Table 9-F. High and Low Context Cultures

High Context Cultures	Low Context Cultures
Asia, Africa, and Middle East	North America and Western Europe
Interpersonal relations; non-verbal expression; social circumstances	Spoken and written messages; action oriented; analytical
TV commercial drama with product in context	Illustrated lecture; product comparisons

Some global marketing successes include:

- Coca Cola's "I'd like to teach the world to sing"
- British Airways' "Manhattan Landing" campaign in 35 countries
- Proctor & Gamble's "Even when they're wet they're dry" campaign for Pampers
- IBM's "Little Tramp"

Some global marketing failures include:

- Imperial Margarine's "Magic Crowns" (offensive to monarchies)
- Chevrolet's Nova (the classic failure: "No va" means "doesn't go" in Spanish)
- GM's Body by Fisher (which became "Corpse by Fisher" in Flemish)
- Kentucky Fried Chicken's "finger lickin' good" (translated "eat your fingers off" in Chinese)[9]

Sometimes a national campaign can be carried to global markets if it is somewhat modified. For example, Coca Cola's "Mean Joe Green" campaign substituted local sports figures for the U.S. football player in non-U.S. markets.

Selecting the Media. Publications read by international businesspersons are obvious places to advertise global products. Such publications include the *Financial Times,* the *Wall Street Journal,* the *International Herald Tribune, Le Monde,* and *The Times.* There are problems advertising in local print sources. In some countries, the quality of printed sources is variable, and, more importantly, there is a lack of fixed or published rates and no audited or authenticated circulation data.

In the U.S., published audited circulation figures come from the Audit Bureau of Circulation, advertising expenditures from BAR LNA, and published rates from Standard Rate & Data Service. The U.K.'s advertising reporting service is MEAL. Generally, this type of information is not readily available outside the U.S.

There have been recent changes in broadcast media worldwide with the growth of satellite transmission. Within Europe, deregulation has resulted in new TV stations, new programs, and, therefore, space for more advertising. There are now pan-European satellite systems. MTV is a strong player in the cable market because it does not face traditional language problems.

There is some movement in Europe toward mega-radio stations such as Radio 3 in Luxembourg, with three frequencies and five languages. In many countries, the government still controls much of the broadcast media programming, though this has been changing.

Determining the Budget. How much should a firm budget for advertising in any one country? Theory says put money into advertising as long as the ad dollar returns more than the dollar spent on anything else. Among the different international strategies are:

- **Percent of Sales in a Country**: The more you sell the more you advertise; this depends on whether you are entering a market or expanding, what the competition is doing, and media availability
- **Comparative or Parity**: Match your competition, but host country competition may behave differently from home country competition
- **Objective-and-Task**: Determine your objectives (e.g., sales, brand awareness, or market share); determine the tasks to reach objectives; estimate cost of the tasks
- **Comparative Analysis**: The large company, advertising in many countries, should use categories to group countries

The comparative strategies require access to competitor spending data; information that is not widely disseminated.

Organizing for Advertising. In organizing for advertising, the firm determines where the decisions are to be made. Again, there is a continuum from centralization in the home market to decentralization in each market and the decision is not dependent on secondary data sources.

Other Marketing Issues

Personal selling in foreign markets at a national level may be important. Although the sales force may be hired cheaply, sales is often a low prestige job. The challenge is to provide motivation to recruit a quality sales force. The company needs to do an analysis of the market to determine the role of the sales force. There are variations by religion, ethnicity, language, education, and race even within a country. An alternative is to use a distributor or licensee, but then the company gives up control.

Sales promotions, such as contests, coupons, samples, premiums, such as cents/off, and point-of-sale promotions account for 60% of the ad dollar in the United States. The use of these techniques in other countries depends on culture, retailer cooperation, and laws that may restrict premiums. The U.S., U. K., France, and Philippines are considered liberal, while Germany, Switzerland, Italy, and Mexico are considered restrictive.[10]

Other promotional techniques include traveling exhibits, videodiscs, and seminars. Bribery, which is illegal in the United States under the Foreign Corrupt Practices Act, is an accepted form of promotion in many countries. OECD and UNCTAD are working on international codes of ethics, as are various professional organizations.

Public relations is distinguished from forms of advertising in that it is external relations that involve a company's image and its corporate communications. Press releases, consumer service, and participation on local advisory committees are all forms of a company's PR.

INTERNATIONAL MARKETING OF SERVICES

The emphasis in the marketing and exporting literature is on the movement of goods. Services follow goods. The international market for services is fundamentally different from the market in goods; it is more difficult to measure and analyze. In more developed economies, services account for a large percent of GDP. It is estimated by the IMF that about 25% of the world's trade is in services.

Eurostat reports that the European Community was the world's leading exporter and importer of services between 1979 and 1988. Table 9-G shows the international trade in services for 1988.

Table 9-G. Trade in Services in 1988

Region	Exports mil ECUs	Imports mil ECUs
European Community	118,000	108,000
United States	76,000	66,000
Japan	29,000	58,000
World (1)	490,000	512,000
(1) GATT figures—differences due to "asymmetry"		

Source: International Trade in Services, 1991, p. 17

It is more difficult to export services than to export goods. Alternative means to market services internationally include:

• Foreign Direct Investment (in a service company)
• Licensing (a name, a technique)
• Franchising
• Joint Ventures

Certain service industries lend themselves to internationalization. Improved communications networks have resulted in an international financial service industry. As international marketing expands, so does the internationalization of the advertising industry. Consulting organizations and accounting firms operate on a worldwide basis. There is also an internationalization of sports, movies, retail, airlines, insurance, and real estate. (See also Chapter 14, "Industries.")

Source for International Services

International Trade in Services (Eurostat 1989, 1991)

Eurostat has compiled statistics on trade in services. International trade in services is included by definition in balance of trade statistics. The statistics are roughly comparable among countries. But, as with all other data we have examined, there are also problems.

• There is no detailed international classification in services; some countries compile branch statistics in banking
• Valuation methods are not identical; some countries record gross flows, others net
• There is no agreed method of valuing insurance
• Certain transactions are not regarded as services in all countries; some countries consider construction of more than one year to be direct investment

In addition to overview data, the publication includes estimated data for 12 services, including tourism, transport, advertising, and insurance, and for the 12 member countries of the EC.

FRANCHISING

Another marketing alternative is franchising. It is a legal arrangement in which the franchisor grants to the franchisee not only the right to use the product or service and its trademark, but also the right to use the entire system of the business, including support in site selection, training, advertising, and product supply. A key to franchising success is consistency among outlets.

The franchise operation is a contractual relationship between a Franchisor and Franchisee in which the Franchisor offers or is obliged to maintain a continued interest in the business of the Franchisee in such areas as know-how and training; wherein the Franchisee operates under a common trade mark, formation or procedure owned or controlled by the Franchisor, under which the Franchisee has or will make a substantial capital investment in his business from his own resources. (International Franchise Association)

During the past 20 years, U.S. franchisors, especially fast food chains, have made their presence known around the globe.

• McDonald's is in 52 countries
• Holiday Inn is in 51 international markets
• Kentucky Fried Chicken has 3,000 international units in 54 countries

The dramatic changes in Eastern Europe over the past few years have opened that market as well. In general, however, international franchising activities have centered in Western Europe, Japan, and Australia, as illustrated in Table 9-H.

Because franchising is a legal agreement, the franchisor has to understand the legal environment and commercial practices of the target country. In 1990, the United States was the only country that had passed a law concerning the sale of a franchise.

International franchising has been fostered by the International Franchise Association, a U.S.-based organization. It participates in the Council of Multinational Franchisors and Distributors, which provides an international network to people and information. Membership is open to franchisors or distributors having operations in more than one country or plans to have operations in more than one country and who also belong to their national franchise organization.

The European Franchise Federation (EFF), founded in 1972, comprises national franchise groups in Europe and non-European associates. In 1989 it issued a code of ethics.

Sources of Franchising Information

In researching franchises, the two major information needs are:
1. What franchises are located in what countries?
2. What are the laws and regulations affecting franchising in an individual country?

Franchise Opportunities Guide (International Federation—Annual)

The *Franchise Opportunities Guide* lists 20 national franchise associations and the number has been growing. Countries or regions with franchise associations are:

Africa	Denmark	Netherlands
Argentina	Europe	Norway
Austria	Germany	Portugal
Australasia	Ireland	South Africa
Brazil	Italy	Sweden
Britain	Japan	Switzerland
Canada	Mexico	

One drawback to the *Guide* is its lack of an index to those companies franchising internationally, although that information is part of the individual entry.

World Franchise Directory: A Guide Offering Details for Comparing Franchises and Franchise Investment Opportunities Around the World (Gale, 1991)

We were unable to find what we considered a comprehensive directory of international franchisors. In the *World Franchise Directory,* 75% of the franchise locations listed are in the U.S. and many of the entries in the 15 other countries the *Directory* covers are U.S.-based franchises. Data were collected directly from the companies, from brochures, and from secondary sources, such as other directories and news articles. The *Directory* is arranged, like most Gale directories, by broad subject area, with a keyword index, a geographic index, and a personal name index. No updates are planned.

Survey of Foreign Laws and Regulations Affecting International Franchising (American Bar Association, 1989) lists the franchising laws for 24 countries. *International Franchising*, by Alex S. Konigsberg, (Transnational Juris Publications, 1991) covers many of the issues discussed above in relation to selecting a country for franchises. The loose-leaf book is legal in tone and might be useful to the smaller potential franchisor.

International Franchising distinguishes between a license agreement and a franchise agreement. The license agreement is a contractual agreement in which the licensor grants the licensee the right to use the licensor's patents, know-how, and trademarks in connection with manufacturing or distribution of a product, but does not affect how the licensee conducts business. Two types of license agreements are technology transfer and trademark license agreements

The EC also addresses franchises in its regulations and defines a franchise and a franchise agreement. EEC Commission Regulation No. 4087/88, November 30, 1988, Article 3(a) and (b), states:

'franchise' means a package of industrial or intellectual property rights relating to trade marks, trade names, shop signs, utility models, designs, copyrights, know-how or patents, to be exploited for the resale of goods or the provision of services to end users;

"franchise agreement" means an agreement whereby one undertaking, the franchisor, grants the other, the franchisee, in exchange for direct or indirect financial consideration, the right to exploit a franchise for the purpose of

Table 9-H. Worldwide Franchising in 1988

Country	Franchisors	Outlets	Product
France	675 (95% French)	30,000	Clothing & footwear
U.K.	270 (about 24% U.S.)	20,000	Home improvements
Japan	700 (about 10% U.S.)	102,397	Food service
Italy	200 (balanced domestic and foreign)	11,500	Retail distribution

marketing specified types of goods and/or services; it includes at least obligations relating to:

- use of common name or sign and a uniform presentation of contract premises
- communication by franchisor to franchisee of know how
- continual provision by franchise to the franchisee of commercial or technical assistance during the life of the agreement.

SOURCES OF INTERNATIONAL MARKETING INFORMATION

The sources listed here build on the more general country-level sources listed above. These sources focus more on consumer and product, though many also have macro-economic data.

Statistical Compilations

European Marketing Data and Statistics and *International Marketing Data and Statistics* (Euromonitor—Annual)

Euromonitor is one of the leading international publishers of marketing information. It publishes marketing reference books, directories, and market research reports. Its two most widely distributed publications in the U.S. are *European Marketing Data and Statistics (EDMS)*, annual since 1962, and *International Marketing Data and Statistics,* from 1975. These two publications are compendia of statistical information relevant to marketing in many countries. The data are gathered from large international organizations, such as the United Nations, OECD, and International Monetary Fund; from national statistical offices; pan-international and national trade associations; industry associations; unofficial research publishers; and Euromonitor's own statistical databases. As with so many published data sources, the date of the publication does not reflect the date of the data. The 1993 editions, published in the fall of 1992, contain 1990 data.

These publications will not answer all marketing questions. For instance, they will tell how much beer is consumed, per capita in Australia, but won't tell which brands of beer are sold in Australia. The International edition is divided into the following principal sectors:

01	Marketing Geography	05	External Trade by Destination and Commodity
02	Demographic Trends and Forecasts	06	Labour Force Indicators
03	Economic Indicators	07	Industrial Resources and Output
04	Finance and Banking		

08	Energy Resources and Outlook		Costs
09	Defence	16	Households and Household Facilities
10	Environmental Data	17	Health and Living Standards
11	Consumer Expenditure Patterns	18	Literacy and Education
12	Retailing and Retail Distribution	19	Agricultural Resources
13	Advertising Patterns and Media Access	20	Communications
14	Consumer Market Sizes	21	Automotives
15	Consumer Prices and	22	Transport Infrastructure
		23	Tourism and Travel
		24	Cultural Indicators

Notice that the chapter headings match many of the data items discussed above. The data items are presented for one of four time periods.

1. Ten-year trend table, with data for each country from the same source
2. Different period trend based on data availability
3. Latest year available, with years and sources differing for countries
4. Single year, where space does not permit trends or a range of information is provided

Over 150 countries are covered, but the following 25 are considered key:

Argentina	Israel	Singapore
Australia	Japan	South Africa
Brazil	Kuwait	South Korea
Canada	Malaysia	Taiwan
China	Mexico	Thailand
Colombia	New Zealand	U.S.
Hong Kong	Nigeria	Venezuela
India	Philippines	Zimbabwe
Indonesia		

Exhibit 9-3 is an excerpt from a table on consumption in *International Marketing Data and Statistics.*

The sources for the data in Exhibit 9-3 are the International Sugar Organization, OECD, GATT, the International Tea Committee, the national statistical offices, and Euromonitor estimates. Unlike the *Statistical Abstract of the United States*, where the citations to tables serve as finding aids to more up-to-date and detailed data, the citations to Euromonitor tables only direct users toward general publications or publishers.

The *International* volume includes a section entitled "Key International Market Information Sources." It contains the names of the principal international and national organizations that publish statistics.

Euromonitor publications are expensive. However, most libraries with business collections should consider purchasing the two *Marketing Data and Statistics* titles. More specialized Euromonitor publications are described below.

EXHIBIT 9-3. Excerpt from *International Marketing Data and Statistics*

Consumer Market Sizes
Table No:1405
DRINKS
Consumption of Drinks 1989
Per head

	Tea kg	Cocoa kg	Beer litre	Wine litre	Soft drinks litre
Argentina	0.2	0.4	58.0	58.0	
Australia	1.2	1.6	115.0	21.0	80.0
Brazil		0.4	30.0	2.0	36.0
Canada	0.6	1.8	50.0	10.0	75.0
Thailand	1.1		4.0		9.5
United States	0.4	2.0	90.0	8.6	80.5
Venezuela		0.3	75.0	0.7	50.0
Zimbabwe	0.6		16.0		4.0

Source: *International Marketing Data and Statistics*, 1993, p. 456. Reprinted with permission from Euromonitor.

European Compendium of Marketing Information (Euromonitor, 1992)

European Compendium of Marketing Information is a new addition to the Euromonitor publications list. This 1992 publication provides summary trends for a wide variety of consumer markets across Europe, on a pan-European rather than country-by-country basis.

Part 1 is an overview of socio-economic variables, European consumer lifestyles, and retail distribution patterns covering demographic and social trends, spending, advertising, retailing, and marketing. Countries in the EC, EFTA, and former Soviet Bloc are covered.

Part 2 is arranged by 50 consumer markets selected on the basis of importance to consumer spending and interest to marketers. A few services, such as personal finance and travel and tourism, are also included. The tables vary from product to product. Data are at a macro level; very few companies and brands are mentioned.

Data were collected during the second half of 1991 and are reported based on availability and accessibility, as collected from the source. Full details on sources appear in other Euromonitor publications, including *European Directory of Marketing Information Sources*. In some cases, no data are available but Euromonitor's own.

The book answers such questions as:

* How many pieces of direct mail were sent in Denmark in 1989?
* What percent of adults own stocks and shares in Switzerland?
* How many dogs are there in France?

Who should purchase this book? It complements the European Communities industry survey, *Panorama of EC Industry*, discussed in Chapter 14. The compendium incorporates information from Euromonitor Market Direction Reports (*see* discussion of online market research sources in Chapter 10) and *Consumer Europe*, which is organized by specific product and company. The tabular data, though often drawn from the Euromonitor database, are not the same as found in the other publications.

For example, *European Marketing Data and Statistics (EMDS)* has a column for per capita consumption of Confectionery, "Chocolate for all EC and EFTA Countries," using data derived from Euromonitor databases. The *Compendium* has several tables, including total chocolate consumption, imports as a percentage of sales, and growth by product sector.

If you have demand for general information on the European consumer product market, you might consider purchasing the *Compendium* in alternate years with *EMDS*. If you need more than just the numbers of *EMDS* but do not have access to the market reports, you also should consider this publication. If you have requests for general company, product, and brand data, and cannot afford the online sources discussed in Chapter 10, than you may also be interested in the Euromonitor Consumer series.

Table 9-I lists three types of Euromonitor publications and the regions and countries for which there are separate volumes.

Eastern Europe

International marketers immediately recognized the market potential of Eastern Europe with over 400 million inhabitants and consumer spending of about U.S. $1,000 billion per year. They soon also recognized the market limitations both in terms of consumer resources and information resources. Euromonitor estimates the per capita spending power of the region to be no more than $3,000.

Consumer Eastern Europe (Euromonitor, 1992)

Consumer Eastern Europe is a 1992 addition to Euromonitor's Consumer series. Unlike *Consumer USA* and *Consumer Europe*, which are arranged by product and company, *Consumer Eastern Europe* offers a general overview of Eastern European markets and has individual chapters on Bulgaria, Czechoslovakia, eastern Germany, Hungary, Poland, Romania, the former USSR, and the former Yugoslavia. The book is primarily statistical as opposed to analytical, with the data drawn from official sources and subject to "careful scrutiny." This source answers such questions as:

Table 9-I. Sample Titles of Other Euromonitor Marketing Publications

Sample Titles	DIRECTORY AND SOURCEBOOK	CONSUMER XXX	RETAILING XXX
Regions	Europe Eastern Europe Asia Latin America	Europe Eastern Europe Asia Latin America	World Europe Eastern Europe Southeast Asia Latin America
Countries	China	Japan Spain USA	
Non-official Statistical Sources: International and Europe			

- What percent of the households in the former Yugoslavia own dishwashers?
- What was the average annual retail price for a liter of milk in Hungary?

Euromonitor is careful to warn the user of the limitations of the data, stating that there are still false and misleading figures. The handbook presents "fragmented" data from the states of Eastern Europe, tries to standardize it, and then makes its own deductions.

For example, official consumption figures often ignore the free-market stalls. Changes in governmental structure have resulted in changes in statistical collection, which necessitates revisions for time series data. Though published in mid-1992, the data reported are from 1988-1990, while some pan-regional data may be even older. Finally, there has been a problem with exchange rate conversion and inflation. Data, therefore, often appear in local currency; when rates are used, they are 1990 average dollar free-market rates from the IMF.

Chapter subheadings for all countries include demographics, economic indicators, standard of living, advertising and media, and retailing or retail distribution. For most countries, there are tables for consumer expenditure, consumption or apparent consumption, service, and consumer market size. Exhibit 9-4 illustrates a table measuring standard of living.

Eastern Europe: A Directory and Sourcebook (Euromonitor, 1992-)

Eastern Europe is the companion publication to *Consumer Eastern Europe* and has more text than the latter. The book has five parts.

- Section One: Eastern Europe in the 1990s: An Overview
- Section Two: Accessing East European Markets for Czechoslovakia, Former East Germany, Hungary,

EXHIBIT 9-4. *Consumer Eastern Europe*

Standard of Living

TABLE 11.15 THE FORMER YUGOSLAVIA: OWNERSHIP OF SELECTED CONSUMER DURABLES 1988

(% households)	
Radio	60.0
Television	89.1
-of which: colour	40.0
Cassette recorder	35.9
Record player	6.5
Music centre	6.7
Washing machine	67.4
Dishwasher	3.1
Refrigerator	88.6
Freezer	65.8
Vacuum cleaner	66.5
Car	38.5

Source: Consumer Eastern Europe, 1992, p. 285. Reprinted with permission from Euromonitor.

Poland, Romania, the Former USSR and Yugoslavia. Each country has a very short section on economic background, consumer expenditure and retail sales, broad structure of retailing, and outlook.

- Section Three: Major Companies. The emphasis is on companies involved in the production and sale of consumer products. There is little consistency in entries in this section.
- Section Four: Sources of Information
- Section Five: Statistical Datafile

There is an index to companies and information sources. Data were collected during 1991 and early 1992 from national as well as private sources. Data for the USSR and Yugoslavia are before dissolution. Entries from Russia dominate the directory section for the former

USSR, and entries from Serbia and Slovenia dominate for the former Yugoslavia.

Finding Aids for Market Information

Other Euromonitor publications, such as *European Directory of Marketing Information Sources* (2nd ed. 1991); *European Directory of Non-Official Statistical Sources* (2nd ed. 1993); and *International Directory of Non-Official Statistical Sources* (1990) include more complete source listings.

Euromonitor considers *European Directory of Marketing Information Sources* its central reference work. The book features general marketing information, contacts, and sources relevant to all European business needs. Other reference works contain comprehensive listings of sources and business contacts, trade associations, trade journals, and research organizations.

The *European Directory* is divided into 10 sections covering as many as 17 countries—EC members plus Austria, Finland, Norway, Sweden, and Switzerland.

Section	Title	# of Countries Covered
Section 1	Official Sources and Publications	17
Section 2	Libraries and Information Services	17
Section 3	Leading Market Research Companies	16
Section 4	Leading Consumer Research Publishers in Europe	*
Section 5	Information Databases and Databanks	15
Section 6	Abstracts and Indexes	*
Section 7	Major Business and Marketing Journals	17
Section 8	Major Business and Marketing Associations	17
Section 9	European Business Contacts	17
Section 10	Socio-Economic Profiles	17

While many of the sources and much of the data in the socio-economic profile are available in many other sources, it is convenient for the user to have all of it together in one place.

Euromonitor publishes an index to all its publications in print, *Euromonitor Index*. This complete, annotated list of publications can be ordered directly from Euromonitor at 87-88 Turnmill Street, London EC1M 5QU, FAX: 44 71 251 8024.

Information Service Guide to European Market Information: EC Countries (London Business School)

For each EC country, *Information Service Guide* includes major trade associations and annotated entries for business journals, databases, market research reports, newspapers, official statistics, statistical directories, statistical offices, and subscription services. The listings of market research reports and syndicated ser-

vices are useful finding aids. The slimness of the 1991 edition, 129 pages from cover to cover, with many titles appearing under several countries, underlines the absence of a wide range of choices of syndicated services and advertising expenditure data. Gale Research will be publishing the next edition in 1994.

A Guide to Company and Industry Information Sources for European Markets (4th ed. 1992/93, Washington Researchers)
A Guide to Company and Industry Information Sources for Asian Markets (1st ed. 1988-, Washington Researchers)
A Guide to Company and Industry Information Sources for Latin America (1st ed. 1993-, Washington Researchers)

All Washington Researchers Guides have the same basic arrangement. Part 1 lists national and international organizations in the government and private sector. Part 2 lists published sources and databases. There is a high degree of overlap in information presented among the three guides for these sections. Part 3 is country data, including U.S. government offices, officials and sources, associations, and research and transportation organizations.

The books are complied from a U.S. perspective. The Washington Researchers publications are recommended for a general library looking for a single U.S. source of European, Asian, or Latin American information for business clients.

A direct way to find statistical information is to use official publications from the central statistical department of individual countries. These departments all produce basic statistical sources that serve as starting points for country-level marketing information. Most European countries publish a statistical yearbook, an annual bulletin of industry data, and manuals that examine imports and exports in detail. There are also family expenditure surveys and retail trade censuses.

The Future

The successful marketer not only has to understand the present situation but also correctly predict the future. Chapter 13 presents sources of economic forecasts.

Worldcast Product (Predicasts, May 1982—Quarterly)
Worldcasts Regional (Predicasts, April 1984—Quarterly)

These two multi-volume loose-leaf companions to the U.S. *Predicasts Forecasts* are also online on DIALOG File 83—PTS International Forecasts. *Worldcasts* answers both of the following questions:

- What food products are predicted to grow over 10% in Eastern Europe?
- What will be the GDP per capita for Thailand in the year 2000?

As with *Predicasts Forecasts*, the information in print is presented as a spreadsheet, with product code, base, short-term and long-term forecasts and units of measurement, an annual rate of growth, and abbreviated title for the source. Sources for forecasts include standard statistical publications, such as the *World Development Report*, and also forecast data from any of the thousands of publications indexed by Predicasts. When using *Predicasts Forecasts*, checking the source publication is vital for accurate research. To do this with *Worldcasts* often requires using one of Predicasts' online files which may include the text.

CONCLUSION

To succeed in the international marketplace, companies need to research the host country, gathering data on the economy, the culture and lifestyles of the residents, and the political and legal environment. This external data analysis should be combined with internal marketing decisions about the four P's: product, price, place, and promotion. Researchers must depend on secondary data sources, such as those described in this chapter. While compilations exist from international, national, and private sources, the data are often several years old.

Sources of current information at the consumer, product, and company levels are presented in Chapter 10 on international marketing research. Listed below are a few useful reference tips for using the sources described in this chapter.

- Check to see what statistical office publications are in your library or the major research library near you. These publications are relatively inexpensive. Euromonitor suggests that you write to the applicable statistical office and offer to pay for charges, if any. It also warns that you may wait several months for answers from Spain, Portugal, Greece, and Italy; France and Germany send lists of publications unless you are very precise. Disadvantages are that the information is at a general level, will be in the language of the country, and, in the less affluent countries, will not be current.
- Use market research agencies and reports, described in Chapter 10. They may already be publishing statistics based on their analysis of the official statistics.
- Online databases provide a wealth of valuable informa-

tion. However, it may be necessary to access a wide range of international services.
- Contact a trade association. The data the associations provide are a measure of the present market. While some conduct their own studies, many rely on official publications. The available data are usually country-specific. Associations are readily identifiable in Gale's *International Associations*.

SELECTED ARTICLES ON INTERNATIONAL MARKETING

Advertising Theory

Fields, George. "Great Marketing Concepts Are Not Immutable," *Tokyo Business Today 60* (March 1992): 35.
Even major brands differ in one or more of the marketing elements, from positioning and application to distribution techniques. Coca-Cola's premier brand in Japan is Georgia Coffee, not Coke.

Onkvisit, Sak and Shaw, John J. "Standardized International Advertising: A Review and Critical Evaluation of the Theoretical and Empirical Evidence," *Columbia Journal of World Business* (Fall 1987): 43-55.
Includes a review of the literature, discussing standardization, localization, and compromise.

Silverstein, Michael J. "Companies That Meet Higher Ante Will Win Global Marketing Pot," *Marketing News 26* (March 30, 1992): 13.
Primary research, information networks, broadly defined categories, acquisitions, and adapting the world brand to local tastes are signs of a successful global company. Grand Metropolitan is given as an example.

Developing Markets for Western Products

Dominguez, Luis V. and Sequeira, Carlos G. "Strategic Options for LDC Exports to Developed Countries," *International Marketing Review 8* (November 5, 1991): 27-43.
Marketing to developing countries is complex and success is based not only on market conditions, but, according to the authors' survey, the commitment and management focus of the exporting firm.

Guzek, Elizbeta. "Ways of Entering the Polish Market by Foreign Companies," *Journal of Business Research 24* (January 1992): 37-50.
Changes are occurring in the Polish market that are relevant to the foreign marketer. These changes affect the role of intermediaries, marketing channels, and joint ventures.

Nasierowski, Wojciech. "Doing Business in India," *Business Quarterly 56* (Summer 1991): 71-74.
India has an enormous potential market, but complex regulations make entry for foreign companies difficult.

Japan

Conlan-Ayache, Gladys. "European Exports to Japan: Successes and Failures," *European Trends*, no. 3 (1991): 66-69.

According to a 1990 survey of Consumer's Awareness of Imported Goods by the Manufactured Imports Promotion Organization of Japan, good taste, good quality, and good design are the three criteria essential for consumers in Japan. The greatest problem in exporting to Japan remains the distribution system.

Public Relations

Corbett, William J. "EC '92—Communicating in the New Europe," *Public Relations Quarterly 36* (Winter 1991-1992): 7-13.

The EC provides a market of 342 million people and a $4.8 trillion gross national product. This creates an opportunity for U.S. public relations practitioners who need to be better educated and more cultured than before.

Services

Bouchard, Micheline. "International Marketing of Professional Services," *Business Quarterly 56* (Winter 1992): 86-89.

Three penetration strategies that professional services can use to enter a new market are opening an office, making an acquisition, and forming a strategic alliance.

Strategy

Buckley, Peter J., Pass, C.L., and Prescott, Kate. "Foreign Market Servicing Strategies and Competitiveness," *Journal of General Management 17* (Winter 1991): 34-46.

A case study of three different approach strategies to gaining a foreign presence for a sample of U.K. manufacturing firms in pharmaceuticals, scientific instruments, and decorative paints.

King, Elliot. "At Ease Overseas," *Target Marketing 15* (January 1992): 19-20.

Three successful global direct marketing successes are presented: the *Economics Press, Business Week International,* and *Reader's Digest.*

Stonham, Paul. "A Conversation with Michael Porter: International Competitive Strategy from a European Perspective," *European Management Journal 9*(December 1991): 355-60.

Porter's theory states that advantage arises when a company's home base is located in a nation, or even a city within a nation, when the most dynamic environment for innovation is present in that nation.

Trade Shows

Friedlander, Pat. "Flexing the Marketing Muscle of European Trade Shows," *Journal of European Business 3* (January/February 1992): 10-14.

U.S. companies need to understand some key differences between exhibiting in the U.S. and exhibiting in Europe. While U.S. exhibitors are accustomed to sending only salespeople to shows, Europeans expect company senior executives. U.S. attendees at the International Online Meeting in London immediately noticed the difference in the level of both the attendees and the exhibitors.

Bibliographies

Cavusgil, S. Tamer and Nevin, John R. *International Marketing, an Annotated Bibliography.* (Chicago: American Marketing Association, 1983).

Cavusgil, S. Tamer and Tiger, Li. *International Marketing: An Annotated Bibliography* (Chicago: American Marketing Association, 1992).

NOTES

1. Theodore Levitt, "The Globalization of Markets," *Harvard Business Review* (May/June 1983):1.

2. Vern Terpstra and Ravi Sarathy, *International Marketing* (Orlando FL: Dryden Press, 1990), p. 5. This text was used by the author as background for this chapter.

3. Compiled from *Philadelphia Inquirer,* September 19, 1992, p. d1; *Kommersant,* June 29, 1992, p. 12; DATA-STAR, *PROMT,* and *Ecotass,* June 4, 1990. DATA-STAR, *Textline*

4. Michael Porter, "Changing Patterns of International Competition," *California Management Review* 28 (Winter 1986): 9-40. Other related Porter titles are *Competition in Global Industries* (Boston: Harvard Business School Press, 1986) and *The Competitive Advantage of Nations* (New York: Free Press, 1990).

5. Francoise Bourguignon Christian Morrisson, *External Trade and Income Distribution* (Paris: OECD, 1989).

6. *Foreign Economic Trends Thailand* (January 1993).

7. "Global Advertisers Should Pay Heed to Contextual Variation," *Marketing News* (February 13,1987): 18.

8. Milton Pierce, "How to Write Direct Mail Copy for Overseas Use," *Direct Marketing* (May 1988): 132-33.

9. Peter R. Klein, "Advertising: Does Research Find a Cross-Cultural Effect?," *Applied Marketing Research 31* (Spring/Summer 1991): 17-26.

10. Terpstra and Sarathy, *International Marketing,* p. 506.

CHAPTER 10
International Marketing Research

MAJOR SOURCES DISCUSSED

- *Euromonitor Market Direction* Reports
- Frost & Sullivan
- Predicasts Files
- *Findex: The Worldwide Directory of Market Research Reports*
- *Textline*
- M ■ A ■ I ■ D
- ULI *Market Profiles*

INTRODUCTION

Marketing research involves gathering and analyzing the information needed to solve marketing problems. Large firms usually do their own marketing research and have the capability to collect their own primary data. Middle-sized firms often use marketing research firms to do the data collection and analysis for them. Smaller firms often rely totally on secondary data sources.

The specific tasks to be performed by a market researcher or information specialist are set out in Table 10-A. In the previous chapter, we examined the data needs and sources for the first three steps in Table 10-A. In this chapter, we will look at the more specific consumer and product information required for step four.

PROBLEMS IN INTERNATIONAL MARKET RESEARCH

There are several difficulties in collecting and using international market research data. Data are needed for many countries, but data items may not be available for individual countries. When data items are available, they may not be comparable across borders. There is often an absence of secondary data and difficulty gathering primary data. Data quality, data categories, and data consistency are all potential problems. Will we be able to find data in the demographic categories for the geographic level over the period of time that we need? Related questions are:

- What age breakdowns and income ranges are available?
- Are there data for cities, regions, or postal codes within countries?
- Are there time series and forecasts for the items we need?

Evaluating Secondary Information Quality

The key elements in evaluating secondary information quality are its timeliness, accuracy, comparability, and cost.

1. *Timeliness* is data dependent. Current macro-economic data may be two or more years old; useful consumer data should be more recent.
2. *Accuracy* of the data depends on clarity and consistency in item definitions and objectivity of the collection organization.
3. *Comparability* of data among countries is difficult at best. Even organizations such as the EC and OECD, which report data in standard formats, caution the user that the data have been collected by individual countries in non-standard formats.

Table 10-A. The Tasks of International Marketing Research

Marketing Decision	Intelligence Needed
1. Go international or remain a domestic marketer? *Screen potential markets*	1. Assessment of global market demands and firm's potential share in it, in view of local and international competition and compared to domestic opportunities
2. Which markets to enter? *Assess targeted markets*	2. A ranking of world markets according to market potential, local competition, and the political situation
3. How to enter target markets?	3. Size of market, international trade barriers, transport costs, local competition, government requirements, and political stability
4. How to market in target markets?	4. For each market: buyer behavior, competitive practice, distribution channels, promotional media and practice, and company experience there and in other markets

Source: Vern Terpstra and Ravi Sarathy, *International Marketing* (Orlando, FL: Dryden Press, 1990), p. 207

4. *Cost* of the information is relative to the needs and budget of the organization. Generally, the less expensive the data, the older and less specific they are.

Difficulties with Primary Data Collection

In addition to being more costly than secondary data collection, primary data collection is also sensitive to environmental and cultural factors in individual countries. The following are some of the problems associated with international primary data collection.

1. *Survey Design (phone, mail, door-to-door).* The same data collection instrument often cannot be used in different countries. Very few countries have as many household telephones as the United States. Response rates will vary. Many people are reluctant to speak with market researchers using any method.
2. *Questioning the Correct Individual and Getting the Correct Response.* An outsider often does not know who the decision maker is in a culture. In some cultures, interviewees do not want to offend the interviewer with a critical response.
3. *Language (meaning and translation).* An English language firm first has to translate the survey instrument into the local language and then have the responses translated back. If the survey is being conducted in more than one country, the translations may not be consistent.

The solutions for problems of primary data collection will depend on the country. For example, the *Overseas Business Report* for Thailand suggests that an individual having an extensive knowledge of the Thai culture and its characteristics write the survey instrument. A solution for developing countries is to use macro-level data to build models based on known variables for similar products or countries. Improvisation is the technique in Eastern Europe, where strategies might include:

- Talking with official importing organizations
- Attending exhibitions and trade fairs
- Contacting state committees
- Establishing local offices
- Participating in intergovernmental groups

MARKET RESEARCH REPORTS

The macro-economic data used in country-level analysis are available and well documented in print. The data might not be as timely as we would like or in the categories we prefer, but we often have a choice of sources, and often can find time series data for one country or comparable categories of data for several countries.

However, information on market share, consumer demographics, or advertising expenditures is fragmented, often expensive, and of questionable reliability. We cannot access one international source and find comparable information for a range of data items across products, countries, and companies. Compiling this information from a variety of sources takes time, patience, money, and luck.

Print Sources

One way to get at needed information and analysis is to use market research reports. Market research reports are written reports describing the market for a given product or service and its industry. These reports include analysis, forecasts, and recommendations. They describe the structure of the industry, size of the market, major players, characteristics of end-users or consumers, and external factors such as government regulations.

Commercially prepared market research reports for sale to the public are referred to as "off-the-shelf" reports. Off-the-shelf reports are provided by many publishers, such as the Economist Intelligence Unit, Euromonitor, Financial Times, Mintel, and ICC Key Note in Great Britain, and Frost and Sullivan and the U.S. International Trade Administration in the United States.

Market research reports may be expensive, costing from several hundred to several thousand dollars. Full reports can be purchased directly from the publisher. While the reports may provide excellent information, they are not tailored to the needs of the individual and are often several months or years old.

Market research reports answer such specific questions as:

- What is the size of the German beer market?
- What are the consumption and purchasing trends in the Italian healthcare market?
- What are future uses for lithium batteries worldwide?

Electronic Sources

Many market research reports are available in full-text online databases. Table 10-B lists online sources of market research reports and other full-text reports that provide information for market research.

Researchers weigh the relative costs of purchasing

Table 10-B. Electronic Sources of Market Research Reports

Source	Content
Datamonitor	Analysis and forecasts for over 400 market sectors in the U.K., Europe, and the U.S.
Euromonitor	Marketing information on consumer product sectors in the U.K., France, Italy, Germany, Spain, and the U.S.
Freedonia Industry & Business	New to online as of August 1992; over 150 reports on industrial products
Frost & Sullivan	Provides analysis and forecasts of technical and market trends for European and U.S. markets.
ICC Key Note	Detailed marketing information reports on consumer and industrial products, mainly in the U.K.
Investext	Company and industry reports produced by major international investment analysts
ICC International Business Research	Brokerage House reports from the U.K. and rest of the world; primarily U.K. companies

an off-the-shelf report, accessing reports or parts of reports online, or conducting primary research. For example, one individual Euromonitor report may be a reasonable $120. But a full 200-page "World" Freedonia report is prohibitive both in terms of cost and time online. If you are retrieving reports online, narrow your search. Instead of retrieving the entire European Beer Report, only screen for those records with information about consumer profiles.

Euromonitor. In addition to publishing reference and statistical sources, Euromonitor publishes international marketing reports and will provide custom reports. There are a series of published reports on the international market for a wide range of consumer products, from "In-Car Entertainment" to "Ice Cream, Yoghurt & Chilled Desserts," with most costing around $2,400.

Euromonitor Market Direction is an online file of full-text market research reports on consumer product sectors in the U.K., France, Italy, Germany, Spain, and the U.S. Japan is being added. Examples of online titles include:

AIR FRESHENERS AND INSECTICIDES
ANALGESICS
AUDIO PRODUCTS
BABY CARE
BEER
BOOKS
CDS, RECORDS AND TAPES
DAIRY PRODUCTS
HEALTH, SLIMMING AND DIETETIC FOODS
MAIL ORDER AND HOME SHOPPING

For ease of comparison, each report has a standard format with the following sections:
- Market Overview
- Sources of Supply
- Consumption and Purchasing Patterns
- Advertising and Promotion
- Future Outlook
- Total Market Size
- Market Sectors
- Prices and Margins
- Brands and Manufacturers
- Retail Distribution

Data are collected through interviews with manufacturers in all product sectors and countries. In addition, information is taken from trade journals, manufacturer and trade associations, and Euromonitor's original market analysis and forecasts. Each report is updated twice a year to incorporate the latest data. For example, all reports include advertising expenditure data complied from such local sources as:

Country	Local Data Source
U.K.	MEAL
Germany	Media Analysen GmbH or Schmidt und Pohlmann
France	Trade press after Secodip
Italy	Distribuzione Organizzata/Agb Italia

Euromonitor reports are available online on DATA-STAR (*MONI*), on DIALOG (File 762 and MARKETFULL) and on M ■ A ■ I ■ D.

Datamonitor. Datamonitor focusses on market research reports and does not provide the published data and source materials associated with Euromonitor. The databases often have reports on the same subjects. Table 10-C compares industries covered by Euromonitor and Datamonitor on DATA-STAR.

Datamonitor reports are predominately on the U.K. market. By the beginning of 1993, Datamonitor had issued both pan-European and world reports. Online, Euromonitor provides an individual report for each of six countries. A Datamonitor pan-European report, in contrast, takes one product and divides it into individual segments. The segments are individual subjects, country, or company reports. Most European titles are divided into the following separate reports: Belgium, Netherlands, U.K. 1 and 2, Spain, Italy, Germany, France, Competitive Analysis, Executive Summary, Market Opportunities, and Questionnaires.

The online file contains the full text of reports that cover a wide range of products, from stockbroking to egg boilers. Each report analyzes the major changes that occurred in the market during the previous year and provides detailed four-year market forecasts. In addition, the reports provide recent historical data on market size, segments, brand shares, advertising, trade, distribution, and consumer profiles; and contain analysis based on business school and Datamonitor models.

Table 10-C. Comparison of Industries Covered by Euromonitor and Datamonitor on DATA-STAR

Euromonitor	Datamonitor
Consumer Electronics	Automotive
Consumer Services	Industry to Industry
Cosmetics and Toiletries	Personal Products
Drinks	Drink
Foods	Foods
Electrical Appliances	Home Products
Healthcare	Financial
Household Cleaning	Retail/Mail Order
Leisure Goods	Leisure/Media
Tobacco	Telecommunications

Data are collected through trade interviews and exclusive surveys from GALLUP. Additional data are gathered from published sources, including stockbroker reports, trade press, government statistics, and MEAL, and from the trade associations, consumer panels, and storechecks.

Sample Datamonitor titles include:

European Magazines: Introduction
European Radio: Market Analysis 2
European Dietary Supplements: UK
European Commercial Vehicles: Italy
European Electricals Companies (30 individual company reports)
European Casualwear: Competitive Analysis
European Retail Banking
World Central Nervous System Markets: Forecasts
World Endocrine Market

Datamonitor reports are available on DATA-STAR (*DMON*), on DIALOG (File 761 and MARKETFULL), and on M ■ A ■ I ■ D.

Frost & Sullivan. Frost & Sullivan reports are widely respected. They are available in print or as full-text online files from DATA-STAR (*FSMR*) and M ■ A ■ I ■ D. Half the reports are from the U.S. and half are pan-European. Many of the reports cover very specific hi-tech, industrial products. The cost of these reports will be prohibitive for many users. The online cost for a full report may be even more than for the print version.

Sample Frost & Sullivan titles are:

- *The European Market for Lithium Batteries* (NO E1657/J, Summer 1992, pp. 250+ , $3,900) with forecasts through 1997
- *The Market for Satellite Communications in Developing Countries* (NO W1597/C, Winter 1991/1992, pp. 500, $3,700)

Other representative titles are *Business Development Opportunities in the European Clinical Diagnostics Market* and *The European Market for PC-Lan Hardware, Software, File Servers and Value Added Services in the Office Environment.* There is also a database of abstracts to Frost & Sullivan reports on DATA-STAR (*FSFS*), including all titles still in print.

Freedonia. *Freedonia's Industry Studies, Business Research Reports and Corporate Intelligence* is another, less familiar, source of market information. The file contains the full text of studies/reports published by the Freedonia Group, Inc. Geographically, 80% of the studies/reports deal with the U.S., 10% with North America (U.S. and Canada), and the remaining 10% with the rest of the world by country.

Each study/report contains analysis of economic environment, products and technology, end-use markets, marketing patterns, channels of distribution, competitive strategies, industry structure and market share, and company profile of leading participants. Also included are analyses and tables of detailed product/market data. Reports often contain product histories and forecasts to the year 2000.

Major industry groupings covered are:

Chemicals	Environment	Household Goods
Plastics & Plastic Materials	Health Care	Security Systems
	Construction	Electronics
Packaging	Industrial	Communications
Paper & Textiles	Components	Transportation
Metals	Producer Durables	

Examples of Freedonia reports on world markets include:

WORLD CARBON BLACK TO 1996
WORLD PHARMACEUTICALS
WORLD TITANIUM DIOXIDE TO 1995
WORLD DIAMOND THIN FILM & COATINGS
WORLD RUBBER AND TIRE TO 1995
WORLD LIGHT VEHICLES TO 1995
WORLD PLASTICS TO 1995
WORLD ADVANCED CERAMICS
WORLD HEALTH CARE TO 2000 (DEVELOPED COUNTRIES)
WORLD HEALTH CARE TO 2000 (DEVELOPING COUNTRIES)

Freedonia is available on DATA-STAR (*TFGI*) and on DIALOG (File 763 and MARKETFULL).

MARKETFULL. MARKETFULL, a collection of full-text market research reports on DIALOG, combines the Datamonitor, Euromonitor, and Freedonia databases. Each record represents a part of the report. Records may be anywhere from one computer screen, to more than 10 screens. Reports vary from 10 records for a single-country Euromonitor report, to more than 100 pages for a European Datamonitor report or more than 200 pages for Freedonia World Reports. Datamonitor, Euromonitor, and Freedonia, either separately or in MARKETFULL, cost $1.60 per minute ($96 an hour) and $10 per online record on DIALOG.

Investment Bank Reports as Market Research Reports

Another source for market information about both companies and industries is investment bank reports. Investment bank reports differ from market research reports in that their primary application is the financial analysis of quoted companies and the industries of which they are a part. Therefore, much of the information in these reports focusses on the financial and stock market performance of the companies analyzed. However, investment reports also contain information of value to the market researcher. The reports are good sources of competitive intelligence and may include market share information as part of their analysis.

Individual investment banks conduct research on the companies and industries they follow for their clients. Although available in print, these reports must be searched through full-text databases online or ondisc.

Electronic Sources of Investment Bank Reports. Investext is a product of Thomson Financial Network. Though originally U.S. in scope, it now includes reports from non-U.S. sources and about non-U.S. activities. It is available on many time-sharing hosts, including Thomson's own network, as well a CD-ROM provided by the Information Access Group.

A second time-sharing source is *ICC Stockbroker Research,* which includes the full text of U.K. and international reports. About 70% of the reports are related to U.K. companies and industries. In addition to online access, the *ICC Stockbroker Research Reports* for U.K. traded companies are on the DIALOG ONDISC*UK Factfinder* CD-ROM. A second ICC source, *ICC KeyNotes,* provides market analysis of key U.K. industrial sectors.

Ark Information Services, which became a subsidiary of Thomson Financial Services at the end of 1992, offers *The Research Bank*, full-text image reports. The European edition has over 30,000 company, industry, and economic reports from more than 50 participating brokers. *Investext* reports are being added to produce a Global Edition with up to 260 contributors worldwide. Search software accompanies the image reports.

Industry Reports as Market Research Reports

Industry reports, discussed more fully in Chapter 14, are also excellent sources for the market researcher. The *Financial Times Business Reports* on DATA-STAR and FT PROFILE has market analysis for a wide range of industries, such as biotechnology, telecommunications, and pharmaceuticals. The information comes from the *Financial Times'* newsletters and management and conference reports. The individual reports are also available on *Financial Times'* special surveys which often include useful information for the market researcher. For example, "The Survey of India" in 1992 has interesting information from Marg, India's largest market research organization, on the huge potential Indian market in rural and semi-rural areas. Marg sees the rapid penetration of television into the rural areas as the major factor behind greater product awareness.[1] The *Reports* are available online on DATA-STAR, FT PROFILE, and the LEXIS AND NEXIS SERVICES.

Newsletters

Specialized newsletters may be excellent sources for the market researcher. But because of their expense and narrow focus, it is more efficient to search newsletters online if they are needed only occasionally. Sources for newsletters are NEWSNET, and the newsletter files on DIALOG, DATA-STAR, and LEXIS AND NEXIS SERVICES.

Predicasts Files

The Predicasts files are an important source of market information. They contain excerpts from market reports in addition to abstracts and the full text of newspapers, trade publications, and business magazines. Predicasts files are available as print indexes, CD-ROMs, and online databases. The breadth and depth of the information, covering thousands of individual products from hundreds of countries, make Predicasts an essential source for marketing research. Euromonitor and Datamonitor reports only cover consumer products. Investment bank reports cover broad industry groups consisting of public companies. Predicasts' coverage is much broader. It describes industrial as well as consumer products to the 7-digit product level.

Sections of *Investext* and Euromonitor reports appear as part of the online *PROMT* file. *PROMT* also extracts material from two other marketing publications, "Eurofood" and "Research Studies Market Assessment." Two interesting new print newsletters, *Market Europe* and *Market Asia Pacific*, are part of Predicasts' newsletter file. Exhibit 10-1 is a sample Predicasts record, pointing to a market research report.

EXHIBIT 10-1. Sample Predicasts Record from *PROMT*

PTSP a *Euromonitor* publication costs $850
SO   Market-Research-Europe, April, 1992, PAGE 20,
TI   Table 13 FORECAST SALES OF ICE CREAM, YOGHURTS AND CHILLED/
AT   Europe: Sales of ice cream, yogurt and chilled desserts tabulated for 1990-95 by country.

Source: Promt on DATA-STAR, November 1992. PTS PROMT™ © 1993 by Information Access Company. Reprinted with permission.

ITA Market Reports

In Chapters 12 and 14 on exporting and industries we discuss the *National Trade Data Bank (NTDB)* and the market reports written by the U.S. International Trade Administration. Printed reports may be purchased or searched on the NTDB CD-ROM or through the LEXIS AND NEXIS SERVICES. Several thousand reports have been published for individual products in individual countries. They may also be made available on Internet.

Finding Aids for Market Research Reports

Findex: The Worldwide Directory of Market Research Reports, Studies and Surveys (Cambridge Information Group, 1993, 15th ed.—Annual, with mid-year supplement)

Findex has abstracts and indexes for some 12,500 off-the-shelf reports. Reports are of different types and include audits, syndicated, and multiclient studies. Most entries are market research reports arranged under 12 major industry groupings, with a separate section for reports about companies. The reports come from more than 500 U.S. and non-U.S. publishers. *Findex* is indexed by publisher, title, subject, country, and company name. *Findex* abstracts are searchable on DIALOG (File 196).

Sample titles from *Findex* that indicate the range of prices and subjects include *China Drug Purchase Audit*; this quarterly publication on Western-type pharmaceuticals sold to a sample of hospitals and clinics in the People's Republic of China costs $17,500. Another sample title is the one-time "Tights and Stockings"; this report, with forecasts to the year 2000, covers a segment of the hosiery industry in the U.K. and costs less than $200.

Marketsearch (Arlington Management Publications and the British Overseas Trade Board—Annual)

Formerly the *International Directory of Published Market Research*, *Marketsearch* has a brief summary of 20,000 published market research studies. Countries are in the summaries, but index access is to publisher and corporate author.

WORLDWIDE MARKET SHARE

Many commonly asked marketing questions concern "market share." The question must be clearly defined to be answerable. A question such as "What is Nestle's market share?" is too ambiguous for an answer.

Market share requires a defined product or service, a defined geographic region, and a defined unit of measurement. Market share is now expressed globally, regionally, nationally, or locally. It can be measured by sales or volume, consumption or production, dollars or units (e.g., barrels or bottles). To calculate a meaningful share, the entire market quantity should be known. The answer is usually expressed as a percentage.

Market share can be measured at the level of broad industry grouping:

- What is Nestle's share of the world food market?

For a product line:

- What is Nestle's share of the European coffee market?

For a specific line of business:

- What is Nestle's share of the U.S. decaffeinated coffee market?

For a specific brand:

- What share of the coffee market is held by Decaf Nescafe?

Because of the elusiveness of the definition of *market* for each situation, no one source, printed or online, can be relied upon to answer market share questions.

Market Share Reporter: An Annual Compilation of Reported Market Share Data on Companies, Products and Services, Arsen J. Darnay and Marlita A. Reddy (Gale Research, 3rd ed., 1993)

The *Reporter* presents market share data that have been published in other sources. There are more than 2,000 entries, arranged by 2- and then 4-digit U.S. SIC codes with indexes to sources, place names, products, services and issues, companies, and brands. The data are selected from newspapers, trade publications, and business magazines as well as from the *Investext* database. Sources are primarily from the U.S. but also may come from Canada, Europe, or Asia. *The Market Share Reporter* is a file in the Market Library on the LEXIS AND NEXIS SERVICE.

Use the *Market Share Reporter* with caution and primarily as a finding aid. Its limitations include the highly selective nature of the entries, which often appear random; the lack of underlying market information; and the age of the information. The burden is on the user to determine the reliability of the source and to examine the source document.

Researchers with access to *Investext* and to the other online and CD-ROM databases mentioned below would be much better served searching for market share information directly. Searching electronic sources is often

expensive, but there is also a cost attached to providing partial, dated, or misleading information.

In mid-1993, Gale announced the *European Market Share Reporter.* According to the publicity brochure, the book will have over 1,500 entries from over 80 countries. Its format and arrangement will be similar to the U.S. counterpart. The book will be published biennially.

Electronic Access to Market Share Information

To find other market share data in print, it is usually necessary to begin by searching online or on CD-ROM. In addition to market research and investment bank reports, multi-purpose databases such as *ABI/Inform, Textline,* and Predicasts *PROMT* all contain worldwide market share data. The most specific and far ranging market share information appears in the Predicasts' files. Table 10-D lists selected databases that provide market share information.

Table 10-D. Selected Databases with Market Share Information

PREDICASTS	F&S Index + Text CD-ROM (International and U.S. discs)
	PROMT
	Predicasts Newsletter Database
	PTS MARS (Marketing and Advertising Reference Service)
REUTERS	TEXTLINE
UMI	ABI/INFORM

Predicasts Files. A diverse range of articles with market share data appear in the online *PROMT* database and the *F&S Index Plus Text International* CD-ROM. The print versions of the F&S indexes and *PROMT* cannot provide the same level of access to articles containing market share data. Many of the Predicasts international sources are difficult to obtain, but Predicasts has been adding more full text to its electronic files. Because many of the publications Predicasts indexes may be unfamiliar, and because the original source of the data is often not included, much of this data should be used judiciously. Exhibit 10-2 is an article from *PROMT* that includes examples of important marketing concepts.

Other representative titles relating to market share in *PROMT* include:

- Condition & prospects of automotive industry in Indonesia: Isuzu Panther enters the market for Category I cars. *Indonesian Commercial Newsletter*

EXHIBIT 10-2. Excerpts from Predicasts *PROMT*

AN　3751725 PROMT 920511.
SO　East-Europe-Agriculture-and-Food, March, 1992, PAGE N/A, ISSN 0263-3205.
DT　920300.
LG　EN.
PN　Bulk-Fluid-Milk (P2026100). Cheese (P2022000). Butter (P2021000).
EN　Foreign-Trade (E64).
CN　**Poland** (C6POL).
TI　INCREASING IMPORTS AFFECTING POLISH DAIRY SECTOR.
AT　Poland: Imports 137.8 mil L of milk in 1990, with further large imports in 1991; discusses taste for Western prods.
AV　*FULL TEXT AVAILABLE IN FORMAT 'ALL'*.
LE　WORD COUNT: 571.
TX　Polish **consumers** have rapidly developed a **taste** for western dairy products, despite the higher **prices** which they attract on the retail market. Official statistics show that Poland imported as much as 137.8 million litres of milk in 1990, mostly from France, Belgium, Germany and Denmark, with further large imports in 1991. The reason for the increase in the huge difference in **product quality**, especially for cheeses, which has attracted consumers to pay a large **premium** for imported products. These developments have been held in check to some extent by limits on imports of milk and dairyproducts from Western Europe. These include the **administrative barriers and customs duties** which, as from March 1 1992, have been adjusted in accordance with the Poland-EC Association Agreement. In addition, these is only a limited number of more **affluent consumers** in Poland who can afford to buy Western milk. Thus the **market share** of imported milk and dairy products in 1991 remained at 10%. Overall consumption falling. . .

There is also a general tendency towards decreased **consumption** of milk and dairy products in Poland . . . The **structure** of the Polish **dairy industry** is far from satisfactory . . .

Market prices rising . . . liquid milk sold in the shops for between 4 400 and 5 200 slotys per litre ($1 = 13 200 slotys) . . .
Polish dairy exports in Jan-Sep 1991
According to the latest available data from the **Central Statistical Office**, imports of milk and selected dairy products the end-September 1991 stood at:

Milk (hectolitres)		Cheese (tonnes)		Butter (tonnes)	
France	5 934	Holland	126.8	Germany	1 052.0
Belgium	821	Hong Kong	20.0	Austria	439.7
		Switzerland	15.0	France	364.7
		France	12.0	Holland	315.0
		Germany	9.0	Czecho-Slovakia	86.4

Source: Monthly Statistical Bulletin of GUS (Polish Central Statistical Office) 1992, No. 1
Table details Poland's imports of milk and selected dairy products as end-Sept 1991 by type and country.
THIS IS THE FULL TEXT: Copyright 1992 Agra Europe (London) Ltd.

Source: F & S Index + Text International, SilverPlatter CD-ROM, November 1992. Copyright © 1993 by Information Access Company. Reprinted with permission.

- Aegyptens Klimageraetemarkt hart umkaempft. AT Koldair: Currently holds 70% mkt shr of wall mounted air-conditioning mkt. *Nachrichten fur Aussenhandel*
- The OTC Market in Czechoslovakia: ANALGESICS & SEDATIVES—Future Trends. Research Studies— Nicholas Hall & Company

Textline. Reuters *Textline* has well over 100,000 records with market share information. Some sample titles on market share for beer are presented below:

- **Spain:** Catalan based brewer Damm reports improved results for 1991. *La-Vanguardia*

- **Europe:** Leading brewers increase combined market share to 46% in 1990. *The Grocer*, 6/20/92 p. 28.

Predicasts products and *Textline* are good sources for very specific products. *ABI/Inform* references market share information on a more global scale. Examples of *ABI/Inform* citations are shown in Exhibit 10-3.

M ■ A ■ I ■ D. Market Analysis and Information Database (MAID) is a specialized online system comprised of full-text market research reports, syndicated demographic data, and advertising expenditures. It also accesses the Predicasts and *Textline* files. Formerly available through Pergamon Financial Database Services, it is

---

EXHIBIT 10-3. Market Share Information on *ABI/Inform*

Anonymous. GEA: Making Things Happen - Open Door Policy. Appliance Manufacturer; Jan 1992; v40 (n1): GEA2-GEA5.
General Electric Co.'s GE Appliances (Louisville, Kentucky) . . . Speed is required in capturing a larger **share of the global market . . . .** Approximately 30% of GE Appliances' (GEA) $5.7 billion in 1990 sales came from outside the US. The company currently markets appliances on 5 continents and in 150 world markets.

Drynan, David; Jeanes; David. Global Data Networking with DPN-100. Telesis; 1991; 93: 36-45.
During the past 2 years, Northern Telecom's DPN-100 data networking system - which commands the largest **global share in its market -** . . .

Ekberg, Kent F. The Bright Future of Optical Storage. Document Image Automation; May-Jun 1991; 11(n3): 170-173..
Today, Pioneer is widely known as the LaserDisc company and commands a **worldwide market share greater than 65% of total units sold** in both the consumer and industrial markets.

Hoggan, Karen. Kellogg: A Cereal Killing? Marketing.; Oct 31, 1991: 22-24.
The power of the Kellogg name extends beyond the US into 130 other countries, where it markets more than 40 brands. It has cornered **51% of the worldwide market outside the US,. . . .**

Levin, Gary. Co-Branding Trend Takes Credit Cards. Advertising Age.; Nov 11, 1991; 62(n48): 69. . .
Visa dominates the **worldwide general-purpose credit card market** with a 50.9% share.

Reprinted with permission from UMI.

now an independent time-sharing system. It markets itself as "the biggest source of market information."[2]

M ■ A ■ I ■ D is produced in the United Kingdom; while giving special emphasis to Western Europe, its coverage is worldwide. Its scope is consumer products, retail services, and industrial products.

Publisher of reports found on M ■ A ■ I ■ D include:

Advertising Age	Euromonitor	MEAL
BAR-LNA	Find/SVP	Mintel
Datamonitor	Frost & Sullivan	Packaged Facts
EIU	ICC Key Note	Simmons

Access points are market sector, company or brand, country, publisher or publication, and "scope of reports."

Advertising and Promotion	Foreign Trade
Brand Shares	Market Structure
Consumer Profiles	Mergers and Acquisitions
Distribution	Prices

These reports contain a wealth of useful information for the corporate marketer. The system is expensive to access, but if your organization requires a wide range of secondary market data, than this is a databank to consider.[3]

MARKETING RESEARCH AS AN INDUSTRY

Marketing Research is an industry in itself. ESOMAR, the European Society for Opinion and Marketing Re-

search, started collecting data on the market for market research in 1989. The data are collected from national market research societies and trade associations and measure turnover (sales) only from external market research companies or institutes. Almost half the marketing research value in the world is centered in Europe, primarily in France, Germany, and the United Kingdom. The European strength in this area is reflected in U.S. access to commercial secondary market research material, since much of it is from European firms such as Euromonitor.

In Europe, about 90% of research is conducted for local clients. Consumer product companies accounted for over 50% of the European total expenditures. Exhibit 10-4 gives estimates of the world market for market research.

Data on the world's top 10 market research companies is compiled by ESOMAR from a variety of sources, and the figures are "reasonably accurate" (p. 218). These companies collect primary data to sell to individual clients and also offer syndicated services. Exhibit 10-5 lists the largest market research companies in 1991.

Sources of Information about Market Research Companies

Marketing News (American Marketing Association) published a *Directory of International Marketing Research Firms* as a supplement to its March 1, 1993 issue. This 10-page publication arranges research firms by country. All entries include name, address, and phone numbers. FAX numbers and a contact name and title may

Exhibit 10-4. Market Research Markets in 1991

	Value (million ECU)	%	Index
EC 12	2,364	39	106[1]
Other Europe[2]	294	5	105[1]
Total Europe	**2,658**	**44**	**106[1]**
USA	2,171	36	113
Japan	518	9	110[1]
Other[3]	610	11	107

ECU 1=$1.23

[1] absolute figures (value) not comparable with last year's reported results; the index figures for EC12, Other Europe, Total Europe, and Japan have been based on corrected market size data for 1990

[2] excluding Poland, Bulgaria, Hungary, Albania, Rumania, but including estimates for Czechoslovakia and the former Yugoslavian states.

[3] no complete data available for *'other'* parts of the world; this analysis is based on an assumed annual growth rate of 5% since 1989

(Sources: ESOMAR, trade associations and estimates, Advertising Age.

Source: Permission to report these tables from ESOMAR Annual Market Study on 1991 Market Statistics has been granted by ESOMAR, Amsterdam, Tel +31-20-664-2141. Fax +31-20-664-2922.

also be provided. If companies have additional offices, the offices are shown under the main listing and also in a special table.

ESOMAR publishes a *Directory of ESOMAR Members* and a *Directory of Research Organizations*. It also publishes multi-lingual glossaries of market research terms and monographs, in addition to sponsoring conferences throughout Europe. Members abide by the ICC/ ESOMAR International Code of Marketing and Social Research Practice, adopted by over 50 associations in 26 countries. ESOMAR also publishes a quarterly journal, *Marketing and Research Today*, which lists the summary results of the "ESOMAR Annual Market Study: The State of the Art in Marketing Research."

Euromonitor's *Directories of Marketing Information Sources* have sections on leading market research companies, arranged by country. Each entry has name, address, and telecommunications, and most also indicate research services available. Complete entries also have parent or subsidiaries, countries reached, turnover and employees. The Washington Researchers *Market Guides* have limited lists of research organizations for some countries with name, address, telecommunications, and a one-line description. Individual *OBRs* discuss marketing research within the country and provide the names of some of the major firms. The standard directory sources for U.S. market research firms also include a few international market research companies.

Bradford's Directory of Marketing Research Agencies and Management Consultants in the United States and the World (Bradford—Biannual)

Bradford's has a brief international section. Entries have the company name, address, contact name, and telecommunications. Other than the company name, nothing in this directory distinguishes marketing firms from management consulting firms.

Exhibit 10-5. Largest Market Research Companies 1991

World Top Market Research Companies, 1991

Research Company	Turnover (million ECU)[1]	Countries with office[2]	Head office	Ownership
1. A.C. Nielsen	986	27	US	Dun & Bradstreet, USA
2. IMS Internat	414	62	US/UK	Dun & Bradstreet, USA
3. IRI	169	4	US	Public Company, USA
4. GfK	154	24	D	Public Company, D
5. Arbitron	153	1	US	Control Data Corp, USA
6. Sofrès/Cecodis[3]	118	8	F	Fimalac-led Group, F
7. Research International	101	36	UK	WPP, UK
8. Infratest/Burke	81	12	D	Private Company, D
9. Video Research	79	1	J	Dentsu el al, J
10. MRB	78	8	UK	WPP, UK

1) excluding associates

2) including associates

3) combined 1991 turnover shown for entities merged in 1992

(Sources: Research companies, ESOMAR, J. Honomichl, Research International Estimates)

Source: Permission to report these tables from ESOMAR Annual Market Study on 1991 Market Statistics has been granted by ESOMAR, Amsterdam, Tel +31-20-664-2141. Fax +31-20-664-2922.

International Directory of Marketing Research Companies and Services (New York Chapter, American Marketing Association—Annual)

Known informally as the Green Book, the *International Directory* has a geographical index to companies listed alphabetically in the body of the book. In addition to name, address, and telecommunications, several contacts are given and, more importantly, each entry has an abstract describing the company's activities.

A final place to look for marketing research companies is in company online databases such as the D&B files.

DEMOGRAPHICS

For U.S. marketers, accustomed to readily available data at zip code (postal code), city, country, and Metropolitan Statistical Area level, international demographic research can be tedious and frustrating. The type and detail of demographic data necessary for regional marketing, new business locations, or real estate investments are not readily available on the international scene. Almost all of the printed demographic data we have located are at a country level.

Even large market research organizations have difficulty obtaining detailed international demographic data. In October 1991, Donnelley Demographics, a major U.S. provider of demographic information, began negotiations with a European organization to provide detailed demographics for one European country. The target date was 1993. Donnelley has now put the project on hold because of the problems it encountered getting and verifying data.

Syndicated Data

Marketing analysts use demographic data to answer such questions such as:

- How many people live in Germany?
- How many people living in Germany are between the ages of 18 and 34?
- How many people living in Germany between the ages of 18 and 34 drink imported beer?
- How many people living in Germany between the ages of 18 and 34 had a Budweiser in the last seven days?
- Are people living in the postal code for the Sorbonne more likely to play tennis than the average for a French postal code?
- What is the median home value in Osaka?

Answers to similar questions are available for the U.S. market. But for the rest of the world, the available data, if any, are scattered, and most often part of a market research report.

One exception is the United Kingdom, where Target Group Index, the U.K.'s largest product and media survey, samples 24,000 adults per year. Many market researchers in the U.S. still request data from the Target Group Index, even though in the U.S. it has been merged with the Simmons *Study of Media and Markets*. Target Group Index results are included in marketing journals accessible through *Textline, PROMT,* and *Infomat*. The data are published in conjunction with the British Market Research Bureau, a part of the international WPP group. Almost 400 ICC *Key Note* market reports include such TGI data as Breweries and the Beer Market, UK Travel and Tourism, and Supermarkets and Superstores. Demographic data include age and sex breakdowns, but also tables by major geographic region and "Social Grade." Exhibit 10-6 is an extract from the report on the U.K. confectionery industry.

ICC *Key Note Reports* are also available on DATA-STAR, FT PROFILE, ESA (European Space Agency), and direct from ICC.

Euromonitor publishes data supplied by *Public Attitude Surveys* in its U.K. beer reports. PAS operates continuous monitoring on 20,000 adults and counts among its clients major brewers and retailers. Data are reproduced in the Euromonitor reports with the permission of PAS. Researchers cannot directly access the PAS data themselves.

The data resemble those reported in the U.S. in *The . . . Study of Media and Markets* from Simmons Market Research Bureau, as illustrated in Exhibit 10-7.

International organizations, regional organizations, and individual countries produce demographic data of varying depth, scope, and quality. The MRI project, an attempt to provide Europe-wide consumer research along the lines of Target Group Index, failed to materialize because of a lack of support from sponsors.[4]

We found no printed postal code demographic data such as CACI's *Sourcebook of Zip Code Demographics*. In Europe, EC privacy issues, discussed in more detail in Chapter 11 in our discussion of direct mail, affect the public dissemination of this type of data. Many of the databases listed in Chapter 6 can be used to create mailing lists at a postal code level, in a manner similar to the Dun's Market Identifier Files.

Consumer Confidence

Consumer confidence surveys question consumers on their buying intentions. Market researchers use the

EXHIBIT 10-6. Target Market Index Data in *ICC Key Note Report*: Extract from "KEY NOTE REPORT CONFECTIONARY"

TABLE 17:   PROFILE OF PURCHASERS OF CONFECTIONERY BY SOCIAL GRADE (% OF RESPONDENTS), 1992

	AB	C1	C2	D	E
Chocolate assortments and other boxed chocolates	20.4	25.4	26.3	16.8	11.1
Other chocolate items	18.0	24.6	27.4	17.7	12.1
Mints	17.1	24.6	27.5	17.7	12.5
Bars of chocolate	17.7	24.5	27.6	17.6	12.6
Sweets in tubes and sweets for children	16.6	23.6	28.1	18.8	12.9
Toffee and caramels	15.8	23.9	26.9	18.9	14.5
Chewing gum	13.8	22.8	30.0	21.2	12.2

Source: Target Group Index. BMRM International, 1992

Source: ICC *Key Note Report Confectionery,* March 1993, from LEXIS AND NEXIS SERVICES. Reprinted with permission from ICC.

EXHIBIT 10-7. PAS Attitude Survey on Beer Drinkers in Euromonitor U.K. Beer Report 1992

Of those respondents drinking any beer in the week prior to interview, 73% were male. Just over half (57%) were over 35, and 60% were from social groups C2DE. Slightly more women had drunk packaged beer than had drunk draught; by age group there was little distinction between the two categories. Packaged beer drinkers were marginally more up-market than draught beer drinkers; 42% of respondents who had drunk packaged beer in the previous week were from social gropus ABC1, compared with 39% for draught beer.

93% of respondents who had drunk draught bitter were male; 65% were over 35. The social profile of draught bitter drinkers was even, except that ABs were slightly overrepresented.

TABLE 4.15   PROFILE OF BEER DRINKERS 1989
Based on % drinking any of specified beer types in week prior to interview

	SEX		AGE				CLASS			
	M	W	18-24	25-34	35-49	50+	AB	C1	C2	DE
Any beer	73	27	19	24	27	30	18	22	30	30
Draught	79	21	21	25	27	27	17	22	31	30
Packaged	73	27	20	26	26	28	19	23	30	28
Dr bitter	93	7	14	21	30	35	21	21	30	28
Dr lager	69	31	30	29	25	16	15	23	32	30
Dr mild	96	4	11	17	32	40	10	19	34	37
Packaged lager	70	30	23	29	27	21	19	23	30	28
Packaged LPE/bitter	89	11	12	21	30	37	24	23	28	25

Source: PAS Drinks Market Survey 1989

Source: Beer Market in the U.K. from *MONI* on DATA-STAR. Reprinted with permission from Euromonitor.

surveys as predictors of buying plans. The Conference Board publishes a Consumer Confidence Survey for the U.S., the EC, Japan, and Canada. Present data and expectations are part of all the surveys. The EC and Canadian surveys also examine present buying conditions for major purchases. These data are available online on DATASTREAM.

General Sources for Demographic Data

Demographic information is available at a general country level from international and regional organizations.

Demographic Yearbook (Statistical Office of the United Nations, 1948—Annual)

The United Nations collects and compiles demographic data for more than 160 countries. Data items include population by age, sex, and urban/rural designation. Each table is well documented, with the data items defined and the data quality issues enumerated.

Social Indicators of Development (World Bank—Annual)

Though compiled by the World Bank to measure human welfare in more than 170 countries, including the U.S., EC, and Japan, the information given for each country on social indicators of development is also useful for the potential market entrant. In addition to a "Current Conditions Table" for the world, up to 94 indicators are prepared for each country, depending on time series availability. Each country has a two-page entry. A table gives the year of the last census and official estimates for each country included.

Per capita income and income distribution are supplemented with infrastructure data, including fuel and power, transport (population per car), road length, and population per telephone. Data on education include percent of students beyond high school enrolled in science and engineering. Other pertinent data items are percent of population in urban areas, urban/rural growth and birth rate differentials, labor force participation information, and natural resources.

Social Indicators is issued annually in paper and on diskette. It contains time-series data from 1965 in the present edition. The indicators used correspond to the United Nations' recommended fields from the *Handbook of Social Indicators*. The data are compiled mainly from other international agency publications.

World Market Atlas (Business International, 1992)

World Market Atlas has a limited amount of data with marketing applications for 150 countries. Each country has a minimum of 8 graphs and could have as many as 16. Important to market researchers are forecasts, demographic trends from 1985 to 2000, and age group trends from 1990 to 2000. Data from a variety of published sources and other Business International research are included.

Demographics in the European Community

In 1991, all countries in the EC conducted a census of population. Some macro-level data were released in 1992. Because of the EC's concern with individual privacy, it is uncertain at what level of detail the data will be released.

The EC is moving toward "Eurodemographics," a harmonized system of demographics used in *Eurobarometer*. *Eurobarometer* public opinion surveys have been conducted for the Commission of the European Communities each spring and autumn since September 1973. The results have been published since 1974.

An identical set of questions is asked of a sample of people aged 15 and over in each EC country. The former East Germany was added with *Eurobarometer 34*. Most of the questions are about the respondents' attitudes toward the EC. The surveys are carried out by national institutes that are members of ESOMAR, the European Society for Opinion and Marketing Research.

EC depository libraries receive these reports, and nondepository libraries have access to some reports on *Textline*. Online records come from *European Community Press Releases,* publication of which precedes the printed versions. Results of the new *Eurobarometer* opinion surveys of Eastern Europe are also released online.

ESOMAR has created a system of Harmonisation of Demographic Classifications which is being adapted by the EC as a common classification system in *Eurobarometer* surveys. The "Recommended Questionnaire" and definitions and comments are available directly from ESOMAR (Central Secretariat J.J. Viottastraat 29, 1071 JP Amsterdam, The Netherlands, FAX: 31-20-664-29 22).

One of the items ESOMAR has developed is an "economic status scale" based on the number of households in a country owning each of 10 durable goods, from color TVs to second homes. This effort is supported by the EAAA, the European Association of Advertising Agencies. The questions are available in English, French, and German.

Demographic Statistics (Eurostat—Annual)

An example of a regional publication is Eurostat's *Demographic Statistics*. In 1990, Eurostat organized the data to allow for inter-country comparisons in an attempt to satisfy the growing interest in demographic statistics. The contents include:

A. Population Change
B. Population Structure, including age pyramids for each country
C. European Community and Its Regions
D. European Community in the World
E. Fertility
F. Marriage and Divorce
G. Mortality
H. Foreign Residents
I. Population projections (1990 through 2020)

Exhibit 10-8 is a table from *Demographic Statistics* that gives detailed age data with country breakdowns for men and women in the EC.

Rapid Reports: Population and Social Conditions (Eurostat, 1987—Irregular)

This series of reports contains statistical information of interest to the market analyst. It uses the harmonized nomenclature of ESOMAR, but often suffers from old data. Issue 7 from 1991 was available at the end of 1992; it presents data from "Household Consumption Expenditure for Eight Member States of the European Commu-

EXHIBIT 10-8. Table from *Demographic Statistics*

B-5

Population by sex and age
on 1 January 1989 (1000)

AGE	B		DK	
	Males Hommes	Females Femmes	Males Hommes	Females Femmes
0	60.8	57.8	30.3	28.5
1	60.3	57.2	29.1	27.3
2	60.6	57.1	28.6	27.1
3	58.8	55.9	27.8	26.7
4	59.5	56.9	26.9	25.7
0-4	**300.0**	**284.9**	**142.8**	**135.4**
5	60.3	57.3	26.3	25.3
6	61.8	58.8	27.4	26.1
7	63.8	60.4	27.3	26.4
8	63.4	60.9	29.5	28.4
9	63.6	59.7	30.6	29.3
5-9	**312.7**	**296.9**	**141.0**	**135.4**
...				
35	75.1	71.9	38.4	36.7
36	75.2	71.5	37.7	36.4
37	72.0	69.4	37.3	35.6
38	72.6	70.0	38.1	37.3
39	72.6	69.5	38.2	37.1
35-39	**367.5**	**352.3**	**189.8**	**183.1**

Source: Demographic Statistics, 1990, p. 112. Reprinted with permission.

nity in 1988," which is based on data collected between 1986 and 1988. The results are reported in ECUs and PPS (Purchasing Power Standard) by country. The European Community also issues *Rapid Reports: Regions*, which began in 1989 and also appears irregularly.

The Regions in the 1990s (Eurostat, 1991)

Regions in the 1990s: Social and Economic Situation and Development of the Regions of the Community is the fourth report on European demographics from the Office for Official Publications of the European Communities. It is the closest EC equivalent to U.S. metropolitan area data. Exhibit 10-9 displays extracts from Table A24 in *The Regions in the 1990s.*

The Book of European Regions: Key Facts and Figures for Business (Euromonitor, 1992)

Euromonitor has compiled EC information plus regional data from some additional sources in *The Book of European Regions: Key Facts and Figures for Business.* The book covers 152 regions in the EC and EFTA, and 48 regions in Eastern Europe. Regional coverage by country in *The Book of European Regions* is illustrated in Table 10-E.

Each West European region has a one-page discussion of demographic trends and economic activity and also details of the major companies within the region. Statistics for most regions include:

EXHIBIT 10-9. *The Regions in the 1990s*

Regions of the Community Ranked according to their level of GDP per head (average 1986-87-88, In PPS, EUR 12=100

Rank	Region	GDP/head in PPS, average (1986-88) EUR 12 14 730 =100	Unemployment rate, average (1988-90) EUR 12 (9.1%) =100	Population 1988	
				total (mil)	cumulative % share
1	Voreio Aigaio (GR)	39	63.6	0.2	0.1
35	Puglia (I)	72.5	165.9	4	18.6
141	Haute-Normandie (F)	115.7	116.7	1.7	73.5
168	Greater London (UK)	164.0	80.8	6.8	96.0
169	Ile-de-France (F)	165.6	84.3	10.3	99.2
170	Hamburg (D)	182.7	97.2	1.6	99.7
171	Groningen (NL)	183.1	135.0	0.6	99.8

Source: The Regions in the 1990s, pp. 109-111. Reprinted with permission from the Office for Official Publications of the European Communities.

Table 10-E. Regional Coverage in *The Book of European Regions: Key Facts and Figures for Business*

REGIONS PER COUNTRY					
Country	No of Regions	Country	No of Regions	Country	No of Regions
Western Europe:					
Austria	9	Iceland	1	Portugal	4
Belgium	3	Ireland	1	Spain	18
Denmark	3	Italy	20	Sweden	7
Finland	3	Luxembourg	1	Switzerland	5
France	22	Netherlands	12	Turkey	8
Germany	16	Norway	5	United Kingdom	11
Greece	3				
Eastern Europe:					
Albania	1	Hungary	7	Former USSR	9
Bulgaria	9	Poland	8	Former Yugoslavia	6
Czechoslovakia	4	Romania	4		

- Land Area
- Demographic Data
  - Population Total, Change, Density and Structure
  - Sub-Regional Population Totals
  - Major Town Population Totals
- Economic Data
  - Number employed, unemployment rate
  - Employment Structure: agriculture, industry and services, construction
  - GDP per capita
- Miscellaneous Data
  - Households
  - Cars

Despite the promise of the title, the book does not provide enough unique information to make it worth purchasing if you have other EC publications.

Special Sources

Some specialized publications are either too narrow in scope or too expensive for most collections. One example of an expensive product is from Demosphere International Inc, located in Virginia and Japan. It uses personal computer applications to help consumer marketers analyze markets, segment population, evaluate media, and target direct mail. *JapanSite* is a mapping program for 150 items at the neighborhood level for the Tokyo metropolitan area. Main subject areas are households, labor force, population (by age and sex), and establishments (by type, number of employees, and age of establishment). It is not as sophisticated as comparable U.S. products, such as Donnelley's, but the Demosphere product should be considered by institutions needing detailed data on the Asian market.

Demosphere also has data for over 200 countries of the world. Complete data for South Africa, including cluster segmentation, suburbs, and roads, was priced at $40,000 in 1992.

Market Europe and *Market Asia*, published by W-Two Publications of Ithaca, New York, often mention companies that have compiled demographic information. Searches of the online databases suggested for other marketing topics will also retrieve demographic information.

REAL ESTATE

Information about space, availability, price, and utilization rates for the housing, retail, office, and industrial real estate markets are all important to the market re-

searcher in determining site selection. One source of limited international information answers such questions as:

- What is the standard land price per acre for an industrial park in Bangkok?
- How many condominiums are there in Frankfort?
- What is the standard rent for a new two bedroom apartment in Sydney?

ULI *Market Profiles* (Urban Land Institute—Annual)

U.S. business researchers use ULI publications for real estate research and also as sources for regional demographic data. ULI has added international cities to its *Market Profiles*. Table 10-F lists the cities for which there is a 1992 or 1993 *Market Profile*. Not all cities are updated every year. The publication appeared in two volumes for the first time in 1993.

A ULI report provides statistical data and analysis on the housing market (*see* Exhibit 10-10), shopping center market, office market, and industrial market, with a map of developmental activity for the city, its central business district, and the greater metropolitan area. Each city's report is written by a regional real estate expert.

CONCLUSION

International market research is both expensive and time consuming. Much of the information is collected locally and is not publicly available to an international audience.

Table 10-F. ULI *Market Profiles*—International Markets, 1992-93

Volume 1 Eastern North America and Europe	Volume 2 Western North America and Pacific Rim
Barcelona	Bangkok
Berlin	Hong Kong
Brussels	Kuala Lumpur
Budapest	Sydney
Frankfort	Tokyo
London	
Mexico City *	
Montreal *	
Moscow	
Paris	
Prague	
Warsaw*	
* In the 1992 edition but not in the 1993 edition	

EXHIBIT 10-10. ULI *Market Profiles* for Bangkok, 1992

TABLE 72.2   **HOUSING MARKET**

(All dollar figures based on 1991 exchange rate)

	1988	1989	1990	1991[1]
Total Households	1,750,000	1,800,000	1,860,000	1,920,000
Housing Inventory				
Total Units	1,374,000	1,454,000	1,556,000	1,683,000
Single-Family	205,000	255,000	319,000	370,000
Condos/Apts	59,000	66,000	78,000	92,000
Annual Construction[2]				
Total Units	67,450	80,031	102,335	127,555
Detached				
Single-Family	36,574	40,844	38,693	37,534
Semidetached				
Single-Family	455	845	805	1,274
Townhouses	26,741	31,280	42,510	52,087
Condos/Apts	3,680	7,062	20,327	36,660
Standard New-Unit Sale Prices				
Detached				
Single-Family[a]	110,000	145,000	177,000	195,000
Townhouses[b]	16,700	22,500	32,000	43,000
Apartments[c]	79,000	101,400	102,000	125,000
Standard New-Unit Rents				
One-Bedroom[d]	$580	$610	$650	$715
Two-Bedroom[e]	$980	$1,170	$1,400	$1,470
Standard Lot Prices				
Single-Family				
Lot[13]	$156,500	$239,000	$266,000	$274,000

Notes 1 through 13 can be found on page 438. Where report authors changed standard (numbered table notes, a lettered author's note has been substituted. This table is therefore missing one or more note numbers. Standard notes 3 through 7 do not apply to this table. [a]A new, 2,700-square-foot, three bedroom, two-bathroom unit in a 3,500-square-foot lot in an upper-income area. [b]A new, 1,000-square-foot, two-story, two-bedroom, two-bathroom unit on a 900-square-foot lot in an average-income area. [c]A new, 900-square-foot, 2½-bedroom condominium in an upper-middle-income area. [d]Monthly rent for a furnished, 450-square-foot, one-bedroom apartment. [e]Monthly rent for a furnished, 900-square-foot, two-bedroom apartment. Sources: Government Housing Bank; and Richard Ellis Research.

Source: ULI *Market Profiles,* 1992, p. 401. Reprinted with permission from ULI.

Off-the-shelf market research reports may be purchased, but often cost over $1000, and the reports are rarely for the exact situation that the researcher needs. Primary data collection, on the other hand, in host countries, also has problems. Market share and consumer demographic data are also hard to find at the level of specificity to which the U.S. marketer is accustomed.

Use finding aids from companies such as Euromonitor and Washington Researchers to identify marketing research services in the host country in conjunction with secondary data from the research reports, trade publications, and newsletters.

SELECTED ARTICLES ON MARKET RESEARCH

Miller, Richard. "First Steps to Selling Abroad," *Target Marketing* v (February 1992): 39–40.

Basic international research steps and sources are presented: geopolitical. socioeconomic, and strategical-logistical.

Oostveen, Jan and Wouters, Joost. "The ESOMAR Annual Market Study: The State of the Art of Marketing Research," *Marketing & Research Today 19* (November 1991): 214–18.

This article includes a summary of the European Society for Opinion and Marketing Research (ESOMAR) report on the size of the market for market research.

Stacey, Robert T. "Canadians, Eh! Similar but Different," *Direct Marketing* 54 (December 1991): 68–69.

Despite the geographic proximity and some demographic similarities, Canadians are different from both Americans and Europeans.

NOTES

1. David Housego, "Survey of India," *Financial Times* (June 26, 1992).

2. M ■ A ■ I ■ D brochure, April 1993.

3. Michael Halperin, "M.A.I.D. for Marketing, " *Online 12* (January 1988): 51–52

4. "EUROPE: Lack of Support Kills Off MRI Research," *Media-Week* (July 27, 1990): 15; from DATA-STAR, *Textline*.

CHAPTER 11
Advertising, Direct Marketing, and Media

TOPICS COVERED

1. Advertising Agencies
2. Advertising Expenditures
3. Advertising Rates
4. Advertising Regulation
5. Advertising Organizations
6. Broadcasting and Advertising
7. Direct Marketing
8. Selected Sources of Information
9. Conclusion
10. Notes

MAJOR SOURCES DISCUSSED

- *Advertising Age*
- *Survey of World Advertising Expenditures*
- *Business Publications Rates and Data*
- *Standard Directory of International Advertisers and Agencies*
- *European Advertising, Marketing and Media Data: Directory and Sourcebook*
- *Direct Marketing in Europe*

Advertising is both an important part of international marketing and an important international service industry. Three facets of international advertising are examined in this book. The first is advertising as a part of international marketing strategy.

- How do you advertise internationally? Do you use the same ad in Singapore as in Chicago?

The second is advertising as an international industry.

- Who are the major advertising agencies? What is the structure of the local media?

The third is advertising regulations.

- What restrictions do governments put on advertising?

The first facet of international advertising is discussed in Chapter 9, within the section entitled "The International Four P's." The second and third facets are discussed in this chapter.

ADVERTISING AGENCIES

International Agencies

Advertising Age (Crain Communications—Weekly)
   Advertising Age publishes a special report on the world's top advertising agencies each year in the spring. The article reports income for the largest agencies worldwide. It gives the ranking, the U.S.-based agency, its headquarters, the worldwide gross income, and the change from the previous year. In 1992, five out of the top ten agencies were not headquartered in the U.S. and the agency showing the greatest increase in revenues was the Tokyo-based Dentsu.

   The same *Advertising Age* issue also lists leading agencies, by gross income, arranged by country. Gross income, percent change, billings, and the exchange rate used are the entry items reported for each locally based agency as well as its affiliation, if any, with worldwide agencies. For example, the leading agencies in Argentina include affiliates of Young & Rubicam, J. Walter Thompson, and a locally based agency, Lautrec/SSA.

   A second *Advertising Age* special report, issued in July, focuses on world brands. This report is arranged by agency. For each agency, a chart indicates which brands the agency handles in which countries. Accounts served in at least four countries two weeks before publication are included and combined client business must total at least $5 million.

   This listing indicates how worldwide advertising has become. It presents agencies advertising in more than 31 countries and gives the number of countries in which an agency is located, the number of international brands it handles, its major international brand, and the number of countries in which that brand is advertised. For example, McCann-Erickson Worldwide handles the account for Coca Cola in 82 different countries while both Lintas Worldwide and J. Walter Thompson handle Unilever products in more than 45 countries. There is an additional listing for agencies operating in less than 31 countries.

A second *Advertising Age* special report on world-wide agencies focuses on world brands. This report is arranged by agency. For each agency, a chart indicates which brands the agency handles in which countries. Accounts served in at least four countries two weeks before publication are included and combined client business must total at least $5 million.

Regional Agencies

Mergers and acquisitions within the advertising sector have resulted in a few large, dominant firms. To compete with these large multinational agencies, small agencies in Europe have set up independent agency networks. Examples of such networks are Alliance International Group in London, with gross income of $106 million and 18 members, and ComVort GmbH in Berlin, with $44 million in billings and 18 members.

Public Relations Firms

Many companies seek promotion through public relations, nonpaid publicity, as well as advertising. Globalization of public relations firms has taken the shape of "voluntary networks" of firms rather than the global agencies that exist in advertising. The largest independent international network, International Connections, is a loose affiliate grouping. A listing of the top 10, from the U.K. publication *PR-Week*, is presented in Exhibit 11-1.

ADVERTISING EXPENDITURES

Advertising Age is the standard source for world-wide agency and advertiser data. However, it does not include data about the different advertising media used in individual countries.

Survey of World Advertising Expenditures (Starch INRA Hooper and the International Advertising Association—Annual)

Survey of World Advertising Expenditures has been the standard source for aggregate country-level advertising data since 1960. The survey report is sponsored by Starch INRA Hooper and the International Advertising Association. It is designed to facilitate comparisons among countries. The top 10 advertisers for reporting countries are an added feature.

The publication has gone through a series of changes in name and publication schedule. In the spring of 1993, the 1990 *Survey* was the most current available. Starch was unable to give an estimate of when the 1991 edition would be available.

The 53 countries or territories for which data were available in 1990 are reported, based on survey results. Economic data, including exchange rates, are provided

---

EXHIBIT 11-1. Europe's Top PR Consultancies, *PR-Week*

Rank (#)	PR Network	UK member	Income 1991 (pounds)
1	Countrywide International	Countrywide Communications	32,100,000
2	International Connections	Charles Barker	22,500,000(a)
3	Entente International Communication	Communication Group	20,550,000
4	Ketchum PR	Group PR	15,000,000(a)
5	European Communication Partners	Pielle and Company	13,676,100
6	Manning Selvage and Lee	Manning Selvage and Lee	12,882,198
7	PR Organisation Intl	Edson Evers & Associates	10,650,000
8	Europrism	Vox Prism	10,440,000
9	PRX International	Infopress	7,821,000
10	Europe On-Line	Cornerstone Communications	5,622,877

Key (a) denotes organisation's own estimate.

Source: "Top 50 PR Consultancies—Europe's Uncertain Partnerships," *PR-Week*, May 28, 1992, p. 22. Reprinted with permission from Routledge, Chapman and Hall, Inc.

by the World Bank and International Monetary Fund. The introduction states that "fluctuations in currency exchange rates and inflation frequently contribute more to year-to-year changes than increases or decreases in actual advertising volume." Therefore, different tables are presented in *current* or *constant* currency and in U.S. dollars or local currency. Listed below are examples from the *Survey* of each reporting situation:

- **Constant U.S. dollars:** Table 7 presents television advertising expenditures for 1986-1990
- **Constant and current local currency units:** Tables 2A and 2B present total advertising expenditures
- **Current U.S. dollars:** Table 9 presents 1990 advertising expenditures in various media

Table 3 in the *Survey* presents 1990 per capita advertising expenditures. While the U.S., with expenditures of more than $128 billion, spent as much on advertising as the next 19 countries combined, Switzerland had a higher per capita figure, $612.60 to $512.60.

Table 9 includes spending for print, television, radio, cinema, outdoor transit, direct advertising, and miscellaneous. This table illustrates the differences in advertising spending among media in various countries. Exhibit 11-2 includes a few examples from Table 9.

ADVERTISING RATES

A standard advertising question is the cost of advertising in commercial media.

- How much does it cost for one full-page black-and-white ad in the Asia/Pacific edition of the *Economist*?

The sources listed below provide advertising rates for some international publications.

Business Publications Rates **and** *Data* **(Part III)** and *Consumer Publications Rates and Data* (Standard Rate and Data Service—Monthly)

Standard Rate and Data Service publications, the standard U.S. sources for advertising rates and circulation figures, now include a few international publications. At the end of 1992, *Business Publications* had 170 international titles under 60 subject groupings. The subject groups are the same as those used for the U.S. SRDS plans to expand the list as more publications conform to their format and policies. Both audited and nonaudited publications are included. "International" covers non-U.S. publications and U.S. publications with international circulation.

Entries for international publications are the same as for U.S. titles, with the addition of language of publication and currency of rates. All entries are uniform. Introductory material has journal title, address, frequency, publisher, brief content note, and, for audited journals, the insignia of the auditing agency. Each entry may contain any of these additional data items.

1. Personnel
2. Representatives or Branch Offices
3. Commission and Cash Discount
4. General Rate Policy
5. Black/White Rates
6. Color Rates
7. Covers
8. Inserts
9. Bleed
10. Special Position
11. Classified/Mail Order
12. Split Run
13. Special Issue Rates
13a. Geographic and/or Demographic Editions
14. Contract and Copy Regulations
15. General Requirements; also see SRDS Print Media Production Data
16. Issue and Closing Dates
17. Special Services
18. Circulation and Establishment Date

The non-U.S. audit bureaus used in the SRDS publications include:

EXHIBIT 11-2. *Survey of World Advertising Expenditures*: **Extract of Table 9**

1990 ADVERTISING EXPENDITURES IN VARIOUS MEDIA
(Millions of U.S. Dollars)

Country	Total	Print	Television	Radio	Cinema	Outdoor Transit	Direct Advert.	Miscellaneous
Argentina	829.7	202.3	250.9	72.4	27.2	79.6	58.4	78.6
Bahrain	11.0	6.1	4.9	-	-	-	-	-
China, PR	523	159.7	117.4	19.1	.5	-	126	100.4
Germany FR	13,944.4	8,429,8	1,708.2	550.8	136.2	420.9	2,698.5	-
Hong Kong	861.4	363	421.9	37.9	11.2	27.3	-	-
Norway	1,233.3	730.9	20	8	9.6	17.6	447.3	-
United States	128,640	42,174	28,405	8,726	-	1,084	23,370	24,881

Source: *Survey of World Advertising Expenditures,* 1990, pp. 36-37, published by Starch INRA Hooper in cooperation with the International Advertising Association. Reprinted with permission.

ABC	Audit Bureau of Circulations Ltd.	U.K.
ojd	Office de Justice de la Diffusion	France
IVC	Insituteo Verificador de Circulacao	Brazil
IVW	Informationsgemeinschaft zur	Germany
	Festtellung der Verbreitung von	
	Werbertrageme	
CCAB	Canadian Circulations Audit Board	Canada

SRDS placed the following warning on page 1609 of the December 1992 issue of *Business Publications Rates and Data:*

CAUTION—CAUTION—CAUTION

Devaluation of the many national currencies now floating in relation to the dollar, such as the British pound sterling, West German deutschemarks, Italian lire, Swiss and French francs, etc., suggests caution should be exercised in determining billing arrangements for space placed in International publications whose rate structures are reported in U.S. dollars.

SRDS recommends that buyers of media consult the nearest U.S. advertising sales office of each International publication—for current procedures and arrangements.

ADVERTISING REGULATION

When we discussed accounting in Chapter 2, we examined the work of international and regional organizations toward harmonization. The development of advertising codes within a framework of international and regional organizations has met with limited success. There is no international code on advertising.

History of Regulation

Advertising regulation, taking the form of consumer protection, can be traced back to Roman law; in the U.S., advertising regulation dates from the Sherman Anti-Trust Act of 1890 and the formation of the Food and Drug Administration in 1906. The Federal Trade Commission (FTC) was created as part of the Federal Trade Commission Act of 1914 and had the authority to prohibit unfair practices, such as advertising that injured competitors. The FTC authority was extended in 1938 to include advertising that adversely affected consumers. In the late 1960s and early 1970s, legislation for consumer protection was enacted in Western Europe. In the rest of the world, most advertising regulations, until the 1970s, were based on the prevailing colonial background.

Today, host countries regulate advertising within their borders, including advertisements originating outside their borders. As with accounting and financial practice, the underlying legal culture determines the direction of national advertising regulations. Advertising regulations can be categorized as civil law or common law, and also as socialist law; Islamic law; Confucian law, which is based on human rather than legal relationships; and traditional or unwritten law (for more on the distiction between code and civil law countries, see Chapter 2).

Regulation in the EC

As with other areas of regulation, much of the attempt at harmonization has been taking place within the European Community. The EC has passed directives that affect advertising. The two major ones are the Misleading Advertising Directive and the Cross-frontier Broadcasting Directive.

The text of the 1984 directive concerning misleading advertising is printed in the EC *Official Journal* No. L 250, 19/09/84 P. 0017. The text is also online in *CELEX* and updated information on implementation is in *CELEX* and *Spearhead* (84/450/EEC: Council Directive of 10 September 1984 Relating to the Approximation of the Laws, Regulations and Administrative Provisions of the Member States Concerning Misleading Advertising). For EC purposes, the following definitions for advertising and misleading advertising are used:

Advertising means the making of a representation in any form in connection with a trade, business, craft or profession in order to promote the supply of goods or services, including immovable property, rights and obligations; 2. Misleading advertising means any advertising which in any way, including its presentation, deceives or is likely to deceive the persons to whom it is addressed or whom it reaches and which, by reason of its deceptive nature, is likely to affect their economic behaviour or which, for those reasons, injures or is likely to injure a competitor.

The Misleading Advertising Directive was passed in 1984 and all EC countries enacted it by 1992. The Council justified involvement in advertising by arguing that misleading advertising impedes fair competition.

The Cross-frontier Directive provides a limited harmonization of member states' laws in relation to television broadcasting activities, including advertising and the protection of children (*Official Journal* Reference L298 of 17 October 1989). Advertising restrictions concern

- duration of advertising
- the form of interruption
- ethical considerations (particularly for children)

- advertisements for alcohol
(Council Directive 89/552/EEC of 3 October 1989 on the co-ordination of certain provisions laid down by law, regulation or administrative action in Member States concerning the pursuit of broadcasting activities).

In March 1992, the Council enacted a wide ranging directive that addressed advertising of medicines, Council Directive 92/28/EEC on the advertising of medicinal products for human use. It appeared in the *Official Journal* Reference L113 of 30 April 1992. "Advertising" includes advertisements and information of any kind directed both to the public or health care professionals that may promote the prescription, supply, or sale of medicinal products. The activities of pharmaceutical company sales representatives are also subject to certain requirements. Enactment was scheduled for January 1993 (from *Spearhead*).

Seven key advertising areas are under consideration within EC countries.

1. **Alcohol:** Various restrictions exist in most member states. The "Loi Evin" banned a large proportion of alcohol and tobacco advertising in France as of January 1, 1993.
2. **Tobacco:** All television tobacco advertising has been banned in the U.K. and several other EC states since October 1991. The Commission gave the tobacco industry until January 1, 1994 to come up with self-regulatory measures.
3. **Food:** The four main framework directives for food advertising cover labelling, food for particular nutritional purposes, additives, and materials and articles in contact with foodstuffs.
4. **Comparative Ads:** Eight EC member states permit comparative advertising under various conditions and four prohibit it (Italy, Belgium, Germany, Luxembourg). The debate centers on providing consumers with better information, improving competition, and cross-border advertising. In the U.S. comparative advertising has been encouraged by the FTC.
5. **Pharmaceutical Ads:** All EC member states prohibit the advertising of prescription-only pharmaceuticals. Nine members permit advertising of nonprescription medicinal products.
6. **Distance Selling (direct mail):** A draft proposal, by the EC Commission's Consumer Policy Service, is currently under discussion. It covers information overload, right of refusal, inertia sales, contract terms, membership of a recognized guarantee fund, unaddressed offers, and confusion over delivery dates.
7. **Data Protection (privacy):** The key issue here is the protection of individuals regarding automatic processing of personal data. EC directives have concentrated on the storage, processing, and transmission of data; the rights of the data subject (prior consent, right to information, right to access, right to rectification, right to opposition); and data quality and security.[1]

Other Advertising Regulations

Various bodies of the United Nations have been active in areas related to advertising and consumer protection. The Centre for Transnational Corporations focuses on consumer protection, while the World Health Organization and the Food and Agricultural Organization are concerned about health affects of multinational activities. UNESCO is concerned with the cultural effects of global advertising, and advertising is one topic in the GATT discussions.

ADVERTISING ORGANIZATIONS

Self-regulation began in 1904 with the formation of the Associate Advertising Clubs of America. The group established a National Vigilance Committee that became the Better Business Bureau in 1915. Self-regulation took a step forward in 1938 when the International Chamber of Commerce issued a Code of Standards of Advertising Practice. Also in 1938, the Export Advertising Association of New York was founded and grew into the International Advertising Association in 1954.

Some industry associations have also created bodies to monitor advertising and marketing behavior. One example is the International Federation of Pharmaceutical Manufactures. Selected organizations, and their focus, when known, are presented in Table 11-A.

The Institute of Practitioners in Advertising (IPA) supports an agreement with the European Association of Advertising Agencies (EAAA) to set common standards for advertising production costs, the benchmark "European Production Contract."[2]

The European advertising industry established a cross-border self-regulatory system in June 1992. It attempts to monitor and regulate media that originate in one country for consumption in another. The arrangement handles complaints from the public and from competitor companies. The framework will be overseen from Brussels by the European Advertising Standards Alliance (EASA), an association of national bodies. The Alliance has members in all EC member states except Denmark and Luxembourg, plus members in Austria, Switzerland, and Sweden.

One issue facing EASA is varying tastes among countries and how to judge an advertisement originating in one country and disseminated in a country with different standards. For instance, in France bare bottoms are acceptable, but in the U.K. the same ads draw complaints. The authorities in individual countries will continue to monitor internal complaints.

Table 11-A. Selected Government and Industry Regulatory Bodies

ORGANIZATION	LOCATION	FUNCTION or FOCUS
Institute of Practitioners in Advertising (IPA)	Europe	Production costs
European Association of Advertising Agencies (EAAA)	Europe	
European Advertising Standards Alliance (ESEA)	Europe	Industry Association
Advertising Standards Authority (ASA)	U.K.	Code of Advertising; Regulatory body
Committee of Advertising Practice (CAP)	U.K.	Guidelines on offensiveness
Advertising Standards Authority	South Africa	Arbitration of complaints
Hungarian Complaints Board-Regulatory	Hungary	Fines
Advertising Federation of Australia	Australia	
Australian Association of National Advertisers	Australia	
Advertising Standards Authority-Regulatory	New Zealand	
GCC Advertising Association	Bahrain & Gulf	
Advertising Department	China	Regulatory
National Advertising Council	Mexico	Industry Association

The U.K. Advertising Standards Authority (ASA) monitors advertisements to make sure they comply with the U.K. Code of Advertising Practice and rules on complaints within the U.K. For example, a Bacardi ad from Westbay showed a bar with the caption: "Don't be shy, who's first up for Karaoke? " The ASA agreed with the complainant that its code had been broken because the ad suggested that drinking could remove inhibitions in social situations.[3]

Another issue is advertising and children. The European Association of Advertising Agencies' Advertising and Children Committee has accepted a self-regulation code. The 12-point code allows children to appear in ads but not verbally endorse a product or act as presenters.

The direct marketing industry is lobbying for more involvement in drafting regulations. The industry in the U.K. formed the Direct Marketing Association. Self-regulation is an important step for the Association in order to stem consumer criticism and potentially harsh legislation.

Advertising and Media Organizations

There is an interdependence between advertising and media that includes both TV and print publications (newspapers, consumer and business publications).

Several organizations, called tripartite organizations, represent advertisers, advertising agencies, and the media in which they advertise. Some of these organizations are:

International Advertising Association (IAA)	International
European Advertising Tripartite (EAT)	Europe
Advertising Association (AA)	U.K.
ZAW	Germany
American Advertising Federation (AAF)	U.S.

The IAA is the global tripartite association representing the common interests of advertisers, agencies, and the media. Its principal objectives are to protect freedom of commercial speech and consumer choice, promote the value of advertising, encourage self-regulation, and foster professional development through education and training. It has 3,000 members in 87 countries. Its members account for 97% of global advertising expenditures. The World Secretariat is located in New York City. IAA coordinates its activities with the other major advertising tripartite organizations listed above.

BROADCASTING AND ADVERTISING

The structure of a country's advertising expenditures depends on the availability of media. In the U.S., we take for granted the large number of television and radio stations, most of which survive on advertising revenue. In other countries, the government may regulate the number of stations, the programming, and the amount and content of advertising.

Television has been a major factor in the globalization of the world market. Now the TV market itself is becoming global with the rapid growth of satellite TV.

- There are more than one billion TV sets in the world.
- TV sets are more common in Japanese homes than flush toilets.

- Most Mexican households have a TV while only half have telephones.
- 1994 is the target date for Europesat, the pan-European satellite.

The satellite dish has replaced the TV antenna. There are more than 300 satellite-delivered TV services worldwide. At the end of 1992, CNN was viewed in 137 countries. Satellite TV is viewed as the "holy grail" of marketing, making instant global advertising a reality.[4]

Within recent years, there has been a move toward deregulation of television worldwide, resulting in more stations and more outlets for advertising. Appendix H on TV availability in OECD countries shows that countries have different broadcast models and that there is a trend toward liberalization.

DIRECT MARKETING

Direct marketing refers to both a distribution method and a promotion technique between supplier and customer. It refers to the way some companies, e.g., L.L. Bean, do business, and to the manner in which companies promote their products and services.

- Direct Marketing: distribution
- Direct Advertising: promotional technique
- Direct Mail along with Telemarketing: two types of direct marketing or direct advertising

There are many examples of international direct marketing:

- The Lands' End catalog is shipped to more than 100 countries and most international sales come from Canada, Western Europe, and Japan.[5]
- U.S. catalogers are featured in printer R.R. Donnelley's *American Showcase,* a cooperative catalog mailed to 50,000 Japanese households.
- Harrods ran an international 800 phone number for U.S. customers in a full-page ad in *The New York Times* to advertise items that could be bought via the phone.

Direct marketing grew rapidly in the 1980s though it has flattened in the early 1990s. NAFTA should open up the Canadian market. In Europe, the U.K. is accustomed to direct marketing. The Germans order through the mail and have begun ordering through toll-free telephone lines. The catalog business is new to Japan.

Two types of lists are available to the international direct marketer: multinational and indigenous. Multinational lists are files of list owners who have small quantities of names in many different countries. Presently, sources of consumer lists often come from U.S. magazines with subscribers abroad, such as *Business Week, Fortune,* or the *International Herald Tribune.* These may be useful for testing which foreign markets are interested in an offer. Indigenous lists are country-specific and would be used for mail campaigns within a particular country.

Telemarketing and the use of "800" and "900" numbers is predicted to be the growth segment of international marketing, but it is not widely used now.[6] The estimates for percentage of catalog orders taken by phone in Europe vary greatly by country.

Country	Catalog Orders Taken by Phone
France	25%
Italy	25%
Germany	35%
Sweden	60%
United Kingdom	70%

Some of the differences among countries can be explained by more restrictive environments in France, Italy, and Germany. Also, it is estimated that less than 25% of all French people have credit cards.[7, 8]

Direct Marketing Agencies and Organizations

In doing research for this chapter, we found an overlap between conventional advertising and direct marketing at one end of the scale, and direct marketing and sales promotion at the other. The traditional distinctions between marketing disciplines are breaking down.

This is reflected in the structure of the industry. While direct marketing services are provided by direct marketing agencies, many of these are now part of advertising agency groups. Prominent multinational agencies include Ogilvy & Mather, Young & Rubicam, Watson Ward Albert Varndell, Wunderman, Evans Hunt Scott (Eurocom), and McCann-Erickson.

The European Direct Marketing Association (EDMA) is taking a strong position on self-regulation in response to the EC Directive on Data Protection. EDMA's "Single Market Campaign" includes a List Forum for list brokers and creation of EURODIP, a standard address layout.

The EC directive is designed to give European citizens rights over use of personal data, even beyond the boundaries of the EC. In the U.S., anyone may use names and addresses unless individuals make the effort to have their names removed from the list. The situation in the EC is the reverse. The EC directive presently gives individuals the right to express consent to use their names in a file. This means that a company has to obtain permission each time it wants to rent a customer's name or run information about the customer through a profiling program. The EC will not allow data exchange with countries that do not have adequate levels of protection of privacy.[9]

SELECTED SOURCES OF INFORMATION

Directories of Advertisers and Agencies

Standard Directory of International Advertisers and Agencies (National Register Publishing: A Reed Reference Publishing Company, 1984—Annual with updates)

International Advertisers and Agencies has profiles of more than 2,000 international advertisers and more than 2,000 international agencies from more than 90 countries. This is a companion to the U.S. *Standard Directory of Advertisers* and *Standard Directory of Advertising Agencies* described in detail in the second edition of Michael Lavin's *Business Information,* pp. 120-121.

In addition to extensive listings of advertisers and agencies, *International Advertisers & Agencies* has several interesting special features. It contains a list of country advertising associations that are part of the International Advertising Association. It also has a brief country synopsis of advertising restrictions.

> In most countries, virtually all advertising is controlled in some way. Following are specific restrictions. For additional information, please contact the country's advertising association. (A-47)

The largest part of the book is devoted to advertisers. There is an alphabetical index to all company names. The body of the directory is arranged alphabetically by parent company. This arrangement is different from the U.S. version, which is arranged by broad product grouping.

A standard listing may include the following elements, also present in the U.S. counterpart:

* - Company provided information
Name, address, telecommunications
Approximate Sales and Employees
Fiscal year-end
Year founded
Computer system used
Business description with SIC codes
Key personnel
Subsidiary information (directory and sales, sic, executive)
Agency
    Possibly products advertised and account executive
Month of advertising budget
Type of media used (coded)
Distribution of products/services, e.g., national, international, direct

There are geographic indexes of advertisers and agencies, U.S. SIC codes, a trade names index, and, finally, "Who's Where in International Advertising and Marketing, a listing of personnel, their titles, company, and country.

Though designed for marketing applications, *International Advertisers & Agencies* provides a long list of subsidiaries, both domestic and foreign, which is also available in the publisher's international volume of *Corporate Affiliations* (1993-). Many of the companies are international divisions of U.S. firms. The actual advertising data for each company varies greatly, from the name and address of one agency to a complete breakdown of advertising expenditures. Exhibit 11-3 shows an example of agency data from Avon Thailand.

The second part of the book has agency information that again is similar to the U.S. Agency Red Book. A sample entry appears in Exhibit 11-4.

EXHIBIT 11-3. *Standard Directory of International Advertisers and Agencies:* **Extract of an Advertiser Entry**

* 64530041	MEDIA TYPES INCLUDE:
	12 Network Radio
AVON COSMETICS (THAILAND)LTD ...	13 Spot Radio
	14 Network T.V.
Advertising Agency:	15 Spot T.V.
	16 Exhibits
Dentsu, Young & Rubicam/Bangkok...	17 Product Samples
	18 Yellow Pages
18 Yellow Pages	19 Point of Purchase
(Advertising Appropriations: $1,360,000;	20 Newsp. Dist. mags
Consumer Mags. $720,000; Premiums,	23 Cable T.V.
Novelties $480,000; Network T.V. $160,000)	
(Media:1-2-3-4-9-10-14-15-16-17)	
Distr: Natl; Direct to Consumer	

Source: Reprinted from *Standard Directory of International Advertisers and Agencies,* 1993, p. 53

EXHIBIT **11-4.** *Standard Directory of International Advertisers and Agencies*: Agency Entry

BBDO Marketing   027406537
        Hydometeorology Pavillion "Nauka"
        Exhibition Center, VDNX, Moscow USSR
        12933
Tel: 95-181-9997
Telefax: 95-187-8295

Employees: 13   Year Founded: 1989

Agency specialized in: Marketing, Advertising,
        Public Relations & Direct Marketing
Nikolai Romanenko....Deputy Dir. Gen. & Print
        Production...

Creative Dirs: Ivan Chimburov, Igor Lutz
Mktg Research Dirs. Igor Litvin, Alexander Titov

Clients:
Avon Products Inc, New York NY Cosmetic Prods...
Wrigley GmbH, Unterhaching, Germany
        Chewing Gum

Source: Reprinted from *Standard Directory of International Advertisers and Agencies,* 1992, p. 650

There are inconsistencies in the entries. Under *Advertisers*, for example, there are only two brief listings for McDonalds, one in Germany and the other in the U.K; several pages of listings for Nestle conclude with a note that operating companies handle their own advertising, but information is not provided for the operating companies. Under *Agencies*, from Exhibit 11-4, there is no entry under *Advertisers* for Wrigley GmbH. Another client, Gold-Star, is listed under parent Lucky-Star (Korean) but there is no reference to the Moscow agency.

le Dossier des Agences Conseil en Communication
(Publications Professionelles Francaises, 20th ed., 1992—Annual)

This French directory of advertising agencies is a glossy edition, with color examples of advertisements for each agency and a full page of information that includes establishment date, officers, major clients, prizes, associated agencies, and philosophy.

Statistical Information and Sourcebooks

European Advertising, Marketing and Media Data: Directory and Sourcebook (Euromonitor, 2nd ed., 1992).

European Advertising, Marketing and Media Data is a mix of data and sources for Europe's advertising and media markets. While some of the information is found in other Euromonitor titles, there are also unique

media and advertising statistics. Seventeen countries are covered, with advertising data, media data, and directories of advertising agencies, leading newspaper and magazine publishers, television stations, radio stations, cable and satellite TV systems, cinemas, and outdoor operators projected for each. National advertising associations and research firms are also listed.

A chart given for each country indicates advertising restrictions and regulations for selected categories of products. The categories include tobacco, spirits, beer and wine, pharmaceuticals, food, ads aimed at children, toys, records, and travel services, and financial services. The restrictions vary by country although usually advertising for tobacco and spirits is banned on TV and radio. In Norway there is almost no advertising on TV at all. Finally, national "Stat/Packs" supply hard-to-find data from national syndicated sources. The Stat/Pack for France has data on:

- Total Advertising expenditure by product or service (8 sectors)
- Press expenditure detail
- 50 Leading advertisers by media (press, radio, TV, outdoor, cinema)
- Cinema number and attendance; monthly variation; daily attendance
- Radio ownership by type of owner
- Radio audience
- TV ownership
- VCR ownership
- TV audience (total and housewives)
- Press readership demographics
- Readership of national newspapers and dailies
- Magazine readership (number and penetration)

There is also some useful summary media data in Euromonitor's *European Directory of Marketing Information Sources*, described in detail in Chapter 9. Not only are the standard numbers of TVs, radios, etc. included, but also presented is legislation on television advertising and advertising regulations, newspaper circulation, and advertising expenditure by type. Exhibit 11-5 displays a socio-economic profile for Spain from the *European Directory of Marketing Information Sources.*

Sources for Advertising Regulations

International Advertising Handbook: A User's Guide to Rules and Regulations, Barbara Sundberg Baudot (Lexington Books, 1989)

Published in 1989, this handbook is the most recent treatment of the subject of international advertising regu-

---

EXHIBIT 11-5. *European Directory of Marketing Information Sources*

SOCIO-ECONOMIC PROFILE/SPAIN

Media availability (1988)

Number of TV sets (million)	12.5
Number of radio sets (million)	11.5
Dailies	120
Consumer magazines	900
Cinemas (number of screens)	2,309

Source: Euromonitor

Television advertising

Legislation introduced in 1988 created three new national channels, ending the monopoly of the state-run Television Espanola. Henceforth, the system will be regulated by the Red Tecnica Espanola de Television (Retelevision). All channels accept advertising.

TV channels are as follows:
-Canal Sur (started 1989): Andalucia
-Euscan Telebista (started 1983): northern Spain
-Television de Galicia: Galicia
-TV3
-Televisio de Catalunya (entirely Catalan language)
-Sky, Superchannel and Galavision can all be received

Advertising regulations: There are restrictions on tobacco and alcoholic beverages (both of which are banned on radio and TV) and on medicinal products and financial services.

Source: *European Directory of Marketing Information Sources*, 1992, p. 607. Reprinted with permission from Euromonitor.

---

lations for business we could find and much of it still accurately reflects the advertising regulatory environment.

The book is arranged in six parts: Background; Industrialized Market-Economy Countries (United States, Europe by parts and Community, and Japan); Socialist Countries (Eastern Europe, China, and Socialist Asia); Third World Countries (Arab Middle East, Latin America and the Caribbean, Third World Asia, categorized by income level); and Africa South of the Sahara. The final section is on international controls with guidelines and standards.

Each group of countries has a Regulatory Profile table that includes, among other categories, legal system and ad regulation. For example, the profile for "High-Income Latin American" reports significant regulation of advertising, while the table for "Low Income Asia" reports moderate regulation based on the British system.

Another source of advertising regulations is Business International's *Investing, Licensing & Trading*, discussed in Chapter 12.

Sources of Direct Marketing Information

Direct Marketing in Europe (ELC, 1st ed., 1991-)

Direct Marketing in Europe is sponsored by the European Direct Marketing Association (EDMA) and distributed in the U.S. by Dun & Bradstreet. The book is a directory of direct marketing organizations in 15 European countries. Non-EC countries are Austria, Finland, Norway, Sweden, and Switzerland. Greece, where there is no direct marketing activity, and Luxembourg, where the activity comes from the surrounding countries, are not included.

The book is arranged by country. For each country, there is a one-page overview of the direct marketing industry, including the status of data protection legislation. Availability of statistics varies widely; the statistical bases are not the same among countries, and some estimates are for direct marketing, while others are for direct mail. Within each country, companies are arranged by the type of service they provide, from full service agency to telemarketing. Entries include name, address, telecommunications, business activities, contact names, parent company, year established, number of employees, turnover in local currency, and geographical markets. Part 2 is an alphabetical index to all companies. Text is in English, French, and German.

Direct Mail List Rates and Data (Standard Rate and Data) has a small section on established Canadian lists and established international lists. *Scientific American* and *Time* both provide international consumer lists. Many of the business lists are also based on circulation records or established databases.

Online Databases

If you have access to the LEXIS AND NEXIS SERVICES, a consistently good source of information on the media at a country level is Walden Publishing's *Country Reports,* described in detail in Chapter 13. Each country report includes information about broadcast media, and also lists newspapers with their circulation, indicating which figures are audited.

For some countries, recent data are not available and for other countries no data are available. For example, the report for Malaysia, updated January 20, 1993, presents audited circulation figures from the Audit Bureau of Circulation Malaysia as of November 1987. The English language Malaysia business newspaper, *Business Times,* did not have audited figures. In Pakistan, the government ceased including aggregated data on the country's print media in 1987. Pakistani newspapers do not announce their revenues. The Audit Bureau of Circulation (ABC) of the Ministry of Information and Broadcasting in Pakistan monitors the circulation of newspapers to fix their advertising rates, but does not disclose the circulation figures.

Using online databases such as *Textline,* or Predicasts *MARS* (Marketing and Advertising) is the best way to keep up on advertising regulations worldwide. Some examples of the direction regulation has been taking, based on online searches, are presented below.

- Vietnam is concerned about billboard advertising, the most popular form of advertising in the country.[10]
- The Hungarian Competition Board fined Unilever for "deceptive" detergent advertisements.[11]
- China issued four advertising regulations in 1992, in an attempt to clean up malpractice in the industry. The regulations cover the advertising of medicines, medical apparatus, treatment, and temporary advertising activities for sports events. Rules will be administered by the Advertising Department under the State Administration of Industry and Commerce (SAIC). Advertisers have been accused of promoting fake products and services, such as height-raising devices and an English vocabulary memory enhancer. SAIC also will draft

China's first advertising law, which is to be based on similar legislation in other countries. China has more than 10,000 advertising agencies employing 125,000 people. Their business turnover was expected to exceed 4 billion yuan ($732.6 million) in 1992.[12]

- There has been an expansion of advertising in countries in Asia and Oceania with growing middle classes. Local companies now account for 70% of a typical ad agency's revenues, with billings from multinational clients now making up 30% of revenues. Deregulation of the television industry in Indonesia led to 60% growth in ad spending in 1991. Thailand saw ad billings growth of 26% in 1991. Hong Kong's ad industry grew 14% in 1991, and ad spending in Singapore is expected to improve upon the 15% growth experienced in 1991.[13]
- Mexico's ad industry is lobbying the Office for Control of Advertising in the government's Health Secretariat to relax proposed regulations on tobacco, liquor, and food advertising. Tobacco and liquor TV spots would have to carry written warnings for the entire commercial, similar to those already on packages. The regulations also affect sponsorship of special events and use of children in ads. They would also eliminate some other restrictions. Working with the National Advertising Council, advertisers, media, and agencies have been lobbying the Secretariat for a compromise.[14]

CONCLUSION

Advertising in the host country is an important facet of international marketing. The choice of agency, message, and media are made by a company but affected by local custom and regulation. This chapter has provided information about the advertising industry worldwide and sources of agency information, advertising regulations, the role of the EC in regulating advertising, and the interaction between advertising and media. Standard advertising print sources are described and online databases are recommended as the best method of monitoring ongoing changes in regulations.

NOTES

1. "Campaign Report," *Campaign* (September 9, 1992): 41. DATA-STAR, *Textline*
2. "Europe: Institute of Practitioners in Advertising Welcomes European Deal on Product Costs," *Marketing* (November 6, 1992): 10. DATA-STAR, *Textline*
3. "UK: Advertising Standards Authority Upholds Complaints Against Several Drinks Companies," *Off License News* (November 6, 1992): 8. DATA-STAR, *Textline.*

4. John Lippman, "How Television Is Reshaping the World's Culture," *Toronto Star* (December 31, 1992): A21. LEXIS/NEXIS SERVICES, CURRNT

5. Mark Poirier, "Lands' End Looks Abroad to Expand Sales," *Catalog Age 9* (January 1992): 30. *ABI/Inform*

6. "Telemarketing Grows," *Market Europe* (March, 1992). DATA-STAR, *PROMT*

7. "Telemarketing Opportunities in the EC," *Market Europe* (January 1991). DATA-STAR, *PROMT*

8. Michael Violanti, "International Telemarketing," *Direct Marketing 52* (April 1990): 24-26. *ABI/Inform*

9. EC Directive Draft Proposals on Information Technology Data Protection: Proposal for a Council Directive Concerning the Protection of Individuals in Relation to the Processing of Personal Data. COM (90). 314 (*Official Journal* Reference C277 of 5 November 1990) as amended by COM (92) 422 (*OJ* No. C311 of 27 November 1992). DATA-STAR, *Spearhead*

10. "Vietnam: Ads in Ho Chi Minh City About to be Controlled," *Bangkok Post* (May 5, 1992): 16. DATA-STAR, *Textline*

11. "Unilever Rises 5pc in First Quarter," *The Daily Telegraph* (May 16, 1992): 19. LEXIS/NEXIS SERVICES, *CURRNT*

12. "China to Issue Regulations on Advertising," *Xinhua News Agency News Bulletin* (April 9, 1992). LEXIS/NEXIS SERVICES, *CURRNT*

13. "Asian Advertising Agencies Benefit from Expansion," *Asian Wall Street Journal Weekly* (May 11, 1992): 18. LEXIS/NEXIS SERVICES, *CURRNT*

14. Elisabeth Malkin, "Ad Groups Fight Proposed Mexican Rules," *Advertising Age* (October 26, 1992): 16. DIALOG *PTS MARS* (File 570)

CHAPTER 12
Exporting and Importing

EXPORTING AND THE ECONOMY

Exporting is the sale of goods or services in another country; importing is the purchasing of goods or services from another country. As noted in Chapter 9 on international marketing, exporting is one type of market entry strategy. When a company decides to manufacture at home, but sell abroad, this company is an exporter.

Exporting is important to the U.S. economy. According to a report issued by the U.S. Department of Commerce in January 1993 the goods from 1989 export shipments generated $287.4 billion, and along with revenue come jobs.[1]

- More than six million full-time jobs in the U.S. were directly or indirectly related to the export of manufactured goods in 1989.
- Exports accounted for 15.5% of all manufacturing employment, and export-related jobs represented 5.1% of all civilian employment in 1989.
- The largest number of export-related jobs were in industries manufacturing industrial machinery and equipment, electronic and other electrical equipment, and transportation equipment.

In the U.S., the Department of Commerce and the Small Business Administration encourage small companies and entrepreneurs to consider exporting to improve business. The small businessperson is usually unfamiliar with library sources and research techniques and least able to pay the price for published market research reports or online database searches. This chapter is designed for this group of users.

- I make specialty boxes for chocolates and I would like to start selling them abroad. Is Germany a good place to do this?
- What's the market for push pins in South Africa?
- How do I sell cosmetics in Thailand?

Why Export?

There are many reasons why companies of all sizes export. The U.S. Department of Commerce encourages exporting to improve the U.S. balance of trade and to create jobs in the U.S. The Commerce Department estimates that every $45,000 in exports creates one job—more than double the rate of job creation from domestic sales. For individual companies, exporting will:

- Broaden their market base
- Increase overall sales
- Improve profit/sales ratio by lowering costs through improved economies of scale
- Extend product life cycle

Who Exports?

It is difficult to get a good count of the number of companies actively involved in exporting. Less than 15% of U.S. companies are reported to be exporters, and 15% of these account for 85% of the value of U.S.

manufactured exports. Half of the exporters sell to only one market. There is no complete list of U.S. exporters. The *Directory of U.S. Exporters* lists only 19,000 exporters and Duns Market Identifiers (File 518) identifies about 50,000 companies as exporters.

This chapter is divided into four major parts. The first part lists referral sources, which in many cases are as important as in-house library resources. The second part describes the process of planning and financing export. The third part discusses importing, but in less detail. The fourth part describes library sources for the exporter and importer.

REFERRAL SOURCES

In all the other chapters, understanding the topic and sources has been of primary importance. In this chapter, knowing where to send your clients is of primary importance.

International Trade Administration

The International Trade Administration (ITA) is part of the Department of Commerce and the primary agency for promoting exporting and offering information on markets and trade practices worldwide. A listing of export services appear annually in an issue of ITA's journal, *Business America*.

One arm of the ITA, the Trade Development Unit, promotes U.S. trade interests. It is arranged in seven major industry sectors: aerospace, automotive affairs and consumer goods, basic industries, capital goods and international construction, science and electronics, ser-

vices and textiles, and apparel. Potential exporters can contact the appropriate industry desk officer. The Trade Information and Analysis Unit provides data useful for exporters.

Another arm, the U.S. and Foreign Commercial Service (US&FCS), has 47 district offices and 20 branch offices in cities throughout the United States and Puerto Rico. These offices help businesses through stages of the exporting process by offering individual counseling, seminars, and educational programming. Examples of US&FCS programs are:

- **Export Mailing List Service (EMLS):** Provides custom mailing lists as labels or tape and trade lists of companies by country or by product
- **Trade Opportunities Program (TOP):** US&FCS officers in over 60 countries seek out trade opportunities and disseminate the information daily or weekly through TOP
- **Agent/Distributor Service(A/DS):** Provides custom searches for overseas import agents and distributors
- ***Commercial News USA* Export Promotion Catalog-Magazine:** Published monthly by US&FCS. U.S. providers of newly manufactured single products or services pay from $250 to $5000 to have their products promoted in overseas markets. Three programs are New Product Information Service (NPIS): the product is described in *Commercial News* with pictures and sometimes promoted on Voice of America (VOA); International Market Search (IMS): a special issue of *Commercial News* is devoted to one technology, product, or service; and Worldwide Services Program (WPS): for service firms

Table 12-A lists the product groupings covered in *Commercial News USA.*

Table 12-A. Product Groupings Promoted in *Commercial News USA*

1. Agricultural machinery equipment, supplies	18. Food processing/packaging equipment & supplies
2. American handcrafts	19. Forestry
3. Audiovisual	20. General industrial
4. Automotive	21. Health care
5. Aviation	22. Housewares/hardware
6. Business & office	23. Laboratory & scientific
7. Chemical & petrochemical	24. Land transportation
8. Communications	25. Marine
9. Computers, peripherals, software	26. Metalworking
10. Construction	27. Mining & heavy construction
11. Consumer goods	28. Pollution control
12. Consumer service supplies	29. Printing & graphic arts
13. Electronic components	30. Production
14. Electronics industry production & test equipment	31. Restaurant, hotel, catering equipment & supplies
15. Energy: Electricity, fossil fuel	32. Safety & security
16. Energy: Solar, wind-generated & other	33. Sports, recreation, hobby
17. Fishery & seafood	34. Trade & technical literature

Other ITA Programs

Listed below are other important programs provided to exporters by the International Trade Administration.

- The ITA has *Export Development Offices* located abroad. The Commerce Department also has country desk officers and industry and country specialists.
- The *Export Hotline* (1-800-USA-XPORT) allows businesspeople to obtain country and industry reports directly from ITA by dialing the *Export Hotline* through a FAX. The system is available 24 hours a day, seven days a week from any FAX machine anywhere in the world. The calls and reports are free.
- The *Export Hotline Directory*, an electronic yellow pages, was added to the FAX service in January 1993 to facilitate the North American Free Trade Agreement. Companies in the U.S., Canada, and Mexico may list themselves in the *Directory*. Access to company listings is through Harmonized Codes. Companies are not limited in the number of codes they assign themselves. There is a small fee for listing and no fee for FAX retrieval.
- The *Trade Information Center,* (1-800-USA-TRADE) is an interagency hotline designed to assist the exporter in identifying programs from the 19 federal agencies that are members of the Trade Promotion Coordinating Committee. Information is available on such topics as how to export, where to find financing, and how to conduct foreign market research.
- Special assistance in exporting is provided for minority-owned businesses through the *Minority Business Development Agency* (MBDA).
- A complete "Directory of U.S. Government Export Services" is published in the bi-weekly *Business America* (v113 n9, pp. 2-5, 1992).
- Another listing of the government's programs is in *Export Programs: A Business Directory of U.S. Government Resources*, prepared by the Trade Promotion Coordinating Committee (call 1-800-USA-TRADE).

Other Governmental Programs

Listed below are programs run by other government departments and agencies that assist exporters.

The *Department of State* provides commercial services in 84 embassies and maintains regional bureaus and country desk officers.

- The *Small Business Administration* offers export counseling services, training, financial assistance, and legal advice.
- The *Foreign Agricultural Service* of the Department of Agriculture has several major export programs: the Commodity and Marketing Programs (CMP) for six commodities; the Export Programs Division (EPD); the

Export Incentives Program (EIP); and Agricultural Information and Marketing Services(AIMS). AIMS serves as the liaison between U.S. companies and foreign buyers of U.S. food and agricultural products. It provides trade leads, publicity, contacts, and statistical information.

- *State and Local Governments* are actively involved in supporting export development. For example, California has a World Trade Commission with an office of Export Development and Export Finance.

Nongovernmental Sources

Private agencies also offer information and support for exporters. Among them are:

- More than 300 commercial banks with international banking departments
- Chambers of Commerce both in the U.S. and abroad
- Trade associations
- Export intermediaries

Trade Fairs

Trade fairs have long been an important element of European business, with the first recorded fair at St. Denis near Paris in 710 A.D. Today there are over 1,000 fairs in Europe each year. Probably the best known is the Hannover Industrial Trade Fair, held annually in the spring. In 1990, there were over 6,000 exhibitors from 51 nations at Hannover.

In the U.S., the first World Trade Week observance was in 1926. Since then, a week has been designated every spring to focus attention on the importance of exporting to the U.S. economy. The objective is to make the American business community more aware of the opportunities in overseas markets, and the services offered by U.S. government agencies to help U.S. companies penetrate those markets. Some of those services include:

- **Certified Trade Fair Program**: The Department of Commerce has a Certified Trade Fair Program that helps U.S. companies participate in shows abroad. Organizers of trade fairs may receive certification if the fair organizer meets the Department's standards.
- **Foreign Buyers Program**: Foreign buyers are encouraged to attend U.S. shows through the work of the US&FCS.
- **Trade Missions**: Planned visits to potential buyers and clients overseas are sponsored by the Department of Commerce.

There are several sources of trade fair listings in print and in electronic form. *Business America* lists upcoming fairs for the next year in its last yearly issue.

European Trade Fairs: A Key to the World for U.S. Exporters (U.S. International Trade Administration, 1991)

European Trade Fairs lists major trade fairs by product and country and also provides information on successful participation in European fairs.

Trade Shows Worldwide: An International Directory of Events, Facilities and Suppliers (Gale—Annual)

Trade Shows Worldwide publishes information about upcoming trade fairs. The 1993 edition included more than 2,600 events in 64 countries outside the United States and includes U.S. contacts for the shows. A sample record, shown in Exhibit 12-1, provides entry number; trade fair name; contact information, including the exhibit management and the U.S. contact; and descriptive information such as frequency, date, audience, attendance, space rental, principle exhibits, number of exhibits and exhibition space, and dates and locations for three years.

EXHIBIT 12-1. *Trade Shows Worldwide: An International Directory of Events, Facilities and Suppliers*

2310 **Hannover Fair Industry**
            Contact Information
Exhibition management company: Deutsche Messe AG Messegelande, D-3000 Hannover 82 Germany. Phone: 511 8933120. Telex: 922728. Facsimile: 511 8932626
  U.S. Contact: Hannover Fairs USA, 103 Carnegie Center PO Box 7066, Princeton, NJ 08540. Phone: (609) 987-1202. Telex: 5101011751. Facsimile: (609) 987-0092.
  Descriptive Information
  Frequency: Annual. Always held at the Exhibition Centre in Hannover, Germany. **Founding**
date: 1947
  Audience: Experts from industry, commerce,
  and general public. **Attendance:**386,888
  Space rental: DM 80-220/sq.m.
  Principal exhibits: Electrical engineering and electronic equipment, supplies and services; lighting equipment, supplies, and services; computer technologies for manufacturing; plant engineering equipment supplies and services; research and technology innovations; advertising and public relations information; energy, air conditions, and environmenta technology; technical optics and laser technology; new materials, including metals, polymeters, and ceramics; surface treatment supplies; factory equipment; robotics; and handling technology.
  Number of exhibits: 6026
  Exhibition space: 345,000 sq. m.
  Dates and Locations
  1993 Apr 21-28; Hannover, Germany; Exhibition Centre
  1994 Apr 20-27; Hannover, Germany; Exhibition Centre

Source: *Trade Shows Worldwide: An International Directory of Events, Facilities and Suppliers*, 1993, p. 275. Reprinted with permission from Gale Research.

Fairbase (FAIR), an online database available through DATA-STAR, BRS, and the German databank FIZ Technik, contains information on more than 2,400 trade fairs and exhibits worldwide through the year 2000. An organization requiring infrequent access to trade fair information or one that wants to scan for fairs meeting a variety of criteria should select *Fairbase* over Gale's *Trade Shows Worldwide.* Exhibit 12-2 displays a sample record from *Fairbase.*

EXPORTING

Export Planning

Since exporting is one international marketing strategy, many of the same considerations discussed in Chapter 9 on international marketing apply to exporting. A *Basic Guide to Exporting* lists the different steps involved in creating an export marketing plan.

Basic Guide to Exporting (U.S. International Trade Administration, 1992)

Basic Guide simplifies the process for potential exporters by recommending that they use third parties as sources of information. Such third parties can include U.S. government agencies, export intermediaries, and banks or freight forwarders.

The *Guide* recommends that exporters first define the market, which it breaks down into a four-step process that recommends use of many of the information sources discussed in the marketing, industry, and country chapters of this book. Many are also basic sources that most libraries already have in their collections. The four steps the *Basic Guide* recommends for defining a market are:

- Step 1. Classify your product
- Step 2. Research many countries
- Step 3. Access a handful of markets you want to target with more specific information
- Step 4. Select the market you want to enter

General sources discussed below, such as *Exporters' Encyclopaedia* or the *Official Export Guide*, provide basic information for most of the factors listed above. Once a market has been selected, the type of in-depth information available from the ITA's country desk officers or from expensive print or online services, such as Business International's *IL&T* (Investing, Licensing & Trading) should be consulted.

Any library that receives any export questions should own *Basic Guide to Exporting.* Some libraries will be able to help the exporter in stage 1 with printed directories, such as *Directory of U.S. Importers* and *Directory*

EXHIBIT 12-2. *Fairbase* on DATA-STAR: Chocolate Shows in 1993

	1 FAIR
AN	07743392 9205.
TI	INTERSUC 93, SALON DE LA CONFISERIE,
	CHOCOLATERIE, PATISSERIE, BISCUITERIE
	INTL. CONFECTIONERY, CHOCOLATE, BISCUIT AND PASTRY TRADE EXHIB.
LO	PARIS: PARC DES EXPOSITIONS PARIS NORD.
DT	FROM SATURDAY, JANUARY 30, 1993,TO MONDAY, FEBRUARY 22, 1993.
TE	E.
AG	INTERSUC
	103, RUE LA FAYETTE
	F-75481 PARIS CEDEX 10
	FRANCE
	Countryphone: +33
	TEL: (1) 42 85 18 20
	FAX: (1) 40 16 01 45
	TLX: 633 166 PRCOM.
CN	C4FRANCE, FRANKREICH, FRANCE, FR, WESTERN-EUROPE, WEST- EUROPA, EUROPE-OCCIDENTALE.
PN	FOOD-PRODUCTS, CONFECTIONERY, CHOCOLATE, BISCUIT, PASTRY, ICE-CREAM, SWEETS, SNACKS,
	MATERIALS-FOR-CONFECTIONERY- PRODUCTION, CONFECTIONERY-EQUIPMENT,
	LABORATORY-EQUIPMENT, FOOD-TECHNOLOGY, FOOD- PACKAGING.
PC	P206, CONFECTIONERY, SUESSWAREN, CONFISERIE.
NT	ANNUAL, TRADE ONLY.
	STATISTICS OF 1991 CHECKED BY OJS:
	VISITORS: 19332
	EXHIBTRS: 201
	TOT-SQMT: 19000
	NET-SQMT: 4487
	COSTSQMT: 1460
	CURRENCY: FRF.

Source: *Fairbase* on DATA-STAR, November 1992. Reprinted with permission.

of U.S. Exporters. More specialized libraries and information centers with access to online databases and CD-ROMS should be able to answer most research needs. Other recommended sources include trade associations, current customers, and suppliers and competitors.

Export Methods

The Commerce Department identifies several different methods of exporting: 1) export directly; 2) export indirectly through intermediaries; 3) use foreign-based agents; and 4) fill orders for domestic companies who then export your product as part of their product line. The first three methods have many variations which are presented in list form below.

- **Export directly.** A company can market directly overseas although this method is not recommended for small businesses. It is the most expensive method and requires the most expertise on the part of the exporter, but gives the exporter the most control. The following distribution channels are available to the direct marketer:

1. *Sales representatives* are the equivalent of the domestic manufacturer's representative; the rep often handles noncompeting complementary lines. He/she works on a commission and has no risk or responsibility.
2. *Agents/representatives* have authority to make commitments for the firms they represent.
3. *Distributors* purchase merchandise from the domestic exporters (often at a discount). The distributor provides parts and servicing.
4. *Foreign retailers* purchase directly from the domestic supplier; requires use of a traveling sales force.
5. *Direct sales to end users* who are identified through trade fairs, industry publications, or contract programs.

- **Export indirectly** through intermediaries. This approach is recommended for small to medium sized manufacturers who are new to exporting or who do not have the expertise or financial resources to cope with exporting on their own. Larger companies may use these intermediaries to break into new geographical areas. The disadvantage is that the company turns over control to the intermediary. There are many types of intermediaries.

1. *Brokers and commission agents* set up deals.
2. *Exporting service companies* specialize in marketing U.S. products and services abroad.

U.S. export trading companies differ from French and Japanese companies both in their smaller size and their focus just on exporting. There are two major types of export intermediaries, though the distinctions are blurring and the terms are often used interchangeably.

a) *Export Management Companies* (EMCs) are private firms that act as the export department for several companies, help with the overseas marketing functions on an exclusive basis, and arrange financing and shipping. EMCs work closely with the supplier. They generally specialize in a particular geographical region or country or a particular product category and provide individualized service. They may take title, work on commission, or on retainer.

The EMC and the company develop a marketing plan and share the overseas marketing costs, with the supplier providing the product information. A usual contract is three years. There are about 2,000 in the U.S. The *Directory of Leading U.S. Export Management Companies* has more information about EMCs in addition to a listing of EMCs.

> A Washington, DC, EMC deals exclusively with 10 U.S. suppliers of orthopedic equipment, marketing the products primarily in developed countries. It takes title to 90% of the goods it sells.[2]

b) *Export Trading Companies* (ETCs) are similar to EMCs but most take title to the goods and pay the exporter directly. They act as independent distributors and provide a broader range of services. They also work with a large range of products and may identify U.S. companies for overseas clients.

> A Chicago company identifies products in demand and buyers then find U.S. suppliers. It buys and sells a variety of industrial products, from several manufacturers.

c) *ETC Cooperatives,* a third method using intermediaries, are networks of export-oriented companies with similar products, primarily industrial and agricultural

3. *Piggyback arrangements* describes a situation in which one company uses the distribution channels of another, usually larger, company that often takes title to the goods.
4. *Foreign Trading Companies* may provide the export services for a U.S. company. They are European, Japanese, and Korean. In Japan they are extremely large conglomerates called *Sogo-shosha*. For example, Mitsubishi, the world's largest, has offices in the United States.

- Use **foreign-based** agents or distributors.
    1. *Foreign agents* are like manufacturer's representatives working on commissions. They check local laws and develop marketing strategy
    2. *Foreign distributors* work either on commission or buy goods for resale. The product is kept in inventory and sold off the shelf. Marketing may be a joint effort but the distributor handles service. When using a foreign distributor, exporters should define responsibilities and know the local laws.
    3. *State-controlled trading companies* still exist in some countries. For example, imports of such products as rice, medicines, building materials, and fishing equipment into the Maldives is through the State Trading Organization.

The U.S. government passed the Export Trading Act in 1982 to stimulate U.S. exports by encouraging the formation of EMCs and ETCs in the public as well as the private sector to facilitate export financing and remove antitrust disincentives to export. For example, as a result of this act, the New York-New Jersey Port Authority operates an ETC subsidiary, XPORT.

The government set up an Office of Export Trading Company Affairs (OETCA) within ITA to inform businesses of the benefits of exporting through intermediaries. To this end, OETCA publishes the *Export Trading Company Guidebook,* which is for sale through the GPO. OETCA also maintains a database of more than 12,000 firms involved in foreign trade. The list of firms is published annually as *Export Yellow Pages* and is available free of charge while supplies last. *Export Yellow Pages* is also on the *National Trade Data Bank* (disc 2).

Service Exporting

As noted in Chapter 9, most attention is given to the export of goods rather than services. The Department of Commerce has made the Office of Service Industries responsible for analyzing and promoting service trade. Divisions of the Office include Information Industry; Transportation, Tourism, and Marketing; and the Finance and Management Industries. Firms may list their services in *Commercial News USA*.

Export Financing

There are also many options for methods of payment and sources of funds. This section details the methods and describes some government programs.

The *Basic Guide to Exporting* lists the following items (p. 45) to consider when making the financing decision:

- The need for financing to make the sale: the exporter may need financing to produce; the importer may need financing to purchase
- The cost of different methods of financing and the effect this cost has on the overall cost of the deal
- The length of time that financing is required; the longer the time, the higher the costs
- The risk involved
- The company's financial resources

Methods of Payment. There are a variety of payment methods. The first three methods listed below involve a high level of risk. Therefore, new exporters or exporters dealing with new clients tend not to use them.

- **Advance Payment**: The buyer pays before delivery; this method is rarely used because it is too risky for the buyer
- **Open Account**: The buyer pays after delivery without guarantees; this method is too risky for seller (*see* forfaiting and factoring, below, under "Alternative Means of Payment," as two means of handling open accounts)
- **Consignment**: The seller gets paid after resale; this method is riskier yet for the seller

The next two methods, documentary collection and letters of credit, require a third party, often a bank, which acts as intermediary, or two banks, one in each country. The banks charge percentage fees for handling the payments. Usually the buyer is expected to pay the charges for the letter of credit.

Documentary collection (bill of exchange or draft) involves an unconditional written order from the *drawer* (seller) to the *drawee* (buyer) directing the drawee to pay a specified amount to the drawer at a fixed or determinable future date, a transaction analogous to giving a personal check. Title is transferred through the drawee's bank. The drawee pays the bank in his/her country and then receives the documents necessary to collect the goods. There are two types of drafts: *sight drafts* (payment before goods are released to the buyer) and *time or date drafts* (payment after goods are received by the buyer).

Letters of credit involve three parties, buyer, seller, and the buyer's bank, which guarantees payment. The following steps are part of the letter of credit transaction:

1. The buyer arranges to open a letter of credit at his/her bank after the terms of the deal have been set with the seller.
2. The buyer's bank prepared the letter of credit, including all shipping instructions and sends the letter to the seller's bank.
3. The seller's bank prepared a letter confirmation for the seller's review.
4. The seller arranges with a freight forwarder for delivery and the forwarder completes the necessary documentation.
5. The seller or forwarder presents the documents of compliance to the seller's bank. If the documents are in order, the bank issues the seller a check; the documents are forwarded to the buyer's bank.
6. The buyer or his/her agent get the documents needed to claim the goods.

Table 12-B categorizes the different methods of payment.

Table 12-B. Payment Methods

(in order of decreasing risk to exporter and increasing risk to importer)

Method	Goods Available to Buyers	Usual Time of Payment	Exporter Risk	Importer Risk
Open account	Before payment	As agreed	Riskiest; relies on importer to pay account	Least
Consignment	Before payment	After sold	Maximum; exporter retains title	Minor; inventory cost
Time draft	Before payment	On maturity of draft	High; relies on importer to pay draft	Minimal; check of quantity/quality
Sight draft	After payment	On presenting draft	Be careful of recourse	Little if inspection report required
Letter of credit	After payment	When documents are available	None	None if inspection report required
Cash	After payment	Before shipment	Least	Most

Source: "Table 4-1 Payment Methods" from Carl A. Nelson, *Import/Export: How to Get Started in International Trade* (New York: McGraw-Hall, 1990).

Exporters or their representatives should do a credit check on the buyer. In addition to the private sources mentioned in the section on credit in Chapter 8, the Department of Commerce will provide a World Traders Data Report for a fee of $100. The reports include trade and financial references.

Sources of Funds. For the U.S. exporter and his/ her import partner, the primary government funding agency is the Export-Import Bank of the US (Eximbank), in existence since 1934. Eximbank supports exports by using loans, guarantees, and insurance programs. In 1991 it supported $12.5 billion in U.S. exports and intended to increase the amount to $15 billion in 1992.

Programs are designed for lenders, overseas borrowers, or both. The bank reorganized in the spring of 1992 to offer more support to small businesses and allow presidential discretion in opening up loans for deals in former Eastern Bloc nations.

For example, the Working Capital Guarantee is for 100% of the principal and interest on commercial loans from certified banks to small- and medium-sized companies with a 12-month repayment schedule. Loans can be up to $750,000.

Other loans go directly to foreign buyers of U.S. capital equipment and services. Not all countries are eligible for loans and special conditions apply in many countries. For example, no coverage is allowed for Afghanistan or Albania; discretionary short-term insurance is offered to Latvia and Lithuania; the allowable coverage for new countries such as Slovenia and Tajikistan had not been determined by July 1992; and no special conditions exist in most industrialized countries and Asian NICS.[3]

Eximbank also works with 19 states, 2 cities, and Puerto Rico to facilitate use of the bank's financing programs. Eximbank provides insurance policies to foreign buyers, protecting them against political and commercial risks resulting in economic deterioration in a buyer's market area, fluctuations in demand, shifts in tariffs, or technological change. The insurance had been written by a private agent, FCIA Management Companies Inc.; but in January 1993, Eximbank began administering its own credit insurance program.

Two special policies for small businesses are the *new-to export* program and the *umbrella* program. The former covers 95% of commercial risks and 100% of political risks. The umbrella policy is given to an administrator who acts as the exporter's representative.

The bank conducts one-day, two-day, and four-day seminars throughout the year in Washington, costing from $25 to $100, plus occasional three-day sessions outside of Washington. Any bank listed on its *Bank Referral List* must have had a representative attend a three- or four-day session. Both the World Bank and Inter-American Development Banks hold briefings to coordinate with Eximbank. Eximbank programs are outlined in Table 12-C.

Other government-related funding sources include:

- **Private Export Funding Corporation (PEFCO):** This corporation is owned by commercial banks, industrial corporations, and an investment banking firm; it works with Eximbank to provide medium- and long-term loans of $1 million or more.
- **State and Local Governments:** Twenty-two states have laws permitting financial assistance.

Table 12-C. Loan and Guarantee Programs of the Export-Import Bank of the United States

Exports	Appropriate Programs
Short-Term (up to 180 days)	
Consumables, small manufactured items, spare parts, raw materials	Working Capital Guarantee Credit insurance (formerly FCIA)
Medium-Term (181 Days to 5 years)	
Mining, refining, construction, and agricultural equipment; general aviation aircraft; planning and feasibility studies	Commercial Bank Guarantees Small Business Credit Medium-Term Credit Working Capital Guarantee Credit insurance (formerly FCIA)
Long-Term (5 years and longer)	
Power plants, LPG and gas-producing plants, other major projects, commercial jet aircraft or locomotives; other heavy capital goods	Direct loans, Financial Guarantees

Source: Basic Guide to Exporting, pp. 14-16

- **Small Business Administration:** This agency offers an Export Revolving Line of Credit.
- **U.S. Department of Agriculture:** Contained within the Department are the Export Credit Guarantee Program and the Commodity Credit Corporation.
- **Overseas Private Investment Corporation**: This independent, financially self-supporting corporation is fully owned by the U.S. government; it facilitates investment in developing nations and Eastern Europe.

Contact numbers for U.S. government export funding sources are listed in Table 12-D.

Table 12-D. Contact Numbers for U.S. Government Funding Sources

- U.S. Trade and Development Program (TDP) (202) 875-4357
- Export-Import Bank of the United States (Eximbank) (202)566-8873; Online Bulletin Board Access (202) 566-4699
- Small Business Administration (SBA) (202) 653-7794 (The SBA's Export Information System [XIS] reports data based on SITC product codes for the 25 largest importing markets for each product)
- Overseas Private Investment Corporation (OPIC) (202) 457-7200
- Agency for International Development (AID) (202) 663-1451
- U.S. Department of Agriculture (USDA) (202) 447-8732

Finally, when using *commercial banks* with international departments, the exporter should ask the following questions:
- How big is the department?
- Does it have foreign branches or use correspondents?
- What are the charges for preparing documents?
- Does the bank provide credit reports?
- Has it worked with the government finance programs?
- What other services does it offer?

Alternative Means of Payment

Alternative means of payment to government-backed funding or commercial banks include:

- **Countertrade**: payment through a transfer of goods and services
- **Factoring**: transfer of title to the factor in exchange for immediate payment
- **Forfaiting**: exporter forfeits rights to future payment in exchange for immediate cash

Countertrade. Countertrade involves an exchange of goods and services between buyer and seller. For example, Pepsi trades soft drinks for Russian vodka. Ten percent of world trade in 1989 was through

countertrade, and 90 countries mandate countertrade. About half of the U.S. Fortune 500 companies participate in countertrade. The exporter is often from a developed country and the purchaser is from an LDC or non-market economy. However, as the former Eastern Bloc moves toward more private enterprise, its use of countertrade may change.

Vienna is a key location to find countertrade intermediaries. The Department of Trade and Industry in London maintains a list of countertrade companies.

Five types of countertrade are identified by the U.S. International Trade Commission.

1. **Barter**: This type of countertrade involves a contractual direct exchange of goods or services between two principals without the use of currencies. Barter agreements often take place within a year. One contract is used. Barter is used where foreign currency is a problem. It is estimated that over 150,000 U.S. companies are swapping goods and services.[4] Several firms called "barter-brokers" or "match makers" have appeared to facilitate barter deals.

   Clearing agreements are barter agreements between governments. Two nations decide the types and quantities of goods to exchange at a predetermined exchange ratio. Any imbalance at the end of the contract, usually one year, is compensated for in cash.

   Switch trading involves a third party, usually a trading house. This method is used when the exporter wants nothing that the customer is supplying as payment.

2. **Compensation or Buyback**: The original export consists of plant and technology such as turnkey construction projects. Part of the payment to the exporter is the output from the project. It involves one contract. For example, an Australian company provides anthracite coal handling equipment to Vietnam and the expertise to use it; in return, Vietnam's National Coal Export-Import & Material Supply Corporation will pay with the coal extracted to be sold by the Australian firm on international markets.[5]

3. **Counterpurchase (parallel barter):** This method involves reciprocal buying to be fulfilled over some time period in the future, with flexibility as to the actual goods to be purchased. The products offered by the buyer are unrelated to the products being sold by the exporter. The majority of the price may be in cash. The time period is generally one to five years. The value of goods offered is usually less than the full contract amount. There is one contract for each product. For example, Beijing Capital Iron and Steel imports equipment from Northern Telecom Canada to build a 5,000 port, program-controlled telephone switchboard system valued at $12 million. Northern Telecom agrees to counterpurchase $8 million in Chinese steel products.[6] Exhibit 12-3 displays an example of a countertrade deal from *Countertrade Outlook*.
   a) Philips France, an electrical company in Europe, sold $10 million worth of equipment to an electrical utility in Africa, Tunisian Light Company.

EXHIBIT 12-3. *Countertrade Outlook*—**Example of a Deal**

The deal with Tunisia:

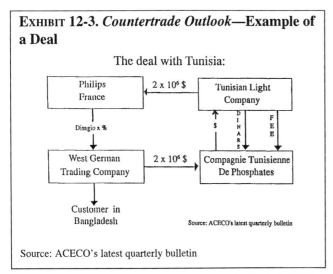

Source: ACECO's latest quarterly bulletin

Source: ACECO's latest quarterly bulletin

Source: Flow chart derived from *Countertrade Outlook,* Fairfax Station, VA 22039-7188, Vol. X No. 34, September 14, 1992, p. 3-4. Reprinted with permission.

b)   The Light Company paid in dollars which it purchased in local currency from a North African mining company, Compagnie Tunisienne De Phosphates.

c)   Philips France purchased an equivalent amount of minerals to make up the hard currency account.

d)   Philips France then transferred the obligation to the West German Trading Company which actually purchased the minerals and sold them to a company in Bangladesh.

4. **Offset:** This method is used in defense-related contracts, such as aircraft sales and other priority items for the buyer government. The supplier is required by the buyer government to assist in or arrange for the marketing of goods produced in the buyer country.

5. **Evidence Accounts**: These accounts are usually used in deals with Eastern European countries and other countries without sources of foreign exchange. Use of these accounts implies a long-term relationship.

Countertrade is used when other more conventional means of finance are not available, e.g., if your foreign partner cannot get foreign exchange. It is also used to gain a presence in another country. For small businesses, countertrade is not recommended unless normal financing channels are not available. Barter is the most common form of countertrade used in Egypt, while counterpurchase is used in China.

The weekly newsletter *Countertrade Outlook* and the daily newspaper *Financial Times* are the major sources of information on global countertrade transactions.

Countertrade Outlook (DP Publications—Weekly)

Countertrade Outlook, published in Fairfax Station, Virginia, covers countertrade deals by individual

companies, country policy, meetings, and revisions to DP Publications' *Directory of Organizations Providing CT Services.* This is a specialized and unique source for organizations that need to scan countertrade.

Factoring. Factoring is discounting a foreign account receivable without using a draft. Factoring has been used commercially since 1790, but it didn't appear on the international scene until the 1970s. According to Factors Chain International (FCI), an association of factors in 30 countries on five continents, export factoring growth is now exceeding domestic factoring growth. However, in 1991, it accounted for only 6% of the $266 billion factoring business. Three of the leading export factoring countries, the Netherlands, Germany, and Belgium, account for 30% of the foreign volume. Japan, which has had a relatively inactive domestic factor market, contributed 3.3% to the international factor market. Only seven firms offer international factoring services in Japan.[7]

Financing through a factor involves the following steps:

1. Sellers turn over goods to the factor who assumes full responsibility for credit and collection.
2. Seller receives cash at a 2% to 4% discount.
3. Seller's factor selects a foreign factor from FCI and gives the foreign factor information about the importer.
4. Foreign factor checks the buyer's credit and establishes a line of credit.
5. Seller's factor turns over receivables to foreign factor.
6. Foreign factor collects and remits funds to seller's factor by wire transfer.

Factoring is suitable for exporters who sell relatively small amounts of goods to the same customers on open account terms. It isn't used in developing countries and non-market economies. The availability of export credit insurance, through Eximbank and FCI in the U.S. and the Export Credit Guarantee Department in the U.K., has reduced demand for factoring by small businesses in these countries.

Forfaiting. Forfaiting is derived from the French term *à forfait,* which means "without recourse." The forfaiter buys from the exporter (at a discount) an importer's fixed rate letters of credit or bills of exchange. The seller receives immediate cash from the forfaiting institution. The forfaiting institution will collect from the buyer in the future. Forfaiting institutions may be subsidiaries of large international banks or companies specializing in international trade financing.

The deal is usually arranged between the seller's and buyer's banks. The seller's bank, or forfaiting institution, takes over the right to the seller's bills of exchange or buyer's promissory notes. There are therefore four parties involved.

- Exporter, seller, or supplier of the goods or services
- Importer, buyer, or purchaser of the goods or services
- Guarantor for the importer
- Forfaiter

Forfaiting has been used in Europe for a long time, beginning with Finanz AG of Frankfurt and Union Bank of Switzerland. It only appeared in the U.S. and U.K. in the 1980s. There are 30 main providers of forfait finance in London. In 1988 it was estimated that about 1% of world trade, or $30 billion, was financed with forfaiting.[8]

Financing through a forfaiter involves the following steps:

1. The seller makes a sale to a foreign buyer.
2. The seller receives bills of exchange or promissory notes for future payment at a fixed rate.
3. The seller sells the bills or notes to its bank at a discount from face value and receives immediate cash.
4. The bank assumes full responsibility for collection.
5. The notes or bills are guaranteed by the importer's forfaiting institution; the guarantee is often unconditional and irrevocable.
6. The importer pays for the purchase over time (2 to 5 years).[9]

Typical sales range from $200,000 to $5 million and carry a fixed rate of interest. Forfaiting is used most frequently in deals by capital goods manufacturers and distributors of commodities. The risk is on the exporter's bank.

The advantage of this type of deal is that the exporter receives payment immediately while the buyer gets extended payment terms. The popularity of forfaiting as an export financing mechanism is sensitive to interest rates. Rising interest rates discourage forfaiting.

We have identified no one directory for countertrade, factoring, or forfaiting houses. However, these companies are listed in a variety of different databases, especially those covering the U.K., Germany, and Austria.

Financing Deals with Lesser Developed Countries

Many of the financing arrangements we have discussed require the participation of a bank and guarantees and insurance. Many U.S. banks no longer offer loans to LDCs because of defaults. Possible alternative forms of financing include:

- **Confirmed Letters of Credit:** Banks in many of these countries are not well known, but some U.S. banks will confirm the letter of credit for a fee. Some banks will confirm letters from one country, i.e., Thailand or Poland, but not others, such as Pakistan.
- **Export Credit Insurance**: This insurance was formerly underwritten by the FCIA and by private insurers, but is now offered directly by Eximbank. Buyers might prefer this method.
- **Forfaiting:** This is a competitive finance method for short- to medium-range dealings with the less risky developing countries.
- **Sales through Trading Companies:** Certain trading companies specialize in less developed countries.

One way to determine the types of financing available in a country is through the monthly charts in Euromoney's *Project and Trade Finance,* formerly called *Trade Finance.* Monthly reports are divided among Asia, Eastern Europe and the Middle East, and Latin America. Exhibit 12-4 displays an entry from *Project and Trade Finance.*

Export/Import Regulations

Goods and services leaving a country must comply with the export regulations of the home country, any international agreements, and with import regulations of the host company.

The following are some important U.S. requirements and regulations:

- **Export Licenses:** These licenses are necessary for all sales except those to be made under the North American Free Trade Agreement. Licenses are governed by the Export Administration Act as reported in the Export Administration Regulations. The type of license required depends on the type and destination of the product. Exporters should check with the Export Assistance Division of the Department of Commerce to determine the type of license needed.

  In April 1992, President George Bush implemented new rules that eliminated the need for prior government approval to export more than 2,000 items that account for about $2.5 billion in export sales annually. Validated export licenses are no longer needed to sell semiconductor manufacturing equipment, materials technology, certain computers and aircraft, and helicopters and their engines to nations that re-export those goods to other nations that are under existing U.S. export controls.

  Licenses still are required for the export of supercomputers, high-speed streak cameras, and flash discharge X-ray equipment, which can be used in developing nuclear weapons; cryptographic equipment, which can be used to encode and

EXHIBIT 12-4. Euromoney's *Project and Trade Finance*

The exporter's guide to Eastern Europe and the Middle East

Country/population	Remarks	Aid\Credit lines	Consensus group
Slovenia	The economy is still recovering from the shock of separating Yugoslavia. FX reserves are tight due to the loss to Belgrade $1.9bn in bank deposits. However, debt obligations are fairly small and it seems likely that as exports increase and tourists return the FX position should improve	Little information available at present	II

Exim short term/ Medium term	**NCM Credit Risk/** Pre-credit Risk	**Private market**	**Transfer position** Paris Club date	**Non-recourse** finance-index
No cover available	No credit cover available. MRA £0.15 pre-credit risks	Some cover now available on secure terms (L/C Ljubjanska Bank). No long term cover	Little data	A

Source: *Project and Trade Finance*, 1993, pp. 62-63; prepared by Jardine Insurance Brokers. Reprinted with permission from Euromoney.

decode military and intelligence data; night-vision equipment, which can be used in combat systems; and items that are controlled to curb missile proliferation.

- **Antidiversion, Antiboycott, and Antitrust Requirements:** Goods may go only to destinations legally authorized by the U.S. government. Goods may go to countries friendly to the U.S. who are being boycotted by other countries. U.S. antitrust rules apply to international as well as national trade. The Foreign Corrupt Practices Act has special relevance for international trade (*see* Chapter 9).
- **FDA and EPA Restrictions:** An item for foreign export need only meet the standards of the importing country. While the EPA does not control any aspect of exporting, it requires notification of the export of hazardous waste.
- **Tax Incentives:** Under provisions of the Tax Reform Act of 1984, special U.S. income tax treatment is given to Foreign Sales Corporations. An FSC is a corporation set up in certain foreign countries or U.S. possessions (except Puerto Rico) that shares tax information with the U.S. In 1991, 29 countries qualified, but most FSCs are incorporated in Guam or the U.S. Virgin Islands. The FSC must have both export sales and at least one foreign director. Fifteen percent of the profit attributable to export sales is not taxed in the U.S. There are separate incentives for small FSCs, which do not have to meet the same requirements.

- **Drawback of Customs Duties:** This specialized form of tax relief is available to U.S. firms that import materials and components that they process and then re-export. The import duties are refunded as drawbacks. Drawback is a refund of 99% of all ordinary customs duties and internal revenue taxes. Drawbacks were initially authorized by the first tariff act of the United States in 1789. A *direct identification drawback* is given on imported merchandise that is partially or totally used in the manufacture of an exported article. A *substitution drawback* is given on designated imported merchandise upon exportation of articles manufactured or produced with use of substituted domestic or imported merchandise that is of the same kind and quality as the designated imported merchandise.
- **Foreign Trade Zones**: U.S. foreign trade zones are 180 domestic port sites that provide customs privileges. The zones are considered outside the United States. Exported goods become imports to the home country and face another set of regulations.
- **Import Regulations of the Destination's Government:** Every country has its own set of import regulations.
- **Carnet:** When bringing samples or professional equipment into another country for trade fairs, exhibits, or demonstration or promotion purposes, arrange for an ATA Carnet, or Admission Temporariare/Temporary Admission. This is a special customs document for the business traveler that guarantees customs payments if the goods are not re-exported.

- **Intergovernmental Regulations:** The United Nation's Convention on Contracts for the International Sale of Goods became law in the United States in 1988. It applies automatically to all contracts between sellers and buyers in countries that have signed the Convention. Over 25 countries are signatories, including most of the EC countries, a few of the newly independent republics, and China.

Transportation

Additional information is needed to arrange for transporting goods in an international deal. Issues include size of shipment, shipping terms, packaging, labeling, insurance, and documentation.

The size of the shipment may determine the method of shipment. Small shipments use air express or integrated carriers—air and ground service. Large shipments use ocean or regular freight. The daily *Journal of Commerce* provides lists of shippers, rates, and individual ships arriving each month.

When negotiating the export sale, shipping terms are part of the agreement; they determine who pays for shipping costs and who is responsible for damage. There are two published sets of shipping terms:

- *Guide to Incoterms, 1990* by Jan Ramberg (International Commercial Terms, International Chamber of Commerce, 1991)
- *Revised American Foreign Trade Definitions* (originally published in 1941 by Chamber of Commerce of the United States, National Council of American Council of Importers, and National Foreign Trade Council)

Table 12-E lists 13 trading terms identified in *Guide to Incoterms* that specify the obligations of buyer and seller in an international transaction.

Table 12-E. International Trading Terms from *Guide to Incoterms*

EXW	Ex Works
FCA	Free Carrier
FAS	Free Alongside Ship
FOB	Freight on Board
CFR	Cost and Freight
CIF	Cost, Insurance, and Freight
CPT	Carriage Paid To
CIP	Carriage and Insurance Paid To
DAF	Delivered At Frontier
DES	Delivered Ex Ship
DEQ	Delivered Ex Quay (Duty Paid)
DDU	Delivered Duty Unpaid
DDP	Delivered Duty Paid

Source: International Chamber of Commerce Brochure, 1992

In addition to selecting the means and payment of transport, the exporter also has to use correct packaging, labeling, insurance, and documentation.

- **Packing** problems involve breakage, moisture, weight, and theft.
- **Labeling** involves specific markings used to meet shipping regulations, assure proper handling, conceal the identity of the contents, help receivers identify shipments, and meet country requirements. Marks include port marks, customer identification, origin, weights, and dimensions. For example, products ranging from liquid gas to sample must be labeled in metric units to be imported into Thailand. Labels may show either Thai or Arabic numerals, but Thai script must be used.
- **Insurance:** Cargo insurance is arranged by buyer or seller, depending on the deal.
- **Documents:** Table 12-F lists the 10 most common documents required in the movement of goods between countries.

Each country of destination has different requirements. Some requirements are listed in *Exporters' Encyclopaedia* or *Official Export Guide*. A more specialized source is *International Trade Report Export Reference Manual* (formerly *Export Shipping Manual*) from BNA (Bureau of National Affairs).

Freight Forwarders are service companies who design and implement international shipping programs for exporters for compensation. They use common carriers and serve different roles based on the type of carries. For example, for ocean freight, the freight forwarders act as the exporter's agent; for air freight, freight forwarders consolidate shipments and are licensed by the U.S. Civil Aeronautics Board (CAB) or International Air Transport Association (IATA). The forwarders are also among the best sources of information and assistance on export regulations and documentation, foreign import regulations, and shipping methods.

Exporting in the United Kingdom*

Many governments encourage and support export initiatives. In fact, the U.S. has been slow to export compared to many other countries. In the United Kingdom, the Department of Trade and Industry's (DTI) Export Initiative Program provides practical help and support for exporters. Through the British Overseas Trade Board, which has over 200 businesspeople helping exporters and the diplomatic service posts overseas, DTI provides services to British business.

Like the U.S. Department of Commerce, DTI has produced a *Guide to Exporting*, which includes a step-

* The information in this section is based on Sell's *Products and Services Directory,* 1991.

Table 12-F. Documents Required for the Movement of Goods Between Countries

Transportation	Government Control	Commercial	Banking/Payment Method
Ocean bill-of lading Dock receipt Delivery instruction Insurance certificate Transmittal letter	Export declaration Consular invoice Certificate of origin	Commercial invoice	Letter of credit (for example)

Source: Port Authority of New York-New Jersey in *The World Is Your Market* (Washington, DC: Braddock Communications, 1990), pp. 68-69

by-step approach to the export process and provides exporters with contacts at DTI. DTI services include:

- Export Development Advisers in regional offices
- Consultancy initiatives providing private sector advise to firms of less than 500 employees in any two of the following areas: Marketing, Designing, Quality, Manufacturing Systems, Business Planning, and Financial and Information Systems
- Export Market Information Centre, with access to the British Overseas Trade Board's (BOT) online database BOTIS
- Export Intelligence Service on trade opportunities
- Technical Help to Exporters (THE), operated by the British Standards Institution
- Other DTI services include promoting new products from Great Britain; assistance in finding an agent, "outward" and "inward" missions, and trade fairs and seminars

The Export Credits Guarantee Program insures exporters against not receiving payment and will guarantee exporters to banks so the exporters can receive credit themselves.

Contacts at the Department of Trade and Industry include:

- DTI 1 Victoria Street London SW1H 0ET—call regional desks
- Export Market Information Centre 1 Victoria St. 215 8444/4, The Linford Wood, Milton Keynes MK14 6LE (0908) 220022
- Export Credits Guarantees, P.O. Box 272, 50 Ludgate Hill, London SW1E 6SW 71-215-8070

Barclays Guide to International Trade for the Small Business (Blackwell, 1990)

Barclays Guide is an introductory source for U.K. potential exporters. In addition to the how-to's and the contacts, the book also lists recommended online information providers and services in the U.K. These recommended sources include Export Network Ltd. and Barclay's own Trade Development Service.

Chambers of Commerce are important sources and facilitators of export and import throughout Europe. Those from France, Italy, and Spain are actively involved in soliciting business from the information industry. Chambers of Commerce are also beginning to play major roles in newly independent countries. For example, the Slovenian Chamber of Commerce has developed a floppy disk with a listing of potential partners.

IMPORTING

As we have seen, the U.S. government actively encourages exporting because it views exporting as vital to the health of the U.S. economy. The goal of any country is to become a net exporter. Exporting is therefore treated as a marketing tool.

Importing, on the other hand, is not encouraged. Therefore, the government does not allot resources to help companies import. Importing is treated as a legal issue centering on customs. Table 12-G diagrams the structure of the U.S. Customs Service.

There are also U.S. Custom Officers stationed in 16 countries in Europe, Asia, and South America.

Customs invokes the same level of uneasiness as the Internal Revenue Service; both services are under the U.S. Department of the Treasury and both have collection and protection of revenue as their primary goal. However, U.S. Customs employs only 16,000 people, a small staff by government standards.

Import Laws and Regulations

Customs laws are found in Title 19 of the *United States Code* and customs regulations in Title 19 of the *Code of Federal Regulations*. Customs enforces not only its own laws and regulations, but also those of 40 other federal agencies that have interest in imported merchandise.

Table 12-G. Structure of the U.S. Customs Service

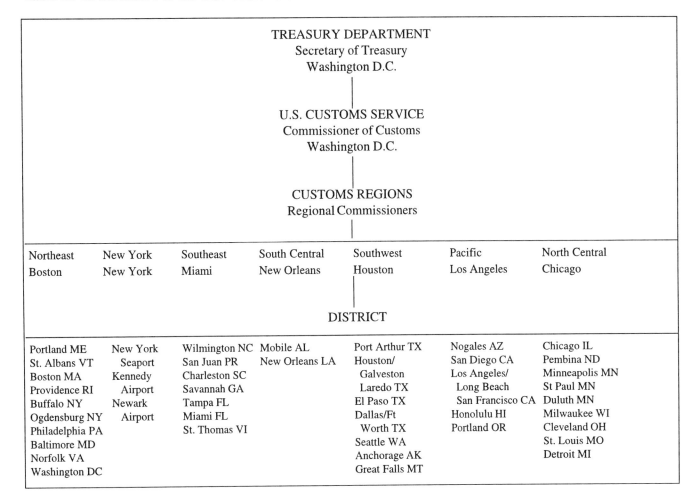

The customs employees who work most closely with importers and import brokers are the *import specialists*. These individuals classify the goods, appraise them, determine import duties, and generally ensure that imports meet all other legal requirements.

There are six fundamental rules that importers into the United States are responsible for knowing:[10]

Rule 1. Goods that are allowed in:
   Importing is not a right and certain goods may be excluded
Rule 2. How Revenue Officers make decisions:
• Protect the revenue
• Resolve all doubts in the government's favor.
   If two different rates might apply, the Customs officers will always choose the higher
Rule 3. Voluntary Compliance (the burden rests with the importer)
   U.S. Customs assumes that importers have:
 • Read the Customs rules and regulations and know which apply to their merchandise
 • Done everything to ensure that they have complied with these laws and regulations

Rule 4. Duty Due on All Imports, Unless Exempt
   Importers should assume that they will pay duties on foreign and domestic items
Rule 5. Duty Exemptions—Burden of Proof
   Importers must prove, beyond doubt, that they qualify for exemptions
Rule 6. Items Purchased in the United States may be Foreign Made
   This refers to situations where merchandise may be made in the U.S., assembled offshore, and re-imported at reduced rates. There must be proof that the original item was indeed made in the U.S.

Importing, like everything else in business, begins at the planning stage. Potential importers in any country should take the same preliminary planning steps as the potential exporter.

Planning for Importing

Several factors are important to importing and importing research.

The Product. The importer must consider not only if there is a demand for the product in the country, but also if there will be special duties or restrictions and regulations.

- Is the product a raw material or component for the manufacturing process?
- Is it a finished product for resale?
- Is it a spare part?
- Is it subject to special import restrictions?

For example, fruits, vegetables, and nuts must meet United States import requirements relating to grade, size, quality, and maturity.

Volume. Not only do regulations vary based on what is being imported, but regulations also vary based on how much is being imported. When planning for importing, it is necessary to consider the size of the shipment. Formal international purchase agreements and entry procedures must be followed for the importation of large quantities.

Country sourcing refers to finding the best place from which to import a product. Obviously, importing minerals and natural resources is limited to those countries where they are mined or grown. However, manufactured products are available in many countries. Identifying the low-cost countries based upon proximity to raw materials, labor costs of manufacturing, current exchange rates, or transportation costs may require considerable study and analysis. This information is not always easy to obtain. Since the U.S. government is more interested in promoting exports, it does not regularly collect and make available such information to U.S. companies wishing to import.[11]

Sources of local import information include:

- Foreign chambers of commerce in the importer's country
- Foreign trade associations
- Foreign banks operating in the U.S. or U.S. banks with foreign branches

Identification of Suppliers. Finding suppliers requires many of the same techniques as finding buyers, such as attending trade fairs, accessing listings of potential sellers, performing credit checks, and visiting facilities, which, if possible, is recommended by the American Management Association (AMACOM).

Compliance with Foreign Law. Suppliers often overlook some basics, so the importer should check with a bank or attorney for such items as:

- **Foreign Export Controls:** Coordinating Committee (COCOM) is in 16 countries, mainly EC and the United States
- **Exchange Control Licenses:** Many countries control foreign exchange or methods of payment
- **Export Quotas:** These quotes come generally from the

importing country; however, the U.S. has brought pressure to bear on some countries to control exports through voluntary restraint agreements

Compliance with Domestic Law. Importers should also check carefully the following domestic considerations:

- Customs Regulations and Procedures
- Import Quotas
- Antidumping, Countervailing, and Other Special Duties that apply to imports as well as exports
- Classification—correctly categorizing a product using the Harmonized Tariff codes

An import quota is a quantity control on imported merchandise for a certain period that serves to protect domestic industries. There are two general categories: absolute tariffs and differential tariff rates. *Absolute tariffs* are quantitative, that is, only a fixed amount is allowed in per year. They may be worldwide or country dependent. Examples in the U.S. include certain types of chocolate, ice cream, textiles, and watches. These tariffs are administered by the Commerce and Interior Departments. Some quotas have *differential tariff rates*. There is no limitation to the amount of the product that may enter during the quota period, but quantities in excess of the quota for the period are subject to higher rates. Examples include tuna fish, certain sugars, brooms, and olives.

Import Marketing, Packaging, and Labelling. The issues are similar to export considerations. In the United States, customs laws require that articles produced abroad for import be marked with the country of origin. Some products, such as eggs, screws, or Christmas trees, are on an excepted list and do not require marking on the product itself, while other products, for example watch movements, require additional markings.

Domestic Commercial Considerations. These considerations include:

- Prevailing market price
- Government policy, i.e., "Buy American"
- Industry standards, i.e., auto emissions

Shipping Terms. Since a good being imported has been exported from its country of origin, it bears the international trading terms listed in Table 12-E, such as FOB or CIF.

Tariffs

Goods leaving a country are subject to export controls and regulations. Goods entering a country are subject to tariffs. Tariffs are dependent on the good itself,

EXHIBIT 12-5. *Harmonized Tariff Schedule of the United States (1992)—Supplement 1*

Heading/ Subheading	Stat. Suf. & cd	Article Description	Units of Quantity	RATES General	OF Special	DUTY 2
2203.00.00		Beer made from malt . .	. . . .	1.6¢/ liter 2/	Free(A*,E,IL J) 2/ 0.9¢/liter (CA) 2/	13.2¢/ liter 2/
		In containers each holding not over 4 liters:				
	30 5	In glass containers . .	liters			
	60 8	Other	liters			
	90 2	In containers each holding over 4 liters	liters			

2/ Imports under this subheading are subject to a Federal Excise Tax(26 U.S.C. 5051) of $18 per barrel of 31 gallons and at a like rate for any other qunatity or for fractional parts of a barrel.
(A) If containing distilled spirits, a tax of $13.50 per proof gallon and a proportionate tax at the like rate of all fractional parts of a proof gallon . . .

Source: Harmonized Tariff Schedule of the United States (1992)—Supplement 1, pp. IV, 22-2.

its quantity, its country of origin, and what stage of processing it is in when it leaves and/or arrives in the destination country.

Restrictions are placed on some products to protect local industry. For example, U.S. sugar prices are kept well above market level through tight restrictions on the importation of sugar into the United States. In 1985, frozen Israeli kosher pizzas were stopped from entering the United States based on sugar regulations, although the pizzas contained less than 1% sugar! President Reagan later signed a law allowing packaged food items for retail sale into the United States if they contain less than 10% sugar, which released the 20,000 pizzas.

To facilitate the tracking of goods between countries, most nations of the world have adopted the Harmonized Commodity Coding System, which was introduced in 1988. The coding system is derived from the United Nations SITC codes and is in harmony with Schedule B of the United States and the European Community NACE codes. The code that a good receives when it leaves its home country should be the same as the one it receives when it reaches its destinations.

Just determining the tariff that will be placed on an item coming into the United States can be confusing and, as in the case of the Israeli pizzas, potentially bankrupting to a company that has failed to understand the laws. The new Harmonized Tariff is still providing problems for the textile industry, which falls under provision 9802 dealing with the duties paid on items fabricated in the United States but assembled in another country and then brought back into the United States.

The tariff schedule is used for the classification of imported merchandise for rate of duty and statistical purposes. An example of regulations is presented in Exhibit 12-5.

Exhibit 12-6 lists the different Harmonized Tariff codes for sugar.

EXHIBIT 12-6. Alphabetical Listing of the Tariff Codes for Sugar

SUGAR...Ch. 17, 17-US3(a)-(ij)
   chemically pure, except sucrose, lactose
   maltose, glucose, fructose.. 2940.00
   confectionaries 1704.10-90
   raw 17-S1, 1701-1702
   refined 1701-1702
   wastes 2303.20
SUGAR BEET 1212.91
SUGAR BEET SEED 1209.11
SUGAR CANE 1212.92
SUGAR CONFECTIONARY .... Ch. 17
   containing cocoa 18-2 1806

Source: Harmonized Tariff Schedule of the United States (1992): annotated for Statistical Reporting Purposes, p. 63.

The information in these tables is printed annually by the U.S. International Trade Commission and reprinted in the commercial source, *Official Custom House Guide.*

The tariff schedule for the different types of sugar are preceded by three pages of notes and include quotas for different country groupings.

The Customs Process

The Customs Service annually publishes *Importing into the United States*, which outlines the requirements and procedures for bringing goods into the United States. There is a four-step formal entry process for all goods valued at more than $1000.

1. **File Documents** (includes getting an Importer's Number)
2. **Post Bond:** A Customs bond is purchased from a surety company. The importer pays a fee to the surety company to obtain the bond, which guarantees that all duties and fees assessed by Customs will be paid. The importer has to go through a credit check to get bonded.
3. **Undergo a Custom's Examination to Determine Tariff:** The exam determines whether the goods are what they claim to be and the transaction value of the goods (price plus shipping, insurance, etc.). Valuation for importing has its own foreign exchange rule. U.S. Customs must use the rates of exchange determined and certified by the Federal Reserve Bank of New York, based on the first business day of each calendar quarter except on days where rates fluctuate more than 5%. The date of exportation of the goods is the date used to determine the applicable exchange rate. The classification category is determined by the importer based on Harmonized Tariff Codes.
4. **Liquidation:** This is the legal term used to indicate that Customs' decisions regarding entry of the goods have been completed and the goods will be released to the importer after payment of the required duty.

To keep up with changes in Customs rulings, quota status, and daily exchange rates, you can access the *Customs Electronic Bulletin Board* at no charge either by phone (202-343-7715; FAX 202-566-2134) or modem (202-535-5059).

The Guide to United States Customs and Trade Laws (Kluwer, 1991)

This legal publication is recommended in the *International Trade Reporter* (BNA, February 2, 1992) for use by customs brokers, freight forwarders, in-house legal counsel, and others who must deal with complex U.S. customs regulations.

Import Support Companies

Parallel to the exporter's freight forwarder is the importer's customhouse broker. Customhouse brokers in the U.S. are regulated by the Treasury Department and must take a qualifying examination. They act as the importer's agent. The brokers prepare documents, obtain bonds, deposit duties, and arrange for the release and delivery of goods for the importer.

A listing of these brokers appears in *National Directory of Customs Brokers*, published by Adele Falco in Red Bank, NJ, 201-530-9668.

SOURCES OF INFORMATION FOR EXPORTING AND IMPORTING

U.S. Government Publications

Basic Guide to Exporting (U.S. Department of Commerce in cooperation with Federal Express Corporation, 1992)

Basic Guide to Exporting is an introductory source that is a must for any library with small businesspersons as patrons. The book is designed for companies that will be exporting either through intermediaries or directly. It emphasizes government sources and contacts and gives addresses, phone numbers, and prices of print government publications.

The importance of planning is stressed and a table containing management issues for the export decision, plus an outline for an export plan, are given in the first chapter. Exhibit 12-7 contains sections of the outline plus sample questions. Additional planning tips from the *Basic Guide* are found in Appendix I.

EXHIBIT 12-7. *Basic Guide to Exporting*

TABLE 1-1
Management Issues Involved in the Export Decision

I. **Experience**
   - With what countries has business already been conducted (or from what countries have inquiries already been received?
   - What general and specific lessons have been learned from past export experiences?

II. **Management & Personnel**
   - What in-house international expertise does the firm have?
   - Who will follow through after the planning is accomplished?

III. **Production Capacity**
   - How is the present capacity used?
   - What would be required to design and package products specifically for export?

IV. **Financial Capacity**
   - What amount of capital can be committed to export productions and marketing?
   - By what date must an export effort pay for itself?

Source: Basic Guide to Exporting, 1992, p. 1-5

Table 1-2 of the *Basic Guide to Exporting* contains the "Sample Outline for an Export Plan," with the Table of Contents and a one- or two-page executive summary.

Business America (U.S. Department of Commerce, International Trade Administration—Biweekly)

Business America bills itself as the official U.S. government trade magazine. It was first published, under another name, by the U.S. State Department in 1880; its mission has always been to help American companies sell their products overseas. In addition to articles, issues have listings of trade fairs in the U.S. for overseas traders and Commerce Department promotions abroad for U.S. traders. A listing of ITA/US&FCS District Offices is also included. The World Trade Week Issue (vol. 114, No. 9 in 1993) lists country and industry specialists, individual state international trade contacts, and other export services. For the 1993 prices of $61 in the U.S. or $71.25 abroad, this publication is a good buy for any organization with clientele interested in U.S. exporting. Articles from *Business America* are available online in databases from IAC, in *ABI/Inform,* and on the *National Trade Data Bank (NTDB).*

U.S. Government Trade Information on CD-ROM

National Trade Data Bank (United States Department of Commerce, ITA—Monthly)

Any discussion of United States import/export information sources must include the *National Trade Data Bank (NTDB).* A review of the database is in the July 1991 *CD-ROM Professional.* For $35 a month, or $360 for a year's subscription, anyone can own this comprehensive two-disc CD-ROM database. We recommend *NTDB* for libraries throughout the world because it contains the complete text of many useful U.S. government publications.

Access to information on disc one is by Source, Topic, Program, Subject, or Item. *NTDB* is made up of documents from about 20 different U.S. government sources, all having some relationship to international trade or activity. Disc two has two directories: *Export Yellow Pages* and *Foreign Traders Index,* discussed below.

NTDB uses menu-driven software. Exhibit 12-8 is the *NTDB* source menu and Exhibit 12-9 is the *NTDB* International Trade Administration menu.

The most efficient way to search the *NTDB* discs is not obvious. However, whether you begin in the Source, Topic, Program, or Subject menu, you will eventually arrive at the documents you need.

One of the strengths of *NTDB* is its series of more than 6,000 market reports. The reports have market information and data on selected products and industries in "countries offering opportunities for U.S. goods." Included are Market Insight Reports, Industry Sub-sector Analysis, and Country Marketing Plans, in addition to the more widely available "Foreign Economic Trends" and "Overseas Business Reports." These reports can be

---

EXHIBIT 12-8. Source Menu for *National Trade Data Bank* CD-ROM

5	BOARD OF GOVERNORS OF THE FEDERAL RESERVE SYSTEM
2	CENTRAL INTELLIGENCE AGENCY
1	EXPORT-IMPORT BANK OF THE UNITED STATES
3	OFFICE OF THE U.S. TRADE REPRESENTATIVE
1	OVERSEAS PRIVATE INVESTMENT CORPORATION
5	U.S. DEPARTMENT OF STATE
1	U.S. INTERNATIONAL TRADE COMMISSION
1	U.S. SMALL BUSINESS ADMINISTRATION
1	UNIVERSITY OF MASSACHUSETTS
1	USDA, FOREIGN AGRICULTURAL SERVICE
13	USDOC, BUREAU OF ECONOMIC ANALYSIS
3	USDOC, BUREAU OF EXPORT ADMINISTRATION
7	USDOC, BUREAU OF THE CENSUS
18	**USDOC, INTERNATIONAL TRADE ADMINISTRATION**
3	USDOC, NATIONAL INSTITUTE OF STANDARDS AND TECHNOLOGY
1	USDOC, OFFICE OF ADMINISTRATION
2	USDOC, OFFICE OF BUSINESS ANALYSIS
1	USDOE, ENERGY INFORMATION ADMINISTRATION
2	USDOL, BUREAU OF LABOR STATISTICS

EXHIBIT 12-9. USDOC, International Trade Administration Menu

24	A BASIC GUIDE TO EXPORTING
448	BUSINESS AMERICA
24	DOMESTIC & INTERNATIONAL COAL ISSUES & MARKETS
21	EASTERN EUROPE LOOKS FOR PARTNERS
213	EC 1992: A COMMERCE DEPT. ANALYSIS OF EC DIRECTIVES
5	EUROPE NOW: A REPORT
8	EXPORT PROGRAMS:A BUSINESS DIRECTORY OF U.S. GOVERNMENT RESOURCES
224	EXPORT PROMOTION CALENDAR
17	FOREIGN DIRECT INVESTMENT IN THE U.S.—ANNUAL TRANSACTIONS
2	INVESTMENT GUIDES
3	LEXICON OF TRADE TERMS
6324	**MARKET RESEARCH REPORTS**
29	NORTH AMERICAN FREE TRADE AGREEMENT INFORMATION
1	TRADE OPPORTUNITY PROGRAM (ON ECONOMIC BULLETIN BOARD)
23	UNDERSTANDING U.S. FOREIGN TRADE DATA
44	U.S. FOREIGN TRADE HIGHLIGHTS
14	U.S. FOREIGN TRADE UPDATE—MONTHLY ANALYSIS
60	U.S. INDUSTRIAL OUTLOOK
30	U.S. MANUFACTURERS TRADE PERFORMANCE—QUARTERLY REPORT

Source: October 1992 *NTDB* disc

called up by country or product and include a wide range of subjects. Some are directly related to trading, such as *Kenya—New Import Regulations—IMI920911*. Others are related to individual products in regions or countries. One example of a regional report is *Baltic States—Microcomputer Systems—ISA9103*, covering Estonia, Latvia, Lithuania, and the Confederation of Independent States.

Commercial Sources

Finding Aids. Listed below are two important finding aids to import/export information.

Global Trade White Pages (Carroll Publishers, 1991—Annual)

Global Trade White Pages lists national, state, county, and international contacts, with contact names. The book looks a lot fuller than it is because its white pages contain so much white space!

Trade Directories of the World (Croner, Loose-leaf Update)

For the most complete print listing of trade directories, by country, with access by trade or profession, use *Trade Directories of the World*. This book also has an index to export and import directories arranged by country. What *Trade Directories* cannot easily do is provide a list of directories of importers or exporters for a given product.

Directories of Exporters and Importers. Listed below are several valuable commercial directories of exporters and importers.

Directory of United States Importers and *Directory of United States Exporters* (Journal of Commerce—Annual)

The *Directory of United States Importers* and the *Directory of United States Exporters* are similar in form, content, and price. The stated purposes of the two directories are:

- To provide a geographical listings of *all* U.S. exporters and importers
- To provide an alphabetical listing of products by Harmonized Commodity Codes
- To provide information on Customs regulations and export procedures

Arrangement in both publications is the same. The main company entries are arranged alphabetically by company within states. There is an alphabetical company listing, an alphabetical product index using the harmo-

nized tariff coding schedule, and listings of American consulates and embassies abroad, associations, banks, foreign consulates and embassies in the United States, foreign trade zones, trade commissions, and world ports. The banks are international banks in the United States that provide loan packages, letters of credit, and assistance with foreign exchange transactions. There is a lot of duplication of basic information in the two directories. The information on how to export, in the *Directory of United States Exporters* is taken from the *Basic Guide to Exporting*. Exhibit 12-10 displays an entry from the *Directory of United States Importers*. Note, that the designations (S), (L), and (A) are used for mode of transportation—by sea, land, or air.

EXHIBIT 12-10. *Directory of United States Importers*

Banana Republic (S)
  1 Harrison St. 1st Fl San Francisco,
  CA 94105
  TEL: 415-777-0250
  President-Robert J Fisher
  Ports of Entry -Long Beach, Los Angeles, New York,
    Oakland, Port Everglades, Tacoma
  Women's Leather Zipper Portfolios, Men's Wool
    Nylon Woven Jackets, Women's Leather Wallets,
    Textile Piece Goods, Women's Wool Jackets,
    Men's Shorts, Women's Cotton Pants, Men's
    Cotton T-Shirts, Men's Cotton Shirts, Women's
    Cotton Blouses, Cotton Readymade Garments,
    General Merchandise, Wearing Apparel, Container
    Cargo—Australia Hong Kong, India, Indonesia,
    Japan, Korea, Macau, Malaysia, People's Republic
    of China, Philippines, Singapore, Sri Lanka,
    Taiwan, Thailand, United Kingdom

Source: *Directory of U.S. Importers*, 1993, p. 409. Reprinted with permission from Journal of Commerce.

Other information that may be in a record includes import manager, traffic manager, customhouse broker, establishment date, and the value of the import/export. The directories are not lists of *all* companies that import or export. Companies fill in questionnaires to be listed in the directories. Additional firms shipping goods via U.S. ports, identified in the *PIERS* (Port Import Export Reporting Services) *Database*, have also been included.

Directory of U.S. Importers & Exporters CD-ROM (DIALOG ONDISC, December 1992—Semi-annual)

The books do *not* easily answer many of the more specific directory questions local libraries tend to get.

- What companies in the Delaware Valley are exporting computer equipment to the Middle East?
- Who's importing T-shirts from Thailand?

However, the DIALOG ONDISC *Directory of U.S. Importers & Exporters* does answer these questions and many others easily.

- What New Jersey companies are exporting through the Port of Philadelphia?
- What Customs House Brokers are being used by companies exporting food products to countries in Asia?

The disc has over 45,000 U.S. companies. It incorporates shipping information from the *Journal of Commerce's PIERS* Databases (Dialog Files 571-574, discussed in Chapter 15) with the directory information from the two print publications. Exhibit 12-11 is a sample record from the CD-ROM, with the product list shortened. Additional information on the CD-ROM includes the number of shipments and tonnage and also the date of the last record update. Some records on the disc were up to three years old.

Many of the standard print sources discussed in Chapter 4 indicate if a company is an exporter or importer. Regional business directories also may include these designations.

International Directory of Importers (Interdata)

International Directory of Importers is a series of eight volumes arranged by continent. The entire set is listed in Table 12-H. Volumes are arranged by country and then by product. All countries have classified lists of importers and general and statistical information, while some countries also have an expanded company information section. Interdata uses its own product classifications.

The basic entry is company name and mailing address. The "expanded" company information adds a contact name, telecommunications numbers, establishment date, number of employees, and a list of products the company imports.

Many other export and import directories cover U.S. regional geographical areas, such as the ones listed below:

- *International Trade Directory: A Guide to International Trade for the Delaware Valley and Mid-Atlantic Region/Wharton Export Network* (Wharton Export Network, 1991, 196p.)
- *Pennsylvania International Trade Directory for the Food, Agricultural and Forest Products Industry* (Pennsylvania Department of Agriculture, Domestic and International Trade Division, 1989-90)
- *California Agricultural Export Directory 1990-1991* (Database Publishing Co., 1990-)

EXHIBIT 12-11. *Directory of Importers & Exporters CD-ROM*

00004238   Record Last Updated On: 08/01/92

Banana Republic
1 Harrison St., 1st Fl.
San Francisco, CA 94105
USA

Telephone: 415-777-0250
Import/Export Indicator: IMPORTER

Import/Export Country:

Australia
Hong Kong
India
Indonesia
Japan
Korea
Macau
Malaysia
People's Republic of China
Philippines
Singapore
Sri Lanka
Taiwan
Thailand
United Kingdom

Shipment Information

Number of Shipments: 668
Aggregated Tonnage: 149,909
Ports: New York, Port Everglades, Oakland, Long Beach, Los Angeles, Tacoma

Officers

President: Robert J. Fisher

Products
966900	Container Cargo
621142	Cotton Readymade Garments
960100	General Merchandise
620520	Men's Cotton Shirts
620520	Men's Cotton T-Shirts
620349	Men's Shorts...

Source: DIALOG ONDISC, searched May 1993. Reprinted with permission from Journal of Commerce.

Chambers of Commerce, government departments of trade and industry, industry associations, and commercial publishers all provide directories from various other countries.

World Chamber of Commerce Directory (World Chamber of Commerce Directory—Annual)

Table 12-H. *International Directory of Importers* **Coverage**

Region	No. of Vols.	No. of Ed.	No. of Companies	No. of Countries	Latest Ed. Date	Cost
Europe	2	6th	40,000	24	1991/92	275
North America	1	6th r	24,000	2	1992/93	150
Middle East	1	7th	14,000	17	1992/93	150
Asia/Pacific	2	5th r	30,000	14	1992/93	275
South/Central America	1	5th r	16,000	18	1991/92	150
Africa	1	5th r	12,000	40	1991/92	150

Source: Interdata brochure, January 1993

Chambers of Commerce are excellent sources for locating import/export information. In many European countries, such as France or Spain, they are the best source of information and offer online and CD-ROM databases. Chambers of Commerce provide free or low cost print directories of members and other publications as well. Use this directory to locate Chambers of Commerce.

1992 Canadian Trade Index (Canadian Manufacturers' Association—Annual)

Canadian Trade Index, published since 1900, is an example of an industry association publication. The directory itself contains Canadian manufacturing companies that have more than local distribution for their products. Volume 2 has an Exports Section that lists companies by product name. Information includes address, telecommunications numbers, geographic areas exported to, and a contact name, as shown in Exhibit 12-12.

EXHIBIT 12-12. *1992 Canadian Trade Index*

PAPERBOARDS...
Peterboro Cardboards Limited, Peterborough, Ont.
Tel. 705-742-8444
(S.M.) Ian Blaiklock
Export: N Central USA, S Central USA, N.W. USA, S.W. USA, China/Hong Kong, Australia, New Zealand, S.E. Asia, South America

---

Source: 1992 Canadian Trade Index, p. D-142

A wide of range of directories is published, but the countries they cover, their frequency of publication, and their availability are scattered at best. Most are arranged by country. Table 12-I contains a sampling of other titles from an RLIN search for "export(ers/ing)" and "directories."

Few libraries have the resources needed to buy and store all the existing trade directories. Beyond the standard sources, it is difficult to anticipate what directories a library will need to stock. In addition, printed directo-

Table 12-I. Range of Directories of Exporters Available

** PAPUA NEW GUINEA DIRECTORY OF PRODUCERS AND EXPORTERS.
* DIRECTORIO DE EXPORTADORES (MONTEVIDEO, URUGUAY)
* DIRECTORY OF TAIWAN'S LEADING EXPORTERS
* TAIWAN IMPORTERS DIRECTORY
* CHUNG-KUO WAI HSIANG HSING CHI YEH NIEN CHIEN. SHANG-HAI
* EXPORTERS' DIRECTORY OF NORTHERN GREECE
** PAKISTAN RED PAGES BUSINESS DIRECTORY.
* MEXICAN EXPORT REGISTER. American Chamber of Commerce of Mexico,)
** THAILAND EXPORT-IMPORT MONITOR.
* MADE IN MALTA
** CARIBBEAN EXPORTERS, IMPORTERS, AND BUSINESS SERVICES DIRECTORY.

[**—Export and Import]

There are a few product-specific directories:
* AMERICAN FOOD AND AG EXPORTER. Vol. 2, issue 6 (Oct. 1990)-
* U.S. INDUSTRIAL EXPORT DIRECTORY.
* THE INTERNATIONAL DIRECTORY OF IMPORTERS. WORLDWIDE FASHION ACCESSORIES IMPORTING FIRMS.
* DIRECTORY OF PHILIPPINE GARMENTS & TEXTILE EXPORTERS.

Sample associations include:

Canadian Importers Association. MEMBERSHIP DIRECTORY.

American Association of Exporters and Importers. MEMBERSHIP DIRECTORY

---

ries do not have the flexibility needed to answer specific questions concerning line of business and geographical regions. We recommend using the online databases listed in Table 12-J, as substitutes for printed directories.

Selected Export/Import Directories. Given below is a selection of important and useful export/import directories.

Table 12-J. Databases on DATA-STAR and DIALOG with Exporters/Importers

Label	Database	Field
EURE	ABC Europe: European Export Industry	RP
BDIE	BDI German Industry	RP
BUSI	Business Opportunities	MJ, MN
DBZZ	D & B Market Identifiers -European Files	HI
F 518, F521, F522	D & B International, Europe, Asia-Pacific	SF
FRIE	French Import/Export	CN
ABCE	German Business & Industry Directory	RP
E1X1	German Buyers' Guide	
HOAU, HOEA, HOPE	Hoppenstedt Austria, East Germany, Germany	IE
BNLU	Hoppenstedt Benelex	EX, IM, FT
ITIE/SDOE	Italian Trading Companies	IE
JPCO	Japanese Company Directory	DE
JORD	JordanWatch -UK Companies	RE
F590, F591	KOMPASS Europe, UK	FT
F592	KOMPASS Asia/Pacific	PX
KSVA	Kreditschutzverband -Austrian Companies	RC
UKIM, UKIA	UK Importers	
WGZW	wer gehört zu wem	CC
WLWE	Who Supplies What?	
ZVIE	ZVEE	RP

3W Register of Chinese Business (3W International Digital Publishing, 1991—Annual)

The *Register* includes more than 30,000 Chinese companies. Each company entry consists of name, address, telecommunications, officers, assets, year started, employees, sales in U.S. dollars, import and export products, and ISIC codes. The book is arranged alphabetically by company with ISIC code index and product name index. The Table of Contents is in five languages. The information is also available on CD-ROM or floppy disc, with semi-annual updates.

Directory of American Business in Hong Kong (GTE 1990).

The *Directory* describes the import/export trade with Hong Kong. It lists American holidays and services in Hong Kong, gives an overview of the Hong Kong economy, and provides an alphabetical listing of American companies. Entries include local English name, telecommunications, address, major products and services, parent company, parent headquarters, and may also include company logo. There are also indexes and listings of products and services.

Directory of Leading U.S. Export Management Companies, 3rd ed. (Bergano Book Co. and Johnston International Publishing Co., 1991)

This *Directory* is arranged alphabetically by company within state, and includes indexes by general product grouping and company name. Entries include company name, address, telecommunications, principal, geo-

graphic areas covered, languages spoken, and product area.

General Trade Index & Business Guide, Poland (Business Foundation Co., 1991)

This is a directory of 3,500 Polish businesses and firms seeking trade opportunities; it includes a section on the Polish economy and laws, banking and finance, and culture. Entries include trade names, full name, address, year of establishment, contact person and language spoken, line of business, number of employees, and estimated turnover. The *Directory* uses EC classification codes and includes advertising.

Trading Company Sourcebook (National Federal of Export Associations, 1992)

The *Sourcebook* is both a yearbook, with articles and information about export management and export trading companies, and a directory for NFEA member companies. Each directory entry has name, address, contact, telecommunications, and products handled.

World Business Directory (Gale and World Trade Centers Association, 1992)

The *Directory* includes companies associated with the World Trade Center Association. The emphasis is on import/export firms and the number of companies per country is proportionate to that country's participation in world trade (*see* Chapter 4 for a complete description of this publication).

Sources on How to Export and Import. A number of valuable sources of information on how to import and export are described below.

Exporters' Encyclopaedia (Dun & Bradstreet—Annual, with semi-monthly updates)

Dun and Bradstreet's *Exporters' Encyclopaedia* is a comprehensive guide to all phases of exporting. It includes the standard export information similar to the *Basic Guide*. It also has communications data, transportation information, and contacts. The majority of the *Encyclopaedia* comprises information about export markets. The Market section is divided into Country Profile, Communications, Key Contacts, Trade Regulations, Documentation, Marketing Data, Transportation, and Business Travel. The 1992 *Encyclopaedia* cost $445. The Country Profile overview includes a section on "Best U.S. Export Prospects," shown in Exhibit 12-13.

EXHIBIT 12-13. Sample of Best U.S. Export Prospects from *Exporters' Encyclopaedia*

Thailand

COUNTRY PROFILE

Best U.S. Export Prospects: Computers and peripherals, medical equipment, and supplies; telecommunications equipment, pollution control equipment, analytical and scientific equipment, food processing and packaging equipment, and agricultural products.

Source: Exporters' Enclodpaedia 1992/1993, p. 1377. Copyright © 1993 Dun & Bradstreet Inc. All rights reserved. Reprinted with permission.

The Trade Regulations section includes summary information on import licensing, exchange regulations and controls, taxes, and countertrade. Guidelines are given for necessary documentation.

The Marketing Data section includes legal requirements regarding importer/agents. For example, in Thailand there are four categories.

1. Expatriate firms with strong resources and large turnover
2. Smaller importers specializing in one line of business and/or more government departments
3. New companies that have technical and modern marketing know-how; recommended for medium-sized exporters
4. Private Thai international trading companies, which are generally granted special privileges

This section also contains information on procurement, standards, environmental protection/pollution control, food/health, safety regulation, marking and labeling, patents and trademarks, advertising, media, and market research.

The Business Travel section covers business etiquette.

Official Export Guide and ***U.S. Customs House Guide*** (North American Publishing—Annual, with updates)

The *Official Export Guide* and the *U.S. Customs House Guide* are two other standard library sources. Each costs about $300. The *Official Export Guide* contains the exporting information from *Basic Guide to Exporting*, a country profiles section that includes the U.S., and service directories with transport, automation, and financial services as well as free-trade zones. A list of contacts is also included.

The unique feature of this resource is that it contains the official U.S. Export Administration Regulations, with the product coding schedule B, the actual regulations, and additional regulations on hazardous materials and export documents.

The country profiles in this book are divided into seven sections.

1. Documentation—marking, labeling
2. Trade Data—tariff rates, licenses, prohibited goods, distribution channels
3. Best Prospects
4. Profile—country level statistical data
5. General Information—business hours, etc.
6. Key Contacts
7. Shipping Information

The U.S. Custom House Guide, the companion to the *Export Guide,* published its 130th annual edition for 1993. It claims to "provide all the information you need—whether it's a HTSUSA number, a government import regulation, a sample document or port information." It includes a guide on how to import with information on the North American Free Trade Agreement, customs audits, and insurance.

Other informational chapters include preferential tariff treatment, trade agreements, marking, insurance, quotas, ports, and services. The *Guide* also includes the Harmonized Tariff Schedules and sample import documents.

The Ports section is arranged alphabetically by port. The volume also includes U.S. government agencies, Chambers of Commerce, airports, rail service and sea ports, free-trade zones, and a listing of companies serving the port.

Both the U.S. Export Regulations and the Harmonized Tariff Schedule are available through the U.S. Government Printing Office.

• *Export Administration Regulations* (U.S. Office of Export Administration) Kept up to date by a supplement, *Export Administration Bulletin.*

- *Harmonized Tariff Schedule of the United States* (United States International Trade Commission) Kept up to date between editions by sequentially numbered supplements.

Investing Licensing & Trading Conditions Abroad
(Business International—Annual loose-leaf)

For those who can afford it, a useful service for potential exporters and investors is Business International's *Investing Licensing & Trading Conditions Abroad. IL&T* is divided into three loose-leaf volumes, which may be purchased separately: Latin America, Europe—Middle East—Africa, and Asia-Pacific. The entire set costs close to $4000. For each country covered, the volumes lay out most of the basic regulations necessary for trading there. In 1992 the Eastern European countries were added to this valuable service.

Reports are divided into 13 sections with a number of subsections, covering such items as the role of the state in industry, price controls, licensing, corporate and personal taxes, incentives, capital sources, labor, and foreign trade. *IL&T* is also available online on the LEXIS AND NEXIS SERVICES (INLITR) as part of the regional libraries, and on DIALOG (File 627). An advantage of using the online version is that you can find those countries whose reports discuss specific issues, for example, misleading advertising.

The McGraw-Hill Handbook of Global Trade and Investment Financing, Lawrence W. Thuller (McGraw-Hill, 1992)

This handbook has chapters on general financing methods, such as countertrade and United States private and government-sponsored export trade finance. A series of chapters covers regional finance options: the Caribbean and Central America; Mexico and South America; the European Community; Eastern Europe and the former Soviet Republics; Japan; South Korea; Taiwan; Southeast Asia; Singapore and Hong Kong; China, Pakistan, and India; Sub-Saharan Africa; and the Middle East. Appendixes include referral information found in other export sources.

Like all handbooks, the entries per country are short. Not all countries are included. Explanations for financing terms are clear but superficial. A useful feature is a list of credit reporting agencies throughout the world. The handbook would be a worthwhile purchase for a small export collection.

Export Profits: A Guide for Small Business (Upstart Publishing, 1992)

Export Profits, by Jack Wolf, is an example of the many basic books designed for the small businessperson that are built on the uncopyrighted material from government sources. *Export Profits* is fairly well done. In some ways, it is arranged like this book. It discusses a topic, for example, "Finding and Choosing Intermediaries," and also has an annotated list of sources for each topic. It has many of the same lists, i.e., ports, government contacts, Chambers of Commerce, and sample documents, as well as many more expensive sources.

This type of book is appealing because it is about one-tenth the price of any of the individual reference sources we cite. It is very readable, but also ages rapidly. Rules and regulations are modified, desk officers are replaced, new sources are added, old sources modify their names and prices, and the way in which the government offers information changes. All libraries' first choice for a introductory export guide should be the *Basic Guide to Exporting*. A book such as *Export Profits* is a good $20 investment today for small businesspeople who want to own their own source.

Journal of Commerce (Knight Ridder—Weekdays)

The *Journal of Commerce*, published since 1827, is a daily commercial source of export information. It includes articles of interest to international trade, trade fairs, a major section on shipping, and business opportunities, discussed below.

Electronic Sources

Only online databases and CD-ROM products, often from foreign chambers of commerce, can provide very specific levels of detail. Many of the databases discussed in Chapters 4 and 6 have fields identifying companies that export or import. Some also give the geographical areas in which companies are active. Dun & Bradstreet's *Market Identifiers* (in different versions on DIALOG, DOW JONES, and DATA-STAR) can be used to identify importers and exporters.

The results of using file 516 on DIALOG to generate a list of companies with sales of $100,000 or less that list themselves as importers are shown in Exhibit 12-14, sorted in ascending order.

The databases listed in Table 12-J have searchable fields that indicate if a company is an importer or exporter.

Table 12-K gives us a sense of how many import and export companies are listed in DIALOG directory databases. Note the high number of European companies.

Some databases identify the countries with which a company deals as well as the names of exporters and

EXHIBIT 12-14. Dun & Bradstreet File 516—U.S. Companies Listed as Importers with Sales<=100000 (October 1992)

Company Name	City	ST	Sales $	Total Employees	Primary SIC
A B S	Mount Clemens	MI	1000	1	5122
Suridi-Impex Inc	Hackensack	NJ	1000	6	5136
Equator International Import E	Seattle	WA	1000	1	5199
Aero-Medical Consultants Inc	Largo	FL	2800	3	2731
Post-Ambient Motion	Omaha	NE	4000	1	3652
Quikbyte Software Inc	Torrance	CA	4332	3	7373
Powers Industries	Flagstaff	AZ	4456	2	3694
Gupta Imports	Scottsdale	AZ	4902	2	5023
Sharif, Masoud	Herndon	VA	5000	1	7389
Map Ventures	Pflugerville	TX	5000	2	2754
Jesena, Mae S & Co	Daly City	CA	5000	2	5199
H-V-H Co Inc	Providence	RI	5000	3	3471
Thompson Fabrication	Little Falls	NJ	5000	3	3444
Nod Narb Enterprises	Denver	CO	5000	3	5199
Cortes Rios, Luis F	Arecibo	PR	5100	1	0912
Timber Exports Inc	Edmonds	WA	6294	2	5031
Vmz Puerto Rico Trading Corp	Bayamon	PR	6824	4	5137
Kobayashi Enterprises	San Francisco	CA	8000	2	5131
B & M Industries	Paterson	NJ	8000	2	5092
Megha Corp	Brooklyn	NY	8025	4	5149

Source: Dun and Bradstreet's *Market Identifiers*, File 516 on DIALOG, October 1992. Copyright © 1993 Dun & Bradstreet Inc. All rights reserved. Reprinted with permission.

EXHIBIT 12-15. *ABC Europe* **on DATA-STAR**

	1 EURE
DB	EURE, FIZ Technik Frankfurt: ABC Europe, (C)1993/05 ABC-Verlag.
AN	E40784740.
AS	Annoni & Figli, S.a.s., Attilio, di Luigi Annoni & C.
	Via N. Bettoni, 2.
	I-20125 Milano
	Italy.
TL	Telephone: (02) 6709309
	Telex: 311271.
PE	Non-alcoholic beverages.
	Beer.
	Dietetic preparations.
	Chocolate.
	Soya bean products . . .
RP	Exports to: Spain, Germany, Malta, Turkey, Cyprus, United Arab Emirates, Libya, Australia, Singapore.
	Imports from: Europe, USA.

Source: ABC Europe from DATA-STAR, May 1993. Reprinted with permission from ABC Europe.

Table 12-K. Number of Exporters and Importers on DIALOG Databases

File	Database Label	Date	Exporters	Importers
516	D&B United States -DMI	Q1/93	51,756	35,418
518	D&B International -IDMI	5/93	293,029	333,964
521	D&B Europe	5/93	247,699	246,564
522	D&B Asia-Pacific	4/93	49,423	63,586
529	Hoppenstedt German Companies	2/93	20,224	11,418
590	KOMPASS Europe	12/92	123,563	43,462
591	KOMPASS UK	1/93	15,203	2,002
592	KOMPASS Asia/Pacific	12/92	42,760	14,892

Source: DIALOG, May 1993

importers. Exhibit 12-15 is an example of this type of database from the *European Export Directory*, *ABC Europe* on DATA-STAR. It answers the question:

- Are there any European companies importing chocolate from the United States?

Selected Online Export/Import Sources

CD-Export (Telexport, Cerved, ICEX)

CD-Export contains the databases on exporting companies published in France by Telexport, in Italy by Cerved, and in Spain by ICEX. The three databases have 130,000 companies with the following information: company name, address, company type, industry codes, NACE product codes, turnover and export figures, employees, exported products (NACE), and contact names. The database is searchable in French, Italian, Spanish, and English, using Bureau Van Dijk software.

FIRMIMPORT/FIRMEXPORT (Chambre de Commerce et d'Industrie de Paris—Quarterly updates with annual revision)

The *FIRMIMPORT/FIRMEXPORT* database provides information on 30,000 French companies and businesses that export or import. Entries include company's full name, address, telecommunications numbers, manager, legal status, broad industry grouping, list of products using EC harmonized tariff code, countries traded with, and, where available, sales, values for imports and exports, and number of employees. The database is available from Telexport and DATA-STAR.

TELEXPORT (Chambre de Commerce ed d'Industrie de Paris)

Telexport provides a full range of corporate and regulatory information of interest to French companies involved in foreign trade. The *TELEXPORT* databank comprises the following files:

- EXPORT-AFFAIRES—covers approximately 2,000 import-export opportunities and international tenders.

- DOC-EXPORT—provides information on foreign trade regulations for more than 140 countries of export, including principal accompanying documents, rules on the export of merchandise, and descriptions of the foreign trade services offered by the Chambres des Commerce et d'Industrie in France.
- FIRMEXPORT/FIRMIMPORT—(*see* above).
- I-EXPORT—contains addresses of French organizations ready to help exporters.
- DELPHES—covers French and international economy. It is a database of article abstracts that is also available on DIALOG and DATA-STAR.

ABC Europe and *ABC Germany* (ABC der Deutschen Wirtschaft Verlagsgesellschaft mbH—ABC Publishing Group)

ABC Europe and *ABC West Germany* are from the German-language print directories, *European Export Industry* and *German Buyers' and Sellers' Guide*. The publications and the corresponding databases have records for about 150,000 exporting manufacturers in Western and Eastern European countries. Entries include address and contact numbers, product types, industry classification, association memberships, sales representatives, banks, management registration, and capital. Records also provide export destinations. They are online in English on DATA-STAR, in German on FIZ Technik, and a subset is on CD-ROM.

BDI—The German Industry—Made in Germany (Verlag W Sacjpm GmbH & Co.)

BDIE/BDID can be searched in English or German. The database has records on German manufacturers involved in export trade. Data items include address and contact numbers, numbers of employees, names and addresses of subsidiaries, and business data (e.g., capital, sales volume). The print equivalent is *BDI—Die Deutsche Industrie*. The database is available on DATA-STAR and the German databanks FIZ Technik and GENIOS.

Selected Online Bulletin Boards. When we think of online services, we generally think of the commercial time-sharing systems. However, there are several services that have both voice and electronic access for export and import information. We have mentioned three U.S. government services: *Economic Bulletin Board* (U.S. Department of Commerce), *US Customs Electronic Bulletin Board* (U.S. Customs Service), and *Eximbank Bulletin Board.* Check with your state to see if it provides bulletin board access. There are also private sources, which generally repackage government information. Test these services before entering a subscription.

Business Opportunities

In addition to directories that identify importers and exporters, some sources are designed to identify specific business opportunities. Governments put out bids for projects or individual companies advertise themselves as potential trade patterns. They answer such question as:

- We would like to invest in Thailand, especially in a resort. Are there any projects needing financial or technical assistance?
- Are there any library construction projects in Europe?
- Are any Slovenian shoe manufacturers looking for foreign partners?

Several sources of online information list potential partners for the exporter or importer and their representatives. Table 12-L lists sources of business opportunities.

Foreign Trade Opportunities (U.S. Department of Commerce)

TOP covers sales opportunities and leads compiled by U.S embassies abroad for specific products, projects, government tenders, representation, joint ventures, direct sale for resale or end-users, and barter arrangements being sought by foreign companies, governments, or organizations. Information provided includes a description of the opportunity, a contact name, address, phone, FAX and telex numbers, and a five-digit harmonized tariff code. Over 100 countries contribute to *TOP*.

The Trade Opportunity Program is disseminated in several different forms. The daily leads are available, along with over 700 other files, online through the Commerce Department's Economic Bulletin Board (EBB)(Modem access: 202-377-3870). Each day at approximately 1:00 p.m., Eastern Time, two files are made available for downloading by subscribers. One file contains private sector opportunities and the other contains government tender opportunities. A one-year subscription is $35, including a $12 credit for connect time with the system. An even newer service is EBB FAX (900-786-2329).

District offices of the Commerce Department also receive the leads daily and have them on file for the public. Government tenders are printed in the *Commerce Business Daily* (U.S. Department of Commerce), the source of U.S. government procurement announcements. Corporate requests are published in the commercial *Journal of Commerce. TOP* is also online on LEXIS/

Table 12-L. Sources for Business Opportunities

Program	Compiling Body	Target Countries	Availability
Foreign Trade Opportunities TOP	U.S. Dept. of Commerce	Worldwide government and commercial	Commerce Business Daily; Journal of Commerce; EBB; L/N; D-S
Foreign Traders Index	U.S. Dept. of Commerce	Worldwide companies	NTDB; L/N
Overseas Private Investment Corporation—OPIC	U.S. OPIC	Worldwide projects	Direct; L/N
Tenders Electronic Daily TED	EC	EC, GATT, U.S., Japan, Canada	L/N; D-S; Echo
DunsContract	D&B	U.K., private contractors, Eastern Europe	Fee-based; DunsNet
Business—BUSI	European banks	Worldwide commercial	D-S; F-T; online direct
Advertise—ADVE	Germany	Mainly European commercial	D-S
Scan-A-Bid	UN	Noncommerical construction	United Nations; D-S
Bisnis	U.S. Dept of Commerce	Eastern Europe	Newsletters

L/N—LEXIS/NEXIS SERVICES; D-S—DATA-STAR; F-T—FIZ Technik; EBB—Electronic Bulletin Board

NEXIS SERVICES in the regional files, in BUSOPP, and as FTO.

Foreign Traders Index (U.S. Department of Commerce)

Foreign Traders Index lists foreign companies, organizations, government entities, banks, associations, and institutes in about 60 selected countries served by the U.S. and Foreign Commercial Service that have some interest in importing goods or services from the U.S.

Information for each entry includes the name of the organization or business, year established, a contact name and address, number of employees, and description of the product or service needed with a four-digit code. The *Index* is available electronically on *NTDB* CD-ROM disc 2 (*see* Exhibit 12-16) and on the LEXIS

AND NEXIS SERVICES in the regional files, in BUSOPP, and as FTI.

OPIC (Overseas Private Investment Corp. Opportunity Bank)

The Overseas Private Investment Corporation, a U.S. government corporation chartered by Congress, provides political risk and other insurance and investment services to U.S. corporations. OPIC operates an "Opportunity Bank" as part of its effort to promote U.S. direct investment in the developing world. The databank enables U.S. firms and overseas project sponsors to register their respective investment interests and requirements and "find each other." At present there are approximately 2,400 records from 100 countries. The Opportunity Bank contains two types of information:

Exhibit 12-16. *Foreign Traders Index* on *NTDB*: **Search for "Beer"**

National Trade Data Bank—The Export Connection (R)

ITEM ID	: IT FTI 1220801741A
DATE	: Oct 2, 1992
AGENCY	: USDOC, International Trade Administration
PROGRAM	: Foreign Traders Index
TITLE	: Wine-Art Inc.

<ADDRESS>
John Arthurs
Vice President
Wine-Art Inc.
250 West Beaver Creek Road
Richmond Hill, Ontario L4B 1C7
Canada

<OTHER COMPANY INFORMATION>
PHONE: (416) 881-7025
YEAR ESTABLISHED: 1959
NO. OF EMPLOYEES: 70
RELATIVE SIZE: SMALL
INFORMATION DATE: 05/15/91
CABLE ADDR: (416) 881-5105 (FAX)

<PRODUCT INFORMATION>

HARMONIZED CODE	PRODUCT/SERVICE DESCRIPTION
1901	MALT EXT; FOOD PREP OF FLOUR ETC UN 50% COCOA ETC
	Manufacturer or Producer of
	Retailer of
	Distributor or Wholesaler of
	Importer of ...
S518	BEER, WINE & DISTILLED ALCOHOLIC BEVERAGES
	Manufacturer or Producer of
	Retailer of
	Distributor or Wholesaler of
	Importer of

Source: Foreign Traders Index on *NTDB*, January 1993

- U.S. Company profiles: Descriptions of companies interested in investing overseas
- Investment Project Profiles: Descriptions of projects worldwide that are seeking U.S. investment

Application forms to register a company or project with OPIC are available directly from Opportunity Bank Project Profile, 1516 M Street, N.W., Washington, D.C. 20527; phone in the U.S.: (202) 457-7010; FAX: (202) 331-4234; Telex: 493-8219. The forms are also available as part of the online file on LEXIS/NEXIS. The file is available in the regional libraries, BUSOPP and as OPIC.

Tenders Electronic Daily (Office for Official Publications of the European Communities BP 2373 L-1023 Luxembourg B-1049)

Governments, local authorities, and utilities are required by an EC directive to advertise contracts in excess of about $150,000 The information appears in *TED*, *Tenders Electronic Daily*, the official publication of the European Communities. *TED* contains the full text of requests for bids published in supplement "S" of the *Official Journal* of the European Communities.

In addition to EC countries, about 60 participants in GATT, the U.S., Japan, and Canada submit tenders exceeding $300,000. Tenders cover electrical and mechanical engineering, consumer goods, catering, hotel management, printing, fuel supply, and a wide array of other items. The EC maintains *TED* on its own databank ECHO, and other online services access it, including the British Export Network Limited, Cerved, DATA-STAR (TEDA), Dun & Bradstreet, and LEXIS AND NEXIS SERVICES in the regional libraries, BUSOPP and as TED. Exhibit 12-17 displays a record from *Tenders Electronic Daily* from LEXIS/NEXIS.

Business (Business DATENBANKEN GMBH, Heidelberg 1, Federal Republic of Germany)

BUSINESS (BUSI) on DATA-STAR, FIZ Technik, and GENIOS is a European database with worldwide business opportunities. It is a joint venture among European banks, information providers, and the EC. It contains worldwide trade opportunities and business contacts in such areas as imports and exports, sales, services, representation (e.g., general, agency, distributorship), research and development, technology, and cooperative ventures in manufacturing, marketing, and investment. It also includes activity and interest profiles of firms, research institutes, and service organizations. Sources include published exchanges, bulletins from trade promotion agencies, manufacturers' lists, exhibition catalogs, directories, new product announcements, and original company entries

DunsContract (Dun & Bradstreet Ltd.)

DunsContract, from D&B Europe, is a database and network with information on public and private contracts. It includes *TED* and D&B's proprietary Contract Information Database (CID). CID has tender information in the public sector outside the EC's threshold, private contractors wishing to advertise, and World Bank projects for Eastern Europe and the developing countries. Organizations advertising on CID pay no fees. For individuals who do not search online, Duns has a Contract Monitoring Service.

ADVERTISE (Deutscher Sparkassenverlag, the publisher for German Savings Banks)

ADVE contains business opportunities for small to medium-sized companies. Companies pay to be listed. Information is valid for one year. Non-German companies often include a German contact. The database is in German. *ADVE* uses Predicasts country codes and shortened Predicasts product codes. *ADVE* lists 10 types of opportunities: Wanted, For sale/on offer, Representation, License, Trade opportunity, Import request, Distribution/sale, Customers, Buying, and Selling. In addition to being offered on commercial time-sharing systems, it is available in Germany as part of S-Database Services, a fee-based information system offered by German savings bank and state banks.

Scan-a-Bid (United Nations, Development Business/Development Forum)

Scan-a-Bid contains requests for quotations on major construction projects worldwide financed by international organizations. Included are name of the project, country, type of project (e.g., highway), building materials required, amount of money allocated for the project, and name of person and organization to contact for further information. It also contains the complete text of monthly operational summaries of the World Bank and the Inter-American Development Bank. World Bank construction contract awards are also included. An annual subscription to *Development Business* is required for either the print version from the United Nations or the online version on DATA-STAR.

BISNIS (U.S. Department of Commerce)

BISNIS is the acronym for the Commerce Department's Business Information Service for the Newly Independent States. *BISNIS* publishes several newsletters, such as *BISNIS Bulletin,* which contains news and practical advice on doing business in the former Soviet Union. *BISNIS Bulletin* is also available on the *National Trade Data Bank* CD-ROM.

BISNIS Search for Partners is a newsletter designed to help U.S. companies find business opportunities in

Exhibit 12-17. *Tenders Electronic Daily* **from LEXIS/NEXIS**

Copyright (c) 1993 Commission of the European Communities
TED (Tenders Electronic Daily)
April 21, 1993

TYPE OF DOCUMENT: Invitation to tender
LENGTH: 880 words
TITLE OF DOCUMENT: F-Poitiers: multimedia library (Only the original text is
authentic)
AWARD AUTHORITY: Local authorities
KEYWORDS: 5011—GENERAL BUILDING CONTACTORS; 5031—GENERAL INSTALLATION WORK;
5041—GENERAL BUILDING COMPLETION WORK

BODY:
Doc. No: 17319-93; Cite: JO S 077; Page: 0007; Date: April 21, 1993
Type of Procurement: Open procedure
Regulation of Procurement: EEC
Type of Bid Required: Not specified
Award Criteria: Not specified

1. Awarding authority: Ville de Poitiers, service des batiments communaux, hotel de ville, F-86021 Poitiers. Tel. 49 88 82 07.
2. (a) Award procedure: Public invitation to tender. National legislation applicable: CMP art. 295-300, RPAO. (b)
3. (a) Site: Poitiers. (b) Works: Multimedia library. 6 floors. Total surface: 10 209 m**2. 31 lots. (c) (d)
4. Completion deadline: 17 months.
5. (a) Documents from: Applications in writing. As in 1, direction generale des services techniques, M. le Maire. (b) Fee: Deposit in the form of a cheque. FF 800. Payee: Mme le Tresorier principal municipal de Poitiers. Fee will be refunded to bona fide tenderers.
6. (a) Deadline for receipt of tenders: 4. 6. 1993 (17.00). (b) Address: As in 1, secretariat de la direction generale des services techniques. Tenders must be submitted in a double sealed envelope. Tenders to be submitted by registered post with form for advice of receipt or by hand, in which case a receipt will be issued. (c) Language (s): French.
7. (a) (b)
8. Deposits and guarantees: 5 %.
9. Financing and payment: Progress payments as indicated in contract documents.
10.
11. Qualifications: See notice in original language.
12. Tenders may lapse after: 120 days.
13.
14.
15. Other information: M. Tourneboeuf ou M.Masse, tel. 49 88 82 07.
16.
17. Notice postmarked: 13. 4. 1993.
18. Notice received on: 13. 4. 1993.
DATE RECEIVED: April 13, 1993
DEADLINE FOR TENDER: April 13, 1993
COUNTRY: FRANCE

Source: *TED* on LEXIS/NEXIS SERVICES, May 1993. Reprinted with permission.

the states of the former Soviet Union. Each issue focuses on long- and medium-term trade leads in one country. Exhibit 12-18 displays a *BISNIS Search for Partners* entry dealing with the Ukraine.

EXHIBIT 12-18. *BISNIS Search for Partners*

Company: A. Ukspirit

Ukspirit is the state-owned concern responsible for international sales of Ukrainian spirits for many associated enterprises. Ukspirit produces more than ten nationally registered brands of vodka. While these brands do not have the international recognition that Pepsi has built for Stolichnaya, Ukraine does have the right and interest to market these brands. Ukspirit is currently looking for distribution and sales opportunities abroad.

Contact: Mr. Mykola Semerina. President

Ukraine

252190 Kiev

9/12 vul. Baumana

A. Ukspirit

Tel (0 11-7-044) 449- 9556

Fax (0 11-7-044) 443-3221

Source: US&FCS/Kiev. Mr. Stephan Wasylko, SCO

Date Received: January 1993

Source: *BISNIS Search for Partners*, March 1993

BISNIS Commercial Opportunities gives information on export and joint venture opportunities that are time sensitive. Exhibit 12-19 displays a sample entry.

EXHIBIT 12-19. *BISNIS Commercial Opportunities*

PARTNER SOUGHT TO CONVERT ST.
PETERSBURG PALACE INTO HOTEL

A Russian company, Nauka-Service, and a Finnish firm, European Policy Advisors (EPA), are interested in working with a U.S company on a project involving the management and reconstruction of a palace in the city of St. Petersburg. Nauka-Service and EPA are interested in reconstructing the palace so that it could be rented to companies or used as a hotel (with a capacity of about 50 guest rooms).

The building, which was initially constructed as a palace for the Grand Duke Vladimir Alexandrovich in 1872, consists of stone structures of three-to-five stories. The area of the building is approximately 11,000 square meters.

The building is located on Millionaya Street 27, 191065 St. Petersburg (approximately 300 meters from the Hermitage).

For additional information, contact:

Anders Kranck

Director

European Policy Advisors

Bernhardinkatu 7A 8 00130

Helsinki

Tel: 358-0629-177

Fax: 358-0629-316

Source: *BISNIS Commercial Opportunities*, March 19, 1993

Short-term trade leads are also available online through the U.S. Department of Commerce's Electronic Bulletin Board. *BISNIS* will also fax trade leads, trade statistics, lists of upcoming trade promotional events, and other commercial information on the states of the former Soviet Union.

NOTES

1. *Exports from Manufacturing Establishment* (U.S. Department of Commerce, Bureau of the Census, January 6, 1993). This report supplies statistics on the contribution of exporting to the U.S. economy.

2. Richard Barovick and Patricia Anderson, "EMCs/ETCs: What They Are, How They Work," *Business America 113* (July 13, 1992): 2-5. Includes some cases.

3. "Eximbank Targets Small Business: Seeks Charter Changes to Help Exports," *BNA International Finance Daily* (April 16, 1992); from LEXIS/NEXIS search. Outlines changes to three major Eximbank programs: Working Capital Guarantee, New-to-Exporting Insurance and Umbrella Insurance.

4. Nigel M. Healey, "A Beginner's Guide to Corporate Barter," *Illinois Business Review 48* (Spring 1991): 13-15.

5. Aspy Pailia and P. Shenkar, "Countertrade Practices in China," *Industrial Marketing Management 20* (February 1991): 357-65. This article includes examples from *Countertrade Outlook* 6 no. 5 (1988), and analyses 80 countertrade transactions with China.

6. Pailia and Shenkar, "Countertrade Practices in China," pp. 357-65.

7. Charles Batchelor, "Survey of Factoring," *Financial Times* (April 1, 1992): 16; from LEXIS/NEXIS search. Statistics and state of international factoring.

8. Frank Gray, "Forfaiting: London's Where the Skill Is," *Euromoney* (February 1988): S2-S6. This article explains how forfaiting is done.

9. Adapted from R. Michael Rice, " Four Ways to Finance Your Exports," *Journal of Business Strategy 9* (July/August 1988): 30–33. This article provides brief descriptions of forfaiting, factoring, the Export-Import Bank, and insurance underwriting.

10. Michael J. Horton, *Import and Customs Law Handbook* (New York: Quorum Books, 1992). This book provides guidance to those whose jobs make them responsible for handling U.S. Customs matters. Although the book deals with the legal aspects of Customs, it is is understandable to a layperson.

11. Thomas E. Johnson, *Export/Import Procedures and Documentation* (New York: AMACOM, 1991). Published by the American Management Association Communications Division, this introductory guide to importing and exporting has extensive sample documents.

PART IV
Industrial and Economic Statistics

CHAPTER 13
Economic Statistics

TOPICS COVERED

MAJOR SOURCES DISCUSSED

- *National Accounts Statistics*
- *World Economic Outlook*
- *Monthly Bulletin of Statistics*
- *International Financial Statistics*
- *Main Aggregates and Detailed Tables*
- *National Accounts ESA*
- *Bulletin of Labour Statistics*
- *EUROSTAT CD-ROM*

INTRODUCTION

Economic statistics are the basic indicators of a nation's economic well-being. They include measures of national income, employment, price levels, and industrial output. They are used to gauge an economy's performance and to predict future conditions. In this chapter, we examine some of the issues concerning the use of economic statistics in an international setting as well as describe general sources of economic data. We use economic statistics in a broad sense and include in our discussion national finance, labor statistics, and energy. Trade statistics are discussed separately in Chapter 15.

Economic data are available in three basic forms. The first form is a time-series, numbers reported at a regular interval over time. The monthly consumer price index for Canada for the past three years would be a time series. The second form is cross-sectional data, several economic characteristics described for a particular time. An example would be a country's industrial production by industry group for the current year. The third form for economic data is text. An example would be a news story that described Japan's trade surplus. In practice, these forms of data are often combined. Cross-sectional data frequently include historical (time-series) as well as current data. Text often combines descriptions of economic variables with tables and graphs of the data.

COUNTRY CLASSIFICATIONS

The individual country is the basic unit for the presentation of comparative international data. Countries are grouped in several ways for analysis.

- by geographic region (e.g., Asia)
- by type of economy (e.g., market)
- by stage of economic development (e.g., "least developed")
- by political organization (e.g., EC)

Economic Classifications

There is no standard economic classification scheme for countries. Recent publications by the UN categorize countries by economic development into three groups: "developed market economies," "developing countries," and "economies in transition." Earlier terminology used "industrialized countries," "less developed countries," and "non-market economies." Developed market economies would include North America, Southern and Western Europe (excluding Cyprus, Malta, and the former

Yugoslavia), Australia, Japan, New Zealand, and South Africa. Developing countries are found in Latin America and the Caribbean, Africa (other than South Africa), Asia and the Pacific (excluding Australia, Japan, and New Zealand), Cyprus, Malta, and the former Yugoslavia. Economies in transition include the countries of the former USSR and the former Soviet Bloc countries of Eastern Europe (excluding Yugoslavia).

Other country classifications that are frequently used include:

- **Group of Seven (G-7):** These are the seven largest developed market economies: Canada, France, Germany, Italy, Japan, the U.K., and the U.S. Before 1987 you will see references to the "G-5." When the size of Italy's GDP overtook Great Britain's in 1987, the group was expanded to include both Italy and Canada, and it may expand again because Spain's GDP exceeded Canada's in 1992.[1] There are several other "groups" of countries; the Group of 10 (G-10), for example, consists of the 10 wealthiest countries in the IMF.
- **Newly Industrialized Countries:** "Newly industrialized countries" or "nearly industrialized countries" (NICs) is a category widely used in economic analysis. It describe countries with rapidly expanding market economies that are heavily engaged in international trade. There is some disagreement on which countries should be included. Hong Kong, Singapore, South Korea, Taiwan, Argentina, Brazil, and Mexico are the countries most identified with the group. Israel, Venezuela, and China are sometimes included.

There are a host of informal names for other country groups. For example, Hong Kong, South Korea, Singapore, and Taiwan are sometimes referred to collectively as the "Four Dragons" or the "Four Tigers." The U.S., Japan, and the EC are called the "Triad" in discussions of international trade.

Formal Economic Groups

There are a number of formally constituted economic country groups. The following groups are among the most important:

- **EC (European Community):** The members of the EC are Belgium, Denmark, France, Germany, Greece, Ireland, Italy, Luxembourg, the Netherlands, Portugal, Spain, and the United Kingdom. The EC is a supranational body, and ranks with the U.S. and Japan as one of the world's leading economic powers. The EC's goal is to join its member nations in a political, economic, and monetary union.
- **EFTA (European Free Trade Association):** EFTA was set up in 1960 as a common market. It has elimi-

nated all customs duties and quota restrictions on industrial products between members and with the EC. Members of EFTA are Austria, Finland, Iceland, Norway, Sweden, and Switzerland.

- **OPEC (Organization of Petroleum Exporting Countries):** OPEC is a group of countries that are net exporters of petroleum. All the countries in the group are "developing countries." Several important oil exporting countries, such as Bahrain and Mexico, are not part of OPEC. The category "net energy exporters" is sometimes used to include all oil exporting nations. The members of OPEC are Algeria, Gabon, Indonesia, Iran, Iraq, Kuwait, Libya, Nigeria, Qatar, Saudia Arabia, United Arab Emirates, and Venezuela.
- **OECD (Organization for Economic Cooperation and Development):** The OECD is an international organization for industrialized market-economy countries. It is a forum where officials from member countries exchange information and coordinate policy. OECD members include the EC and EFTA, Turkey, Canada, the U.S., Australia, Japan, and New Zealand. The organization gathers a wide range of statistical information from member states, processes it for comparability, and distributes it to the public.

A useful source for descriptions of country groups is the CIA's *World Factbook*, described below. Eurostat's *Europe in Figures* gives a clear description of the evolution and present situation of the EC.

NATIONAL ACCOUNTS

National accounts are a compilation of the data needed to estimate the money value of goods and services produced by a country. This measure is usually expressed as gross national product (GNP) or gross domestic product (GDP).

Gross national product is the market value of all goods and services produced during a particular period by the residents of a country. In the United States, for example, GNP is the sum of the market value of all goods and services produced by individuals, businesses, and government. GNP *includes* income earned by U.S.-owned corporations overseas and U.S. residents working abroad. For example, U.S. GNP *includes* income earned by General Motors in the United Kingdom. GNP *excludes* income earned in the U.S. by residents of the rest of the world. For example, U.S. GNP *excludes* income earned by the Honda Corporation in the United States.

Gross domestic product is the market value of all goods and services produced by people in a country whether or not they are citizens. For example, profits earned by foreign-owned businesses in the U.S. are included in U.S. GDP but not in U.S. GNP. In contrast, profits earned by U.S. firms abroad are included in U.S. GNP but not in U.S. GDP.

Most countries and international organizations reporting national accounts use GDP. There are some important exceptions; Japan, for example, reports GNP. Until 1991 when it switched to GDP, the U.S. used GNP as its main measure of national economic output.

For the U.S., the difference between GNP and GDP is very small—a few billion dollars in a $6 trillion economy. Few U.S. residents work abroad and U.S. earnings on foreign investments are about the same as foreign earnings on investment in the U.S. Countries that have workers in foreign countries often have a GNP that is higher than their GDP. Turkey's GNP, for example, is about 1% above its GDP. Countries that have more foreign investment in their country than they have abroad often have a higher GDP than GNP. Canada's GDP is about 4% higher than its GNP.[2]

Because GDP is a key variable in the analysis of a country's economy, there is interest in several aspects of this measure. In addition to examining the trend in GDP over time and determining differences in GDP by region and country, researchers often want such details as the following:

1. **GDP at Constant Prices:** GDP is measured in a country's currency. Because currencies are subject to changes in value, GDP must be adjusted for inflation. GDP price deflators (general measures of an economy's inflation rate) are used to convert GDP measured in current prices to constant prices.

2. **The Contributions of Economic Sectors to GDP:** One method of calculating GDP is to add up the value-added contribution of a country's economic sectors. As a result, it is possible to determine each sector's contribution to total GDP. One could, for instance, determine the share of the Italian service sector in the total Italian GDP.

3. **GDP by Type of Expenditure:** GDP represents the use of goods and services produced by an economy. GDP is used by consumers (households), governments, and businesses (investment). Determining the changes in final uses of GDP over time, or the differences in final uses among countries is often of research interest. For example, the expenditures by households is one indication of a country's standard of living.

4. **The Relation of GDP to Other Economic Variables:** A nation's GDP divided by its population equals per capita GDP. This measure allows a direct comparison of the economic strengths of countries with unequal populations. A nation's expenditures or debt is sometimes expressed as a percentage of GDP. Examples would be defense expenditures as a percentage of GDP (Expenditures/GDP) or budget deficit as a percentage of GDP (Debt/GDP).

5. **The Effect of the Underground Economy on GDP:** Not all income in an economy is recorded by governments. Unreported economic activities range from fees collected for child care to the activities of organized crime. There are no firm statistics for the underground economy. Estimates of the underground economy in the U.S. range between 5% and 15% of GDP.[3] Some estimates of the underground economy in developing countries are as high as 50% of reported GDP.[4]

Sources for National Accounts

National Accounts Statistics (United Nations—Annual)

The United Nations System of National Accounts (SNA) was first formulated in 1952. It provides the framework for the display of the national accounts of more than 170 countries. It is used extensively by individual countries and by international organizations in their national accounts reporting. The EC's European System of Integrated Economic Accounts (ESA) is based on the UN system. The U.S. will adopt the United Nations system of national accounts in the mid-1990s.

The UN's annual two-part *National Accounts Statistics* is an essential resource, particularly for its coverage of countries that are not part of the OECD or the EC. Part One of the series, *National Accounts Statistics: Analysis of Main Aggregates*, gives general measures of GDP for 170 countries for the past 20 years. The measures include total and per capita GDP, GDP by type of expenditure and by kind of economic activity, and implicit price deflators. The overall GDP figures are given in current prices using the national currency. Details of economic activity and type of expenditures are given as percentages of total GDP. The section on price deflators gives GDP as index numbers in current and constant U.S. dollars. The UN converts GDP to U.S. dollars using the annual average of market rates as reported by the IMF. For countries not part of the IMF, conversion rates are the annual average of the United Nation's operational rates of exchange. The UN plans to use alternative methods of currency conversion, such as using purchasing power parities, in future presentations of GDP. Part Two of the series, *National Accounts Statistics: Main Aggregates and Detailed Tables,* gives detailed breakdowns of GDP expenditures in both current and constant national currency prices. The notes that begin each country's entry give the source of information for the accounts. In most cases this consists of the name of the statistical office in the country together with the name of the published volume containing the account. Exhibit 13-1 displays a sample page from *National Accounts Statistics*.

Exhibit 13-1. *National Accounts Statistics*

Austria

1.2 Expenditure on the Gross Domestic Product, in Constant Prices

Thousand Million Austrian schillings

	1970	1980	1981	1982	1983	1984	1985	1986	1987	1988	1989	1990
		1978				**At constant prices of:** **1983**						
1 Government final consumption expenditure	100.71	212.27	216.99	221.97	226.89	227.38	231.80	235.65	236.59	237.37	239.24	242.82
2 Private final consumption expenditure	309.31	651.89	653.97	661.88	694.84	694.31	710.86	723.43	746.14	771.05	792.67	821.10
3 Gross capital formation	160.37	328.50	295.34	269.26	263.73	295.71	301.29	307.53	316.39	345.71	364.49	401.70
A Increase in stocks [a]	16.72	29.17	0.14	-1.84	-5.82	20.47	12.28	7.88	7.40	18.04	18.99	39.97
B Gross fixed capital formation	143.65	299.33[b]	295.21[b]	271.10[b]	269.55[b]	275.24[b]	289.01[b]	299.65[b]	309.00[b]	327.67[b]	345.50[b]	361.73[b]
Residential buildings	30.76	62.99	64.23	62.72	61.58	61.11	60.09	61.47	62.89	68.15	67.84	67.65
Non-residential buildings	47.40	98.19	94.81	81.29	83.41	85.03	87.94	91.48	98.35	103.39	111.23	123.29
Other construction and land improvement etc.												
Other	57.28	121.24	119.48	110.94	107.98	112.83	124.21	129.00	130.22	137.56	147.52	151.70
4 Exports of goods and services	159.33	404.61[c]	424.34[c]	435.79[c]	449.69[c]	477.07[c]	509.96[c]	496.14[c]	507.91[c]	553.22[c]	609.87[c]	669.15[c]
5 Less: Imports of goods and services	158.25	428.60[c]	425.35[c]	411.15[c]	433.93[c]	476.90[c]	506.37[c]	500.45[c]	523.82[c]	572.87[c]	622.05[c]	682.29[c]
Statistical discrepancy	-	...	.	.	.	.	.	.	.	.	.	.
Equals: Gross Domestic Product	571.47	1168.66	1165.29	1177.75	1201.22	1217.57	1247.54	1262.30	1283.23	1334.47	1384.23	1452.47

a) Item 'Increase in stocks' includes breeding stock, draught animals and a statistical discrepancy. These estimates are shown separately as 'Statistical discrepancy' in tables 2.7, 2.8, 2.9, 2.10 and 2.11.
b) Item 'Gross fixed capital formation' includes value added tax on investments of investors not entitled to deduct invoiced value added tax. This component is not included in the sub-items. For c) The estimates on transit trade are on a net basis. years 1973-1975, 1977 and 1978 of the current prices table, special investment tax is included.

1.3 Cost Components of the Gross Domestic Product

Thousand Million Austrian schillings

	1970	1980	1981	1982	1983	1984	1985	1986	1987	1988	1989	1990
1 Indirect taxes, net	55.16	132.77	142.31	150.70	161.69	180.15	186.73	188.00	197.77	209.81	226.30	240.79
A Indirect taxes	61.68	162.83	174.40	184.98	197.08	216.09	225.93	234.04	245.15	254.89	271.41	288.72
B Less: Subsidies	6.52	30.05	32.09	34.28	35.39	35.93	39.20	46.05	47.38	45.08	45.11	47.93
2 Consumption of fixed capital	43.85	116.10	128.51	140.76	149.24	158.19	167.53	176.20	183.87	194.11	205.63	218.49
3 Compensation of employees paid by resident producers to:	175.82	545.63	589.01	616.85	642.44	676.33	717.09	761.25	792.73	822.36	875.85	942.66
4 Operating surplus	101.05	200.20	196.14	225.22	247.86	262.10	277.08	297.05	307.01	335.42	356.11	387.45
Statistical discrepancy	-	-	-	-	-	-	-	-	-	-	-	-
Equals: Gross Domestic Product	375.88	994.70	1055.97	1133.54	1201.22	1276.76	1348.43	1422.50	1481.39	1561.70	1663.89	1789.39

1.4 General Government Current Receipts and Disbursements

Thousand Million Austrian schillings

	1970	1980	1981	1982	1983	1984	1985	1986	1987	1988	1989	1990
					Receipts							
1 Operating surplus	...	...	...	...	...	...	...	...	...	...	...	...
2 Property and entrepreneurial income	4.45	18.49	22.42	22.67	22.40	23.06	26.15	25.91	29.44	30.72	33.34	35.79
3 Taxes, fees and contributions	136.41	418.68	455.32	477.61	502.93	549.42	591.18	617.66	635.78	665.26	694.57	752.85
A Indirect taxes	61.68	162.83	174.40	184.98	197.08	216.09	225.93	234.04	245.15	254.89	271.41	288.72
B Direct taxes	41.11	128.39	144.21	149.48	156.64	173.77	193.63	203.77	203.36	214.46	214.47	239.17
C Social security contributions	32.91	124.58	133.36	139.76	145.46	155.46	167.80	175.99	183.34	191.82	204.28	220.18
D Compulsory fees, fines and penalties	0.71	2.89	3.36	3.39	3.75	4.10	3.82	3.86	3.93	4.10	4.42	4.78
4 Other current transfers	8.34	24.44	26.62	29.59	31.74	33.67	36.19	38.51	40.49	42.02	44.42	46.97
Total Current Receipts of General Government	149.20	461.62	504.36	529.87	557.06	606.14	653.53	682.08	705.71	738.00	772.33	835.61
					Disbursements							
1 Government final consumption expenditure	55.22	178.70	195.25	214.30	226.89	237.76	255.00	270.66	280.44	288.35	302.88	321.24

Source: National Accounts Statistics: Main Aggregates and Detailed Tables, 1990, page 1355 (United Nations publication, Sales No. E. 93. XVII.3). Reprinted with permission.

Main Aggregates and Detailed Tables (Organization for Economic Cooperation and Development—Annual)

The national accounts published by the EC and OECD are similar to the UN's *National Accounts Statistics,* but much more limited in their national scope. The OECD publishes statistical accounts in *Main Aggregates and Detailed Tables.* The information is updated in *Quarterly National Accounts.* These OECD publications are unique in presenting constant dollar GDP figures calculated on the basis of both market exchange rates and purchasing power parity rates.

National Accounts ESA (European Community—Annual)

EC national accounts publications have more detail than the publications of the UN or OECD. Four EC annual publications are *National Accounts ESA—Aggregates, National Accounts ESA—Detailed Tables by Branch, National Accounts ESA—Detailed Tables by Sector,* and *General Government Accounts and Statistics.* The EC defines "sectors" as economic units such as households or businesses that have similar economic behavior. Statistics for the EC as a whole are given in ECUs. Individual nations' accounts are in their national currency. The data are available online through the EC's statistical databank CRONOS.

Table 13-A compares some of the main features of the national account statistics prepared by the UN, the EC, and the OECD.

Table 13-A. National Accounts Publications of International Organizations

	UN	EC	OECD
Publication lag	3 Years	4 Years	2 Years
Currency Used	National & U.S. Dollar	National & U.S. Dollar	National & U.S. Dollar
Update	NA	Quarterly	Quarterly
Countries Reported	170	12	24
Years Covered (Main Aggregates)	20	17	30
Years Covered (Detailed Tables)	20	17	12

COMPARATIVE ECONOMIC STATISTICS

Researchers are often interested in comparing the economic statistics of countries.

- Compare the growth of GDP in France with GDP growth in Germany
- Compare the unemployment rate in Mexico with the U.S. unemployment rate
- Compare the consumer price index of the U.K. with Japan's CPI

In Chapter 8, we discussed the problems associated with the international ranking of companies and their products. These problems include foreign exchange conversions, the definition of products, and the frequency of data collection. A similar set of problems is involved in making economic comparisons among countries. The *Statistical Abstracts of the U.S.* in its section on international statistics gives a succinct statement of the pitfalls of using economic statistics for international comparisons.

> The bases, methods of estimating, methods of data collection, extent of coverage, precision of definition, scope of territory, and margins of error may vary for different items within a particular country and for like items for different countries.[5]

Economic data come from such a variety of sources that international comparisons should be undertaken with caution. Economic data are usually collected by individual countries. International agencies such as the UN often simply report the data they receive from national sources. An example of this reporting is seen in the *Bulletin of Labour Statistics'* summary of unemployment statistics. The figures vary by country in frequency, currency, and detail. Every country's entry is footnoted to show the variations in the definitions of "unemployed."

The states of the former Soviet Bloc present the researcher with a special set of problems. As discussed in Chapter 8, international research becomes complicated when there is little agreement on the name of a country. The former Soviet Union was not a member of several key international organizations, including the International Monetary Fund, the OECD, and GATT. Consequently, the long time series of economic and financial variables in such sources as the *IMF Yearbook* do not include most of the countries of Eastern Europe. When statistics are available, they are often sketchy. For example, in the UN's *National Account Statistics,* the USSR's national accounts take up four pages and the U.S. accounts occupy 60 pages. A further complication was that the Soviet Union and other centrally planned economies reported their national accounts as "Material Product Balances" (MPS) rather than as GNP or GDP. The MPS measure, among other things, excluded most services from national accounts.

With a few exceptions, such as the former Yugoslavia, the socialist countries of Eastern Europe regarded most economic data as state secrets. In the U.S., the CIA made estimates of basic economic production statistics for Eastern Europe, as it turned out, with rather low accuracy. Even basic economic statistics such as GNP were estimates. GNP per capita estimates for the USSR in 1989 ranged from $1,780 by the World Bank to $9,230 by the CIA.

Although much less secretive than in the past, Russia is still not forthcoming in its publication of data. The *Economist* notes that Russian statistical services do not publish tabular data but instead issue monthly textual bulletins in which numbers are sprinkled. There seems to be little consistency or reason for the numbers chosen. Mayonnaise prices may be available every month but statistics on foreign exchange are not.[6] All the countries that made up the USSR have applied for membership in the International Monetary Fund. As a result, we can expect to see increasing consistency in data collection and presentation from the countries of the former Soviet Union and other Eastern European nations. In 1992, the IMF began publishing reports on the individual states of the former Soviet Union.

Data on foreign direct investment in Central and Eastern Europe are available in Volume 2 of the *World Investment Directory,* which covers Central and Eastern Europe. This source also supplies lists of the largest foreign affiliates in the host countries and the largest transnational corporations aboard together with some information on sales and exports. The *World Investment Directory* is described in more detail in Chapter 15.

Two additional sources of information on "economies in transition" are the monthly reports of *PlanEcon* and the quarterly *Russian Economic Trends.* Both are described below.

Currency Conversion

A central issue in the use of international data is how to compare statistics denominated in national currencies. We are often required to compare the wages, prices, or output of one country with another. Examples might be comparing the average wage in Japan to that in the U.S., ranking the countries of the world by their per capita GDP, or comparing the price of gasoline in Japan with the price in the U.S. Making these kinds of comparisons depends fundamentally on comparing the values of currencies. For example, to compare the wages of Japanese and American workers, we must convert the wages to a common currency such as dollars or yen. The market exchange rate frequently is used to make the conversion. Let's assume that the average hourly Japanese wage is 1,535 yen per hour and that the average U.S. wage is $10.34. Assume further that the wage rates were calculated for the same period and for the same

group of occupations. We can use the exchange rate to find the average Japanese wage in terms of dollars. If the exchange rate is 133 yen per dollar, then Japanese workers make the equivalent of $11.54 per hour, $1.20 more than their U.S. counterparts.

However, market exchange rates often do not reflect accurately the purchasing power of a currency within a country. A more accurate way to compare currencies is to use exchange rates based on purchasing power parity (PPP). The relation between goods and services prices and exchange rates is known as purchasing power parity. The PPP-based exchange rates are, therefore, the rates of currency conversion that equalize the real purchasing power of different currencies. This means that a given sum of money when converted into different currencies at the PPP rates will buy the same basket of goods and services in all countries.

As an example of how purchasing power parity operates, look at the "Big Mac Purchasing Power Parity" devised by the *Economist.* The "Big Mac" exchange rate is the rate that makes the price of a Big Mac the same in all countries. Here, our basket of goods and services is reduced to one item, a Big Mac hamburger. In 1992, the average price of a Big Mac in four American cities was $2.19. In Japan, a Big Mac cost 380 yen ($2.86 at the market exchange rate of 133 yen per dollar). If we divide the yen price of a Big Mac by the dollar price, we get an exchange rate of $1 = 174 yen. If the actual (market) dollar foreign exchange rate was $1 = 133 yen, then the dollar was undervalued by 24% against the yen.[7]

Let's return to our example of U.S. vs. Japanese wages and adjust the wages using the Big Mac exchange rate. If the U.S. dollar equals the buying power of 174 yen, then the average Japanese wage of 1,535 yen per hour is equal to $8.82, not $11.54 per hour as indicated by the market exchange rate. The average Japanese worker by this calculation makes $1.52 less than the average American worker, not $1.20 more.

Obviously, using purchasing power parity for currency conversion requires analyzing more than the price of Big Macs. The OECD calculates purchasing power parities for 24 member countries. In 1990, this involved collecting data on 2,150 consumer goods and services; 30 government, education, and health services; 350 types of equipment goods; and 23 construction projects.[8]

When we rank countries on such economic measures as GDP, investment, or wages, the results will depend on whether we use the PPP-based exchange rates or market exchange rates to convert currencies. For example, Tables 13-B and 13-C show the difference in country rankings of GDP per capita as the result of using market exchange rates or purchasing power parity rates. Table 13-B shows the ranking of countries by their per capita GDP or GNP in 1989 U.S. dollars (exchange rate basis).[9]

Table 13-B. Countries Ranked by Per Capita GDP/GNP (Exchange Rate Basis)

Rank	per capita GDP/GNP U.S. dollars, 1989
1 Switzerland	$30,050
2 Luxembourg	$26,220
3 Japan	$24,240
4 Finland	$22,120
5 Sweden	$21,580
6 Iceland	$20,940
7 Norway	$20,940
8 United States	$20,850
9 Denmark	$20,740
10 West Germany	$20,450

Source: *Fortune,* July 27, 1992, "How the Nations Rank," p. 71

Table 13-C shows GDP per capita adjusted for purchasing power in 1989 U.S. dollars.

Table 13-C. Countries Ranked by Per Capita GDP/GNP (PPP Basis)

Rank	per capita GDP/GNP adjusted for purchasing power U.S. dollars, 1989
1 United Arab Emirates	$23,798
2 United States	$20,998
3 Canada	$18,635
4 Switzerland	$18,590
5 Norway	$16,838
6 Luxembourg	$16,537
7 Kuwait	$15,984
8 Australia	$15,266
9 Hong Kong	$15,180
10 Singapore	$15,108

Source: *Fortune,* July 27, 1992, "How the Nations Rank," p. 71

The differences in the lists are striking. All the ranks have changed and only four of the ten nations in Table 13-B are in Table 13-C.

The effects of using the PPP-based exchange rates versus market exchange rates can be shown for individual items. In 1991 the average price of a liter of gasoline in Japan using the foreign exchange rate was .94 U.S. dollars. The cost of a liter of gasoline was .66 dollars using purchasing power parity exchange rates. The cost of a liter of gasoline in the U.S. was .30 dollars in 1991. Was the cost of gasoline in Japan two or three times its cost in the U.S. in 1991?

The International Monetary Fund and the World Bank are beginning to use purchasing power parities to calculate national income figures. The effect on individual countries' GDP figures has been dramatic. The developing countries' share of world output is now estimated to be 34% rather than 18% as calculated using market exchange rates. Estimates by the *Economist* rank China as the second largest economy in the world, behind the U.S. but ahead of Japan and Germany. China, India, Brazil, and Mexico are estimated to have larger GDPs than Canada.[10]

Which method of conversion (purchasing power parity or market exchange rates) is more accurate? Purchasing power parities are more realistic in adjusting for what money can buy in an individual country, particularly when market exchange rates are changing rapidly. Market exchange rates are more accurate in showing what a country's money will buy in the world's marketplace. Because many economic variables such as wages and housing costs reflect mostly domestic rather than international spending, purchasing power parity rates are, in general, a more accurate way to compare currencies.

SOURCES FOR ECONOMIC STATISTICS

There are thousands of economic data series. Table 13-D lists a few of the series that are generally available for many countries. The series are available as pure number databases in electronic format; as printed statistical publications, often accompanied by graphs; and as part of textual reports on a broad range of topics. Economic statistics are published in confusing abundance by national governments, international organizations, and commercial publishers. The most authoritative sources of statistics are usually the official national statistical reports of a country. The practical problems of language barriers, multiplicity of sources, and the need to compare series from several countries over time make using primary sources difficult. Fortunately, the UN, the EC, and the OECD and their agencies collect and make available thousands of economic data series in scores of serial publications and through electronic media. The series frequently overlap among the organizations. Basic data on national accounts, labor statistics, and trade and finance can be found in the publications of all three groups. The series often overlap as well within one organization. A statistical series gathered by one agency may appear in several publications. For example, expenditure on the gross domestic product in purchasers' values at current prices is furnished by the

United Nations Statistical Office and is published in the Statistical Office's *Yearbook of National Accounts Statistics,* the *Statistical Yearbook,* and the *Monthly Bulletin of Statistics.* In addition, these data appear in the publications of other agencies, such as the IMF's *International Financial Statistics.*

The data are often expressed in different units by the various agencies. A series may be presented as an index number by the U.N., in U.S. dollars by the OECD, and in ECUs by the EC. When series are expressed as index numbers, the base years used by the agencies are often different. The *Index to International Statistics (IIS),* described in Chapter 1, is a general index to the statistical publications of international organizations.

Table 13-D. Economic Time Series

Business Failures	Housing Starts
Capacity Utilization	Import/Export Price Index
Capital Appropriations	Industrial Production Index
Consumer Confidence	Interest Rates
Consumer Credit	International Investment
Consumer Price Index	Position
Distribution of Income	Manufacturers Orders
Employment/	Money Supply
Unemployment	Personal income and savings
Flow of Funds	Plant & Equipment Expendi-
Government Budget and	tures
Debt	Producer Price Index
Gross Domestic Product	Productivity
	Unit Labor Cost

To make our discussion of economic statistics sources more coherent, we have divided the sources into several categories.

- Current and Forecast Time Series
- World, Regional, and National Summaries
- Special Subjects
- Computer Readable Data

Because of their importance, we pay particular attention to the topics of national accounts, price indices, and labor statistics.

Current Statistics

Economic statistics usually appear at less frequent intervals than do financial statistics. A nation's GDP figures, for example, usually are published quarterly. The foreign exchange value of a nation's currency, however, changes continuously. Despite the slower pace at which economic statistics appear, we want to be able to secure the most recent data available.

Three useful monthly publications for general economic data are the UN's *Monthly Bulletin,* the OECD's *Main Economic Indicators,* and the EC's *Eurostatistics.* The publications all give country breakdowns for the current year in months or in quarters. They typically provide annual statistics for the past four or five years. In general, the greater the country coverage (as in the publications of the UN) the less detailed the data. Table 13-E shows the principle economic series they present. In the Table, "Currency" refers to the currency of individual countries. Table 13-E is designed to show the variety of data presentations as well as gaps in coverage among these publications. *Eurostatistics* gives data for the U.S. and Japan in addition to the EC member countries.

Because they depend on statistics gathering by individual countries, the data in these publications vary greatly in timeliness. The *Monthly Bulletin of Statistics* has the greatest variability, with some series being two or more years out of date. Consumer price indexes for many countries, in contrast, are current within one month.

Forecasts

Economic forecasts are used by governments and industry to estimate the effect of policy changes and to project capital and labor requirements. The forecasts may be based on mathematical models of an economy. The most detailed econometric models are available on time-sharing systems such as WEFA and DRI. Given below are brief summaries of print sources of international economic forecasts.

International Economic Outlook (Basil Blackwell— Twice a year)

The forecasts contained in the journal *International Economic Outlook* are based on the global model maintained by the London Business School and the U.K.'s national Institute of Economic and Social Research. Eight year forecasts are given for output and demand of the industrial countries. A narrative description of the outlook for the world's economy is a useful feature of each issue.

World Economic Outlook (International Monetary Fund—Annual)

World Economic Outlook gives an overview of the performance and prospects for the global economy. It includes approximately 50 tables of 10-year time series of economic variables with short-range (one year) projections. Medium-range (two to four years) projections are given for a few measures such as GDP. The tables are divided into industrial countries and developing

Table 13-E. Monthly Economic Publications of the UN, OECD, and EC

	UN Monthly Bulletin	*OECD Main Economic Indicators*	*EC Eurostatistics*
Agricultural Products	Index		ECUs
Balance of Payments		Currency	
Business Failures			Index
Business Surveys		Percent	Percent
Consumer Price Index	Index	Index	Index
Employment	Number	Index	Index
Exchange Rates		Dollars	ECU & Dollars
Exports	Currency	Dollars	ECUs
GDP		Index	Index
GDP Deflator		Index	
Hourly Earnings			Index
Hours Worked	Number		
Housing Starts		Number	
Imports		Dollars	
Industrial Production	Index	Index	Volume
Interest Rates	Percent	Percent	Percent
International Reserves	Dollars		
Leading Indicators		Index	
Money Supply	Currency	Index	Currency
National Accounts		Currency	Index
Passenger Cars Produced		Number	Index
Producer Prices	Index	Index	Index
Retail Sales		Index	
Share Prices	Index	Index	Index
Trade Balance	Dollars	Dollars	
Unemployment		Percent	Percent

countries. Country detail is available only for the G-7 industrial nations. *World Economic Outlook* includes a series of "annexes" that contain brief discussions of specialized economic topics. The 1992 report, for example, contained a discussion of the Maastrict Agreement on economic and monetary union and a paper on the accuracy of *World Economic Outlook* projections.

OECD Economic Outlook (Organization for Economic Cooperation and Development—Twice a year)

This publication gives analyses of the latest economic trends and approximately 50 tables of short-term (one year) projections for OECD countries. The projections include components of GDP, public debt, balance of payments, employee compensation, and unit labor costs. Additional tables of "reference statistics" give 20-year time series for national accounts, prices, unemployment, balance of payments, and exchange rates.

Economic and Financial Outlook (National Westminster Bank—Monthly)

This newsletter published in the U.K. gives up to four-year projections for several key economic and fi-

nancial variables, including GDP, consumer prices, balance of payments, interest rates, stock exchange indices, commodity prices, exchange rates, and bond yields. The number of countries for which projections are made varies; typically, OECD members are included. Purchasing power parity estimates for major currencies, difficult to find pieces of information, are also provided.

Global Forecasting Service (Economic Intelligence Unit—Quarterly)

This service gives five-year forecasts for 55 countries. Forecasts include GDP and its components, population, consumer prices, exchange rate, external trade, and foreign indebtedness.

The Book of European Forecasts (Euromonitor—1992)

This 300-page compendium of forecasts on every facet of European life includes an extensive array of forecasts for macroeconomics, labor force, industrial development, trade, and energy. Most of the forecasts are to the year 2000 and were made between late 1989 and late 1991. The sources are a combination of published data and Euromonitor's own estimates. Many of the sources are described in a final section of the book. The book's main subject divisions are listed below.

Demographic Trends	Market Penetration
Macro-Economic Trends	Advertising Marketing and Media
Labor Force and Media	Retail Distribution
Employment	Consumer Expenditure
Extern Trade	Drinks Consumption and
Energy	Expenditure
Defence	Tobacco
Technology	OTC Healthcare
Household Structure	Personal Care
Electrical Goods	Footwear
Catering	Travel, Transport and
Single European Market	Tourism
Eastern Europe	German Unification

Country Data Forecasts (Bank of America—Twice a year)

Twenty-three key economic variables are presented for 80 countries. Six years of historical statistics, the current year and five years of forecasts, are also included. Variables include income per capita, growth and size of the economy, inflation rates, trade performance indebtedness, and exchange rates.

Consensus Forecasts (Consensus Economics, Inc.—Monthly)

Consensus Forecasts surveys 200 financial and economic forecasters each month for their estimates of key variables. The forecasters constitute the world's major investment banking and economic research centers. The projections are for the next six quarters. Individual country forecasts are given for 35 countries (industrialized countries plus several newly industrialized countries). Detailed forecasts are given for the U.S., Japan, Germany, France, the U.K., Italy, Canada, and Australia. The detailed forecasts include the specific forecasts of individual institutions. For all countries, forecasts are made for GDP, consumer prices, current account, and exchange rates. In addition, detailed forecasts include projections of private consumption, business investments, industrial production, unemployment, and both short-term (three months) and long-term (10 years) interest rates.

World and Regional Summaries

The world and regional summaries of economic data produced by the UN and other international bodies are useful for their consistent presentation of long time series. However, the data they provide are limited in detail and frequently dated.

World Tables (World Bank—Annual)

World Tables gives 20-year economic time series data for more than 130 countries. The series are presented both by subject and by country. The data are derived mostly from national account statistics. The topical pages are updated semiannually. In the basic volume, the latest year of data is usually two years behind the date of publication. The information in the semiannual update is one year behind the publication date.

Statistical Yearbook (United Nations—Annual)

The UN's *Statistical Yearbook* for 1992 presents country data and world and regional aggregates on a broad range of economic, demographic, and social topics. It includes 10-year time series on national accounts, balance of payments, international trade, industrial production, agriculture, and energy. Most of the world aggregates are expressed as index numbers. The latest information is about three years behind the date of publication.

World Bank Atlas (World Bank—Annual)

This compact reference to basic economic and social statistics on 185 countries includes GNP, GNP per capita, growth rates of GNP, population, fertility rates, illiteracy, life expectancy, and daily calorie supply. Each country is ranked on the variables. The information is also presented in color coded maps. The data are about one year behind the publication date.

Basic Statistics of the Community (Eurostat—Annual)

Eurostat's *Basic Statistics* contains 300 tables of annual data on all aspects of the EC's economy. Included are data on national accounts, balance of payments, labor statistics, energy, agriculture, foreign trade, environment, and demographics. Some of the tables include information on the U.S., Canada, Japan, and selected non-EC European countries. The information is usually one year behind the date of publication.

Country Statistics

Publications of central banks and country statistical abstracts are excellent sources of data, if you can read them. Clearly the publications of the U.K. Central Statistical Office will not be a problem. The publications of the Statistisches Bundesamt may be. Some countries publish their statistics with English overlays. Three examples of statistical sources that attempt to bridge the language gap are given below.

Economic Statistics Monthly (Bank of Japan—Monthly)

Despite its name, this publication contains mostly financial data. All the material in this publication, including the introduction, table of contents, and all the statistical tables and their notes, are in both Japanese and English.

Census of Commerce (Ministry of Internal Trade and Industry, Japan—Triennial)

Japan's *Census of Commerce* has been conducted every three years since 1976. From 1952 to 1976 it was conducted every two years. It reports on all Japanese wholesale and retail establishments with the exception of eating and drinking places, which are covered in a separate volume released in 1990. The *Census of Commerce* has many points in common with the U.S. *Census of Wholesalers* or *Census of Retailers*. It reports the number of establishments, number of employees, and total annual sales. It gives breakdowns by Japanese industrial classification and geographically (cities, towns, and villages). General table headings are given both in Japanese and English. Detailed headings are in Japanese only, but English language templates are provided in the introduction.

Statistisches Jahrbuch (Federal Statistical Office, Federal Republic of Germany—Annual)

The *Statistisches Jahrbuch* [*Statistical Yearbook*] for the Federal Republic of Germany is a compendium of economic and social statistics. To help the non-German speaker, it is accompanied by a booklet that translates the table headings (*Where to Find What: Statistical Yearbook . . . for the Federal Republic of Germany*). Although this will lead you to the appropriate table, translating the subheadings and table breakdowns will still be a problem.

Country Reports

Compendiums of statistical data are the raw material of analysis. Often we want data that has been shaped by analysis. Economic analysis of countries is abundantly available in books and journals. The material in books tends to be two or more years out of date. Journal articles are more timely but often have a narrow focus. The country analyses in both books and journals will be scattered. The country report series described below overcome these problems. They are timely, provide an overview of the economies, and analyze all countries in a consistent fashion.

Country Profiles and Country Reports (Economist Intelligence Unit—Annual, with Quarterly Updates)

An excellent example of timely economic analysis

from a commercial source, the *Country Profiles* series organizes data from national and international sources into a standard 40-page format. The series contains 92 reports covering 165 countries. The series includes basic macro-economic, political, and demographic data, as well as details of national accounts, wages, prices, employment, industrial production, and foreign trade. The series is updated by quarterly *Country Reports* that present the most recent economic data available and provide short-term forecasts.

Walden Country Reports (Walden Publishers—Twice a year)

Walden Country Reports were formerly distributed by Reuters as part of its country reports service. The series contains 60-page reports on 100 countries. The *Reports* give less emphasis to macro-economic data than do the EIU *Country Profiles*. The *Reports* are a much better source of information on a country's major industries and companies, its labor profile, and its banking and finance. They also include extensive information on demographics, customs, and culture. The *Reports* are available on the LEXIS AND NEXIS SERVICES.

OECD Economic Surveys (Organization for Economic Cooperation and Development—Biannual)

The OECD publishes separate economic surveys on each of its member countries on a two-year cycle. It publishes, in addition, surveys of some Eastern European countries, including Hungary, Poland, and the former Czechoslovakia. The Surveys review the most important economic developments for the past few years, give short-term projections, and include extensive statistical appendices.

Regional Reports

Regional Newsletters (Economist Intelligence Unit—Varies).

The Regional Newsletters are a series of reports designed to provide practical and current business information. The 12-page reports highlight business economic trends, short-term country forecasts, regulatory and policy changes, and specific company and industry developments. Table 13-F lists the specific regional newsletters published and their approximate price. The full text of all the publications in the series are available on the LEXIS AND NEXIS SERVICES, DIALOG, and DATA-STAR.

Table 13-F. EIU Regional Newsletters

Title	Issues Per Year	Approximate Price
Business Africa	24	$ 845
Business Asia	26	$ 620
Business Eastern Europe	51	$1,175
Business Europe	50	$1,150
Business Latin America	50	$ 945
Business China	26	$ 620
Business International	50	$ 675

Social Indicators

Measures such as GDP are good indicators of a nation's economic strength but may be misleading when used to estimate a nation's quality of life. Social measures, such as literacy, health care availability, and political freedom are often combined with economic measures to analyze a country's welfare. Two compendiums of social indicators are described below.

Human Development Report (United Nations Development Programme, Oxford University Press—Annual)

The United Nations Development Programme has developed a Human Development Index (HDI) that attempts to measure a nation's social as well as economic strength. The HDI combines per capita GDP with measures of educational attaintment and life expectancy. The annual *Human Development Report* includes a table ranking 160 countries on human development. In addition to the Index, the *Report* contains more than 40 tables of national data on education, poverty, and health with area and world aggregates.

Social Indicators of Development (World Bank—Annual)

Social Indicators provides data for assessing human welfare in more than 170 countries, including both members and non-members of the World Bank. Up to 94 indicators are reported for each country, depending on the availability of information. Country data are presented in two-page tables that describe income, poverty levels, human capital investment (such as medical care and education), natural resources, labor force, and vital statistics. The volume is particularly useful for its long (25 years) time series.

Developing Economies

Most of the nations of the world fall into the category of "developing economies." Statistical compendiums on developing economies emphasize such measures as GDP growth and the amount of external debt. Two important publications on developing economies are described below.

World Development Report (World Bank—Annual)

World Development Report provides economic, social, and natural resource indicators for 185 economies and various analytical and geographical groups of economies. Each *Report* has a distinctive title, e.g., *Development and the Environment,* published in 1992. The reports are useful for their estimates of world totals of series such as GDP, average annual growth rate of GDP, and per capita energy consumption.

World Debt Tables: External Debt of Developing Countries (World Bank—Annual)

World Debt Tables is a two-volume annual on external public and private debt and debt flows of 107 developing countries, including totals by region and economic groups. It includes data on debt outstanding, debt service projections, loan disbursements, payments, amortization, and interest expressed in U.S. dollars.

MEASURES OF PRICE LEVELS

In the U.S., the Consumer Price Index, the Producer Price Index, and the GDP deflator are standard measures of inflation. Similar price indexes are used worldwide to measure changes in the purchasing power of money. Measures of inflation have several purposes. They are used to gauge the success of economic policy, to adjust wages and pensions for changes in prices, and as a deflator in the calculation of national accounts. Price indexes are also used to compare inflation among countries. Comparing inflation rates across borders raises familiar problems of differences in definitions and data collection methods.

For example, a consumer price index requires data to be collected on a fixed market basket of goods and services. The specific items to be priced are determined by a survey of consumer buying patterns. There is great variation among countries in the population included and in the number of items covered in household income and expenditure surveys.[11]

Once a consumer price index has been constructed, there are again major differences among countries in survey methods. Table 13-G gives the name of the consumer price index for EC countries. The number of items priced in the survey is given in parenthesis. As some of the titles indicate, the population surveyed is often different in the various countries. France, for example, surveys urban households, while the Netherlands surveys the entire population. There are many differences among the indices, including sampling procedure, frequency of survey, and index construction. The EC is attempting to harmonize its consumer price index, but this procedure has yet to be completed.

Table 13-G. Consumer Price Indexes in the EC

Belgium	Consumer Price Index (401)
Denmark	Consumer Price Index (523)
France	Consumer Price Index for Urban Households (296)
Germany	Cost of Living Index for All Private Households (755)
Greece	Consumer Price Index (386)
Ireland	Consumer Price Index (722)
Italy	National Consumer Price Index (878)
Luxembourg	Consumer Price Index (255)
Netherlands	Consumer Price Index for the Whole Population (690)
Portugal	Consumer Price Index (500)
Spain	Consumer Price Index (428)
U.K.	General Index of Retail Prices (394)

Source: *Consumer Price Indices in the European Community,* 1989, p. 48

Sources for Price Level Data

Consumer price indices for most countries of the world are available in the UN's *Monthly Bulletin of Statistics.* The indices have a common base year. The gap between the date of the reported figures and publication of the figures varies, with a three-month lag typical. The UN reports both a general CPI (all items) and a CPI for food. More detailed consumer price indices are reported by the OECD and the EC. The EC's monthly *Eurostatistics* gives CPI broken down by eight categories of consumption.

Note that in comparing the consumer price indexes of two or more countries, we are comparing the rate of inflation for the countries. We are not comparing the relative costs of living in the countries. For example, in July 1992, the consumer price index for Japan was 128.2 and for the U.S. 170.5 (1980=100). The figures tell us that the cost of goods and services have increased 28.2% in Japan since 1980, and 70.5% in the U.S. during the same period. They do not tell us anything about the costs of living in Japan compared to the U.S.

U.S. Department of State Indexes of Living Costs Abroad, Quarters Allowances, and Hardship Differentials (U.S. Department of State—Quarterly)

For U.S. citizens, this is the standard source for comparing living costs among countries. It is used to establish allowances to compensate U.S. government civilian employees for costs and hardships related to assignments abroad. The information is also used by many business firms and other private organizations to assist in establishing private compensation systems. The indexes are computed at the currency exchange rate in effect as of the date of the survey. The index for Washington, D.C., is set at 100. For example, the July 1992 *Indexes* show that the local index for Tokyo was 192. This tells us that it cost about 92% more for an American family to live in Tokyo than in Washington, D.C. The indexes can be adjusted to reflect changes in the exchange rate.

The publication warns that the indexes cannot be used for measuring cost changes over time at a foreign location. In addition, the indexes should not be used to compare living costs of Americans in the U.S. with the living costs of foreign nationals living in their own country, since the indexes reflect only the expenditure pattern and living costs of American families.

Retail Price Indexes Relating to Living Expenditures of United Nations Officials (United Nations—Quarterly)

Appearing four times a year in the *Monthly Bulletin of Statistics,* this publication uses New York City as the base (100), and gives two sets of figures, a total index and an index that excludes housing. The information is keyed to specific cities in more than 160 countries. These indexes relate to United Nations officials whose consumption patterns may differ from the general population of their countries.

The UN also prepares a quarterly "Schedule of Daily Subsistence Allowance Rates of United Nations Officials" that is published in the *Monthly Bulletin of Statistics.* It gives, in dollars and in local currency, the daily amounts required by UN officials in some 800 cities around the world. At the end of 1992, for example, it required $212 a day for a UN official to "subsist" in Paris.

Prices and Earnings Around the Globe (Union Bank of Switzerland—Triennial)
Executive Living Costs Worldwide (Business International—Twice a year)

These two commercial publications compare living costs across borders. *Price and Earnings Around the Globe* compares price levels, wages, working hours, and purchasing power in more than 50 cities. It also gives dollar prices for purchases of a variety of items, including clothing, appliances, and food. *Executive Living Costs Worldwide* gives an index of living costs for 102 cites as well as pricing information for goods, services, transportation, and housing.

Sources for Producer Price Data

Producer price or wholesale price indexes are less available than are consumer price indexes. Annual producer price indexes (wholesale price index) for most countries of the world are included in the *UN Statistical Yearbook*. Unfortunately, they will be at least three years out of date. The details of the indices will vary by country. For example, France reports one index only (for agricultural products). Japan reports 12 producer price indices, including indices for raw material, intermediate products, finished goods, and capital goods. Except for the price of exported goods, producer price information is not updated in the UN's *Monthly Bulletin of Statistics*. Wholesale price indices are reported for some countries in the IMF's *International Financial Statistics*. This publication also includes monthly commodity prices for about 50 products. Monthly producer price indices are reported for most OECD member countries in *Main Economic Indicators*. More detailed producer price indices are reported in the OECD quarterly *Indicators of Industrial Activity*. The EC reports producer prices in the monthly *Industrial Trends*.

LABOR STATISTICS

The size and quality of a country's labor force is crucial to its economy. Labor force statistics are used to gauge an economy's efficiency and to measure a country's standard of living. Some of the important labor statistics series are described below.

- Economically Active Population (all persons who furnish the supply of labor for the production of goods and services)
- Employment (all persons above a specified age who were for a certain period either self-employed or a paid employee)
- Unemployment (all persons above a specified age who during a particular period were without work and currently available for work and seeking work)
- Hours of Work (hours actually worked)
- Earnings (wages, salaries, bonuses, and gratuities)
- Labor Cost (cost incurred by the employer in the employment of labor)
- Occupational Injuries (deaths, personal injuries, and disease resulting from work accidents)
- Strikes and Lockouts (temporary work stoppages by workers or employers attempting to enforce or resist a demand or to express a grievance)

In addition, we often require breakdowns by sex, age, industry, or occupation for many of these variables. For example, we may be interested in employment cat-egorized by sex or unemployment broken down by age group.

There is great variation in the timeliness, availability, and detail of labor statistics among countries. Some of the gaps in reporting may seem surprising. The general definitions of labor terms have been framed by the International Labour Organization and are in wide use. However, the details of these definitions vary among countries. For example, the age that people are included in the "economically active population" varies from 6 years and older in countries such as Egypt and Peru to 15 or 16 years and older in many industrialized countries.

Methods and frequency of data collection vary as well. Collecting data on unemployment according to the ILO definition requires labor force surveys. Many countries do not conduct labor force surveys but calculate unemployment (if at all) based on registrations at an employment office. The registration method invariably undercounts the unemployed. Among OECD countries, for example, monthly labor force surveys are carried out in Canada, the U.S., Japan, Australia, Finland, and Sweden. Quarterly surveys are carried out in New Zealand, Italy, Norway, Portugal, and Spain. Annual surveys are used in the U.K., Ireland, Switzerland, France, Germany, and Austria. The OECD estimates quarterly unemployment figures for the countries that use annual surveys.

As in the case of national accounts reporting, the UN (through the International Labour Organization), the OECD, and the EC all publish extensive data on labor. The International Labour Organization's *Year Book of Labour Statistics* and its update *Bulletin of Labour Statistics* have the broadest coverage and are described below in some detail. The OECD's annual *Labour Force Statistics* and its update *Quarterly Labour Force Statistics* give more detailed statistics for its 24 members.

Year Book of Labour Statistics (International Labour Organization—Annual)

Published by the ILO since 1936, the *Year Book* presents labor statistics for more than 180 countries and territories for the preceding 10 years. The subjects covered include employment, unemployment, wages, hours of work, industrial disputes, and price indices. Data by industry are grouped by major divisions of International Standard Industrial Classification (ISIC) code. Data for occupations are arranged by the major groups of the International Standard Classification of Occupations.

Bulletin of Labour Statistics (International Labour Organization—Quarterly)

Issued in March, June, September, and December of each year, the *Bulletin* gives recent time series on employment, unemployment, hours of work, wages, and the consumer price index. Information is given for the most current year and three previous years. The *Bulletin* is updated four times a year by a *Supplement*. The information in each *Supplement* is then incorporated in the following issue of the *Bulletin*. The data in the *Supplement* often are surprisingly current. For example, the third quarter supplement for 1992 (published in October 1992) had consumer prices for countries such as Chile, Sri Lanka, and Thailand through August 1992. Compared to many statistical publications of the UN, this is "real time" availability.

Each October, a separate issue of the *Bulletin* is published called the "October Inquiry Results." It contains the result of an annual worldwide (150 country) survey of wages, hours of work, and retail prices. In the survey published in 1991 with data for 1989 and 1990, the wages and hours reported details from 159 occupations in 49 industries. The retail prices covered 93 food items. For some countries, the prices are given for individual cities. We can find details such as the price of a kilogram of oranges in Bangkok (17.6 baht in October 1990). Prices and wages are reported in national currencies.

Foreign Labor Trends (U.S. Department of Labor—Annual)

Foreign Labor Trends is prepared by the U.S. embassies in 80 countries. It provides key labor statistics (including employment, prices, and wages) as well as descriptions of the labor market and union organization. This source is useful for addresses of foreign unions, labor market organization, and government offices.

Monthly Labor Review (U.S. Bureau of Labor Statistics—Monthly)

Although the *Monthly Labor Review* is primarily a source for U.S. labor, it does include foreign labor statistics as part of its coverage. Annual data with 10 years of historical data are provided for G-7 countries plus Australia, Sweden, and the Netherlands. The series are:

- Civilian Labor Force (number)
- Employment Participation Rate (percent)
- Employment (number)
- Participation Rates (percent)
- Unemployment (percent)

Annual indexes of manufacturing productivity and related measures are given for G-7 countries plus Belgium, Denmark, the Netherlands, Norway, and Sweden. The series are:

- Compensation Per Hour (index)
- Output Per Hour (index)
- Total Hours (index)
- Unit Labor Cost (index)

FINANCIAL DATA

Financial and economic data overlap to some extent. Economic measures such as consumer prices and national income frequently are included with financial data. Financial measures such as money supply and interest rates often are included with economic data. The economic and financial researcher, however, often has a different focus. The economist is often interested in longer range trends with data available at most with monthly frequency. The financial researcher is often concerned with daily or intra-day changes in data.

International Financial Statistics (International Monetary Fund—Monthly)

Published since January 1948, this principal statistical publication of the IMF contains country tables for each of the approximately 150 members of the IMF. It includes data on a country's exchange rates, international liquidity, money and banking, interest rates, production, prices, international banking, and trade. In addition, it includes data on both GNP and GDP. It also presents world and area tables listing major data series broken down by country. The series include exchange rates, interest rates, consumer prices, imports, exports, and industrial production. The most recent data are two months behind the publication date. For most series, monthly data are given for the current year, quarterly data are included for the previous six quarters, and annual data are presented for the previous seven years. The *International Financial Statistics Yearbook* presents the same data as 30-year annual time series.

Although its emphasis is on financial data, *International Financial Statistics* is a convenient source of current information on several standard economic series, including consumer prices, discount rates, and both GNP and GDP. The data series in the publication are available on CD-ROM and through commercial time-sharing systems such DATASTREAM. Exhibit 13-2 displays a sample page from *International Financial Statistics*.

Government Finance Statistics Yearbook (International Monetary Fund—Annual)

The *Yearbook* gives data on the income and expenditures of central governments. It has three parts. *World Tables* lists IMF member countries and shows in detail the components of income and expenditures as percentages of GDP and of total expenditure. The data are for the most current available year. *Statistical Tables for Individual Countries* presents additional details as a 10-year time series for each country. Expenditures are given in the national currency. *Institutional Tables for*

EXHIBIT 13-2. *International Financial Statistics*

Belgium 124		1986	1987	1988	1989	1990	1991	1992	1990 I	II	III	IV	1991 I	II	III	IV
Exchange Rates																*Francs per SDR:*
Market Rate..................aa = ...	wa	49.429	47.032	50.255	46.994	44.078	44.730	45.623	45.607	45.459	44.900	44.078	47.515	49.104	46.854	44.730
																Francs per US Dollar:
Market Rate..................ac = ...	we	40.410	33.153	37.345	35.760	30.983	31.270	33.180	35.060	34.338	32.243	30.983	35.293	37.355	34.250	31.270
Market Rate..................rf = ...	wf	44.672	37.334	36.768	39.404	33.418	34.148	32.150	35.294	34.612	32.783	30.983	31.519	35.665	35.922	33.487
																Francs per ECU:
ECU Rate	ea	43.233	43.154	43.576	42.592	42.184	41.931	40.178	42.313	42.403	42.407	42.184	42.369	42.288	42.181	41.931
ECU Rate	eb	43.803	43.039	43.427	43.378	42.423	42.222	41.604	42.550	42.301	42.491	42.350	42.220	42.350	42.258	42.062
																Index Numbers (1985=100):
Market Rate..	ahx	132.5	158.1	160.6	149.7	176.8	173.2	183.7	167.0	170.3	179.9	190.2	187.3	165.3	164.2	176.2
Nominal Effective Exchange Rate....	neu	104.7	108.4	107.1	106.3	111.2	111.1	113.2	110.2	111.3	111.4	112.0	112.4	110.2	110.2	111.6
Real Effective Exchange Rate...........	reu	104.1	105.9	102.7	101.8	105.1	103.5	....	105.1	106.0	105.6	105.0	106.3	101.9	102.8	104.2
Fund Position																*Millions of SDRs:*
Quota..	2f.s	2,080	2,080	2,080	2,080	2,080	2,080	3,102	2,080	2,080	2,080	2,080	2,080	2,080	2,080	2,080
SDRs..	1b.s	280	494	418	423	398	411	124	412	391	403	398	418	418	400	411
Reserve Position in the Fund...........	1c.s	462	392	345	342	326	367	586	320	329	315	326	391	384	370	367
of which: Outstg.Fund Borrowing.....	2c	1	—	—	—	—	—	—	—	—	—	—	—	—	—	—
International Liquidity																*Millions of US Dollars Unless Otherwise Indicated:*
Total Reserves minus Gold	1l.d	5,538	9,620	9,333	10,766	12,151	12,180	*13,801*	10,888	11,762	11,593	12,151	10,541	10,094	11,169	12,180
SDRs..	1b.d	342	700	563	556	566	588	171	536	518	562	566	563	550	548	588
Reserve Position in the Fund.........	1c.d	565	557	464	449	464	524	806	417	436	438	464	527	505	507	524
Foreign Exchange	1d.d	4,630	8,363	8,306	9,760	11,121	11,068	*12,825*	9,935	10,809	10,593	11,121	9,451	9,039	10,115	11,068
Gold (Million Fine Troy Ounces)....	1ad	34.18	33.63	33.67	30.23	30.23	30.23	25.04	30.26	30.22	30.23	30.23	30.23	30.23	30.23	30.23
Gold (National Valuation)..............	1and	1,443	1,421	1,421	1,277	1,277	10,774	8,321	1,277	1,277	1,277	1,277	11,739	11,739	11,739	10,774
Monetary Authorities:Other Assets..	3..d	109	82	86	512	609	254	165	402	613	632	609	577	222	259	254
Other Liab......	4..d	144	151	273	131	274	339	241	180	172	211	274	269	182	298	339
Deposit Money Banks: Assets..........	7a.d	117,926	149,126	150,374	164,516	192,031	192,024	188,522	166,030	170,373	174,282	192,031	176,087	182,134	175,412	192,024
of which: Claims on Nonbanks.....	7add	33,143	38,923	39,175	43,451	52,856	52,076	54,688	46,318	46,780	50,437	52,856	49,399	48,500	50,144	52,076
Deposit Money Banks: Liabilities....	7b.d	144,838	184,795	186,432	205,526	239,787	229,933	226,055	208,123	214,844	222,256	239,787	212,430	214,498	212,295	229,933
of which: Liab. to Nonbanks.........	7bdd	18,243	24,420	27,672	34,723	44,361	49,937	56,127	36,891	38,171	43,961	44,361	43,271	40,377	45,822	49,937
Monetary Authorities																*Billions of Francs:*
Foreign Assets	11	272.9	365.6	393.5	446.5	447.4	752.1	731.7	443.3	473.9	446.1	447.4	770.1	765.7	759.2	752.1
Claims on Central Government	12a	88.8	91.9	95.6	98.8	103.3	48.9	*51.9*	103.3	103.3	103.3	103.3	49.1	49.4	55.2	48.9
Reserve Money.....................................	14	415.6	426.9	431.2	443.6	429.0	432.0	430.4	417.4	435.5	416.0	429.0	418.3	445.7	422.1	432.0
of which: Currency Outside DMBs	14a	400.5	410.7	415.0	422.6	408.6	412.2	410.2	402.1	418.5	399.7	408.6	401.9	427.1	404.4	412.2
Other Items (Net)	17r	-53.9	30.6	57.8	101.5	122.0	369.1	353.3	129.2	141.5	133.3	122.0	400.8	371.6	392.2	369.1
Deposit Money Banks																
Commercial Banks																*Billions of Francs:*
Reserves...	20	22.9	21.6	20.9	23.2	23.2	....	....	17.4	16.6	16.9	23.2	....	....	....	....
Foreign Assets	21	4,765.4	4,943.9	5,615.7	5,883.1	5,949.6	....	....	5,821.0	5,850.2	5,619.3	5,949.6	....	....	....	....
Claims on Central Government	22a	1,558.2	1,655.8	1,711.7	1,811.5	1,942.7	....	....	2,020.4	2,022.6	2,049.4	1,942.7	....	....	....	....
Claims on Official Entities..............	22bx	433.7	528.9	426.9	420.9	401.5	....	....	436.2	399.3	378.8	401.5	....	....	....	....
Claims on Private Sector..................	22d	1,342.4	1,493.8	1,769.5	2,220.8	2,327.6	....	....	2,126.5	2,219.5	2,293.4	2,327.6	....	....	....	....
Demand Deposits..................................	24	468.4	502.6	545.6	574.9	584.8	....	....	555.2	601.2	525.2	584.8	....	....	....	....
Time & Foreign Currency Deposits ...	25	1,328.8	1,495.0	1,573.0	1,787.4	1,900.2	....	....	1,926.0	1,842.8	1,870.8	1,900.2	....	....	....	....
Bonds	26ab	451.1	461.4	468.7	530.0	676.1	....	....	543.5	603.0	657.6	676.1	....	....	....	....
Foreign Liabilities..............................	26c	5,852.9	6,126.4	6,962.3	7,349.6	7,429.2	....	....	7,296.8	7,377.2	7,166.1	7,429.2	....	....	....	....
Other Items (Net)	27r	21.7	58.4	-5.0	117.2	54.1	....	....	99.7	83.5	137.8	54.1	....	....	....	....
Other Monetary Institutions																*Billions of Francs:*
Claims on Central Government......	22a.j	109.6	105.8	108.0	121.3	115.6	....	....	130.6	129.2	128.2	115.6	....	....	....	....
Claims on Nonfin.Pub.Enterprise..	22bxj	45.7	52.6	64.6	72.8	91.4	....	....	67.5	70.9	63.7	91.4	....	....	....	....
Claims on Private Sector................	22d.j	.3	—	—	—	—	....	....	1.6	—	—	—	....	....	....	....
Monetary Liabilities	24..j	178.4	180.3	192.4	215.0	228.6	....	....	228.0	226.5	219.1	228.6	....	....	....	....
of which: To Private Sector	24x.j	131.2	128.6	132.9	157.3	160.2	....	....	167.6	173.2	165.6	160.2	....	....	....	....
To Govt. & Off. Ent.	24y.j	36.5	43.1	51.9	52.1	63.0	....	....	55.2	50.8	49.4	63.0	....	....	....	....
Other Items (Net)............................	27r.j	-22.8	-21.8	-19.9	-20.9	-21.5	....	....	-28.3	-26.4	-27.2	-21.5	....	....	....	....
Monetary Survey																*Billions of Francs:*
Foreign Assets (Net)	31n	-819.2	-821.9	-963.3	-1,024.7	-1,040.7	....	....	-1,036.4	-1,059.0	-1,107.5	-1,040.7	....	....	....	....
Domestic Credit	32	3,579.8	3,929.8	4,177.1	4,764.0	4,997.6	....	....	4,892.8	4,967.2	5,036.5	4,997.6	....	....	....	....
Claims on Central Govt. (Net).....	32an	1,756.6	1,853.5	1,915.3	2,031.6	2,161.6	....	....	2,254.3	2,255.1	2,280.9	2,161.6	....	....	....	....
Claims on Official Entities............	32bx	480.5	582.5	492.3	494.5	493.5	....	....	504.4	470.8	443.1	493.5	....	....	....	....
Claims on Private Sector.................	32d	1,342.7	1,493.8	1,769.5	2,237.9	2,342.5	....	....	2,134.1	2,241.3	2,312.5	2,342.5	....	....	....	....
Money..	34	1,037.3	1,086.0	1,145.9	1,207.4	1,217.0	....	....	1,180.9	1,244.3	1,140.3	1,217.0	....	....	....	....
Quasi-Money..	35	1,328.8	1,495.0	1,573.0	1,787.4	1,900.2	....	....	1,926.0	1,842.8	1,870.8	1,900.2	....	....	....	....
Other Items (Net)	37r	394.8	526.8	494.6	743.9	839.9	....	....	749.2	820.4	917.5	839.9	....	....	....	....
Money, Seasonally Adjusted	34..b	1,040.4	1,088.2	1,145.9	1,206.2	1,215.8	....	....	1,203.8	1,191.9	1,166.0	1,215.8	....	....	....	....
Interest Rates																*Percent Per Annum*
Discount Rate *(End of Period)*..........	60	8.00	7.00	7.75	10.25	10.50	8.50	7.75	10.25	10.25	10.25	10.50	....	7.50	8.00	8.50
Money Market Rate..........................	60b	6.64	5.67	5.04	7.00	8.29	I9.38	9.38	8.45	8.23	8.46	8.04	I9.67	9.17	9.22	9.46
Deposit Rate..	60l	5.33	5.00	4.54	5.13	6.13	6.25	6.25	5.75	6.25	6.25	6.25	6.25	6.25	6.25	6.25
Lending Rate	60p	10.44	9.33	8.92	11.08	13.00	12.88	13.00	13.08	13.25	12.75	12.92	13.08	12.75	12.75	12.92
Government Bond Yield.....................	61	7.93	7.83	7.85	8.64	10.06	9.28	8.64	10.27	9.91	10.05	10.00	9.45	9.22	9.33	9.13
Prices and Production																*Index Numbers (1985=100):*
Industrial Share Prices........................	62	144	170	168	194	179	174	170	190	189	177	161	168	183	177	169
Producer Prices																
Home and Import Goods..................	63	88.5	84.1	85.5	91.1	90.2	89.3	87.7	90.3	89.1	90.0	91.4	89.5	88.8	89.3	89.5
Industrial Production Prices	63b	90.9	86.9	88.0	93.0	93.6	92.6	92.8	93.2	92.8	94.1	94.3	92.1	92.4	92.9	92.9
Consumer Prices..................................	64	101.3	102.9	I104.1	107.3	*114.1*	114.6	117.3	*122.0*	*110.3*	*111.5*	*112.8*	113.5	113.8	115.1	115.8
Wages: Hourly Earnings......................	65	102.8	I104.8	105.6	111.6	116.4	122.3	127.7	113.3	116.3	115.8	120.3	119.8	120.7	121.4	127.4
Industrial Production, Seas. Adj.	66..b	101.0	103.5	109.6	113.5	117.5	115.2	*115.0*	121.4	117.7	115.3	119.5	116.2	116.3	112.8	115.4

EXHIBIT 13-2. *International Financial Statistics (continued)*

Belgium
124

	1992			1993			1992					1993			
I	II	III	IV	I	Aug	Sept	Oct	Nov	Dec	Jan	Feb	Mar	Apr	May	
End of Period															**Exchange Rates**
46.351	44.939	42.830	45.623	46.461	43.118	42.830	44.393	45.475	45.623	45.274	46.526	46.461	46.282	*47.025*	Market Rate ......aa= ...... wa
End of Period (we) Period Average (wf)															
33.790	31.400	29.080	33.180	33.240	29.078	29.080	31.575	32.978	33.180	32.763	33.810	33.240	32.515	*32.920*	Market Rate ......ae= ...... we
33.332	33.220	30.149	31.896	33.675	29.880	29.868	30.475	32.683	32.531	33.256	33.843	33.927	32.850	*33.040*	Market Rate ......rf= ...... wf
End of Period (ca) Period Average (cb)															
42.037	42.174	40.612	40.178	39.957	41.808	40.612	40.450	40.325	40.178	40.162	39.858	39.957	40.185	*40.066*	ECU Rate ...... ea
42.045	42.211	41.765	40.397	40.113	41.913	41.307	40.440	40.446	40.303	40.311	40.050	39.977	40.102	*40.192*	ECU Rate ...... eb
Period Averages															
176.9	177.5	195.6	185.0	175.0	197.3	197.5	193.5	180.3	181.2	177.2	174.1	173.7	179.4	*178.4*	Market Rate ahx
111.7	111.6	113.7	115.9	116.1	113.7	114.6	116.5	115.3	116.1	116.0	116.2	116.2	116.1	....	Nominal Effective Exchange Rate neu
102.5	103.5	108.4	....	....	108.8	109.6	111.4	110.4	110.4	109.1	108.5	109.1	109.7	....	Real Effective Exchange Rate reu
End of Period															**Fund Position**
2,080	2,080	2,080	3,102	3,102	2,080	2,080	2,080	3,102	3,102	3,102	3,102	3,102	3,102	*3,102*	Quota 2f.s
407	403	395	124	124	405	395	395	124	124	124	124	124	124	125	SDRs 1b.s
345	366	347	586	568	364	347	348	603	586	591	583	568	568	568	Reserve Position in the Fund 1c.s
—	—	—	—	—	—	—	—	—	—	—	—	—	—	—	of which: Outstg.Fund Borrowing 2c
End of Period															**International Liquidity**
11,135	14.642	12.838	*13,801*	13,223	14,940	12,838	11,499	9,851	*13,801*	*13,617*	*13,945*	13,223	14,070	*13,976*	Total Reserves minus Gold 11.d
558	577	582	171	173	600	582	555	171	171	172	171	173	176	*178*	SDRs 1b.d
473	524	512	806	793	540	512	489	832	806	817	803	793	808	*811*	Reserve Position in the Fund 1c.d
10,104	13,541	11,745	*12,825*	12,256	13,800	11,745	10,455	8,849	*12,825*	*12,629*	*12,972*	12,256	13,086	*12,987*	Foreign Exchange 1d.d
30.23	23.75	25.04	25.04	25.04	25.04	25.04	25.04	25.04	25.04	25.04	25.04	25.04	25.04	25.04	Gold (Million Fine Troy Ounces) 1ad
10,675	8,385	8,842	8,321	*8,345*	8,842	8,842	8,842	8,842	8,321	*8,345*	*8,345*	*8,345*	7,842	....	Gold (National Valuation) 1and
252	272	288	165	176	302	288	275	248	165	194	164	176	*192*	209	Monetary Authorities:Other Assets 3..d
287	268	282	241	....	279	282	257	227	241	....	....	....	....	....	Other Liab. 4..d
179.705	197.925	212.243	188.522	....	223.518	212.243	216.025	210.515	188.522	....	....	....	....	....	Deposit Money Banks: Assets 7a.d
51.686	55.556	59.314	54.688	....	59.722	59.314	57.564	56.124	54.688	....	....	....	....	....	of which: Claims on Nonbanks 7add
217.557	238.866	257.975	226.055	....	265.473	257.975	257.028	250.579	226.055	....	....	....	....	....	Deposit Money Banks: Liabilities 7b.d
48.243	54.917	60.579	56.127	....	61.974	60.579	59.456	59.772	56.127	....	....	....	....	....	of which: Liab. to Nonbanks 7bdd
End of Period															**Monetary Authorities**
745.8	762.1	754.3	731.7	....	732.7	754.3	739.2	760.5	731.7	....	....	....	....	....	Foreign Assets 11
47.0	50.9	42.1	*51.9*	....	42.5	42.1	34.3	43.7	*51.9*	....	....	....	....	....	Claims on Central Government 12a
412.9	439.1	414.0	430.4	....	423.1	414.0	417.3	417.5	430.4	....	....	....	....	....	Reserve Money 14
396.9	421.3	398.0	410.2	....	405.7	398.0	400.1	399.8	410.2	....	....	....	....	....	of which: Currency Outside DMBs 14a
379.7	374.1	382.3	353.3	....	352.1	382.3	356.0	386.6	353.3	....	....	....	....	....	Other Items (Net) 17r
End of Period															**Deposit Money Banks** / **Commercial Banks**
....	....	....	....	....	....	....	....	....	....	....	....	....	....	....	Reserves 20
....	....	....	....	....	....	....	....	....	....	....	....	....	....	....	Foreign Assets 21
....	....	....	....	....	....	....	....	....	....	....	....	....	....	....	Claims on Central Government 22a
....	....	....	....	....	....	....	....	....	....	....	....	....	....	....	Claims on Official Entities 22bx
....	....	....	....	....	....	....	....	....	....	....	....	....	....	....	Claims on Private Sector 22d
....	....	....	....	....	....	....	....	....	....	....	....	....	....	....	Demand Deposits 24
....	....	....	....	....	....	....	....	....	....	....	....	....	....	....	Time & Foreign Currency Deposits 25
....	....	....	....	....	....	....	....	....	....	....	....	....	....	....	Bonds 26ab
....	....	....	....	....	....	....	....	....	....	....	....	....	....	....	Foreign Liabilities 26c
....	....	....	....	....	....	....	....	....	....	....	....	....	....	....	Other Items (Net) 27r
End of Period															**Other Monetary Institutions**
....	....	....	....	....	....	....	....	....	....	....	....	....	....	....	Claims on Central Government 22a.j
....	....	....	....	....	....	....	....	....	....	....	....	....	....	....	Claims on Nonfin.Pub.Enterprise 22bxj
....	....	....	....	....	....	....	....	....	....	....	....	....	....	....	Claims on Private Sector 22d.j
....	....	....	....	....	....	....	....	....	....	....	....	....	....	....	Monetary Liabilities 24.j
....	....	....	....	....	....	....	....	....	....	....	....	....	....	....	of which: To Private Sector 24x.j
....	....	....	....	....	....	....	....	....	....	....	....	....	....	....	To Govt. & Off. Ent. 24y.j
....	....	....	....	....	....	....	....	....	....	....	....	....	....	....	Other Items (Net) 27r.j
End of Period															**Monetary Survey**
....	....	....	....	....	....	....	....	....	....	....	....	....	....	....	Foreign Assets (Net) 31n
....	....	....	....	....	....	....	....	....	....	....	....	....	....	....	Domestic Credit 32
....	....	....	....	....	....	....	....	....	....	....	....	....	....	....	Claims on Central Govt. (Net) 32an
....	....	....	....	....	....	....	....	....	....	....	....	....	....	....	Claims on Official Entities 32bx
....	....	....	....	....	....	....	....	....	....	....	....	....	....	....	Claims on Private Sector 32d
....	....	....	....	....	....	....	....	....	....	....	....	....	....	....	Money 34
....	....	....	....	....	....	....	....	....	....	....	....	....	....	....	Quasi-Money 35
....	....	....	....	....	....	....	....	....	....	....	....	....	....	....	Other Items (Net) 37r
....	....	....	....	....	....	....	....	....	....	....	....	....	....	....	*Money, Seasonally Adjusted* 34..b
Percent Per Annum															**Interest Rates**
8.50	8.50	8.00	7.75	7.00	8.50	8.00	7.75	7.75	7.75	7.50	7.50	7.00	6.75	*6.25*	Discount Rate *(End of Period)* 60
9.55	9.57	9.64	8.76	8.51	9.78	9.53	8.80	8.73	8.74	8.28	8.92	8.34	8.02	*7.22*	Money Market Rate 60b
6.25	6.25	6.25	6.25	6.25	6.25	6.25	6.25	6.25	6.25	6.25	6.25	6.25	6.25	*6.25*	Deposit Rate 60l
13.25	13.25	13.25	12.25	12.17	13.25	13.25	12.25	12.25	12.25	11.75	12.75	12.00	11.50	*11.00*	Lending Rate 60p
8.76	8.88	8.96	7.95	7.49	9.13	8.66	8.13	8.02	7.71	7.53	7.54	7.40	7.54	*7.31*	Government Bond Yield 61
Period Averages															**Prices and Production**
174	178	167	159	*167*	168	157	157	159	161	162	*166*	*173*	*178*	....	Industrial Share Prices 62
															Producer Prices
88.6	88.5	87.3	86.6	....	86.8	87.4	87.0	86.6	86.4	....	....	....	....	....	Home and Import Goods 63
92.4	93.4	92.8	92.4	....	92.3	92.8	92.8	92.6	91.7	....	....	....	....	....	Industrial Production Prices 63b
116.3	116.9	117.8	118.4	*119.6*	117.7	117.9	118.1	118.5	118.5	119.3	119.6	*119.8*	*119.9*	*120.1*	Consumer Prices 64
124.5	128.4	127.3	130.8	....	....	....	....	....	....	....	....	....	....	....	Wages: Hourly Earnings 65
117.8	*115.3*	*114.6*	*111.9*	....	*108.4*	*117.9*	*111.5*	*109.4*	*115.0*	*106.2*	*111.7*	....	....	....	Industrial Production, Seas. Adj. 66..b

Source: International Financial Statistics, July 1993 (Washington, D.C.: International Monetary Fund), pp. 108-109. Reprinted with permission.

Individual Countries describes the units of government, lists government accounts and funds, and supplies a list of reports that form the source of the data.

Money and Finance (Eurostat—Quarterly)

Money and Finance summarizes the various financial statistics covering the countries in the EC, the U.S., and Japan. The first part presents a 10-year time series set of indicators, such as money supply and interest rates, designed to show basic trends. The second part deals mainly with current information on the working of the European monetary system and the private use of the ECU as an instrument of investment. The third part groups together financial indicators used in current economic analysis.

Risk Assessment

Estimating the risk associated with lending or investing in a foreign country is essential for doing business abroad. Country risk assessment is a combination of economic and political analysis. The economic analysis includes examining a country's economic performance, its access to bank lending and capital markets, and its past repayment of debt. Political analysis requires an estimation of a country's future stability and its openness to foreign investment.

Euromoney (Euromoney PLC)

The September issue of this journal gives country risk rankings for about 170 countries based on nine political and economic factors. The same issue includes a "Global Economic Projections" table that estimates real GNP growth for the coming year for 160 countries.

Country Risk Service (Economist Intelligence Unit—Quarterly)

This service gives two-year economic projections and risk assessments for more than 80 of the world's most highly indebted and developing countries. Its emphasis is on predicting growth, budget deficits, and current accounts. *Country Risk Service* is available online through the LEXIS AND NEXIS SERVICES.

International Country Risk Guide (International Reports/IBC—Monthly)

International Country Risk Guide examines the politics, economic policy, financial conditions, and economic trends for 130 countries. It provides a current assessment and one-year forecast of political, financial, and economic risk. It is available online through the LEXIS AND NEXIS SERVICES and DATA-STAR.

Energy

The consumption and production of energy affects all aspects of economic life, but transportation and industry in particular. Statistics of energy typically include the following categories:

*   Energy Sources (e.g., coal, petroleum, natural gas, nuclear)
*   Energy Produced and Consumed
*   Energy Prices
*   Energy Imports and Exports

A confusing feature in the presentation of energy statistics is the variety of units used to express energy consumption and production. In addition to familiar units such as barrels of oil, energy use is expressed variously in quadrillion BTUs, tetra joules, and thousands of metric tons of coal equivalent. The UN, the OECD, the EC, and the U.S. Energy Information Administration all publish multi-national data on energy.

Energy Statistics Yearbook (United Nations—Annual)

This comprehensive compendium of energy statistics is designed to provide a global framework of comparable data on the supply of commercial forms of energy. Data for each type of fuel and aggregate data for all fuels are shown for individual countries and areas and are summarized into regional and world totals. The data are two years behind the date of publication.

Energy Prices and Taxes (International Energy Agency—Quarterly)

The International Energy Agency is an autonomous body established within the OECD. In addition to OECD member countries, it includes statistics from the Czech Republic, Hungary, India, Mexico, Poland, South Korea, and Taiwan. The publication contains country statistics on energy prices and taxes for all energy sources and main consuming sectors. Detailed country statistics are given in national currency. General country statistics are given in U.S. dollars. The publication is a convenient source of spot prices for oil and gasoline. It gives the most recent 18 months of data and annual data for the previous 17 years. The International Energy Agency also publishes the annual *Energy Statistics of OECD Countries*.

International Energy Annual (U.S. Energy Information Administration—Annual)

This U.S. government publication presents current information on world energy production and consumption for petroleum, natural gas, coal, hydroelectric, and nuclear power. Trade and reserves are shown for petroleum, natural gas, and coal. Prices are given for major petroleum products. Country breakdowns are given by regions and for the 50 largest energy producers and consumers. In addition to its data, *International Energy Annual* is useful for its list of international sources of energy information. Data lag one year behind publication date.

Computer Readable Sources

Many of the print sources for economics that we have described have computer readable counterparts. The OECD, the UN, and the World Bank make much of their data available on magnetic disk and on diskettes. The International Monetary Fund publishes its data on CD-ROM as well as magnetic tape. Some of the risk services and country profile services have their text online through commercial databanks such as Mead's LEXIS AND NEXIS SERVICES and through DATA-STAR.

The EC provides access to more than one million macro-economic time series through its CRONOS databank. Another EC data bank is COMEXT, which contains statistics on trade between the member states and between member states and non-EC countries. Both the CRONOS and COMEXT databases are available in the U.S. through the WEFA system. A small part of the WEFA database is available on DIALOG as EconBase (File 565), which has economic time series and some projections on key variables from about 15 countries. The EC-sponsored ECHO (European Commission Host Organization) databases are accessible through the Internet. Their Internet address is 192.87.45.4 or tel echo.lu. There is no charge for access although you must obtain a password. ECHO has about 20 databases. Most of the ECHO databases deal with research and development issues. Another source of EC data is available on *EUROSTAT CD-ROM,* which is described in detail below.

The data sets of the OECD, the UN, the World Bank, and the IMF are retrievable online through commercial time-sharing systems. A comprehensive source of this material is Data Resources (DRI). DRI makes available the data series from the OECD's *National Accounts and Main Economic Indicators* and the IMF's *Direction of Trade and International Financial Statistics*. In addition, DRI maintains several regional and country economic databases based on data from national sources, central banks, and trade organizations. These include the NIKKEI macro-economic statistics database from Japan, the DRI Developing Countries database, and the DRI European database. DRI also makes available economic forecasts, with quarterly up-

dates for 50 countries and seven regions, including a world forecast.

Another commercial source for online economic data is DATASTREAM, which includes national government series from each of the G-7 countries and Australia, Hong Kong, and Taiwan as well as IMF and OECD statistics. These series include statistics on labor, trade, prices, industrial activities, finances, exchange rates, balance of payments, and national accounts. DATASTREAM has the entire data set of the Deutsches Bundesbank (the German central bank), some 15,000 individual series of data.

EUROSTAT CD-ROM (Eurostat—Annual)

Described as the "electronic statistical yearbook of the European Community," the *EUROSTAT CD-ROM* contains statistical information on macro-economics, regional indicators, and trade flows. Trade flow and regional indicators are annual. The macro-economic statistics may be annual, quarterly, or monthly. The data can be displayed as two-dimensional tables or as graphs. The system allows calculation and sorting.

Macro-economic statistics cover the economy, finance, population, energy, industry, agriculture, transport, and tourism. The statistics cover each of the member states, the EC aggregate, and often the U.S. and Japan.

Regional data are broken down according to the Nomenclature of Territorial Units for Statistics. In addition, maps and regional information notes describing the economic strengths of the regions are provided.

Trade flows are classified under both the CN (Combined Nomenclature) and the SITC (Standard International Trade Classification). The trade of the EC as a whole or of any of its member nations with any of 200 other nations is also provided. The data can be expressed as annual imports, exports, or trade balances, and can be shown as value (ECUs) or volume.

The database's lists of nomenclatures are useful. Included are NACE (Nomenclature of Economic Activity), NACE-CLIO (Input-Output categories), CN (Combined Nomenclature), and SITC and NUTS (Nomenclature of Territorial Units for Statistics). Exhibit 13-3 is an example of a table retrieved for the balance of trade data for the two-digit CN number for civil aircraft and parts.

ADDITIONAL SOURCES

Numerous additional sources of international economic statistics are described below.

European Trade Unions in Figures Visser, Jelle (Kluwer Law and Taxation Publishers, 1989).

EXHIBIT 13-3. EC Balance of Trade for Civil Aircraft in 1991

Products : 88 Flow : BALANCE
Periods : 1991 Units : 1000 ECU

Reporting Countries		Partner Countries		
	USA	WORLD	INTRA-EC	EXTRA-EC
EUR 12	-8185511	845461	440698	-2338500
BELGIQUE/BELGIE-LUXE	-621618	-384210	179653	-580313
DANMARK	-362766	-370886	-65883	-304999
DEUTSCHLAND	-2750620	-2714190	-65462	-2648718
ELLADA	-171085	-253043	-82829	-170089
ESPAÑA	-734188	-1040755	-375569	-665192
FRANCE	-2885263	3348380	929778	2477899
IRELAND	-195855	-221937	-25997	-195936
ITALIA	-401003	-431254	-45652	-385647
NEDERLAND	-56989	127900	-185	128082
PORTUGAL	-5089	-7196	-9681	2420
UNITED KINGDOM	-1035	2792652	2525	3993

Reprinted with permission from Eurostat.

This study of trade unions in 10 European countries (Austria, Denmark, France, Germany, Italy, the Netherlands, Norway, Sweden, Switzerland, and the United Kingdom) presents extensive and detailed time series of union membership from 1913 through 1985. Although primarily of historical interest, the book is useful for its extensive listing of national labor sources and for its attempt to frame a comparable cross-border definition of union membership.

International Economic Conditions (St. Louis Federal Reserve Bank—Annual)

International Economic Conditions presents economic data for the G-7 countries and Switzerland. It gives annual rates of change for GDP, GDP deflator, CPI, employment, exports, imports, and money supply for the previous 20 quarters. In addition, the publication includes tables of cross-country comparisons for interest rates, stock market indexes, unemployment rates, and indexes of leading indicators.

Russian Economic Trends (Whurr—Quarterly)

This analysis of the Russian economy is produced by the Centre for Economic Reform, Government of the Russian Federation, with the assistance of the Centre for Economic Performance, London School of Economics. Based on published and unpublished Russian sources, it provides a discussion of Russian economic strategy, and of the main measures of economic activity (e.g., budget, money, prices, wages, production, and employment). The statistical appendix contains data on economic variables that would be difficult to find elsewhere. These data include income distribution, con-

sumer and wholesale prices, unemployment, wages, distribution of wages, income distribution, and details of consumer expenditures.

PlanEcon Report (PlanEcon, Inc.—Monthly)

Subtitled *Developments in the Economies of Eastern Europe and the former USSR*, this monthly report combines official data sources with estimates by the PlanEcon staff. PlanEcon also publishes two annuals (*Review* and *Outlook*) that include four-year forecasts of economic developments in Eastern Europe and the former Soviet republics. *PlanEcon Report* is a good source of information on privatization in Eastern Europe.

World Competitiveness Report (World Economic Forum—Annual)

The World Economic Forum is a Swiss not-for-profit foundation. The *Report* is an analysis of how national economic environments are conducive or detrimental to the domestic and global competition of enterprises. Thirty-four countries are investigated on several criteria, including industrial efficiency, market orientation, future orientation, and socio-political stability. The countries are ranked on such criteria as military expenditures, total tax revenues as a percent of GDP, fiscal treatment of enterprises, and government responsiveness to business.

World Factbook (U.S. Central Intelligence Agency—Annual)

The *World Factbook* includes one-page economic, social, political, and demographic descriptions for every nation in the world plus descriptions of dependent areas (e.g., Puerto Rico). The *World Factbook* also describes areas such as the West Bank and Antarctica. Particularly useful is the one-page summary for "The World." Estimates of many hard-to-find economic and demographic aggregates can be found here, including "Gross World Product" (an estimated $25 trillion in 1991), world literacy, and infant mortality. In an appendix, the *World Factbook* includes capsule descriptions of formal and informal international organizations. The *World Factbook* is available in print, microfiche, magnetic tape, and diskettes; as a time-sharing database through the Internet; and as part of the *National Trade Data Bank CD-ROM.*

CONCLUSION

In this chapter we have examined some of the issues concerning the use of international economic statistics and have described general sources of economic data. We included in our discussion national finance, labor statistics, and energy, as well as standard macro-economic topics such as national accounts. Economic data are usually collected by individual countries. The methods of collection and definition of terms vary greatly among nations. International organizations, such as the World Bank and the IMF, are beginning to change their methods of comparing national output. For these reasons, use caution when making cross-border economic comparisons.

NOTES

1. "There were seven in the bed...," *The Economist* (February 27, 1993): 72.
2. "Gross Domestic Product as a Measure of U.S. Production," *Survey of Current Business* (August 1991): 8.
3. Joel F. Houston, "The Underground Economy: A Troubling Issue for Policymakers," *Business Review* (Federal Reserve Bank of Philadelphia) (September/October 1987): 3-12.
4. "No Room for the Faint-Hearted," *Euromoney* (March 1989): 71.
5. *Statistical Abstracts of the U.S.,* 1992, p. 817.
6. "Russian Statistics: Magic Numbers," *The Economist* (August 29, 1992): 63.
7. "Big MacCurrencies," *Economist* (April 18, 1992): 81.
8. *Purchasing Power Parities and Real Expenditures* (Paris: Organization for Economic Co-operation and Development, 1992), p. 5.
9. "How the Nations Rank," *Fortune* (July 27, 1992): 68.
10. "Chinese Puzzles: Developing Countries are Less Poor than Official Figures Suggest," *The Economist* (May 15, 1993): 83.
11. *ILO Statistical Sources and Methods.* Vol. 6: *Household Income and Expenditure Surveys* (Geneva: International Labour Office, 1990).

CHAPTER 14
Industry Information

TOPICS COVERED

1. Coding and Structure of Industries
2. Researching Industries
3. Sources of Industry Statistics
4. Industry and Country Averages: Ratios
5. Selected Supplemental Sources
6. Conclusion
7. Notes

MAJOR SOURCES DISCUSSED

- *Encyclopedia of Association—International Organizations*
- *Panorama of EC Industry*
- *Industrial Statistics Yearbook*
- *Industrial Structure Statistics*
- *Price Prospects for Major Primary Commodities, 1990-2005*
- *Some Statistics on Services—1988*
- *FAO Yearbook: Production*

In preceding chapters we discussed product codes, rankings, and market share. These aspects of industry analysis focus on individual companies. This chapter examines the concepts and sources that address industries and their structures. Practical applications for industry analysis include company intelligence, financial and economic analysis, exporting, and marketing.

We may be interested in a global industry.
- What is the structure of the steel industry?

We may be interested in many industries in many countries.
- What services industries are growing fastest in the EC?

We may be interested in one industry in one country.
- What is the outlook for the British plastics industry?

In this chapter, we use the term *industry* to refer to all categories of economic activity. Described on the basis of the U.S. Standard Industrial Classification Code (SIC), we are interested in industries grouped under major categories (1-digit level), major groups (2-digit), industry groups (3-digit), and finally industries themselves (4-digits).

The definition of an industry for U.S. SIC classification is a group of establishments primarily engaged in an activity that meets criteria of economic significance based on number of establishments, employment, payroll, value added, and value of shipments or receipts.

According to Michael Porter, "an industry (whether product or service) is a group of competitors producing products or services that compete directly with each other."[1]

Older descriptions of industry centered on "manufacturing." The EC gets around this double meaning of industry by using the term *sector* in its classification scheme, NACE. NACE is the official general industrial classification of the economic activities within the EC. NACE was established by Eurostat in 1970. The NACE system divides economic activity into 10 broad sectors (1-digit); subdivided into more detailed classes (2-digit); and further divided into groups (3-digit) or sub-groups (4-digit); and finally into items (5-digit). NACE is most often applied at the enterprise level.

Sector - Transport equipment	NACE 35/36
Subsector - Aerospace equipment	NACE 364

The manufacturing sectors often are covered more completely in sources of "industrial" statistics. It is far easier to find worldwide statistics on the steel industry than the recreation industry. However, as non-manufacturing economic activity continues to grow in value and employment, the statistical collection and reporting mechanisms probably will improve.

When evaluating sources of industry information, we need to be aware of three general concepts.

1. At what level of business activity are the data being collected, for example, establishment or enterprise?
2. At what level of aggregation is the industry being defined? 2-digit? 4-digit?
3. What is being measured?

In gathering and reporting data, agencies make distinctions between physical entities such as "establishments" (local economic units), and "enterprises" (legal entities). They also make distinctions between industry data and product data. These distinctions are based on how the data are collected and reported.

In the U.S., the Economic Census data are collected at the establishment or local unit level. An establishment is usually one physical location engaged predominately in one type of economic activity. For example, a U.S. textile manufacturing establishment (U.S. SIC 23) produces both men's (2321) and women's (2322) shirts. If 60% of the value added in the manufacturing of the products comes from women's shirts, this establishment is classified in industry 2322 and *all* value added and employment from this establishment are included in SIC 2322.

Product level data refer to the total value of the product, wherever the activity occurs. For example, if the sale of meat (SIC 5411) is 11% of a grocery establishment sales and 67% of a butcher store sales (5421), the sales from both establishments will be included in the product level value of meat sales. Statistics from official bodies are often at the enterprise or establishment level, rather than the product level.

CODING AND STRUCTURE OF INDUSTRIES

Coding of Industries

Coding systems usually group industries in a hierarchy. At the top of the hierarchy are the "major industry groups." Some sources of industry data divide companies into three groups: manufacturing, service, and "trading." "Trading" companies are in either wholesale or retail trade. *Fortune* uses broad industry groupings in the "Industrial" and "Service" Fortune 500 lists.

A more detailed industry classification is seen in the financial services *Worldscope* and CIFAR. They group companies by industry class according to differences in accounting practices. Groups such as industrials, transportation, utilities, banking, and insurance each have a distinct financial template. *Worldscope* further subdivides industries by group (e.g., aerospace) and then by U.S. SIC code. A classification for an individual company in *Worldscope* would look like this:

AMSTRAD PLC
    INDUSTRY CLASS: INDUSTRIAL
    MAJOR INDUSTRY GROUP: ELECTRONICS
    MINOR INDUSTRY GROUP: ELECTRONIC DATA
      PROCESSING EQUIPMENT
    INDUSTRY AVERAGE CATEGORY: ELECTRON-
      ICS - UNITED KINGDOM

Three standard coding systems are used by most providers of international industry data: the U.S. SIC codes and the two major international systems, the EC's NACE and the UN's International Standard Industrial Classification (ISIC). Outlines for these systems are given in Table 14-A. Note the similarity between NACE and the ISIC. Many countries also have their own individual systems.

NACE classifies economic activity on the basis of the goods and services produced, or by the nature of the production process employed. NACE was officially revised in late 1990 and the revision will be used for data collection within the next few years.

The original version of the International Standard Industrial Classification of All Economic Activities was adopted in 1948. It is used by the United Nations to classify data according to kind of economic activity in fields such as production and employment. The latest revision was 1989.

These coding schemes are designed to describe the business activity within a country; therefore, they differ from the Harmonized System of Codes and the SITC system described in Chapter 15, which classify goods traded among countries. Annex III in the 1989 *Industrial Statistics Yearbook* (c. 1991), is a preliminary table of correspondence among ISIC-based codes, SITC, and HS codes.

Table 14-B illustrates the different codes assigned by SIC, NACE, and ISIC to two product classes. Definitions differ among the coding systems for "Spinning and Weaving."

The level of coding used by a researcher should be appropriate to the needs of the analysis. Economist Michael Porter, for one, believes that a grouping such as banking or chemicals is too broad to be useful strategically or for practical applications.

The definitions of industries and products are different for each of the international and national classification schemes. Euromonitor warns that comparisons among product classification codes are difficult. While trade statistics now conform to an international classification scheme, product statistics do not and are not compatible, either with the country's own trade statistics or with industry figures for other countries.[2] Table 14-C

Table 14-A. Industry Classification Schemes

U.S. SIC Division	EC NACE Sector	UN ISIC Major Division
01 Agriculture, forestry & fishing		
10 Mining	1 Energy and water	1 Agriculture, forestry & fishing
15 Construction		
20-39 Manufacturing	2 Extraction & processing of non-energy-producing minerals & derivatives	2 Mining and quarrying
	3 Metal manufacture	3 Manufacturing
40 Transport, communications, electric, gas & sanitary services	4 Other manufacturing	4 Electricity, gas and water
50 Wholesale trade	5 Building & civil engineering	5 Construction
52 Retail trade		
60 Finance, insurance & real estate	6 Distributive trade, hotel catering, repairs	6 Wholesale & retail trade; Restaurants and hotels
70-80 Services	7 Transport & communication	7 Transport, storage & communication
	8 Banking & finance: insurance, business services, renting	8 Financing, insurance, real estate & business services
90 Public Administration	9 Other services	9 Community, social & personal services
9999 Nonclassifiable		

Table 14-B. Sample Coding with U.S. SIC, NACE, and ISIC

	SIC	NACE	ISIC
Textile Mills	22	43	321
Spinning & Weaving *	228	434	3211
Chemicals	28	25	35
Industrial Chemicals	281	251	351
Pharmaceutical	2834	257	3522
*Definitions differ			

lists the codes used by European countries for industries and products. The new CD-ROM *amadeus* has an extensive cross-reference among industry coding schemes.

Structure of Industries

The structure of an industry is often of interest to researchers. Some of the questions concerning industry structure are:

- What is the scope of the industry? Is it global or domestic?
- How does the industry contribute to the GNP/GDP of a country?
- What is the relationship between large and small enterprises in the industry?

When companies in an industry compete worldwide, the industry is described as "global." Automobiles and semiconductors are in this category. Other industries, because of the nature of their products or services, are domestic. Competition among companies in a domestic industry is within the nation. When we examine industry structure, we often use data that measure an activity within one country. European sources, however, include trade data as a part of their industry data.

One point of interest in examining industry structure is the contribution of the industry to the economy. Table 14-D measures the percent each industry group contributed to total manufacturing in four countries.

Another useful concept for industry analysis is "industry concentration." It shows the degree to which large companies dominate an industry. Industry concentration is measured by a *concentration ratio* that is the percentage of total business in an industry handled by a specified number of the largest firms. Concentration ratios are often expressed as the percentage of sales, assets, or profits accounted for by the largest three to twenty firms in an industry.

For example, the top five companies in the European transport equipment sector account for 51% of the sales. For the precast cement industry, however, small production units still dominate, with a trend toward increased concentration that varies from country to country.[3]

A knowledge of the geographical distribution of establishments helps us understand the structure of an industry, especially a global one. Some industries are

Table 14-C. Industry and Product Classification Systems Used in Selected European Countries

Country	Industry Code	Product Code
Belgium	NACE	Import/Export:HS
Denmark	ISIC	Import/Export:HS
	DSE (Danmarks Statistiks Occupational Classification)	
France	A.P.E. (Activité Principale Exercée)	Import/Export:HS
	Production: NAP (Nomenclature des Activités et Produits)	
Germany	WZ (Systematik der deutschen Wirtschaftszweige	Import/Export:HS
	- Statistishes Bundesamt) Production:GP (Systematisches	
	Guterverzeichnis für die Produktion)	
Ireland	Production:NACE	Import/Export:SITC
Italy	Repertorio Merceologico	Import/Export:HS
	Codice Attivita	
Netherlands	Dutch SIC Codes	Import/Export:HS
Spain	NACE	Import/Export:HS
U.K.	U.K. SIC	Import/Export:HS

Source: Karen Beesley, "Researching European Markets," presented at the London Business School, December 11, 1992

Table 14-D. Structure of Manufacturing Industries 1987

Percent of contribution to total manufacturing				
	U.S.	*Japan*	*U.K.*	*W. Germany*
Food	14.2	11.7	18.2	12.1
Textiles	5.7	5	5.7	4.8
Wood	3.3	2.7	3	2.6
Paper	9.6	6.8	8.1	4.4
Chemical	18.4	14.8	20.7	20.7
Nonmetal	2.6	3.5	3.7	2.8
Basic Metal	4.5	7	5.3	5.5
Machinery	40.6	47.1	34.5	46.6
Other	1.2	1.4	0.5	0.5

Source: From OECD *Industrial Structure Statistics,* 1987, in *Statistical Abstracts of the U.S.*, 1992, Table No. 1469,   p. 851

concentrated in particular countries. For example, more than 85% of the EC production of transport equipment is concentrated in four countries.[4]

Table 14-E shows the geographic concentration of several industries (based on export value in 1985).

Table 14-E. Geographic Concentration of Industries

Industry	Country	Share of Total World Exports
Aircraft	U.S.	77.5
Building Stones	Italy	62.62
Motorcycles	Japan	82.0
Rotary Printing Presses	Germany	51.1
Rough Unsorted Diamonds	Switzerland	89.3

Source: Michael Porter, *Competition Among Nations,* appendix

RESEARCHING INDUSTRIES

Research for U.S. industry information might begin with Gale's *Encyclopedia of Associations* for its list of industry organizations and publications. For aggregate U.S. industry data, the *U.S. Industrial Outlook* is a good source. For major U.S. industries with large publicly traded companies, turn to Standard & Poor's *Industry Surveys*. For detailed U.S. industry statistics, use the quinquinnial Economic Census data or the *Annual Survey of Manufactures*. International industry research could follow a similar path.

Encyclopedia of Associations—International Organizations (Gale—Annual)

Multinational and non-U.S. national associations can be found in Gale's *Encyclopedia of Associations—International Organizations,* which lists more than 11,000 associations located in more than 180 geographical areas. It is available as a two-volume set, as part of File 114 on DIALOG, and on the CD-ROM produced by Gale Research. Table 14-F gives some examples of the range of associations and publications represented in this source.

Industry information is available in a variety of statistical sources and in scattered analytic reports written by international government bodies, private publishers, or investment banks.

Statistical information is compiled and published by such international organizations as the United Nations, the World Bank, the Organization for European Cooperation and Development (OECD), and the European Community as well as by industry associations, individual countries, and private organizations. The best source for locating statistics from international organi-

Table 14-F. Sample Industry Associations and Publications in Gale's *Encyclopedia of Associations—* *International Organizations*

Industry	Publication
International: International Federation of Fruit Juice Producers	*International Directory of Fruit Juices* (periodic)
Regional: East African Tea Trade Association	*East African Trade Association. Directory.* (biennial)
European Association of Fatty Acid Producing Companies	*Compendium of Analytical Methods* (statistics,etc.)
Country: Bangladesh Jute Spinners Association	*Annual Report* (Bengali) *Spinners News* (English, monthly)
Federation of Egyptian Industries	*Industrial Egypt Year Book* (semiannual)

zations is the *Index to International Statistics*, described in Chapter 1.

Several useful measurements that are in any industry source regardless of the publisher and the countries described include:

- **How many:** total number of establishments, number of establishments by size arranged by employees or value, number of establishments by geographic breakdown, number of employees
- **How much:** value of shipments/receipts, value added, payroll
- **How good:** production indexes, price indexes, productivity measures

Panorama of EC Industry (Office for Official Publications of the European Communities—Annual)

The closest international parallel to the *U.S. Industrial Outlook* is *Panorama of EC Industry*, prepared by Eurostat, the Statistical Office of the European Community. First published in 1989, it covers 150 major industry sectors.

Panorama of EC Industry is the key source to EC industry information and should be owned by all libraries that receive questions about European industries and services. It gives an overview of manufacturing and service sectors in the European Community. The special issue chapter examines the global scene. Industry reviews provide micro-economic surveys for each sector, covering production, employment, trade and structural changes with detailed statistical data and forecasts. The 1993 edition was written during the second and third quarters of 1992. Time series cover the period 1982-1991, with 1992 being estimates. *EC Panorama* uses the NACE coding system; however, some of the service sectors do not have codes. The two main sources of data and analysis are Eurostat and professional associations. Other EC organizations and DRI/Europe also contributed.

Transport Equipment is an example of a sector described in *Panorama of EC Industry;* it is divided into the following subsectors:

Subsectors	NACE numbers
Motor Vehicles	351-352
Motor Vehicle Parts & Accessories	353
Shipbuilding	361
Railway Rolling Stock	362
Mopeds and Motorcycles	363
Aerospace Equipment	364

While similar to *U.S. Industrial Outlook* in general purpose, *Panorama* differs in content.
- It covers all countries in the EC, with individual country data.
- It includes names of individual companies.
- It includes far fewer industries.
- It is not based on a formal economic census.

Manufacturing industry tables in general include main indicators, trends in EC exports and imports, share of employment and production by country, largest companies in the EC, and a five-year forecast.

Table 14-G lists the tables included in *Panorama of EC Industry* for the 1991 aerospace equipment sector.

Industry and Development: Global Report (United Nations Industrial Development Organization, 1985—Irregular)

UNIDO's *Industry and Development: Global Report* provides an overview of industrialization and industrial performance in 10 regions of the world as well as industry surveys for manufacturing industry groups. Each *Report* covers a different set of industries. The 1990/91 *Report* analyzed the following industries:

A. Chemicals	I. Engineering Plastics
B. Shipbuilding	J. Consumer and Industrial
C. Textile Machinery	Tissue Paper
D. Phosphates	K. Paper and Board for Corrugated Boxes
E. Copper	gated Boxes
F. Ironmaking	L. Leathermaking and
G. Forging	Shoemaking Machinery
H. Petroleum Refining	M. Soft Drinks

The industry surveys are based on ISIC codes. For example, "Paper and board for corrugated boxes" covers ISIC 341137-341141 and draws on data from industry

Table 14-G. Statistical Tables in *Panorama of EC Industry*

Table	Time	Data Element

1: Main indicators	1980-89
	1990 estimate
		EC-sales
		Net export
		  Production
		  Employees

2: Production, added
  value and investments
	1980-89
	1990 estimate
		For EC, U.S., and Japan:
		  Production (current prices and index 1985=100)
		For EC:
		  Production (constant prices) and index
		  Added value (constant prices) and index
		  Productivity (ECUs) and index
		  Investments (current prices) and index

3: EC external trade
  (current prices)
	1980-89
	1990 estimate
		Extra EC-exports and index
		Extra EC-imports and index
		  Exports/imports in %
		  Import quota %
		  Export quota %
		  Intra EC-Trade and index
		  Share in export total %

4: Turnover according
  to product group
	1980, 1988,
	annual change
		For civil, military and
		  Total by product in million ECU and share total
		  turnover, i.e.
		  Aircraft construction
		  Space segment
		  Engines

5: Turnover according
  to market segments
	1980, 1988
	annual change
		In million ECU for civil
		  military, total, i.e.
		  Public authority R&D
		  Modifications, repairs, maintenance
		  Extra EC-sales

6: 20 Biggest manufactures	1989	Turnover in domestic base: U.S., Europe, Japan Employees

publications, in this case Pulp and Paper's *Fact and Price Book*. Data include production, imports and exports, capacity and capacity utilization, consumption by country or region, and major companies at the "global" level with sales figures and worldwide market share. A separate table lists largest companies from the "South," i.e., Brazil, India, or Taiwan. For the industries included, these are useful summary surveys.

Unfortunately, there is no good international parallel to Standard & Poor's *Industry Surveys*.

SOURCES OF INDUSTRY STATISTICS

International Sources

Industrial Statistics Yearbook (United Nations—Annual)

This two-volume set provides data for almost 100 countries. The 1989 edition, published in 1991, is the 23rd in a series of annual industrial compilations. The first seven editions were entitled *The Growth of World Industry* and the 1974-81 editions were called *Yearbook of Industrial Statistics*. The *Yearbook* answers such questions as:

- What is the average number of employees engaged in the rubber industry in Malaysia?
- What coding scheme is used in Singapore
- Does Nepal have an economic census?

Volume I includes general industrial statistics, arranged by country. Part 1 of Volume I provides up to five years of basic data on industrial activity and structure for individual countries. Part 2 contains indexes arranged by country that provide up to 10 years of data on industrial production and employment for the world and large regions. Data are collected at the establishment level. Volume II presents data arranged by product or commodity. Arranged by commodity, Volume II provides up to 10 years of data at the commodities level for more than

550 commodities and 200 countries or areas. Data are also available on computer tape.

In Volume I, up to 15 data items are reported per country per industry grouping.

A. Number of establishments or enterprises
B. Number of persons engaged
C. Number of employees
D. Wages and salaries of employees
E. Supplements to wages and salaries
F. Number of operatives
G. Wages and salaries of operatives
H. Hours or days worked by operatives
I. Quantity of electricity consumed
J. Output
K. Value added
L. Gross fixed capital formation—total
M. Gross fixed capital formation—machinery and equipment
N. Value of stock—total
O. Index numbers of industrial production

Each measurement is defined in the introduction. For example, the United Nations makes the following distinctions among number of persons engaged, employees, and operatives.

Number of Persons Engaged: Total number of persons who worked in or for the establishment during the reference year, excluding homeworker

Number of Employees: All persons engaged other than working proprietors, active   business partners, and unpaid   family workers

Operatives: Employees directly engaged in production or the related   activities, including clerical and supervisory personnel supporting the production process

The coding system used in the present version is a 3-digit ISIC, supplemented by several 4-digit groups. For most countries, data are collected at the establishment level, but for Eastern Europe, data are collected for the enterprise.

The data are collected by a questionnaire issued from a central agency in each country in the survey. For example, the data from Malaysia, except the indices, are based on the reply to the United Nations Questionnaire on General Industrial Statistics from the Jabatan Parangkaan (Department of Statistics), Kuala Lumpur (*see* Exhibit 14-1). The concepts, definitions, and classification by branches of industry are generally according to United Nations standards. Note that the data items listed in Exhibit 14-1 are similar to those used in the U.S. Economic Census.

Volume II presents annual data for specific industrial "commodities." The term "commodities" as used here refers to mining, manufacturing, and utilities. There is a table for each commodity that presents production figures over a 10-year time span, as illustrated in Exhibit 14-2.

Regional Sources

Industrial Structure Statistics (Organization for Economic Cooperation and Development—Annual)

The 1989/90 edition was published in 1992 and combined the 8th and 9th editions. Classification is by ISIC, Revision 2. The annual is supplemented by the quarterly *Indicators of Industrial Activity*. It can answer the following type of questions:

•   How many manhours were employed in the Norwegian industrial chemical industry in 1989? How does that compare to Germany?

The data are presented in two sections. Section one contains industrial survey data collected from national statistical organizations' samples. It also includes foreign trade data derived from customs' figures. Eighteen member states are represented in this section.

Section two gives estimates from national accounts, disaggregated by industry. OECD refers to this as the "top down" approach. Seven member states are represented in this section. Only three countries, Finland, Norway, and Sweden, are represented in both sections.

Industrial Structure Statistics contains an individual listing for each country giving the country's coding system and sources of industrial data. All series published are available on magnetic tape and on a $350 diskette.

As many as 15 data items are presented for each of the OECD countries with up to 10 years of data. However, not all items are reported for each country and very few countries have 10 years worth of data. The data items collected from 1981-1990 are:

Production	Investment (m&e)	Manhours*
Value Added	Wages & Salaries	Exports (current prices)
Employment	Supplements to W&S	Imports (current prices)
Employees	Social Costs	Exports (80 prices)
Investment	Establishments*	Imports (80 prices)

*Collected from 1985-1989
m&e - machinery and equipment

Exhibit 14-3 is an extract from a country entry in *Industrial Structure Statistics.*

Exhibit 14-1. *Industrial Statistics Yearbook,* **Volume I**

MALAYSIA

MALAYSIA

	1. NUMBER OF ESTABLISHMENTS a/ (NUMBER)		3. AVERAGE NUMBER OF EMPLOYEE a/b/ (THOUSANDS)		10. VALUE ADDED IN FACTOR VALUES a/ (MILLION RINGGITS)	
ISIC INDUSTRY	1985	1988	1985	1988	1985	1988
210 Coal mining	...	...	...	...	...	...
220 Petroleum and gas . . .	5	5	5.8	5.7	9759	8757
230 Metal ore mining . . .	756	369	25.2	15.5	597	430
290 Other mining	226	187	10	8.1	285	199
2 Mining, quarrying	...	...	...	...	...	...
11/2 Food products	1241	1298	61.4	70.1	1745	2276
313 Beverages	65	62	5.7	4.8	303	322
314 Tobacco	18	18	4.5	3.3	509	378
321 Textiles	185	200	27.3	32.4	329	589
3211 Spinning, weaving, etc.	91	93	18.4	18.8	243	410
322 Wearing apparel . . .	202	214	31.1	46.2	249	471
323 Leather and products . .	22	21	0.6	0.7	6	6
324 Footwear	11	9	0.9	0.8	12	12
331 Wood products	649	618	54.3	64	654	1000
355 Rubber products . . .	228	312	28	46.9	621	1336
390 Other industries . . .	120	114	8.2	11.1	96	135
Manufacturing	5820	5782	473.3	595.6	12115	16259
4 Electricity, gas etc.	...	...	...	...	...	...
2-4 All industry	...	...	...	...	...	...

a/ Manufacturing: selected industries (see country note)

b/At 31 December or last pay period of the year indicated

Source: Extracted from United Nation's publication *Industrial Statistics Yearbook*, vol. I, 1989, pp. 373, 374, 375. Reprinted with permission.

Exhibit 14-2. *Industrial Statistics Yearbook,* **Volume II**

ISIC-BASED CODE

3844-04   **Bicycles—Cycles**

Unit: Thousand Units   unite: en milliers

Country or area	1980	1981 ...	1988	1989	
America North	8 242	8 043	6 146	5 867	Amérique du Nord
Asia	26 540	30 985	71 903	60 054	Asie
Bangladesh (2)	46	28	20	30	Bangladesh
China	13 024	17 543	44 401	36	768 Chine
Bulgaria	120	124	92	92	Bulgarie
Byelorussian SSR	*695*	*714*	*845*	*850*	*RSS de Biélorussie*

    (2) Twelve months ending on June 30 of year stated

Source: Extracted from United Nation's publication *Industrial Statistics Yearbook*, vol. II, 1989, Commodity Production Statistics, pp. 788-89; annual data from 1980-89. Reprinted with permission.

EXHIBIT 14-3. Extract from *Industrial Structure Statistics*

Millions of MK   Table FN.2 FINLAND (Current Prices) p. 48
                                              VALUE ADDED

		1981	1982 ..	1989	1990
31	Food, Beverages & Tobacco	7,347	8,189	12,555	12,840
311,2	Food	6,183	6,390	9,566	9,580
313	Beverages	920	1,027	2,476	2,570
314	Tobacco	244	233	512	678
32	Textiles, Apparel & Leather	4,904	4,408	4,263	3,583
321	Textiles	1,880	1,839	1,790	1,508
3213	Knitting mills	781	757	646	562
322	Wearing Apparel	2,243	2,319	1,868	1,573
323	Leather & Products	201	193	186	164
324	Footwear	580	648	419	345
33	Wood Product & Furniture	4,774	4,408	7,988	7,995
39	Other Manufacturing nes	441	503	676	689
3901	Jewelry	92	125	172	206
3000	Total Manufacturing	59,203	63,924	105,467	102,309
1000	Agri., Hunt., Forest., Fish	...	...	. ...	...
2000	Mining & Quarrying	931	1,079	1,941	1,532
3000	Total Manufacturing	59,203	63,924	105,467	102,309
4000	Electricity, Gas & Water	7,059	8,388	11,705	11,342
5000	Construction	...	...	...	...
6.90	Services	...	...	...	...
0000 Grand Total		67,193	73,391	119,114	116,217

Source: Reprinted from *Industrial Structure Statistics*, 1992, p. 84

Industry Statistical Yearbook (Statistical Office of the European Communities—Annual)

First published in 1985, this Eurostat compilation covers industries in the EC, the U.S., and Japan. The object of the *Yearbook* is to provide a "clear and comprehensive" overview of industry in the EC, to set a picture of industrial activity and structure in the Community and its member states, and to compare it to the U.S. and Japan. The questions it can answer include:

• What has been the trend in motor vehicle production in France between 1970 and 1988?

• How many workers in Stuttgart are employed in the food, drink, and tobacco industry?

Data are derived from a variety of sources, such as social statistics, Integrated Economic Accounts, and OECD publications.

The *Yearbook* is divided into eight chapters, each of which has several tables, arranged by country. The industrial products chapter contains more than 40 individual product groupings including chemicals, durable goods, food and beverages, and materials. Chapter headings are:

1. Industry in the European Community, the USA and Japan
2. Employment in Industry
3. Structure and Activity of Industry
4. Data by Size of Enterprise
5. Industrial Products: Production and External Trade
6. Index of Industrial Production for 24 Major Industry Groupings
7. Regional Industrial Statistics
8. Energy and Raw Materials

The *Yearbook* is updated quarterly by *Industrial Production* and monthly by *Industrial Trends*. These EC industry publications are based on data supplied by member states. Part A has harmonized statistics on the following sectors: textiles; leather and footwear; pulp, paper, and board; data-processing equipment; domestic electrical appliances; mechanical engineering products; and electric and electronic construction. Part B has non-harmonized data from the mining, chemical, transport equipment, and food and drink industries.

Industrial Trends includes macro-level data and graphs for the EC and countries in the EC, with the U.S. and Japan included for comparison. It has production and price indices for capital goods, intermediate goods, and consumer goods. It also has production and indices, turnover, and number of employees for major industry sectors (2- and combined 3-digit) NACE levels.

Results of the Business Survey Carried Out Among Managements in the Community (Commission of the European Community—Monthly)

This survey measures the expectations of members of the EC manufacturing and mining communities. Started in 1962, the publication surveys 20,000 enterprises each month, using a harmonized questionnaire across the EC.

Each month, respondents are asked whether they expect production trends, production expectations, and selling price expectations to go up, down, or stay unchanged. They are also asked if they expect order-books, export order-books, and stocks of finished products to be normal, above normal, or below normal. Additional questions about employment, new orders, and capacity are asked quarterly. This survey does not publish industrial statistics, and it presents survey responses as percentages.

For example, in May 1992, 98% of the respondents in the food, drink, and tobacco industry in Luxembourg believed that product trends in the month ahead would be unchanged. In the same period, 2% believed that production would go down. On the other hand, only 60% of the Dutch respondents thought production trends would be unchanged. Of the remaining 40%, 21% expected production trends to go up while 19% expected them to go down, for a net balance of 2% up.

Selected Industry-Specific Sources from International Organizations

We will examine the following examples of specific industry sources from governmental organizations:

Steel	UN Economic Commission for Europe
Iron and Steel	Eurostat
Cocoa	UNCTAD
Pulp and Paper	OECD

Steel is an industry that is monitored by both the United Nations and the European Community. In fact, the United Nations publishes two serials specifically about steel.

Steel Market in . . . [*year*] (latest edition 92/93) has been published annually since 1953 by the United Nations Economic Commission for Europe (ECE). It is a review of the steel market, with analysis of international developments and national developments. Information is based on statistics from governments, oral statements, and the work of the ECE Steel Committee. There are

more than 20 individual country reports as well as regional and worldwide data.

- What is the trend in steel consumption in Czechoslovakia?
- How many tons of steel were used in the manufacture of private cars in Czechoslovakia in 1989?

At the country level, there are four years of data with general economic trends, trends in iron and steel production, foreign trade, trend by demand (sectors), and deliveries by sectors and products. Also provided are employment figures, cost indexes, and base prices. Text supports the data.

Statistics of World Trade in Steel is also published by the United Nations Economic Commission for Europe. The purpose of this publication is to provide basic data on exports of semi-finished and finished steel products from European and other steel exporting countries in the world.

- How many tons of Japanese steel does the United States import?
- How much of this is used for railway track material?
- What country is the world's largest importer of semi-finished steel products?

Iron and Steel: Yearly Statistics is compiled by the Statistical Office of the European Communities. This publication differs from the other two in that it is purely statistical and covers only the EC countries. Data items are included for production, consumption, prices, and trade.

- How many tons of steel were consumed in the manufacture of wire rods for the EC countries?
- Which EC country employed the most foreign workers in the iron and steel industry in 1990? Has the pattern changed since 1970?

Prospects for the World Cocoa Market Until the Year 2005 (1991) is an example of a United Nations Conference on Trade and Development report. Prepared in conjunction with the International Cocoa Organization, an active industry association, *Prospects for the World Cocoa Market* has in-depth analysis of trends in the supply of and demand for cocoa at world and country levels.

- What country had the highest per capita chocolate confectionery consumption in 1987?
- What percent of Swiss chocolate sales are filled chocolate?
- How much chocolate was it estimated that the Ukraine would produce in 1990?

The OECD publishes an annual industry-specific serial, *Pulp and Paper Industry in the OECD Member*

Countries, that has quality data on production and consumption of pulp and paper products. It includes production capacity, utilization, and foreign trade for 33 pulp and paper products or groups of products by partner country. The data series are for 1982 to 1989 with forecasts to 1994.

The U.N.'s Economic Commission for Europe (ECE) and Conference on Trade and Development (UNCTAD) also publish more technical reports, which provide comprehensive analysis of a few industries. One example from the ECE is the *Annual Review of Engineering Industries and Automation*, first published in 1979. The 1992 edition analyzes developments in the ECE region, with reference to the United States, Japan, and Eastern Europe for the year 1990. Data are based on a questionnaire sent out jointly by ECE and OECD; robotics information is supplied by the International Federation of Robotics.

Five sectors of the engineering industry are reviewed: metal products except machinery, non-electrical machinery, electrical machinery, transport equipment, and precision instruments. Each sector is then further subdivided into subsectors. The content of each subsector is dependent on the product.

Country level data, as well as company-specific information, is included. For example, the chapter on manufacture of electrical machinery provides market share data on the 10 leading semiconductor companies for 1979 and 1990. Volume II has statistical tables.

The *Annual Review of the Chemical Industry*, also from the Economic Commission for Europe, is arranged by country overview and then by about 50 specific chemicals for which production and import/export data are given.

A third publication of the ECE is *Food-Processing Machinery* which includes information about the food industry and packaging techniques. This excellent analysis of the industry describes structure and trends in selected countries.

UNCTAD (United Nations Conference on Trade and Development) is another arm of the United Nations that issues industry studies. *Structural Changes in the Automobile and Components Industry During the 1980s with Particular Reference to Developing Countries* and a companion publication, *Structural Changes in the Electronic Industry . . .*, are two examples of recent titles. These studies grew out of the UNCTAD Committee on Manufactures' decision to consider supply, demand, trends, comparative advantage, and market access to specific sectors of export interest to developing countries. These two reports are primarily analytical, based

on data from other UN published sources, the OECD, and the *Panorama of EC Industry*.

Other titles from UNCTAD include *Trade and Development Aspects and Implications of New and Emerging Technologies: The Case of Biotechnology* and *Iron Ore Statistics,* an annual publication. The latter has detailed production, import, and export data for 10 years. Forty countries are represented in the 1991 edition.

The main problem for librarians regarding UNCTAD publications is finding them. We located these titles by using the *Index to International Statistics*. Some are on microfiche and some in paper. Libraries often do not catalog these publications.

Sources for Commodities. *The Commodities Yearbook* is the standard source for commodities information in the United States. It examines commodities primarily from the perspective of the futures trader.

Price Prospects for Major Primary Commodities, 1990-2005 (World Bank, 1989—Annual)

A very different source from *The Commodities Yearbook* is the World Bank's *Price Prospects for Major Primary Commodities 1990-2005*, a two-volume publication giving forecasts of production, consumption, and prices. Volume I contains a summary and covers the energy and metals and minerals field. Volume II covers agricultural products, fertilizers, and tropical timber. Sample data from *Price Prospects* appears in Exhibit 14-4.

Chapters in Volume I include a summary, demand and supply outlook, and price outlook. Chapters in Volume II have a summary, consumption and price history, and outlook. For example, the price of sugar is given annually in constant and current U.S. dollars per ton between 1950 and 1989 with projections for 1990-2005. Sources of information include the commodity's international organization, the FAO, and the World Bank. The annual *Price Prospects* is supplemented by the periodical *Quarterly Review of Commodity Markets*.

Sources for Services. According to Eurostat, services accounted for about 60% of both employment and value added in the EC in 1988 (based on nine countries). But information about services is hard to obtain, despite their growing importance in the world economy. Eurostat states that enterprise level data are most significant at the small to medium enterprise level, especially for service industries. Yet this is the area for which the least data are available.

Some Statistics on Services—1988 (Eurostat, 1991)

In 1991, Eurostat published the first edition of *Some Statistics on Services—1988*. A main aim of the data gathering for this publication was to set up a system of

EXHIBIT 14-4. Extract from *Price Prospects for Major Primary Commodities 1990-2005*

Table 1. Commodity Prices and Price Projections in 1985 Constant Dollars/a

| | | ——— Actual ——— | | | ——— Projections ——— | | | |
| | | | | | — Short-term — | | — Long-term— | |
		1970	1980 ...	1989	1990 ..	1995	2000	2005
Energy								
Petroleum	$/bbl	3.6	29.1	11.8	14.7	12.3	15.2	14.5
Coal	$/mt	n.a.	29 ...	29	29	28	30	30
Food								
Coffee	¢/kg	314	328	172	135	164	207	207
Cocoa	¢/kg	185	248	90	86	94	109	126
Tea	¢/kg	300	213	146	139	153	147	166
Sugar	$/mt	222	602	204	188	200	223	227
Beef	¢/kg	357	263	186	174	179	189	160

/a Computed from unrounded data and deflated by MUV(1985=100) manufacturing unit value

Source: *Price Prospects for Major Primary Commodities 1990-2005.* Reprinted with permission from the World Bank.

statistical information on services called MERCURE.

The data contained at present in MERCURE and, consequently the figures presented in this publication, often leave something to be desired in terms of comparability, availability and continuity. (p. 9)

The data in *Some Statistics on Services—1988* are compiled from:

• Non-harmonized data from EC member states
• Eurostat projects with "services" components
• Projects carried out by Eurostat and other EC departments

The introduction to the publication describes the services and the methodology used. The six major service groupings that were used are:

• Distributive trades, including wholesale and retail
• HORECA—travel agencies
• Transport activities
• Credit institutions, including banks
• Insurance
• Information, communication, and business services

For each sector, a brief summary describes the sector and its importance; the NACE codes with definitions are also provided. All sectors but insurance have the following three sections:

Section 1. Tables by branch (from national accounts statistics) for all EC countries plus the U.S. and Japan for 1975, 1980, and 1985-1988.

Data elements in this section include:

• Value added at 1985 market price
• Share of value added at 1985 market prices on total branches
• Gross fixed capital formation at 1985 market prices
• Share of gross fixed capital; 1985 prices
• Total employment
• Share of total employment on total branches
• Wage and salary earners
• Compensation of employees

Section 2. Business statistics

2.1 Comparative tables for the EC 12 for most current year available by 2-, 3-, 4-, and 5-digit NACE code. Sample data elements are shown in Exhibit 14-5.

Note that for most of the NACE codes, there is even more missing data than for advertising.

2.2 Detailed Tables, not printed in the book but available from Eurostat

Section 3. Sectoral tables

For example, the information category has data for telecommunications, post, and advertising for 1975, 1980, and 1985-1988. Data are arranged under sector by country. Data items vary by sector. For advertising, potential data are provided for total advertising expenditure for five media: press, television, radio, cinema, and outdoor/transport. Definitions used are from the Nace CLIO25. For example, the information sector is defined as "Communication, computer and business services," Nace 79, 83, 84, 85. Because 1970 NACE is not detailed enough, additional headings are taken from ISIC Revision 3. Data are presented at the enterprise level and the local unit level (establishments).

EXHIBIT 14-5. *Some Statistics on Services*—**VII.2.1 Comparative Tables for Advertising**

		Number of enterprise	Turnover (excl. VAT) Mio ECU	Gross Value Added Market Prices Mio ECU	Number of Persons Employed
NACE 8380—Advertising					
EUR 12		:	:	:	:
Belgique/Belgie	1987	5 803	1 661.30	:	(1) 6 487
Danmark	1983	:	:	:	4 016
BR Deutschland	1986	23 996	9 336.79	:	(2) 58 20
Ellas	1978	(4) 349	:	:	1 622
Espana	1987	2 000	:	:	(5) 9470
France	1988	12 200	12 593.55	3 120.28	104 383
Ireland	1987	53	172.93	864.00	:
Italia	1981	5 231	:	:	21 061
Luxembourg	1987	99	41.61	:	(6) 349
Nederland	1987	5 431	2 211.82	477.66	19 756
Portugal		:	:	:	:
United Kingdom	1987	8 292	7 806.39	:	:

(1) Number of wage and salary earners.   (5) 1980.
(2) Number of wage and salary earners 1988.   (6) 1985.
(3) Number of wage and salary earners 1984/88.

Source: *Some Statistics on Services—1988*, 1991, p. 276. Reprinted with permission from Eurostat.

Sources of Agriculture. An important source of worldwide agricultural statistics is described below.

FAO Yearbook (Food and Agricultural Organization of the United Nations—Annual)

The principal agency publishing worldwide agricultural statistics is the Food and Agricultural Organization of the United Nations. The 1990 *FAO Yearbook: Production*, published in late 1991, is the 44th edition. The date range for the data is from 1979-81 to 1990, including FAO estimates for the current calendar year. Data are compiled from FAO questionnaires to national governments.

As with all data providers mentioned here, FAO warns the user that definitions of categories differ among participating countries. There are 90 different crops and more than 200 different geographical entities. The number of countries varies per crop. Data for individual crops are given by country, region, continent, and world. The aggregated totals include only those countries listed for that particular crop.

- What countries in the world provide buffalo meat?
- What country in Europe has the highest percent of its economically active population engaged in agriculture?
- How has the world's per capita production of food changed over the past 10 years?

Exhibit 14-6 is an extract containing data from the *FAO Yearbook: Production.*

Reports on over 20 individual fruits and vegetables, ranging from apples to kiwis to unshelled walnuts, are published by the OECD in its *International Standardization of Fruit and Vegetables* series.

Country Statistics

All of the previous examples have been drawn from international and pan-regional sources. Most of the data have been drawn from the data collected by the participating countries. These countries also have their own statistical publications.

Norway is an example of a country with sets of industry data available to the public. *Industristatistikk* comprises two volumes of manufacturing statistics and commodity statistics. Volume 1 includes figures by industry, group of employees, and county. The purpose of the set is to give detailed structural figures. Another set of industry data, *Regnskapsstatistikk*, contains retail trade data. Norway also provides quarterly, monthly, and weekly data.

The international publications generally list the country level agencies or publications with industry statistics that they have used. Researchers needing more information can use these lists as finding aids to locating more specific country level sources. Some of these sources are listed in Table 14-H. Additional sources and coding schemes for OECD countries are in Appendix J.

EXHIBIT 14-6. *FAO Yearbook: Production*

Table
Tableau **17**
Cuadro

	Rice, Paddy		Riz, Paddy		Arroz En Cascara	
	Area Harv 1000HA Sup Recoltee Sup Cosechad		Yield KG/HA Rendement Rendimento		Production 1000MT Production Production	
	1979–81 . . .	1990	1979–81 . . .	1990	1979–81 . . .	1990
Asia	128237	131470	2807	3641	360080	478691
Afghanistan	210	214F	2182	2009	458	430F
Bangladesh	10310	10600*	1952	2655	20125	28140*
Bhutan	28	26F	2017	1654	56	43F
. . .						
Thailand	8986	9700*	1887	1959	16967	19000F
Turkey	67	50F	4706	4700	314	235
Viet Nam	5579	5900F	2117	3119	11812	18400F

* Unofficial figure; F-FAO estimate

Source: *FAO Yearbook: Production,* 1991, pp. 72-73. Reprinted with permission.

Table 14-H. Official Country Sources of Industrial Statistics

	Agency Collecting Industry Information	
COUNTRY	*INDUSTRIAL STATISTICS*	*BUSINESS SURVEYS*
Belgium	Institut national de Statistique, from VAT and Social Security	Banque Nationale de Belgique
Denmark	Danmarks Stattisik; VAT and workplace registers	Danmarks Statistik
Greece	National Statistical Service from 78 and 84 censuses	IEIR-Institute of Economic and Industrial Research
Spain	Instituto National de Estadistica; internal such as 1980 census and private sources and other governmental sources	MIE-Ministerio de Industria y Energia
France	Institut national de la Statistique et des Etudes economiques (INSEE); 3 enterprise level surveys	INSEE
Ireland	Central Statistical Office; 1986 census	CIL-Confederation of Irish Industry
Italy	Istituto Centrale di Statistica; 1981 economic census; generally enterprise level	ISCO -Insituto Nazionale per lo Studio della Congiuntura
Luxembourg	Service central de la Statistique et des Etudes economicques; from registery and 1975 census	STATEC
Netherlands	Central Bureau voor de Statistiek; annual sample surveys	CBS
Portugal	Instituto Nacional de Estatistica; 1982 census or enterprises; annlus hotel survey Empresas de Construcao e	INE AECOPS—Associacao de Obras Publicas do Sul
United Kingdom	Business Statistics Office; various sources	CBI-Confederation of British Industry BSO-Business Statistics Office

Commercial Sources of Industry Information

In addition to the data and analysis from international, regional, and national agencies, there are commercial sources of industry information.

D&B Europa (Duns International Ltd.—Annual)

D&B Europa provides a breakdown of the 60,000 companies in the directory (*see* Chapter 3) arranged by size in terms of sales range and by 2-digit U.S. SIC code, as shown in Exhibit 14-7. Over 50% of the companies fall into the 10 to 49.9 million ECU range. The largest industry groupings are for wholesale trade, with a total of 22% in durable and nondurable wholesaling.

Similar data are provided for each country in the directory. For example, over half the 895 Turkish companies in the directory are in the 1 to 9.9 million ECU range and the largest number of companies is in SIC 22—Textile Mill products. The companies in *D&B Europa* have been selected for their size and their importance to international trade.

Many of the commercial sources of industry information are specialized. One example is *World Automotive Market*, published by Auto & Truck International. The 61st edition was published in 1991. Vehicle production for individual manufactures in 35 countries, vehicle registration in almost 150 countries, and import/export movements are the important features of this volume. *World Automotive Market* can answer such questions as:

- How many trucks and buses did Iraq import from the U.S. and Canada in 1990?
- How many Buick Centurys were produced or assembled in Mexico?

Individual investment bank reports, available through *Investext* or in the ICC Brokerage Reports database, provide in-depth information for many industries. Although the focus of these reports is often on the financial performance of individual companies, they frequently include industry analysis, performance, and forecasts. Online investment bank reports are expensive, a fact that limits their usefulness.

ICC's *KeyNotes* analyzes 175 U.K. industry sectors. Information includes industry structure, market size and trends, major companies, market and brand shares, advertising expenditures, and recent and future developments. A feature that makes these reports more valuable is an extensive list of additional sources, including industry associations, periodicals, directories, general sources, government publications, and non-U.K. sources. Chapter 10 contains a more detailed description of *KeyNotes.*

McCarthy Cards have been providing an industry "clipping service" to U.K. libraries for many years and continue to do so even in an electronic age. A sample industry grouping is "Beer & Lager Brewing & Sales." The cards dated January 10, 1992 are numbered 603–605, indicating that 602 cards have gone before. A sample card appears to be a cut-and-paste photocopy of articles from U.K. papers, in this case the *Daily Telegraph* of December 23, 1991, the *Times* from December 31, 1992, and the *Financial Times* of January 2, 1992. The articles cover an increase in sales of full-bodied beers at Christmas, as well as the U.S. action against Canadian beer. *McCarthy* is also available online through FT PROFILE.

Selected Sources of Commercial Industry Reports. Jordan & Sons Limited is a British information company that collects U.K. company information and makes it available in a variety of print and electronic formats. In conjunction with individual consultants, it also provides a series of industry reports.

One example is the 1990 *British Plastics Industry,* priced at £150. It extracts establishment and enterprise data from the U.K. 1987 Census of Production and from the industry association, Plastics Processing Industry Training Board, with limited comparative data from other EC counties and the U.S.

Different types of plastics are defined and the major participants are named. Concentration ratios are not calculated; however, the reader can determine that the six establishments with 1,000 or more employees account for less than 8% of net output. Geographical distribution is also given: 26.7% of total employment is in South East England. Individual company data are also provided for both listed and unlisted companies. There are no calculated ratios.

British drinks, sporting goods, airlines, and franchises are other industries analyzed by Jordan & Sons. The surveys cost under $500 and are also available on diskette.

Another source of industry reports is the *Financial Times Business Reports.* Covering a wide range of issues, some of the *Reports* are organized around individual industries such as banking, pharmaceuticals, and hazardous waste management. The *Reports* are targeted for top management and are nontechnical. They are designed to fill the gap between a book and a detailed consultant's report. An individual report costs approximately $300.

The *Financial Times Business Reports* are also available online. DATA-STAR contains one database for energy and the environment (FTNV), one for technology and communications (FTTC), one labelled industry reports, covering industries such as biotechnology and pharmaceuticals (FTIN), and one including all the FT

Exhibit 14-7. Size of Companies in *D&B Europa*

STATISTICAL PROFILE FOR EUROPE - SALES AND S.I.C.

Sales Ranges in Million ECU

		1-9.9	10-49.9	50-74.9	75-99.9	100-249.9	250-499.9	500-749.9	750-999.9	1,000+	Total
01	Agricultural Production - Crops	11	75	17	3	12	1			2	121
02	Agricultural Production - Livestock	1	110	24	12	18	4			1	170
07	Agricultural Services	1	47	10	5	9	3		1		76
08	Forestry	1	7	4	2	3	1				18
09	Fishing, Hunting, & Trapping	1	20	3	1	3	1				29
10	Metal Mining	3	35	13	3	7	7	2	2	2	74
11	Anthracite Mining		3	1	2	3	3	1		1	14
12	Bituminous Coal & Lignite Mining	1	15	9		4	3		1	5	38
13	Oil & Gas Extraction	4	40	12	7	18	17	7	8	29	142
14	Nonmetallic Mineral Mining, Except Fuels	4	84	42	9	17	8	2	1	5	172
15	General Building Contractors	37	719	209	85	167	53	19	7	25	1,321
16	Construction other than Bldg Contractors	9	475	105	48	96	41	10	8	15	807
17	Special Trade Construction Contractors	24	523	90	46	92	18	4	3	5	805
20	Food & Kindred Products Manufacturers	82	2,209	547	309	581	212	56	38	85	4,119
21	Tobacco Manufacturers	3	32	8	2	22	6	4	2	14	93
22	Textile Mill Products	96	958	151	69	89	15	3	8	6	1,395
23	Apparel/ other Finished Fabric Pdts Mfrs	92	529	92	46	55	14	3	3	2	836
24	Lumber & Wood Product Mfrs, Ex Furniture	15	350	54	27	30	23	8	3	1	511
25	Furniture & Fixture Manufacturers	9	455	81	38	36	7	3		1	630
26	Paper & Allied Product Manufacturers	21	535	144	76	161	59	9	5	19	1,029
27	Printing, Publishing & Allied Industries	20	708	166	76	126	40	6	7	12	1,161
28	Chemicals & Allied Product Manufacturers	46	1,220	344	213	418	144	57	19	67	2,528
29	Petroleum Refining & Related Industries	1	71	21	9	38	13	12	6	38	209
30	Rubber & Misc Plastics Product Mfrs	31	689	134	53	104	36	9	2	13	1,071
31	Leather & Leather Product Manufacturers	17	217	34	13	21	3	2	2	1	310
32	Stone, Clay, Glass & Concrete Product Mfrs	35	664	130	64	127	31	17	8	13	1,089
33	Primary Metal Industries	32	679	151	92	212	53	18	11	43	1,291
34	Fabricated Metal Pdt Mfrs, Ex Machinery	53	1,185	233	108	172	47	13	8	13	1,832
35	Machinery Mfrs, Except Electrical	44	1,733	386	200	375	125	35	18	51	2,967
36	Electrical Equipment & Machinery Mfrs	60	1,211	273	148	310	110	36	17	67	2,232
37	Transportation Equipment Manufacturers	12	592	141	78	189	62	27	16	69	1,186
38	Measuring & Photo/ Medical Equip & Clocks	13	363	83	45	61	16	8	4	14	607
39	Miscellaneous Manufacturing Industries	12	297	48	23	40	10	1	1	3	435
40	Railway Transportation		16	4	3	5	1	2		10	41
41	Local Public Transport & Intercity Buses	22	167	22	16	23	4	5	1	2	262
42	Haulage & Warehousing	6	461	80	49	71	22	9	4	6	708
43	Postal Service							2		8	10
44	Water Transportation	11	237	67	34	59	22	6	6	7	449
45	Air Transportation	5	63	28	10	41	24	6	5	12	194
46	Pipe Lines, Except Natural Gas	2	5	3	1						11
47	Transportation Services	17	524	123	64	104	28	10	6	12	888
48	Communication		39	13	11	32	23	6	3	12	139
49	Electric, Gas & Sanitary Services	10	326	83	74	155	75	36	24	56	839
50	Wholesale Trade - Durable Goods	65	3,741	795	388	718	219	72	39	73	6,110
51	Wholesale Trade - Nondurable Goods	68	3,889	907	417	836	254	98	56	116	6,641
52	Building & Garden Supply Retailers	3	63	9	3	16	6	1	2	2	105
53	General Merchandise Retailers	9	492	94	41	107	62	20	12	57	894
54	Food Retailers	11	215	60	33	56	32	15	7	26	455
55	Motor Vehicle Dealers & Petrol Stations	12	829	132	51	92	31	5	5	8	1,165
56	Clothing & Accessory Retailers	6	222	49	19	51	18	4		4	373
57	Home Furnishing/ Equipment Retailers	4	183	46	25	51	9	4	3	8	333
58	Eating & Drinking Establishments	23	130	22	8	29	10	5	1	1	229
59	Miscellaneous Retail Trade	8	267	62	29	73	28	10	4	17	498
62	Security & Commod Brokers/ Dealers/ Svcs	5	99	16	11	25	9	4	1	7	177
64	Insurance Agents, Brokers & Services	26	112	28	15	33	12	4	2	6	238
65	Real Estate	29	481	105	46	94	26	13	7	10	811
66	Comb of Real Estate/ Insurance/ Loans/ Law		29	7	1	7	2	1	3	1	51
67	Holding & other Investment Offices	58	348	107	49	179	99	35	33	103	1,011
70	Hotels/ Rooming Houses/ Camps/ Lodgings	27	155	33	15	27	4	2	1	4	268
72	Personal Services	9	120	28	9	27	3	3		3	202
73	Business Services	84	1,372	313	182	292	107	29	18	42	2,439
75	Automotive Repair, Services, & Garages	8	135	25	11	26	10	6	2	6	229
76	Miscellaneous Repair Services	5	24	5	5	3	3				45
78	Motion Pictures	2	58	12	5	9	7		3	2	98
79	Amusement & Recreation Svcs, Ex Cinemas	12	88	18	7	14	13	4	4	8	168
80	Health Services	10	71	7	4	9	5	1		1	108
81	Legal Services	1	1			2				1	5
82	Educational Services		19	2	1	4					26
83	Social Services	2	14		1	1			1		19
84	Museums/ Art Galleries/ Bot. & Zool. Gdns		1								1
86	Membership Organisations	4	22	6	2	9	6	1	1	1	52
88	Private Households		1								1
89	Miscellaneous Services	17	227	51	28	59	14	7		8	411
	Total	1,372	32,096	7,122	3,580	6,955	2,376	796	463	1,262	56,022

reports (FTBR). Coverage begins in 1992 and is updated weekly.

Economist Intelligence Unit (EIU), another U.K. information provider, has a series of industry reports on major groupings including:

Automotive	Energy
Commodities	Textiles
Consumer Goods	Travel and Tourism

For example, for the automotive industry, EIU has a monthly *Automotive Intelligence Service,* quarterly publications such as *Japanese Motor Business,* and many special topics such as *The Motor Industry of South-East-East Asia: Prospects to 2000.* The cost of these reports varies but typically ranges between $500 and $1000.

Worldscope is a new entrant into the industry report arena. Worldscope introduced Worldscope Industry Studies in the fall of 1992. These studies, which are better suited for financial analysis than industry analysis, are discussed in Chapter 5.

Online Sources of Industry Information. Table 14-I lists some commercial databases on DIALOG or DATA-STAR that cover industries. The codes are DIALOG file numbers and DATA-STAR mnemonics.

Industry-Specific News from Reuters. *Reuter Insurance Briefing* is a new online end user product for the individual who needs up-to-date worldwide information on the insurance industry. It is menu driven and runs in a Windows environment. The service is divided into two parts, current and archives. Current includes articles published within the past two to three days (with a few minutes delay) that may be accessed by country or the following general subjects: all news, economic news, political news, general news, sports news, insurance news, risk news—Reuters, casualty wire from Lloyd's Information. The annual archives of articles may be searched by countries, industries, companies, topics such as acquisitions or contracts, and sources, such as insurance publications like *Lloyd's List* or *Reinsurance.*

Users may combine menu choices with a keyword, for example *typhoon,* and also select a date range: one week; one, three, or six months; one year; or a specific time.

Articles are translated from 15 languages into English and presented in full text or as an abstract. Two or more translated articles may be integrated into one story by Reuters' editors; all sources will be listed.

INDUSTRY AND COUNTRY AVERAGES: RATIOS

Researchers often require country or industry financial "averages." For U.S. industries, this type of information is available in print sources such as Dun and Bradstreet's *Industry Norms and Key Business Ratios* or the Robert Morris & Associates publication *Annual*

Table 14-I. Online Databases with Industry Information

Code	Name of File	Type
AINS	Automotive Information and News Service	AB
CBNB or 319	Chemical Business Newsbase (75% Europe)	AB
164	Coffeeline	AB
CISS	Computer Industry Software, Services and Products	TX
CNEW	European Chemical News	TX, D
EECM	East European Chemical Monitor	TX
269	Materials Business File	AB
240	Paperchem	AB
PLST	CHEM-INTELL Trade & Production Statistics	TX, D
VWWW	Volkswagen AG	AB(German)
67	World Textiles	AB
GENERAL DATABASES WITH INDUSTRY INFORMATION		
	Infomat International Business	AB
	Predicasts	AB, TX, EX
	Textline	TX
	Trade and Industry	AB, TX

AB-Abstract; TX-Full text; D-Directory; EX -Extract

Statement Studies. Often this information is used to compare a company to its peer group.

Here are examples of typical requests for average balance sheet ratios:

- For all companies worldwide in the aerospace industry
- For all U.K. companies
- For all companies in the aerospace industry in the U.K.

There is no global equivalent to *Industry Norms* or *Annual Statement Studies.* However, global industry ratios are available for major traded companies. In Chapter 5, we describe CIFAR's *Global Company Handbook* as a source for worldwide company financial information and rankings. Volume 1 also includes 12 industry averages for up to 20 industries in 48 countries. All reports include:

- Profit Margin (OPMG)
- Debt to Equity Ratio (D/E%)
- Return on Assets (ROA%)
- Price/Earnings Ratio (P/EX)
- Return on Shareholder's Equity (ROE%)
- Price to Book Value Ratio (PBVSx)
- Market Value to Cash Flow (PCF%)
- Shareholders Rate of Return (holding period of return) (ROR%)
- Market Value to Sales (P/Sx)
- Current Ratio (CR%)
- Dividend Yield (DY%)

Two additional ratios are calculated for industrials, banks, insurance, and other financial services. A weighted average technique based on sales in U.S. dollars for industrials and total assets for financial companies is used.

Listed below are four examples from the *Global Company Handbook* of tables using ratios. They illustrate the differences in performance standards among countries, among industries, and by year. Exhibit 14-8 provides samples of examples 1 to 3.

- Example 1: Table R.1 Ratios for one industry in one country for several years
- Example 2: Table R.2 Using ratios to compare two industries in one country
- Example 3: Table R.3 Comparing the same industry in different countries
- Example 4: Table R.4 Comparing all industries in different countries

How should we evaluate this information? Many of the same problems we have encountered before in evaluating the comparability of data apply here as well. Two important issues are these:

1. **Fiscal Year-End Differences among Countries.** The data from which the country averages are calculated rep-

resent different time periods. For example, the fiscal year for the U.S. is usually January to December. In Japan, the reporting year runs from April 1 to March 31.

2. **Classification of a Company within a Product Grouping.** There is surprisingly little agreement among information providers on assigning industry classification codes to individual companies.

In Table R.1. in Exhibit 14-8, notice how the figures for the U.K. utilities/transportation industry vary from year to year. Shareholders rate of return (ROR) went from more than 50% in 1989 to below 13% in 1990. The debt to equity ratio (D/E) increased 230% in the five-year period while the current ratio (CR) has remained the same. When the figures are this volatile, it is risky to compare current year figures with published industry averages.

Also notice in Table R.2 the difference among industries within the same country. Generally, the industry average profile for the U.K. construction industry, especially in profit margin, market value to sales, and return on equity is different from either the utilities or electronics groups.

Finally, in Table R.3 there are large differences in country norms, even for the same industry. The U.K. debt/equity ratio for the utilities industry is less than 25% of that for Japan, while its return on investment is five times greater. National differences are less pronounced for all industries, R.4, but finally notice that the country averages for all industries also differ from the country averages for an individual industry.

Worldscope and CFAR products calculate industry averages and country averages and some industry averages for individual countries. There is one record for each country and industry on *Worldscope* CD-ROM and additional industry records if there are enough companies in an individual country, as in Exhibit 14-9.

The average records are a separate section in *Cfarbase.* Select the specific data items you want and receive an individual report for each one. There is no single record for all data items. Selection choices include Country/Worldwide; Industry—33 groupings, including NONE and OTHER; and Type of Account— each individual line item. Exhibit 14-10 is an example of one time period for one industry in one country.

ICC Information Group calculates 30 ratios for the individual companies in its database. Ten of these are also calculated for the 4-digit U.K. SIC code industry grouping, presenting lower median and upper quartile.

The ratios are published in the U.K. as special industry reports. Users can also access these ratios from the ICC British Company Financial Database, available on DATA-STAR, DIALOG, and direct from ICC and in

Exhibit 14-8. *Global Company Handbook*—**Industry Averages**

Table R.1 UK Utilities/Transportation

Averages of Key Financial Ratios

	Year	OPMG	D/E%	P/Ex	PBVSx	PCFx	P/Sx	DY%	ROA%	ROE%	ROR%	CR%
United Kingdom												
Industry related	1990	12.4	**66.4**	10.0	2.8	7.0	0.92	4.6	6.4	27.9	-13.6	**1.2**
Averages in	1989	14.0	64.8	11.5	3.5	11.5	0.89	3.5	7.5	34.9	50.4	1.1
a country	1988	13.8	61.9	9.4	2.6	6.2	0.63	3.3	8.1	32.1	28.0	1.1
Utilities/Trans	1987	12.7	52.6	14.0	2.5	5.7	0.44	3.6	7.6	21.8	26.6	1.3
# of companies: 19	1986	10.8	**20.1**	14.3	2.2	6.7	0.39	3.9	5.8	23.2	27.1	1.2

Table R.2: UK- Construction and Electronics

Comparing Two Industries in a Country

	# Cos	Year	OPMG	D/E%	P/Ex	PBVSx	PCFx	P/Sx	DY%	ROA%	ROE%	ROR%	CR%
Construction	45	1990	**4.1**	50.2	12.3	1.3	5.2	**0.28**	6.1	2.2	**9.3**	-26.3	1.4
Elec Equip.	51	1990	**10.5**	23.8	10.0	2.9	5.9	**0.71**	3.8	6.9	**24.5**	-17.6	1.5

Table R.3 Utilities/Transportation 1990

Comparing the Same Industry in Different Countries

Country Averages	U.K.	JAPAN	GERMANY	U.S.
No. of companies	19	81	35	48
Debt/Equity (D/E%)	66.4	246.8	94.4	112.0
Return on Equity (ROE)	27.9	5.1	-1.6	9.1
Price Earnings(P/EX)	10.0	66.8	81.7	14.2

Table R.4 Japan Country Average 1986–1990

Average of Key Financial Ratios over Time

Averages of Key Financial Ratios

	Year	OPMG	D/E%	P/Ex	PBVSx	PCFx	P/Sx	DY%	ROA%	ROE%	ROR%
Japan	1990	7.5	136.3	48.2	3.5	31.5	1.55	0.5	1.0	15.8	-0.1
Country Averages	1989	9.3	147.1	48.2	4.1	35.1	1.79	0.5	1.2	16.5	12.1
	1988	9.0	151.6	52.7	4.3	35.4	1.87	0.5	1.1	16.8	21.4
	1987	9.0	160.0	54.1	4.4	35.4	1.63	0.6	1.1	15.3	49.6
Number of	1986	7.1	175.8	40.9	3.2	25.3	0.97	0.9	1.1	13.7	26.8
Companies: 1,532											

Source: Global Company Handbook, 1992, vol. 1, IV Industry and Company Averages, pp. 19, 29, 56. Reprinted with permission from Center for International Financial Analysis & Research, Inc. (CIFAR).

the ICC financial records on DIALOG ONDISC's *UK Company Factfinder*. Ratio categories are profitability (4), revenue (4), credit (5), gearing, i.e., debt (4), productivity (7), value added (4), and auditor's fee (2).

The example in Exhibit 14-11 compares Cadbury Schweppes to the confectionery industry in the U.K.

Other even more specialized databases, such as the financial CD-ROMs*Diane* and*Fame,* using Bureau Van Dijk software, have ratio information and the capability to compare companies with their industries or companies with any set the user creates.

SELECTED SUPPLEMENTAL SOURCES

Other sources of industry information are published regularly by both governmental organizations and private organizations. The United Nations Statistical Office publishes such annual titles as *Construction Statistics Yearbook, Energy Statistics Yearbook,* and *Energy Balances and Electricity Profiles.* For a full range of Statistical Office publications check the *United Nations Publications Catalog.*

The United Nations Industrial Development Organization publishes special reports on industries and countries. One set of reports is the "Industrial Development Review Series," which examines the state of industry in

EXHIBIT 14-9. Extracted *Worldscope* Industry Average Record AEROSPACE / FRANCE

CURRENT EXCHANGE RATE: 0.17892 U.S. Dollars per French Franc
INDUSTRY CLASS: INDUSTRIAL
MAJOR INDUSTRY GROUP: AEROSPACE
INDUSTRY AVERAGE CATEGORY: AEROSPACE - FRANCE
NUMBER OF EMPLOYEES: 18,919 (SOURCE: 12/31/89)

FISCAL YEAR END: 12/31
LATEST ANNUAL FINANCIAL DATE: 12/31/89

Profitability Ratios—Annual

Fiscal Year Ending	12/31/89	12/31/88	12/31/87	12/31/86	12/31/85	12/31/84
Cash Flow/Sales	10.05	6.08	7.42	9.76	9.36	15.71
Cogs/Sales	82.63	82.13	73.10	107.05	105.12	99.94
Gross Profit Margin	9.15	9.78	16.92	-18.96	-16.09	-11.57
SG & A/Sales	NA	NA	NA	NA	NA	NA
R & D/Sales	NA	26.52	27.59	25.01	23.47	15.01
Pretax Margin %	3.18	1.77	0.66	1.63	2.56	1.84
Effective Tax Rate %	26.57	46.64	104.15	35.34	35.65	35.77
Net Margin %	1.68	0.84	-0.05	0.89	1.53	1.15
Sales/Employee (Mil)	0.9468	0.8498	0.7448	0.6934	0.6879	0.7171
Effective Int Rate	8.52	10.95	13.59	11.73	13.90	13.18
Oper Inc/Total Capital	-5.58	11.31	-7.69	-5.81	-1.52	5.85
Return on Invt Cap %	7.16	6.73	6.00	6.28	6.63	7.68
Return on Equity per Share	10.32	7.23	-0.39	7.84	13.95	11.07
Return on Equity	11.26	6.88	-0.41	7.45	13.02	10.69
Return on Assets	2.70	2.55	2.57	2.53	2.80	3.19
Oper Profit Margin	-2.25	4.31	-5.34	-3.48	-0.97	3.08
Cash Earnings ROE	67.47	49.96	58.73	81.70	79.60	146.61

Source: *Worldscope*® CD-ROM, November 1992. Reprinted with permission from Worldscope/Disclosure

EXHIBIT 14-10. *Cfarbase* CD-ROM: Sample Average Record

Record Return on Equity for the French Aerospace Industry
YEARLY AND 5-YEAR AVERAGES

Country/Worldwide	France
Industry	Aerospace
Type of Account	Return on Equity

YEAR	AVERAGE VALUE
90:	0.000
89:	16.171
88:	10.716
87:	-3.698
86:	7.231
85:	14.623
84:	10.242

5 YR. AVER./ANNUAL GROWTH

90:	6.084
89:	9.009
88:	7.823
87:	5.825
86:	7.410

Source: *Cfarbase* CD-ROM, February 1992. Reprinted with permission from Center for International Financial Analysis & Research, Inc. (CIFAR).

developing countries. Blackwell began publishing this series for UNIDO in 1992.

This book has discussed many sources published by United States government agencies. One of note for industry research is a series entitled *Competitive Assessment. . .*, published since the early 1980s by the U.S. Department of Commerce International Trade Administration. Each report examines the worldwide competitiveness of a different U.S. industry segment. The most recent title is *Competitive Assessment of the U.S. Power Tool Industry* published in 1992. Another ITA series is *Industry Sector Analysis,* annual reports for 67 countries selling for $10 each from Commercial Information Management System and also available on NTDB CD-ROM.

For information specifically on the mineral industry worldwide, researchers can use publications from the U.S. Bureau of Mines. *The Minerals Yearbook* has volumes for Africa, Asia, and the Middle East. There are also "Minerals Availability Circulars" for market economy countries.

GATT (General Agreement on Trade and Tariffs) publishes analyses of agricultural markets. One example

Exhibit 14-11. ICC *British Company Financial Database:* ICC Industry Comparisons

SIC Code: 4214 (Cocoa, chocolate and sugar confectionery)

Year to: 31.12.91

		Lower Quartile	Median	Upper	CADBURY SCHWEPPES PLC
Profitability:					
Profit/Capital Emp.	%	1.5	10.6	24.1	19.5
Profit/Total Assets	%	.0	4.8	11.1	11.9
Profit/Sales	%	.1	3.3	7.9	9.8
Revenue					
Sales/Total Assets	%	120.8	160.9	203.9	121.8
Credit					
Credit Period	Days	66.7	50.4	31.6	48.5
Liquidity	R	.8	1.1	1.8	1.2
Value added					
Value Added/Employee	UKL	NA	NA	NA	2909.6
Productivity					
Average Remuneration	UKL	6,102.2	7,216.6	8,609.0	14257
Sales/Employee	UKL	24,604.7	37,263.2	48,994.6	91390.2
Wages/Sales	%	26.8	22.0	17.1	15.6

Source: ICC File 561 on DIALOG. Reprinted with permission from ICC.

is the annual *International Markets for Meat*, an in-depth analysis prepared by the GATT secretariat based on the work of the International Meat Council. Each annual includes data for publication year and forecasts for the following year; data items include numbers for slaughter levels, production, prices, imports, consumption, and exports in the bovine meat sector. There is summary data on pigs, poultry, and sheep. Information also comes from the OECD, IMF, and industry and private sources. *International Markets for Meat* covers 18 countries and the EC. GATT also publishes the *World Market for Dairy Products*, based on the International Dairy Arrangement.

Individual countries publish a wide range of statistical data. Statistics Canada is an example. The *Quarterly Financial Statistics for Enterprises* presents industry level data for more than 30 industry groupings, including financial services that are part of the business sector. It uses vertical integration of industry categories. An example is presenting data for food together with data for food retailing or the manufacture of electronic equipment and computer services. Data are collected at enterprise level. A Canadian coding scheme, the Standard Industrial Classification for Companies and Enterprises 1980 (SIC-C) is used. Detailed information is available on request. Data are collected from questionnaires and sampling. Data include balance sheet information for five quarters, income statement, and five selected ratios: return on capital employed, ROE, profit margin, debt/equity, and working capital ratio.

Coffee Annual from Coffee Publications is a sample commercial industry book. While most of the data refer to the internal United States coffee market, *Coffee Annual* does have imports of green coffee into consuming countries from producing companies.

ICC annually publishes *Industrial Performance Analysis* and *ICC Business Ratio Report: An Industry Sector Analysis*. The *Report* calls itself the guide to profitability and efficiency in British industry. It is a U.K. equivalent of Duns ratio publications. The series includes one industrywide compilation plus individual industry reports. Data items include balance sheet and profit and loss statistics for each industry and its sector, graphic representation of return on capital by sector, key ratios, statistics for industry and sector, and employee-based rations in matrix format for sectors. The ratios are also available in ICC online British company database (*see* Exhibit 14-11).

In this chapter, we have examined concepts about industries and sectors and factors affecting their structure. We introduced a variety of industrial coding schemes, such as U.S. SIC Codes, NACE, and United Nations SITC codes, as ways of organizing establishments or enterprises within industries.

CONCLUSION

This chapter describes the basic tools for industry research. Most of the sources that we presented are compilations of data about industry groups and come from governmental and non-governmental organizations such as the United Nations, EC, and OECD. Some of these sources compile data for all industries in specific regions. Industry data are used heavily in conjunction with the market research data discussed in Chapters 10 and 11.

NOTES

1. Michael Porter, *The Competitive Advantage of Nations* (New York: Free Press, 1990), p. 33.

2. *European Directory of Marketing Information Sources* (Euromonitor, 1992), p. 14.

3. *Panorama of EC Industry* (Office for Official Publications of the European Communities), pp.13-4, 5-26.

4. *Panorama*, p.13-6.

PART V
International Transactions

CHAPTER 15
International Trade and Payments

The world economy is fueled by trillions of dollars of international investments and international purchases of goods and services. In tracing these international economic transactions, the researcher is faced with the problems of multiple monetary systems, economic policies, government regulations, and languages. In this chapter we present the main concepts and sources for international trade and payments. We use the categories of the balance of payments as the framework for our discussion.

BALANCE OF PAYMENTS

International economic transactions involve payment by residents of one country to the residents of another. The payment may be in one of three forms.

- Barter (goods or services exchanged for other goods or services)
- Exchange of goods or services for money or other financial instruments
- Exchange of financial claims (e.g., stocks exchanged for money)[1]

Residents include governments, companies, and individuals. U.S. residents, for example, include persons residing and pursuing economic interests in the U.S. Corporations are defined as residents of the country in which they are incorporated. In contrast, the foreign branches and subsidiaries of corporations are considered the residents of the country in which they are located.

International economic transactions are often divided into four types.

1. Merchandise Trade (international transfer of physical goods)
2. International Service Transactions (international transfers of intangibles such as transportation and insurance)
3. Capital Flows (international financial transfers such as direct foreign investment and purchase of foreign financial instruments)
4. Official Reserves Transactions (transfers by governments of foreign exchange, special drawing rights, and monetary gold)

Together, merchandise trade, service transactions, capital flows, and official reserves transactions make up the economic series called the *balance of payments*.

The balance of payments provides a useful framework for understanding several economic concepts, including international trade, foreign direct investment, and international debt. The balance of payments is a statistical statement for a given period (usually a year) showing a country's trade in goods, services, and financial assets with the rest of the world. The transactions are usually presented in the national currency of the compiling country. Payments are "balanced" in the sense that every transaction is entered on both sides of the balance sheet, as a *credit* and a *debit*, based on double entry bookkeeping. Debits are transactions that either increase a country's assets (items owned) or decrease its liabilities. Credits are transactions that either decrease assets or increase liabilities.

For example, here is the effect on the U.S. balance of payments when a resident of the U.S. purchases a car manufactured in Japan.

1. The transaction is recorded in the U.S. balance of payments as a debit. The acquisition of the automobile increases U.S. assets. The U.S. now has an additional automobile.
2. The transaction is also recorded in the U.S. balance of payments as a credit. The payment of dollars to the Japanese manufacturer increases U.S. dollar liabilities to Japan. The U.S. owes Japan several thousand dollars in payment for the car

The effect on the Japanese balance of payments is the opposite.

1. The export of the automobile is recorded in Japan as a credit. Japan has one less automobile, a decrease in its assets.
2. The payment xceived in dollars is recorded as a debit. Japan has decreased its foreign currency claim liabilities.

We can better understand how the transaction is recorded by examining the balance of payments concept in more detail. Exhibit 15-1 shows the main categories of the balance of payments.

The balance of payments is often arranged into three subaccounts.

1. The *current account* groups all international transfers of goods and services as well as unilateral transfers. Unilateral transfers by governments and private individuals refer to transfers of money for which there is no direct economic benefit. An example of a private unilateral transfer would be a Turkish worker in Germany sending money to her family in Turkey. An example of a public unilateral transfer would be the Canadian government sending aid to Somalia. Unilateral transfers are described as "unrequited transfers" in IMF publications. We frequently see more detailed subdivisions of the current account balance. The *merchandise trade balance* (the balance of trade) is a country's total exports of merchandise minus its total imports of merchandise for a given period. The *balance on goods and services* is a country's total exports of both merchandise and services minus its total imports of merchandise and services.
2. The *capital account* includes all financial transactions with the exception of reserve transfers. It consists of direct foreign investment, portfolio investment, and short-term capital flows. Foreign direct investment is the ownership of enterprises located in one country by the residents of another country. Portfolio investment includes cross-border loans, bank deposits, and the purchase of stock. Short-term capital is capital payable on demand or with a maturity of one year or less.
3. *Reserve transfers* are the official financial transfers of a nation's monetary authority. A nation's monetary authority (frequently the central bank) has the exclusive right to use gold, special drawing rights from the IMF, and foreign currency holdings to finance the balance of payments transactions.

EXHIBIT 15-1. Balance of Payments Categories

	CREDITS	DEBITS
Current Account	Merchandise Exports	Merchandise Imports
	Service Exports	Service Imports
	Private Unilateral	Private Unilateral
	Transfers (nonresidents)	Transfers (residents)
	Official Unilateral	Official Unilateral
	Transfers by foreign governments	Transfers by national governments
Capital Account	Foreign Direct Investment (by nonresidents)	Foreign Direct Investment (by residents)
	Portfolio Investment	Portfolio Investment
	by nonresidents	abroad by residents
	Other Long-term Capital Inflow	Other Long-term Capital Outflow
	Short-term Capital Inflow	Short-term Capital Outflow
Reserve Account	Net Change in Reserve	

Source: World Bank. Reprinted with permission.

Let's return to our example of the Japanese automobile exported to the U.S. to illustrate the effect of such a transaction on those balance of payments subaccounts.

- The balance of payments for the U.S. records the transaction as both a debit in the current account and a credit in the short-term capital account.
- The balance of payments for Japan records the transaction as both a credit in the current account and a debit in the short-term capital account.

In practice, individual international transactions are not recorded in a country's balance of payments ledger. However, total transactions are represented in the manner we have described. Thus, all imports of automobiles into the U.S. would be represented as both a debit in the U.S. current account and a credit in the short-term capital account.

Because the balance of payments is a key economic series, there is much interest in its components: merchandise trade, trade in services, and capital flows. Extensive detailed data on merchandise trade are available. The quality of this data is mixed; the import data for a country are generally of higher quality than the country's export data. For trade in services, the data are sketchy and often of poor quality. Capital flow data are described by many economists as positively misleading.

FOREIGN TRADE

Foreign trade is the physical movement of merchandise across international borders. Exports are goods shipped from a country. Imports are goods shipped into a country. Foreign trade is an important component of a country's balance of payments. For many countries foreign trade constitutes a critical part of their economy. Import/export data are used by governments to assess their economic policy and by companies to evaluate foreign competition and to identify market opportunities. Merchandise trade is highly concentrated; about 80% of world trade is generated by 25 countries.

Trade between countries is mutually profitable when one country can produce a particular product more efficiently than another country. Economic theory demonstrates that this efficiency does not have to be absolute but only comparative. For example, Japan may be more efficient than all other countries in producing both automobiles and airplanes. If Japan is relatively more efficient in producing automobiles than airplanes, Japan will maximize its gains by producing automobiles exclusively and purchasing airplanes from other countries.

The dollar value of world trade has increased 60-fold since 1950. The increase is the result of international agreements designed to improve world trade. Economists agree that the prosperity of individual nations improves with an increase in international trade. The degree to which trade can be improved depends on the following conditions:

1. Stable exchange rates
2. Improved employment and production in less developed countries
3. Removal of trade barriers

Following the collapse of trade in the depression of the 1930s and the destruction of World War II, the international community created three key agencies that have affected world trade: the International Monetary Fund (IMF), the International Bank for Reconstruction and Development (the World Bank), and the General Agreement on Tariffs and Trade (GATT)

The IMF and the World Bank were established at the Bretton Woods Conference in July 1944. The purpose of the IMF was to reduce the disruption in trade caused by unstable exchange rates. The member nations of the IMF agreed to peg their exchange rates to either the U.S. dollar or to gold. A country was not allowed to change the value of its currency except to correct a severe problem in its balance of payments. Since 1973, currencies of IMF member countries have been allowed to "float." The currencies need not be pegged to the U.S. dollar or to gold. Market forces of supply and demand set a currency's value. The IMF helps nations maintain their currency's exchange values by allowing members to borrow Special Drawing Rights (SDRs), IMF quotas, or the currencies of other countries.

The International Bank for Reconstruction and Development (the World Bank) was established to provide short-term capital for postwar reconstruction and long-term policies for providing a larger flow of international private investments. The World Bank was established to operate with the IMF. Each member of the IMF subscribes to the World Bank's stocks and each member is given 250 votes and an additional vote for each stock held. The World Bank promotes international private investments by providing guarantees, or by participating in loans when there is a need and private capital is not forthcoming. Loans are made for specific projects. Borrowers must be able to repay the loans.

GATT (the General Agreement on Tariffs and Trade) is a multilateral agreement drafted in 1947. It sets rules of conduct for trade among signatory countries. GATT both sets rules governing international trade and provides a forum for trade negotiations and dispute resolution. Originally signed by 12 developed and 11 developing countries, GATT membership reached 100 signatories in

1990. An additional seven countries have applied for membership.

GATT members have engaged in a series of eight negotiations, called "rounds," since 1948. The first round led to GATT's establishment. The most recent round, called the Uruguay round, began in 1986 in Punta del Este with the object of expanding and improving multilateral trading. As of 1993, the Uruguay negotiators were unable to break a deadlock concerning agricultural subsidies by the EC. The Uruguay round has gone on for so long, that pundits refer to the GATT as the "general agreement to talk and talk."

In addition to the GATT, several other international organizations deal with trade issues. They include the Organization for Economic Cooperation and Development (OECD), the United Nations Conference on Trade and Development, and the EC.

Trade Data

World merchandise trade involves over 200 countries, tens of thousands of product categories, and $3.5 trillion annually. With this level of complexity, it is not surprising that trade data are sometimes incomplete and often inconsistent. One inconsistency in merchandise trade data is that exports are usually under-reported. For example, exports of merchandise from the U.S. to Canada should equal Canada's imports of merchandise from the U.S., but they seldom do. Canada's imports are usually higher than the corresponding export figures from the U.S. On a worldwide basis, there are about $150 billion less exports reported than imports. There are several reasons for this. Customs officials may be less diligent about reporting exports than imports. Exporting companies do not report transactions that are restricted or banned under law. Exporting companies also have incentives to understate export sales to reduce taxable income and to pay lower duties to importing countries.

Trade Classification

In order for nations to compare their international trade, they must agree on a classification scheme. The UN created the Standard International Trade Classification (SITC) in 1950. All member nations must submit their own foreign trade statistics to the UN based on this system, which uses five-digit codes grouped into 10 major categories. The SITC, with about 3,000 headings, is a useful classification system for international comparisons of trade. However, it may not be detailed enough to serve as a substitute for an individual country's import and export classification schedule. To meet the need for detailed and consistent schedules, many countries adopted the Harmonized Commodity Description and Coding System developed in 1985. The U.S. adopted the Harmonized System (HS) in 1989. It is important to realize that the SITC and the Harmonized System are completely different classification schemes. The *National Trade Data Bank* (CD-ROM) has cross-classification tables that give equivalent numbers for the Harmonized System, the SITC, and U.S. SIC numbers.

Developed by the Customs Cooperation Council, the HS classification consists of approximately 5,000 six-digit numbers arranged in 96 categories. Most countries, as well as the EC, have modified the HS classification for their own use. The EC uses the Combined Nomenclature, which contains about 16,000 headings. The U.S. has extended the classification to the 10-digit level. The U.S. uses separate classifications for imports and exports. The classifications are the same for the first six digits. For example, Table 15-A shows the import and export classifications for computer printers. The import schedule gives a specific 10-digit code for laser printers. The export code has only an eight-digit code for printer units (and it is different from the import code).

Table 15-A. Comparison of U.S. Export and Import Classifications

Imports
8471 Automatic data processing machines and units thereof
  8471.92 Input or output units
    8471.92.65 Printer units
      8471.92.6560 Laser printers
Exports
  8471 Automatic data processing machines and units
      thereof
  8471.92 Input or output units
    8471.92.75 Printer units

Countries often use different codes beyond the basic six digits. For example, the U.S. and Canada both compile their merchandise trade statistics according to the Harmonized System. About 80% of the U.S. Schedule B Export Classification is directly comparable to Canadian import classifications. There are a few cases where U.S. and Canadian Customs do not agree on the first six digits of the code.[2]

Regulation of International Trade

"Free trade" is the unrestricted exchange of goods and services between countries. No country allows completely free trade. Signatories to the GATT agree to provide one another with most-favored-nation status. Most-favored-nation treatment requires that any tariff concession granted by one country to any other country is automatically extended to all other countries. In spite of their international agreements to improve the flow of trade, all governments attempt to regulate the international trade of their countries. Some of the principal reasons for this policy are:

- To improve the country's balance of trade. The "balance on merchandise trade" (imports minus exports) is an important component of balance of trade statistics. When exports exceed imports, countries are said to be running a positive trade balance. A positive trade balance often makes a country's currency more valuable abroad. This fact, in turn, can help reduce interest rates domestically.
- To protect national industries. Import protection can be designed to help industries survive, to prevent unemployment, or to counter "dumping" by foreign competitors. Dumping occurs when foreign suppliers sell imports at less than their home market price. The practice can drive domestic firms out of business.
- To respond to national pressure groups. Interest groups within a country often view imports as an economic threat. For example, the EC imposes import duties on imported agricultural products to protect internal farm prices in response to a strong EC agricultural block.
- To protect national security. Countries restrict the export of products they believe to be vital to their national defense. The United States government, for example, will not allow the export of "stealth" technology.

Trade Restrictions

Governments use several techniques to control foreign trade. The most common device is the tariff, which is a tax on goods imported into a country. Bilateral treaties, multi-country trading arrangements such as the EC, and the General Agreement on Tariffs and Trade (GATT) have sharply reduced tariffs worldwide. However, countries use a variety of nontariff barriers, including:

- Import Quotas (quantitative restrictions on imports). For example, Canada has annual global import quotas for chickens, turkeys, and table eggs.
- Import Licensing. Countries may prohibit imports without a license and then restrict the issuance of licenses.
- Export Subsidies. The EC grants export subsidies on many agricultural products. This allows EC agricultural producers to sell on the world market below world market prices.
- Voluntary Export Restraints. A country may ask a trading partner to restrict the exports of a particular product. The U.S. has asked Japan to restrict its exports of automobiles to the U.S.

- Customs Valuation Procedures. By valuing imports at a higher price than market price, customs increases the duty payable.
- Local Content Regulations. Countries may require imported manufactured products to contain a certain percentage of domestic parts to escape tariffs.

SERVICES

Merchandise trade deals in tangible goods such as machinery, food, and textiles. Services, in contrast, are intangible. They have been described as "the things that one can buy and sell, but not drop on one's foot."[3] Services include such activities as wholesale and retail trade, transportation, communication, banking, finance, insurance, real estate, and business services. Trade in services is much more difficult to measure than is merchandise trade. Although services are recorded by all countries as part of their balance of payments statistics, comparison between countries and between types of services is difficult for the following reasons:

- There is no detailed international classification of trade in services.
- The methods used to value services are not identical in all countries.
- There is little agreement on valuing certain services such as insurance operations.
- Certain transactions are not regarded as services by all nations. For example, construction operations carried out abroad and lasting more than a year are treated as direct investment rather than services by some countries.[4]

Despite the problems of data collection and comparison, some information concerning international transfer of services is available.

CAPITAL FLOWS

Capital flows refer to transactions in financial assets between residents of different countries. Capital flows include foreign direct investment, portfolio investment, and long-term and short-term capital investment.

- *Foreign direct investment* is the ownership of enterprises located in one country by the residents of another country. Countries often use some percentage of foreign ownership of a business to define foreign investment. In the U.S., foreign direct investment is defined as the ownership of 10% or more of the voting securities of an incorporated business enterprise or an equivalent interest in an unincorporated business. A U.S. firm meeting these criteria is considered a domestic affiliate of a foreign investor. All investment transactions between parent organizations and their foreign affiliates are direct investment flows. For example, Honda's establishment of a manufacturing plant in the U.S. is an example of a foreign direct investment. *Flows* of foreign direct investment refer to the amounts invested by foreign parent companies in affiliates during a time period, usually a year. A *stock* of foreign direct investment refers to the cumulative outstanding value of direct investment at any point in time, usually the end of a year. Most countries report only flows of direct foreign investment.

* *Portfolio investment* includes cross-border loans, bank deposits, drafts, and the purchase of security equities. Portfolio investments are, by definition, not large enough to qualify as direct foreign investment. An example of a portfolio investment would be the purchase of 100 shares of IBM stock by a citizen of Germany.

* *Long-term capital* is capital payable with a maturity of more than one year.

* *Short-term capital* is capital payable on demand or with a maturity of one year or less. Short-term capital includes the cross-border transfer of currency (cash).

With the explosion in direct and portfolio investments across national boundaries in the 1980s, the values of capital flows have come to surpass those of trade flows. The measurement of capital flows is important for a nation in several respects. For example, such measurements allow a country to assess the impact of foreign direct investment on the domestic economy and to estimate the amount of foreign indebtedness.[5]

Of all data on international economic transactions, capital flow statistics are most subject to errors and gaps. Clive Crook, the economics editor of the *Economist*, refers to "lies, damned lies and capital flows"[6] and notes that any attempt to measure capital flows quickly runs into acute difficulties. For example, the IMF reports that in 1990 all countries contributed $229 billion to direct investment, but only $179 billion was reported as received by countries in which the money was invested. Fifty billion dollars appears to have been lost in transit. Instant cross-border electronic transfer of funds makes it difficult for nations to keep track of capital flows. Moreover, countries use different methods to measure flows and have no agreement on definitions, such as what constitutes foreign direct investment. John Dunning and John Cantwell were the first to deal systematically with capital flow statistics in their work, *IRM Directory of Statistics of International Investment and Production,* described below.

We can describe two types of transactions between a nation's companies (for example, U.S. firms) and the companies of the rest of the world: cross-border transactions and affiliates' transactions. Cross-border transac-

tions, as diagramed in Exhibit 15-2, are imports or exports of goods, services, or financial assets.

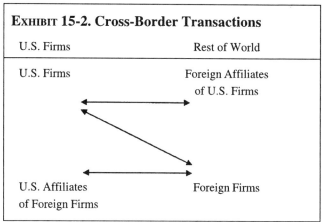

EXHIBIT 15-2. Cross-Border Transactions

U.S. Firms	Rest of World
U.S. Firms	Foreign Affiliates of U.S. Firms
U.S. Affiliates of Foreign Firms	Foreign Firms

Source: Adapted with permission from *Behind the Numbers: U.S. Trade in the World Economy,* Anne Y. Kester, editor. National Academy Press, 1992, p. 38. Copyright © 1992 by the National Academy of Sciences. Courtesy of the National Academy Press, Washington, D.C.

Information regarding the details of cross-border transactions is available with varying degrees of detail from balance of payments statistics.

Affiliates' transactions are outlined in Exhibit 15-3. They consist of sales or purchases within a country.

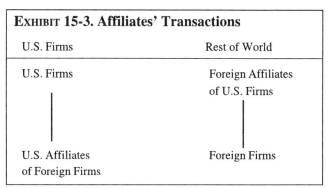

EXHIBIT 15-3. Affiliates' Transactions

U.S. Firms	Rest of World
U.S. Firms	Foreign Affiliates of U.S. Firms
U.S. Affiliates of Foreign Firms	Foreign Firms

Source: Adapted with permission from *Behind the Numbers: U.S. Trade in the World Economy,* Anne Y. Kester, editor. National Academy Press, 1992, p. 38. Copyright © 1992 by the National Academy of Sciences. Courtesy of the National Academy Press, Washington, D.C.

Information about affiliates' transactions is not part of the balance of payments framework. Consequently, data about this aspect of international business are often not available.[7]

SOURCES FOR BALANCE OF PAYMENTS STATISTICS

We begin our discussion of sources with a description of balance of payments statistics. The most comprehensive general source of balance of payments statistics is the IMF's *Balance of Payments Yearbook*. The data are based on reports sent to the IMF by member countries.

Volume 1 consists of country sections containing both a general (aggregated) presentation of the transaction data, as well as a detailed presentation. Figures are in U.S. dollars. Monthly and quarterly data are given if available. Data are shown for the eight or nine most recent periods. For some of the industrial countries, stock data are given for the capital and reserve accounts in addition to transactions data.

Volume 2 of the *Yearbook* aggregates the data by balance of payments category and breaks down the data by country group. In addition to print, the *Yearbook* is also available on CD-ROM and computer tape. Summaries of balance of payments data also can be found in the IMF publication, *International Financial Statistics*. Exhibit 15-4 displays a sample page from the *Balance of Payments Yearbook*.

The *Balance of Payments Yearbook* did not include data from the states of the former Soviet Union in its 1992 edition. The IMF publication, *Economic Review Russian Federation*, gives estimates of summary balance of payments statistics for both Russia and the former U.S.S.R. for 1990 and 1991.

The OECD and the EC also publish detailed balance of payments statistics for their member nations. Their publications are briefly described under "Additional Sources," below.

The primary sources for balance of payments statistics are the publications of individual countries. A useful listing of these publications can be found in the *Balance of Payments Yearbook* "notes" to the country sections. Often a country's central bank is responsible for collecting balance of payment data.

Current estimates of international transactions of the U.S., including estimates of merchandise trade, are reported in the March, June, September, and December issues of the *Survey of Current Business*. Estimates of the international investment position of the United States appear in the June *Survey*.

Balance of payments data for individual countries are available as well in several online (time-sharing) databases, including WEFA and DATASTREAM. *Econbase*, a subset of the WEFA database that is available on DIALOG, can sometimes be used as an inexpensive substitute for the more specialized economic online sources. *Econbase* contains current account balances and capital account balances for about 20 nations from 1970. Forecast data are available for the current account balances of many of these countries.

SOURCES FOR MERCHANDISE TRADE STATISTICS

Foreign trade data are compiled by individual countries, by several international organizations, and by commercial database producers. The international organizations include the EC, the OECD, and the UN with its specialized agencies such as the International Monetary Fund.

The foreign trade publications of international organizations have several common characteristics. The first is long delays before the information is published. In general, the more commodity and country detail required, the longer the wait for it.

A second characteristic of foreign trade data published by international organizations is a lack of product detail. The EC's annual *External Trade Statistics,* with eight-digit harmonized code product descriptions, is an exception. The details of product descriptions in the other sources vary from none at all (in the publications of the IMF) to five-digit SITC descriptions in some UN publications. In comparison, the Harmonized System used by many countries in their individual foreign trade reports gives seven- to ten-digit classifications of products. The lack of product detail is not necessarily a shortcoming. We often want aggregate statistics. In addition, detail product listings of trade among many countries is cumbersome in a book format. The eight-digit detail presented by the EC requires 26 volumes a year as well as minuscule print.

A final characteristic of the publications of international organizations is that they provide a consistent format and valuation method over time. With the exception of the EC, all these international organizations use the SITC classification. Although the SITC system has been revised in 1960, 1976, and again in 1988, its main features are constant. All the publications use the U.S. dollar as the measure of value with the exception of the EC, which uses the ECU.

Table 15-B shows the characteristics of several standard foreign trade publications of international organizations.

One of the complications of finding import/export statistics is the variety of variables that may be used to present the data. These variables include:

- Product Type: Ranging from "all products" to 10-digit code detail
- Measurement: Price (for individual units of products), quantity (such as kilograms), and value (price times quantity)
- Classification Variety: Standard International Trade Classification (SITC) or Harmonized Code

EXHIBIT 15-4. *Balance of Payments Yearbook*

Japan
158

Table 1.   AGGREGATED PRESENTATION: TRANSACTIONS DATA, 1984–91

(In billions of U.S. dollars)

	Code	1984	1985	1986	1987	1988	1989	1990	1991
A. Current Account, excl. Group E	A . . C A	**35.00**	**49.17**	**85.83**	**87.02**	**79.61**	**56.99**	**35.87**	**72.91**
Merchandise: exports f.o.b.	1 A . A 4	168.29	174.02	205.59	224.62	259.77	269.55	280.35	306.58
Merchandise: imports f.o.b.	1 A . B 4	−124.03	−118.03	−112.77	−128.20	−164.77	−192.66	−216.77	−203.49
Trade balance	1 A . C 4	44.26	55.99	92.82	96.42	95.00	76.89	63.58	103.09
Services: credit	1 V . A 4	22.48	22.47	23.54	28.85	35.03	39.70	40.83	44.65
Shipment and other transportation	1 P . A 4	*12.88*	*12.44*	*11.32*	*12.94*	*15.54*	*18.15*	*18.16*	*19.67*
Travel	1 D . A 4	*.97*	*1.14*	*1.46*	*2.09*	*2.89*	*3.15*	*3.59*	*3.44*
Other	1 V . A Y	*8.63*	*8.89*	*10.76*	*13.82*	*16.60*	*18.40*	*19.08*	*21.54*
Services: debit	1 V . B 4	−32.80	−32.74	−35.45	−48.42	−63.53	−75.01	−81.97	−85.04
Shipment and other transportation	1 P . B 4	*−15.92*	*−15.09*	*−13.85*	*−19.05*	*−22.98*	*−25.90*	*−27.65*	*−29.93*
Travel	1 D . B 4	*−4.61*	*−4.82*	*−7.23*	*−10.76*	*−18.67*	*−22.50*	*−24.93*	*−24.00*
Other	1 V . B Y	*−12.27*	*−12.83*	*−14.37*	*−18.61*	*−21.88*	*−26.61*	*−29.39*	*−31.11*
Income: credit	1 Q . A 4	19.67	23.04	30.16	50.81	76.75	104.21	125.13	143.94
Income: debit	1 Q . B 4	−17.10	−17.94	−23.18	−36.96	−59.52	−84.52	−106.18	−121.24
Total: goods, services, and income	1 T . C 4	36.51	50.82	87.89	90.70	83.73	61.27	41.39	85.40
Private unrequited transfers	1 K . C 4	−.13	−.28	−.59	−.99	−1.12	−.99	−1.01	−.66
Total, excl. official unrequited transfers	1 U . C 4	36.38	50.54	87.30	89.71	82.61	60.28	40.38	84.74
Official unrequited transfers	1 H . C A	−1.38	−1.37	−1.47	−2.69	−3.00	−3.29	−4.51	−11.84
B. Direct Investment and Other Long-Term									
Capital, excl. Groups E through G	9 Z 1 X A	**−50.01**	**−63.26**	**−132.08**	**−133.98**	**−117.09**	**−93.76**	**−53.08**	**31.39**
Direct investment	3 . . X A	−5.97	−5.81	−14.25	−18.35	−34.73	−45.22	−46.29	−29.37
Portfolio investment	6 Z 1 X A	−23.96	−41.75	−102.04	−91.33	−52.75	−32.53	−14.49	35.45
Gensaki transactions	6 Y 1 X Y	*−.36*	*1.32*	*−.66*	*3.04*	*13.36*	*−3.77*	*−9.68*	*−4.21*
Other	6 . 1 X Y	*−23.60*	*−43.07*	*−101.38*	*−94.37*	*−66.11*	*−28.76*	*−4.81*	*39.66*
Other long-term capital									
Resident official sector	4 Z 1 X A	−3.44	−1.74	−2.73	−4.10	−6.91	−8.51	−10.41	−11.27
Deposit money banks	5 Z 1 X A	−8.71	−7.66	−6.60	−9.69	−6.07	−4.90	−6.04	1.52
Other sectors	8 Z 1 X A	−7.93	−6.30	−6.46	−10.51	−16.63	−2.60	24.15	35.06
Total, Groups A plus B	B 1 . X A	**−15.01**	**−14.09**	**−46.25**	**−46.96**	**−37.48**	**−36.77**	**−17.21**	**104.30**
C. Other Short-Term Capital, excl. Groups E									
through G	9 Z 2 X A	**13.44**	**9.73**	**58.60**	**88.61**	**50.87**	**45.83**	**31.54**	**−103.24**
Resident official sector	4 Z 2 X A	.79	1.33	1.28	−3.77	1.50	11.55	14.39	9.89
Deposit money banks	5 Z 2 X A	17.56	10.85	58.51	71.80	44.46	8.58	−13.66	−93.46
Assets	5 L 2 X A	*−5.77*	*−24.70*	*−81.56*	*−107.07*	*−147.47*	*−133.88*	*−56.01*	*37.86*
Liabilities	5 Y 2 X A	*23.33*	*35.55*	*140.07*	*178.87*	*191.93*	*142.46*	*42.35*	*−131.32*
Other sectors	8 Z 2 X A	−4.91	−2.45	−1.19	20.58	4.91	25.70	30.81	−19.67
D. Net Errors and Omissions	. A . X 4	**3.69**	**3.78**	**2.49**	**−3.71**	**3.13**	**−21.82**	**−20.92**	**−7.68**
Total, Groups A through D	D 1 . X A	**2.12**	**−.58**	**14.84**	**37.94**	**16.52**	**−12.76**	**−6.59**	**−6.63**
E. Exceptional Financing	. Y . X B	—	—	—	—	—	—	—	—
Total, Groups A through E	E 1 . X 4	**2.12**	**−.58**	**14.84**	**37.94**	**16.52**	**−12.76**	**−6.59**	**−6.63**
F. Liabilities Constituting Foreign Authorities'									
Reserves	9 W . X 4	...	...	...	...	...	...	...	...
Total, Groups A through F	F 1 . X 4	**2.12**	**−.58**	**14.84**	**37.94**	**16.52**	**−12.76**	**−6.59**	**−6.63**
G. Reserves	2 . . X 4	**−2.12**	**.58**	**−14.84**	**−37.94**	**−16.52**	**12.76**	**6.59**	**6.63**
Monetary gold	2 A . X 4	—	—	—	—	—	—	—	—
SDRs	2 B . X 4	−.12	.06	.14	.10	−.61	.42	−.38	.47
Reserve position in the Fund	2 C . X 4	−.07	.20	.14	−.07	−.57	−.31	−2.04	−1.68
Foreign exchange assets	2 D . X 4	−1.93	.33	−15.12	−37.97	−15.34	12.66	9.01	7.83
Other claims	2 E . X 4	—	—	—	—	—	—	—	—
Use of Fund credit and loans	2 Y . X 4	—	—	—	—	—	—	—	—
Memorandum items									
Total change in reserves	2 . . R 4	*−1.83*	*−.29*	*−15.54*	*−38.72*	*−15.76*	*12.77*	*5.46*	*6.44*
of which: revaluations	2 . . B 4	*.29*	*−.87*	*−.70*	*−.78*	*.76*	*.01*	*−1.13*	*−.19*
Conversion rates: yen per U.S. dollar	. . R F 4	**237.52**	**238.54**	**168.52**	**144.64**	**128.15**	**137.96**	**144.79**	**134.71**

Reprinted with permission from the IMF.

Table 15-B. Characteristics of Foreign Trade Publications

Publication	Lag	Numeric Detail	First Published
Direction of Trade (IMF)	1 Yr	-	1964
Direction of Trade Annual (IMF)	2 Yrs	-	1962
Eurostat Annual External Trade (EC)	2 Yrs	8	1964
Eurostat Monthly External Trade (EC)	1 Yr	2	1964
Foreign Trade by Commodities (OECD)	1 Yr	2	1960
Monthly Stats of Foreign Trade (OECD)	4 Mths	2	1960
Commodity Trade (UN)	2 Yrs	4	1951
International Trade Statistics (UN)	3 Yrs	5	1952
World Trade Annual (UN)	5 Yrs	5	1963

- Country/Geographic Area/Political Group: e.g., Japan, EC, non-oil exporting nations, Central America, Massachusetts
- Time Period: e.g., Current month, year-to-date, annual trade
- Valuation: e.g., CIF, FOB, or FAS

In addition, we may want reports in a particular format, such as a ranking by value or as an import/export matrix of countries. We may want quantities expressed in nonstandard forms (e.g., export volume expressed as "pairs of shoes" rather than weight of shoes). We may be interested in the details of "re-exports" and "re-imports" or in the volume of trade passing through a particular port.

An important consideration is the different methods of measuring the value of trade. The value of imports for most countries is recorded as CIF (the cost of the item plus the cost of insurance and freight required to ship the item to its port of entry). The value of exports for most countries are recorded as FOB (Free on Board). This includes the cost of the item, plus the cost of loading, but does not include insurance or ongoing freight charges. The United States is an exception to this rule, valuing its exports FAS (Free Alongside Ship). This includes the cost of the commodity plus all costs associated with getting the product to a shipping point.

The IMF and the UN both publish merchandise trade data. The IMF statistics are general trade figures between countries that are IMF members. The UN statistics give detailed commodity descriptions of trade between UN member countries. GATT (another UN agency) publishes detailed studies of the trade practices of individual countries. The major trade publications of the IMF, the UN, and GATT will be discussed here in some detail.

The EC and the OECD also publish trade statistics for their member states. These publications are described in "Additional Sources," below.

IMF Trade Publications

Direction of Trade Statistics (International Monetary Fund—Quarterly)

Direction of Trade Statistics (DOT) was first published in 1964. It gives current figures on the value of merchandise exports and imports in dollars for 135 countries, including details of trade with a country's major trading partners arranged by country and area. The reported data are supplemented by estimates whenever the data are not current or unavailable. In addition to tables for individual countries, *DOT* publishes the following aggregate tables:

- World Aggregates comprising all countries, including about 30 small countries for which individual country tables are not presented
- Industrial Country Aggregates
- Developing Countries Aggregates

Exhibit 15-5 displays a sample page from *Direction of Trade Statistics.*

A companion IMF publication, the *Direction of Trade Statistics Yearbook,* presents time series covering a seven-year period of merchandise trade for about 160 countries. For each country, the *Yearbook* gives dollar value of trade for major trading partners and percent distribution and annual percent change for the individual country's trade by geographic area. It also includes aggregate tables for the world and for geographic regions. The *Yearbook* was first published in 1962.

United Nations Trade Publications

Commodity Trade Statistics (United Nations—Annual)

This publication combines product detail (mostly four-digit SITC) with comprehensive country coverage (almost all UN members are included). The information is reported to the UN annually by member countries and

Exhibit 15-5. *Direction of Trade Statistics*

Portugal(182)

	Exports *Millions of U.S. Dollars*							Imports *Millions of U.S. Dollars*						
	III 1991	IV 1991	I 1992	II 1992	III 1992	Sep 1992	Oct 1992	III 1991	IV 1991	I 1992	II 1992	III 1992	Sep 1992	Oct 1992
IFS World Total	3,729.0	4,314.5	4,670.7	4,245.2	4,862.2	1,547.3	1,566.2	5,968.2	6,757.7	7,214.1	7,181.9	8,018.8	2,537.0	2,534.6
DOTS World Total 001	3,614.7	4,540.4	4,643.6	4,453.4	4,581.6	1,631.8	1,784.9	5,913.5	6,954.8	7,045.6	7,651.5	7,548.2	2,647.3	2,752.3
Industrial Countries 110	3,225.3	3,927.2	4,230.9	3,941.4	4,030.1	1,369.6	1,444.2	4,891.3	5,926.7	6,107.5	6,643.2	6,433.4	2,224.3	2,353.2
United States 111	144.7	169.0	143.7	152.0	176.6	64.4	62.0E	199.3	220.7	235.6	234.8	225.8	82.7E	80.9E
Canada 156	29.2	28.3	30.5	33.0	42.9	16.5	17.4*	41.2	29.1	50.8	47.8	40.4	16.0	17.4*
Australia 193	10.9	10.5	9.3	9.4	12.2	4.3	3.3*	7.1	7.8	9.0	7.1	8.8	1.8	1.3*
Japan 158	24.7	41.5	37.5	33.3	30.7	9.8	8.1*	175.3	202.0	198.3	239.3	231.9	79.3	74.8*
New Zealand 196	2.1	2.4	2.4	2.1	1.8	.6	.8*	9.5	6.3	4.8	6.9	9.2	3.6	1.8*
Austria 122	47.5	47.6	44.5	45.4	55.6	22.3	28.3*	40.6	55.4	54.7	60.5	62.5	22.5	23.9*
Belgium-Luxembourg 126	112.9	135.7	168.1	138.0	145.8	52.0	49.7E	230.2	264.4	259.8	294.2	277.5	97.8	96.9E
Denmark 128	80.5	85.9	96.0	96.2	105.4	42.5	31.5E	46.3	57.0	55.6	57.8	64.4	28.4	20.9E
Finland 172	51.7	61.6	63.0	54.6	51.9	14.7	17.4*	48.2	38.8	46.3	49.4	57.8	22.7	17.6*
France 132	484.7	615.2	673.9	643.8	600.3	190.5	205.9*	674.6	817.6	924.2	973.9	923.1	300.0	358.2*
Germany 134	681.5	785.6	887.5	821.0	848.9	291.4	347.2*	834.5	1,067.3	1,020.4	1,119.6	1,105.2	389.6	525.6*
Greece 174	13.8	20.2	23.3	25.4	23.4	6.0	7.4E	4.8	5.6	6.9	6.5	6.2	2.5	2.0E
Ireland 178	18.3	20.9	21.6	19.3	19.2	7.3	7.7E	23.6	31.3	26.0	27.2	31.8	11.7	11.5E
Italy 136	138.7	172.2	190.1	175.2	178.5	60.5	63.1E	593.9	735.9	713.6	784.6	753.9	249.8	269.8E
Netherlands 138	205.5	250.2	279.0	232.2	263.1	88.7	62.2*	369.5	425.4	450.3	545.8	542.1	181.5	128.9*
Norway 142	47.1	52.3	54.8	48.1	56.1	19.1	27.6*	75.8	81.8	115.3	142.4	113.2	43.1	23.4*
Spain 184	530.6	697.9	749.5	684.5	640.7	214.6E	255.9E	911.1	1,128.3	1,200.9	1,261.6	1,225.9	423.9E	413.7E
Sweden 144	150.9	151.6	164.9	146.0	170.5	62.7	55.6E	75.1	90.6	84.4	104.2	99.6	40.1	33.2E
Switzerland 146	71.2	84.3	83.9	82.0	83.6	28.8	22.6*	101.5	132.4	112.0	127.4	126.9	44.4	57.2*
United Kingdom 112	376.9	492.1	504.9	498.2	521.1	172.4	169.9*	407.5	522.6	527.3	539.3	514.1	174.4	191.7*
Developing Countries 200	304.5	437.4	355.1	422.0	544.4	261.2	154.3	991.7	989.9	901.6	965.4	1,068.8	399.5	369.7
Africa 605	189.5	293.7	222.2	279.5	401.8	214.1	107.9	288.1	327.7	365.8	324.5	341.1	122.4	120.1
Algeria 612	8.0	1.6	.9	.3	4.7	4.6	.6E	51.7	92.4	69.8	44.6	52.4	17.0	33.9E
Angola 614	120.3	211.4	149.6	208.4	244.7	101.8	77.5E	15.4	34.4	42.5	27.8	38.1	13.6	12.6E
Cape Verde 624	11.3	14.7	15.0	14.8	12.8	4.3	5.4E	.4	1.0	.7	.8	.8	.2	.4E
Côte d'Ivoire 662	.4	2.6	4.3	.5	.8	—	1.0E	5.0	6.2	7.4	6.8	6.1	1.7	2.3E
Congo 634	.2	.4	.4	.4	.4	.1	.1E	8.2	7.9	8.0	9.0	10.5	2.3	2.9E
Guinea-Bissau 654	5.5	9.3	5.4	7.1	6.6	1.4	3.4E	1.1	1.6	.9	1.2	1.0	.2	.6E
Morocco 686	8.9	12.9	15.9	12.0	13.4	4.6	4.7E	8.8	12.7	5.7	5.5	5.4	2.4	4.6E
Mozambique 688	7.9	9.2	6.6	8.3	6.8	3.2	3.4E	4.3	6.7	9.2	9.9	6.7	2.8	2.5E
Nigeria 694	1.4	5.0	2.7	3.0	2.8	.8	1.8E	78.0	68.0	109.1	112.0	93.7	32.4	24.9E
Sao Tome & Principe 716	2.7	3.2	2.9	2.9	2.4	.6	1.2E	.1	—	—	.2	.3	—	—E
Senegal 722	1.2	.9	.5	.8	.4	.2	.3E	1.7	1.3	1.5	1.4	1.5	.6	.5E
South Africa 199	10.3	10.7	8.7	9.9	8.8	2.6	3.9E	37.8	29.9	29.1	38.8	47.0	23.2	11.0E
Sudan 732	—	—	.7	1.0	.2	.1	.4E	.1	.1	—	.1	.3	—	—E
Tanzania 738	1.9	1.0	1.2	1.3	1.1	.3	.4*	4.3	4.7	6.6	6.8	6.3	1.7	1.7E
Tunisia 744	.4	.6						.5	.8	.9	.7	.8	.4	.4*
Zaire 636	.4	—	.1	.2	.2	—	—E	3.7	6.2	6.5	4.2	6.7	2.3	2.3E
Zimbabwe 698	4.4	—	2.6	3.3	3.3	.1	—E	6.6	7.0	4.0	2.3	1.3	.5	2.6E
Asia 505	37.8	57.0	48.3	47.7	45.6	13.2	17.0	156.5	171.7	169.1	194.4	193.6	72.4	69.9
China, People's Rep. 924	7.4	14.7	.9	2.0	2.9	.6	1.6*	17.1	19.3	19.0	25.3	28.8	11.4	4.2*
Hong Kong 532	4.7	5.5	5.6	6.3	5.2	1.8	1.2*	9.7	12.7	9.5	10.5	9.9	3.8	13.4*
India 534	.6	.9	8.1	5.5	6.8	.7	.3E	12.7	12.0	17.6	18.2	14.7	5.0	4.4E
Indonesia 536	.9	.5	—	—	—	—	.2E	8.0	1.5	2.1	4.1	6.1	2.1	.5E
Macao 546	3.9	3.1	2.5	6.1	5.9	2.1	2.3*	2.3	2.3	1.2	.8	2.1	1.3	.4*
Malaysia 548	4.9	5.2	5.0	7.2	5.8	1.3	1.9E	6.4	8.6	9.3	10.9	13.3	6.0	3.2E
Pakistan 564	1.0	1.7	.4	.8	.6	.1	.1*	11.4	7.5	12.5	13.2	11.6	4.0	4.2*
Philippines 566	.3	1.2	.7	1.2	1.5	.4	.4E	3.0	3.3	2.6	3.0	2.8	1.0	1.2E
Singapore 576	3.6	5.9	5.0	5.1	5.1	1.4	2.1E	9.4	9.8	10.1	11.0	11.2	4.1	3.6E
Thailand 578	1.6	4.0	3.9	4.2	4.1	1.9	1.5E	23.6	33.4	31.1	33.7	32.2	12.7	12.2E
Europe 170	13.9	15.8	21.8	22.5	30.4	10.7	5.8	27.5	32.3	29.5	32.0	39.0	14.4	11.9
Poland 964	1.0	1.2	1.0	.9	.8	.2	.4E	5.8	5.7	3.6	3.9	3.8	1.7	2.1E
Romania 968	.5	—	4.0	1.5	2.9	—	—E	1.4	.5	.2	.7	1.1	.3	.2E
Turkey 186	2.7	4.4	3.3	5.9	14.3	5.9	1.6E	8.9	13.7	12.8	10.7	10.9	4.4	5.0E
Yugoslavia 188	.7	1.5	2.1	4.1	1.5	.4	.5E	4.4	4.3	4.1	5.6	5.1	1.4	1.6E
Middle East 405	38.6	40.2	39.7	48.4	41.1	13.4	12.4	275.1	253.9	144.3	203.6	263.5	115.5	92.9
Egypt 469	1.7	3.3	2.6	2.6	2.1	.8	1.2E	44.4	54.1	39.9	70.3	88.2	28.1	19.8E
Iran, I.R. of 429	1.4	2.6	2.3	6.6	11.1	2.6	.9E	64.0	69.8	14.3	27.2	60.3	34.0	25.6E
Iraq 433	—	—	—	7.8	—	—	—E	—	—	—	30.5	—	—	—E
Israel 436	12.4	17.6	15.0	14.6	14.8	5.5	4.5*	8.4	7.0	8.9	8.7	9.2	3.3	2.4*
Kuwait 443	.7	1.0	.9	1.2	.9	.3	—E	—	—	—	—	—	—	—E
Libya 672	.1	.6	2.3	1.0	.8	—	.2E	42.4	16.7	10.8	12.8	31.6	14.6	6.1E
Qatar 453	.6	.1	.2	1.2	—	—	—E	—	—	—	—	—	—	—E
Saudi Arabia 456	6.6	7.2	10.4	7.6	5.7	2.1	2.6E	52.5	81.2	42.5	40.4	68.5	35.1	29.8E
Syrian Arab Republic 463	.6	.3	.4	.5	.8	.6	.1E	.6	5.1	1.2	3.2	5.4	.4	1.9E
United Arab Emirates 466	7.7	2.8	2.7	2.3	2.4	.9	1.0E	62.7	19.8	26.6	10.4	.1	—	7.3E
Western Hemisphere 205	24.8	30.8	23.1	23.8	25.5	9.9	11.3	244.6	204.3	192.9	211.0	231.6	74.7	74.9
Argentina 213	1.6	3.8	.8	2.9	2.4	.6	1.4E	72.3	32.7	28.5	30.5	33.3	16.1	12.0E
Brazil 223	10.9	12.3	6.6	7.6	8.0	3.6	4.5E	75.3	78.5	68.8	84.8	106.5	32.6	28.8E
Chile 228	2.4	1.6	2.4	3.0	3.0	1.8	.6E	19.0	15.7	16.1	16.8	9.6	3.2	5.8E
Colombia 233	.3	.3	.2	.1	.2	—	.1E	8.3	13.6	10.9	8.0	7.4	4.4	5.0E
Mexico 273	2.4	2.3	2.3	1.8	2.0	.8	.8E	30.3	28.5	29.1	34.2	32.3	1.1	10.4E
Netherlands Antilles 353	.5	.2	.2	.2	.3	—	.1E	—	—	—	—	2.4	2.3	—E
Panama 283	.2	.4	.7	.6	1.2	.4	.1E	6.9	.8	4.4	1.7	1.6	.2	.3E
Paraguay 288	.1	.2	.1	.1	.1	—	.1E	8.7	8.2	5.6	7.6	8.0	1.9	3.0E
Peru 293	.2	.8	.9	.2	.2	.1	.3E	4.0	6.0	3.7	4.3	5.4	1.0	2.2E
Venezuela 299	2.6	2.4	1.5	2.0	2.5	1.0	.9E	1.9	6.4	1.9	2.8	11.0	9.6	2.3E
Other countries n.i.e. 910	1.7	9.4	17.4	15.8	7.1	.9	3.5	20.5	17.1	33.1	36.6	46.0	23.5	6.3
Cuba 928	.2	.5	.1	.1	.5	.5	.2E	3.0	1.3	9.2	8.1	9.0	3.4	.5E
U.S.S.R. (former) 974	1.0	7.3	14.9	13.8	5.5	.5	2.7E	16.1	14.6	23.4	27.3	35.7	19.7	5.4E
Memorandum Items Oil Exporting Countries 999	30.1	23.9	23.9	33.1	31.5	12.5	8.4	361.3	356.0	277.1	284.9	323.8	144.8	130.5
Non-Oil Developing Countries 201	274.3	413.5	331.2	388.9	512.9	248.8	145.9	630.5	633.9	624.4	680.5	745.0	254.7	239.2

Reprinted with permission from the IMF.

converted to a common format that allows direct comparisons to be made between countries over time. Values are in thousands of U.S. dollars. The lowest published value is $100,000. The conversion into U.S. dollars has been made using weighted exchange rates. Quantities when available are expressed in metric units. Exhibit 15-6 shows the general form of the statistics. In this table, 885 is an SITC number. The numbers following areas and countries are values in thousands of U.S. dollars. The abbreviation "EC" stands for "economies" not the organization, which is given as "EEC." Other tables may include measures of quanity, e.g., weight in kilograms.

EXHIBIT 15-6. Imports of Austria, January-December, 1991

885 WATCHES AND CLOCKS

WORLD	152452
DEVELOPED EC	114209
DVELOPING EC	37924
OTHER	318
NORTHRN.AMER	647
N.AMER.DEVPO	647
USA	645
ASIA	47318
ASIA DEV'PED	9568
JAPAN	9564
ASIA DEV'PNG	37749
OTHER ASIA	37745
CHINA	5062
HONG KONG	28787
KOREA REP.	901
•	•
•	•
EUROPE	104354
EUROPE DEV'PED	103990
EEC	36284
BELGIUM-LUX	406
•	•
•	•

Source: Reprinted from *Commodity Trade Statistics* (Austria), Series D, January-December, 1991, p. 165

World Trade Annual (United Nations—Annual)

Published annually since 1963, the *World Trade Annual* provides detailed and summary trade statistics by commodity by nation for 23 industrial countries, using SITC classifications to the five-digit level. The *Supplement to the World Trade Annual* gives trade of the industrialized nations with developing countries. It is arranged by country. The *World Trade Annual* and its *Supplement* are very slow in publication; the 1987 edition, for example, appeared in 1992.

International Trade Statistics Yearbook (United Nations—Annual)

The *Yearbook* is published in two volumes. It provides trade statistics on more than 150 countries. The first volume gives:

- The total value of imports and exports by country for each year since 1954
- Imports and exports expressed as a percentage of total value for broad industry groups for the previous seven years
- Trade by principal countries of origin and last destination for the previous five years
- The value of the country's trade, for the previous 10 years, as a percentage of the country's world trade for major trading partners, political groups, and geographic areas
- General exports and imports by commodity group in U.S. dollars and in weight for the previous four years, given in up to five-digit SITC detail
- Several special tables, including world exports by commodity classes and by regions, and export price index numbers of primary commodities

The second volume contains:

- Import/export value by product broken down by country, political group, and geographic area for the past five years; product detail is three-, four-, and five-digit SITC groups
- The value of the product's trade, for the previous 10 years, as a percentage of the product's world trade for major industrial countries, political groups, and geographic areas
- Commodity matrix tables for the year of publication that show the trade between countries for specific three-digit SITC product groups; 22 exporting countries and 20 importing countries are ranked for value for each commodity

The *International Trade Statistics Yearbook* is useful for time series of trade by product or by country. It is less complete than the *Commodity Trade Statistics* or *World Trade Annual* in providing details of product trade among countries.

GATT Trade Publications

Trade Policy Review (General Agreement on Tariffs and Trade—Frequency varies)

Under GATT, the trade policies of all contracting parties are subject to periodic review. The four largest "trading entities" (countries and trading blocs such as the EC) by world market share, counting the European Community as one, are reviewed every two years. GATT reviews the next largest 26 trading entities every four years, and others every six years. Reviews are conducted by the GATT council on the basis of two reports, one presented by the contracting party under review and another drawn up by the GATT secretariat. The reports are published after each review.

The two-volume *Trade Policy Review Austria* is a typical example of GATT's review. The first volume contains the report of the GATT secretariat, which consists of a description of Austria's role in world trade, a description of its economic environment, and its trade policy regime. Most of the volume is devoted to a detailed description of Austria's trade policy. The second volume is written by the government of Austria. Its purpose is to answer questions raised by GATT in the first volume and to supply additional information concerning Austria's trade policies.

The annual *GATT International Trade* provides a broad overview of world trade and its impact on individual economies. It is useful for the general picture it gives of world trade and the product composition of world trade for the past 20 years.

Trade Statistics from Individual Countries

The foreign trade statistics published by individual countries are more accessible than most country-specific data sources. Language differences may not be a serious problem in using an individual nation's printed trade statistics. There is little text and the sources often use the Harmonized Code to categorize products. In addition, the trade statistics of many non-English-speaking countries include English translations. The main drawback to the use of these sources for purposes of comparison is the lack of a standard currency unit.

The main sources for U.S. import/export statistics are described clearly in the second edition of Michael Lavin's *Business Information* (Oryx, 1992). An important U.S. source that was not widely available until after the publication of *Business Information* is the *PIERS* database. A commercial version of U.S. trade statistics, the *World Trade Atlas* on CD-ROM, is scheduled for release. Both products are described in the next section.

Online Sources for Merchandise Trade Statistics

The printed sources we have described often have machine-readable equivalents. *Direction of Trade*, for example, is available in CD-ROM and on magnetic tape. The machine-readable formats will have the same shortcomings of the printed products, lack of product detail and lack of timeliness. The trade publications of international organizations are useful mainly as economic indicators and for historical research. The identification of

trade opportunities, the monitoring of specific product imports and exports, and the identification of potential trade partners require electronic sources that are timely and detailed.

TRADSTAT (DATA-STAR)

TRADSTAT is a world trade statistics database that provides official government import/export information on all reported commodities traded by 24 countries. In addition, the database can create aggregate import or export reports for the European Community. Available through the DATA-STAR online system, *TRADSTAT* includes about 90% of world trade. *TRADSTAT* obtains its data tapes directly from official government statistical or customs offices. The monthly data are usually received within four to ten weeks of the trading month. The data are stored by detailed customs product code representing more than 60,000 traded commodities. Monthly data for the latest 25 months are stored online for all reporting countries. Annual data are available from 1982 for many of the countries in the file. Table 15-C lists the countries in the database, the year from which data are first available, and the year in which the data can be searched by Harmonized Code number.

Table 15-C. Countries and Years of Coverage in *TRADSTAT*

Country	Beginning Year Online	Harmonized Code
Argentina	1986	1990
Austria	1982	1988
Belgium/Lux	1982	1988
Brazil	1985	1989
Canada	1982	1988
Denmark	1982	1988
Finland	1988	1988
France	1982	1988
Germany*	1982	1988
Greece	1985	1988
Hong Kong	1985	1988
Ireland	1981	1988
Italy	1982	1988
Japan	1982	1988
Netherlands	1982	1988
Norway	1981	1988
Portugal	1986	1988
Spain	1984	1988
Sweden	1981	1988
Switzerland	1981	1988
Taiwan	1986	1989
Venezuela	1981	1990
United Kingdom	1982	1988
United States	1982	1989
*East Germany included from January 1, 1991		

The product codes for individual countries can be searched online, but there are several complications. The Harmonized Code is used only from 1988/89 to date. Before this date countries use their national trade classifications. The amount of product detail varies. Some countries do not use English for their product descriptions. Product classifications vary in detail over time and among countries. For example, the U.S. uses a 10-digit code after 1989 and seven-digit code before that date.

An insight into the problems of trade data quality and availability is given by *TRADSTAT's* attempt to use trade figures from Mexico and India in 1992. The data provided by the Mexican authorities were poor (e.g., product codes with extra characters and symbols, and no corresponding descriptions). The Indian authorities would only publish data for 50 commodities out of several thousand commodities traded. Consequently, *TRADSTAT* was unable to make the data from the two countries available.

TRADSTAT allows flexibility in the selection and presentation of data. The database has 24 formats for the creation of import/export reports. The currency of any of the 24 countries in the database can be used to display price and value. The unit of quantity can be requested in the units used by each country or can be converted to a unit of your choice. You can search the database for a product or product group using either the Harmonized Code or natural language. Some examples of reports include:

- Import/export figures for the current month and year-to-date trade between a reporting country and all its trading partners
- Year-to-date trade between a reporting country and its key trading partners (quantity value and price) by imports or exports
- Ranking of the value of imports or exports between a reporting country and its partners for a product
- Ten-year annual trend reports between a country and selected trading partners

Exhibit 15-7 is an example of a *TRADSTAT* report that ranks the first 10 countries importing shampoo into Spain based on quantity. Currency is shown in U.S. dollars.

An important feature of the database is its ability to produce "deduced reports" for countries that do not supply figures to *TRADSTAT*. Imports and exports are mirror images of trade. One country's imports are another's exports. For example, the figures for Poland's import of shampoo can be estimated from the export figures for shampoo reported to the 24 countries in the database. China's exports of plastic dolls can be deduced from the corresponding import figures of plastic dolls

from China. It is also possible to produce deduced trade reports for each of the new states created after the break-up of the Soviet Union and Yugoslavia.

For the U.S., *TRADSTAT* includes the names of the ports through which products were exported or imported. The U.S. port data should be identical to the information available on CD-ROM (U.S. Exports and Imports of Merchandise). The data include reporting district (e.g., New York City), the product, and the country of destination or origin.

PIERS Exports/PIERS Imports (Journal of Commerce)

Available online through DIALOG, the *PIERS* databases contain compilations of manifests of vessels loading international cargo at 62 U.S. seaports. The compilations cover all maritime movement into and out of the continental U.S. and Puerto Rico. The records contain the details of each shipment—approximately six million transactions a year.

A search of the *PIERS Imports* database for imports of Chilean grapes into the port of Philadelphia retrieved more than 100 records in the current year. Exhibit 15-8 is a sample record from the *PIERS Imports* database.

Unfortunately, the records do not tell us the value of the shipments. The *PIERS* product code is unique to the database, and is neither an SITC nor a Harmonized System code.

The database allows us to create a report that will total the amount shipped by a variable of our choice. Exhibit 15-9 shows the first few lines of a report of the Philadelphia importers of Chilean grapes sorted by name of importer.

World Trade Atlas (Global Trade Information Service— Monthly)

Anyone who has used the U.S. import/export statistics supplied by the U.S. Commerce Department on CD-ROM will welcome this new product. *World Trade Atlas* contains the same data as the government disc, but uses much better software. Exhibit 15-10 is a sample report from the *World Trade Atlas* ranking countries by U.S. exports. The disc is updated monthly.

PROMT (Predicasts)

The online version of *PROMT* is primarily a bibliographic/full-text file, but it can often be used as a convenient source of merchandise trade data appearing in trade publications. *PROMT* is available on several time-sharing systems, including DIALOG and DATA-STAR. Exhibit 15-11 shows a search for tabular information about Japan's exports of automobiles. The database has the useful feature of allowing us to search for all information in tables. In the DIALOG system, the command is S SF=TABLE.

EXHIBIT 15-7. *TRADSTAT* **Report: Spanish Imports of Shampoo**

TRADSTAT World Trade Statistics   PAGE 1

R3 - IMPORT RANKING   MONTH : 12/92
RUN DATE: 10/05/93

PRODUCT : (HS)33051000

   (HS) SHAMPOOS

REPORTING COUNTRY : SPAIN

COUNTRY IMPORTED FROM	YEAR TO DATE QUANTITY	PERCENTAGE OF TOTAL QUANTITY	YEAR TO DATE VALUE	PRICE
001 FRANCE	5404184	56.39	13737382	2.54
006 U.K.	1514423	15.80	4760175	3.14
	14340	88.66		331.95
010 PORTUGAL	888785	9.27	927293	1.04
004 GERMANY	700927	7.31	2875589	4.10
	1200	7.42		2396.32
400 U.S.A	363940	3.80	1547048	4.25
	128	0.79		12086.31
003 NETHERLANDS	349226	3.64	909005	2.60
005 ITALY	180167	1.88	733386	4.07
	15	0.09		48892.41
002 BELGIUM-LUXEMBOURG	72317	0.75	240096	3.32
404 CANADA	30000	0.31	89418	2.98
007 IRELAND	16124	0.17	117955	7.32
OTHER COUNTRIES	62753	0.65	292034	4.65
	492	3.04		593.57
CALCULATED TOTALS	9582846	100.00	26229382	2.74
	16175	100.00		1621.60

*****QUANTITY OPTIONS: PRIMARY QUANTITY IS SHOWN IN KILOGRAMS
                          NO CONVERSION FACTOR WAS USED
                          A FILTER WAS USED FOR TOP 10 TRADING COUNTRIES
                          LINE 2 SHOWS QUANTITY IN SUPPLEMENTARY UNITS
*****CURRENCY OPTIONS: CURRENCY IS SHOWN IN US DOLLARS
                          CONVERSION FACTOR FROM ORIGINAL UNITS WAS 112.48391

Reprinted with permission from *TRADSTAT*.

EXHIBIT 15-8. Sample Record from *PIERS Imports* Database

10612307
   Product Imported: FRESH GRAPES MIXED
   Product Code: 1461000 (FRUIT)
      Weight of Cargo: 27646 POUNDS
      Number of Units of Cargo: 1140 CASES
Date of Arrival (YY/MM/DD): 920607
Exporter: SISTAGRO
      Company Location: NA, CHILE (337)
U.S.-Based Importer: HILLCREST SALES
      Company Location: BALA CYNWYD, PA
Point of Origin: VALPARAISO (33797), CHILE (337)
U.S. Port of Discharge: PHILADELPHIA (1101)

Reprinted with permission from Journal of Commerce.

EXHIBIT 15-9. Report from *PIERS Imports* Database

PHILADELPHIA IMPORTERS OF GRAPES

1. WILLIAM H KOPKE, LK SUCCESS, NY

Product Description	Country of Origin	Arrival Date	Weight (Pounds)	Quantity
FRESH GRAPES	CHILE	920503	114971	5418 MIX
Exporter: RIO BLANCO EXPORTS, NA, NA				
FRESH GRAPES	CHILE	920503	951296	45030 MIX
Exporter: RIO BLANCO EXPORTS, NA, NA				
FRESH GRAPES	CHILE	920512	6742	312 CASES
Exporter: AGRICOLA & IND LAILHACAR, NA, NA				
•				
•				
•				
FRESH GRAPES	CHILE	920512	2053	96 CASES
Exporter: EXPORTS RIO BLANCO, NA, NA				
>>>Total shipped			1,197,722 pounds	

2. PANDOL BROTHERS, DELANO, CA

Product Description	Country of Origin	Arrival Date	Weight (Pounds)	Quantity
FRESH GRAPES	CHILE	920503	146076	7202 MIX
Exporter: C & D COMMERCIAL, NA, NA				

Reprinted with permission from Journal of Commerce.

EXHIBIT 15-10. Sample Report from *World Trade Atlas*

Global Trade Information Service
World Trade Atlas
Total U.S. Exports

	CALENDAR YEAR				Percent
	Millions of U.S. Dollars		Percent	Share	Change
Rank Country	1991	1992	1991	1992	1992/1991
THE WORLD	421,730	447,471	100	100	6.1
1 CANADA	85,150	90,156	10.1	10.07	5.88
2 JAPAN	48,125	47,764	5.71	5.34	-0.75
3 MEXICO	33,277	40,597	3.95	4.54	22
4 UNITED KINGDOM	22,046	22,808	2.61	2.55	3.46
5 GERMANY	21,302	21,236	2.53	2.37	-0.31
6 TAIWAN	13,182	15,205	1.56	1.7	15.34
7 SOUTH KOREA	15,505	14,630	1.84	1.63	-5.64
8 FRANCE	15,345	14,575	1.82	1.63	-5.02
9 NETHERLANDS	13,511	13,740	1.6	1.54	1.7
10 BELGIUM	10,572	9,779	1.25	1.09	-7.5
11 SINGAPORE	8,804	9,624	1.04	1.08	9.31
12 HONG KONG	8,137	9,069	0.96	1.01	11.45
13 AUSTRALIA	8,404	8,913	1	1	6.05
14 ITALY	8,570	8,698	1.02	0.97	1.5

Reprinted with permission from Global Trade Information Service.

EXHIBIT 15-11. Export Data from *PROMT*

Japan: Auto exports to US (car units)

Company	exports FY91	ceiling FY92e
Toyota	510,489	480,000
Nissan	324,132	290,000
Honda	339,959	320,000
Mazda	210,208	200,000
Mitsubishi	165,284	160,000
Isuzu	93,100	100,000
Fuji Heavy	51,158	70,000
Suzuki	30,236	30,000
Daihatsu	5,910	—

Note: Fiscal years end in March

Source: *Nikkei Weekly,* May 2, 1992, p. 8. Reprinted with permission from Predicasts/IAC.

CHEM-INTELL Production and Trade Statistics (Chemical Intelligence Services)

Available on both DATA-STAR and DIALOG (File 318), this database is a useful source of data for quantity and value of merchandise trade of chemical products. Produced by the U.K.-based Chemical Intelligence Services, it contains annual production and trade totals from 1979 to date as well as trade breakdowns by major trading partner from 1988 to date. Updated monthly, the file contains annual trade and production figures for over 100 organic and inorganic chemicals worldwide, including petrochemicals, fertilizers, polymers, and rubbers. The database reports on:

- production quantities for the latest available 10 years
- import and export figures (quantity and value totals) for the latest available 10 years
- breakdowns of trade for the past two years reported, showing up to 11 major trading partners
- standardised units for quantities (metric tons) and values ('000 U.S. dollars)
- local currency exchange rates showing average rate used to convert from local currency to U.S. dollars

The information in the file is derived from national and international statistical office publications, trade associations, and selected periodicals and research reports. The records are amended as new information becomes available. Exhibit 15-12 is a sample record from the DATA-STAR version of the database reporting on Japanese trade in sulfuric acid. Notice the British spelling of "sulfuric."

SOURCES FOR INTERNATIONAL TRADE IN SERVICES

GATT estimated that the worldwide value of trade in services was $810 billion in 1990, about 20% of the value of merchandise trade. Unlike merchandise trade, the details of international trade in services are scarce. For many countries the only information concerning trade in services is given in their balance of payments figures. It consists of three items: transport, travel (tourism), and other services.

For the U.S., international services transaction statistics are published annually in the September *Survey of Current Business*. The *Survey* provides data in 25 broad categories for some 40 countries and areas. The detailed information presented in the *Survey* is then highly condensed for reporting as part of the quarterly U.S. balance of payments. The U.S. has exceptionally detailed information on service trade.

International Trade in Services: EUR 12, from 1979-1988 (Eurostat, 1991)

Outlined below is Eurostat's classification for trade in services:

Transport
    Sea Freight
    Sea Passenger Transport
    Air Freight
    Air Passenger Transport
    Other Transport
Travel/Tourism
Other Services
    Insurance
    Trade Earnings (merchandising fees)
    Banking (financial institution fees)
    Advertising
    Business Services (e.g., engineering, legal, management)
    Construction
    Communications (postal and telecommunication services)
    Films/Television
    Income from Patents
    Miscellaneous Services

Eurostat has developed data for each of these categories for all EC countries, Japan, and the U.S. for the period 1979 to 1988. Eurostat warns that the figures should be interpreted with caution and trends should be analyzed rather than absolute figures.

Services: Statistics on International Transactions 1970-1989 (Organization for Economic Cooperation and Development, 1992)

The OECD has compiled and assessed data for member countries' international trade in services. The

EXHIBIT 15-12. Sample Record from *CHEM-INTELL Production and Trade Statistics*

PN   Product   076 SULPHURIC ACID
        INORGANICS
CN   Reporting Country   JAPAN
                          ASIA & OCEANIA OECD
YR   91.
TX   Production: as 100% H2SO4.
        Trade: inc oleum.
        Imports: none reported 1981 or 1990.

Year	Annual Production	IMPORTS Quantity	IMPORTS Value	EXPORTS Quantity	EXPORTS Value	Exchange Rate
1982	6530897	4	10	788953	16849	249.0500
1983	6661754	2	2	723322	13794	237.5200
1984	6457509	8901	348	199052	3895	237.5200
1985	6580213	5	13	322568	6323	238.5275
1986	6562434	13	68	500421	9307	168.5175
1987	6541300	58	46	510209	10274	144.6670
1988	6766400	46	27	526032	14684	128.2220
1989	6885500	17	9	800441	17560	138.0600
1990	6887000			731543	20984	144.2780
1991	7057000	17	16	846442	42651	125.2000

TRADE BREAKDOWN

IMPORTS 1991

Country	QTY	%	Value
KOREA, SOUTH	16	95	8
USA	1	5	8

EXPORTS 1990

Country	QTY	%	Value
KOREA, SOUTH	153883	21	13611
TAIWAN	203784	28	2032
THAILAND	20470	3	542
PHILIPPINES	158334	22	1646
INDONESIA	79646	11	1569
USSR	449		181
USA	31023	4	409
CHILE	41992	6	324
BRAZIL	4	3	
GUINEA	11		119
1622			
AUSTRALIA	41933	6	514
OTHERS	14		35

EXPORTS 1991

Country	QTY	%	Value
KOREA, SOUTH	162780	19	15044
KOREA, NORTH	8		9
TAIWAN	195104	23	3414
THAILAND	17522	2	491
PHILIPPINES	131748	16	5194
INDONESIA	40093	5	1435
USSR	200		93
USA	109014	13	6473
MEXICO	126275	15	8674
CHILE	42268		5
AUSTRALIA	21424	3	165
OTHERS	8		38

QUANTITIES IN METRIC TONS, VALUES IN THOUSAND US DOLLARS

series represent balance of payments data between residents of the reporting countries and nonresidents. Section A of the report presents data for the whole OECD area and for the main services categories. The structure of this section is derived from the standard components of the balance of payments. Section B presents data for individual countries. Data are shown in both national currency and U.S. dollars.

SOURCES FOR CAPITAL FLOW STATISTICS

Worldwide, foreign direct investment totals over $225 billion annually and represents an investment stock of about $1.7 trillion The investment is highly concentrated; about three-fourths of world investment flows take place among developed countries, in particular the

U.S., the EC, and Japan. About two-thirds of all investment flows to developing countries are directed to just 10 countries.

The source for the above information is the annual *World Investment Report,* a publication of the United Nation's Transnational Corporations and Management Division. Published since 1991, each *World Investment Report* has a distinctive title and theme. The 1991 edition was subtitled *The Triad in Foreign Direct Investment.* The 1992 edition was subtitled *Transnational Corporations as Engines of Growth.* The "Annex Tables" in the 1992 edition provide information concerning international comparisons of direct foreign investment. Examples of the tables include:

- Foreign direct investment inward flows, by region and economy, 1980-1990
- Average annual inflows of foreign direct investment to the 10 largest developing economies receiving foreign direct investment
- Pattern of foreign direct investment from the U.S., Japan, and the EC to developing and Central and Eastern European countries, 1989 and 1985-89
- The relative importance of foreign direct investment in host countries
- Changes in main national legislation relating to foreign direct investment in 1991

A related series by the UN's Transnational Corporations and Management Division are the six volumes of the *World Investment Directory.* The volumes in the series are:

Volume 1. *Asia and the Pacific*
Volume 2. *Central and Eastern Europe*
Volume 3. *Developed Countries*
Volume 4. *Latin America and the Caribbean*
Volume 5. *Africa and West Asia*
Volume 6. *Global Trends*

Collectively, the series has data for approximately 100 countries. The directories give data on foreign direct investment, basic data on businesses, the legal framework for investment, and extensive bibliographic sources. Each directory cautions that foreign direct investment statistics suffer from a lack of comparability and advise users to read the technical introduction and explanatory notes carefully.

The detail of the data presented varies by country. The following series are often available for a country:

- Number of foreign affiliates
- Sectoral distribution of foreign investment
- Industrial distribution of foreign investment
- Geographic distribution for foreign investment
- List of largest foreign affiliates in the country
- Largest transnational corporation abroad

The data on direct investment flows are presented as 10-year time series, although for many countries most of the series may be absent. Exhibit 15-13 is a summary table for Poland from the *World Investment Directory.*

The *World Investment Directory* is designed to be an update and an extension of the *IRM Directory of Statistics of International Investment and Production* by John Dunning and John Cantwell. The *IRM Directory* assembled data on the international direct investment position of 80 countries in a systematic and comparable way. Although dated (1985), the *IRM Directory* was the first source to address issues of data quality and comparability of balance of payments statistics.

In the U.S., the Bureau of Economic Analysis (BEA) has the major role in collecting data on foreign direct investment. The BEA conducts quarterly, annual, and benchmark surveys of U.S. direct investment abroad and of foreign direct investment in the U.S. The information often appears initially in the *Survey of Current Business.* The major information series on foreign direct investment contained in the *Survey* and the month they appear are listed below:

- Direct investment position and flows of capital, income, royalties and license fees between parent companies and affiliates (June issue)
- Capital expenditures by majority-owned foreign affiliates of U.S. companies (March and September issues)
- Financial structure and operations of U.S. parent companies and their foreign affiliates (month varies; August in 1992)
- Financial structure and operations of U.S. affiliates of foreign companies (May issue)
- U.S. business enterprises acquired or established by foreign direct investors (May issue)

In 1992, the Bureau of Economic Analysis in cooperation with the Bureau of the Census published highly detailed establishment level data on foreign direct investment in the United States. The data give the number, employment, payroll, and sales of the establishments of U.S. affiliates of foreign companies in 1987. In 1993 expanded information will be published for 1989 and 1990 on the manufacturing establishments of U.S. affiliates. The information was published in summary form in the October 1992 *Survey of Current Business* and as a 650-page publication entitled *Foreign Direct Investment in the United States: Establishment Data for 1987.*

CAVEATS FOR RESEARCHERS

The balance of payments and its components can generate many research questions. Before beginning our

EXHIBIT **15-13. Poland's International Investment Position**

Table 1. Summary of international investment position
(Millions of dollars)

Variable	Inward	Outward
1. Flow of foreign direct investment '86 -'91 (annual av.)	111.7[b]	2.7[c]
2. Flow of foreign direct investment as percentage of GDCF	—	—
3. Foreign direct- investment stock 1991	670.0[b]	146.1[d]
4. Foreign direct- investment stock as percentage of GDP	—	—
5. Employment in foreign affiliates, 1990	85249	27[e]
6. Sales of foreign affiliates, 1990	1380.8[f]	4200.8
7. Number of foreign affiliates, 1991	15100	202[g]
8. Number of transnational corporations	—	58

Source: United Nations, Economic Commission for Europe, ECE database on East-West joint ventures; United Nations Department of Economic and Social Development, Transnational Corporation and Management Division, the *East-West Business Directory 1991/1992* (United Nations publication, Sales Nol. E.92.II A.20); and Carleton University, East-West Project database.

  a Excludes "Polnia" investments.

  b As of the end of the third quarter 1991.

  c Includes only 1980-1990 annual average investment in developed countries.

  d Includes only investments in operational foreign affiliates in developed countries, end-1990.

  e Average estimated employment in foreign affiliates located in developed countries, per company, 1990.

  f Sales of 1,119 operational foreign affiliates, end-1990.

  g Number of operational foreign affiliates only, end-1990.

Source: UNCTC World Investment Directory, (New York: UN, 1992). Reprinted with permission.

research, we should be aware of the issues of data comparability between countries and data availability from individual countries. Here are examples of plausible sounding questions, tasks for which it will be difficult or impossible to find information in secondary sources or which have hidden assumptions in the data available.

- *Compare the amount of direct foreign investment in the U.K. with the amount of direct foreign investment in the U.S.* These figures can be found in the IMF *Balance of Payments Yearbook* and other sources. However they should be used with care. The U.K. and the U.S. have different definitions of direct foreign investment. The U.K. defines foreign investment as ownership of 20% or more voting shares of all directly and indirectly owned subsidiary companies. The U.S. uses 10% ownership. In addition, the two countries use different accounting principles to compile financial data and have different methods of collecting the data.
- *What is the total annual value of laser printers exported from South Korea?* South Korea does not publish detailed export statistics. Statistics from international organizations will report trade statistics from South Korea. None will be detailed enough to capture a product as specific as laser printers. Sometimes we can derive the exports from nonreporting countries from the corresponding imports of countries that do report. For example, we can determine South Korea's exports of laser printers to the U.S. from the U.S.'s imports of laser printers from South Korea.

- *What are the annual sales by U.S.-owned firms to U.S. affiliates of foreign firms in the U.S? What are the sales of foreign-owned firms abroad to foreign affiliates of U.S. firms abroad? How much U.S. currency is held by non-U.S. residents?* These three questions are examples of gaps in the collection of data for the balance of payments. Exact numbers are not available.[8]

ADDITIONAL SOURCES

Balance of Payments

Balance of Payments Manual (International Monetary Fund, 1977, 4th ed.)

This guidebook for member countries reporting balance of payments statistics is also used as a model by the OECD and the EC. It is a convenient source for definitions of the components of the balance of payments.

Merchandise Trade

Handbook of International Trade and Development Statistics (United Nations—Annual)

The *Handbook* presents merchandise data analytically. The tables emphasize growth rates, rank order, and extended time series.

Foreign Trade by Commodities (Organization for Economic Cooperation and Development—Annual)

This annual comprises multiple volumes, each of which contains import/export data at the 2-digit SITC level for six OECD member countries. A final volume contains data arranged by country groups (the OECD, North America, Europe, the EC).

External Trade Analytical Tables (Eurostat—Annual)

The *Tables* give breakdowns by 8-digit Harmonized Code category by country for EC member countries for imports and exports. A second breakdown of country by 2-digit code is also presented. The EC began using the Harmonized Code to report trade statistics in 1988. Before 1988, they used the Nomenclature of Goods for the External Trade Statistics of the Community (NIMEXE). Eurostat publishes CD-ROM versions of the EC's annual and monthly trade as well as historical data on CD-ROM (external trade 1976-87).

National Trade Estimate Report on Foreign Trade Barriers (Office of the U.S. Trade Representative—Annual)

The *Report* supplies an inventory of the most important foreign barriers to U.S. exports of goods and services and barriers affecting U.S. investment and intellectual property rights. The publication gives quantitative estimates of the impact of these foreign practices on the value of U.S. exports. The trade barriers include laws, regulations, and policies that either protect domestic products from foreign competition or artificially stimulate exports of particular domestic products. The *Report* covers more than 40 countries and the EC.

The Year in Trade: Operation of the Trade Agreements Program (U.S. International Trade Commission—Annual)

This report provides factual information on U.S. trade policy and its administration together with an historical record of major trade-related activities of the past year. It is an excellent source of information on the activities of GATT and of other trade-related organizations, such as the OECD, the Customs Cooperation Council, and the UN Conference on Trade and Develop-

ment. It gives a good overview of existing U.S. trade agreements, such as the U.S.-Canada Free Trade Agreement, and pending legislation, in particular NAFTA (North American Free Trade Agreement). Chapters are devoted to developments with the major U.S. trading partners (the EC, Canada, Japan, Mexico, South Korea, Taiwan, and Brazil).

Behind the Numbers: U.S. Trade in the World Economy (National Academy Press, 1992).

This book gives a clear statement of the problems of international data collection for the balance of payments with proposals for improvements.

CONCLUSION

This chapter discussed the concepts and sources of information for international trade and payments. The balance of trade was used as a framework to discuss merchandise trade, international service transaction, and capital flow. There is great variation in the quantity and quality of data available for international trade and payments. A country's import data, for example, are often detailed and of good quality. Capital flow data, in contrast, are sketchy and of poor quality.

NOTES

1. Franklin R. Root, *International Trade and Investment* (Cincinnati: South Western Publication, 1990), p. 349.
2. *U.S. Merchandise Trade: Exports, General Imports, and Imports for Consumption* (U.S. Department of Commerce, May 1992), p. 5.
3. *Foreign Direct Investment and Transnational Corporations in Services* (United Nations, 1989), p. 4.
4. Marie-Paule Benassi,*International Trade in Services: Eur 12, from 1979 to 1988.* (Luxembourg: Office for Official Publications of the European Communities, 1991).
5. *Behind the Numbers:U.S. Trade in the World Economy* (Washington, DC: National Academy Press, 1992), pp. 156-57.
6. Clive Crook, "Fear of Finance," *Economist* (September 19, 1992), p. 6.
7. *Behind the Numbers*, p. 38.
8. *Behind the Numbers*, pp. 33-40.

CHAPTER 16
International Financial Markets

TOPICS COVERED

MAJOR SOURCES DISCUSSED

- DATASTREAM
- *European Directory of Financial Information Sources*
- *G.T. Guide to World Equity Markets*
- *Emerging Markets Factbook*
- *Moody's International Manual*
- *Morgan Stanley Capital International Perspective*
- *Quarterly Review of Emerging Stock Markets*
- REUTERLINK
- *Tradeline International*
- *World Financial Markets*
- *World Currency Monitor Annual. U.S. Dollar*
- *World Currency Yearbook*

INTRODUCTION

Financial markets are concerned with the purchase or sale of one or more types of financial instruments, such as stocks or bonds. International financial markets are involved with financial transactions that cross national frontiers. Financial markets sometimes operate through exchanges, physical locations, such as the New York or London stock exchanges. Financial exchanges involve members who purchase the right to trade securities. Alternatively, financial markets may be communication networks (computer links and telephones) between buyers and sellers. Financial instruments not traded on exchanges are said to trade OTC (Over the Counter). The globalization of financial markets may be making physical exchanges obsolete as electronic networks allow 24-hour trading around the world.[1]

Table 16-A summarizes the chief types of international financial markets, gives a brief description of their purpose, and lists a typical financial instrument.

International financial markets use many of the same financial instruments employed in domestic markets, including stocks, bonds, options, and futures. However, international markets may denominate these instruments in foreign currencies, in Eurocurrencies, or in composite currencies such as the ECU (European Currency Unit). In addition, there are specialized instruments of international financial markets, such as currency and interest rate swaps and foreign exchange forwards. The market for foreign currency is by its nature international in scope.

Specific factual questions about financial markets are often of two types. The first type concerns the operations and characteristics of the markets as a whole.

- What are the name, address, and principal officers of the Amsterdam exchange?
- What are the types and number of financial instruments traded on the London Stock Exchange?
- What has been the overall performance of the Tokyo Stock Exchange?
- How do the world's stock markets rank by size?

The second type of question concerns the characteristics and performance of specific financial instruments.

- What was the high, low, and close of Sumitomo Corporation's stock on the Tokyo exchange on July 2, 1991? during 1990? for the past 10 years?
- What types of options, if any, are available on Sumitomo Corporation stock?

Table 16-A. International Financial Markets and Instruments

Type of Market	Purpose	Typical Financial Instrument
Stock Market	Purchase or sale of equities	Common Stock
Bond Market	Purchase or sale of long-term debt obligations	Bonds
Money Market	Purchase or sale of short-term debt obligations	Commercial Paper
Foreign Exchange Market	Exchange of one country's currency for another country's	Forward
Commodity Market	Purchase or sale of agreements to take delivery of a commodity often at some date in the future	Future
Options Market	Purchase or sale of rights to buy or sell securities on or before a future date	Put/Call

- What is today's U.S. dollar to Japanese yen exchange rate?
- What is a current rating for the bonds of the Tokyo Electric Power Company?

In this chapter we will briefly describe the principal types of international financial markets and financial instruments and discuss sources of information for both.

FOREIGN EXCHANGE MARKETS

Central to all international transactions is the value of a country's currency in terms of another currency. Consequently, the market that has the greatest effect on all other financial markets is the foreign exchange market. Foreign exchange involves the buying and selling of currencies. Foreign exchange markets are the institutional arrangements through which such purchases and sales are made. They allow the free flow of goods and services among countries by providing a medium of exchange. A foreign exchange rate is the price of one country's currency in terms of another country's currency. In addition, exchange rates are important as economic indicators and as a means for the cross-border comparison of industries and companies.

Although there are no precise statistics on the volume of foreign exchange trading around the world, it is immense, perhaps a trillion dollars a day. Only about 5% of foreign exchange transactions are conducted by traders in goods and services.[2] Most transactions are the result of foreign exchange risk from fluctuations in currency values, or of speculators attempting to profit by the same fluctuations. London is the leading center of foreign exchange transactions with about 25% of the business. About 15% is handled in New York and 10% in Tokyo. The remainder of foreign trade transactions are

spread among several cities, including Frankfurt, Singapore, and Hong Kong.[3] A central part of the foreign exchange operation mechanism is the computer system of the Clearing House Interbank Payments System (CHIPS). Described as "the heart of global capitalism," CHIPS is owned by 11 large New York banks. When currency is converted into or out of dollars, it is often processed through the CHIPS computers because of their speed and low cost.[4]

In the *spot* foreign exchange market, currencies are purchased and sold for immediate delivery within two business days after the day the transaction is agreed upon. In the *forward* market, foreign currencies are purchased and sold for future delivery (usually 30 or 90 days). A foreign exchange *swap* combines a spot purchase of a currency with the simultaneous sale of a forward on the same currency. A swap reduces the risk of switching from one currency to another and back again.

Although there are more than 150 currencies in the world, only about 50 countries have currencies that are actively traded. Key currencies include the U.S. dollar, the British pound, the Deutschmark, and the Japanese yen. In addition to national currencies, there are two important composite currencies: the ECU (European Currency Unit) and the SDR (Special Drawing Right). The ECU is the official currency unit for the European Monetary System, which was established in 1979. The ECU is a weighted average of currencies of EC members. Its value relative to the U.S. dollar is calculated daily. The SDR is an artificial currency created by the International Monetary Fund (IMF). Its value is determined as a weighted average of the U.S. dollar, the German mark, the French franc, the Japanese yen, and the British pound. Both the ECU and the SDR are used as a means of payment and loan. The ECU may be held by private individuals. Ownership of the SDR is confined to governments, although individuals may own financial instruments denominated in SDRs. The ECU is much more widely employed than the SDR.

Countries sometimes link or peg their currency to that of another country or to a basket of currencies. For example, several African nations (Niger, Senegal, Togo) peg their currency to the French franc. These "exchange rate arrangements" are listed in the IMF's monthly *International Financial Statistics*.

Currency Quotations

Currencies can be quoted in terms of the number of units of currency A to currency B (for example, the number of U.S. dollars required to "buy" one Deutschmark) or in terms of the number of units of currency B to currency A (the number of Deutschmarks required to "buy" a U.S. dollar). The two exchange rates are reciprocals. For example, if there are 1.75 Deutschmarks per U.S. dollar (if one dollar will buy 1.75 DM), there are 1/1.75 or .5714 U.S. dollars per Deutschmark (the Deutschmark is worth about 57 cents).

The relative value of two non-U.S. currencies is usually determined by comparison of the value of each against the U.S. dollar. These exchange rates are called "cross rates." If you know the exchange rate of two currencies to the dollar, you can calculate the cross rate. For example, if a U.S. dollar is worth 1.3301 Australian dollars and 1.7232 New Zealand dollars, the exchange rate of the Australian to the New Zealand dollar is:

$$1.7232/1.3301 = 1.2950$$

The Australian dollar is thus worth 1.2950 New Zealand dollars.

Exchange rates are usually quoted to four decimal places. Transactions in these currencies usually involve one million units of currency. Exchange rates may be expressed as a bid price (the price at which a bank is willing to buy the currency) and an asked price (a higher price for which banks are ready to sell a currency). The difference between selling and buying rates is called the spread. Occasionally, rates will be reported as mid-point rates (the mid-point between the bid and asked price). When one price is given as the exchange rate, it is usually the selling price (the asked price).

There are several potential pitfalls in interpreting foreign currency exchange rates. Some issues to be aware of are:

• How was the rate quoted? For example, a weekly U.S. dollar to Japanese yen exchange rate may be calculated as an average of the week or may be the closing rate at the end of the week. A daily rate may be calculated at different times of the day.

• Where was the rate quoted? An exchange rate that represents the daily close in New York may be different from the closing rate for the same day in London.

• What does an exchange rate represent? Exchange rates may be expressed as *bid rates* (the rate at which a dealer is willing to buy a currency), *asked rates* (the rate at which a dealer is willing to sell a currency), or *mid-point rates* (the average of the bid and asked rate).

To clearly define what its exchange rates represent, the *Federal Reserve Bulletin* uses the following footnote in its table of monthly and annual rates: "Averages of certified noon buying rates in New York for cable transfers."

In addition, exchange rates may be expressed as "trade weighted" or as "real exchange rates." Trade weighted exchange rates take into consideration the importance of a country's trading patterns in determining the value of its currency. For the United States, changes in the value of the Canadian dollar (a leading trading partner) would be of more importance (would have a greater weight) than changes in the Italian lira. Real exchange rates adjust nominal exchange rates for the differences in inflation among countries. Trade weighted and real exchange rates are expressed as index numbers. The relation between goods prices and exchange rates is known as purchasing power parity. Purchasing power parity is described in more detail in Chapter 13.

Be aware of devaluations or revaluations of currency rates that you are reporting. Countries with high inflation frequently devalue or revalue their currencies. For example, in December 1989 the exchange rate of the Yugoslavian dinar was about 118,000 to the dollar. In January 1990, a new dinar was issued that was worth 10,000 of the old. Some sources (the *World Currency Monitor Annual*, for example) will show the abrupt transition caused by a revaluation.

Example 1:
Yugoslavian dinars per U.S. dollar
End of Period

	Nov.	Dec.	Jan.
	77,619	118,160	11.8200

Other sources (*International Financial Statistics*, for example) will recalculate the old exchange rates to bring them into line with the revaluation.

Example 2:
Yugoslavian dinars per U.S. dollar
End of Period

	Nov.	Dec.	Jan.
	7.7619	11.816	11.8200

The purpose of retroactively recalculating the exchange rate is to represent the rate of change over time accurately. For example, the value of the Yugoslavian dinar declined about 52% against the U.S. dollar between November 1989 and January 1990. This change can be determined from the figures in the second example shown above. The figures in the first example, by themselves, would indicate that the dinar's value against the dollar *increased* over 6,500% in the same period. However, recalculated exchange rates can be misleading if we need the historical exchange rates for accounting purposes, or if we are unaware that a revaluation has occurred. This is one instance in which printed sources may be superior to machine-readable numeric databases. Printed sources typically explain the details of currency revaluations. Machine-readable sources usually give only the numbers without explanation.

When you are reporting the value of a currency that does not "float" (that is not freely convertible into other currencies and has an exchange rate set by a government), there will be a parallel market ("black market") rate of exchange in addition to an official rate. There also may be more than one official rate. For example, Iran in 1992 was using three different official exchange rates for its currency, the rial. In addition, there was a "black market" rate. At the official exchange rate, the dollar was worth around 70 Iranian rials in January 1992. Iran also used two other rates, one for travelers and one for certain business transactions; these rates valued the rial more closely to its black market rate of about 1,400 rials to the dollar.

Information Sources for Foreign Exchange. Business newspapers are a good, if limited, source of foreign exchange rates. For example, each issue of the *Wall Street Journal* includes currency cross rates for nine major currencies. In addition, the *WSJ* gives the exchange rates of 50 currencies for the previous two days. The equivalents are given both as U.S. dollar equivalents per foreign currency, and foreign currency per U.S. dollar. In addition to exchange rates, the table gives forward rates (for 30, 90, and 180 days) for major world currencies. A weekly table ("World Value of the Dollar") gives the current and previous exchange rate of the dollar against 150 currencies. The same tables are also available online through the DOW JONES NEWS RETRIEVAL System described below.

Foreign Exchange Rates (Federal Reserve Board—Weekly)

The Federal Reserve Board's statistical release *Foreign Exchange Rates* is a widely quoted source of exchange rates. The single sheet release gives rates against the dollar for 31 currencies, including the ECU, for each day of trading during the week. In addition, it gives an

index of U.S. trade weighted exchange value against the currencies of the G-10 countries. Exchange rates from the Federal Reserve Board are available from the U.S. Census Bureau's Electronic Bulletin Board, which is available on the Internet. Exhibit 16-1 shows the Electronic Bulletin Board listing.

EXHIBIT 16-1. U.S. Electronic Bulletin Board Listing of Currency Values

FEDERAL RESERVE BANK
OF NEW YORK

Value of Foreign Currencies

Country	Monetary Unit	Noon Buying Rates for Cable Transfer in N.Y. Value in Foreign Currency Unit
*Australia	Dollar	0.7150
Austria	Schilling	11.2980
Belgium	Franc	33.0400
Brazil	Cruzeiro	N/A
Canada	Dollar	1.2580
China, P.R.	Yuan	N/A
Denmark	Krone	6.1550
*European Curr Unit	ECU	1.2150
Finland	Markka	5.5600
France	Franc	5.4200
Germany	Mark	1.6050
Greece	Drachma	219.3000
Hong Kong	Dollar	7.7302
India	Rupee	31.6000
*Ireland	Pound	1.5185
Israel	Shekel	N/A
Italy	Lira	1532.5000
Japan	Yen	111.1000
Malaysia	Dollar	2.5732
Netherlands	Guilder	1.8040
*New Zealand	Dollar	0.5399
Norway	Krone	6.8025
Philippines	Pesos	N/A
Portugal	Escudo	148.4000
Singapore	Dollar	1.6207
South Africa	Rand	3.1700
South Korea	Won	798.9000
Spain	Peseta	116.3500
Sri Lanka	Rupee	47.8300
Sweden	Krona	7.4275
Switzerland	Franc	1.4620
Taiwan	N.T. Dollar	25.8800
Thailand	Baht	25.2000
*United Kingdom	Pound	1.5363
Venezuela	Bolivar	N/A

* Value in U.S. dollars

The noon buying rates in New York for cable transfers payable in foreign currencies are certified by the Federal Reserve Bank of New York for customs purposes, as required by Section 522 of the amended Tariff Act of 1930. The information is based on data collected by the Federal Reserve Bank of New York from a sample of market participants and is intended only for informational purposes. The data were obtained from sources believed to be reliable but this bank does not guarantee their accuracy, completeness or correctness.

World Currency Monitor Annual. U.S. Dollar (Meckler—Annual)

The *World Currency Monitor* gives weekly values of the U.S. dollar in terms of 99 world currencies. Sponsored by the Bank of America World Information Services, the *Monitor's* 1989 edition covers the period January 5, 1976 through December 25, 1989. The section of the work entitled "Currency Exchange Rate Arrangements" gives the details of currency devaluations and specifies what rate (official or market) is being quoted.

A similar yearbook was published for the British pound (*World Currency Monitor Annual. Pound Sterling*). Although no longer published, this source is useful for its historical time series.

International Financial Statistics (International Monetary Fund—Monthly)

International Financial Statistics gives several time series of exchange rates per U.S. dollars and in terms of SDRs (Special Drawing Rights). The publication will print market values if available, otherwise it gives official rates. The time series give figures for each of the most current seven months, quarterly figures for the past three years, and annual figures for the preceding seven years. In addition to actual exchange rates, the IMF provides indexes of exchange rates adjusted for inflation and for trading patterns. The *International Financial Statistics Yearbook* gives 30 years of annual statistics for many of the same statistics that appear in the monthly publication. Older editions of the *Yearbook* will give series as far back as 1949. The *International Financial Statistics Yearbook* is described in more detail in Chapter 13.

World Currency Yearbook (International Currency Analysis Inc.—Annual)

Formerly titled *Pick's Currency Yearbook,* the *World Currency Yearbook* is a convenient source of historical information *about* currencies. The work gives the history, currency developments, transferability, and currency administration for some 147 nations. Included in each description is a 10-year currency history, official and "black market" exchange rates, and a photograph of the currency. In addition to its descriptions of national currencies, the *World Currency Yearbook* provides useful descriptions and statistics on the Eurocurrency market, currency and trade areas, currency control categories, and the international black market for currency. Appendixes include statistics on currency circulation and money supply per capita, the devaluation of paper money, and a directory of central banks.

Electronic Sources for Exchange Rates. Printed sources of exchange rates are awkward to use if we are dealing with several countries' rates over an extended period. Online databases not only simplify gathering exchange rates, they are essential for much foreign exchange data retrieval. Although many of the printed sources of exchange rates exist as well in machine-readable form, foreign exchange data often exit exclusively in computer form. Because exchange rates are constantly in flux, determining a currency's rate as it changes throughout the day requires access to a time-sharing online system that is continuously updated. Professional foreign exchange dealers use systems such as Telerate and Globex. Access to real-time quotes or intraday quotes is also available through such general time-sharing systems as DIALOG and DOW JONES NEWS RETRIEVAL.

DIALOG/MoneyCenter (DIALOG)

This real-time menu-driven financial database from Knight-Ridder Financial Information includes not only foreign exchange quotes, but also quotes and news from all major U.S. and international cash, futures, and options markets. Exhibit 16-2 is a report on foreign exchange as it appears on *DIALOG/MoneyCenter.* The two rates given are bid and asked.

DOW JONES NEWS RETRIEVAL

DOW JONES NEWS RETRIEVAL reports the value of major currencies throughout the day on its *Wires* database. In addition, it provides a table of over 50 world currencies for the previous two days. The rates represent closing asked quotations in New York at 3 p.m. The tables include forward rates for several currencies as well as SDR and ECU rates. The spot prices of major currencies are updated hourly on the Dow Jones *Futures* database. Exhibit 16-3 shows the format Dow Jones uses for presenting currency spot prices.

EXHIBIT 16-2. *DIALOG/MoneyCenter* **Report**

Fixed Page 804   06/07 10:57 EDT

World Foreign Exchange Cross Rates, US, UK, DM, SF & JY

Currency	US-1	UK-1	DM-1	SF-1	JY-1000
US		1.6720-.6735	.5655-.5658	.6594-.6598	7.1235-.1266
UK	.5976-.5979		.3379-.3383	.3940-.3945	4.2567-.2617
DM	1.7675-.7785	2.9561-.9596		1.1642-.1656	12.587- .599
FF	5.9840-.9855	9.980820.0167	3.3946-.3874	3.9459-.9495	42.627- .653
SF	1.5165-.5165	2.5347-.5479	.8572-.8582		10.806- .817
IL	1308.0-10.0	2188.3-92.9	739.8-41.2	862.6-4.2	9317.6-35.1
CD	1.1469-.1484	1.9191-.9111	.6486-.6491	.7660-.7674	82.705-.770
JY	139.33-44800	234.60-.936	79.37-.45	92.54-.53	
AD	1.3289-.3301	2.2226-.2260	.7516-.7528	.8763-.8877	9.466-.479
BF	36.34-.35	.6080-.6085	20.68-.59	23.96-.98	259.81-.28
NG	1.9910-.9925	3.3209-.3354	1.1261-.1273	1.3130-.3144	14.283-.199
DK	6.7340-.7890	11.367-.379	3.8360-.8410	4.4785-.4835	48.363-.419
NK	6.8825-.8875	1.1526-.1541	3.8999-.9049	4.5363-.5426	49.017-.070
HK	7.7325-.7355	13.035-.048	4.4754-.4796	5.0972-.1026	55.055-.116
NZ	1.7218-.7232	2.8707-.8840	.9741-.9755	1.1451-.1365	12.362-.376
SD	1.7800-.7810	2.9776-.9814	1.0157-.0175	1.1738-.1749	1.2680-.2692

Reprinted with permission from Knight-Ridder Financial Information.

EXHIBIT 16-3. Currency Rates on Dow Jones *Futures* **Database**

AUSTRALIAN DOLLAR-SPOT (IMM); $ PER AD$;

DATE: 6/5/92

	OPEN	HIGH	LOW	LAST	CHANGE
INDX	7625	7630	7625	7627	+ 4

DEUTSCHE MARK-SPOT (IMM): $ PER MARK.;

DATE: 6/5/92

	OPEN	HIGH	LOW	LAST	CHANGE
INDX	6271	6297	6271	6292	+ 44

Copyright © Dow Jones & Company, Inc., 1993. Reprinted with permission. DOW JONES NEWS/RETRIEVAL is a registered trademark of Dow Jones & Company, Inc.

The exchange rates in Exhibit 16-3 require interpretation. The 7627 figure given for the last Australian dollar quote indicates that the exchange is .7627 U.S. dollar per Australian dollar. Spot currency prices are available daily on *DOW JONES NEWS RETRIEVAL* from April 1991 to date.

Econbase (DIALOG).

DIALOG's *Econbase* is a convenient online source for monthly and annual time series of foreign exchange rates of major currencies against the dollar. The database also contains one-year forecasts for annual exchange rates. *Econbase* can be searched by series codes or with natural language. The database contains exchange rates for 21 currencies. Exhibit 16-4 shows the first few entries for the record of the monthly exchange rate of the Japanese yen.

Other Time-Sharing Sources. Long time series of daily data for currencies can be retrieved from several online systems. IDD's *TRADELINE* database, for example, gives historical reports (daily, weekly, monthly, quarterly, or yearly rates) for 154 currencies. In addition, *TRADELINE* allows retrieval of comparison reports (multiple currencies for a single day) and reports showing percent change over time. IDD's database consists of calculated cross rates from the British pound.

The DATASTREAM and ReuterLink online systems are examples of time-sharing databases designed to retrieve multi-year time series of daily data. Both systems give daily rates from major markets worldwide. In addition, the systems are designed to download large quantities of data directly into spreadsheets. DATASTREAM and ReuterLink are described in more detail later in this chapter.

THE WORLD'S FINANCIAL EXCHANGES

Most of the world's exchanges have transactions in stock. In addition to equities, stock exchanges are often involved with the trading of fixed interest instruments such as bonds. However, most bonds are traded OTC and not on exchanges. Some stock exchanges trade options on stocks (so-called "equity options"). Futures and commodity options are usually traded on exchanges that specialize in these instruments. Foreign exchange trans-

---

Exhibit 16-4. *Econbase*—**Japanese Yen Per U.S. Dollar**

Series Code: MF8117
Corp Source: FRB; TABLE 3.28, FEDERAL RESERVE BULLETIN
Start Date: JANUARY, 1971 (7101)
Frequency: MONTHLY
Units: JAPANESE YEN PER US DOLLAR

1992	JAN	125.4600				
1991	JAN	133.7000	FEB	130.5400	MAR	137.3900
	APR	137.1100	MAY	138.2200	JUN	139.7500
	JUL	137.8300	AUG	136.8200	SEP	134.3000
	OCT	130.7700	NOV	129.6300	DEC	128.0400
1990	JAN	144.9800	FEB	145.6900	MAR	153.3100
	APR	158.4600	MAY	154.0400	JUN	153.7000
	JUL	149.0400	AUG	147.4600	SEP	138.4400
	OCT	129.5900	NOV	129.2200	DEC	133.8900
1989	JAN	127.3600	FEB	127.7400	MAR	130.5500

Reprinted with permission of the WEFA Group.

actions in the spot and forward markets and Eurocurrency transactions are conducted among banks and not on formal exchanges.

Stock Markets

The world market value of outstanding equity issues in 1990 was about $10 trillion. There are more than 100 stock markets on which equities are traded. However, the market value of stocks (the value of stock traded on the exchange) is highly concentrated in a few markets. For example, the New York Stock Exchange and the Tokyo exchange together control about 40% of the value of stocks traded worldwide. The 10 largest exchanges ranked by value of outstanding equity issues account for 80% of the value of all equity issues.

In addition to being listed on national exchanges, large companies sometimes list their shares on foreign exchanges as well. A company such as Royal Dutch Shell, for example, is traded on a dozen markets. The requirements for foreign share listing vary greatly among the world's exchanges. In the U.S., a company must meet the requirements of both the exchange (such as the New York Stock Exchange) and the U.S. Securities and Exchange Commission. The expense and reporting requirements that foreign share listing requires has the effect of restricting direct listing in the U.S. to a few hundred companies.

20-F Filings. Foreign companies that list their shares on U.S. exchanges are required to file annual reports with the Securities and Exchange Commission within six months after the end of their fiscal year. These reports, called 20-F, are functionally equivalent to the 10-K reports required by U.S. companies. Approximately 370 companies file 20-F reports; 75 of these are listed on the New York Stock Exchange. A comprehensive list of companies filing 20-F reports together with extensive extracts from the reports is available from Disclosure/SEC on CD-ROM or Disclosure online. Table 16-B is a representative list of companies on the New York Stock Exchange that file 20-F reports.

The complete texts of 20-F filings are available in electronic form from SEC-Online for companies listed on the New York and American stock exchanges. Facsimiles of the reports of all companies filing are available from Disclosure, Inc. on microfiche or in CD-ROM image format.

American Depositary Receipts. Companies sometimes trade their stock in foreign markets without direct listing on an exchange. In the U.S., foreign shares can be listed as American Depositary Receipts (ADRs). U.S. banks accept deposits of foreign shares and issue ADRs in the name of the foreign company. About 850 companies trade ADRs in the U.S. For example, Broken Hill Proprietary Co., Ltd., an Australian company, trades American Depositary Receipts on the New York Stock Exchange. The ADRs were issued by Morgan Guaranty Trust. Each ADR issued after May 28, 1987 represents four shares of Broken Hill Proprietary stock. Companies trading ADRs are listed in *Standard & Poor's Corporation Record* and *Moody's International Manual.* These sources give the details of the initial ADR offering, the price when issued, and the trading range of the ADRs. A source for comprehensive listings of companies issuing ADRs is *Hoover's Handbook of World Business.*

Table 16-B. Representative Companies on the New York Stock Exchange Filing 20-F Reports

COMPANY NAME	CITY	TICKER SYMBOL
AEGON NV	THE HAGUE NETHERLANDS	AEG
ALLIED IRISH BANKS PLC	DUBLIN 4 IRELAND	AIB
AMERICAN BARRICK RESOURCES COR	TORONTO ONTARIO CAN	ABX
ARACRUZ CELLULOSE SA	RIO DE JANEIRO BRAZIL	ARA
AUTOMATED SECURITY HOLDINGS PL	LONDON UNITED KINGDOM	ASI
BANCO BILBAO VIZCAYA SA	48005 BILBAO SPAIN	BBV
BANCO CENTRAL HISPANOAMERICANO	MADRID SPAIN	BCM
BANCO COMERCIAL PORTUGUES SA	1100 LISBON PORTUGAL	BPC
BANK OF SANTANDER SA	SANTANDER SPAIN 39	ADS
BARCLAYS PLC	LONDON EC3N 4HJ ENG	BCS
BASS PLC	LONDON W1M 1PR NG	BAS
BCE INC	MONTREAL QUEBEC CAN	BCE
BENETTON GROUP SPA	PONZANO VENETO 3105	BNG
BENGUET CORP	MANDALUYONG METRO M	BE
BET PLC	PICCADILLY LONDON	BEP
BRITISH AIRWAYS PLC	HOUNSLOW MIDDLESEX	BAB
BRITISH GAS PLC	LONDON SW1V 3JL ENG	BRG
BRITISH PETROLEUM CO PLC	LONDON EC2M 7BA ENG	BP
BRITISH STEEL PLC	LONDON SE1 7SN ENG	BST
BRITISH TELECOMMUNICATIONS PLC	LONDON EC1A 7AJ ENG	BTYP

Source: Disclosure/SEC CD-ROM, March 1993 Disk. Data © Disclosure Incorporated 1993. Compact D/SEC is a trademark of Disclosure Incorporated. Reprinted with permission.

Investment Companies. Another way to invest in foreign stocks and bonds is through investment companies. Many U.S.-based mutual funds invest in non-U.S. markets. The Lipper Analytical Service, which tracks these funds, has defined several types based on their objectives.[5]

- **Global Fund:** A fund that invests at least 25% of its portfolio in securities traded outside the U.S. and may own U.S. securities as well
- **International Fund:** Invests its assets in securities whose primary trading markets are outside the U.S.
- **European Region Fund:** A fund that concentrates its investments in equity securities whose primary trading markets or operations are concentrated within the European region or a single country within this region
- **Pacific Region Fund:** A fund that concentrates its investments in equity securities whose primary trading markets or operation are concentrated within the Western Pacific basin region or a single country within this region

Money Markets

The money market is a wholesale market for low-risk highly liquid short-term IOUs. It is a market for debt securities rather than equities (such as stocks). The money market provides a mechanism by which the surplus funds of cash rich corporations and financial institutions such as pension funds can be channeled to banks, corporations, and governments that need short-term money (money that must be repaid in less than one year). The "money market" is not one market but a collection of markets for several distinct and different instruments, including commercial paper, certificates of deposit, banker's acceptances, and government agency bills and notes.

Eurocurrencies are an important part of the international money market. Eurocurrencies are currencies of one country that are held by the citizens of another country. For example, Eurodollars are U.S. dollar balances held on deposit in a bank located outside the United States. The prefix "euro" is derived from the market's London origins. During the 1950s, interest grew in borrowing and lending offshore dollars free from U.S. government interference.

The Eurocurrency Market (the Euromarket) deals with borrowing and lending Eurocurrencies. It is closely linked with the foreign exchange market. For example, in May 1992 banks were willing to lend Spanish pesetas for three months at 12.5% interest. During the same period banks were prepared to pay 12% interest to borrow Spanish pesetas for 90 days. The *Financial Times* listed this information in a daily table (Euro-Currency Interest Rates) as:

Three
Month
Spanish peseta 12-12 1/2

Closely allied to the Eurocurrency Market is the market for Euro-notes. Euro-notes take various forms, such as Euro-commercial paper, banker's acceptances, and certificates of deposit.[6]

The interest rate for lending on the Euromarket is often based on the London Interbank Offered Rate (LIBOR). This is the interest rate for loans made by banks in London to other London banks. It is calculated as the average of rates quoted by several reference banks. The rate is usually for three or six month loans. Rates for Eurocurrency are expressed as LIBOR plus an additional percentage. Other major financial centers often calculate their own interbank offering rates, such as NYBOR (New York), HKIBOR (Hong Kong), and MIBOR (Madrid).

Bond Markets

About $1.5 trillion of international bonds are outstanding. About $250 billion in new bonds are issued each year.[7] The predominant currency for bonds is the U.S. dollar, followed by the Japanese yen. International and domestic bond markets are closely related. There are important bond markets in Zurich, New York, Tokyo, Frankfurt, London, and Amsterdam. However, most bonds are traded OTC.

There are two general types of international bonds, *foreign bonds* and *Eurobonds*. Foreign bonds are issued by foreign borrowers in another country's capital market using that country's currency. For example, a bond issued by a Japanese company in the U.S. denominated in U.S. dollars is a foreign bond. In the U.S., as in most countries, foreign bonds have different registration and disclosure requirements than do domestic bonds.

Eurobonds are usually issued simultaneously in the capital markets of several countries. Eurobonds differ from foreign bonds in that most countries require pre-offering registration or disclosure requirements for them.

Futures

A futures contract is a commitment (a legally binding agreement) to buy or sell a fixed quantity of a commodity or an underlying financial instrument (such as a group of stocks) during a specified month in the future. For example, on March 4, 1992, dealers on the London Futures and Options Exchange paid 147.8 pounds sterling for the delivery of a ton of potatoes at the end of May. Futures are traded on formal exchanges. Most of these exchanges are so-called "floor traded" markets in which brokers and traders in trading pits shout out the price and quantity at which they want to buy or sell. Other exchanges are "electronic markets." For example, only members of the Osaka Securities Exchange have access to terminals for trading Nikkei futures. Buy and sell orders appear on the screen and all buyers and sellers are anonymous.[8]

There are two types of futures: commodity and financial. Commodity futures are based on such items as agricultural products, metals, and petroleum. Financial futures have as their underlying instruments groups of stocks (represented by a stock index), a currency, or fixed income securities.

Options

The owner of an option has the right to buy or sell a specified amount of a financial instrument for a specified price on or before a particular date. Unlike a futures contract, the owner of an option is not obligated to exercise it. Options are sold on stocks, stock indexes, currencies, and on interest rate instruments. For example, on March 4, 1992, common stock in the Guinness Company closed at 584 pence per share. On the same day, an option to purchase Guinness stock (a call option) at 600 pence before the end of May cost 19 pence per share. On the same day, an option to sell Guinness stock (a put option) at 600 pence before the end of May cost 30.5 pence. This information appeared in the *Financial Times* in this form:

Guinness (584)	May	Aug	Nov
Call 600	19	32.5	45.5
Put 600	30.5	36.5	41.5

Other Derivatives

Futures and options are often called *derivative* financial instruments. An equity option, for example, is derived from an underlying stock. Another important group of derivatives include interest rate and currency rate swaps. The world value of outstanding swaps is estimated to be $3 trillion. Swaps are customized financial arrangements that allow two parties to trade streams of interest payments. They allow corporations to better manage risks associated with interest rates and foreign currency rate fluctuation.

Here is an example of an interest rate swap. A corporation has issued a floating rate note with its interest rate tied to the 6-month LIBOR. The corporation is afraid that interest rates will rise and wants to exchange its floating rate note for a fixed rate note. The corporation makes an agreement with a bank to trade (swap) floating rate payments for fixed rate payments. The corporation pays the bank a fixed rate per year (say 10%) and the bank pays the corporation the prevailing floating rate.

In a currency rate swap, two institutions trade interest rate payments associated with borrowing foreign currency.

SOURCES OF INFORMATION FOR FINANCIAL MARKETS

Finding Aids and Directories

European Directory of Financial Information Sources (Euromonitor, 1990).

This directory describes the source of financial information in 17 major West European countries, including members of EFTA and the EC. It is divided into seven sections.

1. Financial Services in Europe: A New Era: An introductory section that gives an overview of the European financial services sector.
2. Company Information Sources: Describes the main sources of company financial information across Europe and in specific European countries. Each country section includes information on company registration and document filing procedures; selected financial information and credit rating services; online services, discs, and CD-ROMs providing company financial information; selected printed company directories; and official departments involved in the production of financial data.
3. Banking and Financial Information Libraries: Describes the major business libraries that hold large amounts of financial and banking materials.
4. Banking and Financial Trade Journals: Briefly describes the editorial content and gives addresses for some 100 journals.
5. Banking and Finance Associations: Gives the addresses, officers, objectives, and statistical services provided by major banking and finance associations.
6. Financial Operators: This section constitutes about half the volume. It describes the main financial institutions and financial service companies in Western Europe. Each country section includes an introduction to the banking sector and chapters covering the following operators:

   - Major banks
   - Major insurance companies
   - Major accounting firms and tax advisors
   - Major stockbrokers
   - Main stock exchanges
   - Other financial institutions

The company entries in the *Directory* provide address and communication information plus, if available, details of ownership, foreign branches, financial year-end, assets, income, information service, contacts, and publications. The *Directory* has one alphabetic index. Exhibit 16-5 is an example of the introduction to the *Directory* entry on Luxembourg.

EXHIBIT 16-5. *European Directory of Financial Information:* **Headnote for Luxembourg**

The Belgian central bank, Banque Nationale de Belgique (qv), also acts as the central bank for Luxembourg. While the banking laws make a distinction between banking and savings enterprises and credit institutions, all banks in Luxembourg operate generally as universal banks, i.e. as both deposit and merchant banks. Most business is however short-term. All banks may also function as stockbrokers. The banking sector is characterised by the presence of a very large number of foreign banks; Luxembourg is a very important centre for Euro-bonds.

Source: European Directory of Finanicial Information, p. 220. Reprinted with permission from Euromonitor.

G.T. Guide to World Equity Markets (Euromoney/G.T. Management—Annual)

This useful worldwide directory of stock markets has been published by Euromoney and G.T. Management (an international investment management company) annually since 1985. The *Guide* profiles the equity markets of 50 countries. For each country, the following information is given:

- market performance of the exchange for the past five years,
- market indices and their constituents
- brief history and structure of the market
- principal exchange addresses
- market size (as measured by number of listings and market value)
- largest quoted companies
- types of shares, trading systems
- lists of principal brokers and their commissions
- reporting requirements and shareholders protection codes

The Handbook of World Stock and Commodity Exchanges (Basil Blackwell—Annual)

Another source of current information about world stock exchanges, the *Handbook* covers 57 countries and about 225 exchanges. It includes information about such nascent exchanges as the Moscow Stock Exchange and the Moscow Commodity Exchange. For each exchange, it provides the following information:

- brief history and structure
- trading hours

- number of securities traded
- market capitalization
- main indexes
- type of securities traded
- trading system
- settling and clearing process
- commission rates
- investor protection details

Tradeline International (IDD)

The Tradeline International database includes brief descriptions of stock exchanges worldwide. Exhibit 16-6 displays the output from a search on the DIALOG version of *Tradeline International* for information about the Madrid Stock Exchange. We first requested the stock exchange symbols for Spain, and then entered the symbol for Madrid.

EXHIBIT 16-6. *Tradeline International* **Stock Exchange Snapshot**

Stock Exchange Snapshot

Stock Exch Code	Exchange Name	Country
EEB	Barcelona	Spain
EEM	Madrid	Spain
EEA	Bilbao	Spain
EEV	Valencia	Spain

Exchange Name:	Madrid, Spain (EEM)
Hours of operation:	10:00AM–1:00PM
	9:00AM–12:00PM GMT
	4:00AM–7:00AM EST
Days of operation:	Monday–Friday

Usual quotation convention:	High-Low-Close
Major market index:	Madrid S.E. Index (SEDOL 128817)
Issues in database:	1,032

Source: IDD Information Services/Tradeline International. Reprinted with permission.

Individual Exchanges. Individual financial exchanges often publish English language versions of their annual reports and other descriptive materials. The reports typically give such facts as listing requirements, volume of sales, number of issues, and market index composition. Often the material can be obtained for little or no direct cost. Listed below are examples of stock exchange reports and fact books.

- *Athens Stock Exchange—Annual Statistical Bulletin*
- *Federation of German Stock Exchanges—Annual Report*
- *Madrid Stock Exchange—Annual Report*
- *Stockholm Stock Exchange—Annual Report*
- *Tel Aviv Stock Exchange—Annual Report*
- *Tokyo Stock Exchange—Annual Securities Statistics*
- *Vienna Stock Exchange—Yearbook*
- *Zurich Stock Exchange—Facts and Figures*

Market Measures

Every financial market has one or more indexes or averages that describe the movement of the market. For example, the most widely quoted German stock market index is the DAX (the Deutscher Aktienindex), an index of 30 large German companies weighted by market capitalization representing all the country's stock exchanges.

Large stock exchanges, such as the Tokyo and London exchanges, often have several indexes. For example, the Tokyo Stock Exchange calculates a broad general market index (the TSE Stock Price Index) as well as a "blue-chip" index (the Nikkei-Dow Index.). Nikkei (Nihon Keizai Shimbun Inc.) also computes stock indexes for over 30 industry and special subgroups, such as the Nikkei Automobile Stock Index.

In addition to measuring the movement of individual stock markets, market indexes are available that track the performance of stock exchanges aggregated by geographic area and by special groups such as "emerging markets." Two examples of "world indexes" are the Morgan Stanley Capital International Indices and the FT Actuaries Index. They measure the movement of the stock market worldwide.

Several other aggregate measures of market performance and size are frequently of interest to researchers.

- price earnings ratio
- price book value ratio
- dividend yield
- value of stocks traded
- number of companies listed
- index of total return

Market indices for important markets are reported daily in major financial newspapers such as the *Wall Street Journal* and the *Financial Times* (London). The *Financial Times*, for example, gives one or more market measures for 25 exchanges. Information is included for the four previous days plus the high and low for the year. More extensive information is given for the *Financial Times'* own stock indexes, including hourly changes.

The "Special Features Section" of volume one of Moody's *International Manual* is a convenient source for long time series of monthly and annual stock exchange indexes. In Table 16-C we list the indexes in the 1991 edition. Most of the indexes give monthly data.

Table 16-C. Stock Market Indexes in *Moody's International Manual*

Country	Current Index	Approximate Coverage
Australia	All Ordinaries Index	20 years
Austria	Vienna Share Index	30 years
Belgium	Brussels SE Index	10 years
Canada	Toronto 300 Composite	35 years
France	CAC General Index	10 years
Germany	Commerzbank Index	20 years
Hong Kong	Hang Seng	25 years
Italy	Banc Commerciale Index	10 years
Japan	Tokyo Stock Exchange Index	50 years
Netherlands	All Share Index	25 years
Norway	Oslo Stock Exchange Index	10 years
Sao Paulo	Sao Paulo SE	20 years
Singapore	Stock Exchange	10 years
South Africa	Johannesburge SE Industrials	10 years
South Korea	Composite Stock Price Index	15 years
Spain	Madrid SE Index	10 years
Sweden	Affarsvarlden General Index	30 years
Switzerland	SBC Index	30 years
Taiwan	SE	25 years
U.K.	FT/SE 100	10 years

Index Composition. The names of the companies that make up market indexes and averages are often a point of interest. Two sources of this information are described below.

Hoover's Handbook of World Business (Reference Press—Annual)

The 1993 edition of *Hoover's Handbook* lists the names of the companies that make up the following major market indexes and averages:

- Dow Jones Industrials
- Standard and Poor's 500
- Nikkei Index 225 (Japan)
- DAX Index (Germany)
- FT-SE 100 Index (U.K.)
- CAC Index (France)
- Hang Seng Index (Hong Kong)

Straits Times Index (Singapore)
All Ordinaries Index (Australia)

The Handbook of Financial Market Indexes, Averages, and Indicators (Dow Jones-Irwin, 1990)

Written by Howard M. Berlin, the *Handbook* describes 200 market indexes, averages, and indicators in 25 countries. Although most of the measures concern

U.S. markets, there is a chapter on foreign stocks. The *Handbook* describes the stock markets for each country and lists the companies that compose the market index or average. Exhibit 16-7 lists the countries and indexes described.

EXHIBIT 16-7. Foreign Stock Market Indicators

Australia
All Ordinaries Index
Twenty Leaders and Fifty Leaders Indexes

Austria
The Vienna Stock Exchange Share Index
Creditanstalt-Bankverein Index

Belgium
The Cash Market All Share Indexes
The Forward Market Share Indexes

Canada
Toronto Stock Exchange 300 Composite Index-TSE 300
Toronto Stock Exchange High-Technology Index
The Toronto 35-Stock Index

Denmark
General Share Index

Finland
Unitas Share Index
Kansallis-Osake-PankkiIndex-KOP

France
The CAC-240 Index
CAC-40 Index

Germany
Frankfurt Stock Exchange Composite Index
Frankfurter Allgemeine Zeitung Index-FAZ
Commerzbank Index
Borsen Zeitun Index
The German Share Index-DAX

Great Britain
Financial Times 30 Index
Financial Times Stock-Exchange 100-Share Index-FT-SE 100

Hong Kong
The Hong Kong Index
The Hang Seng Index

Italy
MIB General Index
Banca Commerciale Italiana All-Share Index

Japan
Tokyo Price Indexes-TOPIX
Nikkei Stock Averages
Osaka Securities Exchange Indexes

Korea
Korea Stock Exchange-KSE

Luxembourg
>The Luxembourg Shares Index
>The Luxembourg Shares Return Index

The Netherlands
>CBS Index
>EOE Index

New Zealand
>New Zealand Stock Exchange Indexes
>Barclays Industrial Share Index
>Barclays Mining Share Index

Norway
>The Oslo Stock Exchange General Index
>The Custos Finansanalyse Index

Singapore/Malaysia
>Straits Times Index
>Business Times Index
>Kuala Lumpur Stock Exchange Composite
>Index

South Africa
>Johannesburg Stock Exchange-Actuaries Index

Sweden
>Stockholm Stock Exchange Composite
>Index
>Affarsvarlden General Index-AFGX
>Jacobson & Ponsbach Index
>Stockholm Options Market Index-OMX
>SX-l6 Index
>Alfred Berg Nordic Index

Switzerland
>Credit Suisse Index
>Swiss Market Index
>Swiss Performance Index
>Swiss Bank Corporation Indexes
>Swiss National Bank Index

Taiwan
>Taiwan Stock Exchange Weighted Price
>Index

Thailand
>Securities Exchange of Thailand Index-SET
>Book Club Index

World Stock Market Indexes
>Morgan Stanley Indexes
>AMEX International Market Index

Source: Howard Berlin, *The Handbook of Financial Market Indexes, Averages, and Indicators* (Dow Jones-Irwin, 1990). Reprinted with permission.

In addition to its information on foreign market measures, the *Handbook* has much useful and clearly written information on the European Currency Unit (ECU) and on the mathematics of market averages and indexes. Except for graphs, the *Handbook* does not give data for index movements.

Keep in mind that the *Handbook* was written in 1990 and typically reports the make-up of indexes as they were

in 1988. The names of the companies that make up the individual market indices usually change slowly, but they do change as companies merge, change their names, or become financially weak. The DATASTREAM online system, which lists the names of companies that comprise the major stock indexes, is a more current source. DATASTREAM is discussed in some detail below.

Morgan Stanley Capital International Perspective (Morgan Stanley—Monthly and Quarterly)

Morgan Stanley indexes measure the performance of the stock markets of the U.S., Europe, Canada, Mexico, Australia, and the Far East. Morgan Stanley offers 7 international, 20 national, and 38 international industry indices. They appear in *Morgan Stanley Capital International Perspective,* which is published both monthly and quarterly (16 issues a year).

FT-Actuaries World Indices

The *FT-Actuaries World Indices* are complied by the Financial Times; Goldman, Saches; and County NatWest Securities Limited. The indices consist of one world index and 11 regional and 24 national indices, as well as seven economic sectors and 36 industry groups. The indices appear daily in the *Financial Times*. In addition, they appear in the monthly *World Market Review*. The Morgan Stanley Index began over 20 years ago. The FT-Actuaries made its appearance in 1987 and is calculated from 1986. The FT-Actuaries Index is more broadly based (2,500 stocks) than the Morgan Stanley Indexes.

Both *Morgan Stanley Capital International Perspective* and *World Market Review* give measures of valuation in addition to performance for the groups of stocks that comprise their various indices. *The World Market Review*, for example, gives measures such as price earnings ratio and dividend yield for country and industry groups.

Stock Exchange Quarterly with Quality of Markets Review (London Stock Exchange—Quarterly)

The *Stock Exchange Quarterly* is a good source for comparisons of international markets. Each issue contains several statistical tables detailing the size, activity, and composition of stock, commodity, and option markets. Included is a table showing the daily close for 11 major stock market indices for the previous quarter.

Annual Report of the Bank for International Settlements (Bank for International Settlements)

The Bank for International Settlements (BIS) is a private company owned jointly by the central banks of most industrial countries. Dating from 1930, it is the oldest international financial organization. The BIS is a bank for central banks. Its annual report includes chapters on domestic and international financial markets. In addition, it discusses issues relating to international trade, the monetary systems and economic development, and is a good source for detailed descriptions of trends in international markets.

Emerging Markets Factbook (International Finance Corporation—Annual)

The International Finance Corporation (IFC) was established in 1956 to promote the growth of developing countries through private sector investment. The *Emerging Markets Factbook* brings together fundamental market data on the leading stock markets of the developing world. The *Factbook* is based on the IFC's Emerging Market's Data Base begun in 1981 (*see* Table 16-D). Using a sample of stocks in each market, the Data Base includes weekly and monthly statistics on more than 800 stocks from 20 markets, going back as far as 1975. The IFC has created several indexes of price and returns for the stocks in its database. It also publishes details of valuation and performance by region and by individual country.

Table 16-D: Countries in the IFC Emerging Stock Markets Data Base

Argentina	Korea	Turkey
Brazil	Malaysia	Venezuela
Chile	Mexico	Zimbabwe
Colombia	Pakistan	
Greece	Philippines	
India	Portugal	
Indonesia	Taiwan	
Jordan	Thailand	

In addition to the *Emerging Stock Markets Factbook,* the IFC publishes *Quarterly Review of Emerging Stock Markets.* The IFC makes its information available as well on diskette and magnetic tape. Online access to market indexes are available in several financial databases, including *Tradeline International,* REUTERLINK, and DATASTREAM. These systems are described below.

Bond Indexes. Bond indexes (indexes that chart the movement of bond markets) are not as numerous and are less widely published than stock indexes. International bond indexes include the J.P. Morgan Government Bond Index, which gives total return performance and 10-year constant maturity yields for 12 major industrial countries. The J.P. Morgan Government Bond Index is published in *World Financial Markets.* The *Wall Street Journal* gives daily bond index total rates of return for Eurodollar bonds. The *Financial Times* also publishes daily quotes on benchmark bonds representative of major markets

worldwide. The Salomon Brothers Bond Index is published in *Euromoney,* and monthly, quarterly, and annual interest rates on government bonds make up one time series in *International Financial Statistics.*

The DATASTREAM time-sharing system is an excellent online source for bond indices. DATASTREAM has devised indices covering major government bonds markets for 13 European countries, Australia, Japan, and the U.S. The indices are updated daily. In addition to its own indices, DATASTREAM reports a wide variety of other bond measures, including J.P. Morgan World Indices, ECU bonds, and Credit Suisse bond performance indices.

Bond Ratings. *Moody's Bond Record* includes a section that gives ratings on 6,000 international corporate and convertible bonds. In addition, *Moody's* includes information on interest dates and the amount outstanding in millions when issued. Exhibit 16-8 is an extract from *Moody's Bond Record* showing the first few entries for Tokyo Electric Power Company bonds. The first Eurobond described was issued in Canadian dollars. The second was issued in Deutschmarks. The two numbers following the listing of the bond are the interest rate paid by the bond (e.g., 7.625%) and the date the bond matures (e.g., 1997). The rating of Aaa given to the Tokyo Electric Power Company bonds is Moody's highest. These bonds have the smallest degree of investment risk.

Moody's Annual Bond Record describes new issues of bonds and changes in corporate and municipal bond ratings during the previous year. Exhibit 16-9 shows entries for Tokyo Electric Power Company from the 1992 edition.

Standard & Poor's Corporation Records (Standard & Poor's Corporation—Annual, with updates)

S&P includes descriptions of about 200 foreign bonds in the statistical section of its *Corporation Records.* The information provided includes bond ratings, redemption provisions, underwriting provision, amount outstanding, yield to maturity, and prices. Three types of prices are given: a 10-year high and low, a current year high and low, and a month's end price.

Financial Times Credit Ratings International (Financial Times—Quarterly)

This service gives credit ratings for issuers of internationally traded bonds, CDs, and commercial paper. The publication reports the ratings of 12 credit agencies as well as an average rating on about 6,000 company and government issuers. It is arranged both alphabetically and by 37 industrial groups. The 12 rating services are:

* Australian Ratings, Melbourne
* Canadian Bond Rating Service, Montreal

EXHIBIT 16-8. Listing from *Moody's Bond Record*

Issue	Moody's Rating	Interest Dates	Amt Outst Mil$	Issued	Currency
TOKYO ELECTRIC POWER CO.					
eurobonds 7.625 1997.....	Aaa	AUG 6	500.0	7-6-92	C$
eurobonds 7.625 2002[3].....	Aaa	NOV 6		10-13-92	DM
japan bonds 6.10 2004....	Aaa	MAY 25		5-14-92	YEN
japan bonds 5.80 2004....	Aaa	JUL 14	100.0	7-14-92	YEN
japan bonds 5.375 2004[4]...	Aaa	J&D 26	100.0	11-26-92	YEN

Source: Moody's Bond Record. Reprinted with permission from Moody's Investors Service.

EXHIBIT 16-9. Listing from *Moody's Annual Bond Record*

CUSIP	TITLE	ACTION (See following section)	DATE OF ACTION	MOODY'S RATING	PREVIOUS
	TOKYO ELECTRIC POWER CO.				
1>	eurobonds 7.625 8/6/1997	New Issue	7/6	Aaa	
1>	eurobonds 7.625 11/6/2002	New Issue	10/13	Aaa	
1>	japan bonds 6.10 5/25/2004	New Issue	5/14	Aaa	
1>	japan bonds 5.80 7/14/2004	New Issue	7/14	Aaa	
1>	japan bonds 5.375 12/26/2004	New Issue	11/26	Aaa	

Source: Moody's Annual Bond Record. Reprinted with permission from Moody's Investors Service.

- Dominion Bond Rating Service, Toronto
- Duff & Phelps, Chicago
- Fitch Investors Service, New York
- Japan Bond Research Institute, Tokyo
- Japan Credit Rating Agency, Tokyo
- McCarthy, Crisanti & Maffei, New York
- Moodys Investors Service, New York
- Nippon Investors Service, Tokyo
- Standard & Poor's Corporation, New York
- S&P-ADEF, Paris

A useful feature of the service is its detailed descriptions of the methodology used by the various rating agencies.

Prices of Individual Financial Instruments. Hundreds of thousands of financial instruments are traded daily in world markets. Finding price and related information about individual stocks, bonds, options, or futures can be difficult if we are limited to printed sources. Newspaper listings of quotations may be adequate if we need only a few current prices for widely traded issues, but newspapers have several limitations. They typically report only the previous day's transactions. Understandably, financial newspapers concentrate on covering their domestic financial markets and use their local language and currency.

The *Wall Street Journal*, for example, gives quotations for companies on the New York, American, and NASDAQ exchanges (about 6,000 companies), but reports the prices of only a few hundred non-U.S. stocks. Virtually no quotes are given for non-U.S. options, bonds, and futures. The Canadian paper, *The Globe and Mail,* gives good coverage of U.S. securities in addition to its comprehensive coverage of Canadian financial markets. The *Financial Times* (London) is a good source of price information for foreign (i.e., non-U.K.) securities. About half the volume on the London International Stock Exchange is for non-U.K. stock.

Financial newspapers are best used as a source of news stories rather than as data sources for prices. As a practical matter, following the price movements of several financial instruments on a variety of markets requires access to an online financial database.

The automation of the world's financial markets has not only made price information available virtually instantaneously, but has allowed the creation of historical files of data. Online databases of securities prices include real time and historical data. The major supplier of international stock price data is EXTEL Financial Ltd. Several online systems supply historical financial pricing data. They include IDD, Reuters, and DATASTREAM. IDD's *Tradeline International* database is available on Dow Jones, DIALOG, and directly through IDD. The following description is based on the DIALOG version.

The *Tradeline International* database contains historical price quotes for more than 38,000 active and inactive equities and over 1,000 indexes traded on over 90 overseas stock exchanges. Historical price quotes for Canadian companies are included with U.S. companies in separate Tradeline databases. Historical price information can be obtained on daily, weekly, monthly, quarterly, and yearly bases. This information dates back approximately two years. Quotes for active issues are current through the previous day's close. *Tradeline* uses SEDOL numbers (described in Chapter 10) as unique identifiers of securities. The system has an online directory of SEDOL numbers. The default report will be the currency originally reported by the exchange. The user can change this setting to convert prices into any major currency. For example, Exhibit 16-10 shows a report giving the price and volume of Sumitomo Bank stock on the Tokyo exchange in Japanese yen, and the same information converted to U.S. dollars.

Tradeline International's coverage of individual financial instruments is confined to stock prices for the past two years. The DIALOG and DOW JONES versions of the database will not allow the users to download information in a spreadsheet format.

Tradeline adjusts stock prices for stock splits, stock dividends, and currency revaluations. Stock splits and stock dividends dilute stock. If a stock selling for $100 splits two for one, the stock should sell for $50 after the split. The effect of a currency devaluation can be seen in Table 16-E, which shows the unadjusted and adjusted price in Mexican pesos for the Cementos company. The Mexican peso was revalued 1,000 to 1 at the beginning of 1993.

Table 16-E. Price of Cementos (Cemex A) Stock in Mexican Pesos

	Unadjusted Price	Adjusted Price
12-28-92	47000.00	47.00
12-29-92	46900.00	46.90
12-30-92	46900.00	46.90
12-31-92	46900.00	46.90
1-4-93	47.50	47.50
1-5-93	49.30	49.30
1-6-93	49.00	49.00
1-7-93	48.50	48.50

Source: DATASTREAM

REUTERLINK and DATASTREAM are examples of time-sharing systems that have broader coverage of financial instruments and longer time series than does *Tradeline International*. REUTERLINK, for example, gives about eight years of daily data on equities, fixed income securities (bonds), money markets, options, mutual funds, and commodities on markets worldwide. REUTERLINK is designed to download data for further analysis. In fact, users must download; the system will not display or print data while online.

The systems are designed to capture data for additional analysis. As part of the software package needed to operate the systems, REUTERLINK and DATA-STREAM both store the names and mnemonics for the databases' financial instruments on the user's hard disk.

DATASTREAM has equally broad coverage of stocks, bonds, money market instruments, options, and commodities. DATASTREAM can often supply financial information that is difficult to find elsewhere. Examples of specialized financial data on DATASTREAM are:

- Betas (measures of stock volatility) for non-U.S. stocks and industry groups
- Lists of the companies that make up standard stock indices
- Dividend yields, price earnings ratios, and total returns for equity markets

DATASTREAM can be used to screen for financial instruments that meet certain criteria. For example, international bonds can be screened to select those with a particular combination of interest payment type, amortization features, and yields. Exhibit 16-11 shows the first 10 entries of DATASTREAM's listings for Tokyo Electric Company bonds. Exhibit 16-12 shows DATASTREAM's listings of daily prices for Tokyo Electric's 7 5/8% bond issued in 1992. In addition, the DATASTREAM system has several other useful features, including a statistical analysis package, a graphics package, and the ability for users to load and integrate their own data series with DATASTREAM files.

Securities Data Corporation. Securities Data Corporation (SDC) has several unique international financial databases. Their Merger and Joint Venture files were discussed in Chapter 7.

The *U.K. Domestic New Issues Database* provides information on all equity and convertible issues offered in the U.K. domestic market since 1988. More than 500 data items are available on each issue type, including rights issues, institutional placing, vendor placing, offers of sale, and subscription offers. The database is updated daily from London Stock Exchange filings covering the listed, unlisted, and overseas markets.

The *Euroequity* and *Eurobond* databases provide information on nearly 19,000 euro and foreign market transactions dating back to 1983. The databases cover public and private debt, common stock, and preferred stock securities offers.

Exhibit 16-10. Report from *Tradeline International*

685852 SUMITOMO BANK Y50
Tokyo
Equity

Daily adjusted prices 4/20/92 to 5/01/92
Prices in currency as reported by exchange

Date	Volume	High	Low	Close
4/20/92	992000	1440.000 JPY	1380.000 JPY	1380.000 JPY
4/21/92	1360000	1410.000 JPY	1330.000 JPY	1370.000 JPY
4/22/92	1190000	1410.000 JPY	1340.000 JPY	1370.000 JPY
4/23/92	1155000	1440.000 JPY	1370.000 JPY	1440.000 JPY
4/24/92	1409000	1450.000 JPY	1380.000 JPY	1390.000 JPY
4/27/92	839000	1400.000 JPY	1380.000 JPY	1390.000 JPY
4/28/92	623000	1400.000 JPY	1380.000 JPY	1390.000 JPY
4/29/92	NA	NA	NA	1390.000 JPY
4/30/92	805000	1400.000 JPY	1380.000 JPY	1400.000 JPY
5/01/92	597000	1390.000 JPY	1370.000 JPY	1370.000 JPY

685852 SUMITOMO BANK   Y50
Tokyo
Equity

Daily adjusted prices 4/20/92 to 5/01/92
Unit of currency is the U.S. dollar

Date	Volume	High	Low	Close
4/20/92	992000	10.709 USD	10.263 USD	10.263 USD
4/21/92	1360000	10.519 USD	9.922 USD	10.220 USD
4/22/92	1190000	10.514 USD	9.992 USD	10.216 USD
4/23/92	1155000	10.706 USD	10.186 USD	10.706 USD
4/24/92	1409000	10.793 USD	10.271 USD	10.346 USD
4/27/92	839000	10.500 USD	10.350 USD	10.425 USD
4/28/92	623000	10.524 USD	10.374 USD	10.449 USD
4/29/92	NA	NA	NA	10.404 USD
4/30/92	805000	10.509 USD	10.358 USD	10.509 USD
5/01/92	597000	10.441 USD	10.291 USD	10.291 USD

Source: IDD Information Services/Tradeline International. Reprinted with permission.

The *Warrants Database* was created in association with IFR Securities Data Company in London. It provides users with information on over 2,600 international warrant issues since 1989. Coverage includes warrants exercisable into corporate equities, as well as warrants linked to stock indexes, commodities, currency values, debt instruments, and stock baskets. A concise summary of the issue and its exercise provisions includes total value of the issue, warrant price and repayment value, and exercise premium and market price of underlying stock. Details included about the structure of the issue feature relevant dates, issue minimums, and style of the issue.

ADDITIONAL SOURCES

A Guide to Financial Times Statistics (Financial Times Business Information, 1991)

The *Financial Times* (*FT*) has few equals in its coverage of international markets. This guide describes how to read the financial and economic statistics that appear in the *FT*. The *Guide* contains brief chapters with tables on equities, commodities, futures, options, currencies, equity indices, and British economic statistics. An appendix describes how financial averages, indexes, and percentage changes are calculated.

The international edition of the *Financial Times* appears Monday through Friday and differs from the

EXHIBIT 16-11. DATASTREAM Listing of Tokyo Electric Company Bonds

NAME	CODE	MNEMONIC	CUR	NOTES
TOKYO ELECTRIC 2.2% 03-29-02	CV	799964	Y	
TOKYO ELEC.POWER 11% 06-05-01	1991	596230	£	
TOKYO ELEC.POWER 10 1/2% 06-14-01	1991	596342	C$	
TOKYO ELEC.POWER 7 5/8% 08-06-97	1992	381623	C$	
TOKYO ELEC.POWER 9 5/8% 12-20-96	1989	560938	CU	
TOKYO ELEC.POWER 8 3/4% 08-28-98	1991	599025	U$	
TOKYO ELEC.POWER 8 3/4% 08-23-96	1989	560163	U$	
TOKYO ELEC.POWER 10 5/8% 12-20-96	1989	561133	C$	
TOKYO ELEC.POWER 9 3/4% 09-29-93	1988	798629	U$	
TOKYO ELEC.POWER 4 1/2% 08-10-93	1988	796592	SF	

Source: Datastream International. Reprinted with permission.

EXHIBIT 16-12. DATASTREAM Listing of Bond Prices

301V TOKYO ELEC.POWER 1992 7 5/8% 11-06-02
5-3-93

HIGH VALUE 4-30-93	106.00	4-15-93	LOW VALUE	103.85	

WEEK COMMENCING	MONDAY	TUESDAY	WEDNESDAY	THURSDAY	FRIDAY
3-15-93					105.40
3-22-93	105.15	104.95	104.85	104.95	105.10
3-29-93	105.05	105.00	104.80	104.75	104.50
4-5-93	104.70	104.60	104.70	104.90	104.90
4-12-93	104.90	105.35	105.50	106.00	105.45
4-19-93	105.55	105.55	105.40	105.00	105.25
4-26-93	105.00	105.05	104.60	104.25	103.85

Source: Datastream International. Reprinted with permission.

British version. The international edition is printed in Germany, France, the U.S., and Japan. It has greater emphasis on international economic and financial developments as well as more comprehensive prices of non-U.K. stocks.

The World Financial System, Robert Fraser (Longman, 1987)

This is a useful reference source for understanding the history of the world's financial system and for its descriptions of international financial agencies. The first part of the volume is a description of the evolution of the world financial system since 1945. The second part describes 50 major international and regional bodies, such as the IMF, the OECD, and the World Bank.

The Unit Trust Yearbook (Financial Times Business Information)

The *Yearbook* is a directory of management groups that run unit trusts (mutual funds) in the U.K. It provides information about the portfolio distribution, type of fund, minimum investment, and a 10-year record of the trust's price and income. A statistical section gives rankings of management groups and trusts by size, and tables of performance by yield and income.

International Investor's Directory (Asset International—Annual)

International Investor's Directory is a useful compendium of information about the international investment scene. It includes listings of international securities firms and managers, stock analysts, and market makers, as well as descriptions of major financial databases. An important feature is its list of American Depositary Receipts, their stock symbols, country of origin, depository banks, and CUSIP numbers.

Euromoney (Euromoney Publications—Monthly)

Euromoney describes itself as "the journal of the world's capital and money markets." In addition to its articles and columns, *Euromoney* issues several supplements each year. Ranging between 40 and 120 pages, the supplements are an excellent current source of information on the details of financial markets in Europe. Examples of supplements issued by *Euromoney* include *Guide to Currencies, Guide to European Domestic Bond Markets, Guide to European Domestic Money Markets, Guide to Offshore Financial Centres, Borrower's Guide to Financing in Foreign Markets*, and *Guide to the World's Best Credits*.

CONCLUSION

International financial markets are involved with financial transactions that cross national borders. This chapter described the principal types of international financial markets and financial instruments, and discussed the sources of information for both. Financial instruments familiar to us from domestic markets (such as stocks, bonds, options, and futures) are used internationally. In addition, there are specialized instruments of international financial markets, such as currency and interest rate swaps and foreign exchange forwards. Price and related information for individual financial instruments are best obtained from time-sharing databases. The large number of financial instruments and their constantly changing characteristics limit the usefulness of print sources.

NOTES

1. Peter A. Abkin, "Globalization of Stock, Futures, and Options Markets," *Economic Review* (July/August 1991): 19.
2. Roland Leuschel, "Fixed Exchange Rates or Financial Bust," *Wall Street Journal* (June 29, 1991): A14.
3. "The Last of the Good Times," *Economist* (August 5, 1992).
4. Peter Passell, "FAST Money," *New York Times Magazine* (October 18, 1992): 41.
5. *Lipper-Mutual Fund Performance Analysis*, Lipper Analytical Service (June 30, 1992): 2-3.
6. Bruno H. Solnik, *International Investments* (Reading, MA: Addison-Wesley, 1991), p. 87.
7. *Annual Report of the Bank for International Settlements* (Basle, 1992), p. 137.
8. Walmsley, Julian, *The Foreign Exchange and Money Market Guide* (New York: Wiley, 1992).

Appendixes

APPENDIX A
Selecting a Company Directory—A Checklist

Listed below are data elements that may be included in a company sourcebook. When evaluating a new source, either in print or online, use these items as a guide. You may want your source to emphasize the number of data items included or the number of companies described.

You may also be interested in the number of access points, that is the number of ways you can "get at" the information.

For print sources, the arrangement of the basic text and the accompanying indexes and their organization are equally important. Some questions to ask: If you do not know the exact company name, can you still find the company in the source? If you are not sure of the product code, will you still find a listing of companies in the lines of business of interest to you?

Electronic sources will invariably have more access points than printed sources. However, do not assume that because a data element is available in an electronic source it automatically is searchable. For example, Disclosure/Worldscope includes standard numbers for companies, such as the SEDOL and VALOR, but they cannot be searched.

When evaluating a new product, be concerned with the data elements provided for individual records and the number and type of individual entries in the publication.

Data Elements

Different directories have few or almost all of the following data elements. Some will be more important to you than others.

- **Company Name**
  Legal Name
  "Traded Name"
  Entire name or set number of characters
  Name in local language/translated into English/transliterated into English
- **Address**
  Incorporated Address
  Trading Address
  Mailing Address
  Local Postal Code
  Headquarters Location
  Branches
  Country—text or standard code
  Language of country name/English

- **Products**
  Standard Numeric Codes
    U.S. SIC, Predicasts codes, U.K. SIC codes,
    KOMPASS codes, Harmonized tariffs schedule
  Product/Line of Business/Industry
  Language of Country/English
- **People**
  Chief Executive Officer/President/Managing Director
  Board of Directors
  Upper Management
  Trade Contacts
- **Financials**
  Turnover, "Capital"
  Full Financials
  Public Equity/Public Debt
  Local currency/US $/Standard Currency (ECU)
  Annual statement date
  Date of reported data
- **Affiliations**
  Parent/Subsidiary/Division/Mergers & Acquisitions
  Financials—sales for affiliates

- **Standardized Number**
  D-U-N-S Number
  Country Registration Number
  Equity listing number
- **Credit Ratings**
  Available to Public
  Large/Small Companies
- **Ranking**
  Within Industry/Product
  Within Country
  Within Region
- **Import/Export**
  Trading Partner Countries
  Trading Partner Companies
  Contacts

- **How are the financials presented?**
  As Reported/Standardized
  Local Currency of Reporting Country
  Local Currency of Publisher
  Standard Currency (e.g., ECU or $U.S.)
  Users' Option
- **Country coverage**
  One Country
  One Country, but part of a "series"
  One Region
  One Continent
  Worldwide
  Industrial Nations
  Emerging Markets
  Political/Economic Organizations (e.g., the IMF)

Directory Scope and Content—Number and Type of Entries

- **What types of companies are included?**
  Public/Private/Service /Nonprofit
  Active/Defunct
  Large/Medium/Small

APPENDIX B
Glossary—Company Definitions

These definitions have been adapted from Dun's Marketing Services Business definitions.

Branch: A secondary location of a business which reports to its headquarters. Both have the same name.

Company: A general term for all types of businesses.

Corporation: A legal form of business organization in which the company is a separate legal enterprise. Corporations issue shares of equities or bonds to individuals. Most corporations' issues are *not* traded to the public.

Division: A separate operating unit of a corporation. It may have its own officers and name, but it does not issue shares and it is not listed on an exchange.

Enterprise: A legally defined organization that has its own balance sheets, is subject to a directing authority, and has been formed to carry out in one or more places one or more activities for the production of goods and services (EC definition); family of businesses under common ownership and control for which a set of consolidated financial statements is produced (Statistics Canada -Quarterly financial . . . , p. 19).

Establishment: An enterprise or part thereof (whether located separately or not) that carries out a single activity which is characterized by the nature of the goods or services produced or by the essential [identity] of the production process employed, the activity being defined by a single SIC. (LKAU—local kind of activity—EC). In smaller firms, generally under 100 employees, the enterprises and establishments are the same reporting units. Firms having over 500 employees have an average of four establishments each (*Enterprises in the EC*, p. 21). In the U.S., an establishment is a single operating location with at least one employee. Used by the U.S. Bureau of the Census for data gathering.

Headquarters: A business establishment where the executive offices of the corporation are located. In the U.K., this is the "registered office" as opposed to the trade office.

Holding Company: A company that owns or controls others. In the U.K., it implies that the company operates through its subsidiaries.

Listed Company. *See* **Publicly Held Company**

Partnership: A legal form of business enterprise in which two or more persons are co-owners of the business and share the profit and losses. Partners are liable for the actions of the firm.

Privately Held Company: Generally, a U.S. term to designate those enterprises whose shares are not traded openly to the public. Well over 90% of the world's enterprises are "privately held."

Proprietorship: A legal form of business enterprise in which one individual is the sole owner of the company.

Public Company: A company whose securities may be publicly traded. In the U.K., this is a PLC. There is no direct U.S. equivalent.

Publicly Held Company: The U.S. term for companies whose shares are traded on a stock exchange or are available to the public. Often referred to as a "Listed Company" in other countries.

APPENDIX C
Synthesis of Accounting Standards in 48 Countries

INDUSTRIAL COMPANIES				
Country	Revaluation of fixed assets is	Consolidated information provided by	Inventory costing method used by majority	Accounting for Goodwill
US	not allowed	80-100%	mixed	C & A
Canada	allowed	80-100%	mixed	C & A
Mexico	allowed	80-100%	cost or equity	C & A
EUROPE				
Austria	allowed	minority	mixed	C & A
Belgium	allowed	40-80%	mixed	C & A
Denmark	allowed	80-100%	FIFO	C & R
Finland	allowed	80-100%	FIFO	C & A
France	allowed	80-100%	mixed	C & A
Germany	allowed	40-80%	mixed	C & A
Greece	allowed	ND	ND	ND
Ireland	allowed	80-100%	FIFO	Taken to reserves
Italy	allowed	40-80%	mixed	C & A
Luxembourg	allowed	80-100%	mixed	C & A
Netherlands	allowed	80-100%	FIFO	Taken to reserves
Norway	allowed	80-100%	FIFO	C & A
Portugal	allowed	minority	ND	ND
Spain	allowed	80-100%	Average cost	C & A
Sweden	allowed	80-100%	FIFO	Taken to reserves
Switzerland	allowed	40-80%	mixed	Taken to reserves
Turkey		40-80%	Average cost	ND
UK	allowed	80-100%	FIFO	Taken to reserves
ASIA/PACIFIC				
Australia	allowed	80-100%	FIFO	C & A
Hong Kong	allowed	80-100%	Average cost	Taken to reserves
India	allowed	ND	FIFO	C & A
Japan	not allowed	40-80%	mixed	C & A
Malaysia	allowed	80-100%	mixed	C & A
New Zealand	allowed	80-100%	FIFO	C & A
Pakistan	not allowed	minority	Average cost	ND
Philippines	not allowed	40-80%	FIFO	ND

Country	Revaluation of fixed assets is	Consolidated information provided by	Inventory Costing method used by majority	Accounting for Goodwill
Singapore	allowed	80-100%	Average cost	Taken to reserves
South Korea	allowed	40-80%	mixed	C & A
Sri Lanka	not allowed	80-100%	ND	ND
Taiwan	allowed	minority	Average cost	C & A
Thailand	allowed	40-80%	FIFO	C & A
AFRICA/MIDDLE EAST				
Israel	allowed	80-100%	Average cost	C & A
Nigeria	allowed	40-80%	ND	ND
South Africa	not allowed	80-100%	FIFO	Expensed/taken to reserves
SOUTH AMERICA				
Argentina	allowed	minority	ND	ND
Brazil	allowed	80-100%	Average cost	C & A
Chile	allowed	80-100%	mixed	C & A
Colombia	allowed	40-80%	FIFO	ND
Peru	allowed	minority	mixed	ND
Uruguay	allowed	ND	ND	ND
Venezuela	allowed	40-80%	LIFO	ND

Country	Discretionary Non-equity reserves	Gains or Losses from foreign currency translation	Depreciation Method	Excess Depreciation
US	NU	IS and/or SE	Straight line	not allowed
Canada	NU	SE	Straight line	not allowed
Mexico	SPR	IS and/or SE	Straight line	allowed
EUROPE				
Austria	GPR	ND	ND	allowed
Belgium	GPR	IS and/or SE	Straight line	allowed
Denmark	GPR	IS and/or SE	Straight line	allowed
Finland	GPR	IS	SL or accelerated	allowed
France	SPR	IS or SE	Straight line	allowed
Germany	GPR	IS or SE	SL or accelerated	allowed
Greece	SPR	IS	Straight line	ND
Ireland	SPR	IS and/or SE	Straight line	ND
Italy	GPR	SE	Straight line	not allowed
Luxembourg	SPR	SE	Straight line	not allowed
Netherlands	NU	IS and/or SE	Straight line	allowed
Norway	GPR	IS and/or SE	SL or accelerated	allowed
Portugal	SPR	IS and/or DEF	Straight line	ND
Spain	SPR	IS and/or SE	Straight line	not allowed
Sweden	GPR	IS and/or SE	Accelerated	allowed
Switzerland	GPR	SE	Straight line	not allowed
Turkey	GPR	IS	Straight line	ND
UK	SPR	IS and/or SE	Straight line	not allowed

Deferred taxes: GPR—General Purpose Reserves; SPR—Some Specific Reserves; NU—Not generally Used; **Goodwill:** C & A—capitalized and amortized; C & R—capitalized and taken to reserves; ND—not disclosed; **Foreign currency:** IS—Income Statement; SE—Shareholders' equity; DEF—Deferred
Source: Global Company Handbook 1992

Country	Discretionary Non-equity reserves	Gains or Losses from foreign currency translation	Depreciation Method	Excess Depreciation
ASIA/PACIFIC				
Australia	SPR	IS and/or SE	Straight line	not allowed
Hong Kong	SPR	IS and/or SE	Straight line	not allowed
India	SPR	ND	Straight line	allowed
Japan	GPR	IS and/or SE	Accelerated	not allowed
Malaysia	SPR	IS	Straight line	not allowed
New Zealand	SPR	IS and/or SE	Straight line	not allowed
Pakistan	NU	IS	Straight line	ND
Philippines	NU	IS and/or SE	Straight line	not allowed
Singapore	SPR	IS	Straight line	not allowed
South Korea	SPR	IS and/or SE	Accelerated	allowed
Sri Lanka	NU	IS	Straight line	not allowed
Taiwan	NU	IS and/or DEF	Straight line	not allowed
Thailand	NU	IS and/or SE	Straight line	ND
AFRICA/MIDDLE EAST				
Israel	NU	SE	Straight line	ND
Nigeria	GPR	IS	Straight line	ND
South Africa	SPR	IS	Straight line	allowed
SOUTH AMERICA				
Argentina	SPR	ND	Straight line	ND
Brazil	SPR	IS and/or SE	Straight line	allowed
Chile	SPR	IS	Straight line	ND
Colombia	GPR	IS	Straight line	ND
Peru	SPR	IS	Straight line	ND
Uruguay	SPR	IS	Straight line	ND
Venezuela	SPR	SPR	Sraight line	ND

Deferred taxes: GPR—General Purpose Reserves; SPR—Some Specific Reserves; NU—Not generally Used; **Goodwill:** C & A—capitalized and amortized; C & R—capitalized and taken to reserves; ND—not disclosed; **Foreign currency:** IS—Income Statement; SE—Shareholders' equity; DEF—Deferred
Source: Global Company Handbook 1992

APPENDIX D
Sample U.K. and French Balance Sheets

U.K. Company —AMSTRAD PLC

```
Consolidated Balance Sheet at 30th June, 1990
Amstrad plc
-----------------------------------------------------------------
                                  1990            1989
                       Note       £000    £000    £000    £000
Fixed assets
Intangible assets       9                  104             382
Tangible assets        10               41,940          44,428
Investments            11               27,126          44,574
                                        69,170          89,384

Current assets
Stocks                 12     188,415         325,155
Debtors                13     110,692         132,302
Cash at bank and in hand       30,475          44,681
                              329,582         502,138

Creditors amounts falling due
   within one year     15     (81,152)       (276,792)

Net current assets                     248,430         225,346

Total assets less current liabilities  317,600         314,730

Creditors amounts falling due
   after more than one year  16          (6,500)         (3,920)

Net assets                             311,100         310,810

Capital and reserves
Called up share capital 17              28,211          28,419
Share premium account  18               13,950          13,806
Revaluation reserve    20                8,002           9,848
Other reserves         20                1,429           1,204
Profit and loss account 20             259,508         257,533

Shareholders' funds                    311,100         310,810
```

Source: Company annual report on microfiche.

French Company—ALCATEL—1989 Balance Sheet (for the year ended December 31)

Assets [Actifs]	Gross value [Valeur brute]	Amortization Depreciation of Provisions	Net value [Valeur nette]	Notes
Intangible assets				
Start-up expenses	137	137	0	1
Patents, licences and trade marks	106,828	21,090	85,738	2
Goodwill	0	0	0	
Property plant and equipment				3
Land	84,581	141	84,440	
Buildings	324,868	59,151	265,717	
Technical facilities equipment and machinery	478,638	157,931	320,707	
Other tangible assets	245,269	81,594	163,675	
Construction process	43,919	0	43,919	
Allowances and progress payments	6,809	0	6,809	
Investments and long-term receivables				4
Subsidiaries and shareholdings	909,546	101,073	808,473	
Receivables from subsidiaries			0	
and affiliates	300,622	14,343	286,279	
Other securities	5,216	0	5,216	
Loans	35,592	1,000	34,592	
Other investments	8,270	9	8,261	
Total I	**2,550,295**	**436,469**	**2,113,826**	
Inventories and work in process				5
Raw materials and components	685,792	47,677	638,115	
Work in process	1,049,941	4,125	1,045,816	
Intermediate and finished goods	132,210	10,856	121,354	
Advances and progress payments and orders	122,952	9	122,943	6
Operating receivables				6
Accounts receivable and related accounts	3,516,869	42,017	3,474,852	
Other receivables	304,393	154	304,239	
Miscellaneous receivables				
marketable securities	157,381	6,981	150,400	
Other securities	1,401,220	0	1,401,220	
Cash	136,991	0	136,991	
Prepaid expenses	1,945	0	1,945	
Total II	**7,509,694**	**111,819**	**7,395,930**	
Expenses to be shared-out over several fiscal years	69	0	69	
Adjustment accounts	71,216	0	71,216	
Total assets	**10,131,274**	**548,288**	**9,582,986**	

French Company—ALCATEL—1989 Balance Sheet (for the year ended December 31)
(continued)

Liabilities [Passif]	Before distribution	After distribution	Notes
Capital	1,000,000	1,000,000	
Merger premiums and paid-in surplus	23,435	23,435	
Reserves			
Legal reserve		14,003	
Long-term capital gain special reserve			
Retained earnings	(16)	1,056	
Net income for the year	280,075		
Capital Subsidiaries	0	0	
Regulated provisions	64,248	64,248	
Total I	1,367,758	1,102,742	7
Provisions for contingencies and expenses	1,707,509	1,707,509	8
Total II	1,707,509	1,707,509	
Financial debts			9
Borrowings and debts from			
financial institutions	408,600	408,600	
Miscellaneous financial borrowings			
and debts	304,722	304,722	
Advances and progress payments from customers	2,951,833	2,951,833	9
Operating liabilities			9
Trade payables & related accounts	1,477,403	1,477,403	
Taxes, pensions & social liabilit	759,754	759,754	
Opther operating liabilities paya	124,167	124,167	
Miscellaneous debts			9
Liabilites to fixed asset suppliers			
and related accounts	48,236	48,236	
Other debts	416,429	681,429	
Accrued expenses	2,200	2,200	
Total III	6,493,130	6,758,130	
Exchange adjustments	14,250	14,250	
Total liabilities	9,582,647	9,582,647	

Source: Company report presented in English on microfiche.

APPENDIX E
Disclosure Requirements of Major Stock Exchanges

Disclosure Requirement	Toronto	Tokyo	London	NYSE
1. General Information				
(c) Research & Development	No	Yes	Yes	Yes
(f) Corporate social responsiblity	No	Yes	No	Yes
(h) Extent of dependence on major customers	No	Yes	No	Yes
2. Manager and directors				
(a) Salaries of managers	Yes	No	Yes	Yes
(b) Salaries of directors	Yes	No	No	Yes
4. Financial Information				
(d) Interim reports	Q	S-A	S-A	Q
(g) Segment sales or earnings	Both	Sales	Sales	Both
5. Recent developments and prospects				
(c) Profit forecast	Yes	Yes	Yes	No
6. Other requirements for foreign companies				
(a) Differences between accounting principles in country of origin and national accounting principles when former is used	Disclose IAC	Disclose	Disclose IAC	Disclose and Reconcile

Disclosure Differences on Major exchanges: from Choi, pg 5-28, 5-29 by Ajay Adhikari

APPENDIX F
Size of Enterprises

These tables emphasize the fact that most of the world's companies fall into the categories of micro enterprises or small to medium enterprises.

Table 1. *Enterprises in Europe*—Second Report

COUNTRY	Type	Micro	SME	Large	Total	PER CENT Micro	SME	Large
BELGIUM	Employer	498865	26477	447	525789	.949	.050	.001
DENMARK	Legal Units	97705	28260	274	126239	.774	.224	.002
GERMANY	Enterprises	1856502	265924	3360	2125786	.873	.125	.002
GREECE	Establishments*		8340	75	8415	.000	.991	.009
SPAIN	Enterprises	1905882	111660	1053	2018595	.944	.055	.001
FRANCE	Enterprises	1873212	134627	2033	2009872	.932	.067	.001
IRELAND	Establishments*	1870	2855	40	4914	.381	.581	.008
ITALY	Enterprises	1563238	134346	919	1698503	.920	.079	.001
LUXEMBOURG	Enterprises*	12937	1724	23	14684	.881	.117	.002
NETHERLANDS	Economic Units	261316			291282	.897	.000	.000
PORTUGAL	Enterprises	610951	31329	332	642612	.951	.049	.001
U.K.	Enterprises	2450879	175907	3127	2629913	.932	.067	.001
ICELAND	Enterprises	17472	1035	82	18589	.940	.056	.004
NORWAY	Establishments*	7867	4269	219	12355	.637	.346	.018
AUSTRIA	Enterprises	154799	26684	381	181864	.851	.147	.002
FINLAND	Enterprises	103203	15665	259	119127	.866	.131	.002
SWEDEN	Enterprises	134430	9613	2072	146115	.920	.066	.014

```
* Greece - no micros; only industry and repair sectors
*Ireland - Only industry; micro 3-9; 149 classed as "other"
*Luxembourg - 1987 figures
*Norway - 1989 figures; for Industry; different size for other
          NACE sectors
```

Duns International Market Identifiers, File 518 on DIALOG, has approximately 2.5 million companies. We used these files to determine how many SMEs there were worldwide. These figures are approximate and we would expect companies in these commercial databases to be generally larger than the populations as a whole. Therefore, it is interesting to note that only about 2% of all the companies in the D&B files could be classified as "large."

Table 2. Size of Companies in D&B Databases by Number of Employees

		World FILE 518 Per Cent		Europe FILE 521		Canada File 520		Asia-Pacific File 522		United States File 516	
	NA	627177	.25	563501	.28	23858	.07	48621	.20	1399036	.17
Micro	1-9	970151	.39	812176	.40	219475	.65	71995	.29	4707574	.56
Small	10-99	742461	.30	549708	.27	84545	.25	84398	.34	1034220	.12
Medium	100-499	134198	.05	78701	.04	8279	.02	28444	.12	90346	.01
SME	10-499	876659	.35	628409	.31	92824	.27	112842	.46	1124566	.13
Large	>=500	41893	.02	22045	.01	2460	.01	11635	.05	26117	.003
	TOTAL	2515880		202631		338617		245093		8381859	

APPENDIX G
Selecting an International Database

CHECKLIST

Much of the information discussed in this book is available from more than one source. There are multiple directory databases, financial filing databases, and text databases. Which should you use? This appendix presents guidelines as to what to look for in an international database. Some of these criteria will be the same as for print sources; some will be the same as for any database. We have arranged the criteria under the following categories: Time, Data, Searching, Output, Database Provider, and Databank Provider.

1. Time

Currency—How up-to-date is the information?
History—How many years of data are available?
Updates—How frequently is the database updated? How frequently is a directory entry updated?
Loading dates—Does the database indicate when it was reloaded? When an entry was reloaded?

2. Data

Amount of directory information—
How many companies are in the database?
How many countries are included.
How many data items (fields) are there per record?
Amount of textual information—
How many titles of journals, newspapers, etc. are covered?
Accuracy of information—
Are there many typos? These are often easier to spot when browsing on a CD-ROM. Expand a DIALOG country field and notice the variant spellings. One database has more than 10 entries for "European Community."
Do your clients question the data?

Collection of information—
How are the data collected? By phone? Questionnaire? How are the data verified? How long are non-repondants kept in the database?
Uniqueness of information—
Is this information available in other sources? In other formats?
Value added—
what are the benefits of accessing the information in this format?
Depth and/or breadth of information—
Is this a mega-database (*PROMT*)?
Is it boutique (*Delphes*)?
Completeness of information—
For text, are you getting abstracts, extracts, selected full text, or cover to cover full text?

3. Searching

Ease of use—Can you use the database with little training time or preparation? Is it suitable for end-users?
Flexibility—Are there multiple access points? Is there a tradeoff between ease of use and flexibility? How many fields are searchable? sortable? reportable?
Hardware/Software—Do you need special hardware and software or will this run on any machine?
Networking—Can this product be networked? Is it an appropriate product to network?

4. Output

On-screen presentation—Are the data presented in a clear manner?
Report features—Can you create your own reports?
Downloading—If the database is numeric, in what format does it transfer data? How easy is it to import the data into a spreadsheet?

5. Database Provider

Familiarity—Have you used other products either in print or online by this provider?

Reputation—What is the reputation of this provider?

Availability—Does the database provider have a local representative? A toll-free telephone number? A fax? An E-mail address?

Training and documentation—Does the provider have user manuals, code books, and help sheets? Will the database provider come to your institution to give training? Do you have to pay for training?

Knowledge—Does the database provider understand the information?

6. Databank Provider

Familiarity—Do you use other databases on this databank?

Reputation—What is the reputation of the provider? Innovative, helpful?

Availability—Does the databank provider have a local representative ? What hours are help available? London time? U.S. time?

Other complementary databases—Are there other databases that you can access at the same time to answer your question? Can you do a multi-file search?

Training and documentation—Does the provider have user manuals, etc.? What level of training and support does the databank producer provide?

Knowledge—How knowledgeable is the databank provider about the content of the database? Does the databank representative know when to refer you to the database provider?

You might want to build up a core group of international databases that will answer most of your routine questions, e.g., company addresses, industry participants, product/market information, financial information, and stock prices. Look for databases that are multipurpose. These should have field codes for country name or country code, for company name, and for product coding (ideally a standard code like the U.S. or U.K. SIC). Look for families of databases, such as the Dun and Bradstreet databases, the KOMPASS databases, the UMI databases, or the IAC databases. If you can search one, you can search them all.

MULTIPLE DATABANKS, MULTIPLE DATABASES

- Whose data do you use when more than one database has "similar" data on the same system?
- Which databank do you use if a database is available from several providers?

Read the documentation! Talk to your local representatives. Ask for some free practice time or a trial of a CD-ROM. One of the major problems with electronic databases today is that it is just as difficult for the customer service reps to keep up with the changes as it is for us. Databank representatives, though familiar with how to search the system, are not conversant with the content of the databases. International information is complicated. Many CD-ROM providers are not familiar with database content.

When similar information is available from multiple sources, cost becomes a factor in your decision. In determining cost, however, consider the following factors:
- Online costs
- Preparation time
- Searching and output format alternatives

For example, when screening for a list of companies with multiple variables that your client wishes to use in a spreadsheet, DIALOG may be the only online databank to which you have access with these capabilities. However, it might be preferable to retrieve several full-text articles off of DOW JONES Text during evening hours.

- If the database or databank resides in another country, how much information can your local representative provide?
- What is the turnaround time for a question to be answered?

If you have gone online because your patron needs the information now, you need to use a system that can answer the question for you now. According to the U.S. representative for a non-U.S. databank, Americans do not like to make international phone calls—even to the U.K. Can you use E-mail or a FAX?

EVALUATING ONLINE AND CD-ROM

1. When do you decide to get the information on CD-ROM rather than going online or using print?

This decision should be made very carefully. All of the usual CD-ROM decisions that you should have been making, but probably haven't been, become much more important when deciding to purchase a specialized international CD-ROM product. Think of all of the possible international questions you are asked and the possible sources you could use to answer these questions.

2. Is it advantageous to buy one CD-ROM that will answer one type of question or use the same money to go online to a variety of different systems?

Look at alternative pricing with online systems, such as negotiating a fixed price, as alternatives to CD-ROM.

3. Who is your user group?

Do you want to encourage end-user access? Will your users be better off using one of the menu-driven systems, such as DOW JONES, DBC (DIALOG Business Collection), or DATA-STAR's Business Focus? Will the CD-ROM answer the routine questions and leave you free for the more difficult ones? If you intend to buy an international CD-ROM when you are not familiar with the printed directory or the online equivalent, the documentation and the sales rep are again very important to you.

HUMAN RESOURCE ISSUES

For not only those of us who are new to business research, but also those of us who have been involved in business research for many years, the wealth of international information and the wide ranging demand for this information is taking us into unfamiliar territory. We are looking at print products from producers who are unfamiliar and online systems that originate in countries outside our borders. We must understand international business practice and terminology. We have a responsibility to our clients to know what it is we are offering them, in our print sources and our machine-readable ones. We need to have

- Knowledge of source content—Are you and your staff familiar with the online source and printed equivalents?
- Understanding of the question asked—Can you reasonably answer the question? Is the question reasonable?
- Ability to judge results—Do you know enough about the data, the source, and the topic to evaluate the output?

APPENDIX H
Broadcast TV Operators in OECD Countries

	Broadcast TV Operator(s)	Number of over-the-air channels	Status of service	Regulatory body
Australia	ABC plus 52 commercial stations	n.a.	Competitive	Department of Transport and Communications Australian Broadcasting Tribunal
Austria	ORF	2	Monopoly	State Chancellor's Office
Belgium	BRTF; BRT; 3 commercial	4 (+1 scrambled)	Liberalized in mid 1980s	Regional governments
Canada	CBC; Other public broadcasters; 5 main commercial channels	n.a.	Competitive	CRTC
Denmark	Danmarks Radio TV2	2 plus local	Liberalized in 1986	Directorate General of P&T
Finland	Finnish Broadcasting Co.; Maïnos-TV Co. Kolmos-TV Co.	3	Competitive	Council of State
France	TFI,A2,FR3, ARTE, M6 (Canal Plus)	5 (+1 scrambled)	Liberalized in 1986	CSA
Germany	ADR, ZDF + Regional stations	3	Competitive	State governments (Länder)
Greece	ERT1,2,3+ foreign channels;re-broadcast	3	Liberalized since 1989	2 government bodies for "social" and "political " regulation
Iceland	RTE	2	Monopoly	Icelandic Government
Italy	RAI 1,2,3 Commerical channels incl. Canale 5, Rete 4, Italia I	6 main channels	Liberalized since 1976	P&T ministry plus local and district courts
Japan	NHK + 158 regional commerical channels	n.a.	Competitive	Ministry of Posts and Telecommunications
Luxembourg	CLT	4	Private monopoly	2 government commissions for technical and content issues

Appendix H: Broadcast TV Operators in OECD Countries *(continued)*

Netherlands	NOS	3	Open access monopoly	Ministry of Welfare, Health & Culture
New Zealand	TVNZ,TV# plust 7 private channels inc. Sky Network TV	Up to 10	Liberalized in 1987	Broadcasting Commission
Norway	NRK, TV2	2	Liberalized in 1989	National Advisory Council; Ministry of Culture
Portugal	RPT plus 2 commercial channels out to tender	2 (+2)	Liberalized in 1986	Institute of Communications in Portugal (technical) Directorate General for Social Communications (other)
Spain	RTVE plus private channels	Up to 8	Liberalized	Presidential Ministry
Switzerland	SSR Télécinéromanie and others	3 + 1 pay-TV Regional and local	Liberalized in 1992	Federal Council(Executive) Federal Dept. of Transports, Communications & Engery; Independent Authority for radio and TV broadcasts complaints (AIEP)
Turkey	TRT, Magic Box	3	Liberalized in 1989	Ministry of Transport
U. K.	BBC 1,2; Channel 3,4, 5(in 1993); cable	4 (+1)	Competitive since 1950s	ITC Home Office

Source: *Information Computer Communications Policy* 29. "Telecommunications and Broadcasting:Convergence or Collision, " OECD, 1992

Source: Information Computer Communications Policy 29. "Telecommunications and Broadcasting: Convergence or Collision," OECD, 1992

APPENDIX I
Basic Guide to Exporting

TEN KEYS TO EXPORT SUCCESS

1. Obtain qualified export counseling and develop a master international markets plan.
2. Secure a commitment from top management; take a long-range view.
3. Take care in selecting overseas distributors.
4. Establish a basis for profitable operations and orderly growth; don't depend on unsolicited leads.
5. Devote continued attention to export business even when the U.S. market is profitable.
6. Treat international distributors on an equal basis with domestic counterparts. Offer the same incentives.
7. Do not assume that a market technique that works in one country will work in another.
8. Be willing to modify products to meet the regulations or cultural preferences of other countries.
9. Print service, sale, and warranty messages in locally understood languages.
10. Provide readily available servicing or service support for the product. (*Basic Guide,* p. ix)

TWELVE MOST COMMON MISTAKES OF POTENTIAL EXPORTERS

1. Failure to obtain qualified export counseling and to develop a master international marketing plan before starting an export business.
2. Insufficient commitment by top management to overcome the initial difficulties and financial requirements of exporting.
3. Insufficient care in selecting overseas distributors.
4. Chasing orders from around the world instead of establishing a basis for profitable operations and orderly growth within one region.
5. Neglecting export business when the U.S. market booms.
6. Failure to treat international distributors on an equal basis with domestic counterparts.
7. Assuming that a given market technique and product will automatically be successful in all countries.
8. Unwillingness to modify products to meet regulations or cultural preferences of other countries.
9. Failure to print service, sale and warranty messages in locally understood languages.
10. Failure to consider use of an export management company.
11. Failure to consider licensing or joint-venture agreements.
12. Failure to provide readily available servicing for the product. (*Basic Guide,* pp. 85-86)

APPENDIX J
OECD Country Sources and Coding Schemes

COUNTRY	INDUSTRIAL CLASSIFICATION	INDUSTRY CENSUS - Selected Publications
United States	US SIC regrouped to ISIC	Census and Annual Survey of Manufactures
Australia	ASIC - aligned with ISIC	Manufacturing establishments
Austria	Betriebssystematik 1968 - aligned with ISIC	Indrustriestatistik 1. Teil
Canada	CSIC 1970	Annual Census of Manufactures
Denmark	Danish National Codes-DSE -some conformation with ISIC	Industrial Statistics Industrial Accounts Statistics
Finland	Finnish national system follows ISIC	Industrial Statistics
France *	Uses NAP 100-converted to ISIC	Rapport sur les COmptes de la Nation
Germany	National System-SYPRO;converted to ISIC	
Greece	National system -adjusted estimates to ISIC	Annual Industrial Survey
Iceland *	Preceding ISIC	Industrial Statistics
Italy	NACE-not fully convertable	Bollettino Mensile di Statistica, suplmts
Japan	Japanese Standard Industrial Classification	Census of Manufatures
Netherlands	Standard industrial Classification 1974; fully converted to ISIC	Yearly Production Statistics for each major industry group
New Zealand	NZ Standard Industrial Classification (5 digits)converted to ISIC	Annual Business Pattern and 5-year Economy Wide Census Reports
Norway	Close to ISIC	**Industristatistikk**
Portugal	CAE - with links to ISIC	Industrial Statistics
Spain	CNAE 1974; regrouped to ISIC	Encuesta Industrial Annual 1984-1988

Appendix J: OECD Country Sources and Coding Schemes *(continued)*

Sweden	SNI = 1968 4-digit ISIC	Manufacturing, Pt1 and 2 in Offical Statistics
Switzerland **	General Classification of Economic Activity-reclassed	Mitteilungen des SGZZ, 1990
Turkey		from annual manufacturing survey
United Kingdom	Standard Industrial Classification Revised 1980	Census of Production Introductory notes; Annual Abstract of Statistics

* National accounts only; ** Foreign trade only

Source: OECD Publications

Title Index

All acronyms and initialisms are filed as words, whether or not they are pronounced as words. Titles are not indexed if they appear only in a table.

Subject Index